FEMINIST BIBLICAL STUDIES
IN THE TWENTIETH CENTURY

Society of Biblical Literature

The Bible and Women
An Encyclopaedia of Exegesis and Cultural History

Edited by Jorunn Økland, Irmtraud Fischer,
Mercedes Navarro Puerto, and Adriana Valerio

The Bible and Women
The Contemporary Period
Volume 9.1: Feminist Biblical Studies in the Twentieth Century

FEMINIST BIBLICAL STUDIES IN THE TWENTIETH CENTURY

SCHOLARSHIP AND MOVEMENT

Edited by

Elisabeth Schüssler Fiorenza

Society of Biblical Literature
Atlanta

Publication made possible by the support of
the Research Council of Norway.

Library of Congress Cataloging-in-Publication Data

Feminist biblical studies in the twenieth century : scholarship and movement / edited by
Elisabeth Schüssler Fiorenza.
        pages cm. — (The Bible and women ; number 9.1. The twenieth century and the
        present)
    Includes bibliographical references.
    ISBN 978-1-58983-583-2 (paper binding : alk. paper) — ISBN 978-1-58983-921-2
    (electronic format : alk. paper) — ISBN 978-1-58983-922-9 (hardcover binding : alk.
    paper)
    1. Bible—Feminist criticism—History—20th century. I. Schüssler Fiorenza, Elisa-
beth, 1938–. II. Society of Biblical Literature.
    BS521.4.F445 2014
    220.6082—dc23   2014002889

Printed on acid-free, recycled paper conforming to
ANSI/NISO Z39.48-1992 (R1997) and ISO 9706:1994
standards for paper permanence.

Contents

ACKNOWLEDGMENTS

This volume is the product of collegial collaboration. My deepest thanks go to the contributors to this important work, which seeks to chart the beginnings and developments of feminist biblical studies around the globe. I greatly appreciated and enjoyed working with all of you!

This book is part of a multivolume project, The Bible and Women: An Encyclopedia of Exegesis and Cultural History, being published in four languages (German, Italian, Spanish, and English). Special thanks are due to the initiators of this complex and path-breaking encyclopedia project, Irmtraud Fischer and Adriana Valerio, who were joined by Mercedes Navarro Puerto and Jorunn Økland.

Particular thanks to Jorunn Økland, the general editor of the English-language edition, who among other things organized an international research colloquium at the University of Oslo that brought many of the contributors to the volume together for two days of discussions and colleagueship. Without Jorunn's work of fundraising and conference planning, the collegial collaboration of the contributors to this volume would not have been possible. To Jorunn and her assistants Stefanie Schön and Chantal Jackson, my deepest thanks.

Acknowledgements are also due to the research project Canonicity, Gender and Critique: The Hermeneutics of Feminism and Canon Transformations for sponsoring the Oslo colloquium and the translation, to the gender research program in the Norwegian Research Council for funding the Canonicity, Gender and Critique project, and to the Centre for Gender Research of the University of Oslo for hosting the colloquium. I also want to thank the unnamed translators of Amesto Translations and Richard Ratzlaff for translating select chapters of the book from their original languages into English.

We were fortunate that, under the sponsorship of The Journal of Feminist Studies in Religion, an affiliate of the SBL, we were able to have a session at the SBL meeting in New Orleans in 2009 for discussing our work. Jorunn Økland, Dora Mbuwayesango, Renate Jost, and Shelly Matthews initiated the discussion on how to write the history of feminist biblical studies in the twentieth century. After the Oslo colloquium, *JFSR* also sponsored a follow-up seminar session at the SBL Annual Meeting in Atlanta in which Renate Jost, Joseph Marchal, Cynthia Baker, Melanie Johnson-DeBaufre, Jorunn Økland, Elsa Tamez, Dora Mbuwayesango, Denise Buell, Jane Schaberg, and Shelly Matthews participated. Thanks to all of my colleagues who have so greatly contributed to this work.

This volume would not have materialized without the expert guidance of the SBL Director of Publications, Bob Buller. I am deeply grateful for his invaluable collegial assistance and care for the volume. Thanks are also due to the production staff for their meticulous work: copyeditor Patricia K. Tull, publications coordinator and typesetter Lindsay Lingo, and cover designer for the encyclopedia project Kathie Klein. As always, it was a joy to work with Leigh Andersen, who expertly coordinated the project's production.

Last but not least, I want to thank my research assistant Kelsi Morrison-Atkins, who compiled the bibliography and contributor list, expertly proofread the contributions to the volume several times, polished the translations of some of the chapters, and tirelessly worked on the volume for two years. The future of feminist biblical studies is in good hands if it can depend on the work of emerging scholars such as her.

Elisabeth Schüssler Fiorenza

Abbreviations

ANQ	*Andover Newton Quarterly*
ATR	*Anglican Theological Review*
BibInt	*Biblical Interpretation*
BiKi	*Bibel und Kirche*
BTB	*Biblical Theology Bulletin*
BZAW	Beihefte zur Zeitschrift für die alttestamentliche Wissenschaft
CBQ	*Catholic Biblical Quarterly*
CH	*Church History*
CR:BS	*Currents in Research: Biblical Studies*
EATWOT	Ecumenical Association of Third World Theologians
Enc	*Encounter*
ExpTim	*Expository Times*
FTS	Frankfurter theologische Studien
GHAT	Göttinger Handkommentar zum Alten Testament
HThK	Herders Theologischer Kommentar
HTR	*Harvard Theological Review*
HTS	Harvard Theological Studies
INPUT	Interdisziplinäre Paderborner Untersuchungen zur Theologie
IFFTR	Internationale Forschungen in Feministischer Theologie und Religion
JAAR	*Journal of the American Academy of Religion*
JBL	*Journal of Biblical Literature*
JESWTR	*Journal of the European Society of Women in Theological Research*
JFSR	*Journal of Feminist Studies in Religion*
JHS	*Journal of the History of Sexuality*
JITC	*Journal of the Interdenominational Theological Center*
JRT	*Journal of Religious Thought*
JSNT	*Journal for the Study of the New Testament*
JSNTSup	Journal for the Study of the New Testament Supplement Series
JSOT	*Journal for the Study of the Old Testament*

JSOTSup	Journal for the Study of the Old Testament Supplement Series
MQ	Mankind Quarterly
MR	The Massachusetts Review
MWJHR	Muslim World Journal of Human Rights
OBO	Orbis biblicus et orientalis
OBT	Overtures to Biblical Theology
NRTh	Nouvelle revue théologique
QD	Quaestiones Disputatae
RBL	Review of Biblical Literature
RelSRev	Religious Studies Review
RevExp	Review and Expositor
RIBLA	Revista de interpretación bíblica latino-americana
RivB	Rivista Biblica italiana
SBS	Stuttgarter Bibelstudien
SBLGPBS	Society of Biblical Literature Global Perspectives on Biblical Scholarship
StPat	Studia Patavina
TD	Theology Digest
THKNT	Theologischer Handkommentar zum Neuen Testament
ThQ	Theologische Quartalschrift
TP	Theologia Practica
USQR	Union Seminary Quarterly Review
WSQ	Women's Studies Quarterly
WW	Word and World
ZNT	Zeitschrift für die neutestamentliche Wissenschaft und die Kunde der älteren Kirche

Between Movement and Academy: Feminist Biblical Studies in the Twentieth Century

Elisabeth Schüssler Fiorenza
Harvard University Divinity School

According to its main editors, this encyclopedia, Bible and Women, is conceived as a reception-history project in theology and gender research that originated in Europe and developed into an international undertaking. They understand the project as follows:

> This encyclopedia could … be seen as a gender-inclusive display room of what the reception history of the Bible might also be if we include a focus on the reception of gender-relevant texts and interpretations generated by women.… They represent, in fact, an untapped world that we believe biblical scholars should pay more attention to rather than continuing to inhabit only a small part of the "museum."[1]

1. Charting Feminist Biblical Studies in the Twentieth Century

While this is a very important goal, the present volume on the twentieth century seeks more than just to occupy a room in the "museum" of reception history. Rather, it seeks to chart a rupture, or break, in the malestream reception history of the Bible, which includes wo/men's Bible readings, and it does so by reconceptualizing biblical studies in a feminist key. It uses the much controverted term "feminism" not in the narrow sense of women or gender studies but in a "performative" sense that is spelled out and qualified differently

---

1. Jorunn Økland, Irmtraud Fischer, Mercedes Navarro Purto, and Adriana Valerio, "Introduction—Women, Bible, and Reception History: An International Project in Theology and Gender Studies," in *Torah* (Bible and Women 1; Atlanta: Society of Biblical Literature, 2011), 28.

in different social-cultural and theoretical-religious locations. The f-word, "feminist," serves here as an umbrella term for gender, womanist, liberation-ist, postcolonial, Asian, African or indigenous, Latina, queer, interreligious, and transnational studies and many other kyriarchy-critical perspectives and approaches. Moreover, the volume situates the topic "women and the Bible" in the space between wo/men's movements for justice and liberation on the one hand and the academic study of sacred Scriptures on the other.

However, the volume's stated restriction to the twentieth century is some-what misleading, since feminist biblical studies have their roots in the women's movements of the nineteenth century. Beginning in the nineteenth century with works such as Grace Aguilar's *Women of Israel*,[2] newly edited by Mayer I. Gruber, and Elizabeth Cady Stanton's *Woman's Bible*, feminist studies moved in the twentieth century into the academy. It continues to articulate feminist biblical knowledge into the twenty-first century. While the roots of academic feminist biblical studies in the twentieth century wo/men's movements around the globe are unquestionable, it is not certain whether we will use our analytic academic tools to "dismantle the master's house" (Audre Lorde) in the twenty-first century, rather than seeking merely to gain more space in the "master's museum" of the academy. To chart or to map biblical studies in the twentieth century and to foster it into the twenty-first, we need not only to ask what kind of analysis to bring to bear on the biblical text, but we must also continue to ask, in the interest of the wo/men's movements around the globe: "How do we move from analyzing what is or has been to announcing the advent of what might or should be?"[3] When mapping the genealogy of feminist biblical inter-pretation, it becomes evident that much remains to be done.

This collection of essays, therefore, begins this initial work by charting the efforts of feminist biblical studies around the globe, if only in a prelimi-nary way. It does so despite limited written resources and feminist historical scholarship for this task. It is important to chart the terrain of feminist biblical studies so that our feminist history is recorded and not forgotten. We need many more dissertations, research projects, oral histories, and archives to gather and research the beginnings, developments, and institutionalizations of feminist biblical studies in the twentieth century so that it can continue to flourish in the twenty-first. This collection of essays can do so only episodi-cally, since such extensive scientific historiographic work on feminist biblical

---

2. Grace Aguilar, *The Women of Israel* (ed. Mayer I. Gruber; Piscataway, N.J.: Gorgias, 2011); first published in 1851 by Appleton.

3. Virginia Burrus, "Mapping as Metamorphosis: Initial Reflections on Gender and Ancient Religious Discourse," in *Mapping Gender in Ancient Religious Discourses* (ed. Todd Penner and Caroline Vander Stichele; Leiden: Brill: 2007), 1–10, here 3.

studies is still lacking. But it does provide substantive work on the development of feminist biblical studies. Hence, this volume must be seen as a first major step on the road toward a history of feminist biblical interpretation that must be continued and strengthened in the interest of progressive movements around the world.

This initial mapping of feminist biblical studies in the twentieth century seeks to explore four areas of inquiry demanding further investigation. It attempts first to chart the beginnings and developments of feminist biblical studies not only in the U.S. and Europe, but as a conversation among feminists around the world. In a second step, it introduces, reviews, and discusses the hermeneutic religious spaces created by feminist biblical studies, and in a third segment it discusses academic methods of reading and interpretation that were developed to "dismantle the master's house" (Audre Lorde) of androcentric language and kyriarchal authority. The book's fourth, concluding section returns to the first with work that transgresses academic boundaries in order to exemplify the transforming, inspiring, and institutionalizing feminist work that has been and is being done to change religious mindsets of domination and to enable wo/men to engage in a critical reading of the Bible.

The encyclopedia project of which this volume is a part rightly assumes that wo/men[4] have read, understood, and applied biblical texts and ideas to their lives throughout the centuries. What was new in the twentieth century, and what will be highlighted in this volume, is not only that wo/men for the first time were able to join the ranks of biblical scholars, but also that we developed feminist approaches and theories of interpretation. A feminist reception history that traces the interactions between wo/men and the Bible, therefore, cannot be solely interested in how the text has been understood by wo/men and applied throughout history. It also must analyze the powers that have excluded wo/men from the authoritative traditions of interpretation. Thus, we need also to recognize how feminist biblical studies have sought to interrupt and rupture not only the malestream reception history and *Wirkungsgeschichte* of the Bible, but also the structures of domination that determine not only men's but also wo/men's biblical interpretations.

Feminist scholars in religion have not simply joined the long and exclusive "procession" of clergy men and men of letters (Virginia Woolf), but we have insisted that the study of the Bible and its reception history must be changed, since such malestream scholarship has not only theorized and served interests of domination, but has also silenced wo/men as recognized subjects of

---

4. I write wo/men in such a fractured way not only in order to indicate that wo/men are not the same or have an essence in common but also to include disenfranchised men.

interpretation by excluding us from professional biblical studies. Hence, feminist studies have raised the issues of power, exclusion, and domination. In the latter part of the twentieth century, postcolonial, differently abled, and religiously situated African, Asian, and Latin-American critical scholars of emancipation joined in this work.

Engaging the definition of feminism ascribed to Cheris Kramarae and Paula Treichler, which states that "women are people," I understand feminism in a political sense as the radical notion that wo/men are fully entitled and responsible citizens in society, academy, and organized religions. At the SBL meeting in 2010, the authors present adopted the following exposition of the meaning of "feminist," which Monica Melanchthon articulated as follows. Feminist work:

- ▶ must challenge/destabilize/subvert the subordination of wo/men, rather than strengthen or reinforce it;
- ▶ must reflect appreciation of and respect for wo/men's experience by acknowledging wo/men's capacities and agency;
- ▶ must be sensitive to context—both the immediate and possibly the larger context as well;
- ▶ must be critical of the manner in which wo/men have both aided and resisted oppression, subjugation, and violence;
- ▶ must have as its consequence far-reaching changes in religion and society, as well as political and revolutionary significance. Hence, it must be practical, this-worldly, transformative, renewing, and transitional.

Hopefully, other volumes of the encyclopedia will take over these ethical-political imperatives as critical interpretive lenses and criteria, whether or not they adopt the identification "feminist."

In line with this understanding of feminist work, the articles in this volume indicate that feminist biblical studies have their roots in feminist movements for change in religion. This comes to the fore particularly in the reports from Africa, Asia, and Latin America, as well as in those from Europe and the U.S. They also indicate that feminist biblical studies are currently in danger of becoming ensconced in academic readings and debates rather than in developing methods and habits of interpretation that empower wo/men in their struggles for survival, dignity, and rights. This danger can be seen especially in the U.S. and Europe, where wo/men have gained greater access to the academy.

Insofar as feminist biblical studies have gained a foothold in universities and theological schools, they must fulfill institutional requirements and academic standards. Thus, many young feminist scholars no longer have the time and freedom to work with wo/men who read the Bible or to study how wo/men use it. Moreover, they are encouraged to write dissertations and pen articles that are "acceptable" in terms of academic standards and interests, but not in terms of the needs of the movement. This pressure to conform to traditional academic standards has proven costly to the continuation of feminist studies in religion. For instance, we need more dissertations that study the history of the development of feminist movements in religion and ethnographic works that elaborate feminist biblical studies in the contexts of academy and wo/men's conscientization. We are lacking research that focuses, for instance, on the work of leading scholars in the field, and on oral histories of wo/men rabbis and ministers who have shaped the movement.

We also lack institutional spaces and foundations that would sustain the academic and activist work that has been done and that will support such work in the future. We lack critical feminist books and electronic media for children, materials for grammar and high school teaching, and Bible study materials for religious communities. The contributions to this volume celebrate the creative work that has been and is done, but at the same time also indicate the work we have still ahead of us.

Since its contributors seek to record and sustain such work, I want to contextualize this volume by focusing on the theoretical framework articulated in various ways by its contributors and the critical lenses of interpretation that are needed for future work in order to sustain critical feminist biblical studies in the theoretical and practical space "between" movement and academy. Obviously, any articulation and delineation of such a theoretical framework is shaped by each author's own theoretical perspective. Yet, I venture to say that most of the contributions in this volume work with an intersectional analytic of domination, although they may use different nomenclatures, and are rooted in and indebted to wo/men's struggles for justice and change.

2. A Critical Feminist Decolonizing Analytic

Wo/men's studies began by naming the cultural-political power at work in our world as patriarchy, which literally means the father's domination over the members of his household, but was then generally understood as the domination of man over woman.[5] Since the mid-1980s, this key category of feminist analysis has been problematized and replaced by that of gender.

---

5. Ann Oakley, *Sex, Gender, and Society* (New York: Harper & Row, 1972); Rosemary Radford Ruether, "Patriarchy," in *An A to Z of Feminist Theology* (ed. Lisa Isherwood and

2.1. Gender

In the 1970s, women's studies distinguished social gender roles from biological sex, and by the mid-1980s gender studies emerged as a distinct field of inquiry that questions seemingly universal beliefs about woman and man and attempts to unmask the cultural, societal, and political roots of gender.[6] Since then, gender has become a key analytic category alongside race, class, age, and colonialism, an analysis that has led to an "adding up of oppressions" approach, or an adding-up of the diverse structures of domination working alongside each other and constituting different dualistic frameworks of analysis. This dualistic gender analytic has constituted the notion of diversity as an aggregate of such dualistic identity markers. Women's studies scholars first objected to the introduction of this analytic category because it no longer articulated that *wo/men* were the focal point of feminist analysis. It is also interesting to observe that the analytics of gender arrived on the scene at the time when neoliberal globalization and postmodern academic discourses gained ground worldwide. Moreover, by replacing the central analytic categories of *patriarchy* and *androcentrism* (male-centered ideology) with gender, the question of power relations was muted and often eclipsed. Neglecting the question of power relations is also in danger of overlooking the harmful

---

Dorothea McEwan; Sheffield: Sheffield Academic Press, 1996), 173–74; Sylvia Walby, *Theorizing Patriarchy* (Oxford: Basil, 1990). See for instance Ernst Bornemann, *Das Patriarchat: Ursprung und Zukunft unseres Gesellschaftssystems* (Frankfurt: Fischer, 1991); Maria Mies, *Patriarchy and Accumulation on a World Scale: Women in the International Division of Labour* (New York: Palgrave, 1999); Lorraine Code, "Patriarchy," in *Encyclopedia of Feminist Theories* (ed. Lorraine Code; London: Routledge, 2000), 378–79; Pierre Bourdieu, *Masculine Domination* (trans. Richard Nice; Stanford, Calif.: Stanford University Press, 2001).

6. Conversation partners in this section are Marjorie Agosín, ed., *Women, Gender, and Human Rights: A Global Perspective* (New Brunswick, N.J.: Rutgers University Press, 2001); Dennis Baron, *Grammar and Gender* (New Haven: Yale University Press, 1986). Hadumond Bussmann and Renate Hof, eds., *Genus: Geschlechterforschung/Gender Studies in den Kultur- und Sozialwissenschaften: Ein Handbuch* (Stuttgart: A. Kröner, 2005); Judith Butler, *Gender Trouble: Feminism and the Subversion of Identity* (New York: Routledge, 1990); Judith Butler *Undoing Gender* (New York: Routledge, 2004); Teresa de Lauretis, *Technologies of Gender* (Bloomington: Indiana University Press, 1987); bell hooks, *Yearning: Race, Gender, and Cultural Politics* (Boston: South End, 1990); Judith Lorber, *Paradoxes of Gender* (New Haven: Yale University Press, 1990); Stephen D. Moore and Janice Capel Anderson, eds., *New Testament Masculinities* (Semeia Studies 45; Atlanta: Society of Biblical Literature, 2003); and my "Gender, Sprache, und Religion: Feministisch-theologische Anfragen," in *Erträge: 60 Jahre Augustana* (Neuendettelsau: Augustana Hochschule, 2008), 83–90; online: http://www.augustana.de/dokumente/ertraege/ertraege_neu/jubilaeums_sonderheft_2008.pdf.

effects of gendered language. Gendered language articulates power relations and reinscribes cultural-religious gender assumptions. Western androcentric languages and discourses do not just marginalize wo/men or eliminate us from historical records, but as kyriocentric languages they also construct the meaning of being a woman or a man differently. Hence, feminist studies in general, and feminist religious studies in particular, must confront this problem of gendered language.

Grammatically masculine language functions as so-called "generic" language, a "conventional" language function that obscures the presence of wo/men. Wo/men are subsumed under masculine typed language such as "citizens," "presidents," or "chairmen" which is not just male, but also *kyrios*-determined language. In order to lift into consciousness the linguistic violence of so-called generic male-centered language, I use the term "wo/men" and not "men" in an inclusive way. I suggest that whenever we read "wo/men" we understand it in the generic inclusive sense. In English, wo/men includes men, s/he includes he, and fe/male includes male. (However, this wordplay is only possible in English, but not in Spanish or German, making such an inclusive/generic hearing/speaking very difficult in these languages). Feminist studies of language have elaborated that Western androcentric language systems understand language as both generic and as gender-specific. Wo/men always must think at least twice, if not more times, in order to adjudicate whether or not we are meant by "generic" terms such as "men," "humans," "brothers," or "professors."

One can illustrate how such supposedly generic language works with reference to social position in advertisements that read: "University X is an affirmative action institution and invites applications from African, Asian, Hispanic, or Native American, and women candidates," as though these different types of Americans are all men and wo/men are only gendered but do not belong to racial and ethnic minority groups. African, Asian, Hispanic, and Native American wo/men are thus doubly invisible in gendered language systems.

Moreover, it must not be overlooked that the meaning of the gender marker "woman" is unstable and shifting, and depends not so much on its sex/gender relation but on the sociopolitical context of the time and place in which it is used. For example, although the expression "woman" today is used interchangeably with "female," and thus has become a generic sex-based term, until very recently it was applied to lower-class females only. One can perceive the historical ambiguity of the term "woman" much more easily if one compares it with the term "lady," an appellation that readily reveals its race, class, and colonial bias. Not only has "lady" been restricted to wo/men of higher status or educational refinement, it has also symbolized *true womanhood* and *femininity*. A statement such as "slaves were not wo/men" offends our commonsense understanding, whereas a statement such as "slaves were not ladies" makes perfect sense.

The sociopolitical classification of gender, like its grammatical counterpart, does not always correspond to the biological classification of sex. Anthropologists have pointed out that not all cultures and languages know of only two sexes/genders, and historians of gender have argued that even in Western culture the dual sex/gender system is of modern origin. Thomas Laqueur,[7] for instance, has maintained that a decisive shift took place in modernity from the ancient one-sex model to the present dichotomous, two-sex model. Wo/men were once believed to have the same sex and genitals as men except that the wo/men's were inside the body, as opposed to the men's, which were outside. In this one-sex model, the vagina was understood to be an interior penis; the labia the foreskin; the uterus the scrotum; and the ovaries the testicles.

What it meant to be a *man* or a *woman* in the ancient one-sex model was determined by social rank and by one's place in the household, however, and not by sexual organs. As a free man or as a slave woman, one performed a cultural role according to one's social status, and was not thought to be biologically one of two incommensurable sexes. Not sex, but the social status of the free, elite, propertied male head of household determined superior gender status. Hence, the ancients did not need to resort to sexual difference for supporting the claim that freeborn wo/men were inferior to freeborn men. Rather, because freeborn wo/men were subordinates, their "nature" was believed to be inferior.

Beginning with the Enlightenment in the eighteenth century, the two-sex model—the notion that there are two stable, opposite sexes—emerges. In this period, the commonly held notion originates that states that the economic, political, and cultural lives of wo/men and men, or their gender roles, are based on two biologically given sexes. Just as in antiquity the body was seen as reflecting the cosmological order, so in modernity the body and sexuality are seen as representing and legitimating the social-political order. Because the Enlightenment's claims for democracy and equality excluded freeborn wo/men and subordinate men from full citizenship, new arguments had to be fashioned if elite freeborn men were to justify elite wo/men's exclusion from the public domain.

The promise of democracy, that wo/men and disenfranchised men were full citizens, generated new anti-wo/men arguments based on nature, physi-

---

7. Thomas Laqueur, *Making Sex: Body and Gender from the Greeks to Freud* (Cambridge: Harvard University Press, 1990).

ology, and science. For instance, those who opposed the democratic partici-pation of freeborn wo/men sought evidence for wo/men's mental and physi-cal unsuitability for the public sphere by arguing that wo/men's bodies and biology made them unfit to participate. Similar arguments were made with respect to subordinate men and colonized peoples.

The theory of "separate spheres" for men and wo/men thus arose along-side the dual sex/gender model. In Enlightenment discourses, elite wo/men were no longer construed as lesser men but as totally different from and complementary to men, as beings of a "purer race," or an "angelic species" less affected than men by sexual drives and desires. In order to bar wo/men from participation in the new civil society, the physical and moral differ-ences between men and wo/men were conceived to ensure that elite wo/men and subordinate people were excluded from political decision making. Two incommensurable sexes/genders were the result of these ideological practices. However, one must observe that these gendered identity constructs primarily applied to elite bourgeois men and wo/men.

In short, gender is a sociopolitical institution as well as an ideological representation. The assumption of natural sex/gender differences serves as a preconstructed frame of meaning for individuals and cultural institutions. By presenting the sex/gender system of male and female or masculine and femi-nine as universal, this preconstructed frame of meaning obscures the reality that the very notion of two sexes is a sociopolitical construct for maintaining domination and not a biological essence. Sexual differences depend on socio-cultural communicative practices and therefore can be developed differently or changed. Individuals recognize gender and appropriate gender ascriptions because they perceive them as real. Gender is thus a product and process not only of representation but also of self-identification. Understanding gender as a product and process makes it possible to analyze cultural masculinity and femininity with the intention of changing them.

2.2. Intersectionality[8]

Since wo/men's and gender studies have tended to focus on male/mascu-line power over wo/men but not on race, class, heteronormativity, disabil-ity, colonialism, and other structures of domination, a new mode of analysis

---

8. See Helma Lutz, Maria Theresa Herrera Vivar, and Linda Supik, eds., *Fokus Intersektionalität: Bewegungen und Verortungen eines vielschichtigen Konzepts* (Wiesbaden: Springer VS, 2010); Nina Lykke, *Feminist Studies: A Guide to Intersectional Theory, Meth-odology, and Writing* (New York: Routledge, 2010); and Sharon Doetsch-Kidder, *Social Change and Intersectional Activism* (New York: Palgrave, 2012).

has become necessary. When race and colonialism come into view, then the gender dualism of masculine-feminine is generally transposed into the dualisms "First World and Two-Thirds World wo/men" or "white wo/men and wo/men of color." Thus, the dualistic gender identity framework engenders the dichotomy between the space marked "white wo/men/First World wo/men" and the space marked "wo/men of color/Two-Thirds World wo/men." Identity politics claims that white, First World feminists can speak only about and in the name of white, First World wo/men, whereas wo/men of color/ Two-Thirds World wo/men are called to form coalitions and considered able to speak for all wo/men of the so-called Two-Thirds World. Feminist scholars in religion and theologians, so this argument goes, cannot but articulate either a "white/First world" or "a wo/men of color/Two-Thirds World" the*logy and hermeneutics.

Over and against such a discursive identity politics conceptualized in terms of gender, one must recognize that identity is not only constituted by gender but also by immigrant status, class, education, nationality, sexuality, ability, race, religion, and more. Hence, identity must be seen as multiplex and shaped by intersecting structures of dominations. One cannot assume that wo/men's identity is the same whether it is that of wo/men of color or that of white wo/men. If wo/men are not just determined by gender but also by race, class, heteronormativity, imperialism, and many more such structures of domination, it is necessary to develop a critical analytic that is able to deconstruct the global cultural paradigm of the "White Lady" and the power structures she embodies.

Conceptualizing gender as a practice that produces sex differences that are inflected by race, class, sexual preference, culture, religion, age, and nationality allows one to see that individual wo/men are much more than simply gendered. Rather, the intersection of race, class, sexuality, nation, and religion constructs what it means to be a "wo/man" differently in different sociopolitical and cultural contexts. Variegated feminist, postcolonial, and critical race theories have come together, therefore, in developing the analytic of intersectionality as an instrument to analyze the complex situation of global domination and to demonstrate that the structures of heteronormativity, gender, race, and class are inextricably intertwined.[9] These structures are often seen as working alongside each other, but have not been integrated to accomplish a critical intersectional analysis.

---

9. Lynn Weber, *Understanding Race, Class, Gender, and Sexuality: A Conceptual Framework* (2nd ed.; New York: Oxford University Press, 2010), v.

The term *intersectionality* was coined by the legal scholar Kimberly Crenshaw, and entails "the notion that subjectivity is constituted by mutually multiplicative vectors of race, gender, class, sexuality, and imperialism."[10] The theory of intersectionality has been articulated in a threefold way: as a theory of marginalized subjectivity, as a theory of identity, and as a theory of the matrix of oppressions. In the first iteration, intersectional theory refers only to multiply marginalized subjects; in its second iteration, the theory seeks to illuminate how identity is constructed at the intersections of race, gender, class, sexuality, and imperialism. The third iteration stresses intersectional theory as a theory of structures and sites of oppression. Race, sex, gender, class, and imperialism are seen as vectors of dominating power that create co-constitutive social processes that engender the differential simultaneity of dominations and subordinations.

Intersectional theorists usually conceptualize such social and ideological structures of domination as *hierarchical* in order to map and make visible the complex interstructuring of the conflicting status positions of different wo/men. However, I would argue that the label "hierarchy" for such a pyramidal system of domination is a misnomer, since it only targets one specific form of "power over"—power that is religiously sanctioned as sacred (derived from Greek: *hieros* (sacred/holy) and *archein* (rule/dominate). Hence, I have proposed to replace the categories of *patriarchy* and *hierarchy* with the neologism *kyriarchy*,[11] which is taken up by contributors to this volume. The diverse emancipatory articulations of feminist interpretation, I suggest, could work together by adopting a critical intersectional analytics of global domination understood as kyriarchy.[12]

---

10. Jennifer C. Nash, "Rethinking Intersectionality," *Feminist Review* 89 (2008): 3.

11. For a fuller elaboration of kyriarchy/kyriocentrism, see my introduction, "Toward an Intersectional Analytic: Race, Gender, Ethnicity, and Empire in Early Christian Studies," in *Prejudice and Christian Beginnings* (ed. Laura Nasrallah and Elisabeth Schüssler Fiorenza; Minneapolis: Fortress, 2009), 1–24; and my books *Transforming Vision: Explorations in Feminist The*logy* (Minneapolis: Fortress, 2011); and *Changing Horizons: Explorations in Feminist Interpretation* (Minneapolis: Fortress, 2013).

12. For the first development of this analytic, see my *But She Said: Feminist Practices of Biblical Interpretation* (Boston: Beacon, 1992), 103–32; and idem, "Religion, Gender, and Society: Shaping the Discipline of Religious/Theological Studies," in *The Relevance of Theology* (ed. Carl Reinhold Bråckenhielm and Gunhild Winqvist Hollman; Uppsala: Uppsala University Press, 2002), 85–99. While the notion of kyriarchy has not been widely discussed in feminist theoretical works, it has engendered a wide-ranging discussion among young feminists on the internet. See, e.g., http://myecdysis.blogspot.com/2008/04/accepting-kyriarchy-not-apologies.html;http://www.deeplyproblematic.com/2010/08/why-i-use-that-word-that-i-use.html.

A critical intersectional decolonizing feminist analytic therefore does not understand domination as an essentialist, ahistorical, and hierarchical dualistic system. Instead, it articulates domination as kyriarchy, as a *heuristic* concept (derived from the Greek, meaning "to find"), or as a diagnostic, analytic instrument that enables investigation into the multiplicative interactions of gender, race, class, and imperial stratifications, as well as research into their discursive inscriptions and ideological reproductions. Moreover, it highlights that people inhabit several shifting structural positions of race, sex, gender, class, and ethnicity at one and the same time. If one subject position of domination becomes privileged, it constitutes a nodal point. While in any particular historical moment, class or imperialism may be the primary modality through which one experiences class, imperialism, gender, and race, in other circumstances gender may be the privileged position through which one experiences sexuality, imperialism, race, and class.

2.3. KYRIARCHY[13]

The neologism "kyriarchy," understood as a gradated system of dominations, is derived on the one hand from the Greek word *kyrios* (Latin *dominus*)—the emperor, lord, slave master, father, husband, or the propertied freeborn male to whom all the members of the household were subordinated and by whom they were controlled, and on the other hand the verb *archein*—to rule, dominate, and/or control. In antiquity, the sociopolitical system of kyriarchy was institutionalized either as empire or as a democratic political form of ruling that excluded all freeborn and slave wo/men from full citizenship and decision-making powers. In the fourth century B.C.E., the Greek philosopher Aristotle argued that the freeborn, propertied, educated Greek man is the highest of moral beings and that all other members of the human race are defined by their functions in his service. Kyriarchal societies need a "servant class" of people. The existence of a gendered "servant class" is maintained through law, education, socialization, and brute violence. This is sustained by the belief that members of a "servant class" are inferior by nature or by divine decree to those whom they are destined to serve.

Furthermore, according to Hannah Arendt, democracy rests on the distinction between the household and the public space of the *polis*. In contrast to the household, which was given over to necessity and economics, politics

---

13. See also my *The Power of the Word: Scripture and the Rhetoric of Empire* (Minneapolis: Fortress, 2007); and *Democratizing Biblical Studies: Toward an Emancipatory Educational Space* (Louisville: Westminster John Knox, 2009).

was the realm of freedom.[14] Therefore, the household as the realm of necessity was also the realm of domination. Freedom in the classical, Western political sense was exercised by freeborn propertied men only. Only the *kyrios/dominus/gentleman* was the free citizen. Western-type democracy imitates this kyriarchal structure of Greek democracy, which is built on the subordination and enslavement of the subordinated members of household and state.

2.4. A CRITICAL FEMINIST DECOLONIZING ANALYTIC

The intersectional framework developed by Lynn Weber and the renaming of patriarchy as kyriarchy provide a theoretical frame for feminist biblical analysis.[15] But whereas Weber speaks only of race, class, sexuality, and gender as structures of domination, I would extend her list to include heteronormativity, culture, and religion on the one hand, and subsume *sex* under *corporeality*, which is also characterized by age, disability, and other bodily markers, on the other. Thus, the analytic of kyriarchy can be summarized as follows:

▶ Kyriarchy is historically and geographically contextual and political intersectional. Taking a broad historical and global view allows one to register changes over time and place. It is socially constructed and not biologically determined. It is not engendered by biological imperative, inherent inferiority, or by immutable facts or ordained by G*d.

▶ Kyriarchal relationships are power relationships of dominance and subordination. Here the distinction between personal and social-institutionalized power is central. It is important to ask: How do people come to believe and internalize that they have no power in certain situations?

▶ Kyriarchal intersectional systems operate both on the macro level of social institutions and the micro level of individual life. When analyzing a situation, seeing the psychological manifestations of oppression is much easier than recognizing broad macro-level forces, which are more remote and abstract.

▶ Kyriarchal intersecting structures are interlocking axes of power. They operate to shape people's lives, imaginations, communities, and societies at one and the same time. Hence, one needs to analyze

---

14. Hannah Arendt, "What Is Freedom?" in *Between Past and Future: Eight Exercises in Political Thought* (New York: Penguin, 1993), 143–72.

15. Weber, *Understanding Race*, 129–31.

not only the one most obvious structure in the foreground (such as gender), but all structures of domination simultaneously.

3. Religious Symbol-Systems, Biblical Imagination, and Neoliberal Globalization

Feminist theologies and gender studies in religion[16] have sought to bring about a paradigm shift in the way religion and religious texts, traditions, and communities have been seen and studied. We have sought to change and transform the traditions by engaging in a wide-ranging critique of disciplinary presuppositions, methods, and epistemology, as well as through creative reimagination and transformation of religious discourses and institutions. We thereby seek to rediscover and elaborate wo/men's subjectivity and agency within religious histories and contemporary communities. Insofar as feminist theory has revealed the gender encoding of all knowledge, feminist studies in religion has been able to show the gendering of religious knowledge and religious institutions. Feminist scholars in religion have used the theories of gender,[17] intersectionality, and kyriarchy to understand the second-class status of wo/men in religion and its sacred texts.

In many religions, men and masculinity are associated with the divine and the transcendent, whereas wo/men and femininity are seen as immanent, impure, profane, evil, and/or sinful. Many religious traditions, such as Judaism, Christianity, Islam, Hinduism, Taoism, and Buddhism, use binary gender oppositions to construct their symbolic universes. The deity (Jahwe, Allah, or Christ) is not only understood as masculine, but also as all-powerful ruler and judge, whereas wo/men are associated with sin, death and sex (Eve, Lilith, or Kali). As representatives of the divine and religious leaders in the major reli-

---

16. See Mireya Baltodano et al., eds. *Género y Religión* (San José, Costa Rica: Universidad Bíblica Latinoamericana, 2009). See Durre S. Ahmed, ed., *Gendering the Spirit: Women, Religion, and the Postcolonial Response* (New York: Palgrave, 2002); Elizabeth A. Castelli, ed. *Women, Gender and Religion: A Reader* (New York: Palgrave, 2001); Rebecca S. Chopp, *The Power to Speak: Feminism, Language, and God* (New York: Crossroad, 1989); and Darlene M. Juschka, ed., *Feminism in the Study of Religion: A Reader* (New York: Continuum, 2001).

17. I have been puzzled by the enthusiastic reception of gender analysis by feminist the*logians in Latin America at a time when a critique of gender analysis in favor of intersectional analysis emerged in the United States. However, this phenomenon becomes understandable if one takes into account that the intellectual conversation partner on gender in Latin America was liberation the*logy, which eschewed gender analysis, whereas the conversation partners of feminist the*logy in the U.S. and Europe were wo/men's and gender studies.

gions of the world, elite men have excluded wo/men from religious leadership, official teaching, and sacred ritual.

Because religious symbol systems are heavily gendered in masculine terms, they reinforce cultural gender roles and concepts and legitimize them as ordained by God or as the "order of creation." As Judith Plaskow has argued, Christian male theologians have formulated theological concepts in terms of their own cultural experience, insisting on male language relating to God and on a symbolic universe in which wo/men do not appear.[18] Similar observations can be made regarding other world religions.

Since the Industrial Revolution in Europe and America at the beginning of the nineteenth century, religion has been pushed out of the public realm and relegated to the private sphere of individualistic piety, charitable work, and the cultivation of home and family. Thus, religion has become culturally feminized while its leadership has remained predominantly male. Nevertheless, both religion and gender were crucial in shaping Western identity. For instance, as a "missionary religion," Christianity had the same function as the "White Lady." It was to "civilize the savages," who were understood as "untamed nature."

Hence, one must eschew a "woman in the Bible" or a woman's Bible approach. The intellectual tradition inaugurated in the nineteenth century by Elizabeth Cady Stanton's *Woman's Bible* focuses on the conviction that biblical texts about woman need to be interrupted rather than continued.[19] Such a focus on Woman, consciously or not, works with the essentialist notion of "woman" that is culturally elaborated in the Barbie-doll image of the "White Lady." This image of the ideal woman is propagated by the media not only in Western countries, but also around the globe. It must therefore be critically analyzed rather than taken up as an analytic lens.

Feminist scholars insist that religious texts and traditions must be reinterpreted so that wo/men and other "nonpersons" can achieve full citizenship in religion and society, gain full access to decision making powers, and learn how to live out radical equality in religious communities. We argue that differences of sex/gender, race, class, and ethnicity are socioculturally constructed and not willed by God, and therefore must be changed. God, who created people in the divine image, has called every individual differently. The Divine Wisdom is to be found in and among people who are created equal.

---

18. Judith Plaskow, *Sex, Sin, and Grace: Women's Experience and the Theologies of Niebuhr and Tillich* (Washington, D.C.: University Press of America, 1980).

19. See Elisabeth Schüssler Fiorenza, *Searching the Scriptures* (ed. Elisabeth Schüssler Fiorenza with Shelly Matthews; New York: Crossroad, 1997), for one attempt to do so.

Since the authority of the Bible as the "word of G*d" has been, and still is, used to inculcate biblical texts that demand subordination and submission to kyriarchal power, it is necessary to investigate how Scriptures are still used in support of domination and exploitation. The debates around wo/men's reproductive rights and same sex marriage call to mind the biblical texts and injunctions of subordination whose implications are realized and elaborated in contemporary societies.

If kyriarchal power and prejudice is the political context of biblical interpretation, feminist scholars cannot afford to engage in a purely apologetic or positivist reading of the Bible, nor to relegate a critical biblical interpretation to "bourgeois" scholarship addressing the question of the nonbeliever. Rather, feminist biblical interpretations and the*logies need to engage in a critical analysis that seeks to lay open the "politics of prejudice" inscribed in sacred Scriptures. In the last four decades, Christian, Jewish, Muslim, postbiblical, and Goddess feminists have engaged in discussions of prejudice, articulated theoretical structural analyses, and worked toward a feminist transformation of biblical religions. In so doing, we have underscored that in all three so-called Abrahamic religions, sacred Scriptures and traditions have been formulated and interpreted from the perspective of privileged men and therefore reflect neither the perspectives nor the experiences of wo/men, the poor, or enslaved peoples. Religious prohibitions and projections and pious practices have often served to legitimate the*logies and behaviors that marginalize wo/men and other persons categorized as "subhuman," silence them, exclude them, and exploit them. The feminist discussion on prejudice must therefore be solidly anchored in a multifaceted critical interreligious, postcolonial, and anti-racist feminist analysis.

If one does not consciously deconstruct the language of domination in which biblical texts remain caught up, one cannot but valorize and reinscribe such anti-wo/men language. In attempting to rescue holy Scripture as anti-imperial literature, defensive arguments tend to overlook that the language of kyriarchy and the ways in which violence encoded in holy Scriptures has shaped religious self-understanding and cultural ethos throughout the centuries, and still does so today.

Such scriptural language of domination, subordination, and control is not just historical language. Rather, as sacred Scripture, it is performative language that determines religious-biblical identity and praxis. This must be made conscious and critically deconstructed, since the language of "power over" encoded in Scripture has two reference points: Near Eastern and Roman empires as context and social locations of the Bible on the one hand, and contemporary forms of neocolonialist of antidemocratic discourses on the other.

Biblical studies can inspire individuals and groups to support the forces of economic and cultural global dehumanization, or they can abandon their kyriarchal tendencies and together envision and work for a feminist spiritual ethos of global justice. Our scholarship can either foster fundamentalism, exclusivism, and the exploitation of a totalitarian global monoculture, or we can advocate radical democratic spiritual values and visions that celebrate diversity, multiplicity, decision-making power, equality, justice, and well-being for all. Such a the*-ethical-political "either-or" choice does not reinscribe the dualisms created by structures of domination, but struggles to overcome and abolish them. It calls religious wo/men and biblical scholarship to take sides in the global struggles for greater justice, freedom, and the well-being of wo/men and of all of creation.

In conclusion: This volume tries to map the vast field of feminist biblical studies in the twentieth century, but it can do so only by pointing out areas of research that need further development. It seeks to contribute not only to our knowledge about the genealogy of feminist biblical studies in the twentieth century, but also to our imagination of what still needs to be done. It attempts to situate feminist biblical studies in the intersectional activism of wo/men's movements for change, rather than just in the domain of academy and church, synagogue or mosque. Such a social location requires that we develop more fully an interreligious and transnational scope. It remains to be seen whether feminist biblical studies can fruitfully sustain its "in-betweenness" in the years to come, or whether it will withdraw its intellectual energies either to the ivory towers of the academy or to the pastures of organized religions. As long as feminist biblical studies remain committed to social movements for change, they will be able to dismantle the "master's kyriocentric house" in order to imagine and create a different feminist space of biblical interpretation and meaning making.

Part 1
Charting Feminist Biblical Studies
around the Globe

Movement and Emerging Scholarship: Feminist Biblical Scholarship in the 1970s in the United States

Judith Plaskow
Manhattan College

The history of feminist biblical scholarship in the 1970s in the United States cannot be separated from the larger history of the feminist movement. Its emergence was tied to, and was one expression of, the new consciousness that erupted in the late 1960s and early 1970s as women began to question their received roles in family, society, politics, and religion. Meeting in small consciousness-raising groups that sprang up across the country, women began to explore and analyze aspects of their lives that they had previously taken for granted. As they began to make connections between their individual experiences and the larger institutional structures that shaped and constrained them, feminists began to name and challenge the myriad structures that enforced gender-role socialization and perpetuated male dominance. Biology was not destiny; women's subordination was not inevitable. It was a product of social processes that could be examined and understood and therefore resisted and changed. It is difficult to capture the feelings of excitement, energy, celebration, rage, terror, and deep hopefulness that accompanied these insights. Social arrangements that had been in place for millennia were suddenly being questioned. Nothing was exempt from critical inquiry; everything was possible.[1]

---

1. There is ample literature on Second Wave Feminism. For an account in the midst of it, see Judith Hole and Ellen Levine, *Rebirth of Feminism* (New York: Quadrangle, 1971). For an account at a distance, see Gail Collins, *When Everything Changed: The Amazing Journey of American Women from 1960 to the Present* (New York: Little, Brown, 2009).

1. The First Calls for Change

Given the importance of religious institutions, texts, and symbol systems in creating and justifying male dominance, it was impossible that religion not be incorporated into this wide-ranging critique of cultural ideologies and social structures. While for generations women had seemingly accepted their subordination in church and synagogue as simply given, in the course of the 1960s they were increasingly aware of and angry at their marginalization. Two books published at the end of the decade capture the rage and energy of women in the academy and religious institutions. Mary Daly's *The Church and the Second Sex,* published in 1968, offered a compelling indictment of the Catholic Church and a powerful call for change. Beginning with the Bible and moving through the modern period, Daly laid out what she called the "record of contradictions" in the church's attitudes toward women, piling up evidence for ways in which it had inflicted harm. Though Daly later dismissed the book as an artifact of a bygone era, it anticipated some of her later unsparing language, demanding that the church "exorcise" the myth of the "eternal feminine" and condemning the "demonic distortions" it had caused to human relationships and to women's capacity for self-actualization.[2] Sarah Bentley Doely's collection *Women's Liberation and the Church,* published in 1970, brought together Protestant and Catholic authors in order to provide "a written testament and a witness by women to their struggles to be truly free in the Christian church today." Chapter after chapter described the subordination of women in Christian practice and theology and spoke "an unequivocal 'No' to [current] values, norms and structures of the church."[3] Perhaps the best clue to the mood of the period is Peggy Way's concluding essay in the collection, "An Authority of Possibility for Women in the Church." The authority for her ministry, Way argued, is not rooted in Scriptures, church history, or denominational structures but in her own religious experience as it intersects with these realities.[4] These two works, like most that followed in the 1970s, shared the limitations of much early feminist analysis in that they were authored almost entirely by white women, homogenized women's experiences, and focused on gender subordination to the exclusion of race, class, sexuality, and other axes of

---

2. Mary Daly, *The Church and the Second Sex, with a New Feminist Postchristian Introduction* (New York: Harper & Row, 1975), 15, 166–78.

3. Sarah Bentley Doely, "Introduction," in *Women's Liberation and the Church: The New Demand for Freedom in the Life of the Christian Church* (ed. Sarah Bentley Doely; New York: Association, 1970), 11–12.

4. Peggy Way, "Authority of Possibility for Women in the Church," in Doely, *Women's Liberation and the Church,* 91.

oppression. Yet their pioneering feminist insights not only paved the way for later, more complex studies but helped bring about enormous changes in both religious institutions and the academic study of religion.

2. THE EMERGENCE OF FEMINIST STUDIES IN RELIGION

The 1970s was a pivotal decade. In June of 1971, the Alverno Research Center on Women at Alverno College in Milwaukee, Wisconsin, sponsored a two-week conference of women theologians that brought together twenty-two theologians and scholars of religion from various denominations and academic institutions to explore the spiritual and religious experiences of women. Not only was this a first opportunity for feminists who had been working in isolation to share and debate emerging ideas with colleagues, but the conference became the seedbed for the single most important development in the emergence of feminist studies in religion.[5] In the middle of their time together, the participants decided that women in religious studies needed a women's caucus like those being established in other disciplines. Carol P. Christ phoned Harry Buck, then executive director of the American Academy of Religion, and asked him for space on the annual meeting program in 1971.

The women who gathered in Atlanta at the joint meeting of the American Academy of Religion and Society of Biblical Literature in November of 1971 founded both a caucus to take up political and professional issues of concern to women in the academy and a program unit—the Working Group on Women and Religion—to share emerging research. Carol P. Christ (for the AAR) and Elisabeth Schüssler Fiorenza (for the SBL) became co-chairs of the women's caucus, and Mary Daly served as first chair of the working group. The new caucus nominated Christine Downing to run against the single male candidate for AAR president and succeeded in electing her the first woman president of the AAR. Rita Gross captures the significance of these events:

> Before the meeting, isolated, relatively young and unestablished scholars struggled to define what it meant to study women and religion and to demonstrate why it was so important to do so. After the meeting, a strong network of like-minded individuals had been established, and we had begun to make our presence and our agenda known to the AAR and the SBL.[6]

From there on, connections, ideas, and events built rapidly. In June of 1972, a second conference on "Women Exploring Theology," this one sponsored

---

5. Rita Gross, *Feminism and Religion: An Introduction* (Boston: Beacon, 1996), 46–47.
6. Ibid., 47.

by Church Women United, met at Grailville in Loveland, Ohio. Sixty-three women, some from academia, many engaged in ministry, met for a week of work groups, caucuses, liturgies, and large-group experiences. For many of the women present, the opportunity to explore with other women issues of deep personal and professional concern was a life-changing experience. A list of words and phrases that the community generated at one of its last large-group sessions conveys both the impact of the week and the energy and excitement of that historical moment:

> New images/language, commitment … both/and, Yeah/Yeah … dance, spon-taneity, freedom, wholeness, experience as base, up from under … authority from within, transition: confusion frustration, validating our own power, renewal, experimentation … God created my ass as well as my head … ground/ energizing/participating/creating … dreaming dreams, wheeeeeeuuuu whooooshshshshsh (sounds of the spirit) … co-creators of reality.…[7]

November 1972 saw the first sessions of the Working Group on Women and Religion at the annual meeting of the AAR/SBL. Again, it is difficult to capture the intensity of those sessions, the sense on the part of those who packed into meeting rooms that were too small to hold the eager participants that some-thing of great moment was happening, that the field of religious studies would never be the same. Mary Daly delivered the outline of what was to become *Beyond God the Father,* while others addressed such diverse topics as abortion, phallic worship, an image of women in old Buddhist literature, and the ethical implications of women's liberation.[8] The chairs of the working group invited papers from a wide range of areas within religious studies because they took it as their responsibility to transform the entire field. Indeed, in 1974 the work-ing group successfully petitioned the AAR Program Committee for section status—sections were more established program units with more sessions on the program—on the grounds that it had to address the entire subject matter of the AAR. In 1975, the opening panel of the new Women and Religion sec-tion showcased the methodologies that had emerged in four years of work and called for a paradigm shift from an androcentric model of humanity in which only men represent the human to a model in which women and men

---

7. "Brainstorm: The Meaning of the Grailville Conference," in "Women Exploring Theology at Grailville" (packet put together after the event by Church Women United, 1972).

8. See Judith Plaskow and Joan Arnold Romero, eds., *Women and Religion* (rev. ed.; Missoula, Mont.: Working Group on Women and Religion and Scholars Press, 1974).

"are coequally modes of the human, and, therefore, coequally subjects of ... research."[9]

The same period saw an eruption of activity at the grassroots level, manifest in conferences and events and the formation of local groups in both the academy and many religious bodies. In February of 1973, over four hundred women gathered at the McAlpin Hotel in New York City for a conference on The Role of Women in Jewish Life. Organized by the North American Jewish Students' Network, and drawing women from across the Jewish religious spectrum, the conference featured many speakers who were to become prominent names in Jewish feminism. A year later, Network organized a second conference, this time for both women and men. Out of the 1974 conference, the short-lived national Jewish Feminist Organization was born, which demanded "nothing less than the full, direct, and equal participation at all levels of Jewish life—communal, religious, educational, and political." Although the JFO quickly foundered, the two conferences seeded many grassroots initiatives and led to the formation of local study and spirituality groups that met for years.

3. Where Is the Bible?

Attention to the Bible played a definite role in these early developments, but only as one issue among others. Indeed, it is interesting to note some of the places where discussion of the Bible was absent or subordinated to other concerns. In the first feminist articles of Rosemary Radford Ruether, which circulated widely in this period and were avidly discussed, biblical religion is but a moment in a sweeping history of human consciousness and of the growing alienation of the male psyche from body and nature.[10] Peggy Way's essay "An Authority of Possibility for Women in the Church," noted above, dealt with Scripture only to deny its authority.[11] The Alverno College Archive lists no paper on the Bible coming out of the 1971 Conference of Women Theologians, perhaps because the category of "women's experience" so strongly

---

9. Rita Gross, ed., *Beyond Androcentrism: New Essays on Women and Religion* (Missoula, Mont.: Scholars Press for the American Academy of Religion, 1977), 1.

10. See Rosemary Radford Ruether, "Mother Earth and the Megamachine," *Christianity and Crisis* 31 (December 13, 1971): 267–72. In her earlier articles ("The Becoming of Women in Church and Society," *Cross Currents* 17 [fall 1967]: 418–26; and "Women's Liberation in Historical and Theological Perspective," in Doely, *Women's Liberation and the Church*, 26–36), the Bible is scarcely mentioned.

11. Way, "An Authority of Possibility," 78–82.

shaped its agenda.[12] The Bible received somewhat more attention at Grailville in 1972, where "Bible and Theology" was one of five major working groups. That group split into two smaller groups, however, one actually focusing on the Bible and the other exploring consciousness-raising as a religious experience. Significantly, it was the latter group that produced the more substantial reports included in the packet of materials from the conference, though when its members sought to capture the essence of the consciousness-raising experience they chose as their vehicle a midrash on the creation narrative.[13]

Neither the Jewish women's conference in 1973 nor the National Conference on Jewish Women and Men in 1974 had a single session on the Bible. For Jewish women, rabbinic law and interpretation are much more important than the Hebrew Bible in shaping women's roles and status, so feminist calls for change in Jewish religious practice focused largely on rabbinic teaching. The earliest collection of articles by Jewish women, a special issue of *Response* magazine published in 1973, included only one essay on the Bible, Mary Gendler's "The Vindication of Vashti."[14] Elizabeth Koltun's anthology *The Jewish Woman: New Perspectives*, which included papers from both the *Response* issue and the two national conferences, reprinted the Gendler article alongside (Protestant) Phyllis Trible's "Depatriarchalizing in Biblical Interpretation."[15] The fact that there was virtually nothing on the Bible written by Jewish women until the 1980s and 1990s testifies to the way that feminist scholars gravitated to those issues that seemed to hold the most immediate promise of bringing about religious change.

4. The Beginnings of Feminist Biblical Studies

That said, however, both examination of the Bible as a significant cultural force contributing to women's subordination and reinterpretations of the Bible meant to challenge sexist readings were certainly part of feminist discussion early on. Two articles from the early 1970s that were particularly influential and widely circulated and reprinted were Leonard Swidler's "Jesus Was a Feminist" and Phyllis Trible's "Depatriarchalizing in Biblical Interpretation."

---

12. See http://depts.alverno.edu/archives/archome/rcwfindingaid.html.

13. See "Pentecost as a Paradygm [*sic*] for Women's Liberation"; "Bible/Theology Group"; and "The Coming of Lilith: Toward a Feminist Theology," in "Women Exploring Theology at Grailville."

14. Mary Gendler, "The Vindication of Vashti," *Response* 18 (Summer 1973): 154–60. Also published as *The Jewish Woman* (ed. Liz Koltun; Waltham, Mass.: Jewish Educational Ventures, 1973).

15. Elizabeth Koltun, *The Jewish Woman: New Perspectives* (New York: Schocken, 1976).

Swidler's piece, published in *Catholic World* in 1971, argued that Jesus was in favor of and promoted the equality of women and men. The negative evidence for this assertion, Swidler argued, is that there is no recorded saying or action of Jesus that depicts him as treating women as inferior persons. But this negative evidence is raised "exponentially in its significance" when contrasted with the lowly position of Jewish women in Palestine in the first century. Swidler was entirely explicit in linking his claim that "Jesus vigorously promoted the dignity and equality of women in the midst of a very male-dominated society" with an agenda for change in the church. His article began by defining Jesus as "the historical person who lived in Palestine ... whom Christians traditionally acknowledge as Lord and Savior, and whom they should 'imitate' as much as possible," and it ended with the words, "Jesus was a feminist and a very radical one. Can his followers attempt to be anything less...?"[16]

Swidler handed Christian feminists a very powerful tool for challenging sexism in Christian institutions, but it was one that came with a shadow side. As Judith Plaskow pointed out in an article written toward the end of the decade, the "Jesus was a feminist" argument recapitulated a historic anti-Jewish pattern whereby Christians lay at the feet of Judaism characteristics that they sought to deny in themselves. The dramatic contrasts that Swidler drew between Jesus and Judaism rested on a number of fallacies: they used a sixth-century text—the Talmud—as evidence for first-century Palestinian Judaism; they treated rabbinic Judaism as monolithic; they compared the words and actions of an itinerant preacher with laws and sayings formulated in rabbinic academies; and they ignored the fact that Jesus was a Jew and that his behavior and teachings are themselves evidence for the status of women in first-century Judaism.[17] Despite its problematic assumptions, the "Jesus was a feminist" theme became very popular—so popular, in fact, that even the Vatican nodded to it when, in 1976, it reiterated its opposition to the ordination of women.[18] The theme was picked up and expanded on by many authors: by Rachel Conrad Wahlberg in *Jesus according to a Woman*, published in 1975, and by the evangelical feminists Letha Scanzoni and Nancy Hardesty in *All We're Meant to Be*, published in 1974, and Virginia Mollenkott in *Women, Men, and the Bible*, published in 1977.[19] All these writers, and the many others

---

16. Leonard Swidler, "Jesus Was a Feminist," *Catholic World* (January 1971): 177–83; quotations on 178, 177, and 183.

17. Judith Plaskow, "Christian Feminism and Anti-Judaism," *Cross Currents* 33 (fall 1978): 306–9.

18. Sacred Congregation for the Doctrine of the Faith, "Declaration on the Question of the Ordination of Women to the Ministerial Priesthood," 2:10–12.

19. Rachel Conrad Wahlberg, *Jesus according to a Woman* (New York: Paulist, 1975);

who popularized the theme in articles and classes, clearly intended that it serve the cause of greater equality for women in church and society.

By way of contrast, Phyllis Trible's article on depatriarchalizing first appeared not in a popular periodical but in the prestigious *Journal of the American Academy of Religion* in 1973. Yet Trible likewise explicitly linked her attempt to reinterpret the Hebrew Bible with the movement for women's liberation. She acknowledged that patriarchal attitudes and laws were central to scripture but went on to say, "If these views are all which can be said or what primarily must be said, then I am of all women most miserable." But Trible did not find herself forced to choose between the God of the fathers and the God of sisterhood, because the more she participated in the movement, "the more she [discovered her] freedom through the appropriation of biblical symbols."[20] Trible's purpose in "Depatriarchalizing in Biblical Interpretation" was to explore biblical themes that in her view functioned as salvific for both women and men. Probably the best known part of the essay is her detailed exegesis of Gen 2–3, which argued that women were created as helpers equal to men in Gen 2 and that subordination enters into the narrative only as a punishment for sin in Gen 3. But Trible also examined broader motifs that she believed pointed beyond sexism, including the Bible's use of female imagery for God and the joyous mutuality of the male and female lovers in the Song of Songs.[21] She was to expand on all these themes in *God and the Rhetoric of Sexuality*, which appeared at the end of the decade.

The publication of Trible's article in 1973 coincided with early discussions of women and the Bible taking place within the American Academy of Religion. The first-year offerings of the Working Group on Women and Religion included a paper by Winsome Munro on "Patriarchy and Charismatic Community in 'Paul.'"[22] Though it was not much referenced in subsequent discussions, the paper can be read as the opening salvo in the Paul wars, in which various scholars argued about whether Paul was a friend or foe of women's liberation. In its second year, the working group devoted an entire session to *The Woman's Bible*, bringing to its audience an important piece of women's history that had been all but forgotten. While the papers

---

Letha Scanzoni and Nancy Hardesty, *All We're Meant to Be: A Biblical Approach to Women's Liberation* (Waco, Tex.: Word, 1974); and Virginia Mollenkott, *Women, Men, and the Bible* (Nashville: Abingdon, 1977).

20. Phyllis Trible, "Depatriarchalizing in Biblical Interpretation," *JAAR* 41 (March 1973): 31.

21. Ibid, 30–48.

22. Winsome Munro, "Patriarchy and Charismatic Community in 'Paul,'" in Plaskow and Romero, *Women and Religion*, 189–98.

focused largely on the nineteenth-century context and presuppositions of *The Woman's Bible*'s authors, they also made clear the importance of biblical reinterpretation to the project of women's emancipation.[23] The same year, 1973, the AAR/SBL held a plenary session on "Women and the Study of the New Testament" at which Robin Scroggs argued that "far from being a chauvinist," Paul is "the only certain and consistent spokesman for the liberation and equality of women in the New Testament," and Elaine Pagels took issue with a number of Scroggs's claims.[24]

Mary Daly's *Beyond God the Father*, which also appeared in 1973 and which was a watershed volume in the emerging field of feminist studies in religion, mocked all these developments in feminist biblical interpretation. She chided Scroggs for being "more concerned with justifying an author long dead … than with the deep injustice … that is being perpetrated by religion." She joked about the probable length of a depatriarchalized Bible, saying, "Perhaps there would be enough salvageable material to comprise an interesting pamphlet." And she labeled one of the subheads in her book "Jesus Was a Feminist, But So What?" Fine, great, she said, if Jesus was a feminist, "[b]ut even if he wasn't, *I am*." Again, expressing the mood of the period, she argued that women need to give priority to their own experience rather than looking to the past for justification.[25]

Despite Daly's critique, however, feminist biblical studies was quickly becoming an established part of feminist work. The year 1974 saw the publication of Rosemary Ruether's important collection of scholarly essays, *Religion and Sexism,* which explored the role of religion in "shaping the traditional cultural images that have degraded and suppressed women."[26] Phyllis Bird's long and careful essay in the volume, "Images of Women in the Old Testament," became an instant classic. Arguing that "the Old Testament is a collection of writings by males from a society dominated by males" and portraying a man's world, Bird examined the diverse and sometimes conflicting images of women in biblical law, proverbs, and historical writings. She ended rather

---

23. The papers are available in section 3 of Judith Plaskow Goldenberg and Joan Arnold Romero, eds., *Women and Religion: 1973 Proceedings* (Tallahassee, Fla.: American Academy of Religion, 1973).

24. Robin Scroggs, "Paul and the Eschatological Woman," *JAAR* 40 (1972): 283–303, here 283; and Scroggs, "Paul and the Eschatological Woman: Revisited," *JAAR* 42 (1974): 532–37. Elaine Pagels, "Paul and Women: A Response to Recent Discussion," appears in the latter issue, 538–49.

25. Mary Daly, *Beyond God the Father: Toward a Philosophy of Women's Liberation* (Boston: Beacon, 1973), 5, 206 n. 5, 73.

26. Rosemary Radford Ruether, ed., *Religion and Sexism: Images of Women in the Jewish and Christian Traditions* (New York: Simon & Schuster, 1974), 9.

than began her analysis with the creation narratives in order to place them in the larger context of the multitude of Old Testament references to women.[27] Connie Parvey's essay in the same volume, "The Theology and Leadership of Women in the New Testament," focused on the attitudes of the primitive church toward women as reflected in the writings of the New Testament. Contributing her bit both to the Paul wars and to the depiction of Judaism as Christianity's negative foil, Parvey contended that, although Paul was a man of his time, his understanding of the role of women and men in Christ was without precedent in the context of first-century Judaism.[28] The session on methodology in the Women and Religion Section in 1975 further solidified the place of the Bible in feminist scholarship by including biblical studies among the disciplinary perspectives discussed. Mary Wakeman's paper "Biblical Prophecy and Modern Feminism" argued for an analogy between "the prophetic movement in biblical times and the women's movement in our own time," claiming that the prophetic model of cultural change had particular relevance for women's efforts at cultural transformation.[29]

5. The Role of the Bible in Struggles for Ordination

While the academy was the main site for the emergence of feminist scholarship in religion and feminist biblical scholarship in particular, struggles for the ordination of women were an important second locus for the development of feminist biblical studies. By the end of the 1960s, most mainstream Protestant denominations in the United States had admitted women to full ordination. In the early 1970s, however, as women were questioning their received roles in church and society and overturning barriers to full participation in many professions, they still were not ordained to the priesthood in the Episcopal or Roman Catholic churches. Since most opponents of ordination grounded their resistance in the Bible, its proponents likewise needed to turn to the Bible in order to rebut conservative arguments. Fortunately, women were entering seminaries in record numbers during this period, and so there were theologically trained women ready to take up the cudgel.

Krister Stendahl's pamphlet *The Bible and the Role of Women,* which was published in 1958 in the context of a contentious debate over the ordination

---

27. Phyllis Bird, "Images of Women in the Old Testament," in Ruether, *Religion and Sexism*, 42–88.

28. Connie Parvey "The Theology and Leadership of Women in the New Testament," in Ruether, *Religion and Sexism*, esp. 123–35.

29. Mary Wakeman, "Biblical Prophecy and Modern Feminism," in Gross, *Beyond Androcentrism*, 67–86, here 67.

of women as priests in the Church of Sweden and translated into English in 1966, was very influential in the ordination discussion. Stendahl argued that the New Testament is completely uninterested in the question of women's ministry as a problem demanding special attention. Therefore, it makes no sense for people who accept the social emancipation of women to argue for their exclusion from the priesthood on biblical grounds.[30] His claim that women's subordination to men is the *only* biblical argument against ordination was used effectively by Emily Hewitt and Suzanne Hiatt at the height of the Episcopal debate over ordination. Part of the "Philadelphia 11" who in 1974 broke the fifty-year deadlock over ordination to the Episcopal priesthood by getting themselves irregularly ordained, Hewitt and Hiatt wrote *Women Priests: Yes or No?* in 1973 in an attempt to examine and demolish the attitudes and arguments standing in the way of ordination. Two chapters on the Bible at the center of the book examined key biblical passages often used to oppose ordination and argued for the importance of Gal 3:28 ("in Christ … there is neither male nor female") to an understanding of the central New Testament message.[31]

Mounting pressure toward the ordination of women in the Episcopal Church also helped to ignite the Roman Catholic struggle. In 1975, a group of Catholic laywomen organized what they thought would be a small conference of likeminded people to discuss the ordination of women into a renewed priesthood. To their astonishment, more than twelve hundred people showed up, and another five hundred had to be turned away. When in 1976 the Vatican issued its "Declaration on the Question of the Admission of Women to the Ministerial Priesthood," in which it reiterated its longtime opposition to the ordination of women, proponents of ordination were galvanized rather than silenced.[32] One almost immediate response to the Declaration was the publication of *Women Priests: A Catholic Commentary on the Vatican Declaration*, a collection of articles assembled by Leonard and Arlene Swidler that critically examined the Declaration's central arguments. More than a quarter

---

30. Krister Stendahl, *The Bible and the Role of Women* (Philadelphia: Fortress, 1966), ch. 3.

31. Emily C. Hewitt and Suzanne R. Hiatt, *Women Priests: Yes or No?* (New York: Seabury, 1973), chs. 5 and 6.

32. Maureen Fiedler and Dolly Pomerleau, "The Women's Ordination Movement in the Roman Catholic Church," in *Encyclopedia of Women and Religion in North America* (ed. Rosemary Radford Ruether et al.; 3 vols.; Bloomington: Indiana University Press, 2006), 2:952–53; Elisabeth Schüssler Fiorenza, *Discipleship of Equals: A Critical Feminist Ekklesialogy of Liberation* (New York: Crossroad, 1993), 80.

of the essays focused on the New Testament, and their authors represented a Who's Who? of emerging Catholic feminist biblical scholars.[33]

6. Consolidation

By the middle of the 1970s, then, there was a small but significant body of feminist work on the Bible that clearly defined itself as grounded in the struggle for women's dignity and equality in society and in the church. In 1976, Letty Russell published *The Liberating Word*, the first collection of feminist essays devoted exclusively to the Bible. Both the foreword and Russell's introduction to the volume set it in the context of the changing consciousness of women and men and its implications for reading and interpreting Scripture. Four chapters and a study guide offered resources for study and action to the many congregations and denominations working to make the language of Bible study and worship more inclusive of all participants. Chapters by Sharon Ringe, Elisabeth Schüssler Fiorenza, and Joanna Dewey laid out different models of feminist biblical interpretation, while a final essay by Letty Russell focused on inclusive language, arguing for Bible translations that "reflect the gospel mandate of full equality for all human beings."[34] The collection was preparation and provided important theoretical grounding for *An Inclusive Language Lectionary*, the first volume of which appeared in 1980.

Elisabeth Schüssler Fiorenza's contribution to *The Liberating Word* was just one of several ground-breaking essays that she published in the second half of the 1970s. Her writings in this period laid the foundations for *In Memory of Her* (1983) by analyzing and critiquing the androcentric model that had guided most New Testament interpretation, describing an alternative feminist model, and sketching some of the fruits of that model for a new understanding of Christian origins. A number of assumptions that were to remain central to her work were spelled out in these essays: the idea that *all* scholarship on early Christian history is determined by contemporary questions and interests; the notion that singling out "the place of women" in the Bible as a special problem projects contemporary attitudes back onto the New Testament; the insistence that feminist scholars must be willing to criticize the androcentric bias of the New Testament itself, not just of its interpreters; and the conviction that an egalitarian interpretive model can yield a richer and more nuanced picture of women's participation in the early Christian movement. "Although

---

33. Leonard Swidler and Arlene Swidler, eds., *Women Priests: A Catholic Commentary on the Vatican Declaration* (New York: Paulist, 1977).

34. Letty Russell, ed., *The Liberating Word: A Guide to Nonsexist Interpretation of the Bible* (Philadelphia: Westminster, 1976), 85.

studies of women's roles in early Christianity generally conclude that women were marginal figures in the early Christian movement," she argued, in fact "leadership roles were diversified and based on actual function and service."[35]

Three works that appeared toward the end of the decade further solidified the place of biblical studies in feminist scholarship in religion. In 1978, Phyllis Trible published the first full-length feminist scholarly work on the Bible, *God and the Rhetoric of Sexuality*. The book drew on and greatly elaborated themes she had first outlined in her essay "Depatriarchalizing in Biblical Interpretation." Starting from the view that the Bible is "a literary creation with an interlocking structure of words and motifs," Trible explored a number of "clues in [the] text" that point to the image of God as male and female.[36] A very long middle chapter on the creation narrative in Gen 2–3 was preceded by chapters on the metaphor of womb and on female imagery for God and followed by chapters on the Song of Songs and the book of Ruth, both books in which women are of central importance. Though this was clearly a scholarly book with ample notes and other academic apparatus, Trible was not at all shy about rooting her project in a larger feminist critique of culture. Many current discussions of the Bible engage the world as well as communities of faith, she said. Her angle of vision was "a critique of culture in light of misogyny," an issue that intersects with many other liberation struggles.[37]

In 1979, Rosemary Radford Ruether and Eleanor McLaughlin published a companion volume to *Religion and Sexism*, *Women of Spirit: Female Leadership in the Jewish and Christian Traditions*. While *Religion and Sexism* had focused on important male *images* of women in Judaism and Christianity, *Women of Spirit* was concerned with the real-life roles of women as leaders, teachers, and transmitters of religious tradition. The book included a substantial chapter on the Bible written by Elisabeth Schüssler Fiorenza, who used the New Testament as well as other early Christian documents to sketch the roles of women as founders and leaders of congregations, missionaries, prophets,

---

35. Elisabeth Schüssler Fiorenza, "Word, Spirit, and Power: Women in Early Christian Communities," in *Women of Spirit: Female Leadership in the Jewish and Christian Traditions* (ed. Rosemary Radford Ruether and Eleanor McLaughlin; New York: Simon & Schuster, 1979), 30–70, here 30. See also her "Women in the Pre-Pauline and Pauline Churches," *USQR* 33 (1978): 153–66; " 'You Are Not to Be Called Father': Early Christian History in a Feminist Perspective," *Cross Currents* 29 (fall 1978): 301–23; "The Study of Women in Early Christianity: Some Methodological Considerations," in *Critical History and Biblical Faith: New Testament Perspectives* (ed. Thomas J. Ryan; Villanova, Penn.: College Theology Society, 1979), 30–58.

36. Phyllis Trible, *God and the Rhetoric of Sexuality* (Philadelphia: Fortress, 1978), 8, 23.

37. Ibid., 7.

teachers, and apostles.[38] The other important anthology that appeared in 1979 was *Womanspirit Rising*, a feminist reader that brought together and discussed diverse articles in the new and exciting field of feminist studies in religion. In a section entitled "The Past: Does It Hold a Future for Women?" editors Carol P. Christ and Judith Plaskow included two essays on the Bible: one, the section on Genesis from Trible's work on depatriarchalizing, and the other an essay by Elisabeth Schüssler Fiorenza that discussed the evidence for women's multiple roles in the early Christian movement.[39]

Thus, the 1970s saw the emergence of feminist work on the Bible that was explicitly grounded in and supportive of the revolution in women's self-understandings and social roles. As feminists brought new questions to biblical texts, they began both to uncover the lineaments of women's "herstory" buried within androcentric frameworks and to develop exegetical and hermeneutical tools for understanding and evaluating the significance of biblical perspectives on women. The foundations were laid for the flowering of feminist biblical scholarship in the 1980s and 1990s that would see the entry of women of color, out lesbians, and Jewish women into an increasingly rich and multifaceted conversation.

---

38. See n. 35.

39. Phyllis Trible, "Eve and Adam: Genesis 2–3 Reread," in *Womanspirit Rising: A Feminist Reader in Religion* (ed. Carol P. Christ and Judith Plaskow; New York: Harper & Row, 1979), 74–83; Elisabeth Schüssler Fiorenza, "Women in the Early Christian Movement," in Christ and Plaskow, *Womanspirit Rising*, 84–92.

Feminist Biblical Studies in Latin America and the Caribbean

Elsa Tamez
Professor Emerita of the Latin American Biblical University

Today it is possible to find much work in feminist biblical studies in Latin America and the Caribbean, particularly in articles.[1] *La Revista de Interpretación Bíblica Latinoamericana* (*RIBLA*) contains a surprising number of feminist authors. This was not so in the 1980s, when women were timidly beginning to write. Only two decades ago, in the beginning of the 1990s, did the contributions of feminist biblical scholars begin to grow. The objective of this article is to provide an understanding of these contributions, their historical background, exegesis, hermeneutics, focuses, methods, diversity, levels, and obstacles. I privilege the journal *RIBLA* as a source, since it is the most representative, but I do not intend to leave aside other sources and books where feminist biblical scholars have also made contributions.

1. The Beginnings

The feminist biblical-theological movement in Latin America began in the context of revolutions and popular struggles against dictators and limited democracies. At the end of the 1970s and the beginning of the 1980s, shortly after the emergence of liberation theology, women who were studying the Bible and theology began to speak as women who were conscious of being oppressed because of their gender as well as their class. It was at this time that women began to understand themselves as *subjects* of theological work and theology and not just as a topic to be studied.[2] This was a milestone in Latin

---

1. The term *feminist* used here is meant as an ample concept that includes all women who fight against all types of oppression against women and is concerned with their resistance, struggle, and search for liberation.

2. See Elsa Tamez, "La mujer como sujeto de producción teológica," presented at one

American theological studies, because liberation theologians already focused on the economically poor as a starting point of their theology. The few women theologians who were doing liberation theology at this moment very quickly expanded this focus in biblical and theological thought when they began to speak about "the option for women" who were doubly oppressed because of their class and their gender.[3] A little later, in the mid-1980s, this focus was extended to include ethnicity and race.

We need to be clear, however, that these theologians and biblical scholars were not pioneers in the struggle for the rights of women in the church and society; rather, they were late in joining the women's movement. Since the mid-1980s, however, there have been groups of Christian women, Catholic and Protestant, in various countries of the continent who promote the significant participation of women in church and society.[4] These women are also motivated by the secular feminist movements. Unfortunately, there has not been a structured relationship between feminist movements and the organizations of women theologians. In the beginning, this rift was due to ideologization. Women theologians were wary of the intervention of feminist imperialists in Latin America, and feminists were wary of a Christian orientation that subjugated women. This attitude was a great loss for both groups because, on the one hand, the feminist movement could have contributed important theories to the theologians; the theologians, on the other hand, could have helped them understand the religiosity of the majority of women. Today this structural link is still lacking, despite the existence of relationships at an individual level between some feminist theologians and some women from secular feminist movements.

In the 1980s, the term *feminist* was avoided because of prejudices and stigmas from patriarchal society. Women in theology spoke of themselves as biblical scholars of "the oppressed woman," of "women's theology," or of

---

of the first meetings of women theologians, in Mexico in October of 1979, published in the journal *Servir* 88/89 (1980): 461–78.

3. Ivone Gebara, Maria Clara Bingemer, and Ana María Tepedino are three well-known Brazilian women theologians in the field of systematic theology. María José Rosado Nuñes, a sociologist of religion, helped the women with feminist theories, especially on gender. Later, at the beginning of the 1990s, María Pilar Aquino, a theologian who now lives in the U.S.A., made a significant contribution collecting and systematizing the contributions of many women. See *Our Cry for Life: Feminist Theology from Latin America* (Maryknoll, N.Y.: Orbis, 1993; Spanish title: *Clamor por la vida: Teologia latinoamericana desde la perspectiva de la mujer*, 1992). It is worth mentioning here that Rev. Ofelia Ortega from Cuba promoted the theological education of many women from her position at the World Council of Churches.

4. For example: "Mujeres para el diálogo" in Mexico and "Talita Kumi" in Peru.

theology "from a woman's point of view." The term *feminist* was consciously adopted only in the beginning of the 1990s, although this term is rejected even today in many church circles and in the society at large. The term *mujerista*, proposed by Ada María Isasi-Diaz and used by Latinas in the United States, has never been used and is unknown within the women's biblical movement in Latin America and the Caribbean.

2. Living Contexts as Unavoidable Frameworks

The biblical scholarship of Latin American and Caribbean feminists is distinctive because the scholars live on a continent pervaded by poverty and violence. Feminists dream of another society where women are not beaten, raped, or assassinated and where mothers do not need to search for the bones of their daughters or sons assassinated by war, narco-traffic, corruption, delinquency, or the effects of global warming that is wreaking havoc on all the earth. This reality explains why Elisabeth Schüssler Fiorenza's term, *kyriarchy*, fell on fertile ground in this region. Here it is impossible to do feminist theology without considering other oppressions such as class, race, and ethnicity.

It is possible to mark the beginning of feminist biblical studies in the Caribbean and in Meso- and South America in large strokes. The stages that have been experienced here include: dictators, external debt, structural adjustments promoted by neoliberalism, the exclusion of women, migratory movements provoked by the free market, and the devastation of natural resources. Upon being confronted with these realities, women have reacted in distinctive ways. Especially with the crisis in paradigms in the last two decades, there has been a rejection of macrostructural frameworks in order to allow for everyday stories in which women's bodies find themselves confronted with these huge realities to be foregrounded. Resistance is a priority, as are the struggles of women to survive and to transform their own situations, small or large.[5] Since then, feminist biblical work has been tied to these living experiences and has privileged everyday relationships where the stakes are life and death.

---

5. In an article about hermeneutics, I describe the socioeconomic and political stages and how women interpret texts in light of these realities. See Elsa Tamez, "Hermenéutica Feminista en América Latina y el Caribe: Una mirada retrospectiva," in *Religión y género* (vol. 3 of *Enciclopedia Iberoamericana de religiones*; ed. Sylvia Marcos; Madrid: Trotta, 2004), 43–66.

2.1. DIVERSITY IN BIBLICAL APPROACHES AND ACADEMIC LEVELS

In the 1980s, polarized and ideologized by the Cold War, there was a group of women biblical scholars who worked together and resisted any influence from the so-called First World. This situation changed with the fall of the Berlin Wall. Women were moving on and diversifying, being receptive to new paradigms, and many were distancing themselves from liberation theology, whose leadership was dominated by men. Various currents have since arisen within the feminist biblical movement, such as African-descendant feminists who take up racism and blackness as fundamental categories in their analysis of the biblical text; ecofeminists who propose another way to approach reality by breaking with the occidental epistemology; and women who are more interested in the challenges of the feminization of poverty aggravated by the globalization of the free market.[6]

However, within all of these currents the preoccupation with women living in poverty predominates. At the same time, we see a fundamental interest in dealing with daily life and the corporal life of women as the privileged framework of reference in biblical analysis. The question of reproductive rights and abortion is a delicate theme not only in the churches but also in society as a whole. With the exception of the Brazilian theologian Ivone Gevara,[7] feminist theologians are just beginning to touch this issue explicitly in this last decade.[8]

The scarcity of universities that offer a doctorate in biblical-theological studies means that the number of women with a doctorate is small. In fact, when feminist theology started at the end of the 1970s, there was only one woman, an Argentinian, with this degree. Beatriz Melano Cauch is the pioneer in feminist biblical-theological work at this level. In the mid-1980s, various women went to Europe or to the United States to obtain their doctorates. Later the field of biblical studies opened up in Latin America, some at the doctorate level, such as in Brazil and Chile, which made it easier for women to study. Today there is actually a large number of women with a master's or licentiate degree who do excellent work, many of whom are authors in the journal *RIBLA*. This does not mean that universities or seminaries offer courses in

---

6. See the final document from the meeting of biblical scholars in San Leopoldo, Brazil, 2004, sponsored by the women of *RIBLA*.

7. Gebara was silenced by the Vatican after she made declarations in the Brazilian magazine *Veja* in 1993 in favor of the decriminalization of abortion.

8. See *RIBLA* 57 ([2007]: 48–55, 56–64, 70–77), dedicated to reproductive rights, where Elaine Gleci Neuenfeldt, Carmiña Navia, and Adriana Kuhn work on the theme of abortion.

the field of feminist biblical studies. That is far from the case. Women use the methods of biblical studies in general, first specializing in the First or Second Testament, and then women themselves work on the texts from the angle of their own feminist conscience.

There are also many women at the middle level of studies. They are the leaders of the Latin American biblical movement, who do feminist biblical rereadings, work full time in biblical formation workshops at the pastoral level, and are assiduous readers of biblical works. They fulfill a fundamental task in the conscientization of women at the base and are the key to seeing that the women at the base receive the work of feminist biblical scholars. However, it must be recognized that the term *feminist* is not adopted by all women. The stigma is still present, especially in the churches. Men's fear of this word has not disappeared. It is known that many women do not use the "f-word" in church contexts as a strategy, in order not to be rejected nor to undermine their biblical formation projects with church women.

3. Feminist Biblical Publications

The best example of women authoring feminist biblical work is found in *Revista de Interpretación Bíblica Latinoamericana*, which is now published three times a year in Spanish and Portuguese. More than fifty women from different parts of the continent and the Caribbean have written for it. Some have doctorates; others have earned a master's or licentiate in the field. Of the sixty-three issues published from its creation in 1988 until 2009, two hundred and six articles have been written by women biblical scholars addressing very interesting themes and methodological and hermeneutical approaches. It could be said that the journal opened a space for women, a space that was then filled little by little as they were able to prepare academically. For this reason, the first issues had very little participation by women, but in later issues their presence is very strong, almost equal to that of men. [9] More and more women continue to be prepared in this field. Women tend to prefer biblical studies over theology, and we have very few women theologians in the area of systematic theology.

Six issues have been dedicated to the topics of "Woman and the Bible" and "Gender and the Bible." Of these six issues, three have been written only by

---

9. One or two women wrote in the first issue, and there are no women in issues 2 (1989), 3 (1989), 7 (1990), and 10 (1991). Neither are there in issue 34 (1999), dedicated to the book of Revelation. This is strange, because at that time many women were writing in the journal.

women, in 1993, 1997, and 2002.[10] Three issues were written by both men and women because the themes were gender, masculinities, and human reproduction. These were published in 2000 and 2007.[11] The final document, from a meeting of women biblical scholars in 2004 in San Leopoldo, Brazil, was incorporated into the *RIBLA* volume dedicated to the celebration of its fiftieth issue. The document is titled "Respiros ... entre Transpiración y Conspiración" [Sighs ... between perspiration and conspiracy]. This document refers to women's position confronting exegesis and hermeneutics, as I will elaborate below. This inventory is intended to show the advances made by women in biblical studies despite living in an environment that is still hostile to feminist thought. [12] I have consulted other sources where I have found feminist biblical articles, such as the journal *Aportes Bíblicos* in Costa Rica and *Alternativas* in Nicaragua. Both are relatively new journals that include authors from the whole continent.

3.1. THEMES, EXAMPLES, AND ADVANCES

Feminist biblical scholars have explored diverse topics. A great number of articles are dedicated to exploring unknown passages or reconstructing the stories of anonymous women in the Bible. At the beginning, studies of the well-known women such as Judith, Hagar, Ruth, the Shulamite, the Samaritan, Mary Magdalene, Lydia, Second Testament genealogies, and women healed by Jesus were abundant.[13] All of these have been found in the journals

---

10. *Por manos de mujer* (*RIBLA* 15 [1993]); *Mas nostras decimos* (*RIBLA* 25 [1997]); *Las mujeres y la violencia sexista* (*RIBLA* 41 [2002]).

11. *El género en lo cotidiano* (*RIBLA* 37 [2000]); *Imaginando masculinidades* (*RIBLA* 56 [2007]); *Reproducción humana; Complejidad y desafío* (*RIBLA* 57 [2007]).

12. Surely there are various dissertations not considered here because of the impossibility of knowing about them due to the limitations of the region. However, the ample selection analyzed here makes clear the state of feminist biblical studies.

13. For Judith, see Anna María Rizzante Gallazzi, "La mujer sitiada: Lectura de Judit a partir de Dina," *RIBLA* 15 (1993): 47–58. For Hagar, see Mercedes Brancher, "De los ojos de Agar a los ojos de Dios, Gen 16:1–16," *RIBLA* 25 (1997): 11–27; Heydi Galarza, "Agar e Ismael: un estudio de Génesis 21:1–21," *Aportes Bíblicos* 9 (2009): 5–30. For Ruth, see María Antonita Marques, "Los caminos de sobrevivencia. Una lectura del libro de Rut," *RIBLA* 63 (2009): 66–72. For the Shulamite, see Rizzante Gallazzi, "Yo seré para él como aquella que da la paz," *RIBLA* 21 (1996): 91–101. For the Samaritan, see Lucía Weiler, "Jesús y la samaritana," *RIBLA* 15 (1993): 123–30. For Mary Magdalene, see See Maribel Pertuz, "La evangelista de la resurrección en el cuarto evangelio," *RIBLA* 25 (1997): 69–76; Carmiña Navia, "Violencia histórica contra María de Magdala," *RIBLA* 41 (2002): 107–16. For Lydia, see Ivoni Richter Reimer, "Reconstruir historia de mujeres: Reconsideraciones sobre el trabajo y estatus de Lidia en Hechos 16," *RIBLA* 4 (1989): 47–64; Aida Soto, "Lidia, la vendedora de

mentioned above. Very early on, interpretations of women who had been ignored in the history of salvation, especially those in the First Testament, appeared. These include women in the Elisha circle and women hidden within the texts of Leviticus, Numbers, Nehemiah, Ezra, Samuel, Kings, the prophets, and others. Scholars examined texts in which women appear as prophets, witches, mothers defending cadavers of their sons, prostitutes with babies, and desperate widows; they also address the legislation of women's bodies in Leviticus and Numbers. From the Second Testament, stories of women have been reconstructed in the Gospels, Acts, the Epistles, and Revelation.[14] Scholars also have analyzed texts where women appear in the final greetings of Pauline letters, where women prophets are recognized between the lines, and so on.[15]

The reconstruction of stories implies taking different directions of interpretation and often criticizing what the patriarchal biblical tradition has seen as positive. This is the case, for instance, in Alicia Winters's contribution, which recuperates the subversive memory of Rizpah, Saul's widow (2 Sam 21:1–14).[16] Rizpah frightens away the wild birds and animals so they would not eat the cadavers of her sons, thereby "maintaining alive the memory of those assassinated by David's ambition." For the author, the woman's actions have political and subversive repercussions as a protest against the "abuses of David's government." In Rizpah's actions, Winters sees the image of many mothers who struggle against the disappeared and massacred in Colombia, the country in which she writes.

Nancy Cardoso Pereira rereads 1 Kgs 3:16–28 from a perspective completely at odds with tradition.[17] This passage has been praised for Solomon's wisdom in discovering who the real mother was, but Cardoso Pereira gives its interpretation a new twist. Her starting point is women prostitutes and

púrpura, una alternativa de economía doméstica (experiencias bíblicas)," *RIBLA* 51 (2005): 102–5. For Second Testament genealogies, see See Sandra Mansilla, "Hermenéutica de los linajes políticos: Un estudio sobre los discursos en torno a las genealogías y sus implicaciones políticas," *RIBLA* 41 (2002): 83–92. For women healed by Jesus, see Genoveva Nieto, "El cuerpo femenino como texto: La curación de la mujer encorvada, Lc.13:10–17," *Aportes bíblicos* 1 (2005): 5–36.

14. See Violeta Rocha, "Entre la fragilidad y el poder: Mujeres en al Apocalipsis," *RIBLA* 48 (2004): 95–104.

15. See Lilia Dias Mariano, "Profetisas en el antiguo Israel, interfiriendo en el transcurso de la historia," *RIBLA* 60 (2008): 131–46.

16. Alicia Winters, "La Memoria subversiva de una mujer, 2S 21: 1–13," *RIBLA* 13 (1992): 77–86.

17. Nancy Cardoso Pereira, "Prostitutas–madres–mujeres: Obsesiones y profecía en 1R3:16–28," *RIBLA* 25 (1997): 8–40.

sacrificed children, a situation not unrelated to Brazil, where she writes. She does not find comfort in the king's wisdom but prefers to find a solution of the conflict in recognizing the children's bodies. Cordoso Pereira's intention is to "denaturalize" the stereotypes of the maternal instinct of women as prostitutes/mothers, as well as the male's objective judgment. The author does not need the spectacle of the king's wisdom. The real wisdom comes from the woman who knows well the body of her child, and merely seeing this body is sufficient. Cardoso Pereira analyzes the rhetorical situation of the story as the consolidation of the monarchical state and its institutions such as the military, the administration, and the court and its wise men.

In this same line of critiquing traditional readings, Elisabeth Cook rereads Ezra, focusing on the foreign women as victims of an identity conflict between two groups of the *golah* (exiled community).[18] Her analysis leads to the conclusion that the women "are portrayed as a threat to the well-being of the Judean post-exilic community."[19] These women are not really foreigners; their "foreignness" is established by the condition of being a woman, in order to assure the integrity and hegemony of a sector looking to exercise its power, influence, and identity over everyone else. This is so because it is "the masculine political and religious power that defines what is normative, what is pure and acceptable to Yahweh."[20] Her starting point for analyzing the situation is today's migration and the foreignness imposed by dominant cultures, such as North America, on the one side, and the free market of globalization, on the other.

 In the interpretation of such stories, the women are not portrayed as protagonists or as victims, as was often done in the 1970s and 1980s. For example, because of the pervasive problem of militarism within the Latin American and Caribbean context, the Brazilian Tania Mara Sampaio works with the book of Hosea and criticizes traditional readings.[21] She does not look specifically at women but instead at their social groups and their different expressions of social relationships. To make women and their practices visible means to question the structural reality and power relations of the society. It is not sufficient to isolate women as oppressed beings who need to

---

18. Elizabeth Cook, "Las mujeres extranjeras, victimas del conflicto e identidades," in *Ecce Mulier: Homenaje a Irene Foulkes* (ed. Universidad Bíblica Latinoamericana; San José: Sebila, 2005): 105–33.

19. Ibid.

20. Ibid.

21. Tania Mara Sampaio, "El cuerpo excluido de su dignidad," *RIBLA* 25 (1997): 35–45. Sampaio has written various articles about Hosea, products of her doctoral thesis, which was published as *Movementos do corpo prostituido da mulher: Aproximaçães da profecia atribuida a Oséias* (São Paulo: Loyola, 1999).

be liberated. Rather, it is necessary to analyze the processes of exploitation in which they reach their share of power for resistance. Because of this, prostitution in Hosea has to be seen as a political, economic, and religious category. The critique is directed at the priests as agents of the monarchical system that relies on its military force.

Since the beginning, Ivoni Richter Reimer has contributed to the reconstruction of stories in the Second Testament. She has taught us how to "dig out" those texts that are usually not discussed. Using social-historical analysis and reaching out to archaeology, ancient sources, and inscriptions, she has greatly enriched feminist biblical studies. In her reconstruction of Lydia, for example, she proposes to walk on other paths. "The male exegetes," she says, "already have taken liberties with her life: they have her married, widowed, wealthy and transformed into a European, etc." And all of this seems to them as justified, "because one exegete copies another." Therefore, she decided to take the liberty of finding another way, using the contributions of sociohistorical materials and extrabiblical sources.[22] Irene Foulkes also walks in this path. The key to reading, she says, is to know the historical-cultural context of the first century in order to evaluate women's appearance in the Christian communities and other texts as a way of learning about the situation of women in the first Christian communities.[23]

In the last decade, more biblical scholarship has appeared in which patriarchal texts are critically analyzed. Indefensible texts, or "texts of terror," have received attention as unacceptable texts in the Bible. Besides the known "texts of terror," such as stories of the Levite's concubine and the rape of Tamar, women scholars have brought to attention "texts of terror" that express the male chauvinism of patriarchal society in ancient times and are not questioned by the biblical text itself but have passed unnoticed.[24] Work on such texts include Mercedes García Bauchman's, "Un rey muy viejo y una machacha muy linda" [A Very Old King and a Beautiful Young Woman],[25] very clearly referring to King David, and Mercedes Brancher's study that denounces the violence against women called witches (Exod 22:18).[26]

---

22. Richter Reimer, "Reconstruir historia de mujeres."

23. Irene Foulkes, "Invisibles y desaparecidas: Rescatar la historia de las anónimas," *RIBLA* 25 (1997): 41–51.

24. See Elaine Neufel, "Volencia sexual y poder: El caso de Tamar in 2S 13:1–22," *RIBLA* 41 (2002): 39–49.

25. Mercedes García Bauchman, "Un rey muy viejo y una machacha muy linda," *RIBLA* 41 (2002): 50–57.

26. Mercedes Brancher, "La violencia contra las mujeres hechiceras," *RIBLA* 50 (2005): 61–64.

Another task taken on in the last decade has been to denormalize texts in the Second Testament that have been used to resist women's leadership. Two investigative books have appeared on 1 Timothy, one a doctoral thesis by Marga Stroher, and another by Elsa Tamez.[27] In this same vein, Foulkes has worked on the texts of 1 Corinthians and the domestic codes in Ephesians and Colossians.[28] Cristina Conti titles her article on 1 Tim 2:9–15 "Infiel es esta palabra" [This word is unfaithful], making it clear that the text is not normative.[29]

Exegetical studies from the perspective of African-descendant feminists have appeared more frequently in this last decade. Silvia Lima da Silva has been a pioneer in these biblical contributions. She has developed a black hermeneutic since the middle of the 1980s that revalues the inheritance of her ancestors and their non-Christian religion.[30] Tirsa Ventura, an expert on psalms of ascent,[31] rediscovers unknown personalities such as the Cushite Ebed-melech, who speaks as the God of the prophet Jeremiah.[32] New generations of scholars, such as Maricel Mena, have dedicated great effort to analyzing Afro-Asian roots in the Bible and the value of interpreting little-used texts such as the legacy of Egyptian goddesses in the time of the monarchy as a contribution to a black feminist hermeneutic.[33] Betty Ruth Lozano and Bibiana Peñaranda have reread Num 12 from the perspective of black women and have defended

---

27. Marga Stroher, "Caminos de resistencia, en las fronteras del poder normativo: Un estudio de las Cartas Pastorales en la perspectiva feminista" (Ph.D. diss., Escola Superior de Teologia, Instituto Ecumenico de Pós–gradução, São Leopoldo, RS, 2002); Elsa Tamez, *Luchas de Poder en los orígenes del cristianismo: Un estudio de 1 Timoteo* (Santander: Sal Terrae, 2005). This appeared in English as *Struggles for Power in Early Christianity* (Maryknoll, N.Y.: Orbis, 2007).

28. Irene Foulkes, "Conflictos en Corinto: Las mujeres en una iglesia primitiva," *RIBLA* 15 (1993): 107–22; *Problemas pastorales en Corinto* (San José: DEI, 1996), 281–302, 374–82; Irene Foulkes, "Los códigos y deberes domésticos en Colosenses 3:18–31 y Efesios 5:22–6:9: Estrategias persuasivas, reacciones provocadas," *RIBLA* 55 (2006): 41–62.

29. Cristina Conti, "Infiel es esta palabra," *RIBLA* 37 (2000): 41–56.

30. See Silvia Lima da Silva, *En territorio de Frontera: Una lectura de Marcos 7:24–30* (San José: DEI, 2001).

31. See Tirsa Ventura, *Cuerpos Peregrinos: Un estudio desde la opresión y resistencia desde el género, clase y etnia, Salmos 120–134* (San José: DEI, 2008).

32. Tirsa Ventura, "Un cusita habla ¡como el Dios del profeta! Una lectura de Jeremías 38:7–13," *RIBLA* 54 (2006): 48–54.

33. Maricel Mena, "La herencia de las diosas: Egipto y Sabá en el tiempo de la monarquía salomónica," *RIBLA* 54 (2006): 34–47; Mena, "Hermenéutica negra feminista: De invisible a intérprete y artífice de su propia historia," *RIBLA* 50 (2005): 130–34.

Miriam, the sister of Aaron.[34] One issue of *RIBLA*, in which various women participated, was dedicated to the Bible and African-Asian races.[35]

Along with these contributions from the perspective of African-descendant feminists, biblical studies from an intercultural perspective have also appeared. Black and indigenous women, and others who have an interest in indigenous cultures, have begun to dialogue with the biblical text from the perspective of these cultures.[36] Mercedes López rereads the book of Ruth focusing on the presence of two different cultures.[37] Digna Ludeña analyzes Mark 6:30–44 in dialogue with the Quechua culture.[38] Graciela Chamorro rereads Mary, the mother of Jesus, from the perspective of indigenous peoples.[39] Maricel Mena constructs from a black cultural perspective a dialogue between the Catholic Church and Condomble in and through the voices of Mary and Yamanyá.[40]

However, there have been very few ecofeminist interpretations. Such interpretations have been advanced more in theology because of the well-known theologian Ivone Gebara and the Chilean group "Conspirando." In terms of analysis of biblical texts from this angle, however, very little has been published. Mercedes López has entered this area by deconstructing patriarchal images in Prov 8:22–31.[41] María Soavo rereads Isa 34:8–17,[42] and Lilia Días Marianno casts an ecofeminist eye on Genesis, where a woman, water, and the sacred are found.[43]

---

34. Betty Ruth Lozano and Bibiana Peñaranda, "Una relectura de Números 12 desde una perspectiva de mujeres negras," *RIBLA* 50 (2005): 114–16.

35. *RIBLA* 54 (2006).

36. Unfortunately, there are few indigenous women biblical scholars, and they do not often write because of lack of schooling or oral tradition. Therefore, the articles cited from this perspective have been written by Mestizas.

37. Mercedes López, "Alianza por la vida: Una lectura de Rut a partir de las culturas," *RIBLA* 26 (1997): 96–101.

38. The text not only deals with women but also helps explain the methodology that women use in their intercultural analysis. See Digna Ludeña, "La comida compartida: Una lectura de Marcos 6:30–44 en diálogo con la cultura Quechua–Andina," *Aportes Bíblicos* 3 (2006): 3–40.

39. Graciela Chamorro, "Maria en las culturas y religiones amerindias," *RIBLA* 46 (2003): 74–81.

40. Maricel Mena, "¡Amen, Axe! ¡Sarava, aleluya!" *RIBLA* 46 (2003): 64–73.

41. Mercedes López, "Danzando en el universo: Proverbios 8:22–31," *RIBLA* 50 (2005): 65–86.

42. María Soavo, "Nosotras que tenemos alas y sabemos volar: Una hermenéutica ecofeminista de Isaías 34:8–17," *RIBLA* 41 (2002): 64–82.

43. Lilia Días Marianno, "¡Qué alegría! La palabra de Yahveh también vino a la mujer: Un análisis ecofeminista de Génesis 16," *RIBLA* 50 (2005): 49–52.

3.2. Hermeneutics

3.2.1. Problems and Hermeneutical Leaps

Since the beginning (the 1980s and 1990s), women have encountered hermeneutical problems. On one side is the general tendency in the region to read the Bible as a liberating book and the presence of patriarchal texts that contradict this affirmation. On the other side is the diversity of and contradictions within the biblical text itself, some liberating and others oppressive. This has led to the resituation of Latin American hermeneutics and a challenge to it from the reality of women and the African and indigenous cultures, first from intuitions, then from suspicions, and later from exegetical affirmations, as can be seen in the later issues of *RIBLA*.[44]

The most serious problem is the prevalent climate of orthodoxy within the churches and traditionally assumed biblical authority. As we have seen above, women scholars demand the reconstruction of biblical texts and theological concepts that have been elaborated with neoplatonic, dualistic categories and that portray women negatively. The black and indigenous hermeneutic proposes a cosmo-vision that dissents from orthodoxy by once again taking up the ancestral spirituality that sometimes clashes with monotheistic Christianity. Categories outside the framework of Western epistemology come into play. Silvia Regina expresses this very well when, in her article "Fe y Axe," she challenges her readers to begin with life and not with orthodoxy. In order to leave behind concepts elaborated in the great centers of academic-theological study, she invites her readers "to leave the order of orthodoxy and to think from the dis-order of daily life." In this way, she encourages others to think from the margins, "from extreme threats to life, from the border lands, where we find the bricolage and the other."[45] Maricel Mena also challenges Latin American exegesis and hermeneutics from an African-Asian roots perspective. Her attempt has been a target of criticism in the traditional academic

---

44. In 1993 I offered hermeneutical guidelines to understand Gal 3:28 and 1 Cor 14:34. I criticized academic and scientific "prudence," because it often becomes complicit with androcentric readings. See Elsa Tamez, "Pautas hermenéuticas para comprender Gálatas 3:28 y 1 Corintos 14:34," *RIBLA* (1993): 9–18. Silvia Regina de Lima Silva questions popular hermeneutics from the perspective of the black world; see her "Hay zapatos viejos que hacen callos en los pies Ensayo re relectura bíblica a partir de la realidad afroamericana y caribeña," *RIBLA* 19 (1994): 37–45.

45. Silvia Regina de Lima Silva, "Fe y Axe: Sanación como experiencia de encuentro con la fuerza que nos habita," in *Ecce mulier: Homenaje a Irene Foulkes* (San José: Sebila, 2005), 231–45.

world.[46] An example of this conflict is Nancy Cardoso Pereira's debate with the scholar Ciro Flamarion, who calls this type of exegesis "Egyptomania." In her view, this critique is nothing more than violence exerted from the dominant Western model of science and history.[47]

Therefore, the challenge arises not just within academia but also within popular biblical hermeneutics (Leitura Popular da Bíblia) that reads the text from the point of view of social justice and in favor of the poor, but always within the traditional paradigms and within the limits of orthodoxy.[48] Add to that the crisis of the paradigms of modernity, and above all its dichotomist emphasis. In the ninth meeting of Leitura Popular da Bíblia scholars in Buenos Aires in 2003, the women presented reflections from their own experience in dialogue with the Bible as a way of taking on the challenges of today's epistemological paradigms that are still uncommon within the movement. Sandra Mansilla, coordinator of the movement, summed up this form of knowledge that women experience as partial, selective, full of creativity, and provisional.[49]

3.2.2. Final Documents

The issue of *RIBLA* titled *Pero nosotras decimos* [But we women say], written only by women, gathers together the documents from the women biblical scholars who met in Colombia in 1995.[50] This summary produced certain "guiding points" for feminist liberation hermeneutics in the 1990s:

1. The body as a hermeneutical category that offers alternatives to the discourse and invites new nonasymmetric gender relations.
2. The subjects and their everyday stories in the hermeneutical process. These, like the lives of women of today, construct and sustain the social fabric, its changes and resistance.
3. A hermeneutic of construction and deconstruction takes for granted that the text is generically constructed, captive to asymmetric rela-

---

46. Maricel Mena, "Raíces afroasiáticas en el mundo bíblico: Desafíos para la exégesis y hermenéutica latinoamericana," *RIBLA* 56 (2006): 17–33.

47. See Nancy Cardoso Pereira, "Las raíces afro-asiáticas de la Biblia hebrea: ¿Disfraz académico o corriente esotérica?" *RIBLA* 54 (2006): 7–16; 35.

48. See the doctoral thesis of Isabel Aparecida Felix, "Anseio por dançar diferente: Leitura popular da bíblia na ótica da hermenêutica feminista crítica de libertação" (Universidade Metodista de São Paulo, 2010).

49. Sandra Mansilla, "Intuiciones para abrir la historia: Mujeres, conocimiento y Biblia," *RIBLA* 50 (2005): 150–52.

50. *RIBLA* 25 (1997).

tions that subordinate women. Therefore, the interpretative paradigms need to reformulate the text so that it becomes a place of humanization and integration between persons.

4.   A hermeneutic that questions the concept of biblical authority. Revelation is not limited just to the text but includes the possible meeting of the word in the text with the word of God present in the everyday life of the communities, women, men, children ... peoples, cultures, religious traditions.

Later, in 2004, women biblical scholars met again in San Leopoldo and produced another document, which was entitled: "Respiros ... entre transpiración y conspiración."[51] In this meeting, the plurality of biblical studies between the women of Latin America and the Caribbean was adopted. Various leaps were made, and a feminist hermeneutic of liberation, an ethnic-racial feminist hermeneutic, and an ecofeminist hermeneutic clearly emerged. The document itself explains this:

> With this, we have taken qualitative leaps in an epistemological rupture using categories such as "partiality," "provisional," "ambiguity," "diversity," "experience," "simultaneousness" in the critique of the hegemonic-patriarchal-dualist-hierarchy powers. Another rupture appeared in questioning the idea of the linearity of history and conscience, considering different sources, times, spaces, accentuating a renewed process in differentiating levels of circularity-spirituality.[52]

Although the document is written in a poetic tone, in the subtitles it is clear which framework is being worked out. Here I quote again from part of the document:

> *Saberes y sabores* [*Wisdoms and Flavors*] (Epistemological Dimension): Dancing the dances of Life we arrive at this "other place" that we name "partiality," understood as an act of thinking from our distinct conditions because we experience it within our bodies! Therefore we affirm the importance of the impartiality, the ambiguity and the simultaneousness of the intersections in the production of knowledge and reading of the biblical text, from an ethical, political and sacred horizon.
> *Quehaceres y placers* [*Tasks and Pleasures*] (Ethical Dimension): We experience with intensity the complexity of the socio-political and eco-

---

51. "Respiros ... entre transpiración y conspiración: Documento final del encuentro de mujeres en San Leopoldo," *RIBLA* 50 (2005): 109–13.
52. "Respiros," 121.

nomic dimensions whose analysis we renew in our daily lives. Out of this, we perceive there is not just one paradigm of power, but the task always involves an ethical horizon and the commitment we take on in the face of the realities of our bodies, relationships, languages, meta-languages, struggles, tears, pleasures, and celebrations.

Danzas y andanzas [*Dances and Ventures*] (Methodological Dimension): In the recognition of the body and in the provocation of the dance, we move in the construction of our own methods, taking them on as limit and possibility, in an ambiguity that is also visualized as dependence and anatomy in relation to known methods, historical-critical-literary-rhetorical. We do this from our feminist perspective and gender. Therefore, we affirm that in its difference our exegesis, hermeneutics, theology, and pastoral work are serious, legitimate, and exercise authority because they reconstruct Life where it is threatened.

Puertas abiertas! [*Open the Doors!*] (Dimension of Biblical Authority): We reaffirm that the fundamental principle of biblical authority is Life, coming from threatened Life that cries out for Life. This biblical authority is clothed and vested in celebration, in which the doors are always open, gathering in the new, in the transitoriness of the bodies who enter and leave in the experience, nostalgia, desire and in the joy of ample and re-created relationships that feed Life....

3.2.2. Privileged Hermeneutical Categories

Gender theories are most used in the analysis of the text and of reality, in the time of the text as well as in today's realities. This preference can be seen in almost all of the articles, books, and final documents. Feminist biblical scholars are conscious that the term can be an object of manipulation by males. Therefore, they define it carefully as a feminist category of analysis that observes the asymmetric power relations between women and men. Tania Mara Sampaio shows:

> The center is in the mediation of gender as a category of analysis of reality and of those texts. It is to observe the social relations of power between women and men in the everyday life in the story. The proposal of a hermeneutic of gender is not only to make women visible. It tries to confront the power present in the social organization of gender relations in the home, ethnicity, and class that emerge from historical processes and are not purely biological.[53]

---

53. Tania Mara Sampaio, "Consideraciones para una hermenéutica de género del texto bíblico," *RIBLA* 37 (2000): 7–14.

Our daily reality and the body are two other privileged categories in feminist biblical analysis. There are innumerable articles that analyze texts in terms of the body and everyday reality, as can be seen in the various titles mentioned above. It is not the rejection of macrostructural analysis and global projects that struggle to make a new society viable where there is space for all women and men. The problem is that these are seen as limited when the body and everyday realities are not taken seriously. Nancy Cordoso expresses it very well when she analyzes the text about the woman and child in the circle of the prophet Elisha.[54] For her, the idolatrous and sacrificial character of the economy in these texts communicates that "the context of domestic work in the household is presented as a privileged scene for the action of mechanisms of economic oppression that need to control and fetishize the economic relations of the home." It is also of urgent importance to affirm daily life and its relations as a theological and political place that demands the critique of those instruments of analysis used until now. This challenge is to engage in interdisciplinary work that dialogues in a special manner with feminist theories that have been the most engaged in these questions. This means to incorporate the conversations and structures "that are mobilized from the body, and its needs, its beauty, its capacity for epiphany."[55]

4. Methods

Feminist biblical scholars use a variety of methods of biblical analysis. We find useful historical criticism, narrative, semiotics, and social-rhetorical analysis, and social-historical methods, depending on the type of text that is being analyzed. Many times there is a combination of methods that offer the best ways to explore the senses of the texts. As Irene Foulkes says, feminist exegesis has not developed a method that is called "feminist" but rather uses those that already exist. The difference is in the procedure—how they are used, for what reasons, and from which perspective.[56] For example, the textual critique of the historical method is used to test for interpolations or manipulations against the women in the same textual variations. Furthermore, the social-historical method helps to reconstruct daily life through archaeology and ancient extra-biblical documents. Synchronic methods, such as narrative, semantic, and

---

54. Nancy Cordoso, "La mujer y lo cotidiano: La mujer y el niño en el ciclo del profeta Eliseo," *RIBLA* 14 (1993): 7–21.

55. Nancy Cardoso Pereira, "La mujer y lo cotidiano: La mujer y el niño en el ciclo del profeta Eliseo," *RIBLA* 14 (1993): 20.

56. Irene Foulkes, "Praxis exegética feminista: Conceptos, instrumentos, procedimientos," *Alternativas* 36 (2008): 33–58.

social-rhetorical analyses, help to reconstruct texts and to find new meanings in the always polysemic discourse. The analysis is interdisciplinary in dialogue with the social sciences, poetry, or literature. There are many articles that combine poetry with scientific analysis.

A mark of the region is the use of the hermeneutical circle. This involves the concern for the lived experience, the analysis of the text from the context of the text and in dialogue with today's context, and the challenge of a transforming praxis in an impoverished continent where the feminization of poverty and the resistance and struggle of women make it impossible to enact suspicious readings of the Bible. This starting point marks the entrance to the texts. For example, Nancy Cardoso Pereira's study of 2 Kgs 6:24–30, which speaks of devouring babies because of famine, begins:

> It was the first time I went out since my baby daughter was born. A daughter with ten days of life waited for me in the house, and I was in a hurry to return, but the red traffic light kept me from going on. A man passed me selling some things, and he demanded that I look through the car window…. There I saw a woman and a little girl. It was impossible not to see: she was sitting on the island between the lanes washing her child with water she got out of a tin can and rinsed her with an old rag. I remembered my daughter in the house, the boiled water and clean cotton, and looked at the stop light wishing that it would let me go. But, not yet. I turned my eyes toward the woman in the exact moment that she looked at me. Eyes of a mother on a street of San Paulo. It was then that I understood the scandalous biblical reference that marked her desperation. I read 2 Kgs 6:24–30 with shock and fear…. What the mother on the street said to me, and which frightened me, was the verification of the sacrifice of her daughter: "Today my daughter is sacrificed in the middle of the street … and when do we devour yours?" I go to my house saying that my daughter is not going to be food, and what the other replied to me was "But, isn't this what we agreed?" I open the Bible with the commitment to learn the memory of God's people, the words and new actions so that all mothers and children are recognized.[57]

5. Final Words

I have presented important phases and contributions of feminist biblical studies in the last three decades in Latin America and the Caribbean. The analyzed materials have been mostly articles, due to the scarcity of books. The majority of the articles have been footnoted at the bottom of the page so that readers can see by reading the titles where feminist exegesis and herme-

---

57. Cardoso Pereira, "La mujer," 7.

neutics of Latin America and the Caribbean are going. Through the themes and examples presented, it has been possible to observe the preoccupations, priorities, hermeneutical advances, and preferred way to interpret the biblical texts.

"Stirring Up Vital Energies": Feminist Biblical Studies in North America (1980s–2000s)

Susanne Scholz
Perkins School of Theology

1. "Discovering a Largely Unknown Past": From *The Woman's Bible* to *The Women's Bible* in North American Biblical Studies

The rise of feminist biblical studies in North America has been an ocean wave flooding the malestream world of biblical scholarship engendered by the social movements of the time.[1] Early on, feminist biblical scholars believed themselves to be the first to critically examine Christian and Jewish sacred texts with feminist epistemology. They knew little about the accomplishments of previous generations of feminists and even less about the suffragists who opposed the use of the Bible in justification of North American women's secondary status.[2] Only by chance did second-wave feminists discover the first feminist commentary on the Bible, published in the 1890s by U.S. suffragist Elizabeth Cady Stanton and her editorial team.[3] Reading *The Woman's*

---

1. See, for instance, Kathleen M. O'Connor, "The Feminist Movement Meets the Old Testament: One Woman's Perspective," in *Engaging the Bible in a Gendered World: An Introduction to Feminist Biblical Interpretation in Honor of Katharine Doob Sakenfeld* (ed. Linda Day and Carolyn Pressler; Louisville: Westminster John Knox, 2006), 3; Phyllis A. Bird, *Missing Persons and Mistaken Identities: Women and Gender in Ancient Israel* (Minneapolis: Fortress, 1997), 3, 4; Elisabeth Schüssler Fiorenza, *Bread Not Stone: The Challenge of Feminist Biblical Interpretation* (Boston: Beacon, 1984), 2.

2. For a survey on American women reading the Bible in the eighteenth and nineteenth centuries, see Carolyn De Swarte Gifford, "American Women and the Bible: The Nature of Woman as a Hermeneutical Issue," in *Feminist Perspectives on Biblical Scholarship* (ed. Adela Yarbro Collins; Chico, Calif.: Scholars Press, 1985), 11–33.

3. Elizabeth Cady Stanton, ed., *The Woman's Bible* (Boston: Northeastern University Press, 1993). For a history of the leading suffragist in the United States, see, e.g., Kathi Kern, *Mrs. Stanton's Bible* (Ithaca, N.Y.: Cornell University Press, 2001), 7: "In 1974, the

Bible, second-wave feminists learned about the nineteenth-century feminist engagement with religion and the Bible. Similarly, feminist biblical scholars at the end of the twentieth century were inspired by the larger civil rights and social movements of liberation and justice. They initially focused on gender and later connected their work with other forms of oppression, such as race, class, and the globalizing structures of empire.

This chapter describes three developmental phases of feminist biblical studies in North America: the 1980s, when feminist biblical studies expanded and deepened its institutional connections and scholarly perspectives; the 1990s, when the field moved beyond the politics of omission; and the current phase in the early twenty-first century, when intersectionality and dialogical relationships are pronounced as acts of resistance to forces of cooptation into the dominant discourse.[4] Finally, I suggest briefly where feminist biblical scholarship might go in the future. The pioneering phase in the 1970s is not included in this chapter because it receives fuller discussion in Judith Plaskow's contribution in this volume.[5]

2. The Expansion of Sexual Politics and Gender in Feminist Biblical Perspectives during the 1980s

In the 1980s, feminist biblical scholars expanded and deepened the study of the Bible in relation to women, gender, and sexuality. One publication, "The Effects of Women's Studies on Biblical Studies," illustrates the energies that began to manifest in the field. The volume contained the papers from a successful and inspiring panel discussion that had taken place during the 1980 SBL centennial celebration at the annual meeting of the Society of Biblical Literature. The papers were published in 1982 by the British *Journal for the Study of the Old Testament,*[6] not by the SBL's *Journal of Biblical Literature.*

Seattle-based Coalition Task Force on Women and Religion published its edition of *The Woman's Bible,* a reprint made from two volumes that Jane T. Walker of Tacoma, Washington, had inherited from her suffragist mother.... Having enjoyed *The Woman's Bible* herself, Walker wrote to the Coalition Task Force, she was 'glad to share it with my sister women.'"

4. For a slightly different mapping of the phases in feminist biblical studies, see Pamela J. Milne, "Toward Feminist Companionship: The Future of Feminist Biblical Studies and Feminism," in *A Feminist Companion to Reading the Bible: Approaches, Methods, and Strategies* (ed. Athalya Brenner and Carole Fontaine; Sheffield: Sheffield Academic Press, 1997), 39–60.

5. See her chapter entitled "Movement and Emerging Scholarship: Feminist Biblical Scholarship in the 1970s in the United States," in this volume. See also Susanne Scholz, *Introducing the Women's Hebrew Bible* (London: T&T Clark, 2007).

6. Phyllis Trible, ed., "The Effects of Women's Studies on Biblical Studies," *JSOT* 22 (1982): 3–71.

Pamela J. Milne pointed out that it must have been "surely an embarrassment to the SBL" when it became obvious that SBL had missed the mark.[7] The editor of the volume, Phyllis Trible, hinted at this, stating:

> From the beginning, all of us involved in this session, speakers and listeners, knew that we were not celebrating a centennial. In the SBL, as in society at large, women have little, if anything, to celebrate.[8]

During this second phase, the nearly exclusive research focus was on women and gender. Already in 1982, Katherine Doob Sakenfeld acknowledged "the cultural and functional inseparability of racism, sexism, and classism"[9] and saw these issues addressed "on the theological front" but not in biblical studies, where "the literature dealing with these three 'isms' remains on three separate tracks."[10] She recognized that "we Bible specialists have more work to do in this area"[11] of analyzing the intersectionality of gender and other social categories.

One response came from Toinette M. Eugene, an ethicist and womanist scholar, who articulated the parameters of a womanist biblical hermeneutics in 1987. She explained that, due to women of color's "doubly and triply oppressed" status in patriarchal society, it does not suffice to identify patriarchal oppression with androcentrism alone. Sexism must be understood as part of other oppressive ideologies, such as racism, militarism, or imperialism, because "the structures of oppression are all intrinsically linked."[12] She suggested that a feminist biblical hermeneutics has "to articulate an alternative liberating vision and praxis for all oppressed people by utilizing the paradigm of women's experiences of survival and salvation in the struggle against patriarchal oppression and degradation."[13] Yet Eugene's general proposal for the inclusion of other forms of social analysis did not find full articulation in the 1980s. During this phase most feminist biblical scholars focused on

---

7. Milne, "Toward Feminist Companionship," 42.

8. Ibid., 3.

9. Katharine Doob Sakenfeld, "Old Testament Perspectives: Methodological Issues," *JSOT* 22 (1982): 19.

10. Ibid.

11. Ibid.

12. Toinette M. Eugene, "A Hermeneutical Challenge for Womanists: The Interrelation Between the Text and Our Experience," in *Perspectives on Feminist Hermeneutics* (ed. Gayle G. Koontz and Willard Swartley; Elkhart, Ind.: Institute for Mennonite Studies, 1987), 20. For a general discussion of womanist theology, see, e.g., Delores S. Williams, "The Color of Feminism: Or, Speaking the Black Woman's Tongue," *JRT* 43 (1986): 42–58.

13. Eugene, "Hermeneutical Challenge," 25.

gender and androcentrism only. Despite some exceptions, an intersectional analysis was not prominent in feminist biblical publications.[14]

The omission of race, class, and geopolitical dynamics as analytical categories is obvious today because many feminist interpreters embrace intersectional, postcolonial, and dialogical hermeneutics from around the world. Yet in the 1980s, North American feminist biblical scholars were mainly white women, located at departments of religious studies and schools of theology, aiming to establish themselves in academic institutions and in a discipline that defined exegetical work as objective, universal, and value neutral. At the time their exegetical focus on women and gender was in itself a challenge to the mostly white, male, and senior scholars who populated schools and departments and usually had difficulties recognizing feminist research as a legitimate area of scholarship. Yet even then, feminist biblical interpretation challenged modernist notions of objectivity, disinterestedness, and the possibility of extracting an original meaning inherent in the text. From the beginning it has understood its project as the critical analysis of multiaxial power relations in which gender, sexuality, race, ethnicity, nationality, age, physical abilities, and other ideological-theological stances play central roles.

In the 1980s, two feminist biblical publications stand out because they fueled the research agenda for years to come. These books reframed epistemological, hermeneutical, and methodological priorities and lent scholarly legitimacy to women and gender research in biblical studies. Elisabeth Schüssler Fiorenza's *In Memory of Her* is one such book.[15] She explains in the introduction to the tenth anniversary edition that she "set out to explore the problem of women's historical agency in ancient Christianity in light of the theological and historical questions raised by the feminist movements in society and church and to do so in terms of critical biblical studies."[16] Schüssler Fiorenza showed that Christian women and men in the first century attempted to practice "the call to coequal discipleship" with various levels of success. At the time, she worried whether "feminists might label the book as 'male scholarship,' whereas my colleagues in biblical studies might not take it seriously."[17] However, the book was recognized as a milestone accomplishment; for instance, Beverly W. Harrison asserted, "*In Memory of Her* is, I believe, the most ful-

---

14. For a constructive critique of this situation, see, e.g., Nyasha Junior, "Womanist Biblical Interpretation," in Day and Pressler, *Engaging the Bible in a Gendered World*, 44.

15. Elisabeth Schüssler Fiorenza, *In Memory of Her: A Feminist Theological Reconstruction of Christian Origins* (New York: Crossroad, 1994).

16. Ibid., xiv.

17. Ibid.

some proposal we yet possess for a feminist hermeneutics that addresses the full circle of human interpretation."[18]

The other work that galvanized feminist biblical studies came from Phyllis Trible. Her 1984 volume, *Texts of Terror*,[19] presented four biblical women: Hagar, Tamar, an unnamed woman, and the daughter of Jephthah. Informed by a feminist hermeneutic and rhetorical criticism, Trible selected these "ancient tales of terror" because, as she explained, they "speak all too frighteningly of the present."[20] She acknowledged that her study was possible only because of her earlier and more joyous work of 1978, *God and the Rhetoric of Sexuality*.[21] Both volumes unearthed stories about women and gender in the Hebrew Bible that had been mostly neglected in Christian and Jewish communities. Trible's project jolted scholars and lay readers alike into a newfound awareness of these biblical texts and their tremendous significance for discussions on women and gender, with hints toward other forms of oppression, such as nationality and class.[22]

Many important studies appeared in the 1980s exploring the complexities of female characters, topics, and references in biblical literature, history, and tradition. In Hebrew Bible studies they include the works of Phyllis Bird, Peggy L. Day, Tikva Frymer-Kensky, Esther Fuchs, Alice L. Laffey, Carol Meyers, Katharine Doob Sakenfeld, and Renita J. Weems.[23] In early Christian literature they include the studies by Bernadette Brooten, Mary Rose D'Angelo, Jane Schaberg, Sandra M. Schneiders, Luise Schottroff, Mary Ann Tolbert, and Antoinette Wire.[24] The publications of these and other scholars expanded

---

18. Beverly W. Harrison, "Review of *In Memory of Her*, by Elisabeth Schüssler Fiorenza," *Horizons* 11 (1984): 150.

19. Phyllis Trible, *Texts of Terror: Literary-Feminist Readings of Biblical Narratives* (Philadelphia: Fortress, 1984).

20. Ibid., xiii.

21. Phyllis Trible, *God and the Rhetoric of Sexuality* (Fortress: Philadelphia, 1978).

22. See, e.g., ibid., 27. For an early review, see, e.g., Claudia V. Camp, "Review of Texts of Terror: Literary-Feminist Readings of Biblical Narratives, by Phyllis Trible," *JAAR* 54 (1986): 159–61.

23. Renita J. Weems, *Just a Sister Away* (San Diego, Calif.: LuraMedia, 1988); Carol Meyers, *Discovering Eve: Ancient Israelite Women in Context* (New York: Oxford University Press, 1988); Alice L. Laffey, *An Introduction to the Old Testament: A Feminist Perspective* (Philadelphia: Fortress, 1988); Peggy L. Day, ed., *Gender and Difference in Ancient Israel* (Minneapolis: Fortress, 1989).

24. Bernadette Brooten, *Women Leaders in the Ancient Synagogue* (Chico, Calif.: Scholars Press, 1982); Mary Ann Tolbert, ed., *The Bible and Feminist Hermeneutics* (*Semeia* 28; Chico, Calif.: Scholars Press, 1983); Sandra M. Schneiders, *Women and the Word* (New York: Paulist, 1986); Jane Schaberg, *The Illegitimacy of Jesus: A Feminist Theological Interpretation of the Infancy Narratives* (San Francisco: Harper & Row, 1987).

and deepened feminist research beyond anything ever written before. Yet it needs to be remembered that for institutional, hermeneutical, and sociopolitical reasons, feminist interpreters did not usually attend to other intersectional dynamics; in the 1980s, their scholarship practiced, perhaps unconsciously, a politics of omission.

3. Beyond a Politics of Omission and Toward a Differentiation of Feminist-Womanist-*Mujerista* Exegesis in the 1990s

Things changed in the 1990s, when voices of "otherness" became increasingly vocal in biblical studies. For the first time, voices of African American women scholars were joined by exegetes from South Africa and other African countries who criticized white feminist biblical discourse for neglecting race.[25] They preferred the term "womanism" for Christian black women scholarship, from Alice Walker's definition of the term as coming "from womanish.... A black feminist or feminist of color. From the black expression of mothers to female children, 'You acting womanish,' like a woman. Usually referring to outrageous, audacious, courageous or willful behavior."[26]

Womanist theologians stated that racism was as urgent as sexism and demanded that feminist biblical scholarship investigate both gender and race. They wanted biblical interpretations to focus "on *all* historically marginalized persons, women and men, who have been victimized by patriarchal dominance."[27] They advised white feminists to deal with their racist assump-

---

25. See, e.g., Madipoane J. Masenya, "African Womanist Hermeneutics: A Suppressed Voice from South Africa Speaks," *JFSR* 11 (1995): 149–55; Maxine Howell, "Towards a Womanist Pneumatological Pedagogy: Reading and Re-reading the Bible from British Black Women's Perspectives," *Black Theology* 7 (2009): 86–99. For an example of a womanist interpretation on a specific biblical text, see, e.g., Ncumisa Manona, "The Presence of Women in Parables: An Afrocentric Womanist Perspective," *Scriptura* 81 (2002): 408–21; Raquel A. St. Clair, *Call and Consequences: A Womanist Reading of Mark* (Minneapolis: Fortress, 2008).

26. See Alice Walker, *In Search of Our Mothers' Gardens: Womanist Prose* (San Diego: Harcourt Brace Jovanovich, 1983), xi. See also the reference to Walker's definition in Delores S. Williams, "Womanist Theology: Black Women's Voices," in *Black Theology: A Documentary History* (ed. James H. Cone and Gayraud S. Wilmore; 2 vols.; Maryknoll, N.Y.: Orbis, 1993), 2:265. Williams's essay was first published in 1987.

27. Clarice J. Martin, "Womanist Interpretation of the New Testament: The Quest for Holistic and Inclusive Translation and Interpretation," *JFSR* 6 (1990): 53. For a brief historical survey of biblical womanist scholarship, see also Michael Joseph Brown, "The Womanization of Blackness," in *Blackening of the Bible: The Aims of African American Biblical Scholarship* (Harrisburg, Penn.: Trinity, 2004).

tions[28] because "Black women seek to redeem life from patriarchal *and* racist death."[29] Womanists also criticized the binary distinction of female and male, urging feminist biblical scholars to transform not only sociopolitical and cultural-religious structures of oppression based on race but also those based on sexism, classism, sexuality,[30] and geo-politics.[31] Otherwise, they believed feminist scholarship would be "like patriarchal scholarship," "seeking its own perpetuation," and be "doomed."[32]

More recently, some black feminist/womanist biblical scholars acknowledged their ambivalence at being characterized as "womanist." Wilda C. M. Gafney explains that her "primary self-designation" is "a black feminist," a self-definition that reclaims the term *feminism* "from the pale hands of those who infected it with racism and classism."[33] She also acknowledges that in contexts dominated by racism and classism she prefers the term *womanist* "to avoid being coopted by white feminists."[34] Sometimes she considers "a hybridized identifier, fem/womanist" most appropriate because it describes

---

28. See also the challenge by Asian feminist theologian Kwok Pui-lan, "Racism and Ethnocentrism in Feminist Biblical Interpretation," in *Searching the Scriptures: A Feminist Introduction* (ed. Elisabeth Schüssler Fiorenza; New York: Crossroad, 1993), 101–16.

29. Mukti Barton, "The Skin of Miriam Became as White as Snow: The Bible, Western Feminism and Colour Politics," *Feminist Theology* 27 (May 2001): 80, emphasis added. See also Koala Jones-Warsaw, "Toward a Womanist Hermeneutic: A Reading of Judges 19–21," *JITC* 22.1 (1994): 30. For a survey discussion, see Clarice J. Martin, "Womanist Biblical Interpretation," in *Dictionary of Biblical Interpretation* (ed. John H. Hayes; Nashville: Abingdon, 1999), 655–58.

30. See, for example, Renee L. Hill, "Who Are We for Each Other? Sexism, Sexuality and Womanist Theology," in Cone and Wilmore, *Black Theology: A Documentary History*, 2:345–51.

31. For early and influential publications, see Sheila Briggs, "Can an Enslaved God Liberate? Hermeneutical Reflections on Philippians 2:6–11," in *Interpretation for Liberation* (ed. Katie Geneva Cannon and Elisabeth Schüssler Fiorenza; *Semeia* 47; Atlanta: Scholars Press, 1989), 137–53; Martin, "Womanist Interpretations of the New Testament," 4–61; Renita J. Weems, "The Hebrew Women Are Not Like the Egyptian Women: The Ideology of Race, Gender, and Sexual Reproduction in Exodus 1," in *Ideological Criticism of Biblical Texts* (ed. Tina Pippin and David Jobling; *Semeia* 59; Atlanta: Scholars Press, 1992), 25–34.

32. Renita J. Weems, "Womanist Reflections on Biblical Hermeneutics," in Cone and Wilmore, *Black Theology: A Documentary History*, 2:217. More recently, see Raquel St. Clair, "Womanist Biblical Interpretation," in *True to Our Native Land: An African American New Testament Commentary* (ed. Brian K. Blount; Minneapolis: Fortress, 2007), 54–62.

33. Wilda C. M. Gafney, "A Black Feminist Approach to Biblical Studies," *Encounter* 67 (autumn 2006): 397.

34. Ibid.

"the intersection of feminist and womanist practices."[35] New Testament scholar Gay L. Byron also recognizes the complexities of being classified as a "womanist Bible scholar." In a discussion on "my own brand of womanist biblical hermeneutics,"[36] she advises to take seriously the transnational context of black feminism in the U.S. and to develop "a more sustained focus on the common themes that U.S. Black feminists share with women of African descent throughout the world."[37] She urges feminist Bible scholars, particularly in the field of New Testament, "to listen to the voices of those who adhere to 'different' faiths, hail from 'other' cultures, and live in 'distant' lands as we reformulate the methodologies that might lead to a more representative form of global feminist biblical interpretation."[38]

We need to keep in mind that the number of womanist *biblical* scholars has been relatively small. In 2001, only forty-five African American scholars held doctoral degrees in biblical studies. Eleven of them were women, eight of whom specialized in Hebrew Bible and three in New Testament. As a consequence, many womanist *theologians* have published womanist Bible interpretations.[39] They have taken seriously Jacquelyn Grant's 1978 criticism that the black church and theologians "treat Black women as if they were

---

35. Ibid.

36. Gay L. Byron, "The Challenge of 'Blackness' for Rearticulating the Meaning of Global Feminist New Testament Interpretation," in *Feminist New Testament Studies: Global and Future Perspectives* (ed. Kathleen O'Brien Wicker et al.; New York: Palgave Macmillan, 2005), 97.

37. Ibid.

38. Ibid., 95. For another call toward multimethodological, multireligious, and multiperspectival hermeneutics, see, e.g., Cheryl B. Anderson, *Ancient Laws and Contemporary Controversies: The Need for Inclusive Biblical Interpretation* (New York: Oxford University Press, 2009).

39. See, e.g., Kelly Brown Douglas, who acknowledged: "I am a theologian and not a biblical scholar.... It is important for me to approach this timely issue as a theologian and not a biblical scholar." See her article entitled "Marginalized People, Liberating Perspectives: A Womanist Approach to Biblical Interpretation," *ATR* 83 (winter 2001): 41. For a historical survey on the significance of the Bible in African American communities, see Vincent L. Wimbush, "The Bible and African Americans: An Outline of an Interpretative History," in *Stony the Road We Trod: African American Biblical Interpretation* (ed. Cain Hope Felder; Minneapolis: Fortress, 1991), 81–97. For early womanist theological work, see Delores S. Williams, *Sisters in the Wilderness: The Challenge of Womanist God-Talk* (Maryknoll, N.Y.: Orbis, 1993); Katie Geneva Cannon, *Katie's Canon: Womanism and the Soul of the Black Community* (New York: Continuum, 1995). See also Katie Geneva Cannon, "The Emergence of Black Feminist Consciousness," in *Feminist Interpretation of the Bible* (ed. Letty M. Russell; Philadelphia: Westminster, 1985).

invisible creatures" although "Black women represent more than 50% of the Black community and more than 70% of the Black Church."[40]

In the North American context, recognition of diversity among women's social locations was observed not only by womanist scholars but also by *mujerista* theologians. This term is derived from the Spanish word for woman, *mujer*. These theologians stress the distinctiveness of Hispanic women's contexts for the interpretation of the Bible. For instance, Ada María Isasi-Diaz, a trained Christian ethicist, proposed grounding biblical interpretations in the lives of Hispanic women so that the Bible may serve as a direct support system to them. She also proposed that Hispanic women "analyze and test their lives against those sections of the Bible which are life-giving for them."[41] Yet to date a book on *mujerista* biblical interpretation published by a *mujerista* scholar with a doctoral degree in biblical studies does not exist.

Despite the concerns articulated by womanist and *mujerista* theologians, feminist publications of the 1990s focused mostly on androcentrism.[42] The 1992 publication of the *Women's Bible Commentary*, edited by Carol A. Newsom and Sharon H. Ringe, contains interpretations on every biblical book of the Christian canon with a focus on women and gender, and the 1998 expanded edition includes the Apocrypha.[43] The editors explain that "women

---

40. Jacquelyn Grant, "Black Theology and the Black Woman," in *Black Theology: A Documentary History*, 1:334.

41. Ada María Isasi-Diaz, "The Bible and *Mujerista* Theology," in *Lift Every Voice: Constructing Christian Theologies from the Underside* (ed. Susan Brooks Thistlethwaite and Mary Potter Engel; Maryknoll, N.Y.: Orbis, 1998), 274. See also, e.g., Ada Maria Isasi-Diaz, *En la lucha: In the Struggle: A Hispanic Women's Liberation Theology* (Minneapolis: Fortress, 1993).

42. See, for example, Sharon Pace Jeansonne, *The Women of Genesis: From Sarah to Potiphar's Wife* (Minneapolis: Fortress, 1990); Tikva Frymer-Kensky, *In the Wake of the Goddesses: Women, Culture, and the Biblical Pagan Myth* (New York: Free Press, 1992); Danna Nolan Fewell and David M. Gunn, *Gender, Power and Promise: The Subject of the Bible's First Story* (Nashville: Abingdon, 1993); Claudia V. Camp and Carole R. Fontaine, eds., *Women, War, and Metaphor: Language and Society in the Study of the Hebrew Bible* (*Semeia* 61 [1993]); Ilona N. Rashkow, *Taboo or Not Taboo: Sexuality and Family in the Hebrew Bible* (Minneapolis: Fortress, 2000); Claudia V. Camp, *Wise, Strange, and Holy: The Strange Woman and the Making of the Bible* (Sheffield: Sheffield Academic Press, 2000); Joan L. Mitchell, *Beyond Fear and Silence: A Feminist-Literary Reading of Mark* (New York: Continuum, 2001); Dorothy Lee, *Flesh and Glory: Symbol, Gender, and Theology in the Gospel of John* (New York: Crossroad, 2002); Christina Grenholm and Daniel Patte, eds., *Gender, Tradition, and Romans: Shared Ground, Uncertain Borders* (New York: T&T Clark, 2005).

43. Carol A. Newsom and Sharon H. Ringe, eds., *Women's Bible Commentary* (Louisville: Westminster John Knox, 1992; expanded ed., 1998).

have read the Bible for countless generations," but "we have not always been self-conscious about reading as women."[44] They explain that the title of the commentary refers to women in the plural because the editors and contributors recognized the need for intersectional feminist readings even when individual interpretations do not always make such intersectional connections visible. To date, the commentary is the only academically rigorous one-volume publication on all biblical books of the Christian canon that addresses women and gender. Its significance in the history of feminist biblical studies in North America cannot be overemphasized.

The other highly influential publication of the 1990s is the nineteen-volume Feminist Companion series to the Hebrew Bible, edited by Athalya Brenner.[45] Although this series was neither edited nor published in North America, numerous contributors to the first series (1993–2001) and the second series (1998–2002) work and live in North America. The articles explore biblical texts, characters, and topics with historical, literary, and cultural methodologies and represent the diverse range of scholarship on women and gender. Some come from explicitly feminist perspectives, while others remain moderately neutral about their sociopolitical agenda. Although attention to intersectional hermeneutics is minimal, the nineteen volumes have made the extent of research on women and gender in biblical studies more accessible than any other anthology.[46]

---

44. Ibid., xix. A third edition appeared in 2012.

45. The first series was edited by Athalya Brenner from 1993 to 2001 (with the exception of one co-edited volume) and published by Sheffield Academic Press: *A Feminist Companion to Genesis* (1993); *A Feminist Companion to Judges* (1993); *A Feminist Companion to the Song of Songs* (1993); *A Feminist Companion to Ruth* (1993); *A Feminist Companion to Samuel to Kings* (1994); *A Feminist Companion to Wisdom Literature* (1995); *A Feminist Companion to Esther, Judith, and Susannah* (1995); *A Feminist Companion to the Latter Prophets* (1995); *A Feminist Companion to the Hebrew Bible in the New Testament* (1996); Brenner and Carole Fontaine, eds., *A Feminist Companion to Reading of the Bible* (2001). The second series was also published by Athalya Brenner from 1998 to 2002 (with the exception of one co-edited volume) and published with Sheffield Academic Press: *Genesis: A Feminist Companion to the Bible (Second Series)* (1998); *Judges: A Feminist Companion to the Bible (Second Series)* (1999); *Ruth and Esther: A Feminist Companion to the Bible (Second Series)* (1999); *Samuel and Kings: A Feminist Companion to the Bible (Second Series)* (2000); *Exodus and Deuteronomy: A Feminist Companion to the Bible (Second Series)* (1998); *The Song of Songs: A Feminist Companion to the Bible (Second Series)* (2000); *Prophets and Daniel: A Feminist Companion to the Bible (Second Series)* (2002); Brenner and Fontaine, eds., *Wisdom and Psalms: A Feminist Companion to the Bible (Second Series)* (1998). The editor of the New Testament series is Amy-Jill Levine, who has published a growing series since 2000 with T&T Clark.

46. For other anthologies, see, e.g., Day and Pressler, *Engaging the Bible in a Gen-*

In short, the third phase in feminist biblical studies embraced the clarion call toward the inclusion of minoritized voices in history, society, and religion. Yet in practice feminist biblical studies often focused on women and gender at every conceivable level of scholarly discourse and activity— from teaching courses at undergraduate and graduate schools of religious and theological studies to doctoral research projects and scholarly publications. Methodologically, the field also moved toward the development of cultural studies.[47] However, after twenty years of feminist scholarly activities, the institutionalization of a feminist infrastructure in biblical studies has depended largely on individual efforts and hiring practices. Thus the call for a biblical feminist hermeneutics that "empower[s] women to forge strategic bonds with other women—not just with women who share their same demographic profile, but women of differing religious, ethnic, political, class, and geographical identities and locations"[48] represents an ongoing challenge to Bible scholars of all persuasions—feminist, womanist, *mujerista*, and others. By the 1990s, it had become clear that biblical literature needs to be examined with social categories such as gender, race, class, sexual orientation, disability, and geopolitical domination, so that feminist biblical scholarship contributes to the dismantling of the "rhetoric of empire"[49] prevalent in the world today. At the same time, the academic infrastructure for feminist biblical studies was far from securely established, and most feminist biblical scholars continued to function on the margins of the scholarly and institutional establishment.

---

dered World; Alice Bach, ed., *Women in the Hebrew Bible: A Reader* (New York: Routledge, 1999); Harold C. Washington et al., eds., *Escaping Eden: New Feminist Perspectives on the Bible* (New York: New York University Press, 1999); Victor H. Matthews et al., eds., *Gender and Law in the Hebrew Bible and the Ancient Near East* (Sheffield: Sheffield Academic Press, 1998).

47. See, e.g., J. Cheryl Exum, *Plotted, Shot, and Painted: Cultural Representations of Biblical Women* (Sheffield: Sheffield Academic Press, 1996); Exum, ed., *Beyond the Biblical Horizon: The Bible and the Arts* (Leiden: Brill, 1999); Kristen E. Kvam and Linda S. Schearing, eds., *Eve and Adam: Jewish, Christian, and Muslim Readings on Genesis and Gender* (Bloomington: Indiana University Press, 1999); Susanne Scholz, *Rape Plots: A Feminist-Cultural Study of Genesis 34* (New York: Lang, 2000); Yvonne Sherwood, *A Biblical Text and Its Afterlives: The Survival of Jonah in Western Culture* (Cambridge: Cambridge University Press, 2000).

48. Byron, "The Challenge of 'Blackness,'" 96.

49. For this terminology, see Elisabeth Schüssler Fiorenza, *The Power of the Word: Scripture and the Rhetoric of Empire* (Minneapolis: Fortress, 2007).

4. Fostering Global Intersectionality and Dialogical Relationships in the Early Twenty-First Century

In the early years of the second millennium C.E., North American feminist biblical research is dealing with several new challenges, three of which I will discuss in detail here. One challenge is related to the function of feminist biblical scholarship within the institutional boundaries of higher education. Another challenge comes from the Christian Right, which has taken on the issue of women and gender in numerous publications widely distributed to lay audiences. Yet another challenge—probably the most intellectually productive—pushes feminist studies toward investigations of "otherness" of all sorts, such as queer, ethnicity and race, and postcolonial studies.

First, North American feminist biblical scholarship unquestionably developed primarily within institutions of higher education and has become part of some undergraduate and graduate departments of religious and theological studies and seminaries. This development meant that feminist biblical scholars had not only to earn the usual academic credentials and to comply with established standards of tenure and promotion but also to adapt to the dominant academic discourse and scholarly norms in teaching and research projects.[50]

Publications, grants, and the development of feminist knowledge are judged by scholars of the dominant status quo. The feminist call to action—one of the initial drives of feminist scholarship in the 1970s—has all too often become secondary, and, consequently, the impetus toward sociopolitical, economic, and cultural transformation has been neglected. Perhaps unsurprisingly, then, feminist biblical research has turned into increasingly specialized, depoliticized, and coopted projects that comply with dominant standards, norms, and expectations. As Caroline Vander Stichele and Todd Penner observe, the guild of biblical studies "maintains a strong line of male-identified scholarly assessment and production,"[51] and "the difference that is tolerated does not challenge the phallocentric and colonial structures of the guild" but rather contributes to "solidify its hold."[52] Feminist biblical scholar-

---

50. For a critique of the institutional situation, see especially Esther Fuchs, "Points of Resonance," in *On the Cutting Edge: The Study of Women in Biblical Worlds* (ed. Jane Schaberg et al.; New York: Continuum, 2004), esp. 12. See also her work entitled *Sexual Politics in the Biblical Narrative: Reading the Hebrew Bible as a Woman* (Sheffield: Sheffield Academic Press, 2000).

51. Caroline Vander Stichele and Todd Penner, *Contextualizing Gender in Early Christian Discourse: Thinking beyond Thecla* (London: T&T Clark, 2009), 169.

52. Ibid., 170.

ship, like other marginalized discourses by the "excluded other," functions as a "fetish" and "is granted access to the formal structure as a beneficent gesture."[53]

Consequently, in North American institutions of higher education, feminist biblical research often serves as an add-on to the existing academic content management and distribution systems, and feminist biblical scholars must adapt to dominant academic expectations, the evaluation procedures of publishers, and the waning feminist sensibilities of their students. Moreover, as Pamela J. Milne notes, the emergence of feminist biblical studies and the inclusion of "others" into the field of biblical studies has concurrently led to "the devaluing of the field that we can now observe at many institutions." She insists that this development "may well be linked to the fact that what was once a virtually all-male discipline is no longer so."[54] Hector Avalos goes even further. He states that "the SBL is the agent of a dying profession" because it lacks teaching positions at credible academic institutions.[55] In this situation of gradually disappearing teaching positions, the "long-term viability" of feminist biblical scholarship is at stake, because innovation is "endangered or at least impeded."[56] Because of the survival mode in the humanities, the impetus toward maintaining the status quo discourages bold proposals for epistemological and hermeneutical change, including those from feminist biblical scholars.[57] At their best, then, feminist biblical scholars contribute to developing, promoting, and cultivating textual interpretations as "site[s] of struggle"[58] and as focused on issues that are "our own in this present world."[59] In other words, the ongoing marginalization of feminist biblical work in institutions of higher education has dampened the powerful energies that were set free in the 1970s.

Second, the Christian Right and its plethora of publications on women, gender, and the Bible also present considerable challenges to North Ameri-

---

53. Ibid., 169.

54. Milne, "Toward Feminist Companionship."

55. Hector Avalos, *The End of Biblical Studies* (Amherst, N.Y.: Prometheus, 2007), 316.

56. Milne, "Toward Feminist Companionship," 43.

57. See, e.g., Marc Bousquet, *How the University Works: Higher Education and the Low-Wage Nation* (New York: New York University Press, 2008).

58. Schüssler Fiorenza, *Power of the Word*, 254.

59. Vander Stichele and Penner, *Contextualizing Gender*, 173. For books that take seriously contemporary issues of the world today, see, e.g., Anne F. Elvey, *An Ecological Feminist Reading of the Gospel of Luke: A Gestational Paradigm* (Lewiston: Edwin Mellen, 2005); Daryn Guest, *When Deborah Met Jael: Lesbian Biblical Hermeneutics* (London: SCM, 2005); Carole R. Fontaine, *With Eyes of Flesh: The Bible, Gender, and Human Rights* (Sheffield: Sheffield Phoenix, 2008); Susanne Scholz, *Sacred Witness: Rape in the Hebrew Bible* (Minneapolis: Fortress, 2010).

can feminist biblical studies, although it remains largely unacknowledged on either side. Beginning in the 1990s and then forcefully propelled into the public during the new millennium, proponents of conservative-fundamentalist Christianity have published books and anthologies on gender and the Bible. Defining themselves as complementarians, they have taken on writers and theologians within their own religious context and contested egalitarian positions about women and men in church and society. The mostly male and white authors are often powerful leaders in evangelical organizations, particularly the Council of Biblical Manhood and Womanhood.[60]

What is striking about the complementarian Christian Right's discourse on gender and the Bible is its disregard for feminist biblical scholarship as it has emerged in academic discourse since the 1970s. Although many complementarian authors are seminary professors, such as John Piper and Wayne A. Grudem, their books have failed to engage academic feminist and non-feminist biblical scholarship even when they discuss biblical passages such as Gen 1–3, Eph 5:21–33, Col 3:18–19, or 1 Tim 2:11–15. Yet their work is widely accessible to lay audiences.

As a result of the Christian Right's conservative sociopolitical and theological discourse, feminist exegetes continue to combat the most basic and persistent androcentric views on women, gender, and the Bible that they have been deconstructing for more than forty years. The emergence of evangelical publications such as The IVP Women's Bible Commentary, edited by Catherine Clark Kroeger and Mary Evans, contributes to the confusion about the nature, goals, and positions of feminist biblical scholarship.[61] Many lay readers do not distinguish between a women's commentary emerging from an evangelical-theological context and feminist biblical books published within the academic field of biblical studies and descending from the feminist movement of the 1970s. Thus evangelical-conservative books on women, gender, and the Bible remain within the boundaries of a sociotheologically conservative hermeneutics.[62]

---

60. See the online presence of the CBMW at http://www.cbmw.org. For an analysis of the complementarians, see Susanne Scholz, "The Christian Right's Discourse on Gender and the Bible," *JFSR* 21 (spring 2005): 81–100.

61. Catherine Clark Kroeger and Mary J. Evans, eds., *The IVP Women's Bible Commentary* (Downers Grove, Ill.: InterVarsity Press, 2002). A very different commentary was published by Jewish feminist scholars and rabbis; see Tamara Cohn Eskenazi and Andrea L. Weiss, eds., *The Torah: A Women's Commentary* (New York: WRJ/URJ, 2008).

62. See, e.g., recent publications by Baker Publishing Group: Stephen J. Binz, *Women of the Gospels: Friends and Disciples of Jesus* (Grand Rapids: Brazos, 2011); Binz, *Women of the Torah: Matriarchs and Heroes of Israel* (Grand Rapids: Brazos, 2011); Lynn H. Cohick, *Women in the World of the Earliest Christians: Illuminating Ancient Ways of Life* (Grand

Third, investigations on "otherness" related to queer studies, ethnicity and race, and postcolonialism constitute the intellectually most productive challenge to feminist biblical studies in the early twenty-first century. Publications such as the *Queer Bible Commentary* and other anthologies and monographs on queer biblical interpretations have urged feminist biblical scholars to open up to GLBTQ issues.[63] For instance, Deryn Guest observes the prevalence of a "heteropatriarchal framework" in feminist biblical studies that sheds light on women in the Bible but does not explicitly consider lesbian hermeneutical concerns.[64] Ken Stone thus encourages connections between feminist and queer biblical studies because "feminism, too, is devoted to the critical analysis of sex and gender."[65] To him, a critical gender analysis should not be limited to "biblical representations of women" but should extend "to biblical representations of men and of 'masculinity.' "[66] In a way, then, queer biblical studies advances the work in feminist biblical studies as it "problematize[s] normative approaches to sexuality" and deconstructs "such dichotomies as 'homosexual/heterosexual' and 'male/female.' "[67] In short, the goal of LGBTQ exegesis is to disrupt "sex-gender-sexuality norms and academic conventions,

---

Rapids: Baker Academic, 2009); Tammi J. Schneider, *Mothers of Promise: Women in the Book of Genesis* (Grand Rapids: Baker, 2008). See also Robin Gallaher Branch, *Jeroboam's Wife: The Enduring Contributions of the Old Testament's Least-Known Women* (Peabody, Mass.: Hendrickson, 2009).

63. Deryn Guest et al., eds., *The Queer Bible Commentary* (London: SCM, 2006); Robert E. Goss and Mona West, eds., *Take Back the Word: A Queer Reading of the Bible* (Cleveland: Pilgrim, 2000). See also Guest, *When Deborah Met Jael: Lesbian Biblical Hermeneutics* (London: SCM, 2005); Theodore W. Jennings, *Jacob's Wound: Homoerotic Narrative in the Literature of Ancient Israel* (New York: Continuum, 2005); Jennings, *The Man Jesus Loved: Homoerotic Narratives from the New Testament* (Cleveland: Pilgrim, 2003); Robert E. Goss, *Queering Christ: Beyond Jesus Acted Up* (Cleveland: Pilgrim, 2002); Ken Stone, *Queer Commentary and the Hebrew Bible* (Cleveland: Pilgrim, 2001); Stone, *Practicing Safer Texts: Food, Sex, and Bible in Queer Perspective* (London: T&T Clark, 2005); Stephen D. Moore, *God's Beauty Parlor: And Other Queer Spaces in and around the Bible* (Stanford, Calif.: Stanford University Press, 2001); Daniel A. Helminiak, *What the Bible Really Says about Homosexuality* (Tajique, N.M.: Alamo Square, 2000); Stephen D. Moore, *God's Gym: Divine Male Bodies of the Bible* (New York: Routledge, 1996); Bernadette J. Brooten, *Love Between Women: Early Christian Responses to Female Homoeroticism* (Chicago: University of Chicago Press, 1996); Nancy Wilson, *Our Tribe: Queer Folks, God, Jesus, and the Bible* (San Francisco: Harper San Francisco, 1995).

64. Guest, *When Deborah Met Jael*, esp. 107.

65. Stone, *Queer Commentary*, 25.

66. Ibid., 26.

67. Ibid., 27.

playful and at times purposefully irreverent," and to expand feminist research beyond the analysis of "woman" or "women."[68]

Similarly, the emergence of studies on race and ethnicity has opened up feminist exegesis to perspectives from Asian American feminists and feminist scholars from minoritized North American communities.[69] Key in such explorations has been the hermeneutical insight that flesh-and-blood readers are central to the exegetical task of contextualizing biblical meanings in today's world.[70] Combined with postcolonial sensibilities, Mai-Anh Le Tran presents Lot's wife, Ruth, and the Vietnamese figure of Tô Thị as female characters "that liberate rather than dominate."[71] Gale A. Yee also problematizes the methodological, hermeneutical, and political soundness of ethnic/racial identity of biblical readers. She wonders what defines "my Asian Americanness, and how does this identity affect my biblical interpretation?"[72] In addition, postcolonial feminist studies on the Bible have emerged not only from North America but from other contexts as well.[73] A current goal of feminist

---

68. Guest et al., *The Queer Bible Commentary*, xiii.

69. See, e.g., Mary F. Foskett and Jeffrey Kah-Jin Kuan, eds., *Ways of Being, Ways of Reading: Asian American Biblical Interpretation* (St. Louis: Chalice, 2006); Randall C. Bailey, Tat-siong Benny Liew, and Fernando F. Segovia, eds., *They Were All Together in One Place? Toward Minority Biblical Criticism* (Atlanta: Society of Biblical Literature, 2009).

70. For the significance of the flesh-and-blood readers, see already Fernando F. Segovia and Mary Ann Tolbert, eds., *Social Location and Biblical Interpretation in the United States* (vol. 1 of *Reading from This Place*; Minneapolis: Fortress, 1995); and *Social Location and Biblical Interpretation in Global Perspective* (vol. 2 of *Reading from This Place*; Minneapolis: Fortress, 2000).

71. Mai-Anh Le Tran, "Lot's Wife, Ruth, and Tô Thị: Gender and Racial Representation in a Theological Feast of Stories," in Foskett and Kuan, *Ways of Being, Ways of Reading*, 125.

72. This and the following quotes are from Gale A. Yee, "Yin/Yang Is Not Me: An Exploration into an Asian American Biblical Hermeneutics," in Foskett and Kuan, *Ways of Being, Ways of Reading*, 156.

73. For publications from the North American context, see, e.g., Joseph A. Marchal, *The Politics of Heaven: Women, Gender, and Empire in the Study of Paul* (Minneapolis: Fortress, 2008); Hee An Choi and Katheryn Pfisterer Darr, eds., *Engaging the Bible: Critical Readings from Contemporary Women* (Minneapolis: Fortress, 2006); Caroline Vander Stichele and Todd C. Penner, eds., *Her Master's Tools? Feminist and Postcolonial Engagement of Historical-Critical Discourse* (Atlanta: Society of Biblical Literature, 2005). For study from other contexts, see, e.g., Seong Hee Kim, *Mark, Women and Empire: A Korean Postcolonial Perspective* (Sheffield: Sheffield Phoenix, 2010); Jean Kyoung Kim, *Woman and Nation: An Intercontextual Reading of the Gospel of John from a Postcolonial Feminist Perspective* (Boston: Brill, 2004); Musa W. Dube, *Postcolonial Feminist Interpretation of the Bible* (St. Louis: Chalice, 2000). See also Phyllis A. Bird, ed., *Reading the Bible as Women: Perspectives from Africa, Asia, and Latin America* (Atlanta: Scholars Press, 1997).

biblical studies is to bring feminist scholars of different social locations and hermeneutical and methodological assumptions together to find common ground in the academic study of biblical literature, history, and tradition.[74]

5. Toward Quilting Feminist Biblical Meanings: Concluding Comments

Feminist biblical scholars diverge on the future direction of feminist biblical studies. Esther Fuchs suggests that feminist exegetes respect difference and "desire for solidarity and alliance across difference."[75] Because of the diverse array of feminist biblical scholarship, this suggestion is timely. Fuchs also advises that feminist biblical scholarship engage the "very heart of Biblical Studies and the theories that currently shape it" and work "for epistemological transformation," a key goal of feminist theory in general.[76] In Fuchs's view, feminist biblical scholars face the urgent task of "rethinking and re-inventing existing frameworks for the production and dissemination of knowledge."[77]

Another perspective on the future of feminist biblical studies comes from Elisabeth Schüssler Fiorenza.[78] She does not consider academia alone as a viable context to work toward sociopolitical, economic, cultural, and theological transformation of society. In fact, she sees many social institutions as upholders of structures of domination. In her view, only alliances with global feminist movements for change will enable feminist biblical scholars to work toward the elimination of gender, racial, class, and other forms of injustice. Hence, Schüssler Fiorenza demands that feminist biblical scholarship "must be informed by a hunger and thirst for justice"[79] so that feminist interpretations resemble "a critical quilting of meaning" that articulates a "holistic biblical vision of well-being for all."[80]

---

74. See, e.g., Dora Mbuwayesango and Susanne Scholz, "Dialogical Beginnings: A Conversation on the Future of Feminist Biblical Studies," *JFSR* 25.2 (2009): 93–103. See also the ensuing nine responses on pp. 103–43. For an integration of different voices into a single-voiced scholarly account, see, e.g., Barbara E. Reid, *Taking Up the Cross: New Testament Interpretations through Latina and Feminist Eyes* (Minneapolis: Fortress, 2007).

75. Esther Fuchs, "Biblical Feminisms: Knowledge, Theory, and Politics in the Study of Women in the Hebrew Bible," *BibInt* 16 (2008): 224.

76. Ibid., 225.

77. Ibid., 221.

78. Elisabeth Schüssler Fiorenza, "Reaffirming Feminist/Womanist Biblical Scholarship," *Enc* 67 (autumn 2006): 370.

79. Ibid., 372.

80. Ibid.

It seems obvious in the age of corporate economic dominance in North American societies, especially in the United States, that alliances beyond the narrow confines of one's immediate affiliation are essential. Progressive academics, religious leaders, political groups, and social networks need to resist the lure and rewards of what postcolonial theorists call "the empire." At the same time, they will need to articulate theoretical and practical alternatives so that the next generation will be able to continue on. The establishment of institutions that foster such "emancipatory" alternatives remains foremost on the agenda not only of North American feminist biblical studies at the dawn of the twenty-first century.

Feminist Biblical Studies in Africa

Dora Rudo Mbuwayesango
Hood Theological Seminary

African women's interest in the Bible and their recognition of its power began with the first African women's encounters with the Bible. An example of this interest and recognition of power is evidenced in the exchange between Mmahutu (senior wife of chief Mothobi of the BaTlhaping people of South Africa) and the missionary John Campbell and his associates as early as 1813.[1] In the same general sense, feminist biblical studies began with the establishment of Christian churches by missionaries and the indigenous agents who established the African Indigenous churches (AIC). I consider these studies by women as "feminist" in the sense that they were done in women's interests and addressed problems that challenged women's existence and survival.

From the outset, the Bible was seen as a source of consolation and empowerment for overcoming the plight of African women in sub-Saharan Africa, as churchwomen gathered in groups to study the Bible. These studies were not informed by Western scholarly approaches to biblical interpretation, but were strictly related to the contexts of their lives. The Bible was approached as a source for understanding and dealing with the problems and joys they faced in their everyday lives. They were not concerned about what the Bible might have meant originally, but what it meant to them as God's direct word.

This early form of biblical studies by ordinary women in Africa has served consciously or unconsciously as a model for women theologians and biblical scholars in Africa. These women scholars, trained mostly in Western academies, have returned to read or reread the Bible with a focus on the context of the African woman, as their mothers and grandmothers have been

---

1. See a fuller discussion by Gerald West, "(Ac)claiming the (Extra)Ordinary African 'Reader' of the Bible," in *Reading Other-Wise: Socially Engaged Biblical Scholars Reading with Their Local Communities* (ed. Gerald O. West; Atlanta: Society of Biblical Literature, 2007), 29–47, here 32–36.

doing since their conversion to Christianity and their first encounters with the Bible. It is not a surprise, then, that these Western educated African women would like to include in their scholarly endeavors the voices of the "ordinary"[2] women of Africa. This focus and approach continues to be evident in women's church groups all over Africa.[3]

1. Setting the Context

Although this discussion is limited to sub-Saharan Africa, the vastness of the area covered is overwhelming. Africa is a vast continent with a variety of cultures, peoples, and religions. While the whole of Africa experienced Western colonial imperialism, there are regional differences in the ways colonialism was practiced and experienced in the different countries of sub-Saharan Africa. For example, while southern Africa did not experience much of the slave trade that led to the transplantation of Africans from their homeland to Europe and America, it did experience a longer duration of Western colonial domination that only ended with the dismantling of apartheid in South Africa in 1994.

Thus, the cultural context of women's experiences is tremendously diverse. For example, patriarchy is not monolithic in Africa. This cultural diversity is reflected in the fact that issues absolutely urgent in one corner of the continent might be unknown or even insignificant in some other corner. For instance, the notorious problem of female genital mutilation is very problematic in countries like Kenya, while it is not an issue in neighboring countries like Zimbabwe.

One of the other elements that provide a context for the development of feminist biblical studies in Africa is the education of women. In establishing schools, colonialists did not consider girls' education an important need. It took some fifty years after the first boys' school was constructed before girls' schools were established, and these schools were essentially to train women to be good wives for the early African male teachers and administrators. The priority given to males and the exclusion of women in education explains the long absence of African women's voices in theological discourses.

---

2. This practice is recognition that every African woman is an "ordinary" person and an "other" in Western contexts where most of their publications take place. This idea is very evident in the phrase, *Other Ways of Reading…* that is part of the title of the book containing essays by African women published by the Society of Biblical Literature and the World Council Churches in 2001.

3. Mother's Union in the Anglican Church, for example.

2. The Definition and Beginnings of
Feminist Biblical Studies in Africa

Feminist biblical studies is one strand intricately woven into the fabric of African feminist theology. This interweaving is not only explained by the fact that in Africa there is no separation of the discipline of biblical studies from other theological disciplines, but also by the fact that few women in Africa are trained biblical scholars. Hence, feminist theologians double as biblical scholars. In fact, the organizing of feminist theologians into what became known as The Circle of Concerned African Women Theologians (The Circle), spearheaded by Mercy Amba Oduyoye in 1989, marked the emergence of a feminist biblical studies hermeneutic.[4]

African feminist theology, therefore, is a latecomer to the liberation movement in theology that began in the 1970s and developed out of a greater consciousness influenced by socialist ideology to show concern for secular issues.[5] Although this liberation theology was focused on challenging oppression, it was concerned only with political and economic oppression and completely ignored oppression based on gender. In fact, these male liberation theologians valued patriarchy as a legitimate system in African society. Until the formation of The Circle, therefore, theology in Africa had been the domain of foreign and male researchers. African women were conspicuously absent as voices in doing theology, and consequently there was a disregard for issues of concern to them.

Women became increasingly aware of the implication of this absence of women as *subjects* in the "doing of theology." As Musimbi Kanyoro and Oduyoye state, "African women theologians have come to realize that as long as men and foreign researchers remain the authorities on culture, rituals, and religion, African women will continue to be spoken of as if they were dead."[6] African women saw direct results of their absence in African theology in gross marginalization and disregard for women and women's issues in church and society. This negligence needed to be corrected with urgency

---

4. Mercy Amba Oduyoye gathered some eighty women at Trinity College, in Accra Ghana and the proceedings of the meeting are described in *Talitha Qumi! Proceedings of the Convocation of African Women Theologians* (Ibadan: Daystar, 1990).

5. Justine Ukpong, "Developments in Biblical Interpretation in Africa: Historical and Hermeneutical Directions," in *The Bible in Africa: Transactions, Trajectories, and Trends* (Boston: Brill, 2001), 14.

6. Musimbi R. A. Kanyoro and Mercy Amba Oduyoye, "Introduction," in *The Will to Arise: Women, Tradition, and the Church in Africa* (ed. Mercy Amba Oduyoye and Musimbi R. A. Kanyoro; Maryknoll, N.Y.: Orbis, 1992), 1.

and determination. Thus, the mission statement of the Circle, as stated on its website, is "to undertake research and publish theological literature written by African women with special focus on religion and culture."[7] African women were ready to take their rightful place in speaking for themselves and fighting for their own liberation. They were not going to sit passively on the side while others spoke for them as if they were dead. They were going to name their oppressions and struggle to overcome them by finding strategies that were grounded in women's experience. They understood this determination to speak and fight for themselves as "grounded in the challenges of Scriptures and resulting from a new wave of change. African women reading the scriptures have begun to see that God's call for them is not passive. It is compelling and compulsory. It is a call to action and wholeness that challenges the will and intellect."[8]

At the forefront of this formal and systematic African women's theology is the centrality of the Bible as a major resource for empowerment in the search for liberation. In her address to the gathered group of eighty African women who inaugurated The Circle, Nyambura Njorege lifted up Rispah's persistence in seeking dignity in the burial of her sons in spite of King David's refusal (2 Sam 21:9–14) as a model for the way women ought to persist in challenging injustice until justice is granted to them.[9]

This involvement of women in theology was not unique to African women. It was already taking place in North America and Europe at least since the 1960s. In those contexts, the term used in characterizing women's theologizing was "feminism." In Africa, however, women theologians continue to struggle to find an umbrella name that adequately describes their theologizing. The concern for African women theologians is not limited to issues of gender, but extends to the concern for the liberation of the African peoples as a whole. Usually, the African women's approach for interpretation is not specified. It is only the location of the person doing the interpretation that is particularized either by country or ethnicity.[10] According to Teresa Okure,

---

7. See http://www.thecirclecawt.org/.

8. Kanyoro and Oduyoye, "Introduction," 1.

9. Nyambura Njoroge, "A Spirituality of Resistance and Transformation," in Oduyoye and Kanyoro, *Talitha Qumi*, 66–82.

10. Dora R. Mbuwayesango, "Childlessness and Woman-to-Woman Relationships in Genesis and in African Patriarchal Society: A Zimbabwean Woman's Perspective (Gen. 16:1–16; 21:8–21)," *Semeia* 78 (1997): 27–36; Madipoane Masenya, "Proverbs 31:10–31 in a South African Context: A Reading for the Liberation of African (Northern Sotho) Women," *Semeia* 78 (1997): 55–68.

there are two reasons that explain the lack of an umbrella name for African women's interpretative efforts. First,

> African women (and men for that matter) do not as a cultural rule start with the issue of methodology. Their primary consciousness in doing theology is not method but life and life concerns, their own and those of their own peoples. Second, Africa cannot as yet boast of many "professionally trained women biblical scholars."[11]

While it is true that there were, and still are, too few African women in theological studies in general—and even fewer in biblical studies in Africa—to connect an umbrella name to methodology, this does not get at the true reason. Rather, the reason is mainly the vastness of their geographical separation and the multiplicity of languages spoken on the continent. For example, the term "womanist" that is used by both biblical and theological African American scholars is less an approach as it is a "posture."[12]

Although African women theologians struggle to find an umbrella name for what they do as theologians and biblical scholars, it is clear that their work is framed by a belief in and concern for the liberation of women. Malestream African liberation theology had, in general, utilized the Bible as a resource in the struggle against political and economic oppression on the basis of the biblical witness that God does not sanction oppression, but always stands on the side of the oppressed to liberate them. This androcentric reading of the Bible, however, largely ignored patriarchal oppression as a form of oppression that God wanted dismantled. Just as malestream liberation theology uses the Bible as a resource in the struggle to dismantle political and economic oppression, so feminist hermeneutics uses the Bible as a resource for the struggle against the subordination and marginalization of women in contemporary society and church life.

Since the Bible has been used to support their oppression by patriarchy, African feminists see the need for the interpretation of the Bible from women's perspective. Thus, African biblical and cultural hermeneutics is highlighted as one of the four areas of research in African feminist theology.[13]

---

11. Teresa Okure, "Feminist Interpretations in Africa," in *A Feminist Introduction* (vol. 1 of *Searching the Scriptures*; ed. Elisabeth Schüssler Fiorenza with the assistance of Shelly Matthews; New York: Crossroad, 1993), 77.

12. Perhaps the solution will come in an African "Alice Walker" who coins a term that captures the essential posture and attitude of the African Woman and that can easily translate into English, French, and Portuguese.

13. "Report on Circle Study Commissions," Trinity College, Legon, Ghana, March 1998.

The foundational hermeneutic of African feminist theology and feminist biblical studies can be summarized as "reading the Bible from women's perspective." African women's theology, therefore, is unequivocally contextual.

In addition to being contextual, African women's theology is characterized as "a theology of relations" or "society sensitive." [14] In this regard, the ultimate goal of African women theologians is to replace hierarchies with mutuality. This characterization of African women's theology as relational is demonstrated by the ways in which the women of The Circle do their theological reflections. The process of doing theology in The Circle has three stages:

> Women of The Circle proceed from the narrating of the story to analyzing it to show how various actors in the story see themselves, how they interact with others, and how they view their own agency in life as a whole. They ask, 'What is the meaning of the story as a whole?' The next stage is to reflect on the experiences from the perspective of the Christian faith—a conscious implementation of biblical and cultural hermeneutics [is] at work in this process. From this perspective they identify what enhances, transforms or promotes in such a way as to build community and make for life-giving and life-enhancing relationships. This concern is not limited to the articulation of statements of faith. Women do theology to undergird and nourish a spirituality for life. And so from the affirmations of faith, which they make, issue statements of commitment, flows the praxis that gives birth to liberating and life-enhancing visions and further actions and reflections. [15]

So doing theology in general and biblical interpretation in particular involves action. It is a purposeful exercise that calls for contributing to the work of community building. This element of building community is always part of the interpretation of Scripture and calls for grassroots activism.

3. READING THE BIBLE FROM AFRICAN WOMEN'S PERSPECTIVE: CONCERNS AND APPROACHES

In addition to discussing the concern for the absence of women's voices in African theology that was addressed by using the Bible to motivate and empower women to begin to participate fully and vigorously in theological research and publication, I will endeavor to highlight several other concerns, and describe how they influence approaches and methods used in African feminist biblical studies. The first concern is that the interpretations by male

---

14. Mercy Amba Oduyoye, *Introducing African Women's Theology* (Sheffield: Sheffield Academic Press, 2001), 17.

15. Ibid.

theologians, who used historical-critical modes of interpretation developed in Western contexts, are characterized by androcentrism. Such androcentrism ignores the presence of women in the biblical texts, treating them as invisible or misinterpreting and portraying them in negative ways. Either way, the result has been the marginalization of women from full participation in society and church life. These androcentric modes of interpretation have therefore been challenged by African women theologians and biblical scholars. Oduyoye critically asks,

> One can understand how Western missionaries in their eagerness, unfamiliar with African culture and clothed in ethnocentric pride, snatched converts from unconverted culture. Today, though, must this continue? Must the church continue to base its theology on terminology using outdated exegetical methods that enthrone use of biblical texts against women?[16]

African women theologians not only critique the androcentric modes of interpretation, but also engage in corrective readings or rereadings of texts that may have been ignored or misinterpreted. For example, Okure rereads the story of Eve in a way that shows that the story does not portray Eve as inferior to Adam.[17] Similarly, Marie Bernadette Mbuy Beya argues that the Pauline texts so often seen as timeless and universal divine directives should not be read that way, because Paul was dealing with specific situations of disorder in the respective communities to which he wrote.[18] The focus of the reading and rereading of such texts is to distinguish in them "the liberative elements from the divine" and "the oppressive elements from the human."

Another way to counter the negative portrayal of women is by focusing on the texts that depict the positive role of women in the history of salvation or in the life of the church. Thus, Anne Nasimiyu-Wasike analyzes Jesus' teachings, parables, and miracles to show that Jesus had a positive attitude toward women.[19] Joyce Tzabedze likewise finds a positive role for women in the church reflected in 1 Timothy and Ephesians.[20] Similarly, Beya highlights

---

16. Mercy Amba Oduyoye, *Daughters of Anowa: African Women and Patriarchy* (Maryknoll, N.Y.: Orbis, 1995), 176.

17. Teresa Okure, "Women in the Bible," in *With Passion and Compassion: Third World Women Doing Theology* (ed. Virginia Fabella and Mercy Amba Oduyoye; Maryknoll, N.Y.: Orbis, 1988), 47.

18. Marie Bernadette Mbuy Beya, "Doing Theology as African Women," in *Voices from the Third World: EATWOT* 13 (1990): 155–56.

19. Anne Nasimiyu-Wasike, "Christology and African Woman's Experience," in *Faces of Jesus in Africa* (ed. Robert J. Schreiter; Maryknoll, N.Y.: Orbis, 1995), 73–80.

20. Joyce Tzabedze. "Women in the Church (1 Timothy 2:8–15, Ephesians 5:22)," in

the role of women in the history of Israel.[21] The goal of such readings is to present the lives of these women in the Bible as an inspiration for contemporary women in their struggle in a male-dominated society.

Another approach by African women theologians in interpreting the Bible is to seek a basic biblical theological orientation that can function as a guide to interpreting both the negative and the positive biblical texts about women. For example, Oduyoye identifies two such theologies, a theology of creation, which affirms the basic equality of man and woman created in the *imago Dei*, and a theology of community, which calls for the exclusion of violence and discrimination in society. She argues that both theologies are fundamental to all biblical teaching.[22]

The last approach in dealing with the androcentric interpretations of the Bible seeks to interpret biblical texts from African women's experience. For example, Nasimiyu-Wasike reads the stories of polygamy in the Hebrew Bible from African women's experience of polygamy and shows that the Hebrew Bible itself contains a critique of this institution, thus countering the common assumption that it extols it.[23]

The second concern in African women's reading of the Bible is triggered by the nature and origin of the Bible. Although the Bible is seen as a primary source of inspiration by the majority of African women theologians in The Circle, the biblical texts and traditions are undeniably oppressive to women because the texts of the Bible were written in patriarchal contexts. Thus, as a product of men, the Bible was authored from a male point of view characterized by androcentric interests. Women do not generally play a central role in the biblical stories, and even when they do, they are portrayed in ways that serve patriarchal and androcentric interests.

In addition, Christian interpretation of the Bible has been a formidable tool in the support of the African cultural traditions and practices that are oppressive to African women. As Oduyoye states, "Biblical interpretation and Christian theology have had the effect of sacralizing the marginalization of women's experience, even in African religions." In fact, the male Christian interpreters of the Bible and African culture have collaborated to create or perpetuate cultural practices that dehumanize women in all African societies.

New Eyes for Reading Biblical and Theological Reflections by Women from the Third World (ed. John Pobee and Barbel von Wartenberg-Porter; Geneva: WCC, 1986), 76–79.

21. Beya, "Doing Theology," 155–56.

22. Mercy Amba Oduyoye, "Violence against Women: Window on Africa," *Voices from the Third World* 18 (1995): 168–76.

23. Anne Namisiyu-Wasike, "Polygamy: A Feminist Critique," in Oduyoye and Kanyoro, *The Will to Arise,* 108–16.

These practices are scattered all over Africa in a variety of forms that range from "taboos regarding food and relationships, widowhood rites, child betrothals and early marriages, domestic and cultural violence female genital mutilation and lack of access to and control of family and sometimes national resources."[24] These aspects related to the Bible make the Bible a site of struggle in the African women's fight against the injustices of patriarchy that deny them full humanity and participation in society and communities, even church communities.

> The patriarchal nature and context of the Bible complicates its function as a primary resource in African women's struggle against the subjugation and domination of women. African women theologians have developed cultural hermeneutics as an important tool that enables women to interpret their experiences and realities in their own contexts. This cultural hermeneutics involves a critical analysis and a hermeneutic of suspicion of both the context of the Bible and the contemporary cultural contexts in which interpretation takes place. Therefore, African feminist biblical studies, with necessity, involves cultural hermeneutics as an important first step.[25]

As Kanyoro points out, the culture of the reader in Africa has more influence on the way the biblical text is understood and used in communities than the historical facts about the text. Not knowing the nuances of the culture of modern readers of the Bible has more far reaching repercussions on biblical hermeneutics than is normally acknowledged.

Because culture is considered a favorite tool for domination, cultural hermeneutics is an essential hermeneutics of liberation for African women who experience multiple cultures and multiple oppressions, enabling them to see that they have the power to change their plight and to fashion their own destinies. Culture, therefore, is not unchangeable, but a creation of humanity that is continually evolving. Oduyoye provides a definition of culture in the context of African women's theologies as follows: Culture is "what human beings have made from nature, and because of nature and community. All that is not nature has been 'cultivated,' worked upon, devised, dreamed up, and given shape and meaning by the human mind and hands. *Culturing*, therefore, is a continuous activity of the human community, and culture has become the

---

24. Philomen Njeri Mwaura, "Feminist Biblical Interpretation and the Hermeneutics of Liberation: An African Woman's Perspective," in *Feminist Interpretation of the Bible and the Hermeneutics of Liberation* (ed. Silvia Schroer and Sophia Bietenhard; London: Sheffield Academic Press, 2003), 77–85.

25. Musimbi R. A. Kanyoro, "Biblical Hermeneutics: Ancient Palestine and the Contemporary World," *RevExp* 94 (1997): 364.

locus of resistance."[26] The dynamic and evolving nature of culture means that women can and should be involved in effecting cultural change by offering strategies for transforming attitudes, beliefs, and practices. In so doing, African women will no longer be mere victims of oppressive cultures, but may become agents of transformation who are able to identify and promote life-affirming aspects in their culture. There is need, however, to identify the parameters for identifying the cultural elements that are life-affirming for women in Africa. According to Oduyoye, the key to the search for these parameters is "women's full humanity and participation in religion and society."[27]

Cultural hermeneutics, therefore, is an approach utilized by African women theologians to examine the Bible and to scrutinize the multicultural layers embedded in it. Several African women theologians have applied cultural hermeneutics to the interpretation of biblical narratives. Sarojini Nadar reads the character of Ruth in the mindset of the Indian practice of *sati* in order to unleash its mimetic potential to empower single South African women who are "either widowed, divorced or having husbands not living in the residence."[28]

Similarly, Madipoane Masenya reads the story of Ruth in a South African context characterized by racism and patriarchy from a *bosadi* (womanhood) cultural hermeneutics in order to present "Ruth as a model of a person who emerges as a winner, despite the many strikes against her."[29] Kanyoro, reading from the experience of the contemporary African cultural requirement for widows to marry the brothers of their dead husbands, focuses on Orpah, who is written out of the story at its beginning. She sees Orpah as a woman who does not succumb to the cultural expectations of her time. As such, it is women who choose to be Orpahs who have no models of blessing from the Bible. Kanyoro, therefore, asks,

> How do we support Orpahs? What blessings could we imagine for Orpah, especially when compared with the blessings that fell when she [Ruth] succumbed to certain cultural possibilities—a reward that culminates in taking a place in the lineage of salvation (Matt. 1:5)?[30]

---

26. Oduyoye, *Introducing African Women's Theology*, 12.

27. Ibid., 13.

28. Sarojini Nadar, "A South African Indian Womanist Reading of the Character of Ruth," in *Other Ways of Reading: African Women and the Bible* (ed. Musa W. Dube; Atlanta: Society of Biblical Literature, 2001), 159–75.

29. Madipoane Masenya, "Ruth," in *The Global Bible Commentary* (ed. Daniel Patte; Nashville: Abingdon, 2004), 86–91.

30. Musimbi R. A. Kanyoro, "Cultural Hermeneutics: An African Contribution," in Dube, *Other Ways of Reading*, 101–13.

My reading of the narratives of Sarah and Hagar (Gen 16:1–16; 21:8–21) is also a modest attempt at bringing together the Bible and the Shona and Ndebele cultural requirement that women must produce an heir, in order to point out that the barren women in contemporary Shona and Ndebele societies lack models from the Bible, since Sarah eventually gives birth.[31]

An important aspect of cultural hermeneutics is the use of African cultural resources as tools for interpreting the Bible. As with other tools, however, these resources need to be scrutinized first before they are utilized in interpretation. Thus, Oduyoye identifies two forms of oral tradition that are prevalent in Africa but largely ignored in African Christian theology as oral resources in cultural hermeneutics.[32] One type of oral tradition consists of songs and impromptu lyrics sung by Africans to interpret biblical events, to call people to worship, and to teach the young.[33] The second form is a "religious-cultural corpus" in two types: proverbs and "folktalk" (folktales and myths that are the heritage of all people and not just the learned or the elderly).[34] Folktalk is particularly significant as it is "dynamic and malleable, [and] interplays with the changing conditions of life to direct individual self-perceptions and to shape the entire community."[35]

Several hermeneutical principles, significant in making the corpus of folktalk a cultural resource in cultural hermeneutics, are discernible from Oduyoye's critical examination of the corpus. The fifth principle involves the question of how the corpus "reflects or is actually used to shape women's lives and to answer the question, 'What is woman?'"[36] The second principle involves the question of who benefits from the telling of the myths, folktales, and proverbs from generation to generation. For example, she argues that comments in folktalk do not reflect historical reality, but are rhetorical devices aimed at shaping communal values and changing behaviors. Thus she declares,

> For me, African myths are ideological constructions of a bygone age that are used to validate and reinforce societal relations. For this reason, each time I hear "in my culture" or "the elders say" I cannot help asking, for whose benefit? Some person or group or structure must be reaping ease and plenty from whatever follows. So, if that harvest seems to be at my expense, then I

---

31. Mbuwayesango, "Childlessness and Woman-to-Woman Relationships," 27–36.

32. Mercy Amba Oduyoye, *Hearing and Knowing: Theological Reflections on Christianity in Africa* (Maryknoll, N.Y.: Orbis, 1996), 45–50; Oduyoye, *Daughters of Anowa*, 19–76.

33. Oduyoye, *Daughters of Anowa*, 45–50.

34. Oduyoye, *Hearing and Knowing*, 19.

35. Ibid, 20.

36. Ibid.

shall require the proceedings to stop until I am convinced that there is good reason for me to die that others might live.[37]

The third principle involves having the courage to discard some of the folktalk that is harmful and is no longer relevant, and to continue to develop a new tapestry of meanings for women. She argues that since culture is not static, but is constantly open to transformation, women must use their creativity and insight to weave new patterns of meaning for their lives. The new tapestry that will emerge will be multistranded, vibrant, and colorful, reflecting the equal values of women and men and the mutual dependence and reciprocity of human community.[38]

The application of African cultural resources as critical tools in biblical interpretation is not limited to oral traditions—poems, songs, stories, both myth and folktales—but includes the act of storytelling or narrating. According to Isabel Phiri, "The act of storytelling—of delving into the past—encourages introspection and reflection on our experiences. We begin to see our past in a new light and this consequently makes us read the present differently."[39] The aim of storytelling in African feminist theology is to change the role of women "from being observers and victims into participants and actors in history."[40] The sharing of a story, therefore, is a form of witness, practicing a "theology of witness," and consequently taking a step toward encouraging others to share stories and by this sharing to empower one another to transform society.[41]

The other aspect that makes storytelling an important key in African women's theology is the fact that storytelling was traditionally the domain of women in communities. In African society, the function of stories is education—to guide, to warn, to teach, and to lend meaning to events in the listeners' lives. This function in African society leads feminist theologians to opt for storytelling as an important element of their theology. The stories include not just those in the religious-cultural corpus, but also personal stories about women's experiences, many of which are painful. Storytelling is therefore considered to be narrative therapy for the narrator, and a step toward healing.

African women interpreters have begun to develop ways of reading the Bible that utilize African cultural resources as critical tools for interpreting

37. Ibid., 35.

38. Ibid., 74–76.

39. Isabel Phiri, "Introduction," in *Her-Story: The Histories of Women of Faith in Africa* (ed. Isabel Phiri et al.; Pietermaritzburg, South Africa: Cluster, 2002), 6.

40. Ibid., 10.

41. Oduyoye, *Introducing African Women's Theology*, 17.

biblical texts. The first volume of The Circle devoted to the interpretation of the Bible, edited by Musa Dube, includes several readings that specifically use African cultural resources as critical tools. The use of these resources is evident in at least two forms in the book: storytelling and the application of cultural resources.

In a narrative poem, Rose Teteki Abbey retells the story of three biblical women in autobiographical form, using experiences from her own life and the biographies of women living in patriarchal societies. She picks up on the particularities of the experiences of each woman, beginning with the Samaritan woman and the woman caught in adultery, and she highlights Mary's desire to study as the reason she sat at Jesus' feet rather than helping Martha in the kitchen. In addition to exposing the oppression of women in patriarchal societies, she shows that the encounter with Jesus brought a new world of liberation of women from patriarchal cultures and laws. [42]

Similarly, Dube combines three stories—the story of the woman with a hemorrhage (Mark 5:24-43), a southern African resurrection folktale, and a contemporary history of Africa, in order to depict how African women have survived suffering characteristic of all the phases of African history, precolonial, colonial, post-independence, globalization, and the contemporary era of HIV/AIDS. Speaking as Mama Africa, Dube places the experiences of African women, which are often ignored in histories written from male perspectives, at the center of African history.[43] Masenya retells the story of Esther by weaving the biblical text and Northern Sotho folktales to critique global society on ethical issues. She combines the act of storytelling and the use of cultural critical tools as a resource.[44] From a postcolonial perspective, Dube reads the story of Ruth in light of international relations, using the cultural practice of divination prevalent in both African tradition and African Independent Churches. She "divines" the unhealthy relationship between Ruth and Naomi as that between countries.[45]

It is important to highlight how the concern of African women's theology about the survival of all the African peoples—including women, children and men—influences their hermeneutics of the Bible. Life in Africa faces threats from multiple sources, such as past and contemporary imperialism, colonial-

---

42. Rose Teteki Abbey, "I Am the Woman," in Dube, *Other Ways of Reading*, 23–26.

43. Musa W. Dube, "Fifty Years of Bleeding: A Storytelling Feminist Reading of Mark 5:24–43," in Dube, *Others Ways of Reading*, 50–60.

44. Madipoane Masenya, "Esther and Northern Sotho Stories: An African-South African Woman's Commentary," in Dube, *Other Ways of Reading*, 27–49.

45. Musa W. Dube, "Divining Ruth for International Relations," in Dube, *Other Ways of Reading*, 179–95.

ism, neocolonialism, globalization, bad local governance, wars, droughts, and diseases. Thus, African women theologians see the need to read the Bible for decolonization and the empowerment of women. For example, they examine Bible translations to show how those translations contribute to the marginalization of women.[46] Musa Dube has been a pioneer in developing methodologies of reading for decolonization in her development of a feminist postcolonial approach.[47]

African women theologians have also joined in the struggle against HIV/AIDS, and actively participate in grassroots movements to stem the spread of the disease. They examine biblical texts related to issues of violence and justice for children.[48] A collection of essays called *Grant me Justice! HIV/AIDS and Gender Readings of the Bible*, the second book dedicated to biblical interpretation by The Circle, offers "gender-sensitive multi-sectional HIV/AIDS readings of the Bible."[49] In the book, the Bible is brought into conversation with contemporary experiences and understandings of violence, suffering, human sexuality, and stigma. For example, Ackermann's reading of the story of the rape of Tamar (2 Sam 13:1-22) shows how such violence can be read with stories of violence against women in South Africa, and she offers clues for both resistance and hope.[50]

One of the most significant approaches by African women theologians in reading the Bible is "reading with and from nonacademic readers." Such an approach is rooted in their conviction that the Bible is an open book to be

---

46. Dora R. Mbuwayesango, "How Local Divine Powers Were Suppressed: A Case of Mwari of the Shona," in Dube, *Other Ways of Reading*, 63–77; Gomang Seratwa Ntloedibe-Kuswani, "Translating the Divine: The Case of Modimo in the Setwana Bible," in Dube, *Other Ways of Reading*, 78–97; Musa Dube, "Consuming a Colonial Time Bomb: Translating *Badimo* into 'Demons' in Setswana Bible (Matt. 8:28–34,15:2, 10:8)," *JSNT* 73 (1999): 33–59.

47. Musa Dube, *Postcolonial Feminist Interpretation of the Bible* (St. Louis: Chalice, 2000).

48. Sarojini Nadar, "'Texts of Terror': The Conspiracy of Rape in the Bible, Church, and Society: The Case of Esther 2:1–18," in *African Women, Religion, and Health* (ed. Isabel Apawo Phiri and Sarojini Nadar; Maryknoll, N.Y.: Orbis, 2006), 77–95; Dorothy B. E. A. Akoto, "Women and Health in Ghana and the *Trokosi* Practice: An Issue of Women's and Children's Rights in 2 Kings 4:1-7," in Phiri and Nadar, *African Women, Religion, and Health*, 96–110.

49. Musa Dube, "Grant Me Justice: Towards Gender-Sensitive Multi-Sectoral HIV/AIDS Readings of the Bible," in *Grant Me Justice! HIV/AIDS and Gender Readings of the Bible* (ed. Musa Dube and Musimbi Kanyoro; Maryknoll, N.Y.: Orbis, 2004), 13.

50. Denise M. Ackermann, "Tamar's Cry: Re-reading an Ancient Text in the Midst of an HIV and AIDS Pandemic," in Dube and Kanyoro, *Grant Me Justice*, 27–59.

read in community.[51] This community is inclusive, and consists of all types of members. Nonacademic and academic readers, therefore, are partners in finding ways to dismantle all forms of oppression.

As Okure states, "The African women's approach is inclusive of scholars and non-scholars, the rich and the poor; it is inclusive of the "scientific," the creative, and the popular methods."[52] This grassroots aspect of African women's theology is demonstrated by Kanyoro, who reads the book of Ruth with rural women in Kenya to empower them to free themselves from oppressive cultural traditions.[53] Similarly, Gloria Kehilwe Plaatjie reads the story of Anna in Luke 2:36–38 with nonacademic black women of South Africa whose marginalization from positions of power results from apartheid and patriarchy. She suggests that instead of the Bible, which justifies patriarchy and apartheid, the hope for the oppressed women of South Africa is the Post-apartheid South African Constitution.[54]

4. CONCLUSION

Feminist biblical studies in Africa is in the first year of the third decade in the history of its existence. There is reason, therefore, to celebrate. The voices of African women theologians can no longer be ignored. They are clearly demonstrating that they can speak for themselves, and many publications bear witness to this fact. They are making significant contributions in the academy and in the church. They are sharpening their methodology and have come up with at least two clearly definable approaches to the Bible in feminist biblical studies: cultural hermeneutics and postcolonial feminist interpretation.

African feminist scholars are also contributing to the relevance of the Bible in very creative ways. For example, cultural hermeneutics is characterized by the use of resources that are at home in Africa. It has thus succeeded in demonstrating that methods of reading that are based on such resources are not at all inferior to those created in the West. But more importantly, African women theologians' readings make the Bible relevant for the African audience. The challenge remains, however, to train more African women (and men) in these strategies of interpretation.

---

51. For full description of this approach, see Musa Dube, "Introduction," in Dube, *Other Ways of Reading,* 8–11.

52. Okure, "Feminist Interpretations in Africa," 77.

53. Kanyoro, "Biblical Hermeneutics," 363–78.

54. Gloria Kehilwe Plaatjie, "Toward a Post-apartheid Black Feminist Reading of the Bible: A Case of Luke 2:36–38," in Dube, *Other Ways of Reading,* 114–42.

Intercultural Mapping of Feminist Biblical Studies: Southern Europe

Mercedes Navarro Puerto
Madrid, Spain

In this work I intend to construct a map of feminist biblical studies in my own context, Spain, in order to highlight who and what is visible and what this visibility implies in terms of power.[1] This kind of mapping highlights the ways in which feminism, like critical theory, is unable to conceptualize without politicizing. Nonetheless, it should be kept in mind that the map is not the territory.[2]

1. (Historical) Disconnections of a Continent

The distinction between southern and northern Europe is not simply one of difference, but also one of separation and disconnection. During the first half of the last century and even into the second half, Spain had to deal with the powerful belief that because we were different we did not belong to Europe. A kind of polarizing "Catholic" mentality played an essential role in this difference, which is expressed in decisions that are painful for any person who thinks critically.[3] This created a gap in biblical studies within the framework of church-owned schools of theology, as the more intensive focus on education and specialization

---

1. I have taken this contextualization from Denise Ryley. The historical experience of this South is profoundly marked by its concept of catholicism, that is, by the way in which the Christian religion has been understood and developed. This becomes quite evident in Spain starting in the sixteenth century. A problem added to my position is the question of how to avoid creating or re-creating "difference" in this essay.

2. Celia Amorós, "Pensar filosóficamente desde el feminismo," *Debats* 76 (2002): 66–80.

3. Catholicism was the national trademark during the Franco dictatorship, but in the Republic that preceded it catholicism was the "demon" that had to be destroyed. Now, it is the social, political, and economic battleground of a game that is highly calculated in all its parts within a framework that has never ceased to be patriarchal.

of students in biblical studies that developed in the geographical North in conjunction with first- and second-wave feminism (at the end of the 1970s and in the 1980s) was practically unknown in the geographical South. But, Spain and Italy were the loci of the first efforts of feminist thinking within the context of militant activism and thought. Thus, the feminist theological trajectory began with a turning of our gaze in the same direction in which our sister philosophers, sociologists, psychologists, and other feminists were looking—toward what was being produced in the West, particularly the United States and Latin America, which had become a stimulating new world for feminist theory and theology. Feminist theory, like feminist theology, came from the United States and Latin America unimpeded by the expansive distance of the Atlantic Ocean. Although the output of the United States was and continues to be unilateral, this is not the case for Latin America.

Of course, beginning in the late 1970s and continuing into the 1980s, northern Europe had a large number of women with graduate degrees in theology and biblical studies. Professors, departments, and chairs of feminist theology already existed, and developed further in the 1990s. The already numerous publications in German and English expanded greatly, and even those in languages of more limited distribution (those of the Netherlands and Scandinavia, among others) increased with each passing year. Study and research groups formed and expanded. Each of these factors indicates the normalization of feminist theological research and biblical exegesis. The spread of biblical knowledge and the gender and feminist perspective that began in the 1990s has come to form part of the cultural heritage alongside the development of women's studies in other academic disciplines.

In southern Europe during this time, the most significant event was the effort of many women to overcome the difficulties of studying theology and specializing in biblical studies (more than in other theological specializations). The great majority of those who succeeded went into theology after having established themselves in another career, which often enabled them to pay the costs of their theological studies. The change in the decade of the 1990s is noticeable in publications and the establishment of group spaces for research and dissemination. However, feminist theology and exegesis were, and continue to be, minority interests. There are few women professors, and there is no chair or program of feminist theology in any Spanish or Italian university.

The separation/disconnection of these worlds has led historically to a major difference since the time of the Reformation and the Counter-Reformation.[4] Northern Europe is interdenominational and is therefore a world

---

4. I refer the readers to volume 7 of this collection with respect to the reception of

open to religious plurality. Southern Europe is Roman Catholic, and religious homogeneity translates into greater conservatism, less openness, and greater difficulty in achieving coexistence. This reality explains in part the delay in the acceptance of, not to mention the opposition to, feminist theology and biblical exegesis. The repercussions extend to the various forms of gender identity, the establishment of a specific idea of femininity, and the difficulty in normalizing feminist awareness.

In northern Europe, the existence of agents and spaces for research, discussion, and critical awareness favors an equally critical and open reception of feminist theological and biblical research by other women in the field of theology and the humanities. In southern Europe, we feminist theologians have been practically invisible to feminist theory. As a general rule, feminist theoreticians look upon women theologians with suspicion and skepticism, and on more than one occasion have seized upon the religious and Christian aspect without being interested in engaging in serious debate.[5] Many feminist theoreticians show greater interest in a dialogue and debate with Islamic feminism than with Christian theology.[6]

2. Disconnections among Powers

The data available reflects some of the challenges facing women theologians in southern Europe. I have supplied here data from Spain, which will provide a point of reference for mapping feminist theological study in the European context.

In Spain we currently have ten schools of theology, all church-related; that is, they belong to male religious orders or to the Spanish Episcopal Conference (CEE). In addition, there are four Institutes of Theology incorporated into the universities cited, and two supplemental centers. The schools of theology and the centers for advanced studies are directed and managed by men. Many of them, moreover, have established departments of religious science expressly for women and for men who are not candidates for the priesthood.

---

the Bible and its relationship with women during this historical period, since it is very illustrative.

5. In Italy this is clearly the case with Luisa Muraro and in Spain with feminist philosophers such as Celia Amorós and Amelia Valcárcel, who approach religious reality from the perspective of their concern with advancing a conservative ideology extracted from Muslim women.

6. In Spain there is a biennial conference of Muslim feminism that receives financing from public and government establishments and institutions, something that has never existed, in these terms, in the case of (Christian) feminist theology conferences.

In terms of student numbers and percentages, it is clear that the vast majority at all levels of study are men, and almost all of them are candidates for the priesthood (seminarians).[7] The lower figures and percentages for women at the higher levels of study are particularly noteworthy except at the school of theology at the Pontifical University of Comillas, which records the highest numbers at all levels and especially the doctorate level. Thus, the statistics certainly do not point toward a possible future parity in the theological training of men and women. It seems as if women will continue to be a minority group for a long time to come, at least with respect to regular studies and the obtaining of official degrees (always from the point of view of current androcentric Church conditions).

Moreover, there are very few women professors of theology in the Spanish schools of theology. Some of them teach auxiliary rather than traditionally theological subjects. Women professors of biblical studies are very few in number, and there is only one woman teaching the New Testament. The number of women students in theological studies increases very much in the Institutes of Religious Science (ICRs). There are also slightly more women professors at these institutes, some teaching as regular staff and others as guest lecturers. This phenomenon can be ascribed to a multitude of causes and factors, of which I will discuss only the most important here.

The first reason, as already indicated, is the separation between training places for seminarians and for the rest of the interested populace. The schools of theology, in turn, are suffering from a reduction in male student numbers

---

7. In research conducted at the beginning of the 2010–2011 academic year, I contacted the university schools of theology and the theological centers of advanced studies in order to obtain information about students and to filter it through the variables of gender and the levels of courses (the *licenciatura* or basic university degree in church studies, as well as specializations, and doctorate). Five schools of theology (50% of the total) responded. While remaining aware of the incomplete nature of this information, I offer the results obtained as a sampling that is in any case significant. (1) School of Theology of Valencia: *licenciatura* in church studies: 110 men and 20 women, 15.38% women and 84.62% men; specialization: 28 men and 5 women, 15.15% women and 84.85 men; doctorate, 6 men and 1 woman, 14.29% women and 85.71 % men. (2) School of Northern Spain (Burgos): *licenciatura* in church studies: 23 men and 2 women, 8% women (plus 4 auditors) and 92% men; specialization: 7 men, 0 women, 0.00% women, 100% men; doctorate: 45 men, 0 women, 0.00% women and 100% men. (3) School of Theology of Granada: 94 men and 73 women, 43.71% women and 56.29% men. (4) Pontifical University of Comillas (Madrid): *licenciatura* in church studies and specialization: 126 men and 77 women, 37.93% women and 62.07% men; doctorate: 35 men and 17 women, 32.69% women and 67.31% men. (5) Pontifical University of Salamanca: *licenciatura* in church studies, 35 men and 10 women, 22.2% women and 77.78% men; specialization: 16 men and 2 women, 11.11% women and 88.89 % men.

because of the drop-off in vocations to the priesthood. Women who want to study theology are limited by the downgrading of schools of theology to church schools (few in number, and most of them in the major cities), the high cost of studies, the work situation of most women, and the lack of jobs for theological graduates.[8] This situation has particular effects for women who are interested in theology but are not members of religious orders. Women religious, in turn, rarely find in their congregations any stimulus for studying theology and still less for their specialization as instructors or researchers.

Secondly, the Spanish government is not interested in fostering anything that hints at a relationship with Catholicism, since Catholicism appears closely linked with the history of the Franco dictatorship and an episcopacy that is conservative, repressive, controlling of consciences, and profoundly misogynistic. The Spanish episcopacy, in turn, is not willing to allow the government to establish schools of theology in public universities.[9] The Spanish Church not only does not encourage theological training of women (even less, specialization in biblical studies, and not to mention gender and feminist perspectives), but it also tries to ignore the existence of current women theologians and biblical scholars. These theologians and specialists do not count at any level of the church. Rather, they have been rendered invisible and nonexistent even in documents critical of theologians. For example, the episcopal document of 2006 cites and indicts Spanish male theologians, who have been censured by the Holy See.[10] It does not cite women theologians who have been censured for maintaining similarly controversial beliefs.[11]

---

8. The option of teaching religion that some graduate women theologians have chosen has functioned as a corset to confine their thinking, since both public and private teaching of religion is supervised and monitored by the CEE, to which this type of education ultimately reports.

9. Late in the twentieth century, after a hard battle on various fronts (due to the terms of the Concordat between the Spanish government and the Holy See), the Complutense University of Madrid succeeded in establishing an Institute of Religious Science. Degrees earned at this institution are not recognized by the church, either partially or fully, as degrees in theology. The curriculum at this institute includes biblical subjects pertaining to the specialization level, which also are not recognized, and its programs and teaching staff are especially careful to avoid mentioning theology.

10. *Teología y secularización en España: A los cuarenta años de la clausura del Concilio Vaticano II. Instrucción Pastoral* (Madrid, 30 March 2006). The strategy is much harsher than what the Italian episcopacy has, at least, endeavored to showcase with "its own women theologians" of "Christian feminism," and which include, explicitly, prestigious biblical scholars such as Marinella Perroni and Maria-Luisa Rigato, in addition to solid women theologians, such as Cettina Militello and Serena Nocetti, and which provides financial backing for research projects of female theologians, some of whom are openly feminist.

11. We need only mention, by way of example, *Mujeres sacerdotes ¿por qué no?*, by

3. Feminist Connections and disconnections: Feminist Theology and Biblical Studies in Spain

It is obvious that even though they are nonexistent in the eyes of the Spanish episcopacy, there are women theologians and biblical scholars in Spain, many of whom are engaged in theological work, and some appear openly and explicitly as feminist theologians and/or biblical scholars. This minority group has been disconnected from feminist theology and biblical studies in Europe, and has been ignored by academic feminist theoreticians and movements who have been suspicious of feminist theologians.

3.1. Chronology of Significant Events in Feminist Theology and Feminist Biblical Studies in Spain

Here I summarize the short history of feminist theology in Catholic Europe beginning with Spain, and then consider Italy and France. Portugal and other Mediterranean countries are less thoroughly considered, as I have less information concerning these nations.

In Spain, feminist movements emerged in 1975, but Christian feminists and theologians became visible only a decade later. In 1986, the Seminario Fe y Secularidad sobre Teología Feminista (Seminar in Faith and Secularism: on Feminist Theology) was operating under the direction of Felisa Elizondo with several women theologians participating, including Leticia Sánchez, Mercedes Navarro, Margarita Pintos, Esperanza Bautista, and many others. This was also the year when the Mujer y Teología (Women and Theology) groups were established in Madrid under the initiative of Marifé Ramos. The biblical scholar Dolores Aleixandre was particularly noteworthy in this movement.

Continuing into the first decade of the twenty-first century, autonomous regional groups came into being in the peninsula and the islands. Because of the initiative of Margarita Pintos, steps were also taken to include women theologians in the John XXIII Association of Theologians. The Forum for Women's Studies began, under the initiative of Pilar Bellosillo and with the coordination of María Salas. This group is part of the Ecumenical Forum of Christian Women of Europe. Another group that came into being was the Catalan association Col.lectiu de Dones en l'Esglesia (Assembly of Women in the Church). This group established its own "School of Feminist Theology," and, in 2006,

María José Arana and María Salas (Madrid: Claretianas, 1994), as well as the numerous statements made in the media by María José Arana, an openly feminist theologian.

succeeded in introducing feminist theology in Gerona and the public University of Barcelona, where half-yearly courses are taught. This organization also hosted the Second European Synod of Women held in 2003 in Barcelona.

In 1992, Esperanza Bautista, Carmen Bernabé, Isabel Gómez-Acebo, and Mercedes Navarro established the Asociación de Teólogas Españolas (ATE, Association of Spanish Women Theologians). It held its first Conference on Feminist Theology at the University of Comillas of Madrid in 1993. In that same year, Mercedes Navarro edited and published the organization's book, *Diez palabras de Teología Feminista*.[12] The ATE also publishes a bibliographic bulletin two or three times a year.[13] In 2001, it became part of the Coordinadora Española del Lobby Europeo de Mujeres (CELEM, Spanish Coordinator of the European Lobby of Women). It now holds an annual conference and publishes monographs and translations of feminist theology in the *Aletheia* collection of EVD.

In January 2006, Mercedes Arriaga, Mercedes López, and Mercedes Navarro, with the close collaboration of Juana García Domene, founded the Escuela Feminista de Teología de Andalucía (EFETA, Feminist School of Theology of Andalucía). In June the EFETA was legally incorporated and a teaching presence was established in Seville as part of the public courses at the International University of Andalucía (UNIA). Online teaching began in October, and the first of the two courses began a private school degree in Basic Feminist Theology (equivalent in time and content to a master's degree). In 2008, a teaching agreement was signed with the University of Seville for three academic elective credits, and in 2010 an agreement was signed to allow women students from the University of Seville to enroll in EFETA's practical studies program. After unsuccessful efforts with other public universities, including Complutense University of Madrid, steps were taken to establish a possibly permanent academic relationship with Winchester University in the United Kingdom.

The first course in feminist theology at the Menéndez Pelayo International University was held in July 2010 at the central campus in Santander, under the direction of Isabel Gómez Acebo.[14]

---

12. Mercedes Navarro, ed., *Diez palabras de Teología Feminista* [Ten Words of Feminist Theology] (Estella, Spain: Editorial Verbo Divino, 1993).

13. The ATE has been part of the Synod of European Women since 1994, and it participated, through the activity of some of its members, in the preparation and organization of the 1996 meeting in Gmunden, Austria, and, more visibly, with the Col.lectiu de Dones en L'Esglesia, in the Barcelona meeting in 2003.

14. Women's associations and movements exist in other countries of Catholic Europe, with varying degrees of commitment to feminism. The phenomenon of tabooizing the

3.2. Memory, Tradition, and Translation

Amelia Valcárcel, one of our most well-known feminist philosophers, notes that Spanish women of the twentieth century have no personal memory of their predecessors. What they do have is a memory that has been perhaps improperly appropriated. We are not rooted in a received tradition, since we have had to construct our tradition. Women theologians have the same problem: We have appropriated a memory that does not belong to us. Since we were not educated as "successors" of our predecessors, we are not rooted in the soil of history.

Creating our own tradition and appropriating a memory that in fact was never ours has been made possible through reading and translating Ameri-

---

word "feminism" is more visible in these groups than in other academic and even social justice groups. This can be seen in France and in Italy. Portugal has few active groups. One example is the Franco-Belgian group Femmes et Hommes dans L´Église, established in 1970. The Wikipedia entry for this group (11 May 2011) states: "To mention one example, The International Group of Women and Men in the Church (Groupement international Femmes et Hommes dans l'Église) was established in Brussels and Paris in 1970. It made its initial filing with the theologians meeting for the colloquium of the journal *Concilium* in Brussels in September 1970." The international office was soon established in Brussels, around Pierre de Locht and Suzanne van der Mersch of the Centre de pastorale familiale (CEFA, Family Pastoral Center). It includes Louvain professors, theologians, philosophers, and sociologists such as Pierre Delooz, a member of the management team of the Institut Pro Mundi Vita, as well as women who hold positions of responsibility in church associations, including Denise Peeters of the Commission internationale de l'Union Mondiale des Organisations Féminines Catholiques (UMOFC, International Commission of the World Union of Catholic Women's Organizations). In Paris, Yvonne Pellé-Douël–the critically acclaimed author of the 1967 text *Être femme,* a work inspired by Christian Personalism—was the first to encourage Marie-Thérèse van Lunen Chenu (then a member of the Joan of Arc International Alliance) in planning a new group that was to be supported by Reverend M. Dominique Chenu (a Dominican theologian and scholar at Vatican Council II), Marie-Odile Métral, Henri-Jacques Stiker, René Simon (moralist), Sr. Françoise Vandermeersch, Sr. Sabine Villatte des Prugnes, Pauline Archambault, Odile Cadiot (daughter of Marc Sangnier, who founded Le Sillon), Louis Soubise, as well as Chartier, Delarge, Grünenwald, Pagès, Tunc, and others. In the Rhône-Alpes region, contacts were made with Michèle Bauduin, René Shaller, Marie-Jeanne Bérère, Renée Dufour, Dona Singles, and the Effort Diaconal group in Lyon. It catalyzed and pinpointed the criticisms that were beginning to denounce the misogyny of the institution and its monosexual dysfunction. But whereas most of the criticisms were still part of a reformist project, FHE appeared before the theologians assembled in Brussels for the international colloquium of *Concilium* in 1971 with a very different type of criticism: It was no longer a matter of demanding a place for women in the Church, but of asking, "What sort of church do we want?" We shall later examine other areas in which the French have focused on women and feminism in relation to the theology and the Bible, as well as commenting on Italy.

can feminist theologians and biblical scholars. The translation and dissemination of the work of European women theologians came later, mostly thanks to the journal *Concilium*. Still later, we came into contact with Latin American feminist theologians such as Ivone Gebara, María Pilar Aquino, Maria Clara Bingemer, and María Teresa Porcile. Thus, we have constructed our traditions by reading international authors, most often in translation.

The translation of important works of feminist theology and feminist biblical studies has opened doors to the world for inquisitive Spanish women theologians and interested women in general. Once the ideological barriers were broken down, publishers such as Verbo Divino, Desclée de Brouwer, San Pablo, Claretianas, or Herder, all of them denominational, published feminist work despite being targets of the church hierarchy. We also had the support of some nonsectarian publishers, such as Trotta.

3.3. Some Works of Feminist Theology and Biblical Exegesis

Looking at Spanish feminist publications chronologically, I find three main areas of research: examination of the Bible and Judaism, narrative analysis of texts, and reconstruction of the history of the origins of Christianity.

The first line of work is done by authors and researchers on the Bible and Judaism in departments of Hebrew philology and Semitic studies (Targum, midrash, Masorah, rabbinism, Hebrew literature, etc.) at public universities such as Complutense University of Madrid, the Centro Superior de Investigaciones Científicas (CSIC, Advanced Center for Scientific Research) in Madrid, and the University of Granada. The majority of scholars are women, and include María Ángeles Navarro, Carmen Caballero, Olga Ruíz Morell, Aurora Salvatierra, Elvira Martín, and Guadalupe Seijas. Their published works reflect high scientific standards. Because of their specialized nature, however, studies of this type are known and recognized only in small circles. This line of work also includes philological and hermeneutical studies (Nuria Calduch for the former, Pilar de Miguel and Rosa Cursach for the latter), which are better known and accessible to a wider public. Biblical scholars such as María Luisa Melero are less classifiable.

The second area of work includes publications of feminist narrative analysis and interpretation of both the Hebrew and Christian Bibles, and includes the work of scholars such as Mercedes Navarro. Such explicitly feminist publications have had an ambivalent reception in denominational biblical circles, which are less suspicious of gender studies than of explicitly feminist studies.[15]

---

15. Another problem added to this difficult acceptance of narrative exegesis in Spain

The third area of work consists of studies of the historical Jesus, the history of the origins of Christianity, and the reconstruction of historical contexts with a methodological approach appropriate to the history and the cultural anthropology of the ancient Mediterranean. This group of scholars includes authors with a gender perspective (Carmen Bernabé, Elisa Estévez, Ester Miquel, and others) who are connected with and recognized in specialized American circles. Most of them are connected with denominational academic groups and must therefore limit their gender perspective. Within departments of ancient history in the public university system, there are also scholars who have dealt with the history of early Christianity from a feminist perspective (for instance, Amparo Pedregal at the University of Oviedo).

Publications by Spanish women biblical scholars are remarkably numerous, considering how recently they have emerged. These women scholars are authoring doctoral dissertations and monographs, coordinating issues of specialized and informative journals, and appearing as authors in many of these journals (the ABE journals *Estudios Bíblicos*, *Reseña Bíblica* and *Estudios Eclesiásticos* of the University of Comillas, and *Concilium*, to mention just a few). Lastly, they are sponsors and authors of collections that at least bear the mark of a gender perspective, including *En clave de mujer*, published by Desclée de Brouwer, under the direction of Isabel Gómez-Acebo, with editorial contributions from various ATE biblical scholars, the ATE publication *Aletheia*, several volumes in the collection *10 Palabras* in Verbo Divino, and the Colección EFETA, which publishes the feminist theology manuals of that school.[16]

4. Feminist Theology and Biblical Studies in Catholic Europe: A Brief Summary

4.1. Italy: Between History and Interpretation

Italy has many renowned women philologists and historians of classical antiquity, the most noteworthy of whom are found in public universities. The works of Italian women historians on the world of ancient Greece, and particularly on the Roman Empire as the context for the Christian Bible and the early cen-

---

is the appropriation of the method by male and female students in the more conservative academic world, for example, Opus Dei.

16. For a detailed bibliography, see Mercedes Navarro Puerto, "Boletin Bibliográfico: Biblia, mujeres, feminismo. I Parte: Biblia Hebrea," *'Ilu: Revista de Ciencias de las Religiones* 14 (2009): 231–83; and "Boletín Bibliográfico: Biblia, mujeres, feminismo. II Parte: El Nuevo Testamento y el Cristianismo primitivo," *'Ilu: Revista de Ciencias de las Religiones* 15 (2010): 205–86.

turies of Christianity are fundamental. The collaborations between Catholic women biblical scholars, some Jewish scholars, and several scholars within other denominations are frequent and productive, as is demonstrated by the conferences and joint publications of various groups.[17]

The Coordinamento delle Teologhe Italiane (CTI, Coordination of Italian Women Theologians), directed since its inception by the feminist biblical scholar Marinella Perroni, is an initiative seeking to catalyze relations and to sponsor high-level collaborations among women theologians. This group has chosen to give preference to "gender" terminology and its respective categorizations. Not all women theologians, especially those who are working in the various pontifical schools, are members, often because of fear of being closely linked with feminist ideology or gender criticism.[18] It should be noted that the terms "feminism" and "feminist," widely used in American and northern European contexts, have almost always encountered tenacious opposition in secular and (with greater reason) religious academic environments. The word "gender" has not met with a better fate, having been repeatedly challenged at all levels of church teaching.

The Italian panorama is thus a very varied one.[19] We should also keep in mind the active presence of women theologians such as Maria Cristina Bartolomei and Adriana Valerio in various departments of public universities as part of the work of women theologians since the 1960s.[20] I also want to call attention to the interdisciplinary research in gender studies underway for years at the Institute for Religious Science of the Bruno Kessler Foundation in Trento. In recent years, seminars have often featured Italian women theologians as participants. While gender exegesis appears to be advancing very slowly in Italy, progress has been made in collecting the first fruits of years of research and academic encounters with colleagues on an international level.

---

17. I wish to thank the vital collaboration of Marinella Perroni, who provided me with information, references, ideas, and bibliography, and reviewed the text in this paragraph for all references to Italy.

18. This is something they share with the Spanish women, who are in the same situation.

19. In 1965, Maria-Luisa Rigato was admitted as a "special student" to the Pontifical Biblical Institute. For a survey of these presences, see Cettina Militello, "Teologhe," in *Teologhe: In quale Europa* (ed. Sandra Mazzolini and Marinella Perroni; Sui generis; Cantalupa-Torino: Effatá, 2008), 194–204; and the Minutes of the conference on Teologhe a Roma, held in 2000, which offers a survey of the presence of women in Roman theological schools, in *Ricerche Teologiche* 13 (2002).

20. Militello specifically mentions Adriana Zarri and Vilma Occhipinti Gozzini ("Teologhe," 197–98). The names added since the 1970s are too numerous to list here. See the aforementioned collaboration of Cettina Militello, as well as her book *Donne e Chiesa* (Palermo: EdiOftes, 1985).

With respect to biblical exegesis, particularly New Testament exegesis, Italian women specialists suffer greatly from the control of theological institutions, and therefore report to the Holy See or the Episcopal Conference. This situation has led to a proliferation of circumlocutions such as "feminine, women, from the feminine point of view," among other euphemisms easily digestible by Italian male scholars. The document issued by the International Pontifical Biblical Commission entitled *The Interpretation of the Bible in the Church* (1993), which continues to be viewed as nonnegotiable, also includes feminist exegesis among the contextual approaches (E.2). Fortunately, the Protestant publisher Claudine (followed by several Catholic publishing houses, in several publications) has had the foresight to ensure translation of major monographs in the last twenty years of the twentieth century.

In countries outside of Italy, the debate has centered on the discussion between women's/gender studies, on the one hand, and identification of a particular interpretive framework for the feminist-critical reconstruction of biblical history on the other. In Italy, preference has been given to emphasizing the importance of reading sacred scripture from a woman's point of view, but not for developing theoretical frameworks and methodological training for women scholars.

First of all, a compendium of the topical literature is needed, often designated as feminine and/or "from a feminine point of view," which aims at recognition of the role of women in early Christianity. Particularly in New Testament studies, the recognition of the important role of women in early Christianity has challenged the ecclesiastical understanding the role of women.[21]

Among the numerous women who occupy chairs of Sacred Scripture in the Pontifical Universities, only two New Testament scholars have focused explicitly and systematically on issues of gender: Maria-Luisa Rigato from a philological perspective, and Marinella Perroni from a historical-critical perspective.

Maria-Luisa Rigato, a genuine pioneer, has advanced the study of the New Testament texts from a woman's perspective, proposing interesting hypotheses based on meticulous linguistic-literary studies. While her interest in the New Testament has never been limited to questions of the presence and role

---

21. Only the most notable contributions are cited: Elizabeth E. Green, *Dal silenzio alla parola* (Turin: Claudiana, 1995); Carla Ricci, *Maria di Magdala e le molte altre: Donne sul cammino di Gesù* (Naples: D'Auria, 1991); Lilia Sebastiani, *Tra/Sfigurazioni* (Brescia: Queriniana 1992); Sebastiani, *Svolte: Donne negli snodi del cammino di Gesù* (Assisi: Cittadella, 2008); Nuria Calduch-Benages, *Il profumo del vangelo: Gesù incontra le donne* (La parola e la sua ricchezza 11; Milan: Paoline, 2009); Elena Bosetti, *Donne della Bibbia: Bellezza intrighi fede passione* (Assisi: Cittadella Editrice, 2010).

of women,[22] many of her scientific works have been devoted exclusively to the study of women, particularly in the letters of Paul and in the Gospels.[23]

Marinella Perroni studied the feminist exegetical tradition as she prepared her doctoral dissertation on the discipleship of women in the Gospel of Luke.[24] Through works that are methodological in orientation, she has consistently endeavored to sensitize Italian scholars to feminist and gender research.[25] She has also published numerous historical-critical studies that shed light on the contribution of women to the formation of the Gospel traditions and the dissemination of the Christian message.[26]

---

22. See Maria-Luisa Rigato, *Il Titolo Della Croce Di Gesù: Confronto tra i Vangeli e la Tavoletta-reliquia della Basilica Eleniana a Roma* (Tesi Gregoriana; Serie Teologia 100; Rome: 2005); Rigato, *Giovanni: l'enigma il Presbitero il culto il Tempio la cristologia* (Bologna: EDB, 2007); Rigato, *I.N.R.I. Il titolo della Croce* (Bologna: EDB, 2010), 152

23. See, e.g., Maria-Luisa Rigato, "Le figure femminili nel Vangelo secondo Giovanni," in *I laici nel popolo di Dio: Esegesi Biblica* (ed. Vittorio Liberti; Rome: ED, 1990), 173–233; Rigato, "Gesù 'profumato' a Betania da una donna, nella redazione matteana," in *Donna e ministero: Un dibattito ecumenico* (ed. Cettina Militello; Rome: ED, 1991), 497–504; Rigato, "'Lingue come di fuoco' e 'invio' di discepoli/e come profeti-testimoni (At 2,3–4 e Is 6,5–8)," in *Profezia: Modelli e forme nell'esperienza cristiana laicale* (ed. Cettina Militello; Padua: CEDAM, 2000), 81–106; Rigato, "Maria La Maddalena: Ancora riflessioni su colei che fu chiamata 'la Resa-grande' (Lc 8,2; 24,10; Gv 20,1.10–17)," *Studia Patavina* 50 (2003): 727–52. Also, Rigato, along with Jerome Murphy-O'Connor and Cettina Militello, *Paolo e le donne* (Orizzonti biblici; Assisi: Cittadella Editrice, 2006); Rigato, *Discepole di Gesù* (Collana Studi biblici 63; Bologna: EDB, 2011).

24. Marinella Perroni, *Il discepolato delle donne nel Vangelo di Luca: Un contributo all'ecclesiologia neotestamentaria* (Excerptum ex Dissertatione ad Doctoratum Sacrae Theologiae Assequendum in Pontificio Athenaeo S. Anselmi; Romae, 1995).

25. See in this respect Marinella Perroni, "Lettura femminile ed ermeneutica femminista del NT: Status quaestionis," *RivB* 41 (1993): 315–39; Perroni, "Una valutazione dell'esegesi femminista: Verso un senso critico integrale," *StPat* 43 (1996): 67–92; Perroni, "Lettura femminista e lettura spirituale della Bibbia," in *Istituto Superiore di Scienze Religiose delle Venezie: Sede centrale di Padova, Le prolusioni ai corsi degli anni accademici 1994–1996* (Padua: n.p., 1997), 49–77; Perroni, "L'interpretazione biblica femminista tra ricerca sinottica e ermeneutica politica: una rassegna di recenti opere di esegesi femminista," *RivB* 45 (1997): 439–68.

26. Marinella Perroni, "Cristo dice 'donna': La testimonianza del IV vangelo," AA.VV., *Le donne dicono Dio: Quale Dio dicono le donne? E Dio dice le donne? Atti del decimo convegno di studio Progetto Donna (Milan, 26 November 1994)* (Milan: Paoline, 1995), 100–122; Perroni, "Il Cristo Maestro (Lc 10,38–42): L'apoftegma di Marta e Maria: problemi di critica testuale," in *Mysterium Christi: Symbolgegenwart und theologische Bedeutung* (ed. M. Löhrer and E. Salmann; Studia Anselmiana 115; Rome: Anselmiana, 1995), 57–78; Perroni, "L'annuncio pasquale alle/delle donne [Mc 16,1–8]: Alle origini della tradizione kerygmatica," in *Patrimonium fidei: Traditionsgeschichtliches Verstehen am Ende?* (Studia Anselmiana 124; Rome: Anselmiana, 1997), 397–436; Perroni, "Le donne e Maria madre di

The Italian context is marked not only by the academic activity of women professors of biblical studies, but also by scholars whose training has not always been strictly exegetical. While "femininity" and "feminine" elements as well as topical research predominate in these publications, many interesting critical contributions have been made.

Lastly, I wish to emphasize the presence of a small sign of change on the horizon that could finally enable the Italian exegetes to reopen the discussion of the intersection of biblical research, the question of femininity, and gender studies. I refer to the upcoming reprint of a volume by Elisa Salerno (1873–1957) entitled *Critical Commentaries on Anti-feminist Bibliographical Notes: From the First 24 Sacred Books, That Is, from Genesis to the Four Books of Wisdom*, published in 1926, and the first part of a second volume, published that same year, with comments on the antifeminist notes of the last nineteen books of the Old Testament. This book was written in response to the translation of the Bible into Italian with notes by Msgr. Antonio Martini, Archbishop of Florence around 1800. She praises the translation of the Bible by Msgr. Martini, but her praise is tempered by reservation "since his commentary contains erroneous, pernicious, and anti-feminist interpretations." It was Salerno's intention in these two volumes to publish a critical commentary on notes, which were contaminated by anti-feminism.

Salerno asserted that this critical work was necessary because of the propagation of so many heresies against women that have roots in corrupt interpretations of the scriptures. Protestant American suffragists are thus not the

---

Gesù in Luca," in *San Luca evangelista testimone della fede che unisce* (ed. G. Leonardi and F. G. B. Trolese; Atti del Congresso Internazionale; Padua: Istituto per la Storia Ecclesiastica Padovana, 2002), 16–21; Perroni, *I. L'unità letteraria e teologica dell'opera di Luca (Vangelo e Atti degli Apostoli)* (Padua: Istituto per la Storia Ecclesiastica Padovana, 2002), 115–29; Perroni, "L'approccio ermeneutico della teologia femminista ai testi biblico-mariologici," in *L'ermeneutica contemporanea e i testi biblico-mariologici: Verifica e proposte* (ed. Ermanno M. Toniolo; Atti del XIII Simposio Internazionale Mariologico, Rome, 2–6 October 2001; Rome: Edizioni Marianum, 2003), 409–40; Perroni, "Per una pneumatologia femminista: Un contributo biblico," *Servitium* 156 (2004): 731–42; Perroni, " 'Murió y fue sepultado': La contribución de las discípulas de Jesús a la elaboracion de la fe en la resurrección," in *En el umbral: Muerte y Teología en perspectiva de mujeres* (ed. Mercedes Navarro; Bilbao: Desclée de Brouwer, 2006), 147–80; Perroni, "Discepole di Gesù," in *Donne e Bibbia: Storia ed esegesi* (ed. Adriana Valerio; La Bibbia nella storia 21; Bologna: Dehoniane, 2006), 197–240; Perroni, "Canone inverso: La rivoluzione femminista e la maternità di Maria," in *La maternità tra scelta, desiderio e destino* (ed. Saveria Chemotti; Soggetti rivelati 25; Padua: Il poligrafo, 2009), 277–97; Perroni, "Una sessuazione non-segregante: Il 'terzo sesso' interpella la Bibbia," in *L'enigma corporeità: sessualità e religione* (ed. Antonio Autiero and Stefanie Knauss; Scienze religiose. Nuova serie 24; Bologna: EDB, 2010), 55–74.

only "foremothers" of feminist biblical criticism, as Salerno also articulated her personal intellectual and political history in the decades of the first half of the twentieth century. She knew how to answer openly to the "prejudices and absurd and barbarous arguments" that contaminated ecclesiastical interpretations of the Bible with anti-feminist rhetoric.[27]

4.2. FRANCE AND OTHER COUNTRIES

There are few feminist theologians and biblical scholars in France, but there are many women theologians and biblical scholars occupying teaching positions in theological schools and institutes once reserved for men. For example, Veronique Margo was, until very recently, the dean of the school of theology of Angers. In Lille, Thérèse Lebrun is the president and rector of the Catholic Institute, and biblical scholar Bernadette Escaffré is the current vice-dean at the school of theology of Toulouse.[28] Élisabeth Parmentier, a feminist Protestant theologian, is professor of ecumenics at the school of theology of Strasbourg and author of numerous works.

As is the case in Italy and to a great extent in Spain, French biblical scholars are not, and have no intention of becoming, particularly feminist. However, these same specialists often deal with the perspective of women in the Bible and the study of topical questions while also emphasizing their status as women in their teaching of theology and the Bible. Theology students maintain certain numerical gender equality and women students get better results than male students even though they have better conditions for study.

In France, as in the other countries mentioned, women, whether or not they are specialists, tend to band together and join various associations and groups in which they debate theology from their respective points of view, including L'autre parole, a collective of Christian feminist women, as well as other groups mentioned in note 19.

In Portugal, a small number of women scholars in biblical studies teach from a gender perspective at Catholic universities. A slow awakening to feminism among Catholic women, women theologians, and some biblical specialists, can be observed in this country. Some women theologians are members

---

27. Cf. Michela Vaccari, *Lavoratrice del pensiero: Elisa Salerno, una teologa ante litteram* (Sui generis 7; Cantalupa-Torino: Effatà, 2010), 103–12.

28. Bernadette Escaffré (who generously provided me with the information in this paragraph referring to feminist theology and feminist exegesis in France), has noted that because the number of women professors has been decreasing, many of the male members of the faculty council have requested an increase in the number of women.

of a large, deeply rooted, and powerful group of women—the Grail.[29] In the past years, this organization has been incorporating feminist theology into its theological training. The Grail movement arrived in Portugal in 1957, and was established in 1977 as a sociocultural nontrade association, and was recognized in 1985 as a public interest collective. To celebrate the fiftieth anniversary of its inception in Portugal, the group organized a feminist theology conference in collaboration with Mercedes Navarro of Spain. During the summer of 2010, it held a conference on feminist theological education, with the collaboration of Portuguese and Spanish theologians, including Paula Depalma of EFETA. The aim is to make this an annual event in order to promote feminist theology in southern Europe.[30]

This quick panoramic view of the countries considered leads me to suspect that there are more women theologians than meets the eye, and that the women theologians who are visible are not the only ones doing theology. At the same time, women scholars are not always as committed to the critical perspectives of gender and feminism as they would have us believe. These two trends are not contradictory.

5. Conclusions

My survey of the developments in southern Europe leads me to punctuate the map with multifaceted reflections referring to the twentieth century, the first decade of the twenty-first century, and emerging trends for the future. The issues raised can serve as both arrival and starting points.

1. Ambivalences: The twentieth century was an extremely powerful starting point for European feminist interpretation. We have witnessed very rapid advances in research, with major consequences for academic institutions, the Christian churches, and religions. These advances exceed our evaluative ability at the present time, although we are able to perceive some of the inherent phases. Advances in feminist biblical research have led to a change in the representation of basic concepts such as the biblical divine image, the image and dignity of women based on exegetical studies, and relations between the sexes, and their effects on everyday life, values, and sexual ethics. In southern Europe, such effects have been more deconstructive than constructive, and have become only gradually intercultural. The multidisciplinary factor has influenced the multicultural factor, and vice-versa, but

---

29. The reader can obtain more information at www.graal.org.pt.

30. In other, more Eastern, countries of the Mediterranean basin such as Greece and several former Eastern-bloc nations, there are few, if any, feminist scholars because of the various difficulties of their respective countries.

not in a cause-and-effect manner. An extremely important outcome within the Catholic milieu has been the emancipation in biblical hermeneutics and reading by women. While it has kept fears alive and aroused deep resistance, it has also given women authority to practice self-criticism, criticism of texts, and practical encounters.

2. Democratization: The intellectual limitations of Catholic Europe and the countries of the South document the importance of the democratization of the media, specifically, the prospect for access to specific economic and cultural possibilities. The twentieth century teaches us feminist exegetes the importance of medium-term rather than short-term strategies, although in principle this seems to be a slow process. Unfortunately, it has shown us the real possibility of regression, as is evidenced by the ambivalences of later generations of exegetes in the face of feminist and gender studies and the power of the gradual and unstoppable tabooization of terms that are historically impregnated with the struggles and victories of the women who preceded us. The loss of feminist terms forms part of the strategy to eliminate memory. At the present time there is greater fear among women, women students, and women professors of theology and biblical studies than there was twenty and thirty years ago.

3. Secularity: The history of feminist theology and feminist exegesis in southern European countries reveals the importance of the public and secular environments for biblical research that is scientific, free, and creative. It also reveals the need to position oneself simultaneously within and outside of institutions. The challenge is to sustain the ability of women to support and maintain the creation and interrelations of networks, to handle conflicts (which are legitimate, because we are human) in light of personal ambitions, to desire power and acclaim, and to maintain the right to struggle for the cause of women, especially the most disadvantaged women. This means not losing sight of the fact that each personal victory is at the same time a collective victory.

4. Reception: The experiences of biblical women scholars of the Catholic countries of Europe regarding the reception of specialized and also popularizing works indicate the inadequacy of the quality and quantity of the scientific output of women exegetes. Because they wanted to be visible in mixed groups (university faculties, biblical associations, and international seminars, for example), many women exegetes have become invisible or absorbed or have lost power. Twentieth-century feminist exegesis in Europe and the West consists of few names, male or female. Success in transforming the anecdotal and the individual into the political and the collective continues to be the challenge.

5. Production/Dissemination: In southern Europe, we are more aware of the tardy relationship between publication and dissemination in a world that

is changing so rapidly. Hence, I continue to see an urgent need for effective publication and dissemination of feminist biblical studies.

6. Categories: The present is the effect of the past, but only up to a certain point. Each generation is responsible only for itself. This leads us to rethink the immediate past with categories other than those of cause and effect. Such categories and emerging fields are chaos, auto-poiesis, morphic fields, paradoxes, and the like. The findings represent a starting point for the reconstruction of reality. We know, however, that the reality is much more complex. Major work thus remains to be done.

7. Individual/Collective: The experience of Catholic Europe brings with it, from my point of view, the challenge of rethinking everything in terms of both the individual and the collective. Once again, and in the specific environment of feminist scholarship, it is necessary to restate that the personal is the political.

Toward Mapping Feminist Biblical Interpretations in Asia

Monica Jyotsna Melanchthon
University of Divinity, Melbourne, Australia

1. Introduction and Preliminary Considerations

Feminist biblical studies/interpretations in Asia are relatively new. Nevertheless, it is imperative that this introductory section address inclusions and exclusions within this essay, and the problems and questions that may be raised but not adequately answered, in order to indicate some of the directions that future research may profitably take. The mapping or charting of feminist biblical studies in Asia is a complicated affair, particularly because the constitutive elements of the terms "Asian," the "Asian woman," and "feminist" are contested. However, these terms and the complexities that surround can also provide fruitful incitements to discourse.

First, the problem of what constitutes "Asia/Asianness" has been much debated,[1] as the plurality of cultures, religions, languages, ethnic groups, races, socioeconomic conditions, and ideologies begs the question "Who or what makes an interpretation Asian?" Biblical interpreters in Asia represent various population groups involving different geopolitical backgrounds, multiple historical trajectories, and diverse material and discursive formations, often even within a single nation. In questioning the context for exploring, formulating, and mapping feminist biblical interpretations in Asia, one must ask: Which, or whose, works do we draw on to chart this map of Asian women's interpretations of scripture? Which women's experiences have produced interpretations or studies of the Christian scriptures and from what locations? What are the disciplinary parameters of this knowledge? What are the

---

1. Namsoon Kang, "Who/What Is Asian? A Postcolonial Theological Reading of Orientalism and Neo-Orientalism," in *Postcolonial Theologies, Divinities, and Empire* (ed. Catherine Keller et al.; St. Louis: Chalice, 2004), 100–117.

methods used to locate and chart Asian women's interpretations of the Bible? These questions are pertinent as we seek to describe feminist biblical studies in Asia. However, answering these questions and exploring this vast and complex terrain in a way that takes into account both regional differences and disciplinary competencies can hardly be accomplished in the space of a single essay.

Second, since I am interested in sketching out *feminist* biblical studies in Asia, it is imperative that I describe what is meant by the word "feminist" and what makes an interpretation feminist. The terms "feminism" or "feminist" may mean many things. "Feminist" is commonly used to describe those women and men who seek to eliminate women's subordination and marginalization.[2] The root experience of feminism is the realization that cultural "common sense," dominant perspectives, scientific theories, and historical knowledge are all androcentric constructs—that is, male biased and therefore ideological rather than objective. Feminism, therefore, is a social movement rooted in the awareness of women's oppression and exploitation at work both in society and within the family that involves conscious action by women and men to change this situation. In simple terms, feminism is the commitment to work for the political, economic, and social equality of man and woman, girl and boy in every area of life. This commitment takes seriously the interlinkages of gender, race, caste, colonialism, cultural imperialism, religious pluralism, and the violence of women against other women.[3] Therefore, it is essential to delineate the salient factors of feminist biblical interpretation, which must be reflected in a work if it is to be accepted as feminist. Such work must

▶   *reflect appreciation and respect for women's experiences and acknowledgement of women's capacities and agency.* Experience as simply lived and happening is the raw material and matrix for reflection. Feminism engages in the spiritual quest within women's experiences, including the personal and social, women's labor, the experiences of her body, menstruation, pregnancy, and childbirth, as well as women's experiences of subjugation, rejection, and exclusion in society

---

2. See, for example, the statement of purpose of the *Center for Feminist Theology and Ministry*, Japan, which includes the following: "our choice of the term 'feminist' rather than 'human' is intended to make it clear that we understand 'women's' experiences typically reflecting those of the marginalized as 'others' throughout the history of patriarchal societies. Just as situations at the margins are diverse, so too are women's experiences." Online: http://cftmj2000.cocolog-nifty.com/blog/1purpose/index.html.

3. Kwok Pui Lan, *Introducing Asian feminist Theology* (Cleveland: Pilgrim, 2000), 30.

and church,[4] the process of socialization, and being a part of male-dominated religious systems that privilege androcentrism and the maleness of God.

▶ *be sensitive to context; be cognizant of the linguistic, religious, and cultural diversity, as well as the poverty of the majority, the effects of globalization, and the exploitation and abuse of nature and its concomitant results on the Asian people and the land.* The oppressed and the marginalized, namely the women, the dalits, children, the *adivasis*,[5] the *burakumin*, and the tribals, those infected and affected by HIV/AIDS, and the physically and mentally challenged, are people who have been conspicuously absent in biblical interpretation.

▶ *challenge/destabilize/subvert the subordination of women rather than strengthening or reinforcing it.* Some women and men tend to believe that any reading by women is feminist. Challenging patriarchal structures is not easy, considering the fact that we as women are interpreting within the context of patriarchy and therefore experience limitations as we are shaped and influenced by this framework.[6] "An adequate feminist exegetical methodology and perspective, then, must seek to be aware of, and to limit, as far as possible, the influence of patriarchal ideology in its own thought."[7] Interpretations therefore need to be able to subvert patriarchal structures and thought systems that legitimize the subordination of women.

▶ *be self-critical.* Feminists cannot overlook the fact that the critical function of feminist work implies self-criticism and alertness to the ways in which women have both abetted *and* resisted oppression and subjugation. Therefore, feminist work calls for a hermeneutic of suspicion, especially in dealing with texts that appear to be pro-women. It needs also discern and uncover the underlying structures of the texts in order to understand, critique, and challenge the logic of patriarchy.[8]

---

4. Malini Devananda, "Women's Spirituality," *In God's Image: Journal of Asian Women's Resource Centre for Culture and Theology* 24/2 (June 2005): 2–4.

5. Indigenous populations within India (*adi:* original; *vasi:* inhabitant). About 427 of these groups have been listed in the scheduled tribes list of the Indian constitution.

6. Kerry M. Craig and Margaret A. Kristjansson, "Women Reading as Men/Women Reading as Women: A Structural Analysis for the Historical Project," *Semeia* 51 (1990): 119–36, here 120.

7. Ibid.

8. Ibid.

▶   *transform individuals and structures of oppression.* Exegesis of scripture in accordance with the rules of interpretation is not sufficient if the resulting interpretation does not transform the exegete. Indian tradition affirms that "no hermeneutics by itself will yield truth in its fullness without purification of the mind, transformation of the heart, and discipline of the body."[9] Hence, feminist work must have as its goal and consequence far-reaching social changes of political and social revolutionary significance in its society and world. Such changes need to be practical, this-worldly, transformative, renewing, and transitional. In short, an effective hermeneutic is one that is based on a faith response—a hermeneutic of life, of liberation and justice, and a hermeneutic that results in readings that challenge the status quo and transform structures of oppression. This perspective will help us to be cautious about using tools that sift the biblical texts for historical facts (historical critical methods), or about studying the Bible as literature without any sensitivity for its religious visions (literary methods).

▶   *explore the faith dimensions of the Christian gospel.* A majority of the Asian biblical scholars and students are also practicing Christians who find identity and meaning through their involvement in church life. It also has to be borne in mind that Christianity is a minority religion in most of the Asian countries, and that a majority of the educational institutions that make possible the study of the Bible are church-affiliated institutions. Hence, the confessional nature of biblical studies and interpretations cannot be overlooked.[10] Therefore, Christian feminist interpretations must reflect the values of the gospel and contribute to the enhancement of faith.

I have refrained from using the term "studies" in the title because the term carries with it a note of the formality of abstract, academic, and research-oriented work that we experience less often in Asia than in the West. In surveying the material that might be included in this essay, it became clear that in contrast to feminist biblical scholarship in the West, feminist biblical interpretations in Asia have been generated largely by those outside of academic biblical scholarship,

---

9. Stanley J. Samartha, "The Asian Context: Sources and Trends," in *Voices from the Margin: Interpreting the Bible in the Third World* (London: SPCK, 1991), 36–49, here 41.

10. I am aware that there are exceptions, particularly in countries such as China, and that there may be few individual scholars affiliated to secular universities elsewhere in Asia who approach the Bible as a cultural and literary text. But these are more often the exception than the rule.

some with theological training and some without. A major section of women biblical interpreters are not biblical scholars with advanced degrees; some have theological training and some have none. Those not involved in academic biblical studies have made substantial contributions to feminist biblical interpretation, and their work complements that of biblical scholars.

By using the term *interpretations*, I am also extending my inquiries beyond those institutions and practices within which feminist biblical interpretation enjoys a safe, public existence in order to include potentially provocative sites such as art and poetry. My aim is to make space for more wide-ranging approaches towards understanding the issues, the approaches, and the methods employed by feminist interpreters of the Bible in Asia.

2. FEMINIST THEOLOGIZING AND FEMINIST BIBLICAL INTERPRETATION IN ASIA: GENEALOGY

The genesis of feminist theologizing and biblical interpretation in Asia is to be traced back to some landmark publications and events in the 1970s and 1980s that are embedded in the consciousness of those who are its most active participants in different parts of Asia. The project of feminism and feminist theological reflection was initiated by various contributing factors that served as catalysts. I offer here a few examples from select countries that served as catalysts for feminist biblical interpretations in Asia.

Korea: While conversion to Christianity in the 1880s provided the opportunity for Korean women to read and explore the Bible, its egalitarian values also propelled women to affirm themselves[11] in the context of a hierarchical and feudal society. It provided the impetus for women to participate in the struggles against Japanese Occupation in the early 1900s. During the decades that followed, Christianity grew and schisms developed within the churches on issues surrounding the critical study of the Bible and people's participation in addressing social issues. Women were marginalized and became the

---

11. "The reason why Christianity so rapidly became popular among the Korean women and the poor people of the lower class is that Christianity proclaims the equality of all humankind, especially the equality between highborn aristocratic class and the lower class, and between male and female. Many scholars say that because of Christianity, Koreans began to believe that before God, all human beings are equal, and that men and women are equal" (Kyung Sook Lee, "An Old Testament Interpretation in an Era of Globalization: From the Perspective of Korean Feminist Theology" [unpublished manuscript, 2009], 2).

"second sex" in the Korean churches.[12] In 1961, the Korean Association of Old Testament Studies was formed, but it had no women members until 1981.[13] The popularization of Mary Daly's *Beyond God the Father* became a catalyst for awakening the consciousness of women, and this was reinforced by a translation of Kate Millet's, *Sexual Politics* in 1976, and Letty Russell's *Human Liberation in a Feminist Perspective: A Theology* in 1979. In 1977, the Korean Women's Institute was established, and courses in women's studies were being offered at the Ewha Women's University in Seoul. The Liberation movements (Minjung) and the democratic movements in the 1970s in Korea provided the background for the birth of Korean feminist theology.

In 1980, the Korean Association of Women Theologians (KAWT) was formed.[14] In 1985, the Korean Association of Feminist Theologians (KAFT) was also created to promote feminist theological reflection.[15] In 1987, it became a member of the Korean Association of Christian Studies. A journal entitled *Feminist Theological Thought* was also launched, and over the years its issues have also addressed topics related to the Bible and Women. The Korean Association of Old Testament Studies and the Korean Association of New Testament Studies, Ewha Women's Institute for Theological Studies, and the *Ewha Journal of Feminist Theology* are among the various platforms and publications that have provided for women theologians and biblical interpreters the space and opportunity for doing and sharing their feminist work in Korea.

Philippines: In 1978, in a context of martial law and military dictatorship, the Benedictine sister Mary John Mananzan co-founded Filipina. This organization was the first of its kind to address women's issues, particularly the plight of sex workers in the Philippines.[16] She also established the Center for Women's Resources in 1982.[17] Later she headed the well-known GABRIELA organization,[18] a national alliance of grassroots women's organizations

---

12. Ibid., 4.

13. Ibid.

14. Sun Kyung Park, Woo Jung Lee, Sun Ae Ju, Sang Jang, Hwa Sun Jo, Sang Lim Ahn, Suk Ja Jung, and Ok La Kim are some of the founding members (ibid., 5).

15. Ibid.

16. Kwok, *Introducing Asian Feminist Theology,* 26–27.

17. A nonstock, nonprofit nongovernmental women's service institution that provides research, education and training, advocacy and publications, library and data banking service for and about women. See http://cwrweb.com/.

18. Acronym for General Assembly Binding Women for Reforms, Integrity, Equality, Leadership, and Action, which was founded in April, 1984 after ten thousand women marched in Manila, defying a Marcos decree against demonstrations.

in the Philippines, which was founded in 1984 with a focus on issues that affect women.[19] Unlike in other Asian countries, Christianity is the dominant religion in the Philippines, and the church has been actively involved in the politics of the country. Hence, reflecting and interpreting the Bible for the purposes of aiding the Christian church was and remains in the organization's mission to usher in change.

India: The secular women's movement with beginnings in the 1970s[20] was the catalyst that was largely responsible for increasing awareness amongst church women about gender discrimination, equality, and justice in India. As women's studies, the academic arm of the women's movement, developed, it became apparent that religion and theology legitimized patriarchy and sexism in society.

This realization was aided by influences derived from early works of pioneers in the field of feminist theology—Mary Daly, Letty Russell, Elisabeth Schüssler Fiorenza, and Rosemary Radford Reuther—which engendered analysis and critique of the church's tradition from a feminist perspective and from within the church. The secular women's movement therefore fueled the development of "feminist consciousness"[21] in the church and in theological education. In the early 1980s, *Stree,* the newsletter of the All India Council for

---

19. Namely, militarization and women's landlessness; the International Monetary Fund, the World Bank, and the debt crisis; the denial of women's reproductive rights and the gross neglect of health care for women; violence against children, wives, and family life; development aid; prostitution and trafficking of women. See http://www.members.tripod .com/~gabriela_p/.

20. The Secular Women's Movement in India owes its genesis to two landmark events, namely, the publication of the pioneering "Report on the Status of Women" in 1974 and the formation of the "Forum against Rape" in Mumbai in 1979. Since then, women's rights have become a part of the legitimate discourse of mainstream politics. The women's movement has come a long way, agitating a variety of issues from sexual harassment on college campuses to dowry deaths, from female feticide to reservation for women in legislatures, from the use of coercion in population control programs to abuse of the girl child, from *sati* to personal law codes pertaining to marriage, adoption, inheritance and custody, environmental degradation, and from literacy to the demand for prohibition. Five major themes have dominated this post-independence women's movement: legal reform, struggle against violence, social reform, political participation, research, and documentation. Many universities and colleges have established a department of women's studies to promote gender analysis and a feminist reading of issues. Gender has become an established category for social, economic, and political analysis. Even the arts, such as dance, theatre, and literature, have not been left untouched.

21. It refers to the awareness that women's subordination is unnatural and demeaning and inscribed by culture rather than inherent to women's bodies and lives. See Gerda

Christian Women (AICCW), a unit of the National Council of Churches in India, provided the initial space for women within the church to express their thoughts and reflections on women's experiences within church and society.

In 1984, a historic consultation on the theme Towards a Theology of Humanhood was organized by the AICCW. With this consultation and the book that followed in 1987,[22] Indian Christian women along with a few men initiated formal attempts not only to critique the Christian religion and theology for its male-centered, male-authored perspectives derogatory to women, but also to recover and reclaim women's histories and contributions that were either hidden, unnoticed, or devalued, and to reconstruct, revalue, and reshape theological concepts and biblical interpretations in India. In the years that followed, various publications consisting of biblical studies for the use of the church and women were published.[23]

The early years of this new millennium saw more academic and "scholarly" works of the feminist kind by both women and men graduating from theological seminaries.[24] But the limited numbers of Indian women scholars educated in biblical studies[25] provides a significant barrier to the development of *feminist* biblical interpretations, studies, and scholarship generated by biblical scholars, as opposed to lay women, male theologians, other theologically trained women, ethicists, and historians.

Japan: Feminist biblical interpretation has been promoted primarily by the Center for Feminist Theology and Ministry in Japan for the purposes of "doing theology" by integrating Christian theology and ministry from a feminist perspective.[26] The Center was established in 2000, and has since been directed by two New Testament biblical scholars—Satoko Yamaguchi

---

Lerner, *The Creation of Feminist Consciousness: From the Middle Ages to Eighteen-Seventy* (New York: Oxford University Press, 1993).

22. Aruna Gnanadason, ed. *Towards a Theology of Humanhood: Women's Perspectives* (Delhi: ISPCK, 1986).

23. V. Devasahayam, *Biblical Perspectives on Women—Ten Bible Studies* (Chennai: AICCW, 1986); Stella Faria et al., eds., *Biblical Women: Our Foremothers—Women's Perspectives by Anna Vareed Alexander* (Indore: Satprakashan Sanchar Kendra, 1997); Rini Ralte et al., *Envisioning a New Heaven and a New Earth* (New Delhi: ISPCK, 1998); Elizabeth Joy, ed., *Lived Realities: Faith Reflections on Gender Justice* (Bangalore: JWP/CISRS, 1999); Jyotsna Chatterji, *Good News for Women* (Delhi: ISPCK for JWP/CISRS, 1979); idem, *Women in Praise and Struggle* (Delhi: ISPCK for JWP/CISRS, 1982).

24. Through the doctoral program coordinated by the South Asia Theological Research Institute of the Senate of Serampore College (University), India.

25. Only nine so far: seven in Old Testament and two in New Testament.

26. Online: http://cftmj2000.cocolog-nifty.com/about.html.

and Hisako Kinukawa. Able to function only as adjunct lecturers,[27] these two scholars have spearheaded feminist theological reflection in Japan and have succeeded in stirring and drawing like-minded women and students, including women from the Buddhist faith[28] who are interested in learning how the Center attends to and addresses issues pertaining to women in Japan.

3. Emerging Asian Feminist Theologies

The 1970s and early 1980s also saw the emergence of several Asian theologies that were culture specific, context sensitive, and liberative in their intent. Minjung theology, *dalit* theology, and the theological constructions by well-known Asian theologians called for sensitivity to context and culture but failed to acknowledge adequately in their analysis and constructions of theology the minjung, dalit, and Asian woman and the uniqueness of her experience.[29] Therefore, women had to organize and mobilize themselves to meet this theological lacuna.

Their participation in struggles for liberation from dictatorial and military regimes in the Philippines, Korea, and Myanmar, to name a few, and increased networking among groups of Asian women, gave the required impetus. Women were encouraged by developments in secular and religious women's movements, as well as in national and local ones.

Their increased access to biblical knowledge through theological training and opportunities to participate in national and international workshops on feminism, feminist analysis, feminist methodologies and Bible study, paired with networking among Asian women's groups, provided inspiration and grounding. Feminist theological works from the West (both Christian and Jewish) heightened awareness of women's roles and issues, provided insight, and propelled feminist theologizing and interpreting of the biblical text.

The goal of such theologizing was to effect change in the lives of women, their participation in church and society, and the transformation of social and ecclesial structures. As a result, many countries now have national associa-

---

27. See Satoko Yamaguchi, "From Dualistic Thinking toward Inclusive Imagination," in *Mapping and Engaging the Bible in Asian Cultures: Congress of the Society of Asian Biblical Studies 2008 Seoul Conference* (ed. Yeong Mee Lee and Yoon Jong Yoo; Seoul: The Christian Literature Society of Korea, 2009), 55.

28. Buddhist women do not read biblical texts but glean from the readings shared with them strategies for how they might themselves address issues of sexism within their *sanghas*.

29. Kwok, *Introducing Asian Feminist Theology*, 30.

tions or societies of biblical studies.[30] But their level of activity and programs, their women's participation, and their openness to feminist projects on the Bible is varied and open to inquiry.

These developments at the national level were also energized by women's involvement in international movements for change such as the World Student Christian Federation-Asia-Pacific, and the International Movement of Catholic Students Asia-Pacific, both of which organized gender-specific consultations and training programs in which Bible study was a crucial element. The women's regional ecclesial bodies such as the Christian Conference of Asia also contributed to equipping women for a feminist analysis of biblical texts.

The Asian Women's Resource Center for Culture and Theology, conceived at an "Asian Women Doing Theology" conference in November 1987, was established in 1988 in Hong Kong and is now located in Chennai, India. The Center has been fundamental in mobilizing Asian women to articulate a theology that is contextual and feminist in its orientation. *In God's Image: Journal of Asian Women's Resource Centre for Culture and Theology,* the only one of its kind in Asia, has been a valuable avenue for women to share their stories, reflections, and interpretation in diverse forms with other women in Asia and the rest of the world.

Theological institutions and fraternities such as ATESEA Theological Union and the Ecumenical Association of Third World Theologians, and Asian societies such as the Society of Asian Biblical Studies started in 2006 and the Ethnic Chinese Biblical Colloquium are new avenues for women members to present their feminist interpretations of biblical texts.[31]

4. Salient Features of Feminist Biblical Interpretation in Asia

Considering the very significant role that faith and religion play in the lives of Christian women, it is not surprising that women are still hesitant to critique religious traditions and scripture and the role that they play in the subjugation and oppression of women. The act of critiquing religion or articulating an interpretation or theology that is wholly feminine in its language, symbols, and metaphors is akin to the unheard scream of Kunti in the *Mahabaratha* as she gives birth to a son out of wedlock. Because of the fear of being condemned by society, Kunti suppressed that scream of labor pain, which is oth-

---

30. For instance, Korea, Japan, Indonesia, and India.

31. See Satoko Yamaguchi's plenary presentation, "From Dualistic Thinking toward Inclusive Imagination," 53–71, where she appeals for more radically inclusive biblical interpretations.

erwise welcomed and celebrated at the time of childbirth. She was required to bring the child into the world silently. This same sense of fear, of suppression, guilt, and betrayal accompanies the creative efforts of feminist theology and biblical interpretation in Asia.

Like Kunti, the Christian women students and theologians seem to hide the frank expression of their anguish with religion, scripture, and tradition, because it would not be acceptable in society or the church. Women in the church and seminary structures are still excluded outsiders in many parts of Asia, and they lead a precarious existence on the boundaries of both theological institutions and the church. Despite the odds against them, Asian women interpreters recognize that Bible study is an important means of exploring and expanding the religious dimensions of one's life, with implications for one's involvement in family, society, and church. This study is also necessary for social and ecclesial transformation.

The body of feminist work on the Bible is still small in Asia, but becoming increasingly significant. Asian women interpreters acknowledge that the Bible shows a distinct male bias and unabashedly reflects the patriarchal cultures in which its texts were written. In addition, women have been further marginalized by biblical translators and interpreters living in male-dominated societies. They assert that the Bible has been used to maintain the existing order and as a chief instrument in the suppression of women. Yet the Bible carries also a liberating message for women. Interpretations of women in general are full of insights that can contribute to correcting the androcentric worldview of the Bible, especially through their implicit advocacy of the "hermeneutics of suspicion." Asian feminists are working towards helping ordinary church women, men, and young people to reread the Bible in a simple and lively way, "using participatory methods, relating the Bible to our context, and engaging faith with current issues on a worldwide basis."[32]

Some of the salient features of feminist biblical interpretations in Asia are as follows:

▶ *Feminist interpreters are church bound:* Feminist biblical studies in Asia is characterized and influenced by a combination of contextual, academic, and confessional factors. The majority of the interpreters, if not all, are practicing Christians who find identity and meaning through their involvement in church life. While this makes their work and interpretations meaningful, the risks are high and the regulations of the institutional church and seminary restrict women

---

32. Ralte et al., *Envisioning a New Heaven and a New Earth*, xv.

from being radical, frank, and forthright in their interpretations of the biblical texts. Contextual and perspectival studies and readings of the Bible are considered liberal, modern, and nontraditional. Such readings of the Bible are having to go up against the more traditional and loyalist interpretations of individuals and groups influenced by the resurgence of Christian fundamentalism in many quarters of Asia. Hence, the method, the principles of interpretation adopted, the perspectives, and the issues addressed through the interpretation of the biblical text are determined by the confessional leanings and doctrinal stances of the interpreter.

▸ *Feminist biblical interpretations are produced from outside the academy and outside of biblical studies*: In contrast to feminist biblical scholarship in the West, feminist biblical interpretations in Asia have been generated primarily by those outside the academy. Although there is some debate as to what constitutes a feminist approach to biblical texts, feminist biblical interpretation has a diverse, well-developed, and growing body of literature created by a small but growing mass of feminist biblical interpreters. Feminist scholars in nonbiblical fields have also provided notable readings of biblical texts. While those within biblical studies are few, those outside of biblical studies have made substantial contributions to feminist biblical interpretation through artwork, poetry, dramas,[33] and their work complements that of biblical scholars.

▸ *Feminist biblical interpretation in Asia is "liberational" in approach:*[34] Variations in approach arise out of different experiences, training, theological assumptions, caste affiliations and/or positions of feminist thinkers. Yet what unites feminist biblical interpretation in Asia is that the text is read from the vantage point of women's experience and with a commitment to the emancipation and liberation of women. Feminist biblical interpreters in Asia engage with their communities and with other women's lived experiences, which are often ignored within the academy. Thus, their interpretations include the social, cultural, and religious experiences of Asian women within

---

33. See *In God's Image* 7/3 (September 1988): 39–51.

34. They consider the central message of the Bible to be human salvation and liberation found in either in the prophetic tradition or other texts that go beyond androcentricism and patriarchy and witness to the transformation of society. See Carolyn Osiek, "The Feminist and the Bible: Hermeneutical Alternatives," in *Feminist Perspectives on Biblical Scholarships* (ed. Adela Yarbro Collins; SBL Centennial Publications, Chico, Calif.: Scholars Press, 1985): 103–4.

scholarly discourse and draw on the artistic, literary, and intellectual production of these women as resources. It is a critical rereading of the scriptures that employs a liberational approach, enabling them to be read against the grain for the purposes of solidarity and advocacy and for transforming the self and the community. Our task is three-fold—critique, reclaim, and reconstruct.

► *Feminist biblical interpretations are heterogeneous in method and motivated by class, culture, ethnic, and other diversities:* The diversity that characterizes Asia and the difficulty in defining what is "Asian" make it essential that women interpreters pay attention to their immediate contexts—cultures, languages, castes, ethnicities, and traditions. They have definitely found helpful those insights gained from the traditional historical critical methodologies and literary methods. The methods vary, but a majority of the interpretations seem to fall within the arena of cultural criticism or the process that "expressly investigates the interplay between text and reader." Hence, it "has no distinct methodology, no unique statistical, ethnomethodological, or textual analysis to call its own."[35]

The questions, methods, and research strategies that are brought to bear upon the task of interpretation vary greatly depending on the goals of researchers and their disciplines. The "contrapuntal methods" are becoming popular within the context of religious plurality. What seems more important than a fixation on method is the hermeneutical lens through which the text is read and interpreted. The perspective and approach are crucial to feminist readings in Asia. The readings therefore criticize that which is merely theoretical; they validate the experiential, the lived, and the ambiguous.

► *Asian feminist biblical interpretation is interested in addressing multiple social issues:* Feminist biblical interpreters in Asia are aware of the interlocking forms of oppression (between caste, class, and gender), and hence underscore the importance of treating oppression not as universal or exclusive but as multidimensional or multiaxial. In addition, they underscore the overlapping dimensions of experience, particularly regarding gender, caste, and class. The interpretations address issues ranging from various forms of violence (dowry, female infanticide, female feticide, rape, sati, domestic abuse), representa-

---

35. Cary Nelson, Paula A. Treichler, and Lawrence Grossberg, "Cultural Studies: An Introduction," in *Cultural Studies* (ed. Lawrence Grossberg et al.; New York: Routledge, 1992), 2.

tion of women in the media, verbal abuse, "eve teasing," mistreatment of widows, caste violence, women's rights (property/inheritance, abortion, birth control, women's rights to land, food, water, and other basic necessities), women's health, sexuality, marriage, family, interfaith relations, HIV/AIDS, ecology, militarization, globalization, to issues such as women's leadership in church and society, ordination of women, partnership between women and relationship to men, God and the church.

► *Feminist biblical work in Asia is highly dependent on Western feminist scholarship:* In general, feminist biblical interpretation in Asia utilizes the gains of feminist scholarship in the West, but attempts to go beyond a gender-focused analysis to see the interconnections that exist between women's oppression and cultural systems such as caste, religion, ethnicity, and language. Alluding to Western literature inevitably produces a further set of questions, anxieties, and expectations: What about "Asian" theories and methods of biblical interpretation? To begin with "the West" is at once a particular geographical place and a relation. From where we are, this relation is one of extremely complicated domination. But for all intents and purposes, we are effectively located in the West. It is to the credit of feminists in Asia that they refused to be silenced by accusations of being Western-identified and unable to deal with the "real" Asia. In my view, the theoretical questions before us are both more daunting and more exciting. We Asian feminists cannot but draw upon Western theories and methods, since "they determine at an unconscious level, the reading practices we bring to bear" on our work.[36]

In conclusion, feminist biblical interpretation in Asia is an imaginative and creative process that utilizes the experience of women's discrimination and subjectivity to foreground its work and to allow for readings of the text that are liberating and transformative for both society and the church. But, as Brenner has reminded us, imaginative thinking requires theory and "method to complement it, whereas method without imagination accom-

---

36. This description of our relation to Western theories comes from Madhava Prasad's discussion of the problems besetting current analyses of Indian cinema. See Madhava Prasad, *The Ideology of Hindi Cinema: A Historical Construction* (Delhi: Oxford University Press, 1998). For an extended discussion of issues related to the Westernness of theory in the context of feminism, see Mary E. John, *Discrepant Dislocations: Feminism, Theory, and Postcolonial Histories* (Berkeley: University of California Press, 1996).

plishes little."[37] We are still too few to make an impact, but with the development of a critical mass of feminist biblical scholars, we might just be able to equip more women interpreters with the tools of biblical criticism for feminist biblical scholarship.

37.Athalya Brenner, "Who's Afraid of Feminist Criticism? Who's Afraid of Biblical Humor? The Case of the Obtuse Foreign Ruler in the Hebrew Bible," *JSOT* 63 (1994): 38–55, here 40.

Part 2
Creating Feminist Hermeneutical Spaces in Religion

From Androcentric to
Christian Feminist Exegesis: Genesis 1–3

Helen Schüngel-Straumann
Basel, Switzerland

1. Introduction

The background to this paper is the androcentric biblical exegesis in the twentieth century as it continues to have extensive influence on the beginnings of an explicitly feminist exegesis. At early stages of critical interpretation, critical women were already trying to argue against misogynist assertions of certain texts in both popular and theological writings and contexts. However, because women were largely denied access to specialist theological studies in the early twentieth century, they were forced to raise their concerns in other ways, for instance, in letters.

The following explanations focus on the German-speaking area but also cite examples from the Anglo-American area and from northern Europe. By the end of the nineteenth and the beginning of the twentieth century, Germany led the way in developing fruitful new approaches to historical-critical exegesis that continued far into the twentieth century.[1] Some of the major Protestant representatives are used as examples. (Catholic commentators were still forbidden at the time to work with "new" historical-critical methods, and this did not change until the end of World War II.[2]) The period from World War I until after the end of the World War II was not very productive, lim-

---

1. Even in the nineteenth century, there were Genesis commentaries by Julius Wellhausen (1876–1877), Karl Budde (1883), among others, followed by Hermann Gunkel (1901), Otto Procksch (1913), to name just a few important German-language interpreters. For English-language commentaries, see, inter alia, Samuel Rolles Driver (1905) and John Skinner (1910–1912).

2. Due to the papal encyclical "Divinu afflante Spiritu" (1943) and subsequently due to "Humani generis" (1950); see on this Gustave Lambert, "L'Encyclical 'Humani generis' et l'Ecriture Sainte," *NRTh* 73 (1951): 225–43.

ited as it was by the global economic crisis and then by the emergence of the National Socialists in Germany.[3] Therefore, the significant changes brought about by feminist exegesis did not begin until after the middle of the twentieth century.

For the younger generation and for women readers from non-European countries, it cannot be emphasized enough what the tremendous changes brought about by World War II meant in Europe. Whereas scholars before the war "roamed"[4] throughout Europe and there was genuine intellectual exchange between east and west as well as between north and south, after 1945 Europe was split in two parts: east and west. This and the aftermath of the war—even for women referred to as "rubble women" (Trümmerfrauen[5])—caused a relative stalemate in new theological approaches until after 1950. These changes in the history of ideas and political thought cannot be overstated. Relations in Europe once again changed drastically in 1989 due to the fall of the Berlin Wall and the breakdown of the Soviet Union.

As an Old Testament scholar, my explanations are limited to the Hebrew Bible. Even as far back as the Middle Ages, women have constantly been interested in "beginnings," in statements about creation and, in practical terms, in the relationship between men and women as illustrated in Gen 1–3. "Prehistories" are human phenomena that generate identity, and the chapters in Genesis continue to be used to clarify or cement an understanding of the roles of men and women from a positive or negative point of view in both secular and religious contexts. Genesis 1–3 have almost become the prooftexts for the Western Christian image and ideology of woman. For this reason these chapters and their subsequent interpretations in the New Testament need to be critically analyzed. Many statements in Paul's letters are of particular relevance here.[6]

However, it is not only the scholarly papers and commentaries that have continued to pass down and cement misogynist interpretations of the original texts. Religious practice in particular (teaching, preaching) has also worked consistently with oversimplifications and overgeneralizations. Male superiority and female inferiority, weakness, and vulnerability to sin have constantly

---

3. There is, however, a noteworthy new draft at this time: the Jewish commentary by Benno Jacob (1862–1945), *The First Book of the Torah: Genesis* (Stuttgart: Calwer, 2000; first published in 1934), who works with other prerequisites and methods than historical-critical Christian commentators.

4. See the examples below, e.g., Karl Barth (n. 38).

5. These women in Germany were listed who, for years, cleared away, sometimes without an appropriate tool, the detritus of war and reproduced makeshift living conditions.

6. Thus particularly 1 Cor 11, inter alia.

been emphasized. Women's self-appreciation has therefore been undermined for hundreds of years. The catchwords "Eve" or "fall from grace" suffice to recall associations concerning woman as temptress and as a sexually danger-ous creature. The literature on this is boundless. Every reader of exegetical literature is always influenced by such negative texts, whether she wants to be or not.[7]

In the next three parts of my essay (Prefeminist Interpretations; Female Precursors of Feminist Commentators; and Feminist Critique and Reorien-tation), I refer predominantly to examples from German-speaking contexts. These examples make a point of taking into account works that are little known to date. Obviously, such references can never be complete in such a small article, but they are nevertheless representative.

2. PREFEMINIST INTERPRETATIONS

2.1. INDIVIDUAL CONTRIBUTIONS

In the early decades of the twentieth century, scholarly exegesis focused heav-ily on "the woman" in the Old Testament topos. Various works appeared that shall be briefly mentioned. Max Löhr discussed women's proper names in par-ticular alongside the subject of cult.[8] He examined over a hundred women's names in the Old Testament, including *hawwah*, then their social position and in particular the participation of women in the cult (vows, sacrifice, proph-ecy). He did not contribute anything new to the complexities of Gen 1–3.

Georg Beer was likewise more concerned with the social and legal posi-tion of women, despite the fact that they were the property of men who were therefore able to adopt a superior position of power over "their" women, as was prevalent in a patriarchal society.[9] Concerning Gen 2:21, he remarked:

> How gloriously Gen 2:23 rings out from the familiar words of the human race's ancestors: *this* is the bone of my bones and flesh of my flesh! She shall be called *this* Woman because this was taken out of "her" man, the jubilation

---

7. The fact that these destiny texts were also crucial for women in other contexts is demonstrated by the papers in this volume on Africa (Dora Mbuwayesango), Asia and the Pacific region (Monica Melanchthon), and South America (Elsa Tamez).

8. Max Löhr, *Die Stellung des Weibes zu Jahwe-Religion und -Kult* (Beiträge zur Wis-senschaft vom Alten Testament 4; Leipzig: Hinrichs, 1908).

9. Georg Beer, *Die soziale und religiöse Stellung der Frau im isralitischen Altertum* (Tübingen: Mohr Siebeck, 1919).

of the Israelite bridegroom, who found in the wife the half of his being that had been missing until then![10]

The fact that the woman was highly prized as a mother was also emphasized in many examples by Beer, as it was by Löhr.

Johannes Döller went more deeply into the prehistory.[11] He emphasizes even in the first sentences the equality of man and woman and refers to Gen 1:27: "This emphasizes that people are all equal in their relationship to God due to their nature being made in the image of God."[12] Here the limitation "in their relationship to God" is worthy of note. The hierarchical relations "naturally" continued to apply to earthly relationships, because the woman was indeed created expressly for the man and not vice versa:

> A certain *dependence* of woman on man is already expressed in the creation account, insofar as she is there as a helpmeet for his sake alone and is also rooted in the weaker nature of woman. This relationship of dependence is further increased after the fall from grace.[13]

Döller no longer resorted to the original texts in his other explanations but dealt with the names, the cult (forms of) marriage, and legal provisions. The first few sentences on the characterization of women in chapter 5 ("Designation and Evaluation of the Female Sex") are interesting for the image of women that dominated in his time:

> The woman according to her entire physical and mental makeup is the connecting centerpiece between man and child, an adult human in whom some of the characteristics of childhood development have been established, so to speak, which is why she is also so wonderfully suited to bringing the child up to adulthood. Her spiritual being is dominated to a disproportionately higher

---

10. Ibid., 15. Note the language: "Wie prächtig klingt aus den bekannten Worten des Urvaters der Menschheit Gen. 2, 23: *Diese* ist Gebein von meinem Gebein, und Fleisch von meinem Fleische! Darum soll *diese* Männin heißen, denn von 'ihrem' Mann ist genommen *diese*, der Bräutigamsjubel des Israeliten, der in der Gattin die ihm bisher fehlende Hälfte seines Wesens gefunden hat!"

11. Johannes Döller, *Das Weib im Alten Testament* (Münster: Aschendorff, 1920).

12. Ibid., 3, quoting August Dillmann, *Genesis* (6th ed.; Leipzig: Hirzel, 1892), 34: "Was er betont, ist, dass Gott die Menschen in seinem Bilde … geschaffen hat, dass sie in ihrem Verhältniss zu Gott durch ihre gottebenbildliche Natur alle gleich sind."

13. Döller, *Das Weib im Alten Testament*, 6: "Eine gewisse *Abhängigkeit* des Weibes vom Manne kommt schon im Schöpfungsbericht zum Ausdruck, indem sie eine Gehilfin, bloss um seinetwillen da ist, und ist auch in der schwächeren Natur des Weibes begründet. Dieses Abhängigkeitsverhältnis wird nach dem Sündenfall noch gesteigert."

degree than for the man by fantasy and emotion over the quiet contempla-
tion of reason. Thus the woman could be easily overcome by temptation,
which was mainly considered to be due to the excitement of the imagination
and movement of the emotions.[14]

All three works show great interest in the woman as mother, and the clear
subordination of the woman to the man is undisputed.

One further trend should be mentioned here, which extended into the
twentieth century due to misogynist currents in the philosophy of the nineteenth century (Schopenhauer, Moebius, and Nietzsche) and also argued,
inter alia, with the biblical stories of our origins. This trend is exemplified
in a 1910 Halle dissertation that questioned whether women were human.
The title immediately answers that women are not human, and this is argued
using quotations from the creation story.[15] These and similar writings reveal
an image of women in many places that insisted upon the superiority of men
in every area.

2.2. The Commentaries

2.2.1. Genesis 2–3

The division of Genesis into prehistory and histories of the patriarchs is a
common theme in the commentaries of the early twentieth century.[16] The

---

14. Döller, *Das Weib im Alten Testament*, 72, all a quotation from Wilhelm Schmidt,
"Die Uroffenbarung als Anfang der Offenbarung Gottes," in *Religion, Christentum, Kirche*
(ed. Gerhard Esser and Joseph Mausbach; München, 1911), 1:490: "Das Weib ist in seiner
ganzen physischen wie psychischen Veranlagung nach das verbindende Mittelstück zwischen
Mann und Kind, Ein erwachsener Mensch, bei dem ein Teil der Charakteristika der Kind-
heitsstufe gleichsam festgelegt worden ist, weshalb sie auch so wunderbar geeignet ist, das
Kind zum Alter der Erwachsenen heranzuziehen. In ihrem geistigen Wesen dominiert in
ungleich höherem Maße als beim Manne Phantasie und Affekt über die ruhige Erwägung
des Verstandes. So konnte das Weib leichter von einer Versuchung überwunden werden, die
vorzüglich auf die Erregung der Phantasie, die Bewegung der Affekte gelegt war."

15. "A woman did not bring about the fall of Adam; a woman did not seduce the angels
Harut and Marut; a woman did not tempt the pious David to murder Uriah.… And when
God cast Adam and Eve out of Paradise, He directed the question at Adam: 'Why have you
eaten from the forbidden tree?'—Had God acknowledged Eve as a person, however, he
would certainly have directed this question at her as well." Thus Max Funke, "Sind Weiber
Menschen? Mulieres homines non sunt" (Ph.D. diss., Halle, 1910), documented in Elisabeth Gössman, *Ob die Weiber Menschen seyn oder nicht* (Archive for Women's Research
into the History of Philosophy and Theology 4; Munich: Iudicium, 1988), 23–24.

16. For the history of research into Gen 1–11, see the comprehensive statements on

majority of them emanate from a separation of sources in Gen 1–3: in the older texts of Gen 2 and 3 with their author the Yahwist (J), and the more recent source of Priestly writings (P), in which detailed differentiations have also been made. Many orientations were more in terms of literary criticism, while others were directed more at the history of form and genre.[17]

The fact that Gen 2 and 3 must have had a longer prehistory is not really in doubt, even though the dating has always been a matter of great dispute. The Jewish commentary by Jacob admittedly deviates resolutely from this, as he insists on the unity of the texts in their canonical sequence. Separations of sources are irrelevant to him because he wants to lift the "deeper context out of the evidence."[18]

How one understands the first human being created by God is crucial for interpretation. "Adam," the first creature, was interpreted without exception as being a man, while woman was created later. Hence the creation from the so-called "rib" was an important theme. This sequence, which was tied up with certain judgments, already pervaded Christian tradition in its entirety and governed all interpretations right up until the middle of the twentieth century. In the early decades of the twentieth century, there was even an interesting discussion surrounding the term 'ādām.[19] The term's association with 'ădāmâ (red ground) was also discussed, but there was no agreement as to whether this was predominantly a play on words ('ādām taken from the ground, therefore earthly and weak), or whether 'ādām was construed from other Semitic languages (predominantly with the meaning "red").[20] However, the problems of the limitation to a male person, to Adam (proper name!), have never been expounded.[21]

---

the literature by Claus Westermann, *Genesis 1–11* (Neukirchen-Vluyn: Neukirchener, 1974), esp. 97–103, 104–7, 203–19, 245–49.

17. The various methodical approaches would be interesting, but the subjects are not included here. See on this the essays in part 3 of this volume.

18. Jacob, *First Book of the Torah*, 10: "Die Genesis ist ein *einheitliches* Werk, in Einem Geiste entworfen, durchdacht und durchgearbeitet. Zwar gibt es schon einige von dieser unglücklichen Hypothese (gemeint ist die Quellenscheidung) Abtrünnige gelehrten Rufes, aber im allgemeinen beherrscht sie noch immer die Wissenschaft vom Pentateuch."

19. See Claus Westermann, "'Ādām," in *Theological Lexicon of the Old Testament* (ed. Ernst Jenni and Claus Westermann; trans. Mark E. Biddle; 3 vols.; Peabody, Mass.: Hendrickson, 1994), 1:31–42.

20. See on this Theodoor C. Vriezen, "Onderzoek naar de Paradijsvoorstelling bij de oude semietische Volken" (Ph.D. diss., Utrecht, 1937).

21. English-language commentaries are similar in their basic direction: indeed, the woman is not defined in explicitly negative terms, but the androcentric set-up can be felt everywhere. See the commentaries mentioned above in n. 1. Skinner makes a clear

This identification of "man" and "human" is common to all commentators until Westermann's commentary on Genesis.[22] The latter therefore always translates 'ādām as "human" and also explicitly identifies the association with 'ădāmâ (ground); but with the creation of woman, it should be clearly understood that he sees the first created being as man: "What is represented here is an ancient event, and the creation of woman from the rib of the man cannot be put forward any more than the creation of the man from the earth or dust can be."[23]

The difference between "human" and "man" in modern Western languages occurs almost exclusively in German. All the Romance languages in particular have a clear identification, as does the Latin, between the human being in general and the male (homo, homme, uomo, etc.). This course set by Greek antiquity is still evident today.[24] Another play on words occurs with the creation of the woman explicitly recounted in Gen 2, using for the first time the gender-specific terms 'îš and 'iššâ (male/man and female/woman). This chapter explains, in most cases etiologically, the close common bond of man and woman. Almost all the commentaries are clear here about sexual distinction being God's will, a concept rooted in the creation and stipulated as unchanging for all time. It shows the foundation of marriage[25] and thus of monogamy. This admittedly goes against the practical arrangement familiar from the Old Testament, which allowed the man to have several wives.

---

reference to Gunkel. Indeed, he expressly states that 'ādām should be understood generically, not as an individual ("the human race"). He is cautious about what directly concerns misogynist statements, but the commentary taken as a whole is androcentric.

22. A section from Hermann Gunkel is an example (Genesis [4th ed.; HKAT; Göttingen: Vandenhoeck & Ruprecht, 1917], 4–7), where Gunkel continually alternates between meanings. Although he explains that 'ādām (man) is created from 'ădāmâ (ground), he designates the former alternately as man but then as "Ackermann" (= farmer). This alternation is typical of all commentators in the first half of the twentieth century. Woman therefore derives from the term 'ādām!

23. Westermann, Genesis 1–11, 313. "Im laufenden Text gibt er immer wieder zu erkennen, dass er den Erstgeschaffenen als 'Mann' sieht, so z.B. bei Überlegungen über das Verbot in Gen 2 … entsteht die geringe Schwierigkeit, dass das Verbot in V 16f. nur der Mann hörte, während in 3,1ff. auch die Frau es kennt" (265)

24. Indeed, the Greek also has different terms for man and woman (anēr and gynē) and a generic term anthrōpos for "man." This contributes little to the history of impact and reception because, according to understanding in late antiquity, an anthrōpos in the full sense of the term was only the male. This pre-Christian position also limits many statements that apply to humanity as a whole, essentially intended for the male alone—particularly in many statements by Paul.

25. This is also accepted consistently in the various theologies of the Old Testament, one example being Ludwig Köhler, Theologie des Alten Testaments (Tübingen: Mohr Siebeck, 1947).

2.2..2 Genesis 1

The more abstract creation narrative in Gen 1 gives an account of the creation of humans at the end of the sixth day of work. God's action is thereby conceived by his own decision (1:26): "Let us make humanity [*'ādām*] in our own image to rule...." The explanation in verse 27 again refers to the term *'ādām*: "And God created *'ādām* in his own image: in the image of God he created him; male and female he created them." Unlike Gen 2, the gender-specific terms *'îš* and *'iššâ* cannot be found, and thus it is about *'ādām,* man/humanity itself. The division into two genders is not expressly stated until the adjectives "male and female." Gunkel advanced the view here that the text itself does not state what the *Gottebenbildlichkeit* (likeness to God/image of God) consists of, but the continuation of the text in Gen 5:1–3 states: "God created Adam in his own image...." According to this interpretation, the *Gottebenbildlichkeit* is limited to the male, as the ancient apocryphal tradition has emphasized. This denies or limits woman's *Gottebenbildlichkeit*. The major difference between the Old Testament and dogmatics, Gunkel went on to say, is that this statement does not play any specific role in the Bible but is a central locus of dogmatics, in which anthropology as a whole is developed.[26] Such anthropology was essentially androcentric.[27] According to Westermann, the sentence "that God created man/humanity in his own image ... is of such persistent interest as virtually no other place in the entire Old Testament. The literature on this is boundless."[28] One only has to consider the official understanding of women in the pre-Reformation church to get a sense of the immense impact this androcentric combination has had on the Christian image of women that remains in place today.[29]

---

26. Gunkel, *Genesis,* 112.

27. The ancient, to some extent even pre-Christian interpretations of these texts, which are as ever based on the precedence of the man, are well documented by two works: Jacob Jervell, "Imago Dei: Gen 1, 26ff. im Spätjudentum, in der Gnosis und in den paulinischen Briefen" (Ph.D. diss., Göttingen, 1960); and J. B. Schaller, "Gen 1.2 im antiken Judentum" (Ph.D. diss., Göttingen, 1961). On pages 187–90 Schaller provides all the New Testament texts containing references to Gen 1 and 2. The New Testament, particularly Paul (see 1 Cor 11), is also in this exegetical history.

28. Westermann, *Genesis 1–11,* 204: "Dass Gott die Menschen nach seinem Bild geschaffen hat ... ein so beharrliches Interesse wie wohl kaum eine andere Stelle im ganzen AT. Die Literatur dazu ist uferlos."

29. See on this the arguments below with which Catholic women/female theologians fought for the office by rejecting an androcentric anthropology.

3. Female Precursors of Feminist Commentators[30]

The efforts of individual women to read the creation accounts "differently" from the mainstream go back as far as the Middle Ages.[31] A brief overview should outline the most important stages in the German-speaking world, which took place before an explicitly feminist exegesis began in the 1970s.

The first women who defended themselves against an image of women that had been handed down with arguments from the Bible were not in any way academic theologians. (Such women only emerged in the course of the twentieth century.) They were also mostly involved in secular women's movements. In Switzerland, the fact that women's right to vote was not introduced until 1971 made it even more difficult, because women there were more preoccupied than in other German-speaking countries with fighting for their political rights. Thus, even though some of the women in these examples were lawyers, they were still denied access to theological study. To begin with, many resented the New Testament statements about women, particularly those made by Paul.[32] The lack of specialized theological and linguistic knowledge, however, put women who tried to strike back at male dominance at a profound disadvantage. Therefore, the difficult and often unmanageable living conditions allotted to the women in these examples must be taken into account.

The Swiss Helene von Mülinen (1850–1924) was one of the first Protestant women to campaign for women with arguments from the Bible.[33] In

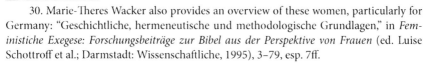

30. Marie-Theres Wacker also provides an overview of these women, particularly for Germany: "Geschichtliche, hermeneutische und methodologische Grundlagen," in *Feministiche Exegese: Forschungsbeiträge zur Bibel aus der Perspektive von Frauen* (ed. Luise Schottroff et al.; Darmstadt: Wissenschaftliche, 1995), 3–79, esp. 7ff.

31. See Elisabeth Gössmann, *Eva Gottes Meisterwerk* (vol. 2 of *Archiv für philosophie- und theologiegeschichtliche Frauenforschung*; Munich: Iudicium, 1985; rev., 2000), and the explanations of the Middle Ages interpretations by Elisabeth Gössmann on the history of impact and reception of Gen 1–3 in the articles on Eve, "Gottebenbildlichkeit," in *Wörterbuch der Feministischen Theologie* (ed. Elisabeth Gössmann et al.; Gütersloh: Gütersloher, 1991), 95–97, 177–81.

32. Reference is made most frequently to 1 Cor 11, where Paul submits a one-sided, misogynist interpretation of Gen 1–3. All those women who reject Paul's equivalent positions therefore also respond indirectly to Gen 1–3.

33. Doris Brodbeck, *Hunger nach Gerechtigkeit: Helene von Mülinen (1850–1924)— Eine Wegbereiterin der Frauenemanzipation* (Zürich: Chronos, 2000), 157. There is also a comprehensive directory of sources and literature here, including copies of numerous letters, for example, letters to Ms. Schlatter, Susanna Schlatter-Schoop (1860–1907), a close friend.

1900, she founded the Bund Schweizerischer Frauenvereine (BSF; League of Swiss Women's Associations). She spoke at the religious and social conference in Bern in 1910 as the first female speaker on the topic "What the Women's Movement Expects from Christianity." She argued that women are just as capable as men of blossoming in God's likeness. Furthermore, she asserted, "I do not think it is asking too much for us to expect the church to give us the space that the Old Testament calls women to fill."

Although she had no broad theological training, as a student of Adolf Schlatter she was not without specialized exegetical knowledge.[34] She also read many theological books, including Harnack's research on women in the early church.[35] In many instances she expressed her delight in Harnack's belief that a woman could have written the letter to the Hebrews. About the expression the "sinful" Eve, on which she had already stumbled earlier, she said: "This concept of guilt may have led in Christianity to the doctrine of Eve's sinfulness and unilaterally incriminated women as a gender." She complained that Christianity "had become crueler than God with this doctrine, a God who according to the Old Testament only wanted to chastise a few generations."[36]

Helene von Mülinen is therefore of particular significance because she succeeded for the first time in linking the women's movement to theological concerns. Her many relations with prominent Protestant theologians of the time who were active throughout the entire German-speaking area also demonstrates how much the subject of women's emancipation in relation to the Bible and the church was discussed in the period before World War I. The women who follow also testify to this.

The altercations of Henriette Visser't Hooft (1899–1968) with Karl Barth (1886–1968) also document this imbalance between educated male theologians and women with no specific specialized study. She came into conflict with the established image of women sanctioned by the church both through her husband[37] and through Barth. Barth, who argued in his *Church Dogmatics* for the superiority of the male in Gen 1,[38] either did not consider her suf-

---

34. Women were already allowed to study in Bern in 1874, but they could not study theology. They were therefore only able to attend the lectures as guest students.

35. Adolf von Harnack, *Mission und Ausbreitung des Christentums* (2 vols.; Leipzig: Hinrichs, 1902).

36. Brodbeck, *Hunger nach Gerechtigkeit*, 182.

37. Willem Adolf Visser't Hooft (1900–1985), first Secretary General of the World Council of Churches from 1938 to 1968.

38. Karl Barth, *Church Dogmatics*, vol. 3.4.

ficiently educated to reply to her letters or curtly cut her off.[39] Like many of her predecessors, Visser't Hooft resented 1 Cor 11. She published an essay in 1934 entitled "Eve, Where Are You?"[40] She fought for a change in the role of women in the church but referred only rarely to the Old Testament texts. One example of her exploration of the negative role of woman in the fall from grace is reproduced from this early essay:

> Woman has sinned against God and against the man/male by acknowledging the superiority of the latter and thus abnegating her own life's work. She has thus saddled herself with a curse: "And your desire shall be for your husband and he shall be your master!" (Gen 3:16). Man wants the totally Other; he wants the eternal male—whatever Goethe says. But woman, too, desires the eternally male. Man must turn to God and subsequently to woman, whereas woman must convert to God and subsequently to herself. Generally, one does not recognize to what extent this curse of Genesis has become a complex "hang-up" in the soul of womanhood as a whole. Here lies the problem of woman in Christianity and, one may add, perhaps also in the divine sense of the Word.[41]

She and Barth never agreed about the main problem, which was the hierarchical order of the sexes.

There were always women who only had an opportunity for employment in association with a male. This was the case, for example, with Maria Richter (1915–1993) in her collaborative work with Prof. Hermann Seifermann (Munich). Both of them worked for decades in lectures and at conferences

---

39. At the World Council of Churches of 1948 in Amsterdam, Barth publicly mocked her. On this, see Jürgen Moltmann, "Henriette Visser't Hooft," in *Gotteslehrerinnen* (ed. Luise Schottroff and Johannes Thiele; Stuttgart: Kreuz, 1989), 169–79.

40. Reprinted in Gudrun Kaper et al., *Eva, wo bist du? Frauen in internationalen Organisationen der Ökumene: Eine Dokumentation* (Gelnhausen: Burckhardthaus-Laetare, 1991), 20–32. Some of the letters exchanged with Barth can also be found here.

41. Visser't Hooft, "Eva, wo bist du," 31. "Die Frau hat gesündigt gegen Gott und gegen den Mann, indem sie die Überlegenheit des letzteren anerkannte und so ihre eigene Lebensaufgabe verneinte. So hat sie einen Fluch auf sich geladen: 'Und dein Verlangen soll nach deinem Manne sein und er soll dein Herr sein!' (1. Mose 3,16). Der Mann will nicht den ganz anderen, er will das ewig männliche—was Goethe auch sagen mag. Aber auch die Frau will das ewig männliche. Der Mann muß sich zu Gott bekehren und nachher zur Frau, während die Frau sich zu Gott bekehren muß und nachher zu sich selbst. Man gibt sich im allgemeinen nicht darüber Rechenschaft, bis zu welchem Grad dieser Fluch der Genesis ein Komplex geworden ist in der Seele der ganzen Weiblichkeit. Hier liegt das Problem der Frau im christlichen Sinn, und man kann vielleicht hinzufügen, auch im göttlichen Sinn des Wortes."

on Old Testament subjects. However, because she was not able to study for a Ph.D. in theology, Maria Richter completed a Ph.D. in history.[42]

The most prominent example of such collaboration was Charlotte von Kirschbaum (1899–1975). Born in Bavaria in 1929, she took up residence in Barth's household as a lifelong colleague and companion. Her part in Barth's theological lifetime achievement can no longer be defined, but it may have been considerable.[43] Although in practice she seemed to accept the "subordination" of women as the "symbolic order"[44] and devoted her whole life to the work and person of Barth, she nevertheless wrote a book about women in the New Testament.[45] In her explanations of 1 Cor 11, she refers to Paul's interpretation of Gen 1–3:[46]

> According to 1 Cor 11:3ff, woman is subordinate in her relationship to man based on the order of creation; man is the head of woman. This is referred to as headship: being a preordained, dominant being. Anyone who is the head has power. As the bearer of power (*exousia*), man is part of the sequence mentioned in verse 3. He represents woman with respect to power and domination. Woman, in contrast, stands at a totally different place, that of subordination. Thus woman has her place in the realm of nature, the place that the community has in the spiritual realm in relation to her Lord. Her very being as woman, totally independent of her particular actions, installs her in the place, which is the place of the community/church in relation to Jesus Christ (Eph 5:23–24).[47]

---

42. See also Wacker, "Geschichtliche, hermeneutische und methodologische Grundlagen," 21. On exact figures and activities "between the wars," see 13–19.

43. See Renate Köbler, *Schattenarbeit: Charlotte von Kirschbaum—Die Theologin an der Seite Karl Barths* (Köln: Pahl-Rugenstein, 1987).

44. See on this Doris Brodbeck, *Unerhörte Worte: Religiöse Gesellschaftskritik von Frauen im 20. Jh* (Bern: eFeF, 2003), 154–59.

45. Charlotte von Kirschbaum, *Die wirkliche Frau* (Zürich: Evangelischer Verlag, 1949). She had argued with Gertrud von Le Fort (1876–1971), *Die ewige Frau* (Munich: Kösel & Pustet, 1960), a book often quoted in Catholic circles, and Simone de Beauvoir (1908–1968), and wanted to develop a Protestant doctrine of woman.

46. See above, n. 32.

47. "Nach 1. Kor 11,3ff steht die Frau auf Grund einer Schöpfungsordnung in ihrem Verhältnis zum Mann in der Unterordnung: der Mann aber ist das Haupt der Frau. Hauptsein heißt: ein Vorgeordnetes, Beherrschendes sein. Wer Haupt ist, hat Macht. Als solcher Träger von Macht (exousia) gehört der Mann in die V 3angeführte Reihe. Er repräsentiert der Frau gegenüber Macht und Herrschaft. Die Frau steht demgegenüber an dem ganz anderen Ort der Unterordnung. Damit aber steht sie im natürlichen Bereich an dem Ort, den im geistlichen Bereich die Gemeinde ihrem Herrn gegenüber einnimmt. In ihrem Sein als Frau, ganz unabhängig von ihrem jeweiligen Verhalten, ist sie an diesen Ort gewiesen,

Of those such as Iris Müller (b. 1930) and Ida Raming (b. 1932) who fought for the priesthood of women in the Catholic Church, Gertrud Heinzelmann (1914–1999), who was involved as a Swiss lawyer with the legal status of women in the Catholic Church, should be mentioned first, chronologically speaking.[48] She was less concerned at the time with the Bible than with Thomas Aquinas, whom she fiercely attacked on account of his misogynistic anthropological theories. Statements of the creation accounts, which she subsequently used, such as "woman is subordinate to man," she regarded as a "time-bound interpretation."[49] Regarding the creation account of Gen 1, she stated in particular, "There is no talk of subordination of the woman to the man.… The woman is therefore inherently judged and placed in every respect as equal to the man, according to P."[50] It is particularly interesting that these statements are derived from the term 'ādām, which is a generic term and should not be limited to the man/male.[51]

Gertrud Heinzelmann was also in contact with another Swiss Catholic lawyer, Hilde Vérène Borsinger (1897–1986).[52] Both were unmarried and fought for the priesthood of women.[53] Gertrud Heinzelmann was known through her petition at Vatican II (1962–1965),[54] in which she entreated the church to fight for equal rights for women. For this intervention she was sometimes belittled and sometimes attacked. Ultimately, she did not succeed.[55]

Ida Raming has been the strongest advocate in Germany for the priesthood of women, producing a corresponding dissertation that was published

---

entspricht sie also exemplarisch der Gemeinde in ihrer Stellung Jesus Christus gegenüber (Eph 5,23f)" (quoted in Brodbeck, *Unerhörte Worte*, 155).

48. Her dissertation (Gertrud Heinzelmann, *Das grundsätzliche Verhältnis von Kirche und Staat in den Konkordaten* [Aarau: Sauerländer, 1943]) did not appear until 1943 due to the lack of paper during World War II.

49. Gertrud Heinzelmann, *Wir schweigen nicht länger: Frauen äussern sich zum II. Vatikanischen Konzil* (Zürich: Interfeminas, 1964), 61–63.

50. Ibid., 63.

51. Ibid., 64.

52. Hilde Vérène Borsinger received a doctorate in 1930 in Zürich on the "Rechtsstellung der Frau in der katholischen Kirche" (Ph.D. diss., Leipzig, 1930). On this, see Doris Brodbeck et al., eds., *Siehe, ich schaffe Neues: Aufbrüche von Frauen in Protestantismus, Katholizismus, Christkatholizismus und Judentum* (Bern: eFeF, 1998), 89ff.

53. Women were forbidden to practice a profession at the time in Switzerland without their husband's permission, and women teachers had to give up their jobs when they married. It is therefore understandable that "academic" women often did not marry in order not to lose their independence.

54. See the 23 May 1962 petition in Heinzelmann, *Wir schweigen nicht länger*, 79–99.

55. Barbara Kopp, *Die Unbeirrbare: Wie Gertrud Heinzelmann den Papst und die Schweiz das Fürchten lehrte* (Zürich: Limmat, 2003).

in 1973.[56] No one at first suspected a discussion of Gen 1–3 in a treatise on church law. However, in an examination of *decretum Gratiani*, one of the most notorious falsifications of church law, she did stumble across the justifications for excluding women from ordination as well as from numerous other cult limitations. These justifications are all associated with misogynist interpretations of Gen 1–3 in late antiquity.[57]

Hence, she added a detailed digression on the patristic evidence for the subordination of women.[58] In an analysis of Old Testament texts, she rejected in particular the limitation of the *Gottebenbildlichkeit* (likeness to God) to man/male as a precondition for the male priesthood. Whereas almost all her predecessors went along with Paul's interpretation in 1 Cor 11, Ida Raming used the source texts to correct subsequent interpretations in the original Hebrew. "Gen 1:27 (as well as Gen 2:7–24) and 1 Cor 11:6–7 are, according to causae 13 and 19, causa 33 questio 5 in Gratian's Decretum, the written evidence for Ambrosiaster's statements that woman is not made in God's own likeness."[59] Prior to any feminist exegesis, she pointed to the sore points in traditional exegesis and anticipated subsequent analyses disputing major exegetical commentaries. This digression is still worth reading today, but it may be overlooked because it appeared in connection with church law.

Although Helga Rusche had already completed a Ph.D. in Protestant theology in Heidelberg in 1943, it was not until after World War II that Catholic women were first allowed to complete studies in theology.[60]

Marga Bührig (1915–2002), who discovered feminist theology relatively late, described her path herself.[61] Like many of her predecessors, she did not avoid the fundamental issues raised by the creation accounts. At the same time, the statements of Gen 2 on the relationship between man and woman were of interest to her not so much with regard to marriage but rather, according to her own way of life, with regard to the relationship of man and woman

---

56. Ida Raming, *Der Ausschluss der Frau vom priesterlichen Amt: Gottgewollte Tradition oder Diskriminierung?* (Köln-Wien: Böhlau, 1973).

57. See n. 27 above.

58. Raming, *Der Ausschluss der Frau*, 166–200.

59. Ibid., 166. "Gen 1,27 (auch Gen 2,7–24) und 1 Kor 11,6f sind nach cc. 13 und 19, C. 33 q.5 im Dekretbuch Gratians der Schriftbeleg für die Aussagen des Ambrosiasters, die Frau sei nicht Gottes Ebenbild."

60. For details, see the chapter by Renate Jost in this volume. There were no exegetical doctoral degrees by female Catholic theologians until the second half of the twentieth century: Annermarie Ohler (1966), Hildegard Gollinger (1968), Helen Schüngel-Straumann (1968/1969), Elisabeth Schüssler Fiorenza (1969/1970), Ingrid Maisch (1970), Iris Müller, etc.

61. Marga Bührig, *Spät habe ich gelernt, gerne Frau zu sein* (Stuttgart: Kreuz, 1987).

professionally, a subject on which she concentrated all her life. She understood the contribution of women as "genuine motherliness," which does not end in biological motherhood.[62] Else Kähler (1917–2011), completed a Ph.D. in 1957 in Kiel on Paul that responded indirectly to Gen 1–3 as it relates to the subordination of women to men.[63] Her view was that the subordination of woman to man cannot be inferred from the genuine letters of Paul. Instead, she advocated for men and women working together in partnership.[64]

4. Feminist Critique and Reorientation

Hardly any of the women involved in the emerging feminist theology avoided the fundamental statements of Gen 1–3. A few of the women already mentioned also continued to be active in the decades after World War II. The first few years, however, were such a difficult time for most women that there was not much space and strength left for new theological approaches.[65] It was not until after they, too, were increasingly able to study academic theology—and not just to impart a rudimentary knowledge—that a broader movement developed, which was motivated still further on the Catholic side by the Second Vatican Council (1962–1965). Numerous women, including Gertrud Heinzelmann, expected the Council to have an impact on the church for a revaluation of women.[66] None of the female commentators gaining doctoral degrees in the 1960s[67] had any explicitly feminist subject at the time.[68] Only gradually did an awareness grow that something was fundamentally not right, and not with women, but with the structures of male-determined scholarship,

---

62. Brodbeck, *Unerhörte Worte*, 212–15. Bührig refers to Gertrud von Le Fort (see n. 45). This basically concerns the fact that men and women were not working against each other but with each other.

63. Else Kähler, *Die Frau in den paulinischen Briefen unter Berücksichtigung des Begriffs der Unterordnung* (Zürich: Gotthelf, 1960). She distinguishes between the real Paul and the Pastoral Letters and identifies a crucial difference: Paul always spoke of a mutual subordination indicating that men and women were equal, whereas the Pastoral Letters emanate entirely from man and demand only subordination for woman.

64. Ruth Epting (born 1919) campaigned more in the field of ecumenism than in Bible study in Basel, Switzerland. She had already become aware early on of ecumenical issues on account of her stronger intermixing between Christian denominations. In 1958, the large women's SAFFA conference was already being held in Zürich. Much of the impetus emanated from there.

65. See n. 5 above on "rubble women."

66. See nn. 48–51 above.

67. See n. 60 above.

68. See, however, the books of Elisabeth Gössmann and Elisabeth Schüssler Fiorenza.

particularly in Christian theology and the church. This new awareness was subsequently articulated clearly at the first women's congresses.[69]

Much of the impetus came from the U.S., as well as from German male commentators. Phyllis Trible's 1973 article on Gen 2–3 should be mentioned first here,[70] followed by Phyllis Bird's 1981 interpretation of Gen 1.[71] Both highlighted the texts in Gen 1–3 that were crucial for women. Trible had already rejected male hegemony in her 1973 article by trying to read the texts in a nonsexist manner. She stripped down the centuries-long interpretations of woman as the subordinate "helpmeet" by examining in detail for the first time the Hebrew term on which it is based. In doing so, she outlined how the masculine word *ʿēzer* in Hebrew is frequently used for God when men are not able to help themselves, thus precluding the understanding that submissive service of woman for man can be understood by this concept. Trible does not, however, eschew criticism but traces parallels in Gen 2 to the Song of Songs, by comparing links between key words and motifs in both texts (garden, trees, etc.). In the process, she also criticizes the juxtaposition of creation with marriage concerning the relationship between the sexes. Like the Song of Songs, Gen 2 is about love itself. Thus, the Song of Songs should be read as a commentary on Gen 2–3. In doing so, she turns the patriarchal interpretation entirely on its head.

Bird, on the other hand, deals with Gen 1:27b by critically reviewing Barth's interpretations in particular.[72] She argues that the creation of man and woman is not to be understood in sociological terms but that, like the animals, they are created as a species. Genesis 1:27 is generically interpreted in this way ("male and female," not "man and woman"). The androcentric orientation of P's text persists, as it is continued later in Gen 5: 1–3 and 9:1. It does not involve reassessing social roles but reevaluating Eros and sexuality as an essential part of creation.[73] It continually emphasizes the fact that the full *Gottebenbildlichkeit* (likeness of God) applies to both sexes.

---

69. The Protestant academies led the way on this in the German-speaking areas.

70. Phyllis Trible, "Eve and Adam: Genesis 2–3 Reread," *ANQ* 13 (1973): 251–58.

71. Phyllis Bird, "'Male and Female He Created Them': Gen 1:27b in the Context of the Priestly Account of Creation," *HTR* 74 (1981): 129–59. On the American commentators, see Judith Plaskow's chapter in this volume.

72. See n. 38 above.

73. "For the priestly account of origins ignores completely the question of the social structuring of roles and of individual and collective responsibility in carrying out the charge addressed to the species" (Bird, "Male and Female," 158).

In a 1976 volume containing various essays, Letty M. Russell scrutinized especially the patriarchal traditions in the Bible.[74] In doing so, she focusd her attention specifically on the problem of androcentric language.[75]

Kari Børresen from Norway takes an entirely different approach with regard to woman's *Gottebenbildlichkeit*. In numerous publications she focuses on the long reception history of this phrase, which she traces from antiquity through the history of theology to today. Throughout this reception history, woman's *Gottebenbildlichkeit* was devalued and/or totally denied in very different ways.[76]

The feminist consideration of the original texts began in the German-speaking world at virtually the same time as the publications in the U.S. One of the first critical publications on this was by Othmar Keel, who touched on the sore points of the interpretation of Gen 2 and 3 irrespective of the American articles by alluding to ancient oriental sources. His starting point is the loneliness of man (*'ādām*). Not until after the creation of woman did the specific term *'îš* occur for the first time. Keel pointed to an interesting difference between Gen 2 and the Epic of Gilgamesh. Whereas woman in the Epic of Gilgamesh is only an episode, Gen 2 sees her as a permanent partner. He asserted, "The characterization of the being to be created as a helpmeet has nothing of the pejorative."[77] He referred to the sayings in Gen 3 as a "description of a state of calamity, which needs to be overcome,"[78] and therefore did not see them as punishment or even as a "curse." With this short essay Keel made the feminist interpretation socially acceptable, as it were. Feminist women commentators were still frequently being ridiculed at the time, and they often had difficulty publishing their articles.[79]

---

74. Letty M. Russell, ed., *The Liberating Word: A Guide to Non-sexist Interpretation of the Bible* (Philadelphia: Westminster, 1976).

75. For the backgrounds to the beginning of American feminist exegesis, see Judith Plaskow's chapter in this volume, where even more detailed examples can be found.

76. Kari E. Børresen, *Subordination et Equivalence: Nature et rôle de la femme d'après Augustin et Thomas d'Aquin* (Oslo: Universitetsforlaget, 1968), published in English as *Subordination and Equivalence: The Nature and Role of Woman in Augustine and Thomas Aquinas* (Kampen: Kok Pharos, 1995). See also Børresen, *From Patristics to Matristics: Selected Articles on Christian Gender Models* (Rome: Herder, 2002).

77. Othmar Keel, "Die Stellung der Frau in Genesis 2 und 3," *Orientierung* 39 (1975): 74.

78. Ibid., 75.

79. In the 1970s, and even in the 1980s, it was relatively difficult for women to publish scholarly studies or essays. Academic periodicals usually did not accept such articles. Many continued to be given out by hand, photocopied, and so on, with the very limited media

Frank Crüsemann's paper regarding the role of woman in Gen 2 and 3, published in 1978, refers to Trible's and Bird's previous essays.[80] The author details the ambivalence of the term *'ādām*, which generally describes humanity. But he asserts that where woman is added (repeatedly in Gen 2 and 3), *'ādām* should be understood as male. The language of the entire text may be androcentric, and therefore the punitive sayings in Gen 3 should be understood etiologically, particularly in order to explain the harder lot of the woman. The sayings therefore should not be misused to legitimize man's domination over woman and in theological terms, and no order of creation should be construed from the punishments. Crüsemann nevertheless rejected Trible's view of woman's superiority and greater activity.

Of the female German theologians who organized the first meetings and conferences, Elisabeth Moltmann-Wendell (b. 1926) must be mentioned, because it was she who set up feminist events such as those in Protestant conference centers and who exerted enormous influence with her biblically influenced themes.[81] She also made translations of American feminist theologians available in German. In her volume *Frauenbefreiung: Biblische und theologische Argumente*, a paper by Phyllis Trible on Gen 2–3 became famous in the German-speaking world.[82] This paper encouraged Helen Schüngel-Straumann, for example, to continue working on this subject. At the end of the 1970s and beginning of the 1980s, conferences of feminist theologians became ever more frequent, and the various conference centers and academies also published reports of the proceedings.[83]

---

resources of the time. The first German-speaking biblical periodical that published an issue on feminist exegesis was *Bibel und Kirche* 39 (1984).

80. Frank Crüsemann, " '…er aber soll dein Herr sein' (Genesis 3, 16): Die Frau in der patriarchalischen Welt des Alten Testaments," in *Als Mann und Frau geschaffen: Exegetische Studien zur Rolle der Frau* (ed. F. Crüsemann and H. Thyen; Gelnhausen: Burckhardthaus, 1978), 15–106, here 52–68.

81. By way of example, see from Elisabeth Moltmann-Wendel's numerous publications *Ein eigener Mensch werden: Frauen um Jesus* (Gütersloh: Gütersloher, 1981); and *Das Land, wo Milch und Honig fließt: Perspektiven einer feministischen Theologie* (Gütersloh: Gütersloher, 1985).

82. Elisabeth Moltmann-Wendel, *Frauenbefreiung: Biblische und theologische Argumente* (2nd ed.; Munich: Kaiser, 1978). There is a history of the German women's movement in the first part (19–77, here 63–77); Phyllis Trible, "Gegen das patriarchalische Prinzip in Bibelinterpretationen," in Moltmann-Wendel, *Frauenbefreiung*, 93–117.

83. The beginnings of feminist theology, particularly in broad practice, have also been gleaned since that time in the biography of Elisabeth Moltmann-Wendel, *Wer die Erde nicht berührt, kann den Himmel nicht erreichen* (Zürich: Benziger, 1997). Feminist theology has been dealing with the influence as well as the discrepancy between theory and practice until today.

The Dutch theologian Catharina Halkes (1920–2011) had enormous influence during this initial period. Although not a biblical scholar, her books, which had been translated into German, encouraged others to continue working on the Genesis texts.[84] One of these women was the Austrian Protestant theologian Evi Krobath (1930–2006), who worked for decades on feminist theology, particularly in biblical studies. Her Jewish ancestors encouraged her to consider the Jewish tradition as well in her works. Her publications, for example, on "Eve and Adam," "Männin und Mann" (woman and man), and many others, are mostly contained in conference transcripts or readers.[85] In feminist ecumenical terms as well as in social, church, and academic circles, she was one of the very many "bridgeheads" at the time between theory and practice.

Elisabeth Gössmann (b. 1928) should be mentioned as one of the first Catholic women theologians to complete her doctoral thesis in 1954 on a subject that would subsequently become an important topic of feminist theology.[86] She had no intention, however, of ending her commitment with the doctoral degree but wanted to pursue her academic work further and qualify as a professor. Because the Catholic laity was still forbidden to take a postdoctoral qualification, she was able to gain a *venia legendi* only in the philosophy faculty in Munich. She was soon producing other publications on the so-called woman's issue.[87] Although she was not a commentator, she primarily dealt with biblical subjects in the history of theology. Particular mention should be made here of her interest in the first few chapters of Genesis, to which she explicitly devoted a volume on "Eva" (Eve) in a ten-volume archive.[88] She has always contested the fact that feminist theology as a whole was an "import" from the U.S., because Europe had its own, independent

---

84. Catharina Halkes, *Gott hat nicht nur starke Söhne: Grundzüge einer feministischen Theologie* (Gütersloh: Gütersloher, 1980); Halkes, *Suchen, was verloren ging: Beiträge zur feministischen Theologie* (Gütersloh: Gütersloher, 1985).

85. See the publication on her seventieth birthday: Maria Halmer, Barbara Heyse Schaefer, and Barbara Rauchwarter, eds., *Anspruch und Widerspruch* (Vienna: Klagenfurth, 2000).

86. Elisabeth Gössmann, *Die Verkündigung an Maria im dogmatischen Verständnis des Mittelalters* (Munich: Hueber, 1957). Since the book was able to appear at the time only with "church permission to print," she had to amend it first in a few places.

87. Elisabeth Gössmann, *Das Bild der Frau Heute* (Düsseldorf: Haus der Katholischen Frauen, 1967); Gössmann, *Die streitbaren Schwestern: Was will die Feministische Theologie?* (Freiburg: Herder, 1981).

88. Gössmann, *Eva Gottes Meisterwerk.*

approaches. The impetus that emanated from Simone de Beauvoir (1908–1968) was just as effective.[89]

The first female doctoral Old Testament scholar who worked on feminist exegesis was the Swiss theologian Helen Schüngel-Straumann. In the early 1980s she published essays on women in the Bible, beginning with Miriam and Deborah, two prophetesses from the dawn of Israel.[90] This was the first work in feminist Old Testament exegesis to unearth the silenced, forgotten, and degraded women of the Bible. Even at the outset of her studies, she regarded the traditional statements on the first woman in the Bible as dubious. It is evident everywhere that the chapters of Gen 1–3 were the crux of all considerations on the role of women and the start of all discrimination against women that penetrated deeply into nonreligious and nontheological contexts. She concentrated particularly on misogynist consequences in the history of theology, including art. No one is able to reinterpret these texts without knowledge of the long history of reception and impact that is firmly embedded in Western culture.

The New Testament, which sometimes interprets Gen 1–3 in a misogynistic manner contrary to the original message of the text, is also part of this reception history. Helen Schüngel-Straumann has not been afraid to reverse the traditional Christian precedence of the New Testament over the Old and to criticize New Testament statements with the original texts in mind.[91] In connection with the practice mentioned in the introduction, it can be shown in proclamation and in the public perception that new interpretations from

---

89. Simone de Beauvoir, *Le deuxième sexe* (Paris: Gallimard, 1949; German ed., 1951) has nothing at all to do with theology but has inspired many women to reflect on their situation in the church as well as theologically.

90. Helen Schüngel-Straumann, "Frauen in der Bibel," *Der evangelische Erzieher* 34 (1982): 496–506. A series of twenty articles on women in the Bible followed (1984), published in the serial *Christ in der Gegenwart*. This series was routinely cited and copied in subsequent years; enquiries to Herder Verlag in Freiburg about turning it into a book were rejected at the time on the grounds that there was "no market." Just a few years later, books mushroomed on women in the Bible. Both publications have been reprinted in Helen Schüngel-Straumann, *Anfänge feministischer Exegese: Gesammelte Beiträge, mit einem orientierenden Nachwort und einer Auswahlbibliographie* (Münster: LIT, 2002), 9–22, 37–59. A major problem at the outset was that papers on feminist exegesis could not be published in the well-known exegetical periodicals or series, so women constantly had to look around to see where they could place their articles. Many were also copied and passed on by hand. The first theological periodical to publish an issue on feminist exegesis was *Bibel und Kirche*: "Frauen lesen die Bibel." The only Old Testament article in it comes from Helen Schüngel-Straumann, "Tamar: Eine Frau verschafft sich ihr Recht," *BiKi* 39 (1984): 148–57.

91. After many public lectures, Helen Schüngel-Straumann, *Die Frau am Anfang: Eva und die Folgen* (Freiburg: Herder, 1989; 3rd ed. Münster: LIT, 1999), appeared in 1989.

a feminist viewpoint are not sufficient. If the long negative history of impact and reception, which was already beginning in the pre-Christian Hellenistic period, is not reclaimed, any reinterpretation will remain piecemeal. Thus in numerous papers and ultimately in the first part of the aforementioned book she attempted to retrace at least the major lines of the effective history of the Genesis text.

The question of woman's *Gottebenbildlichkeit* in Gen 1, however, is theologically more central and more subtle. All previous interpretations of Gen 1–3 assumed that God's first creation (*'ādām*) was male. This assumption was carried over to Gen 1:26–28. However, in Gen 1: 27 it is explicitly stated that both man and woman are created in the image of God. It has been tacitly ignored that the longstanding androcentric interpretation has no basis in the text. Important here is the close connection to the commission to "rule"[92]: if men and women are created in the image of God and *both* are entrusted with rule over the rest of creation, then this statement explicitly precludes valuing man more highly and allowing him to "rule" over woman. Thus, beginning with first pages of the Bible, all statements that woman is secondary and subordinate to man are plainly rejected as wrong.[93] A correction of the fatal consequences of woman's alleged lack of *Gottebenbidlichkeit* still needs to be theologically corrected, particularly in Catholic theology, and this in spite of the clear biblical statements on the matter and the historical studies of Kari Børresen.[94]

This clear statement has consequences not only for anthropology but also for theology as well as for the image of God. If God created man and woman in God's image, then male and female must also be embodied in God's image.

---

92. See Helen Schüngel-Straumann, "Mann und Frau in den Schöpfungstexten von Genesis 1–3 unter Berücksichtigung der innerbiblischen Wirkungsgeschichte," in *Mann und Frau: Grundproblem theologischer Anthropologie* (ed. Theodor Schneider; QD 121; Herder: Freiburg, 1989), 142–66. The reviews of the Conference of Catholic Dogmatics (St. Pölten, 1988) are printed here. All the female theology professors at the time were invited as speakers on the subject: Elisabeth Gössmann, Herlinde Pissarek-Hudelist, Ilona Riedel-Spangenberger, and Helen Schüngel-Straumann. The review by Helen Schüngel-Straumann started a very interesting discussion; no one had considered such an interpretation until that point. This article is published in English: Helen Schüngel-Straumann, "On the Creation of Man and Woman in Genesis 1–3: The History and Reception of the Texts Reconsidered," in *A Feminist Companion to Genesis* (ed. Athalya Brenner; Sheffield Academic Press, 1993), 53–76.

93. See also Helen Schüngel-Straumann, "Die Frage der Gottebenbildlichkeit der Frau," in *Theologie des Alten Testaments aus der Perspektive von Frauen* (ed. Manfred Oeming and Gerd Theissen; Münster: LIT, 2003), 63–76.

94. See n. 76 above.

Schüngel-Straumann has continued to work on this subject of a nonandro-centric image of God.[95]

6. CONCLUSION

In conclusion and as a final summary of the beginnings of feminist exegesis in Europe, reference must be made to a work initiated in the 1980s by Elisabeth Moltmann, the world's first *Dictionary of Feminist Theology*.[96] Numerous overviews and summaries with a heavily biblical focus have been compiled of the first decade of feminist endeavors in exegesis and theology, a treasure trove for all those interested both in history and in feminist exegesis and theology.[97] The eighty or so keywords that first needed to be found in what was a lengthy process show the strategic directions as well as the difficulties of the beginnings.[98]

---

95. On this, see Helen Schüngel-Straumann, "Gott als Mutter in Hosea 11," *ThQ* 166 (1986): 119–34. This paper was edited (and shortened, unfortunately) in English as "God as Mother in Hosea 11," *TD* 34 (1987): 3–8.

96. See also Letty Russell and Shannon Clarkson, eds., *Dictionary of Feminist Theologies* (Louisville: Westminster John Knox, 1996).

97. Elisabeth Gössman et al., eds., *Wörterbuch der Feministischen Theologie* (Gütersloh: Gütersloher, 1991). It was translated into Portuguese and Japanese. See key words, including "Bible," "Eve," "*Gottebenbildlichkeit*," and "creation."

98. Further explanations can be found on this in the chapter by Renate Jost in this volume.

Jewish Feminist Biblical Studies

Cynthia Baker
Bates College

What makes Jewish feminist biblical study Jewish? Several possibilities come immediately to mind: (1) it is feminist biblical study carried out by Jews; (2) it is engaged biblical scholarship by Jewish women for, or on behalf of, a Jewish community or audience; (3) it is feminist Torah/Tanak study as an expression of the transformative feminist movement within and beyond the Jewish community; (4) it is feminist study that engages with the *midrashic* tradition of Jewish biblical interpretation through critical exploration of classical rabbinic midrash and/or through feminist contributions to the midrashic process and genre. A fifth form of Jewish feminist biblical study is perhaps less intuitive but arguably no less significant: namely, the critical feminist study of the Jewishness of earliest Christianity—its protagonists, texts, and contexts—and of the anti-Judaism that pervades the Christian Bible's reception history. The five elements on this list frequently overlap. Each is also open to reasonable contestation as to its "Jewishness," its "feminism," or its "biblicism," and the list itself is likely not exhaustive. Nonetheless, it broadly encompasses what might be called the "field" or "practice" of Jewish feminist biblical studies. Let us consider each of these elements in turn.

1. Feminist Biblical Study Carried Out by Jews

In her 2009 article "Jewish Feminist Approaches to the Bible," Esther Fuchs sets out to "provide an overview of specifically Jewish feminist approaches to the Bible."[1] She begins her discussion of "method" by highlighting her own work in challenging "both the method and conclusions of [the] early

---

1. Esther Fuchs, "Jewish Feminist Approaches to the Bible," in *Women and Judaism: New Insights and Scholarship* (ed. Frederick E. Greenspahn; New York: New York University Press, 2009), 25–40, here 25.

[1970s–1980s] phase of Christian theological interpretation," which she characterizes as problematic attempts "to 'depatriarchalize' the Hebrew Bible by reconstructing it as an egalitarian text," albeit one peppered with misogynist "deviations from biblical social norms."[2] In framing her earliest work and that of other first-generation Jewish feminist scholars as critical reaction and response to Christian feminist biblical interpretations, Fuchs seems to locate the impetus for Jewish feminist biblical scholarship in the Christian community and the reactive impulse felt by feminists within the Jewish community. Others would disagree and point to parallel impulses in the two communities, with the Bible taking secondary priority to halakah[3] for early Jewish feminist scholars. (See Judith Plaskow in this volume.)

Terming her preferred methodology "a deconstructive approach," Fuchs describes the methods practiced by other Jewish feminist biblical scholars.[4] "Carol Meyers promoted a reconstructive approach," which, Fuchs says, "emerged as the dominant interpretive theory in the 1990s" and is shared, with important variations, by scholars such as Ilana Pardes and Tikva Frymer-Kensky.[5] In contrast to these approaches, Fuchs notes Alicia Ostriker's critical psychoanalytic approach and Athalya Brenner's use of "linguistic and philological methodologies."[6]

Under the heading "Postbiblical Scholarship," Fuchs discusses work by Jewish feminist New Testament scholars. The "postbiblical" in the subtitle signals, once again, Jewish difference vis-à-vis Christianity, in which the New Testament is also "biblical." Here, scholarship on antiquity, the New Testament, and the Jewish Apocrypha by Amy-Jill Levine, Adele Reinhartz, and Ross Kraemer falls into Fuchs's "reconstructive" category, whereas Tal Ilan's "critical reconstruction of women's status" is curiously held up as "critical rather than reconstructive" insofar as it "far transcends simplistic Christian

---

2. Ibid., 26. The reference is clearly to the works of Phyllis Trible. See Trible, *God and the Rhetoric of Sexuality* (Philadelphia: Fortress, 1978); and Trible, *Texts of Terror: Literary-Feminist Readings of Biblical Narratives* (Philadelphia: Fortress, 1984).

3. Halakah includes the rabbinically derived practices of traditional Judaism.

4. Fuchs, "Jewish Feminist," 27–30.

5. See Carol Meyers, *Discovering Eve: Ancient Israelite Women in Context* (Oxford: Oxford University Press, 1991); Ilana Pardes, *Countertraditions in the Bible: A Feminist Approach* (Cambridge: Harvard University Press, 1992); Tikva Frymer-Kensky, *In the Wake of the Goddesses: Women, Culture, and Biblical Transformation of Pagan Myth* (New York: Free Press, 1992); and Frymer-Kensky, *Reading the Women of the Bible* (New York: Schocken, 2002).

6. Alicia Suskin Ostriker, *Feminist Revision and the Bible: The Unwritten Volume* (Oxford: Blackwell, 1993); Athalya Brenner, *The Intercourse of Knowledge: On Gendering Desire and "Sexuality" in the Hebrew Bible* (Leiden: Brill, 1997).

binary oppositions between Judaic and Christian communities during both religions' formative era."[7] This latter quality hardly distinguishes Ilan's scholarship, as it is found in Levine's, Reinhartz's, Kraemer's, and many others' works as well.

The same "reconstructive" versus "critical" binary organizes Fuchs's remaining discussions of "feminist midrash" and "modern Hebrew literature" before a final section on "history" recapitulates her account of the centrality of Christian chauvinism to the origins of Jewish feminist biblical studies. To this end, she recounts the story of the nineteenth-century Jewish writer Grace Aguilar, stating, "It is precisely this [Christian] stereotyping of the Hebrew Bible as the less enlightened and more antiquated testament [exemplified by Elizabeth Cady Stanton's *Women's Bible*] that Grace Aguilar sought to debunk in her massive *Women of Israel*," a two-volume tome "which preceded [Stanton's book] by several decades."[8]

By the close of her article, Fuchs acknowledges that "Jewish feminist readings of the Bible are … often indistinguishable from non-Jewish readings."[9] She insists, nonetheless, that biblical scholarship by feminist Jews shares "a unique interpretive philosophy" whose primary characteristic would seem to be that it is not Christian. She argues, "Most apparent is the understanding that the Hebrew Bible is not merely the first act in a two act play but rather the full drama.… It is not considered to be inferior to a sequel or second set of scriptures."[10] Fuchs does not specify how the presence or absence of such a "philosophy" manifests in any particular feminist scholarly article or book in the field of Hebrew Bible.

While troubling in its apparent assertion of non-Christianness as the fundamental nature and character of the Jewishness of biblical scholarship and creative work by feminist Jews, Fuchs's characterization raises key questions and issues at the heart of the enterprise represented by the present chapter, the present volume, and the larger "Bible and Women" project of which these are a part. Fuchs's problematic attempt at articulating an essence or "philosophy"

---

7. Fuchs, "Jewish Feminist," 31–32. See Amy-Jill Levine, *Women Like This: New Perspectives on Jewish Women in the Greco-Roman World* (Atlanta: Scholars Press, 1991); Adele Reinhartz, *Befriending the Beloved Disciple: A Jewish Reading of the Gospel of John* (New York: Continuum, 2001); Ross Shepard Kraemer, *When Aseneth Met Joseph: A Late Antique Tale of the Biblical Patriarch and His Egyptian Wife, Reconsidered* (New York: Oxford University Press, 1998); Tal Ilan, *Integrating Women into Second Temple History* (Tübingen: Mohr Siebeck, 1999).

8. Fuchs, "Jewish Feminist," 35. See Grace Aguilar, *The Women of Israel* (ed. Mayer I. Gruber; Piscataway, N.J.: Gorgias, 2011); first published in 1851 by Appleton.

9. Fuchs, "Jewish Feminist," 37.

10. Ibid.

characteristic of "Jewish feminist approaches to the Bible" serves to reinforce the impression that the "Jewishness" of the scholarly and artistic work she catalogues inheres exclusively in the fact that the creators of these works are Jews. In what ways is this definition meaningful or sufficient? Is "Jewish" whatever Jews do merely by virtue of being Jews (and thereby being "non-Christians")? The question is not a rhetorical one. Indeed it grows, in part, out of reflections by Judith Plaskow—author of some of the earliest and most widely read feminist, biblically engaged writings—about her own early work.

In "Lilith Revisited," a retrospective essay about her famous (1970s-era) retelling of the human saga of Gen 1–3, Plaskow reflects: "Today [in the mid-1990s], when I look at the larger framework within which 'The Coming of Lilith' was initially presented, I am shocked by the Christianness of the religious language that we/I chose to impose on our feminist experiences, describing them in terms of 'conversion,' 'grace,' and 'mission.'"[11] Were she to write the account of her early feminist experiences today, says Plaskow, she would not "impose on them the foreign vocabulary of any particular tradition."[12] At the same time, she avers, "I now see a much closer fit between the shared communal self-understanding of feminism and Judaism than I do between feminism and an individualistic Protestantism," and she observes that the Jewish concept of *tikkun olam,* "the obligation and project of healing the world," better fits the feminist sense of spirituality fused with a commitment to social justice than does her earlier, Christian language of "mission." She continues:

> What is most striking to me in revisiting Lilith, however, and most glaringly absent in terms of Jewish categories and analysis, is any understanding of the story as midrash. In referring to "The Coming of Lilith" in the framing material, I consistently label it a myth. This points to a rather interesting paradox. On the one hand, for all that I was willing to adopt a Protestant vocabulary, when our group's convoluted theological discussion was over and done, I/we returned to the old Jewish mode of storytelling to capture the truths we had arrived at. On the other hand, in doing so, I had no conscious awareness of standing in a long Jewish tradition of using midrash as a way of expressing religious insight and grappling with religious questions.[13]

Plaskow's thoughtful reflections, coupled with Fuchs's analysis and summary, prompt a number of questions related to the "Jewishness" of Jewish feminist

---

11. Judith Plaskow, "Lilith Revisited," in *Eve and Adam: Jewish, Christian, and Muslim Readings on Genesis and Gender* (ed. Kristen Kvam et al.; Bloomington: Indiana University Press, 1999), 425–30, here 427.

12. Ibid.

13. Ibid., 428.

biblical studies and to the "Christianness" of "mainstream," or academic, feminist biblical studies. Surely feminist Hebrew Bible scholars who are not Jews can accord, and often have accorded, their texts the same sense of integrity and sufficiency that Fuchs finds "unique" to biblical scholarship by Jews. And when a Jew writes about "mission," "grace," and the positive potential of feminist "conversion" in the context of retelling a biblical "myth," is that writing properly termed "Jewish" simply by virtue of having been penned by a Jew? What would such a characterization imply?

The greater part of feminist biblical scholarship by Jews comprises "secular" academic study carried out and conveyed according to the canons of historical-critical and/or literary-critical methods, including postcolonial and postmodern critical methods, without confessional voice or stance. Many authors are represented whose work is published by university presses and academic journals. Indeed, some feminist biblical scholars identify as "secular," "atheist," or "agnostic" Jews, and others feel no compulsion to self-identify at all. In what sense, then, could it be meaningful to classify all such biblical scholarship by all such feminist Jews as "Jewish"? How could such identification not eerily echo the claims of Nazi propagandists about a "Jewish essence" somehow manifesting in all works produced by Jews?

In the present volume on "feminist biblical studies in the twentieth century," "biblical" signifies, in virtually every case and every chapter, the *Christian* Bible, with *two Testaments*, just as the academic discipline of biblical studies itself is founded on the study of the *Christian* Bible, *both Testaments*, and is taught as such at all but the handful of Jewish universities and seminaries. What does "Jewish biblical studies," or "secular academic biblical studies," for that matter, signify in such contexts where the unspecified referent "Bible" is fundamentally and inescapably Christian? To interrogate but one example: *Women in Scripture* is a scholarly/popular compendium edited by three feminists: two Jews, one Christian;[14] the translation used throughout is the NRSV, and the "Scriptures" include Hebrew Bible, New Testament, and the Deuterocanonical books of the Christian Bible. What parts or aspects, if any, of this compendium are "Jewish"? The entries by Jews? The entries *about* Jews? In the latter case, many of said Jews (in particular, those featured in the New Testament) would also be considered "Christian."

In a more careful and nuanced attempt to articulate what makes Jewish feminist biblical scholarship "Jewish," Adele Reinhartz offers the following:

---

14. Carol Meyers et al., eds., *Women in Scripture* (Boston: Houghton Mifflin, 2000).

> Jewish women writers on the Bible differ fundamentally from non-Jewish women *to the extent* that they relate in some way to classical Jewish sources as being part of their own heritage; that they in some way or another incorporate Jewish sensibilities or experiences, however these may be defined, into their scholarship and writing; and that they envisage Jews, or more specifically Jewish women, as an important part of their audiences.[15]

Unlike Fuchs, Reinhartz does not claim to perceive an overarching philosophy or impulse unique to biblical scholarship by Jews. Rather, she observes that scholarship by Jews "differs" only when and "to the extent that" an author articulates an active identification with classical Jewish sources, with some kind of Jewish sensibility or experience, and with an explicitly (though not necessarily exclusively) Jewish audience. It is a well-considered, subtle, and compelling formulation, albeit not beyond quibble. And it provides an intriguing framework within which to explore Plaskow's paradox.

Plaskow reflects that, while mobilizing a strongly Protestant Christian vocabulary and remaining unaware of the tradition of midrash as a Jewish biblical interpretive form (and therefore, in Reinhartz's terms, remaining unaware of this "part of [her] own heritage" as a Jew), she, together with her Christian colleagues, nonetheless "returned to the old Jewish mode of story-telling to capture the truths we had arrived at." Did she thereby "incorporate Jewish sensibilities," albeit unconsciously, into her writing? Does this early product of feminist collaboration, then, "differ fundamentally" from the work of non-Jewish feminists engaged with the Bible? Was Plaskow writing *as a Jew* about Lilith and feminism in the early 1970s, or did she come to do so only in her later reflections on that earlier work? If the latter, then as what was she writing before? Plaskow ultimately lets the paradox stand unresolved. To do so is an act of honesty and integrity.

Differences between Jews and non-Jews—especially Christians—can be real, often quite significant, at times celebrated, and at other times hurtful. The ways in which such differences are operative or manifest in our biblical scholarship are sometimes overwhelmingly clear, sometimes barely measurable, and often (in secular, academic biblical scholarship) they seem not to operate or manifest at all. Regardless of (or, rather, because of) our differences, history and human community bind Jews and Christians inextricably together, as do the biblical texts with which we grapple, either directly or by virtue of their (and our) embeddedness in biblically infused cultures around

---

15. Adele Reinhartz, "Jewish Women's Scholarly Writings on the Bible," in *The Jewish Study Bible* (ed. Adele Berlin and Marc Zvi Brettler; Oxford: Oxford University Press, 2004), 2004, emphasis added.

the globe. In contrast to Fuchs's characterization of Jewish feminist biblical studies in reaction and rebuttal to Christian appropriations and prejudices, Reinhartz affirms the complex and particular connections between the two communities. She continues:

> In other ways, however, the concerns and perspectives of Jewish women parallel those of non-Jewish women, *particularly women who explicitly identify themselves as Christian*, who examine issues that arise in Christian contexts and address their studies primarily to Christian women.… Similarities exist because of mutual influence, but also because Jewish and Christian women are engaged in parallel struggles against the ways that the biblical text has been used to restrict women's activities and possibilities.[16]

2. BIBLICAL STUDY BY JEWISH WOMEN IN A JEWISH CONTEXT

Unaccounted for in the above-cited surveys of Jewish feminist biblical scholarship are the number of Jewish men, like Daniel Boyarin, Howard Eilberg-Schwartz, Steven Greenberg, and Lawrence Wills, who have made significant contributions to feminist biblical scholarship.[17] Clearly, their works ought to be counted under the rubric of Jewish feminist biblical scholarship. But ought we also to count *any and all Jewish women* engaged in biblical study for a broad Jewish audience and/or in a public Jewish context, regardless of the degree or absence of critical feminist content and method in their study? For her part, Reinhartz distinguishes among women whose work "partakes of and contributes to the area of feminist criticism," works by women that are "not explicitly … feminist reading[s] of the Bible," and "apologetic works, often written by Orthodox women … with the intention of affirming the traditional separation of gender roles according to which women are relegated to the private, domestic sphere and hence excluded from public roles, particularly within the synagogue service."[18] Of these latter, Reinhartz cannily observes, "Such works reflect the influence of feminism insofar as they focus on the role of women in a way that is not usually apparent in traditional Jewish men's

---

16. Ibid., 2005, emphasis added.

17. Daniel Boyarin, *Intertextuality and the Reading of Midrash* (Bloomington: Indiana University Press, 1990); Howard Eilberg-Schwartz, *The Savage in Judaism: An Anthropology of Israelite Religion and Ancient Judaism* (Bloomington: Indiana University Press, 1990); Steven Greenberg, *Wrestling with God and Men: Homosexuality in the Jewish Tradition* (Madison: University of Wisconsin Press, 2004); Greenberg, "Gender after Feminism," *Lilith* (Fall 2009): 18–20; and Lawrence Wills, *Not God's People: Insiders and Outsiders in the Biblical World* (Lanham, Md.: Rowman & Littlefield, 2008).

18. Reinhartz, "Jewish Women's Scholarly Writings," 2000–2004.

writings on the Bible, but they reject the feminist emphasis on liberation due to its implied critique of traditional Judaism."[19]

The growing number of Orthodox Jews who publicly identify as feminists, and who engage with biblical (and rabbinic) traditions in the interest of benefiting their own and larger communities and empowering their marginalized members, represent a diverse, complex, and variously nuanced practice of feminism and feminist biblical scholarship. The Jewish Orthodox Feminist Alliance, founded by longtime Orthodox feminist activist Blu Greenberg,[20] for example, designs and publishes a "Bible Curriculum" for use in Hebrew day schools that "seeks to give our Imahot (Biblical matriarchs) a voice and encourages students to relate meaningfully to role models among the Imahot while challenging accepted gender stereotypes," according to the organization's website.[21] Other notable Orthodox feminist Torah[22] scholars such as Chana Safrai, Bonna Devora Haberman, and Rabbi Steven Greenberg (see above), have engaged in direct feminist action and education within and beyond the Orthodox world and have published biblical scholarship in popular and academic presses and journals.[23]

The very visible presence of Jewish women in Jewish religious contexts and, in particular, women within Orthodox Jewish communities serving as published biblical scholars and public religious intellectuals is a feminist phenomenon. But the question remains: Does Jewish *women's* biblical scholarship, Orthodox or otherwise, that embodies the "influence of feminism" represent an aspect of Jewish *feminist* biblical studies, regardless of the ideological content of the work and the commitments of its authors?

---

19. Ibid., 2004.

20. Blu Greenberg, "Woman and Judaism," in *Contemporary Jewish Religious Thought* (ed. Arthur A. Cohen and Paul Mendes-Flohr; New York: Scribner, 1987), 1039–53.

21. "JOFA Bible Curriculum: Bereishit," Jewish Orthodox Feminist Alliance. Online: http://www.jofa.org/about.php/programs/jofabiblecur/bereishit.

22. In traditional Jewish understanding, the term "Torah" encompasses the first five books of the Bible, the entire Hebrew Bible (Tanak), and all derived and related rabbinic/Jewish scholarship, including Midrash and Talmud. Orthodox practice always engages the Bible/Torah in this multidimensional fashion.

23. Chana Safrai and Micah Halpern, eds., *Jewish Legal Writings by Women* (Jerusalem: Urim, 1998); Safrai and Halpern, eds., *Women Out Women In* (Hebrew; Tel Aviv: Yedioth Ahronoth, 2008); Bonna Devora Haberman, "'Let My Gender Go!': Jewish Textual Activism," in *Toward a New Heaven and a New Earth* (ed. Fernando Segovia; Maryknoll, N.Y.: Orbis, 2003), 429–42.

3. Feminist Torah/Tanak and the Transformation of Community

Two collections of "women's" Torah commentary provide fruitful frameworks within which to consider this question. *The Women's Torah Commentary* is a collection of *divrei Torah* (homiletic explications) on each of the fifty-four *parashot* (Torah portions traditionally read in synagogues throughout the Jewish year), each of which is composed by a different woman rabbi.[24] The self-contained, essay-format commentaries read as more and less scholarly, more and less homiletic, and the authors are all recognized as ordained rabbis by Judaism's Conservative, Reconstructionist, Reform, and nondenominational communities. The collection begins with a foreword by Rabbi Amy Eilberg and an introduction by the editor, Rabbi Elyse Goldstein. Both are forthright about their own and each contributor's feminism and transformative agenda, and they readily acknowledge the debt owed to feminist movement and the "pathbreakers [who] made it possible for the rest of us to earn the title rabbi."[25] Goldstein notes that each commentary in the volume shares "a feminist vision and a feminist 'spin'" and derives "from a feminist viewpoint," while Eilberg calls on all Jewish women to participate in "the feminization of Judaism" with the intent that "Judaism will be reinterpreted, reappropriated, and transformed."[26] In an epilogue that closes the volume, Rabbi Sally Priesand reflects on "the gifts that feminism has given to all of us over the past thirty years" and the ways "the women's movement has served as catalyst, encouraging us to rethink previous models of leadership," as well as theology and empowerment.[27]

A very different collection, *The Torah: A Women's Commentary*, is also organized according to the weekly *parashot*, and its more than one hundred contributors are all Jewish women, most professional scholars.[28] In this volume each *parasha* receives a short introductory essay followed by Torah text and commentary patterned on the traditional Jewish format of the *Mikraot G'dolot*: the Masoretic Hebrew text with (in this case, English) translation appears toward the top of the page with brief commentaries on significant words and phrases in the lower register of the same page. In these brief notes, words and phrases that involve women are highlighted. This introduc-

---

24. Rabbi Elyse Goldstein, ed., *The Women's Torah Commentary* (Woodstock, Vt.: Jewish Lights, 2000).

25. Ibid., 34–35.

26. Ibid., 34 and 21, respectively.

27. Ibid., 407–8.

28. Tamara Cohn Eskenazi and Andrea L. Weiss, eds., *The Torah: A Women's Commentary* (New York: Women of Reform Judaism/URJ, 2008).

tion and commentary by one scholar is followed by "another view" offered by a second biblical scholar in the form of a brief essay responding to the first commentary or developing, in another vein, a key motif in the *parasha*. A third scholar provides commentary on postbiblical interpretations, most often engaging with classical rabbinic midrashic traditions, while a fourth contributes a contemporary reflection. Each *parasha*'s treatment ends with a collection of "voices," poetry and short prose pieces that invite the reader "to consider how issues and themes in each Torah portion reflect and illuminate women's lives and experiences."[29]

To engage in Torah study means precisely to do what this commentary does and what it invites all readers to do—to engage in close and detailed reading of the text, to consult the rich legacy of traditional Jewish commentary, to ponder the insights that the words can hold for one's own generation and the insights that one's own experience may provide into the text, and to join in partnered dialogue (*havruta*) with others who are doing the same. Although Jewish women by and large have had some access to Bible learning throughout history, they have until very recently been denied access to Torah study in this richer sense by means of a gender system that defined and enforced such study as the purview, privilege, and obligation solely of men. The very fact, then, that so many Jewish women have contributed to this volume as Torah scholars and that countless others are invited and empowered through it to share in and shape the practice of Torah study suggests that this text is not merely the *result* of feminist movement but is, arguably, itself a quintessentially feminist collection and resource. At the same time, the content of the essays, notes, commentaries, and poems in this rich volume (like the aims and commitments of its contributors) falls along the full spectrum from feminist to nonfeminist to apologetic outlined by Reinhartz above.

Both *The Women's Torah Commentary* and *The Torah: A Women's Commentary* highlight the fact that the dialogical, multivocal, and multiperspectival impulses of traditional Jewish Torah study resonate deeply with the best impulses and practices of feminism. "We consider the act of preserving a multiplicity of voices not only a defining feature of the Jewish interpretive tradition, but also an explicit feminist endeavor," the editors of the latter volume assert.[30] In this respect, it might even be observed that the inherently feminist process and project of *The Torah: A Women's Commentary* enables a *more fully Jewish* practice of Torah study than has heretofore been possible. Eilberg offers a similar assessment in her foreword to *The Women's Torah Commentary*. She

---

29. Ibid., lx.
30. Ibid., xxxv.

asserts that prior to the training, ordaining, and empowering of women as full Jews in their own right, "the community was able to tap only half of its resources, half of its creativity, half of its genius."[31]

4. MIDRASHIC STUDY

Jewish feminist midrash and feminist scholarship on midrash certainly satisfy the "Jewish" and "feminist" terms of the present essay's subject matter. But are these fields properly considered "biblical" study? The short answer is that midrash has been, throughout Jewish history, the classic and quintessentially Jewish manner of biblical exegesis. Hence, Jewish biblical study, by definition, includes midrash—the doing and the studying of it in its collected forms. "Just as the [classical] rabbis brought their own questions to the Bible and found there answers that supported their religious world view, so Jewish women are asking new questions of biblical narratives and, in the process of responding, recreating tradition. The flexibility and creativity of midrash, its power to reinvent, easily lends itself to feminist use."[32]

As Plaskow's observation here and her early "Coming of Lilith" both indicate, midrash is a Jewish biblical interpretive tool that has in feminist hands produced an incredibly rich and powerful body of biblically engaged scholarship and creative literature. In Jewish tradition, such midrashic literature is called "oral Torah," and is held to have its origins in divine revelation that accompanied the giving of the "written Torah." The revelatory energy released by feminist midrash has been immense in terms of opening up biblical texts to and through feminists' and women's insights. Insights into the power dynamics and strategies of the Bible's narratives, law codes, and poetry, and into modes of resistance, potential and realized, are among feminist midrashists' most important accomplishments. Feminist midrash has been used for sharp critique of the biblical texts and their reception histories as well as for appropriation of biblical stories and the giving of voice to ancient and contemporary women whose voices have so often been silenced. It has, as well, been harnessed as a way to illuminate critically the fear and self-doubt that seem so often to spur the masculinist will to domination.

Some collections of feminist midrash, like Ellen Frankel's *The Five Books of Miriam* and Athalya Brenner's *I Am...: Biblical Women Tell Their Own Stories*, are single-authored texts that nonetheless attempt to give voice to multiple

---

31. Goldstein, *Women's Torah*, 17.
32. Plaskow, "Lilith Revisited," 429.

characters and their many and differing perspectives.[33] Other collections are anthologies of midrashim by multiple authors. Feminist midrashic practice has become widespread throughout Jewish communities and in schoolrooms, including those of secular colleges and universities throughout the world. Feminist midrash has been adapted as a method of critical reading and empowerment by women in numerous Christian communities as well.

The critical study of classical rabbinic midrash forms another vital component of Jewish feminist biblical studies. Feminist works by Charlotte Elisheva Fonrobert, Judith Baskin, Judith Hauptman, Daniel Boyarin, Galit Hasan-Rokem, Dina Stein, Leila Leah Bronner, and many others have exponentially enriched the understanding of these ancient Hebrew and Aramaic texts that have so strongly shaped Jewish religious life and Jewish biblical study for close to two millennia, while remaining almost entirely inaccessible to the majority of Jews, and to virtually all non-Jews, until mere decades ago.[34] Feminist scholars of rabbinic midrash find preserved in these texts both oppressive androcentric misogyny and potentially liberating countertraditions, patterns of colonial resistance, and alternative models of gender and authority.

Rabbinic midrash is divided into two basic genres, according to the nature of the biblical texts being interpreted. "Aggadic" midrash engages the more specifically narrative and story-based biblical texts; "halakic" midrash expands upon legal materials. Feminist scholars of midrash have more often derived elements of a "usable past" through aggadic midrashim and midrashic method, while finding halakic midrash far less amenable to that aim. Yet, as Charlotte Elisheva Fonrobert aptly cautions,

> We need to take seriously the conservative function of aggadic midrash as a hermeneutic tool, to maintain the basic androcentric structures of the bib-

---

33. Ellen Frankel, *The Five Books of Miriam: A Woman's Commentary on the Torah* (New York: Putnam, 1996); Athalya Brenner, *I Am...: Biblical Women Tell Their Own Stories* (Philadelphia: Fortress, 2005).

34. Charlotte Elisheva Fonrobert, *Menstrual Purity: Rabbinic and Christian Reconstructions of Biblical Gender* (Stanford, Calif.: Stanford University Press, 2000); Judith Baskin, *Midrashic Women: Formations of the Feminine in Rabbinic Literature* (Hanover, N.H.: Brandeis University Press, 2002); Judith Hauptman, *Rereading the Rabbis: A Woman's Voice* (Boulder, Colo.: Westview, 1998); Daniel Boyarin, *Carnal Israel: Reading Sex in Talmudic Culture* (Berkeley: University of California Press, 1993); Galit Hasan-Rokem, *Web of Life: Folklore and Midrash in Rabbinic Literature* (Stanford, Calif.: Stanford University Press, 2000); Dina Stein, "A Maidservant and Her Master's Voice: Discourse, Identity, and Eros in Rabbinic Texts," *Journal of the History of Sexuality* 10 (2001): 375–97; Leila Leah Bronner, *From Eve to Esther: Rabbinic Reconstructions of Biblical Women* (Louisville: Westminster John Knox, 1994).

lical world and to intimately connect rabbinic halakhah with the biblical text.... This is not to say that aggadic midrash as a hermeneutic cannot be used for feminist purposes. But at the same time, I would suggest that the full critical potential of midrash can be enacted only if we reckon with its conservative function. Ultimately, no text and no genre is, in and by itself, more conducive to feminism. The critical potential of texts depends on how they are read and to what use they are put.[35]

For Jewish feminist biblical studies, the critical potential of biblical texts may also depend upon midrashic texts ancient and modern, aggadic and halakic, "usable" and abhorrent, and upon feminist midrashic method informing how they are read and to what use they are put.

5. The Jewishness of the New Testament and Anti-Judaism in Christian Biblical Studies

At the back of *Carnal Israel*, Daniel Boyarin provides an "Index of Primary Jewish Texts" cited throughout his book. Among expected entries such as Genesis, Deuteronomy, and Proverbs and talmudic tractates such as Ketubbot and Kiddushin, one discovers others that some readers might find startling: 1 Corinthians, 2 Corinthians, Galatians, Mark, and Romans. Readers familiar with Boyarin's book on Saint Paul, *A Radical Jew*, or with Pamela Eisenbaum's more recent *Paul Was Not a Christian* will merely nod in recognition.[36] As these examples suggest, there is a growing body of scholarship that treats the many books of the New Testament that were authored by first-century Jews as historically "Jewish texts" and important primary sources for understanding the many movements and focal concerns of early Judaism. This current scholarship differs considerably from earlier (and other current) works that derive much of their data about Jews and Jewish practices from polemics in the Gospels and Epistles, read unselfconsciously as reliable descriptions voiced by "believers" (who were thereby no longer "Jews") who stood in righteous antagonism and opposition to Jews and their practices.

The unimpeachable "Jewishness" of many of the key New Testament authors and the worldviews and characters that animate their writings is becoming increasingly evident with the recovery and fresh examination of

---

35. Charlotte Elisheva Fonrobert, "The Handmaid, the Trickster, and the Birth of the Messiah," in *Current Trends in the Study of Midrash* (ed. Carol Bakhos; Leiden: Brill, 2006), 245–75, here 247.

36. Daniel Boyarin, *A Radical Jew: Paul and the Politics of Identity* (Berkeley: University of California Press, 1994); Pamela Eisenbaum, *Paul Was Not a Christian: The Original Message of a Misunderstood Apostle* (New York: HarperCollins, 2009).

ancient texts and the growing sophistication of critical analytical tools. Feminist criticism has been one such important tool, albeit one that has as often been put to the service of traditional anti-Jewish renderings as it has to this important emerging body of work.

To the extent that the balance is shifting, such change is due in no small measure to the work of Jewish feminist New Testament scholars writing, as often as not, explicitly as Jews. Once again, it is Reinhartz who provides one of the most articulate assessments of how "Jewishness" contributes to the critical power of her feminist scholarship in the field of New Testament studies:

> As a particular Jewish feminist reader of the fourth Gospel, I am particularly sensitive to a number of issues, such as its portrayal of Jews and its use of the term *ioudaios*, the depiction of Jewish-Christian women, the use of the language of wisdom and paternity in Johannine Christology and theology. Yet other issues, such as the parable—or is it allegory?—of the shepherd and the sheep, the structure of the signs stories, the use of prophetic motifs in the characterization of Jesus, are also of interest.

As the daughter of Holocaust survivors, Reinhartz is concerned

> with the contribution of the fourth Gospel, and interpretations thereof, to Christian anti-Judaism. But, though not a Christian, I also care about its implications for the role of women in contemporary Christian life. These contemporary questions do not obscure an intrinsic curiosity about the historical, social and religious setting of the Gospel in the first century CE. In investigating these and other issues I will not hesitate to draw on the range of historical-critical method while acknowledging that the basic facts of my identity, as well as many other factors that may or may not always be visible to me, will shape the exegetical process and its results, just as they have for all readers of this text.[37]

Twice in the past two decades, the *Journal of Feminist Studies in Religion* has called on Jews to initiate a "roundtable" on feminist anti-Judaism. The first, in 1991, on "Feminist Anti-Judaism and the Christian God," was anchored by Judith Plaskow. More recently, in 2004, Amy-Jill Levine, editor of the series *A Feminist Companion to the New Testament and Early Christian Writings*,[38]

---

37. Adele Reinhartz, "Feminist Criticism and Biblical Studies on the Verge of the Twenty-First Century," in *A Feminist Companion to Reading the Bible* (ed. Athalya Brenner and Carole Fontaine; Sheffield: Sheffield Academic Press, 1997), 30–38, here 34–35.

38. Amy-Jill Levine, *A Feminist Companion to the New Testament and Early Christian Writings* (Sheffield: Sheffield Academic Press, 2001).

anchored another on "Anti-Judaism and Postcolonial Biblical Interpretation."[39] Clearly, Jewish scholars play a key role in advancing feminist work in New Testament studies and in sustaining critical dialogue regarding anti-Judaism in Christian biblical scholarship.

They are joined in both endeavors by a growing host of feminist colleagues who are not Jews. Among these, Bernadette J. Brooten emerged as one of the first and most important, and Denise K. Buell stands among the most significant recent contributors to this ongoing scholarship and dialogue.[40]

Whether or not scholars like Reinhartz, Levine, and Boyarin, on the one hand, or Brooten and Buell, on the other, would be described by themselves, their peers, or a wider public as working at least in part in a field called "Jewish feminist biblical studies," there are coherent and reasonable cases to be made for describing each of them so. It is precisely the problematics and perplexities of such characterization that invite potentially transformative reflection on the part of feminist (and nonfeminist) biblical scholars of all stripes.

6. CONCLUSION

Does Jewish feminist biblical study represent a particular methodological approach and theoretical-hermeneutical perspective that distinguishes it from other forms of feminist biblical interpretation, while connecting it to them? And can "biblical" scholarship ever really be "Jewish" in a world and an academy where "the Bible" is so predominantly a Christian construct?

In attempting to pursue these and related questions in a thoughtful and critically reflective manner, one finds one's subjects repeatedly resisting assimilation to the definitions and parameters that the dominant culture provides for them. Is scholarship generated by a Jew thereby "Jewish" scholarship? Such an assertion seems inadequate at best, potentially racist at worst. Wherein does the "Jewishness" of "Jewish" scholarship reside? In the subject matter? Who, and what, and whose is the subject, and how—and to whom—does the subject come to matter? Is "Torah" in its full, rich, multidimensional Jewish sense the same thing as "Bible"? Again, the generalized terms offered by the

---

39. Vols. 7.2 and 20.1, respectively.

40. See, e.g., Bernadette J. Brooten, "Jewish Women's History in the Roman Period: A Task for Christian Theology," *Harvard Theological Review* 79 (1986): 22–30; and Brooten, "Early Christian Women and Their Cultural Context," in *Feminist Perspectives on Biblical Scholarship* (ed. Adela Yarbro Collins; Chico, Calif.: Scholars Press, 1985), 65–91; Denise K. Buell, *Why This New Race? Ethnic Reasoning in Early Christianity* (New York: Columbia University Press, 2005).

dominant discourse seem at times to hang like ill-fitting garments on the subject at hand. They cover but do not quite suit.

Perhaps it is the inevitably discomfiting questions that arise out of such an inquiry that are its most valuable products. The vitality of feminist studies and of biblical studies relies on the continual consideration of new and sometimes troubling perspectives. When these perspectives are met with full-hearted attempts to communicate, comprehend, and make meaning across boundaries that cannot, or ought not, be willed away; and between and among people, cultures, and identities that will not always fit comfortably together, then we might be hopeful that our projects will bear fine fruit and we might be content to live out (and within) our questions and paradoxes. Feminist biblical studies can only stand to gain by such transformations.

A Christian Feminist Hermeneutics of the Bible

Rosa Cursach Salas
Universitat de les Illes Balears (UIB)

1. Introduction

This essay does not claim to cover the entire scope or to provide an overview of feminist biblical hermeneutics. It would be impossible to report fully on its development during the past forty years, since it is the result of a variety of cultural, racial, social, and religious approaches—which accounts for its richness and fullness. For this reason, I decided to limit myself in particular to the contributions made by the work of Elisabeth Schüssler Fiorenza, despite her objections. Since centering her intellectual work on the theoretical framework of feminist biblical interpretation, she has also tried to respond to the various obstacles, problems, and questions that have been raised with regard to Christian feminist biblical hermeneutics. In this chapter I seek especially to explore the theoretical background of her hermeneutics. Following her lead, I shall focus on the method of interpretation proposed by a feminist paradigm of biblical interpretation. While the major part of the essay will focus on the approach of Elisabeth Schüssler Fiorenza, before analyzing her work, I shall address two subjects: the authority of the Bible and the deconstruction and reconstruction of the biblical contexts, particularly those pertaining to the origins of Christianity.

2. Status of the Subject

2.1. Brief Overview

Part of the difficulty of reviewing the status of the feminist hermeneutics of the Bible, as of other fields of feminist theology, lies in the number of authors, investigations, and feminist approaches that have developed over the past forty years. However, there are also convergences and common elements that help us to determine what we mean when we speak of feminist Christian hermeneutics of the Bible.

Biblical interpretation by women is not exclusive to the twentieth century. I will therefore position feminist biblical hermeneutics, understood as the interpretation of sacred text from the point of view of Christian feminist interests, in the second half of the twentieth century. According to Letty M. Russell, what makes feminist interpretation feminist are not the methods and techniques of historical- and literary-critical analysis used, but "the concerns, questions and sensitivities" of the interpreters.[1]

Feminist hermeneutics understands the interpretation of the Bible to be a self-interested task. Feminist hermeneutics abandons any claim of thinking about the possibility of arriving at truth, understood as exact correspondence between the narrative text and the real acts as they happened.[2] Feminist hermeneutics understands its task as engaging with the biblical texts from the perspectives and political investments of feminist movements for change. Mary Ann Tolbert argues that interpretation "is always a subjective activity, in the sense that it is always influenced by the conscious and unconscious concerns of the interpreter."[3]

An interpretation of the Bible in terms of Christian feminist interests can thus be defined as a reading of the Bible that casts light on the oppressive kyriarchal structures of society. Such an approach will therefore also show us how we can understand both the Bible and its interpretations as possibly kyriarchal and therefore oppressive of women. Thus, we conceive of the Bible as a text in which we find both the oppression of women and elements of power that promote the authority of women, elements often concealed and distorted by interpreters.

Mary Ann Tolbert finds that feminist hermeneutics is profoundly paradoxical, since feminist interpreters must struggle against God as enemy with the help of God, and at the same time must reject the Bible as a kyriarchal authority while also using the Bible as liberatory.[4] Pilar de Miguel further explicates the distance covered by feminist hermeneutics between the 1960s and the

---

1. Letty M. Russell, "Introduction: Liberating the Word" in *Feminist Interpretation of the Bible* (ed. Letty M. Russell; Philadelphia: Westminster, 1985), 15.

2. Mercedes Navarro Puerto, *Cuando la Biblia cuenta: Claves de la Narrativa Bíblica* (Madrid: PPC, 2003), 113.

3. Mary Ann Tolbert, "Defining the Problem: The Bible and Feminist Hermeneutics," *Semeia* 28 (1983): 117.

4. Ibid., 120.

1990s.[5] In the 1970s, according to de Miguel, scholars brought forgotten texts to light and reinterpreted others. They focused chiefly on texts in which women appear, often recovering their voices of rebellion against the patriarchal culture as well as recovering and uncovering the oppression and violence suffered by many women. During that period, authors such as Rosemary Radford Ruether and Letty Russell focused their efforts on the possibility of depatriarchalizing the Bible. Pilar de Miguel asserts, "Feminist interpretation presupposes that the Bible continues to be read, listened to, and preached as authoritative text in communities of faith and worship."[6]

Tolbert distinguishes three positions within this reformist stance of the 1980s, although she herself stresses that they cannot be understood rigidly.[7] An initial position may be represented by those biblical scholars, among them Rosemary Radford Ruether, who believe that the texts must be searched for elements of a liberating prophetic tradition.[8] According to this position, the authority of the Bible rests on the fact that the texts are expressions of this tradition. A second reformist position, represented by the work of Phyllis Trible, endeavors to find countercultural impulses in the text as a criterion of biblical "truth" or authority.[9] The third position does not focus on the biblical canon; rather, it tries to reconstruct biblical history and to discover the roles of women within the Jewish and Christian religions.

Feminist interpretation in the 1990s became multilayered. The feminist perspective appears as a critique of the various methods: the historical-critical and sociological methods, narrative analysis, methods of cultural anthropology, and so on. In this context, "Feminist exegesis is a problematizing and a questioning of the basic principles of exegesis and theology."[10] The end of the 1980s and the early 1990s witnessed the eruption of Christian feminist theology and hermeneutics by women from nonwhite, non-Western contexts. The womanist current promoted by African American women emerged; Hispanic theologians contributed the *mujerista* or *Latina feminist* current, and Asian scholars proposed a postcolonial approach. While the latter cur-

---

5. Pilar de Miguel, "La Biblia leída con ojos de mujer," in *La mujer en la teología actual* (ed. Carmen Bernabé et al.; San Sebastián: Publicaciones Idatz, 1996), 47–72.

6. Ibid., 56.

7. Tolbert, "Defining the Problem," 113–26.

8. Rosemary Radford Ruether, *Sexism and God-Talk: Toward a Feminist Theology* (Boston: Beacon, 1993).

9. Phyllis Trible, *Texts of Terror: Literary-Feminist Readings of Biblical Narratives* (Philadelphia: Fortress, 1984); Trible, "Feminist Hermeneutics and Biblical Studies," in *Feminist Theology: A Reader* (ed. Ann Loades; Louisville: Westminster John Knox, 1990), 23–29.

10. Miguel, "La Biblia," 63.

rent of thought developed above all in Great Britain and the United States, postcolonial thought and feminist postcolonialism were promoted chiefly by researchers from Asian countries. Jewish feminists also began to critique Christian feminist theology, particularly feminist Christology and interpretation, which were very often markedly anti-Jewish.[11]

All these movements and currents of investigation led to the questioning of certain feminist categories, for example the classification of "woman" as analytic category. These objections on the one hand remind us of how varied we women are. They also enable us to become aware that, for many women, gender subordination is not the first or the principal oppression that they suffer, since many women are subordinated and exploited because of race, ethnicity, social class, sexual orientation, and so on, in addition to gender subordination. Christian feminist theology and biblical hermeneutics thus became conscious of the various oppressions suffered by women, and their multiplying effects, so that their analysis cannot consist in a simple tallying of oppressions, as if it were a question of making a list of the multiple oppressions that are suffered by many women.

2.2. INTRODUCING ELISABETH SCHÜSSLER FIORENZA: FEMINIST HERMENEUTICS AS CRITIQUE OF IDEOLOGY[12]

The hermeneutical approach that we find throughout the work of Schüssler Fiorenza is theoretical in nature, and therefore not merely a methodology or a criticism of traditional biblical hermeneutics. According to her, the task of theology and biblical interpretation is an eminently political task. Just as Habermas understands the hermeneutical task as a critique of ideologies, so too feminist interpretation of the Bible involves approaching biblical religion with the suspicion that Christian religion has contributed to maintaining the kyriarchal ideology, and working to unveil and transform this reality.[13]

---

11. This essay does not discuss this question because it is raised in another contribution in this volume. For an in-depth study, recommended works include Judith Plaskow, "Christian Feminism and Antijudaism," *Cross Currents* 33 (1978): 306–9; Katharina von Kellenbach, *Anti-Judaism in Feminist Religious Writings* (Atlanta: Scholars Press, 1994); and Elisabeth Schüssler Fiorenza, *Jesus and the Politics of Interpretation* (New York: Continuum, 2000), particularly 115–44, where the question is explicitly discussed.

12. Elisabeth Schüssler Fiorenza, *Hermeneutics*. This work consists of unpublished reflections on hermeneutics. My thanks to Elisabeth Schüssler Fiorenza for providing them to me.

13. Jürgen Habermas, *Coneixement i Interès* (Barcelona: Editorial Acribia, 1996).

The steps in biblical interpretation articulated and developed by Schüssler Fiorenza must be understood as related to this critique of ideologies. Here, ideology is understood as justification or naturalization of a reality constructed on the basis of power relations. This is why feminist hermeneutics is not merely a translation or a way of knowing reality. Rather, it is to be conceived as an emancipatory principle.

Understood as critique of kyriarchal ideologies that are bent on undervaluing women, Christian feminist hermeneutics calls for a hermeneutics that recognizes the justice of the struggle of women for well-being in a variety of ways. Critiquing kyriarchal ideology that treats women as interchangeable, feminist hermeneutics shows that women are not all the same, are not "identical," and that in addition to their gender identity, women's experiences of injustice are influenced by race, class, sexual orientation, and other factors. Contrary to kyriarchal ideology that defines women as "the other," that is, outside the "norm," it enables women to question what and who they have been told they are. Against kyriarchal ideologies that foster the subjugation of women, feminist hermeneutics calls for tools that permit women to decodify and dismantle the messages that humiliate and demonize them. As a critique of kyriarchal ideology that considers women clumsy, stupid, or touchy, a hermeneutics is required that recognizes the perceptiveness of women and their ability to open hitherto unimagined avenues of justice.

Finally, resisting kyriarchal ideology that subjects women to oblivion and renders them invisible urgently requires a hermeneutics of recollection, since it is the memory of women's struggles that has been the herald of the Good News. In her book *In Memory of Her*, Schüssler Fiorenza proposes a reconstruction of Christian beginnings from a critical feminist hermeneutical perspective, a feminist hermeneutics that remembers Her (Mark 14:9).[14] It is the memory of women's historical agency that defines the Gospel as the Good News.

3. ABOVE AND BEYOND AUTHORITY: THE HERMENEUTICS OF SUSPICION

Feminist biblical hermeneutics emerges in dealing with the problem of the authority of the Bible. Feminist women realize that biblical texts and their interpretations contradict our experience of ourselves and our well-being—or lack thereof. This is why the authority of the text is in question.

---

14. Elisabeth Schüssler Fiorenza, *In Memory of Her: A Feminist Theological Reconstruction of Christian Origins* (2nd ed.; New York: Crossroad, 1994).

Christian feminists know that the Bible has been used to ensure the secondary status of women in societies in which biblical religions have, or have had, a marked presence. We are aware that the violence that has been, and is, exercised against women finds justification in biblical texts (e.g., Judg 19). We also know that we can find in the Bible arguments for the recognition of the rights and dignity of wo/men and our struggles for a just distribution of wealth, and our struggle to participate in the spaces of power and the decision-making processes in churches and in society.

It is precisely because of this that Christian feminists question the authority of the Bible. We thus approach the biblical texts and question their authority, because of the role that they have played and may continue to play in the shaping of our societies. Can we continue to believe that the Bible was revealed by God? What type of authority does it possess? Who or what attributed this authority to it? These are some of the questions that must be answered by feminist Christian hermeneutics.

> As a revelation of truth, it [the biblical witness] asks for something less like a submission of will and more like an opening of the imagination—and thence the whole mind and heart. In its own terms, then, it cannot be believed unless it rings true to our deepest capacity for truth and goodness. If it contradicts this, it is not to be believed. If it falsifies this, it cannot be accepted.[15]

Thus, are we to abandon the Bible, or are we instead to understand its authority in a different way?[16]

Various biblical scholars from different theoretical backgrounds have answered this question in different ways. Some scholars seek for a criterion of truth, whether in the scriptures or outside of them, from which we can derive some positive meaning for the life of women. Rosemary Radford Ruether and Letty Russell, for instance, find in the prophetic biblical tradition a correlation between feminist critical principles and a biblical principle. According to Radford Ruether, we find this principle not in a specific corpus of texts; rather, it is a tradition that we find in the Bible itself, the prophetic tradition that consists in correlating the Word of God to new contexts. Thus we could view the forms of feminism and the struggle for equality of women as pro-

---

15. Margaret A. Farley, "Feminist Consciousness and the Interpretation of Scripture," in *Feminist Interpretation of the Bible* (ed. Letty M. Russell; Philadelphia: Westminster, 1985), 41–49, here 43.

16. Katharine Doob Sakenfeld, "Feminist Uses of the Biblical Materials," in Russell, *Feminist Interpretation of the Bible*, 55–64.

phetic voices that denounce the religious and social structures that support inequality.[17]

In raising the question of the authority of the Bible, Schüssler Fiorenza asks what type of authority the Bible can have in the lives of women.[18] According to Anni Tsokkinen, the stance taken by Schüssler Fiorenza is positioned between two trends of feminist hermeneutics: between those who consider the Bible to be an essentially patriarchal book, and those who find that it contains liberating elements.[19] Schüssler Fiorenza represents a third way in that she develops a method of interpretation that seriously considers both the victimizing and the inspiring potential of biblical texts.

Schüssler Fiorenza finds that both groups, those who want the Bible to be accepted as a source of authority and those who believe it should be rejected, understand the Bible as a mythic archetype. As mythic archetypes, the biblical texts are perceived as universal and normative in any place and culture. She proposes that the Bible be understood as a historical prototype. Understood as prototype, the biblical texts will have to be critically evaluated and opened to feminist transformation.[20]

In a first step toward a feminist interpretation of the Bible which understands the Bible as historical prototype, she proposes what she calls a "hermeneutics of suspicion," born of the awareness that the interpretation of reality offered by the biblical texts and the actions that they suggest do not lead to an improvement of life with respect to women.[21] Thus the hermeneutics of suspicion calls the authority of the Bible into question, or at least the ways in which this authority has been interpreted by hegemonic male hermeneutics.

This hermeneutics seeks to undermine what could be called a hermeneutics of respect. We women, above all, have been taught to approach the Bible with respect and obedience. The hermeneutics of suspicion allows us to approach the Bible with the caution needed, so that instead of accepting texts that can be oppressive for women, we may be suspicious of them and may investigate the ideological claims of these biblical texts. To exercise this type of

---

17. Rosemary Radford Ruether, "Feminist Interpretation: A Method of Correlation," in Russell, *Feminist Interpretation of the Bible*, 111–24.

18. Elisabeth Schüssler Fiorenza, *But She Said: Feminist Practices of Biblical Interpretation* (Boston: Beacon, 1992).

19. Anni Tsokkinnen, "Elisabeth Schüssler Fiorenza on the Authority of the Bible," *Yearbook of the European Society of Women in Theological Research* 12 (2004): 134.

20. Elisabeth Schüssler Fiorenza, *Bread Not Stone: The Challenge of Feminist Biblical Interpretation* (Boston: Beacon, 1985), 9–10.

21. Anne-Louise Eriksson, "Radical Hermeneutics and Scriptural Authority," *Yearbook of the European Society of Women in Theological Research* 12 (2004): 47–52.

hermeneutics, it is necessary to liberate ourselves from the male-oriented religious education that we received, which, since it did not provide us with any critical tools, leads us to position ourselves with reverence before the Bible. The "hermeneutics of suspicion" invites us to scrutinize the interpretations of texts and the biblical texts themselves. Thus, the function of this hermeneutics is not so much to unveil the lies of the text or the lies of its interpretations and to re-establish the truth of the text, but rather to try to show the ideological functions of the texts and their interpretations.[22]

Furthermore, the Bible does not have authority in and of itself, outside the community to which it belongs. Schüssler Fiorenza's thinking with respect to the authority of the Bible is thus closely linked with her advancement of the *ekklêsia* of wo/men.[23] She describes the *ekklêsia* of wo/men in this way: It is a rhetorical space from which to assert women's theological authority to determine the interpretation of Christian Scripture, tradition, theology, and community.[24] This is how we must situate authority in the *ekklêsia* of wo/men.

In its first step, this argument is connected with the aim of making visible the fact that we Christian women are, and have always been, the church and not peripheral to it. Subsequently, she argues that this hermeneutical space is not limited to church and religion, but is a radical democratic space.[25] This hermeneutical space is defined on the basis of solidarity with wo/men who suffer multiple oppressions, including sexism, racism, poverty, and other inequalities. These are the women who are at the center of *ekklêsia* of wo/men. This hermeneutical space is a place where a range of feminist public discourses intersect, a space of sociopolitical contradictions in discussion and debate, and an environment in which feminist alternatives are presented. It is a space of heterogeneous feminist discourses through which individual women are able to understand their own histories in dialogue with other women, be they contemporary, historical, or biblical.[26]

---

22. Elisabeth Schüssler Fiorenza, *Sharing Her Word: Feminist Biblical Interpretation in Context* (Boston: Beacon, 1998), 90.

23. In breaking up the category "wo/men," her intention is to construct an inclusive term in which to make room for all women, as well as for men oppressed by patriarchal structures. In using the Greek word *ekklêsia*, she aims to situate feminist theology in the public ground of the assembly or the congress in which all female and male citizens participate on equal footing. See Schüssler Fiorenza, *Jesus: Miriam's Child, Sophia's Prophet: Critical Issues in Feminist Christology* (New York: Continuum, 1994).

24. Schüssler Fiorenza, *But She Said*, 152.

25. Elisabeth Green, *Elisabeth Schüssler Fiorenza* (Brescia: Morcelliana, 2005), 37.

26. See Elizabeth A. Castelli, "The Ekklēsia of Women and/as Utopian Space: Locating the Work of Elisabeth Schüssler Fiorenza in Feminist Utopian Thought," in *On the Cutting*

Therefore, *ekklêsia* of wo/men should be presented as an alternative space to kyriarchal biblical interpretation and to the assumption of many feminists that the feminist hermeneutical task consists in saving the Bible from feminist criticism. It is also proposed as an alternative to postbiblical feminists who reject the Bible in its totality and believe, as has been pointed out, that it is irreconcilable with feminism.

The task of *ekklêsia* of wo/men is to critically evaluate biblical texts and to make the feminist experience of wo/men the center of biblical interpretation and theological reflection. It also has the mission of constructing feminist identity that supports this *ekklêsia* of wo/men, an identity based not on the biological experience of sex or on the "essential" differences of gender, but rather on the common historical experience of women collaborating or struggling in a kyriarchal culture or in biblical history. Thus, "its principle and horizon is a radical democratic vision and movement that creates community in diversity, commonality in solidarity, equality in freedom and love, a world-community that appreciates the 'other' precisely as the other."[27]

4. Debates about Deconstruction and Reconstruction

Schüssler Fiorenza's *In Memory of Her* marks a milestone in feminist interpretation of the Bible. In this book, she uses historico-critical methods, assessments of sociology and critical theory, and the principles of the women's liberation movement to consider the beginnings of Christianity. Here, she posits the need for a reconstruction of early Christianity from the standpoint of the history of women. She conceives of tradition as the legacy of those same women, a tradition that has erased footprints that must be recovered. It will thus be a question of tracking these footprints, raising the possibility of a more significant presence than what has been told to us about the women of early Christianity, as well as questioning assessments that have been made by other Bible researchers, whether postbiblical researchers[28] or the researchers who, operating from an understanding of either positivist historical research or postmodern assumptions, consider it impossible to reconstruct the life and the struggles of women—which is precisely what is achieved by Schüssler Fiorenza in her hermeneutics of remembrance and reconstruction.

Edge: A Study of Women in Biblical Worlds (ed. Jane Schaberg et al.; New York: Continuum, 2003), 36–53.

27. Elisabeth Schüssler Fiorenza, *The Power of the Word: Scripture and the Rhetoric of Empire* (Minneapolis: Fortress, 2007), 79.

28. Daphne Hampson, "On Not Remembering Her," *Feminist Theology* 19 (1998): 63–68.

An understanding of the historical task as a linking together of events is not her starting point. Rather, she compares this task to a quilt or a tapestry created from fragments of information, the final picture of which may vary depending on the model according to which it is woven. She argues for using such remnants for reconstructing a feminist history of Christianity. Initially, this involves searching for documents. In a second phase, assisted by the hermeneutics of suspicion, these documents need to be analyzed. The third step is the reconstruction of history. To reconstruct the origins of Christianity in terms of a feminist reconstructive model, the following factors must be taken into account:

1.   Unless proven otherwise, we must take it for granted that women participated actively in history;

2.   Texts in which the behavior of women is criticized must be read as prescriptive, not as descriptive of reality. If a specific activity is forbidden to women, it is safe to assume that this was necessary because they engaged in it;

3.   Texts must be contextualized in their cultural and religious environments, and must be reconstructed not only from the viewpoint of the dominant ethos but also from that of alternative movements.[29]

On the other hand, operating from a postbiblical standpoint, Daphne Hampson argues that women need not be remembered, an obvious allusion to the title of Schüssler Fiorenza's work. What Hampson questions is the need to turn to the women of early Christianity and their supposed equality within the early Christian communities for support for the contemporary feminist struggle. Her critique of Schüssler Fiorenza must also be understood on the basis of Hampson's proposal to abandon biblical religions, which are essentially patriarchal and contribute nothing to the fight for the emancipation of women. According to Hampson, the women of today have no connection with the women of biblical times, since we are not living in the same situations.

With Marsha Aileen Hewitt, I argue that Hampson ignores the fact that Schüssler Fiorenza conceives of religious movements as emancipating movements.[30] In understanding her feminist proposal in connection with the

---

29. Elisabeth Schüssler Fiorenza, *Wisdom Ways: Introducing Feminist Biblical Interpretation* (Maryknoll, N.Y.: Orbis, 2001).

30. Marsha A. Hewitt, "The Feminist Liberation Theology of Elisabeth Schüssler Fiorenza as a Feminist Critical Theory," in *Toward a New Heaven and a New Earth: Essays in Honor of Elisabeth Schüssler Fiorenza* (ed. Fernando F. Segovia; Maryknoll, N.Y.: Orbis, 2003), 443–58.

movements that are fighting for justice and well-being today, Schüssler Fiorenza seeks to trace in biblical texts and traditions possible counter-discourses or openings that can be drawn upon to transform injustice and thus succeed in rewriting tradition imaginatively from a feminist perspective.

Furthermore, Hampson does not consider the fact that, on the one hand, the hermeneutics of remembrance and reconstruction proposed by Schüssler Fiorenza problematizes the results of positivist historiography and that, on the other hand, her approach is markedly political in nature, since it involves a reclaiming of historical memory similar to what is demanded by the victims of totalitarianism and dictatorships.[31]

The hermeneutics of remembrance and reconstruction enables us to construct our own chronology, so that we do not always have to be reinventing ourselves. Pilar de Miguel emphasizes the importance of chronology, stating:

> I share with Celia Amorós her idea that "there is nothing better than a good chronology." Otherwise, there is a risk that our descendants will believe that this is how things always were, and will forget the passion and the life of struggle of so many women, then and now, as if the conquest of social, political, cultural, economic, and religious rights fell like manna from heaven or were granted by parties who held them as "divine rights," out of benevolence or magnanimity, thus leading them in their innocence to believe that tomorrow will be better and that things happen merely because time passes.[32]

If we divide the hermeneutical strategies proposed by Schüssler Fiorenza into two phases, a deconstructive phase and a reconstructive phase, we can recognize that both phases are interrelated and not successive. We must therefore not view them as temporal in nature, since deconstruction implicitly involves an alternative and reconstruction implies the ruination of something. We shall have to conclude that while there is greater agreement among biblical scholars concerning the deconstructive task, the same is not true of reconstruction. In criticizing Schüssler Fiorenza, it is customary to assume that she wants to rescue the forgotten women of early Christianity and reconstruct an early "golden age." However, this misreading overlooks that the difference is in method and understanding of text. If one adopts an ahistorical method of reading, one can "crash, mimic, and parody the male/

---

31. The "Law of Historical Memory" was approved in Spain in 2007. The purpose of this law was to reestablish the memory of the losing side in the Civil War of 1936 and the victims of the forty years of the Franco dictatorship.

32. Pilar de Miguel, "Los movimientos de mujeres y la teología feminista: Una visión panorámica desde nuestro contexto," *Xirimiri* 12 (2003): 5; online: http://www.ciudaddemujeres.com/articulos/Los-movimientos-de-mujeres-y-la.

masculine text but cannot ultimately comprehend wo/men as speaking subjects and historical agents."[33]

When Schüssler Fiorenza calls for remembrance, her aim is not to tell us about something that happened but has been concealed or forgotten. Rather, she is calling for a possible remembrance, since much of our history has unquestionably been erased. But we can obtain fragments of real or imagined histories that will allow us to construct a genealogy, since we cannot allow ourselves to remain at the mercy of the dogs and the crows, we need to bury our dead women, our forgotten women, since we need to be able to honor them, to lay flowers on their graves.[34]

5. TOWARD A RHETORICO-CRITICAL PARADIGM

Like the Korean theologian Chung Hyun Kyung, who considers engagement in theology to be both a personal and a political activity,[35] in her early works Schüssler Fiorenza expounds the hermeneutical task of scripture and the Christian tradition, taking as its starting point the political, cultural, religious, and theoretical movement of women for liberation. As I have argued, she considers the Bible to be a political book and its interpretation to be an eminently political task. Thus, she starts from the fact that both the Bible and its interpretations are culturally and historically conditioned. Schüssler Fiorenza considers sacred Scripture to be the foundation of a theology rooted in a sexist and kyriarchal culture. Already in her early works, she shows that the hermeneutical task cannot be considered an objective or value-free science. She therefore denies the possibility of an objectivistic investigation of the Bible or of Christian texts. Her hermeneutical purpose is dependent on the emancipatory interest of women.

Schüssler Fiorenza believes that it is a question not only of taking a sociopolitical stance from which to interpret the Bible, but that it is also necessary to become aware, as Elisabeth Cady Stanton and others did, that the Bible is not a neutral book, but rather a political weapon that has been used many times against the liberation of women. When she defends the need for a feminist interpretation of the Bible, she does so for various reasons, which were already articulated by Stanton:

---

33. Schüssler Fiorenza, *Power of the Word,* 19.

34. Sophocles, *Antigone* 441aC.

35. Hyun Kyung Chung, *Struggle to Be the Sun Again: Introducing Asian Women's Theology* (Maryknoll, N.Y.: Orbis, 1990).

▶ First, because, as I have pointed out again and again, the Bible has been used to maintain the subordination of women;

▶ Second, because it is women above all who have taken the Bible as the Word of God; and

▶ Third, because it is not possible to reform one specific area of society without at the same time reforming all areas, given the interdependence of all the social environments. She states: "If feminists think they can neglect the revision of the Bible because there are more pressing political issues, then they do not recognize the political impact of Scripture upon the churches, and society, and also upon the lives of women."[36]

Schüssler Fiorenza considers various hermeneutical models, analyzes them, reveals their weak spots, and calls attention to their successes. For example, she emphasizes the fact that liberation theology has posed an authentic challenge to the supposed neutrality and objectivity of traditional academic theology, since it recognized that, willingly or otherwise, theology is always engaged in favor of or against the oppressed.[37]

Schüssler Fiorenza distances herself from those feminist hermeneutical approaches that seek to identify "a canon within a canon," a central message or text, and a core of liberation content, and criticizes them for reducing to a feminist principle the special features of the texts. They very often recognize the plurality present in scripture, but they try to reduce it to a feminist liberation principle and thereby remain caught up in the question of the authority of the Bible. In short, the aim of Schüssler Fiorenza is to develop a theory and a method, a focus from which to understand and interpret the Bible, while at the same time endeavoring to contribute a feminist articulation of a new model of biblical interpretation and theology.

5.1. HERMENEUTICAL DANCE

5.1.1. Rhetorico-Critical Paradigm

Schüssler Fiorenza positions feminist hermeneutics within the perspective not only of historico-critical but also rhetorical-critical research. Schüssler Fiorenza is not proposing to discover what the Bible really says, to achieve a "final" interpretation of the sacred texts. Rather, as has been mentioned, feminist critical interpretation starts with the struggles of women for their

---

36. Schüssler Fiorenza, *In Memory of Her,* 11.
37. Ibid., 6.

liberation, and from the presupposition that women are a part of the biblical story.

Hence the steps in the hermeneutical dance proposed by Schüssler Fiorenza must be understood in the context of a rhetorico-critical paradigm of interpretation. If texts are understood as rhetorical, they seek to address and persuade not only people in their original historical contexts but also people of today. Hence, she develops the dance of interpretation as a means of conscientization. Through the various steps, people reading or listening to biblical texts need to be enabled to reclaim their intellectual and spiritual authority so that they can evaluate the oppressive or liberating rhetorics of the texts in a specific context.

Schüssler Fiorenza understands Bible research as a rhetorical or communicative task, stating, "Authorial aims, point of view, narrative strategies, persuasive means, and authorial closure, as well as the audience's perceptions and constructions, are rhetorical practices which have determined not only the Bible's production but also its subsequent interpretations."[38] When she proposes a rhetorical hermeneutics of the Bible, she recognizes that the biblical texts are not neutral; rather, they are created to persuade and to influence action and practice. At the same time, her own proposal is rhetorical in nature, since she makes it clear what her aims are.[39] She lays claim to the open nature of her proposal. It is a dance, and as such it will be an unending process. Various choreographies can be composed with the different dance steps, the only requirement being that they be critical and imaginative.

In the composition that Schüssler Fiorenza has been creating throughout her work, by adding and reworking some of the steps initially proposed she constructs a seven-step choreography: *experience* and *social location, analysis of domination, suspicion, evaluation, imagination, remembrance and reconstruction*, all of which take as a goal *social and religious transformation*. We can understand these steps as a feminist revision of the hermeneutics proposed by various thinkers from Schleiermacher to Gadamer, but also of the critical theory of the Frankfurt School.

5.1.2. Sketch of Choreography[40]

Experience and social location: Feminist theology begins with the experience of women or, more specifically, the struggle of women for their survival and

---

38. Schüssler Fiorenza, *But She Said,* 46.

39. Mary Rose D'Angelo and Elizabeth Castelli, "Elisabeth Schüssler Fiorenza on Women in the Gospels and Feminist Christology," *RelSRev* 22 (1996): 293.

40. In the explanation of the steps in the hermeneutical choreography laid out by

their dignity in kyriarchal societies and religions. In the experience of Christian women, the Bible can and has been used against women, their autonomy, and their personal rights. At the same time, for many Christian women, it has also been a tool for struggle, hope, and commitment to their own well-being. Schüssler Fiorenza therefore believes that the feminist interpretation of the Bible is an important task for the feminist movement. In speaking of the hermeneutics of experience as a step in the feminist hermeneutical dance, Schüssler Fiorenza distinguishes feminist experience from the experience of women.

In feminist theology, the experience of women has been used as a benchmark for the interpretation of the Bible, often with a view to rescuing the forgotten voices in the Bible and in tradition. In taking this stance, we are forgetting that these experiences were formed in kyriarchal contexts. Schüssler Fiorenza calls instead for the feminist experience of wo/men, the experience that is created out of the struggles of women and other marginalized persons for their rights and well-being. It is not so much a matter of reading the Bible with a woman's eyes as a matter of reading it with feminist lenses.

Analysis of domination: It is a matter of becoming aware not only of the social, political, and religious position from which we are reading, but also of the position from which the text was written. It is a matter of looking for the ideological functions of the text, elucidating its function of supporting kyriarchy, and also its possibilities for empowering justice. It is a matter of seeing whom the text is promoting and whom it is devaluing, and which values it defends, in order to position the text socially. It requires an intersectional analysis of domination—kyriarchy.

Evaluation: This hermeneutics endeavors to evaluate the rhetoric of the text, using a feminist scale of values. Its intention is not to classify texts as oppressive or liberating, but rather to analyze texts based on a specific feminist scale of values. The particular feature of this step is to ask what effects may be produced by a reading of specific texts in specific contexts. At the same time, the fact that texts were written in specific situations and with specific intentions must be taken into account. This proposed interpretation intends to submit texts to a feminist critical evaluation; it thus sifts the biblical text through the sieve of feminist criteria. Schüssler Fiorenza does not conceive of theology and biblical interpretation as a dogmatic, confessional undertaking,

---

Schüssler Fiorenza, we shall ignore two of them, not because they are less important, but because they have been presented more fully in the preceding paragraphs on suspicion and reconstruction. In this way we shall also be showing how the various steps proposed by Schüssler Fiorenza have their reason for being and shape her understanding of biblical and theological research.

but as a practice that extends beyond sectarian divisions in order to imagine a more just world.[41]

Imagination: This step invites us to imagine and dream of situations of well-being and justice. It requires performing an act of imagination and full freedom. It seeks to bring the silenced into speech. It invites us to reconstruct biblical stories, to perform counter-current readings, and use what could be called the practice of thinking "as if...." The question becomes, "How would this story have been told if the intention had been different?" It is a matter of developing visions that promote well-being and visions of justice, which move us in the direction of its construction, and at the same time interrogating these imaginations and visions with a hermeneutics of suspicion. Imaginative hermeneutics is not a reconstruction of the past; it is a dream of the future in the full knowledge that this dream can also be affected by the kyriarchal limitations of the present on our imagination.

Social and religious transformation: The final objective of the hermeneutical process is change, the transformation of the relations that are supported in structures of domination into relations of equals in a radical democratic space of equals. Every reading of a text in terms of the dance of interpretation has as its goal the transformation of kyriocentric mindsets and kyriarchal structures. In sum, these hermeneutical steps seek to achieve conscientization and to construct a utopia of well-being for all human beings. It is thus a hermeneutics committed to the transformation not only of kyriarchal religions but also of kyriarchal societies, a hermeneutics that does not try to achieve "objectivist" interpretations of the Bible, but is instead committed to revealing the androcentric interests of religious texts and their kyriarchal interpretations.

6. By Way of Conclusion: A Paradigm Change in Biblical Research

It has not been the aim of this essay to explain or provide a thorough analysis of the thinking of Schüssler Fiorenza. Rather, I wanted to point to her work because her research goes beyond a feminist revision of biblical research tools. Rather, it involves a transformation of the very conception of the biblical text as sacred text and biblical exegesis understood as a positivistic scientific task. Moreover, it posits that the meaning of the biblical text must be continually evaluated, not simply accepted, and seeks to give us the tools to do so. Schüssler Fiorenza proposes a change of paradigm. She proposes to contribute a feminist articulation to the creation of a new model of biblical interpretation, a model open to continuous revision.

---

41. Schüssler Fiorenza, *Wisdom Ways.*

In addition, Schüssler Fiorenza brings the feminist interpretation of the Bible closer to the general public. If the Bible is a political book that influences our lives and our societies, its interpretation, study, and research cannot be reserved exclusively for specialists and scholars. Many Christian women listen each week to some passage from the Bible. The principal contribution made by Elisabeth Schüssler Fiorenza to the relationship of women with the Bible is that she has given these women tools for a feminist interpretation so that they can use the Bible for their well-being and not in order to internalize their subordination and second class citizenship.

Rereading the Qur'ān from
a Gender Justice Perspective

Zayn Kassam
Pomona College

> The fact is that those who ache to regulate women are those who invariably violate them, and those who are obsessed with defining the limits for women are those who observe no limits with women. Colonizers always set borders that affirm their power.[1]

Like their monotheistic Jewish and Christian sisters, Muslim women must also consider the patriarchal context of centuries of interpretation of their primary sacred text, which for Muslims is the Qur'ān. Identifying this context, which has driven interpretations of the Qur'ān that women find to be essentialist and unjust, several scholars in the twentieth and twenty-first centuries have sought to reexamine the Qur'ān for its gender justice potential. They have found that the Qur'ān does offer more guidelines for gender justice than medieval Muslim male interpreters could previously imagine, due to their normative patriarchal context.

When considering the issue of qur'ānic interpretation by those who struggle for gender justice in Islam, we must take into account contemporary political realities that frame the discourse on Muslim women. Three observations are appropriate here. The first relates to Chandra M. Mohanty's remarks on our construction of Third World[2] women, for it is in these places where most of the half a billion Muslim women reside:

> An analysis of "sexual difference" in the form of a cross-culturally singular, monolithic notion of patriarchy or male dominance leads to the construc-

---

1. Khaled Abou El Fadl, *The Conference of the Books* (Lanham, Md.: University Press of America, 2001), 153.

2. Now often termed the Two-Thirds World, since developing countries occupy almost two-thirds of the world's land area.

tion of a similarly reductive and homogeneous notion of what I call the "third world difference"—that stable, ahistorical something that apparently oppresses most if not all women in these countries. And it is in the production of this "third world difference" that Western feminisms appropriate and colonize the constitutive complexities which characterize the lives of women in these countries.… While feminist writing in the U.S. is still marginalized (except from the point of view of women of color addressing privileged white women), Western feminist writing on women in the third world must be considered in the context of the global hegemony of Western scholarship—that is, the production, publication, distribution, and consumption of information and ideas.[3]

Second, the cooptation of Western feminists into larger agendas of U.S. hegemonic imperialism was apparent in Western feminist support for the war on Afghanistan, made famous by then First Lady Laura Bush's plea to save Afghan women from fates imposed on them by the Taliban.[4] Both lenses— the one that flattens the world's Muslim women to their religion rather than acknowledging the cultural, economic, social, and legal differences operating among them, as well as that which views all Two-Thirds World women as subject to "male domination and female exploitation"[5]—obscure the agency and autonomy of these women and lead to the pervasive idea among Western feminists and popular media alike that "the third world just has not evolved to the extent that the West has."[6] This assumed superiority of the West sets the stage for a renewed round of economic and cultural colonization of the non-Western world,[7] arguably well underway. Jasmine Zine notes:

> Discourses of race, gender and religion have scripted the terms of engagement in the war on terror. As a result, Muslim feminists and activists must engage with the dual oppressions of 'gendered Islamophobia' … that has re-vitalized Orientalist tropes and representations of backward, oppressed

---

3. Chandra Talpade Mohanty, "Under Western Eyes: Feminist Scholarship and Colonial Discourses," in *Third World Women and the Politics of Feminism* (ed. Chandra Talpade Mohanty et al.; Bloomington: Indiana University Press, 1991), 53–55. This essay was first published in 1984, updated for the 1991 volume, and subsequently revisited in " 'Under Western Eyes' Revisited: Feminist Solidarity through Anticapitalist Struggles," in *Feminism without Borders: Decolonizing Theory, Practicing Solidarity* (ed. Chandra Talpade Mohanty; Durham, N.C.: Duke University Press, 2003), 221–51.

4. See http://georgewbush-whitehouse.archives.gov/news/releases/2001/11/20011117 .html.

5. Chandra Talpade Mohanty, "Under Western Eyes," 66.

6. Ibid., 72.

7. Ibid., 74.

and politically immature women in need of liberation and rescue through imperialist interventions as well as the challenge of religious extremism and puritan discourses that authorize equally limiting narratives of Islamic womanhood and compromise their human rights and liberty.[8]

Third, as Asma Barlas observes, the *burqa* (body veil) has been used to constitute the Muslim Other that serves to construct the non-Muslim Anglo-European self.[9] To her, the representation of the *burqa* is "about the cultural representation of the West to *itself* by way of a detour through the other."[10] And the other suffers for this detour, since it requires that she be "made lacking what the subject has … [but also made] threatening to the stable world of the subject by her radical difference." The Other is thus always already "born accused."[11]

Thus, we must keep in mind the political and cultural implications of studies on the work of Muslim scholar activists who reexamine the Qur'ān for purposes of gender justice. The concerns of such scholar/activists are certainly feminist in their interest in the full and autonomous subjectivity of Muslim women and in advancing gender justice by examining women's status before God and in society within foundational texts in Islam. Nonetheless, Western feminism has historically been coopted, first by colonial regimes, and subsequently by imperialist ambitions, to justify incursions—economic, cultural, and military—into Muslim societies under the rationale of bringing civilization under colonization, bringing trade and neoliberal economic globalization under the ban modernization, and bringing democracy under the "war on terror." Such interactions make the use of the term "feminism" or ideas associated with it, such as autonomy and empowerment, highly political acts for Muslim women. Utilizing these terms suggests complicity both with the Western agendas operating in Muslim societies and the secularist ideologies underpinning much feminist thought. Yet Muslim gender scholar/activists share with their Western, often white, feminist counterparts in other religious traditions the desire and praxis to reclaim women's agency and participation in Islamic discourse production and institutions. Like that of feminists in

---

8. Jasmine Zine, "Between Orientalism and Fundamentalism: The Politics of Muslim Women's Feminist Engagement,"*MWJHR* 3:1 (2006): 1.

9. Asma Barlas, "Does the Qur'an Support Gender Equality? Or, Do I Have the Autonomy to Answer This Question?" Keynote delivered at the University of Groningen, November 24, 2006.

10. Meyda Yegenoglu, *Colonial Fantasies: Toward a Feminist Reading of Orientalism* (Cambridge: Cambridge University Press, 1988), 39.

11. Ibid., 6.

other traditions, their work attempts to move beyond patriarchal constructs by interrogating patriarchal interpretations of sacred texts and the inscription of such interpretations into social institutions, while also proposing liberating alternative interpretations as a means to attaining gender justice.

Contrary to Western, including Western feminist, expectations that gender justice for Muslim women can only come about through dissociation from religion or through the adoption of a secularist perspective, the reality for Muslim women worldwide is that Islam and its values often cannot be divorced from all aspects of life—political, economic, social, cultural, legal, and spiritual. Further, many Muslim women live in Muslim majority societies where the instrument of legal governance is often a blend of sharia law and legal systems left behind by colonial powers or adopted by previous Muslim imperial administrations.

Thus, an additional charge for Muslim gender activists is to work with the legal regimes operating within their geographical location, whether entirely Islamic or not, to bring about gender justice. In this regard, qur'ānic gender hermeneutics will ideally have implications for the legal systems in place and underpin any political action. This can be seen with the work of the Malaysian women's organization, Sisters in Islam (SIS) (to which I return briefly at the end of this chapter), which recognizes that qur'ānic hermeneutics must be a part of any liberating strategy addressing women's issues. I should also point out that a legal system that is not religiously inspired does not guarantee women equity of access or treatment either, given that many of the struggles of early Western feminists also centered around attaining legal rights and fair treatment under the law, such as the struggle for voting rights (Switzerland), wage equity, or the right to a safe abortion (United States), among others.

The purpose of this chapter is to examine the efforts of some key American Muslim gender scholar/activists, all active within the last two decades, who reexamine the Qur'ān's record on women and prevailing interpretations to consider how gender-related verses in the Qur'ān and other authoritative texts might be interpreted differently. Necessarily, this chapter restricts itself to Muslim scholars working within the American academy, although these scholars are themselves transnational in the reach of their scholarly activities. While some of their publications saw the light of day in the first decade of the twenty-first century, I have included them in the twentieth century, where their work could be said to have originated.

A discussion of American Muslim gender scholar/ractivists reexamining the Qur'ān should begin with the writings of Azizah al-Hibri and Riffat Hassan. Azizah al-Hibri published her landmark essay, "Islamic Herstory: Or How Did We Get into This Mess," in 1981 and went on to found Karamah: Muslim Women Lawyers for Human Rights, while Riffat Hassan's reflections on gender issues entered the American scene in 1987 with her essay, "Equal Before Allah? Woman-Man Equality in the Islamic Tradition."[12] Hassan later founded the International Network for the Rights of Female Victims of Violence in Pakistan. Both continue to publish on issues pertaining to gender in Muslim societies, and both argue that the Qur'ān is a scriptural text that offers women dignity and rights that Muslim societies have not always allowed, despite the fact that women are ontologically equal to men in the qur'ānic perspective. While a fuller study of their work is warranted, this chapter will consider four scholars whose entry into the field is more recent but nonetheless extends their analysis: Amina Wadud, Asma Barlas, Nimat Hafez Barazangi, and Khalid Abou El Fadl. Their efforts are important for all Muslims to consider, regardless of sectarian affiliations, when rethinking prior interpretations of the Qur'ān from the perspective of gender justice.

I consider here the aforementioned authors' critique of prior readings of gender in the Qur'ān, and the hermeneutical or programmatic strategies they offer to bring the discourse and treatment of Muslim women more in accord with what they view as consistent with the divine message represented in the Qur'ān. Of necessity, each of these scholars has had to address what may be termed "problematic" verses in the Qur'ān, which have been seized upon by those wishing to affirm male supremacy over women as an Islamic teaching. Each makes the case that the Qur'ān has to be read holistically, and not selectively, and verses should be read as part of the social and historical context in which they were revealed. Thus, gender-related verses must be read within the cultural context of attitudes held toward women in seventh-century Arabia. In doing so, they separate the Qur'ān's principles that they consider eternally valid as a source of guidance for Muslims regardless of time and place from those whose relevance is limited to the specific historical period in which the Qur'ān was revealed.

1. Amina Wadud

Born into a Methodist family in 1952 in Bethseda, Maryland, Amina Wadud converted to Islam in 1972. She earned her doctorate in Islamic Studies and Arabic from the University of Michigan in 1988, and taught at the International Islamic University in Malaysia till 1992. It was there that she became involved with Sisters in Islam, an organization devoted initially to addressing gender

---

12. Azizah al-Hibri, "Islamic Herstory: Or, How Did We Get into This Mess," in *Women and Islam* (ed. Azizah al-Hibri; London: Pergamon, 1981), 208–13; Riffat Hassan, "Equal Before Allah? Woman-Man Equality in the Islamic Tradition," *Harvard Divinity Bulletin* 17 (January–May 1987): 2–4.

issues in Malaysia, and which has since taken on a transnational agenda. At this time, she also published her seminal work entitled *Qur'an and Woman: Rereading the Sacred Text from a Woman's Perspective*, leading Asma Barlas to note, "Wadud is the first [Muslim gender scholar] to acknowledge that people always read from specific sites and that they always bring specific forms of subjectivity into their readings."[13]

Wadud suggests that any qur'ānic hermeneutic must distinguish between the "spirit" of the Qur'ān,[14] by which she means the principles of the Qur'ān, and the socially regulatory verses that spoke to the seventh-century Arabian contexts in which they were revealed. It is on the spirit, she suggests, that we must reflect today in order to retain the Qur'ān's primacy in guiding Muslims. The goal of her work is to read the Qur'ān from "within the female experience and without the stereotypes which have been the framework for many of the male interpretations."[15] Reading the Qur'ān in light of its principles concerning ethics, morals, and social justice opens up the possibility of "adapting the text to a multitude of culturally diverse situations in a constantly changing world of social communities."[16]

To do so, Wadud proposes a hermeneutical model that concerns itself with three aspects of the sacred text: the context, the grammatical composition, and the whole text. For context, she argues against imbuing certain words with universal significance when they should be more precisely translated in terms specific to the cultural context of seventh-century Arabia. She also argues that, according to the rules of Arabic grammar, the masculine plural should be read as gender-inclusive even when the text of the Qur'ān does not specifically address both men and women. With respect to the *Weltanschauung*, or worldview, of the whole text, Wadud argues that "all discussion that the Qur'an contains about matters from the Unseen involve the ineffable: the use of language to discuss what cannot be uttered in language. Such language cannot be interpreted empirically and literally."[17] Further, she argues, a correlation needs to be established between divine guidance and every theme

---

13. Asma Barlas, "Amina Wadud's Hermeneutics of the Qur'an: Women Rereading Sacred Texts," in *Modern Muslim Intellectuals and the Qur'an* (ed. Suha Taji-Farouki; London: Oxford University Press in association with The Institute of Ismaili Studies, 2004), 97.

14. A term invoked by an Indian subcontinental Muslim thinker, Syed Ameer Ali (d. 1928), at the turn of the twentieth century in his landmark book, *The Spirit of Islam* (Piscataway, N.J.: Gorgias, 2001).

15. Amina Wadud, *Qur'an and Woman: Rereading the Sacred Text from a Woman's Perspective* (New York: Oxford University Press, 1999), 3.

16. Ibid., 100.

17. Ibid., 11.

discussed in the Qur'ān, rather than looking at verses individually without considering the rest of the text.

Turning now to some illustrative applications of her hermeneutical principles, Wadud first considers the common assumption that there are essential distinctions between men and women, which are "reflected in creation, capacity and function in society, accessibility to guidance … and in the rewards due to them in the Hereafter."[18] Given that the woman in Muslim societies "is often restricted to functions relating to her biology," she finds that while the Qur'ān acknowledges "the anatomical distinction between male and female," it "does not propose or support a singular role or single definition of a set of roles, for each gender across every culture."[19] To do so, she argues, would be to "reduce the Qur'an from a universal text to a culturally [and historically] specific text—a claim that many have erroneously made."[20] Rather, the Qur'ān's injunctions against certain behaviors were leveled specifically at [seventh-century] Arab cultural perceptions and misconceptions about women, such as infanticide, sexual abuse of slave women, denial of inheritance to women, and divorcing women without allowing them the freedom to remarry. Indeed, she argues, the Qur'ān is "not confined to, or exhausted by, (one) society and its history" but rather, that "each new Islamic society must understand the principles intended by the particulars. Those principles are eternal and can be applied in various social contexts."[21]

Like Hassan, Wadud considers readings of the Qur'anic verses on the creation of human beings that privilege the primacy of males and relegate women to secondary and derivative status to be misinterpretations of the texts, as this distinction is not specified in the Qur'ān. Using linguistic analysis, Wadud asserts that the qur'ānic verses on the creation of the human species reveal that "man and woman are two categories of the human species given the same or equal consideration and endowed with the same or equal potential."[22] Further, "the Qur'an does not support a specific and stereotyped role for its characters, male or female."[23] Piety, not gender, determines how human beings are assessed, for verse 49:13 testifies that God considers the one with the most *taqwa* the most noble among males and females. *Taqwa*, piety, which Wadud renders "consciousness of Allah," underscores the actions and the attitude that

---

18. Ibid., 7.
19. Ibid., 7–8.
20. Ibid., 8.
21. Ibid.
22. Ibid., 15.
23. Ibid., 29.

lead God to judge one's nobility. Therefore, there is no gender distinction in the emulation of piety and God-consciousness.

Both men and women have "the same rights and obligations on the ethico-religious level, and have equally significant responsibilities on the social-functional level."[24] Wadud argues that the equality on the first level has often been overlooked in the second level, leading to the absence of equality in legal and social structures. The goal of social justice necessitates challenging patriarchy and striving for an egalitarian system that "allows and encourages the maximum participation of each member of society" in which "women would have full access to economic, intellectual, and political participation, and men would value and participate fully in home and child care for a more balanced and fair society."[25] To do so would mean that the principle of consultation, or *shura,* would be extended to women in cases of marital conflict, which would impede the creation of oppressive marriages.[26] Only under these conditions can women exercise their rightful religiously authorized place in society in a manner that would translate into social well-being and participation in political activity. It is towards these ideals that Wadud's work strives.

2. Asma Barlas

Pakistani-born Asma Barlas, who worked briefly in the foreign service in Pakistan before seeking asylum in the United States, published her work, *"Believing Women" in Islam: Unreading Patriarchal Interpretations of the Qur'an,* almost exactly ten years after Wadud's. With advanced degrees in International Studies, she is the founding director of the Center for the Study of Culture, Race, and Ethnicity at Ithaca College and teaches in the department of Politics. In recovering the Qur'an's egalitarian and antipatriarchal epistemology, Barlas identifies three hermeneutical moves:

1. To draw upon the principle of textual polysemy: texts can be read in multiple modes, in order to critique interpretive reductionism/essentialism.

2. To argue against interpretive relativism without forsaking textual polysemy on the grounds that not all readings can be accepted as contextually legitimate or theologically sound, especially those that read *zulm,* or injustice, into God's words.

---

24. Ibid., 102.
25. Ibid., 103.
26. Ibid.

3.   To locate the hermeneutical keys for reading the Qur'ān in the nature of divine ontology, according to which God cannot be considered guilty of *zulm* or injustice, nor is God in the Qur'ān conceptualized as father/male, nor does God support theories of father-right or the human male as God's representative on earth.[27]

Barlas's objective is "to show that the family in Islam is not patriarchal inasmuch as the Qur'ān's treatment of women and men in their capacity as parents and spouses is not based in assumptions of male rule/privilege or sexual inequality."[28] Her hermeneutical approach entails showing that the Qur'ān "repudiates the concept of father-right/rule and, to that extent, claims about husband privilege as well."[29] Instead, Barlas argues that "the Qur'ān not only does not link the rights of fathers and husbands in this way, but it also does not appoint either one a ruler or guardian over his wife (and children), or even as the head of the household. Nor does it designate the wife and children as the man's property or require them to be submissive to him."[30]

Barlas also asserts that the Qur'ān's teachings on the family, marriage, and sexual relationships must be viewed against the milieu in which they were revealed. Although historical investigation suggests that women had some freedoms depending on their class, they could not inherit property, but were themselves considered property. Concubinage was unrestricted; slavery and polygyny abounded; sexual abuse of women taken captive in war and as slaves was endemic; and female life was devalued, as evidenced by the killing of baby girls. Against this context, the radicalism of the Qur'ān's teachings is far more apparent, as it considers women to be legal persons rather than chattel, and guarantees women a share in inheritance and grants them several other rights.

Barlas locates marriage and family at the intersection of social and moral-religious spheres. Marriage is social because of its contractual nature, and moral-religious because the laws governing it come from rights and limits placed by God. In addition, family and marriage are also located at the intersection of private and public. In the Western context, feminists have argued that the public sphere has traditionally, and patriarchally, been represented as the domain of freedom, politics, and culture, and has been associated with men, while the private sphere has been associated with women and seen as the domain of necessity, restriction, nature, and family. It is also the domain

---

27. Asma Barlas, *"Believing Women" in Islam: Unreading Patriarchal Interpretations of the Qur'ān* (Austin: University of Texas Press, 2002), 203–4.

28. Ibid., 167.

29. Ibid.

30. Ibid., 167–68.

in which males reign supreme. However, Barlas argues that the Qur'ān "does not define either human beings or social reality in terms of female-male, public-private, nature-culture, politics-family binaries."[31] Rather, the Qur'ān is concerned with whether men and women observe the limits of God, and the only distinction made is between believers and unbelievers. Even the Qur'ān's distinction between individual and community does not distinguish between public institutions and private relations, because God belongs in both spheres, and both must equally observe the limits set down by God in the Qur'ān.[32] Since anything the Qur'ān says on women refers to both public and private spheres, this dichotomy is fruitless in reading the Qur'ān. Nor indeed is the Western feminist utilization of social/sexual division of labor helpful, according to Barlas, for the concept confuses sex with class, and the Qur'ān "does not advocate a specific social or sexual division of labor."[33]

Barlas holds firmly to the position that, although the Qur'ān acknowledges gender differences, it does not privilege males but rather directs most of its provisions to protecting women's interests.[34] She states that "the Qur'ān recognizes that men have the power and authority in patriarchies. However, this does not mean that it either condones patriarchy, or that it is itself a patriarchal text.... Nothing in the Qur'ān suggests that males are the intermediaries between God and women."[35] As a consequence, she holds that the Qur'ān cannot be held "responsible for how a particular social or sexual division of labor has evolved over time."[36] Rather, the failure of Muslims to recognize the ontological equality between men and women or to distinguish between religious and social/legal equality has led to the failure of Muslims to read the Qur'ān in a manner that upholds its timelessness and to acknowledge its gender-egalitarian teachings. In sum, she finds that the Qur'ān "comes closest to articulating sexual relationships in the kind of 'non-oppositional and non-hierarchical' mode that many scholars believe can be liberating for both men and women."[37]

---

31. Ibid., 171.

32. Ibid., 171–72.

33. Ibid., 172.

34. Ibid., 198: parents are to be treated kindly, but mothers even more so, with disobedience to parents sanctioned in matters of faith; both spouses are to find *sukun* or rest in each other; both are held to the same standard of loving behavior; both are treated as legal entities. But the wife's testimony on adultery is privileged, while the male is held responsible as breadwinner, and in the case of female orphans, males are allowed polygyny provided wives are treated justly; otherwise, monogamy is preferable. Female children may not be killed.

35. Ibid.

36. Ibid., 199.

37. Ibid., 202, quoting Jean Bethke Elshtain, *Public Man, Private Woman: Women in*

3. NIMAT HAFEZ BARAZANGI

Nimat Hafez Barazangi was born in Syria and is a research fellow for Feminist, Gender, and Sexuality Studies at Cornell University. In her work, *Woman's Identity and the Qur'an: A New Reading*, she argues that Muslims have oppressed women "by stripping them—perhaps unintentionally—of their self-identity with Islam."[38]

> By assuming that a woman's religio-moral rationality (Din) is the responsibility of her male household, Muslim communities not only denied women the Qur'anic meaning of Din but also violated the very first principle of Islam, the Oneness of the Deity, as the source of value and knowledge. In addition, and because of these assumptions, Muslims built the early structure of Islamic life without including the woman's voice either pedagogically or in policy making, affecting both the construction of 'Islamic' knowledge and that of social fabrics and norms. Eventually, this inability led to women's participating in their own oppression.[39]

Barazangi notes that "most male scholars and religious leaders perceive and propagate the female's role as complementary to that of her male guardian."[40] Doing so "actually contradicts the basic Qur'anic principle of human autonomous trusteeship in the natural order of justice and in mutual domestic consultation."[41] Thus, her central question is, "Who has the authority to reread and interpret the Qur'anic text, and how is it to be done?"[42] She challenges the widespread notion that "only select elite males are authorized (males who bestow upon themselves the exclusive authority) to interpret the text."[43] Arguing that Islamic higher learning is a responsibility for a Muslim woman, Barazangi makes the case that "a woman has a basic right to participate in the interpretation of the Islamic primary sources, the Qur'an and the prophetic tradition, in order to gain and claim her identity with Islam.[44] Indeed, such an engagement with the Islamic primary sources may "bring about and sus-

---

Social and Political Thought (Princeton: Princeton University Press, 1981).

38. Nimat Hafez Barazangi, *Woman's Identity and the Qur'an: A New Reading* (Gainesville: University Press of Florida, 2004), 34.

39. Ibid., 34–35.

40. Ibid., 14.

41. Ibid.

42. Ibid., 5.

43. Ibid.

44. Ibid., 2.

tain fair changes both in the understanding of Muslim women and in their realities."[45]

Noting women's absence from the major commentators on the Qur'ān and the crafters of jurisprudence, Barazangi asserts that any male or female Islam-identified person understands themselves as "a trustee of God on earth (*khalifah*)":[46]

> I also argue that the absence of women from earlier Qur'anic readings is at the root of the misreading of the meaning of Islamic identity and trusteeship, interpreting the principle of *khalifah* stated in the Qur'an—"God said to the angels: I will create a trustee on earth, and God taught Adam the names of all things" (2:30–31)—as if it were limited solely to the male's political and theological leadership, and as if "Adam" were limited to the male human. By this misinterpretation, Muslims also confused human leadership with God's Lordship. Thus, reading and interpretation of a woman who is self-identified Muslim is the only course of action for a change from these conventional readings.[47]

If Barazangi's first hermeneutical move is to suggest that Muslim women's active self-identification with the Qur'ān is their right and responsibility based on the notion of *khalifah* (trusteeship) shared by all humans, then her second move is to justify women's participation in interpreting the Qur'ān based on the ontological equality of men and women. For this, she relies on Q 53:45, "God created the pairs (*al-zwajayn*)—males and females," and 4:1, "O humankind (*ya'ayuha al-nas*), be conscientious of (or in equilibrium with) your Guardian God (*Rabbakum*) who created you of a single [personal] entity (*nafs wahidah*). Created, of the same entity, its [grammatical feminine gender] mate (*zawjaha*)."[48] Such ontological equality makes women's interpretation of the Qur'ān long overdue and a necessary condition for trusteeship.

In a third hermeneutical move, Barazangi attempts to free Muslims from blindly following prior interpretations of the sacred text. Asserting that "the Qur'anic text is God's Word and hence these eternal words cannot be constrained by time, space, or any interpretation that is given to them,"[49] she implies that Muslims may bear earlier interpretations in mind, but a fresh approach is a necessary and morally responsible action in order for Muslims to identify with and benefit from the Qur'ān "as the primary *living* text of

---

45. Ibid., 7.
46. Ibid., 21.
47. Ibid., 25.
48. Ibid. Brackets introduced by Barazangi.
49. Ibid., 27.

Islam."[50] Further, she argues that while the occasion and the context of revelation must be taken into account, interpretations must consider the whole of the Qur'ān within its lexical and linguistic rules. Limitations may be imposed on interpretations of the Qur'ān by either (1) constraining valid interpretations to those of the first century and a half; (2) viewing the Qur'ān through the lens of the Hadith (reports concerning what the Prophet purportedly said or did during his lifetime); (3) imposing juristically determined limits on qur'ānic verses due to imposed chronological orders of revelation; (4) subjecting women's intelligence and interpretation to male authority and omitting or preventing women's interpretations; or (5) viewing the occasion and context of revelation as determinant of meaning. According to Barazangi, all such limitations on interpretation must be lifted in order to privilege reading the Qur'ān through its own internal guidance and wholeness as a text.[51]

The historical excision of women from interpreting the Qur'ān has resulted in exclusion, prevention, and deprivation.[52] The structural change proposed by Barazangi, which calls women actively to participate in the interpretation of the Qur'ān, rests on "making explicit the Qur'anic view of a Muslim's religio-morality that is conditional on the ability of each individual to cognize it autonomously."[53] In this regard, the criterion of the moral, cognizant human being, the *mutaqqi*, one who embodies *taqwa* (morality, piety), is of much more importance than the stated gender of the person. Adam, to whom God taught the names, was assumed by the early Muslims to be male (rather than cognizant humanity). Rather, through understanding Adam to be the representative of primordial humanity, the autonomous religio-morality of the female is restored from under the guardianship of the male members of her household, and with it, the notion that God judges according to moral conduct (*taqwa*) rather than sex.[54]

The key to breaking the stranglehold of Muslim women's erasure from textual interpretation is to "generate new meanings" of religious texts, particularly the Qur'ān.[55] In remaining conscious of socially constructed identities such as gender, ethnicity, race, and class, while reading, interpreting, and applying the Qur'ān's guidelines as an autonomous subject, a woman can gain her self-identity based on the Qur'ān and exercise *taqwa* according to her

---

50. Ibid., 5.
51. Ibid., 27–29.
52. Ibid., 33.
53. Ibid., 48.
54. Ibid., 49.
55. Ibid., 120.

understanding of the Qur'ān's guidance.[56] Ultimately, the changed worldview allows one "to replace human domination of nature with a creative understanding of natural law and of the divine guidance ... [and] replace human domination over other humans by dedicating ourselves to the practicing of *taqwa*, specifically in how we discuss, examine, and engage the different worldviews—be they Islamic or non-Islamic."[57]

4. Khaled M. Abou El Fadl

A Kuwaiti-born legal scholar trained in Islamic jurisprudence in Egypt and Kuwait, Khaled Abou El Fadl studied Islamic and Western legal systems at Yale, Princeton, and the University of Pennsylvania. He currently holds the Omar and Azmeralda Alfi Chair in Islamic Law at the University of California Los Angeles School of Law. Abou El Fadl examines the historical discussions related to gender among the medieval (male) Muslim intellectual Islamic jurists. He shows that the record does not show a juridical consensus on three separate but related concepts pertaining to women: *ḥijāb* (veiling), *fitnah* (causing social chaos), and *'awrah* (what may be considered private parts). Rather, the record suggests that issues relating to gender were debated and puritanical positions contested. Further, he finds that women studied and taught jurisprudence to both men and women (he does not mention whether they actually participated in creating legal works or rulings).

He notes that *ḥijāb*, or veiling, which he understands as the practice of covering the full body with the exception of the hands and face or hands and eyes, "has become one of those sacred territories in Islamic discourses that measure the Islamicity of individuals."[58] The discussions around *ḥijāb* were linked to the question of what is considered *'awrah*, or private parts. In the classical juristic sources, the *ḥijāb* is discussed under the section on prayer, since it is there that the jurists determined what "private parts" need to be covered by both men and women during the state of obligatory prayer, or *ṣalāt*. Thus, the *ḥijāb* "is whatever covers the private parts,"[59] and "presumably, what needs to be covered in prayer also needs to be covered outside of prayer."[60] Abou El Fadl also notes that although contemporary discussions link *ḥijāb* with the notion of *fitnah* (seduction) in that women must be covered in *ḥijāb*

---

56. Ibid., 125.

57. Ibid., 136.

58. Khaled Abou El Fadl, *And God Knows the Soldiers: The Authoritative and Authoritarian in Islamic Discourses* (Lanham, Md.: University Press of America, 2001), 121.

59. Ibid., 123.

60. Ibid.

because they are "a seething source of *fitnah*," early *ḥadith* narratives do not in fact "tie the issue of what eventually becomes known as the *ḥijāb* to the problem of *fitnah*, but they do tie it to social status and the physical safety of women."[61] Thus, he argues that what causes or does not cause sexual entice-ment is largely irrelevant to the discussion on *ḥijāb*, which should more prop-erly be about body parts that need to "be covered because they are private, not because they sexually arouse."[62]

However, he argues, some *ḥadīth* narratives propagate an antiwomen stance, making connections between women and the devil and suggesting that women comprise the majority of the denizens of hell. A woman's power to seduce is contained by marriage and death, as can be seen from the follow-ing narrative: "A woman has two covers of modesty (*sitrān*), marriage and the grave."[63] Narratives such as these, which are considered "weak" and unreliable, nonetheless formed the basis for the celebrated Muslim savant, Abū Ḥāmid al-Ghazālī (d. 1111 c.e.) to argue "that a married woman ought to remain in the depths of her home, not leave her house without permission, and avoid talking to the neighbors."[64] For Abou El Fadl, such views are reflective of the historical milieu that surrounded the early debates on *'awrah*, observing that "traditions, debates, and determinations regarding the *'awrah* are not simply expressions of the Divine Will, but are articulations of social beliefs, con-tentions, and anxieties about the definition of womanhood in early Muslim society."[65] The connections made between *'awrah* and *fitnah* resulted in moves to seclude women and inhibit their movements despite earlier critiques by several scholars such as al-Jāḥiẓ (d. 869 c.e.), who argued that not only was the practice of seclusion unknown in pre-Islamic times, the Qur'ān's rule of seclusion was applicable only to the wives of the Prophet. Indeed, al-Jāḥiẓ pleads, "we must not deny women their rights."[66]

An examination of the historical record shows that juridical opinion and the actual practices and social roles occupied by women did not necessarily coincide. For instance, he notes that several prominent Muslim jurists studied with women scholars and jurists and are listed in biographical dictionaries. He calls for a more extensive examination of the "public role and function of women in various Islamic periods"[67] for, if women were educated by and in

61. Ibid., 125.
62. Ibid., 123.
63. Ibid., 129.
64. Ibid., 129–30.
65. Ibid., 130.
66. Ibid., 136.
67. Ibid., 138.

turn educated men, the association of *ḥijāb* with seclusion, and *fitnah* is called into question.

In the Qur'ān, "women are equal to men because they are rewarded and punished exactly in equal measure, and they have equal access to God's grace and beneficence."[68] He remarks that the Qur'ān consistently makes an effort "to protect women from exploitative situations and from situations in which they are treated inequitably … [and educates] Muslims on how to make incremental but lasting improvements in the condition of women that can only be described as progressive for their time and place."[69] Moreover, these progressive reforms for women came about "as a result of social demands expressed and advocated by women."[70] If the task of *fiqh*, jurisprudence, is to make earthly reality as close as possible to the Divine ideal, or *shari'ah*, and if the Qur'ān illustrates that social change comes about when it is asked for, then surely "women must play the critical role in initiating the processes of change," and further, "the rules of law that apply to women cannot be static and unchanging."[71]

5. Rereading and Its Impact

The examination of the hermeneutical strategies employed by these four gender scholar/activists highlights certain key points. First, to varying degrees, they all argue that the voices and experiences of women have been absent in understanding and implementing the Qur'ān's guidance pertaining to the status, role, and comportment of Muslim women. While Khaled Abou El Fadl acknowledges the role of women as teachers and jurists, the tide of opinion in theological and legal discourses and institutions in curtailing the scope of women's agency and modes of behavior in relation to men, their public mobility, and their forms of dress does not appear to have been stemmed. Wadud argues that women's voices and experiences were excluded from qur'ānic interpretation, and Barlas argues that the patriarchal framework in which Islamic legal institutions were formulated colored the lens through which verses pertaining to women were interpreted, so that they failed to read both the challenges posed to patriarchy and their own social inequities into the text. Barazangi suggests that the radical social restructuring in gender relations brought about by the Qur'ān never really got off the ground, and Abou El

---

68. Khaled Abou El Fadl, *The Great Theft: Wrestling Islam from the Extremists* (San Francisco: Harper San Francisco, 2005), 261.

69. Ibid., 262.

70. Ibid., 263.

71. Ibid.

Fadl argues that Western interventions in Muslim societies as well as puritan strains of thought have resulted in the most narrow and literal readings of the qur'ānic verses, despite the more complex and dynamic picture that emerges from an examination of historical discourses and practices, although they, too, were not entirely free of patriarchal bias.

Each of these scholars views the Qur'ān as an eternally valid source of guidance and a locus of divine self-expression that continues to be relevant to Muslims today, especially with respect to gender. However, they argue, a verse (*āyat*) of the Qur'ān must be read within the context of those surrounding it, as well within the historical contexts in which the verses were revealed. Further, they must be read in concert with the ideals and values articulated in the Qur'ān as a whole, not in isolation from other verses and themes. Interpretation must not be restricted to the literal meaning of the verse. Rather, the *intent* of the verse and its meaning both within the sociocultural modalities of seventh-century Arabia and at present must be considered. Thus, the principles and the spirit of the Qur'ān must be taken into account in interpretation, alongside its historical cultural context. Qur'ānic verses must also be viewed as polysemic, as the meanings of the verses are inexhaustible even if care is taken to ensure that readings are theologically sound and contextually legitimate. Attention must be paid to the grammatical structure and lexical field of significant terms in the Qur'ān. The Qur'ān must be read with sensitivity to time and place, both historically and at present. Finally, all human interpretations must be understood as provisional as the Unseen is ultimately unknowable and ineffable and human interpretations cannot exhaust the possible meanings of a verse.

A constellation of critical concepts also emerges in light of the efforts of these scholars: first, the notion of the ontological equality among human beings, regardless of their sex; second, the idea that women have autonomous moral agency and are able to make decisions for themselves; third, the notion of *taqwa*—piety or moral righteousness—as the quality that distinguishes humans in God's estimation, especially with respect to recompense in the hereafter; fourth, engaging in tyrannical acts (*zulm*) or injustice toward half the human population is not considered fitting for the divine being, who created both males and females as ontologically equal beings; fifth, the observation that the Qur'ān consistently directs its edicts and observations towards ameliorating the status of and benefitting women, concomitant with the qur'ānic notion of "reverencing the wombs" (Qur'ān 4:1); and finally, the need to read, study, and understand the Qur'ān from multiple points of view, embracing differences, and not just from the viewpoint of vested hegemonic male privilege.

Within the larger context of scriptural gender hermeneutics, these scholars make the case that gender justice for Muslim women does not entail having to leave the faith. Rather, they argue that multiple possibilities exist within the rich Islamic scriptural and discursive tradition and Islamic praxis to assure Muslim women a dignified place in Muslim and non-Muslim societies, despite the institutional and historically discursive impediments they face.

In addition to the dissemination of the works of scholars, the twentieth century also witnessed the growth of women's magazines as sites of rethinking authoritative texts and resistance to hitherto accepted patriarchal norms. It also saw the formation of women's organizations employing both discursive and practical strategies to address issues of gender equity and justice. Perhaps one of the most notable women's magazines deserving mention is *Zanan*, founded in Iran in 1992 under the Khatami regime by Shahla Sherkat and closed down under the Ahmadinejad regime in 2008. The magazine created a forum for translating key feminist works into Persian, discussions of topics such as the nature of women's rights, the scope of freedom of the press, new interpretations of Islamic texts, and legal issues. Giving voice to a diversity of viewpoints, the women's press in Iran, and especially *Zanan*, provides

> a forum for the articulation of diverse views, including those that are officially unpopular.... Also noteworthy is that the Islamic feminists who run *Zanan* and *Farzaneh* publish the writings of secular feminists. The rereading of the Islamic texts is a central project of Islamic feminists ... [who] engage in new interpretations of Islamic texts in order to challenge laws and policies that are based on orthodox, literalist, or misogynist interpretations.[72]

In North America, *Azizah*, a magazine that describes itself as being for "the contemporary Muslim woman," was founded in 2000 by Tayyibah Taylor, a Trinidadian who was born to a Christian family and converted to Islam in 1971, and an Indonesian Muslim woman, Marlina Soerakoesoemah. Targeted at the American Muslim woman, *Azizah* has paid special attention to Muslim feminist scholars, who, according to Taylor, "show how 'the beautiful *Qur'anic* ideals [do not support] the oppressive treatment of women in many Muslim societies, [thereby] inventing a feminism that is neither conventionally Eurocentric nor secular in its nature.' In other words, they are shaping an *Islamic* feminist discourse."[73]

---

72. Valentine M. Moghadam, "Islamic Feminism and Its Discontents: Towards a Resolution of the Debate," in *Gender, Politics, and Islam* (ed. Therese Saliba et al.; Chicago: University of Chicago Press, 2002), 15–52, here 35.

73. Jamillah Karim, "Voices of Faith, Faces of Beauty: Connecting American Muslim Women through Azizah," in *Muslim Networks from Hajj to Hip Hop* (ed. Miriam Cooke and Bruce B. Lawrence; Chapel Hill: University of North Carolina Press, 2005), 169–88, here 184.

In addition to the women's press, Muslim women have also formed several transnational organizations that address local, national, and international issues of gender equity. Perhaps the most significant of these is Sisters in Islam (SIS), which included Amina Wadud in its initial discussions at its founding in 1988 in Malaysia. Its mission is to promote "the rights of women within the framework of Islam … based on the principles of equality, justice and freedom enjoined by the Qur'ān."[74] Sisters in Islam's genesis lay in a group of professional women who came together to discuss the discrimination women were facing under the Islamic Family Law Act of 1984, as a subcommittee formed by the Association of Women Lawyers in Malaysia. Recognizing that religion was often the justification given for men's superiority and rights in cases dealing with child custody, polygamy, and domestic violence, the group sought out the guidance of Amina Wadud in order to study for themselves key Islamic texts pertaining to gender. Their studies with Wadud and other renowned U.S.-based scholars such as Abdullahi an-Na'im and Fathi Osman brought home the realization that "injustice toward Muslim women is incompatible with the spirit of compassion and justice in the Qur'ān."[75] In addition to acquiring strategies through which to address such injustice, SIS was able to see that while "the Qur'an is divine, *fiqh* [Islamic jurisprudence] is not,"[76] thereby enabling them to identify the need to "fracture" Islamic discursive and legal hegemony by utilizing feminist methods of engaging Islam in the public sphere. Thus, they began to organize public symposia and to network with Muslim women's organizations nationally and internationally, writing to the media on contested matters such as polygamy. Its website reports:

> SIS research into the texts … shows that a woman's struggle to lead a life of equal worth and dignity to men is clearly located within Islamic teachings. This research has enabled SIS to take the unequivocal position that men and women are equal in Islam, that a Muslim man does not have the right to beat his wife, that polygamy is not an inherent right in Islam but a contract permitted only in the most exceptional circumstances, that one male witness does not equal two female witnesses … and a great deal more.… Research has formed the basis of SIS's arguments for legal reform, the introduction of new policies, and challenges to statements made in the name of Islam that discriminate against women and violate the ethical teachings of the religion.[77]

---

74. "Mission and Objectives"; online: http://www.sistersinislam.org.

75. Azza Basarudin, "In Search of Faithful Citizens in Postcolonial Malaysia," in *Women and Islam* (ed. Zayn R. Kassam; Santa Barbara, Calif.: Praeger, 2010), 93–127, here 103.

76. Ibid.

77. Ibid., under Research.

The combination of research and activism is critical to the work undertaken by the organization. SIS has conducted a multi-year project on the impact of polygamy on the family institution, and is currently drafting a Model Islamic Family Law for Malaysia after producing a 194-page document entitled *Guide to Equality in the Family: A Just and Equitable Family Law for Malaysia* based on work undertaken by the North African women's network, the Collectif 95 Maghreb Egalité, which drafted a *Guide to Equality in the Family in the Maghreb* (Morocco, Tunisia, and Algeria).

SIS has also collaborated with other Muslim women's organizations around the world to create Musawah: A Global Movement for Equality and Justice in the Muslim Family, which was launched at a Global Meeting in Kuala Lumpur in 2009. Musawah predicates its struggle for justice on the axiom that "there cannot be equality in society without equality in the family."[78] As Basarudin observes, "SIS's faith-centered intellectual activism is located within the transnational struggles of Muslim women because it illuminates the local and global as bounded and shared geographical spaces that subscribe to historical specificities yet simultaneously connect women's diverse experiences of negotiating Islam."[79]

In this chapter I have sought to show that there are profound connections between the discursive and the practical in struggling for and realizing gender justice globally and locally for Muslim women in ways perhaps not dissimilar to the intellectual and activist efforts of women in other religious traditions. In this regard, it could be said that the efforts of feminist or woman-centered scholars and activists in every faith tradition during the twentieth century have laid the groundwork for ongoing engagement with the reality of women's lives for the twenty-first century.

---

78. Online: www.musawah.org.
79. Basarudin, "In Search of Faithful Citizens," 116.

STRUGGLING WITH MINDSETS OF DOMINATION

Jacqueline M. Hidalgo
Williams College

In the late twentieth century, a group of indigenous Americans returned the Bible to Pope John Paul II during a visit to Perú. As "Indians of the Andes and America," they relinquished the Bible "because in five centuries it has given us neither love, nor peace, nor justice." They urged, "Please, take your Bible and give it back to our oppressors, because they need its moral precepts more than we.... The Bible came to us as part of imposed colonial change. It was the ideological arm of the colonial assault. The Spanish sword ... by night changed itself into the cross which attacked the Indian soul."[1] Their statements highlight the troublesome connection between biblical reading, Christian missionary activity, and settler colonial violence.

In light of the Bible's historical role in practices of domination (i.e., colonial conquest, slavery, and the Shoah), how, in the twentieth century, did feminists interpret and engage the Bible? Logics of anti-Judaism, Christian-centrism and exceptionalism, Protestant-specific methods of interpretation and standards of canon, antiblack racism and racialization, white supremacy and privilege, imperialist and settler colonialist imperatives and deployments, as well as European- and Euro-North-American-centered norms, all informed early twentieth-century academic biblical scholarship. Thus, Elisabeth Schüssler Fiorenza uses the term kyriarchy in order to elucidate these interlocking, though not coterminous, gendered, anti-Jewish, racist, and

---

1. The Spanish quotation of this statement may be found in Pablo Richard, "Hermenútica bíblica india: Revelación de Dios en las religiones indígenas y en la Biblia (Después de 500 años de dominación)," in *Sentido histórico del V Centenario (1492–1992)* (ed. Guillermo Meléndez; San José: CEHILA-DEI, 1992), 45–62, here 45–46. The translation comes from Elsa Tamez, "The Bible and the Five Hundred Years of Conquest," in *Voices from the Margin: Interpreting the Bible in the Third World* (rev. ed.; ed. R. S. Sugirtharajah; Maryknoll, N.Y.: Orbis, 2006), 13–26, here 18. I thank Neomi DeAnda for her help in tracking down this letter and for her work as a conversation partner and colleague.

colonialist/imperialist[2] patterns of domination.[3] When feminist scholarship tasked itself with challenging gender domination, it was not always attentive to or free from other kyriarchal practices, especially because kyriarchal norms undergirded certain structures of twentieth-century biblical studies. This essay surveys the distinct, yet overlapping, kyriarchal dominations of anti-Judaism, racism, and colonialism/imperialism and some of the challenges different wo/men brought to bear on these kyriarchal practices during the twentieth century.[4]

---

2. According to Edward Said, *imperialism* is a term that considers practices of domination as they stretch out from an imperial center, while *colonialism*, though part of the imperial project, refers to the placement of settlements in a location distant from the imperial center. See Edward W. Said, *Culture and Imperialism* (New York: Vintage, 1994), 9.

3. Schüssler Fiorenza uses the term *kyriarchy*, deriving from the Greek *kyrios*, "to articulate a more comprehensive systemic analysis, to underscore the complex interstructuring of domination, and to locate sexism and misogyny in the political matrix or, better, patrix of a broader range of networks of power." See Elisabeth Schüssler Fiorenza, *Rhetoric and Ethic: The Politics of Biblical Studies* (Minneapolis: Fortress, 1999), 5. Also see Schüssler Fiorenza, "Introduction: Exploring the Intersections of Race, Gender, Status, and Ethnicity in Early Christian Studies," in *Prejudice and Christian Beginnings: Investigating Race, Gender, and Ethnicity in Early Christian Studies* (ed. Laura Nasrallah and Elisabeth Schüssler Fiorenza; Minneapolis: Fortress, 2009), 1–23, especially 5–18, which draws upon intersectionality theory.

4. Some other significant mindsets of domination are outside the purview of this essay, including problems of (dis)ability, age, body shape, cisgender status, class, ecology/environment, education, and sexual orientation. In this essay, I also cannot attend to all of the specific problems and logics of anti-Judaism, racism, and imperialism/colonialism; nor can I address all the feminist responses. As Andrea Smith has shown, the logics of white supremacy alone impact different groups in varying ways even within the limited context of the United States. See Andrea Smith, "Heteropatriarchy and the Three Pillars of White Supremacy," in *The Color of Violence: The Incite! Anthology* (ed. INCITE! Women of Color against Violence; Boston: South End, 2006), 66–73, here 67. This essay thus serves as a nonexhaustive introduction to certain themes and approaches. Although this essay was written for an "encyclopedia," I am not pretending to espouse a universalizing and totalizing perspective on domination. Moreover, I am writing from a particular location. My training has been primarily in the study of "Christianity" and "Christian scriptures." I was born pale-skinned in Costa Rica and of a Roman Catholic religious heritage, and I have spent most of my life in the United States of America, where I speak fluent English. I have been educated and worked primarily at private colleges and universities as well as Protestant seminaries. While I also recognize that much scholarship around the world addresses the themes and problems of this essay (for instance, significant work has been undertaken by German feminists wrestling with anti-Judaism in particular), my training and context within the U.S.A. led me to circumscribe this essay by focusing mostly on scholarship undertaken by those who have trained or been taught in the U.S.A. and published in the English language.

1. TWENTIETH-CENTURY BIBLICAL INTERPRETATION
AND MINDSETS OF DOMINATION

Though I treat anti-Jewish, racist, and colonialist/imperialist mindsets separately in this essay, they intersect even when they have distinct operations and impacts. One hallmark of overlapping kyriarchal mindsets on biblical studies was a presumed universal reader authorized to engage in an "objective," historical critical examination of ancient texts; most historical critical tools, such as source or form criticism, are rooted in a presumed universal reader who was also generally from a very particular background: European/Euro-North-American, white, male, and generally (Protestant) Christian. By the late twentieth century, more scholars turned from this universal reader as they wrestled with the particularity of any reader. Attention to interpretive particularity required reading the reader and the world of the reader in addition to reading the world of a text and the world behind a text.[5]

Although feminist scholars were among those who critiqued the universal generic reader, some presumed a universal female reader, which was in turn critiqued. Following Chandra Mohanty's challenge, feminist scholars sought to examine "woman" as a particularly inflected social category with different performances and meanings in different situations.[6] In this way, Schüssler Fiorenza employs the term "wo/men" so as to enable feminist authors to engage a larger ad hoc political category while including "subordinated men," and to recognize that different kyriarchal structures impact different wo/men in different ways.[7] This awareness of the plural social locations that undergird wo/men also echoes the recognition prevalent among most late twentieth-century feminist biblical interpreters that interpretation is an act informed and inflected by one's particular social location and experiences, especially in relationship to structures of power. At the same time, feminist biblical interpreters in the twentieth century and today disagree about which critical tools are most useful in challenging kyriarchy.[8] In

---

5. I am drawing on Fernando F. Segovia's summary of shifts in the field of biblical studies during the twentieth century. See Fernando F. Segovia, *Decolonizing Biblical Studies: A View from the Margins* (Maryknoll, N.Y.: Orbis, 2000), 7–33.

6. Chandra Talpade Mohanty, *Feminism Without Borders: Decolonizing Theory, Practicing Solidarity* (Durham, N.C.: Duke University Press, 2003), 21–36. This volume reprints her 1986 essay.

7. Although she has elucidated this term in several publications, see especially Elisabeth Schüssler Fiorenza, *Jesus and the Politics of Interpretation* (New York: Continuum, 2000), 4–5, 155–56.

8. Denise Kimber Buell drew my attention to the fact that feminist biblical scholars often divide up into two main camps: those who believe that historical-critical methods

this essay, I look at the three interrelated problems of anti-Judaism, racism, and colonialism/imperialism with a special attention to how feminist biblical scholars, coming from different backgrounds, sought to challenge these frameworks and to envision biblical interpretive paths that break from historical practices of kyriarchal thought.

2. Confronting Anti-Judaism

Anti-Judaism has informed some of the most basic approaches and assumptions of biblical studies, especially among scholars of Christian backgrounds, and this long history is one challenge that feminists confronted in the twentieth century. As Susannah Heschel and Shawn Kelley have demonstrated, eighteenth- and nineteenth-century scholarship developed in relationship to philosophical norms of reading racialized history, norms that elevated the supposed cultural "Aryan"/"Indo-European" ancestors of Western Europe, primarily Greece, while denigrating other peoples, especially Jewish and "Semitic" peoples.[9] Heschel's work on the "Institute for the Study and Eradication of Jewish Influence on German Church Life" underscores how these anti-Jewish biblical interpretive strategies aimed "to create a dejudaized church" that "redefined Christianity as a Germanic religion whose founder, Jesus, was no Jew but rather had fought valiantly to destroy Judaism, falling as victim to that struggle."[10]

Such a view is an extension of interpretive practices and assumptions that have developed over centuries. The long-term permeation of anti-Jewish perspectives in Christian biblical scholarship and theology made Nazi anti-Judaism possible.[11] While the Nazis are an egregious example, anti-Jewish perspectives spread far beyond Nazi Germany and often included many people who had no conscious antagonism toward Judaism or Jewish people. Many Europeans and North Americans never perceived these anti-Jewish assumptions as racism, seeing them instead as "historical or dogmatic truths"

---

can be used for feminist ends and those who look to other approaches, especially those in literary studies. See also the essays by Shelly Matthews and Melanie Johnson-DeBaufre in this volume. I thank Buell more generally for her generous, critical assistance with this essay.

9. See Susannah Heschel, *The Aryan Jesus: Christian Theologians and the Bible in Nazi Germany* (Princeton, N.J.: Princeton University Press, 2008), especially 26–66; and Shawn Kelley, *Racializing Jesus: Race, Ideology, and the Formation of Modern Biblical Scholarship* (New York: Routledge, 2002). Kelley's work traces the impact of Hegelian and Heideggerian racialized thought on contemporary North American Christian biblical scholarship.

10. Heschel, *Aryan Jesus*, 1.

11. Ibid., 7–8.

precisely because of how thoroughly these anti-Jewish perspectives pervaded Christian thought.[12]

Despite strong critiques of scholarly anti-Judaism, these approaches persisted in some areas even into the twenty-first century. For instance, in the context of the quest for the historical Jesus, sayings of Jesus were deemed "authentic" provided they were distinctive from other first-century Jewish thinkers and writers, thus revealing the assumption that Jesus should be differentiated from his Jewish background. Some of these anti-Jewish motifs were all too easily adapted into Christian feminist scholarship, especially studies of the Hebrew Bible that treated the Jewish tradition as the creator and perpetrator of patriarchy that a somehow "non-Jewish" earliest Christianity resisted.[13]

Schüssler Fiorenza asserts that feminist scholars must work against anti-Jewish ideas because "anti-Judaism and antifeminism" are interconnected.[14] Tackling the "Jesus was a feminist" argument, Schüssler Fiorenza finds that such an approach also depends upon a kyriocentric perspective that "places Jesus, the charismatic male leader, into the center and positions wo/men in relation to him."[15] Adele Reinhartz critiques notions of Jewish patriarchy as contrasted with Jesus's egalitarianism by situating Gospel wo/men, such as Mary and Martha, as normal within the context of broader Pharisaic tradition.[16] Moreover, in Reinhartz's view, Christian feminists need to understand Jesus' Judaism "as a positive context … that allowed him to develop his ideas."[17]

To counter anti-Jewish perspectives on early Christianity, feminist scholars have asserted that the history of Christian beginnings must be read differently. Judith Plaskow places Jesus as one of plural possibilities within Judaism in his era and contends that, since some Jewish feminists dispute a narrative of a singular Judaism, Christian feminist scholars should not perpetuate that narrative in order to frame Jesus as a unique feminist.[18] Schüssler Fiorenza

---

12. Ibid., 277–78.

13. For one of the earliest feminist elaborations of this critique of feminist anti-Judaism, see Judith Plaskow, "Christian Feminism and Anti-Judaism," *Cross Currents* 33 (fall 1978): 306–9. This pattern of anti-Jewish thought was especially common in scholars who followed the 1971 Leonard Swidler "Jesus Was a Feminist" argument.

14. Schüssler Fiorenza, *Jesus*, 122.

15. Ibid., 11–12, 136.

16. Adele Reinhartz, "From Narrative to History: The Resurrection of Mary and Martha," in *"Women Like This": New Perspectives on Jewish Women in the Greco-Roman World* (ed. Amy-Jill Levine; Atlanta: Scholars Press, 1991), 161–84. See also Amy-Jill Levine, "Response," *JFSR* 20.1 (2004): 125–32, here 126–27.

17. Adele Reinhartz, "Response," *JFSR* 20.1 (2004): 111–15, here 113.

18. Judith Plaskow, "Feminist Anti-Judaism and the Christian God," *JFSR* 7.2 (fall 1991): 99–108, here 105.

additionally warns of the problem of inscribing "rabbinic Judaism" and "patristic Christianity" onto earlier, plural histories, and she presses the difficulties of constructing the lives and history of Jewish wo/men in pre-70 CE.[19] Reinhartz further affirms certain aspects of "historical criticism" that value situating texts within "their historical, cultural, religious, polemical, and literary contexts" as key to undermining anti-Jewish readings.[20] At the same time, noting the way that certain anti-Jewish strains of biblical interpretation have persisted in different parts of the world, Amy-Jill Levine asserts that institutional training in the United States must change because many seminary and graduate program structures perpetuate anti-Jewish practices and approaches.[21] Jewish feminist scholars have also worked to resituate interpretation of the Tanakh in the broader field of biblical studies so that it is not treated as "merely the first act in a two act play."[22]

The problem of conversation between and among scholars of differing religious traditions has drawn some attention. Plaskow contends that Christian feminist scholars must come to know Judaism as a "living religion" with other expressive lives besides struggles with oppressive anti-Judaism.[23] Kwok Pui-lan would like to imagine a place for Jewish feminists and postcolonial feminists to dialogue without issues being driven by "Eurocentric" projects. Her suggestion is that other frames of reference are possible, that is, "Diasporic Jewish and Diasporic Chinese" dialogue.[24]

Feminists also began to revise the historical narratives of Christianity, from the first centuries onward. Accounts of Christianity's spread often depend upon its portrayal as a universal religion contrasted with the particularity of Judaism. Such a construction relies upon a self/other dichotomy in

---

19. Schüssler Fiorenza, *Jesus*, 116–18. Christian feminist scholars who read rabbinic sources as misogynistic often ignore the historical difference in era and fail to examine the complex and plural composition of the Talmud. See Plaskow, "Feminist Anti-Judaism," 105. She draws on the work undertaken by Judith Wegner, *Chattel or Person? The Status of Women in the Mishnah* (New York: Oxford University Press, 1988).

20. Reinhartz, "Response," 114.

21. See, for instance, Amy-Jill Levine, "Multiculturalism, Women's Studies, and Anti-Judaism," *JFSR* 19.1 (2003): 119–28; and Levine, "The Disease of Postcolonial New Testament Studies and the Hermeneutics of Healing," *JFSR* 20.1 (2004): 91–99, here 95–96.

22. Esther Fuchs, "Jewish Feminist Approaches to the Bible," in *Women and Judaism: New Insights and Scholarship* (ed. Frederick E. Greenspahn; New York: New York University Press, 2009), 25–40, here 37. See further the contribution by Cynthia Baker in this volume.

23. Plaskow, "Feminist Anti-Judaism," 108.

24. Kwok Pui-lan, "Response," *JFSR* 20.1 (2004): 99–106, here 100–102.

which Jews are always a necessary other to constructions of a Christian self.[25] As Denise Kimber Buell reminds readers, attempts to imagine Christianity as a universal religion have had their positive importance, as, for example, in struggles for civil rights. Yet Christian "universalism" has not ended modern racism and has only construed anti-Jewish rhetoric in another manner.[26] The use of anti-Jewish rhetoric, and racializing rhetoric more broadly, in early Christian discourse should be situated amid the competing claims of these plural, often Jewish-identified, factions over and against each other. Sometimes early Christians employed a rhetoric of "universalism" in order "to 'racialize' rival forms" as being overly elitist and particularistic.[27]

3. CONTESTING RACE, RACISM, AND RACIALIZATION

Twentieth-century feminists who sought to undermine the kyriarchal logic of anti-Judaism often confronted other forms of racism and racialization that took up presumptions of white supremacy and privilege in addition to Christian exceptionalism. Readings of the Bible often supported or left unchallenged presumptions of white privilege and white supremacy over peoples deemed a "colored other," whether they shared a scholar's national space or resided in a colonial or postcolonial location.[28]

As with anti-Jewish and colonialist/imperialist interpretive practices, some scholars employed various historical-critical approaches in order to recover what Tat-siong Benny Liew terms "origin(al)" texts or to recreate histories of origin(al) Christians in order to authorize perspectives on an appropriate (and often racialized-as-white) contemporary Christianity.[29] Akin

---

25. See Denise Kimber Buell, *Why This New Race? Ethnic Reasoning in Early Christianity* (New York: Columbia University Press, 2005), 29.

26. Ibid., 11–12.

27. Ibid., 145.

28. See Musa W. Dube, *Postcolonial Feminist Interpretation of the Bible* (St. Louis: Chalice, 2000), 16. For the modern historical engagement between notions of "race" and the Bible, see Colin Kidd, *The Forging of Races: Race and Scripture in the Protestant Atlantic World, 1600–2000* (New York: Cambridge University Press, 2006). See also Kelley's and Heschel's works, cited above. For ways that the Two-Thirds World also attended to the Bible prior to the twentieth century, see discussions in R. S. Sugirtharajah, *The Bible and the Third World: Precolonial, Colonial, and Postcolonial Encounters* (New York: Cambridge University Press, 2001), especially 74–109; and Sylvester A. Johnson, *The Myth of Ham in Nineteenth-Century American Christianity: Race, Heathens, and the People of God* (New York: Palgrave Macmillan, 2004).

29. Liew argues that "the inability to recover the 'origin(al)'—and thus to present an integratable narrative—is also the key not only to endless mourning but also to a truly open

to the logic that sought a "purified," non-Jewish Jesus, purified quests for "authentic," essential origin(al)s demand feminist analysis, including quests to identify a kyriocentric, authorizing figure or era (i.e., the ideal(ized), and racialized, Jesus) followed by a concomitant myth of decline or progress dictated in relationship to that origin(al).

Such quests for an origin(al) often presume an unchallenged, "unified, uniform and consonant" present while a solely antiquarian focus becomes "a fetishization of the text." As Vincent L. Wimbush argues, this approach actually fetishizes "the dominating world that the text helped create."[30] Schüssler Fiorenza connects this attention to fetishized origin(al)s with the rhetoric of scientific objectivism in biblical studies, a rhetoric she places in the context of the colonial roots of the study of religion. Since "religion" was a "feminized" category in European modernity, biblical studies turned into a "scientific" discipline, taking up "positivist factuality" and "antiquarian irrelevancy immune to the concerns of the day" in order to protect its "masculinity" as a field while seeking to mask its Christian-centric, white-privileged, and European/Euro-North-American-normative perspective.[31]

Womanist writers, scholars, and biblical critics especially impacted twentieth-century feminist biblical scholarship in contesting such racialized approaches to biblical texts. Jacquelyn Grant, for instance, confronts liberation theology for its tolerance of sexism while also challenging the "White American" inflected work of feminist theology.[32] On the one hand, Grant critiques feminists who were inattentive to the "interstructuring of oppression" when the problem of sexism is the sole focus, and she finds that feminist analysis too often considered only white sources and white gender construction as an interpretive frame. Grant also elevates the importance of black wo/men reading the Bible with their own experience as a frame that challenges oppressive, authoritative readings.[33] Privileging experience also means privileging other texts as sacred, such as African American women's literature.[34]

---

and inclusive community." Tat-siong Benny Liew, *What Is Asian American Biblical Hermeneutics? Reading the New Testament* (Honolulu: University of Hawai'i Press, 2008), 133–34.

30. Vincent L. Wimbush, "Introduction: Reading Darkness, Reading Scriptures," in *African Americans and the Bible: Sacred Texts and Social Textures* (ed. Vincent L. Wimbush, with the assistance of Rosamond C. Rodman; New York: Continuum, 2000), 1–43, here 10.

31. See Schüssler Fiorenza, *Rhetoric*, 75–78, here 76; also see Schüssler Fiorenza, *Jesus*, 16–19.

32. See Jacquelyn Grant, *White Women's Christ and Black Women's Jesus: Feminist Christology and Womanist Response* (Atlanta: Scholars Press, 1999), especially 109.

33. Ibid., 211.

34. See Katie Geneva Cannon, *Katie's Canon: Womanism and the Soul of the Black Community* (New York: Continuum, 1995).

This approach resonates with the strategies taken up to combat imperialism/colonialism discussed below.

Because womanists critique the sources used in biblical interpretation and contest the practices employed, they have also challenged the very process by which one becomes an "authorized" interpreter of the Bible. As Renita J. Weems highlights in her examination of African American wo/men's biblical engagements, many marginalized readers queried the notions of scientific accuracy, perceiving instead that an "accurate" reading was code for "whose reading is legitimated and enforced by the dominant culture."[35] Weems also asserts that marginalized readers have managed to resist cultural and biblical texts that are "antagonistic" to "identity" and "survival."[36] At the same time, African American wo/men have also sought and found within the biblical texts narratives that affirm their lives and that speak to the survival and liberation of the oppressed and dispossessed.[37] Thus, Weems advocates a hermeneutical approach that seeks, by *"whatever means necessary to recover the voice of the oppressed within biblical texts."*[38]

Despite being critical of how malestream biblical studies have approached the historical project, feminist scholars have not forsaken historical reconstruction. Rather, they have rethought how we read the ancient world and regard our interpretations. For instance, Schüssler Fiorenza has affirmed the "polysemic" nature of critical interpretation as "a performance activity" that transpires under "certain social conditions."[39] Such work brings historical engagement away from a presumed universal reader and origin(al)s and into an engagement with the world in which the critic lives and a recognition that a reader's location impacts interpretation and requires critical reflection. Schüssler Fiorenza also reads the first century through a lens of "'ongoing conflict and struggle' between kyriarchal domination and radical democratic structures and worldviews."[40]

In rethinking the reconstructive project, scholars seek to examine previously unasked questions about the ancient world contexts of biblical texts. For instance, Gay L. Byron's study of "ethno-political rhetorics" in early Christian literary appearances of "Egyptians/Egypt, Ethiopians/Ethiopia, and Blacks/

---

35. Renita J. Weems, "Reading *Her Way* through the Struggle: African American Women and the Bible," in *Stony the Road We Trod: African American Biblical Interpretation* (ed. Cain Hope Felder; Minneapolis: Fortress, 1991), 57–77, here 63.

36. Ibid., 63.

37. Ibid., 70–71.

38. Ibid., 73.

39. Schüssler Fiorenza, *Rhetoric*, 80–81.

40. Schüssler Fiorenza, *Jesus*, 123–24.

blackness," especially including Ethiopian and black women, illuminates how certain questions about African imagery (akin to the omission of the serious study of wo/men in the ancient world) remained unasked in biblical studies because of the impact of racism on the field.[41] Also taking an eye to the questions (un)asked, Buell examines ethnoracial reasoning in early Christian literature. Problematizing contemporary scholarship as well, Buell seeks "to dismantle Christian anti-Judaism" and assumptions of "white privilege" that rest upon separating Christianity from logics of "ethnicity/race."[42] Buell stresses how the rhetorical edges of fixity and fluidity in racial discourse actually work together: both "an essentializing discourse" with its attention to "some inherent, eternal core (fixity)," and "a 'processual' discourse that emphasizes change and transformation of cultural phenomena (fluidity)."[43] Hence, Christianity is a "mutable concept" that should be viewed "not as an essence but as a contested site."[44]

4. Challenging Imperialist/Colonialist Interpretation

The problems of racism and racialization in contemporary biblical interpretation can be disentangled neither from anti-Judaism nor from colonialism/imperialism, and again twentieth-century feminist scholars developed approaches that merge with, while also questioning, colonialist/imperialist interpretive methods. As Colin Kidd observes, the European encounter with the "New World" (a biblically derived name) was treated, in part, as a theological problem because the American hemisphere and its peoples seemed largely unaccounted for in the Bible.[45] In return, the Bible was turned to, interpreted, and debated over as people sought to make sense of perceived racial differences in modernity, leading to a back and forth in which notions of scriptures and the study of scriptures impacted concepts of race and vice

---

41.See Gay L. Byron, *Symbolic Blackness and Ethnic Difference in Early Christian Literature* (New York: Routledge, 2002).

42. Buell, *Why This New Race*, 12.

43. Ibid., 7–8.

44. Ibid., 29. Likewise, Schüssler Fiorenza argues for an approach to biblical studies that "enables us to understand the Bible as a site of struggle over meaning and biblical interpretation and debate and argument rather than as transcript of the unchanging, inerrant Word of G*d." Schüssler Fiorenza then suggests that the future of biblical studies should move toward collaboration and away from metaphors of "battle, combat, and competition." See Elisabeth Schüssler Fiorenza, *The Power of the Word: Scripture and the Rhetoric of Empire* (Minneapolis: Fortress, 2007), 265.

45. Kidd, *Forging of Races*, 56.

versa. Racial and religious otherness were thus complexly bound together in colonial/imperial scriptural reading.[46]

A perspective of Christian exceptionalism has informed anti-Jewish rhetoric and colonial encounters with "religious others" across the globe.[47] Logics of Christian exceptionalism and Eurocentrism converged to mark the Christian Bible as a unique scriptural revelation and as a bar for the measuring of (un)civilization that inscribed other peoples as culturally and intellectually inferior to Europe—childlike, ahistorical, and in need of alteration.[48] Imperialist/colonialist authors frequently marshaled these rhetorics, along with anti-Jewish and racialized readings, to authorize colonialist violence and the settler colonial seizure of land and domination of indigenous peoples.[49] Elsa Tamez observes how Spanish conquerors read the Bible, elevated "the conquest of Canaan," and saw themselves as "the divine instrument" of punishment and liberation that brought salvation from indigenous "idols."[50]

Musa W. Dube turns to imperial/colonial readings of Exodus and Joshua as prime examples of how imperialist/colonialist interpreters "employ female gender to articulate relations of subjugation and domination" and justify settler colonial imperatives.[51] She cultivates "Rahab's reading prism" as a decolonizing, anti-imperial literary and rhetorical approach that can be useful for resistant readers and communities. Rahab may be read as a colonizer's textual fantasy. As a prostitute who represents the land to be colonized, she is readily available; she is in need of a colonizer's civilizing morality; she is ready to believe in a colonizer's superiority; and she desires a colonizer's aid and presence.[52] By decolo-

---

46. Ibid., 73.

47. Buell briefly narrates a history of ethnoracial discourse and the usage of Christianity as the baseline measurement for all religions as deployed in biblical and early Christian historical studies, as well as in the development of the concept of "religion" in the nineteenth century. See Buell, *Why This New Race*, 21–24. Also see Tomoko Masuzawa, *The Invention of World Religions, or, How European Universalism Was Preserved in the Language of Pluralism* (Chicago: University of Chicago Press, 2005).

48. See discussion in Sugirtharajah, *Bible and the Third World*, 61, 68–71. For a thorough discussion of many key colonial hermeneutical practices, see 45–73, especially 61–73.

49. Dube, *Postcolonial Feminist Interpretation*, 16.

50. Tamez, "Bible and the Five Hundred Years," 14–15. Judith Laikin Elkin shows that Spanish colonial discourse drew on anti-Jewish imagery to attack indigenous "idol worship." See Judith Laikin Elkin, "Imagining Idolatry: Missionaries, Indians, and Jews," in *Religion and the Authority of the Past* (ed. Tobin Siebers; Ann Arbor: University of Michigan, 1993), 75–99. Tamez draws connections between these five-hundred-year-old conquest motifs and the motifs used to justify the U.S. invasion of Panama in 1989 (see "Bible and the Five Hundred Years," 17).

51. Dube, *Postcolonial Feminist Interpretation*, 61.

52. Ibid., 76–80, 122. Dube also draws on the notion of the "Pocahontas perplex" in

nizing and resignifying Rahab, Dube engages "concerns over losing control of one's land, subverting the literary genre and language of the colonizer, rereading the master's texts and retelling history, and gender at the decolonization zone."[53]

5. Decolonizing Readings, Canons, and Scriptures

Various twentieth-century feminist readers have used decolonizing literary methodologies to reread imperial power and resistance in the ancient world, as well as to dispute colonial biblical translation and interpretation in the contemporary world while attending to gender. Many of these feminist-decolonizing strategies resonate as responses to anti-Judaism, racism, and colonialism/imperialism. Practices of rereading are often rooted in a commitment to reading with particular communities outside of the academic realm. Dube situates her perspective within interpretive practices of African Independent Churches (AICs) that have sought "to cultivate a space for liberating interdependence."[54] Tamez reads with the poor and engages daily life as a dialogical point of reference for biblical interpretation.[55] In this way, scriptures are treated as "the historic and subversive memory of the poor,"[56] producing interpretations that speak from and to the "concrete" particulars "of political and economic tyranny."[57] She notes that wo/men reading in these communities may resonate with stories of liberation but sometimes feel purposefully excluded and marginalized in certain texts.[58] In response, Tamez suggests that new norms of interpretation must be advocated.[59] Working from examples within Korean *minjung* theology, which privileges the readings of historically dominated groups, Kwok similarly argues that *minjung* commu-

---

colonialist images of gendered subjects. See Rayna Green, "The Pocahontas Perplex: The Image of Indian Women in American Culture," *MR* 16 (1975): 698–714.

53. Dube, *Postcolonial Feminist Interpretation*, 101.

54. Ibid., 42.

55. Elsa Tamez, "Women's Rereading of the Bible," in *Voices from the Margin: Interpreting the Bible in the Third World* (ed. R. S. Sugirtharajah; Maryknoll, N.Y.: Orbis, 1995), 48–57, here 49.

56. Tamez, "Bible and the Five Hundred Years," 20.

57. Elsa Tamez, *The Bible of the Oppressed* (trans. Matthew J. O'Connell; Maryknoll, N.Y.: Orbis, 1979), 3.

58. Tamez, "Women's Rereading," 50.

59. Ibid., 52.

nities must arrive at their own norms of interpretation that are accountable to that community.[60]

Because indigenous traditions of reading and interpretation were subordinated to colonial traditions, some contemporary scholars have sought to recuperate subordinated practices in academic contexts.[61] Elsewhere in this volume, Buell examines feminist challenges to "canon." She underscores canon as phenomenon in terms of what gets read, whether source texts be non-canonical ancient Jewish and Christian texts, religious texts of other traditions, or daily life. Yet Buell also highlights the way that canon refers to rule, as in the norms of interpretation, and she considers how feminists have sought to unravel such norms. For instance, some Jewish feminist scholars recover the use of midrashim as a practice of rethinking female biblical characters.[62] The Circle of Concerned African Women Theologians engages African reading practices of "storytelling and divination" as well as "reading with grassroots or subaltern readers."[63] These approaches privilege community interaction, life-giving relationality, social accountability, and "gender-neutral techniques" that "counteract patriarchal and colonizing ideology," and subvert "exploitative powers."[64] Privileging decolonial, life-giving interpretive practices while looking to communities and daily experience echoes womanist recommendations for subverting racism in biblical studies.

Dube contends that new norms of interpretation must be undertaken with the assumption that readings have international and interreligious implications.[65] Tamez notes that even when Christian churches opt for the poor, they often remain insensitive to the other—especially the religious other.[66] Such a concern pushes canonical boundaries in terms of which texts are read and how authority is granted. Kwok presses for a multifaith hermeneutics, a "dialogical imagination," and a widened fluidity of "the canon" so as to include nonbiblical, non-Jewish, and non-Christian sources of revelation indigenous to an Asian context.[67]

---

60. Kwok Pui-lan, *Discovering the Bible in the Non-biblical World* (Maryknoll, N.Y.: Orbis, 1995), 15, 19.

61. Sugirtharajah, *Bible and the Third World*, 71–72.

62. See Fuchs's further discussion of this method in "Jewish Feminist Approaches," 32–34.

63. Musa W. Dube, "Introduction," in *Other Ways of Reading: African Women and the Bible* (ed. Musa W. Dube; Atlanta: Society of Biblical Literature, 2001), 1–19, here 2.

64. Ibid., 3–4. See also Musa W. Dube, "Divining Ruth for International Relations," in Dube, *Other Ways of Reading*, 179–95, here 184.

65. Dube, *Postcolonial Feminist Interpretation*, 18–19.

66. Tamez, "Bible and the Five Hundred Years," 22–23.

67. Kwok, *Discovering the Bible*, 10, 12–13, 17–18, 23, and 32–43, where she challenges

Kwok is not the only feminist scholar to take up such dialogical practices. In *Other Ways of Reading*, African wo/men incorporate African traditions and texts without privileging the biblical canon.[68] Remarking on the plurality of Latin American religious experiences, Tamez observes that "Syncretism here is not pejorative, but rather a synthesis of spiritual experience that has been present for centuries and has not been recognized as valid."[69] When the Bible and the *Pop Wuj* are read with equal weight in the same liturgy, a dialogical approach to a broadened canon is generally presumed.[70]

Such canon expansions also press at the category of "scriptures" and the canonical bounds of the field of "biblical studies." Wimbush turns toward the "*radical excavation* of the phenomenon of 'scriptures.'"[71] Treating scriptures as phenomena that include certain relationships between human beings and "texts," such radical excavation attends to the power dynamics that surround textual engagements. Thus, radical excavation includes the oral, the performative, and the political. Similarly, Kwok, in taking up the tension between orality and textuality, contends that scriptures must be approached as "dynamic and open-ended, not rigidly fixed by the written word."[72] In broadening these approaches to scriptures, feminist scholars have sought to read for and with the ways that wo/men have engaged, challenged, and subverted imperial/colonial powers and biblical readings.

6. THE STRUGGLES CONTINUE

Meditating on the historical trauma that surrounds indigenous American reception of the Bible, Pablo Richard describes a popular Guatemalan saying: "When the Spanish came, they told us, the indigenous, that we must close our eyes in order to pray. When we opened our eyes, we had their Bible and they had our land."[73] Dube likewise opens her *Postcolonial Feminist Interpretation*

---

the notion of canon and deploys the "dialogical model of interpretation," especially as she picks up Henry Louis Gates's notion of the "talking book."

68. Dube, "Introduction," 14.

69. Tamez, "Bible and the Five Hundred Years," 13.

70. Ibid., 23. See also Elsa Tamez, "Introduction: The Power of the Naked," in *Through Her Eyes: Women's Theology from Latin America* (ed. Elsa Tamez; trans. Jeltje Aukema; Maryknoll, N.Y.: Orbis, 1989), 1–14.

71. Vincent L. Wimbush, "Introduction: TEXTureS, Gestures, Power: Orientation to Radical Excavation," in *Theorizing Scriptures: New Critical Orientations to a Cultural Phenomenon* (ed. Vincent L. Wimbush; New Brunswick, N.J.: Rutgers University Press, 2008), 1–20, here 3.

72. Kwok, *Discovering the Bible*, 51.

73. As quoted in Richard, "Hermenútica," 45–46, my translation.

of the Bible with a similar oral tradition from sub-Saharan Africa: "When the white man came to our country he had the Bible and we had the land. The white man said to us, 'let us pray.' After the prayer, the white man had the land and we had the Bible."[74] Both adages regard the Bible as a tool of imperialist/colonialist expansion and racialized European control, a weapon whose very imperialist deployment is reflected in its Christian-centric inflection. Under colonial/imperial regimes, the Bible was always taught as strictly the Christian Bible, superior to other sacred texts. At the same time, the Christian Bible's own historical creation after Constantine was ignored; in part, the imperialist project attempted to deny the existence of Jewish sacred texts within the Christian Bible and to erase contemporary Jewish readers from scriptural relationship to the Bible. In Spanish, the adage also encodes the feminine gender of the colonized land, something that Dube's sensitive reading of colonial/imperial interpretation also stresses. Such female imagery was often taken up with racialized readings in colonialist/imperialist interpretation in order to subjugate whole peoples.

At the same time, the adages suggest that the Bible also rests in the hands of those it had been used to dominate. In the latter part of the twentieth century, feminist biblical scholarship confronted the role of the Bible in historical practices of domination. Whatever the historical trauma of the Bible's introduction, wo/men have wrestled with how the Bible has been interpreted while seeking out new interpretive paths that break mindsets of domination.

---

74. Dube, *Postcolonial Feminist Interpretation*, 1.

PART 3
READING OTHERWISE: METHODS OF INTERPRETATION

Texts and Readers, Rhetorics and Ethics

Melanie Johnson-DeBaufre
Drew Theological School

Stories are the style and substance of life. They fashion and fill existence....
If without stories we live not, stories live not without us.[1]

— Phyllis Trible

At the heart of rhetoric is both the ethical and the political.[2]

— Elisabeth Schüssler Fiorenza

This chapter focuses on feminist work emerging in the twentieth century in the context of the rise of literary, rhetorical, and ideological criticisms in biblical studies. Exploring the power of the language of the Bible and of its readers, feminist biblical studies has played an important role in developing new critical methods, exposing the politics of the discipline of biblical studies, and promoting conversation about diverse reading communities and the ethics of interpretation.

1. Texts and Readers

Traditionally, religious communities and the academy have approached the Bible as a self-evident source of church doctrine or as window onto the reality of the past. However, with the political challenges of global social movements since the 1960s and the postmodern epistemological critiques of modernity, a different understanding has gained prominence and momentum. This view understands texts as language events rather than as sets of signs that refer directly to stable realities and meanings. As a practice of communication,

---

1. Phyllis Trible, *Texts of Terror: Literary-Feminist Readings of Biblical Narratives* (Philadelphia: Fortress, 1984), 1.
2. Elisabeth Schüssler Fiorenza, *Rhetoric and Ethic: The Politics of Biblical Studies* (Minneapolis: Fortress, 1999), 44.

language has meaning within a specific space and time and shapes meaning within that context. Communication events can be endlessly reused and revised within and across social contexts. Thus, language is a site of struggle over meaning, values, and power. Because speech-acts—oral and written— have their force in relation to material realities, much is at stake in understanding the way that language works and exposing its place in the production and maintenance of power relationships in a society.

This understanding of language dovetails closely with feminist interests. From early on, feminist interpreters have paid attention to the nature of texts and the power of readers, identifying and addressing such problems as: (1) the androcentric or patriarchal (or kyriarchal) nature of the biblical texts;[3] (2) the kyriarchal history of interpretation by ecclesial, academic, and societal authorities; (3) the role of the biblical text in the history of violence and domination; and (4) the exclusion of wo/men from the ranks of authoritative interpreters of the Bible in both religious and academic communities. Implicit in these issues are questions of power and responsibility. Does power and authority lie with the text, the reader, or the history of interpretation? Are interpreters accountable for the Bible's violent history? Is the goal of feminist interpretation to find one, true meaning or effective interpretations that are relevant and productive for wo/men's lives? Raising such questions, feminists entering literary- and rhetorical-critical discussions have developed new interpretations and challenged interpreters to take seriously the hermeneutical and ethical-political implications of their own methods.

2. New Views on Old Stories

As part of the progression in Literary Studies from New Criticism in the 1930s to structuralism and poststructuralism in the 1960s to 1980s, the rise of hermeneutics and reader-response critical methodologies facilitated literary and rhetorical understandings of the biblical text.[4] An influential site

---

3. An androcentric text privileges a male point of view and interests. A patriarchal text espouses a social system that privileges the rule of men over women. A kyriarchal text promotes a structured social system of multiplied oppressions based on the rule of the *kyrios* (Greek for lord, master, father) over hierarchically subordinated women and men. For a summary of this neologism, see Elisabeth Schüssler Fiorenza, *Wisdom Ways: Introducing Feminist Biblical Interpretation* (Maryknoll, N.Y.: Orbis, 2001), 118–24.

4. A literary approach understands a text as literature, produced by culture but also producing culture through its reading. Literary critics usually understand the rhetoric of a text to be the specific mechanics of its meaning-making. Rhetorical critics understand texts themselves as rhetorical, that is, as attempts at persuasion in particular contexts. Although both literary and rhetorical critics attend to rhetorical forms, literary criticism tends to

of interdisciplinarity, literary theory also served as a conduit through which feminists in the 1980s and 1990s drew postmodern, Marxist, and psychoanalytic theory into biblical studies.[5] In biblical studies, literary critics effectively shifted the focus of a notable sector of the discipline from religious/doctrinal questions about the Bible's current meaning and historical questions about its original meaning toward literary and hermeneutical questions about *how the Bible makes meaning.* As with a literary approach more broadly, feminist literary (or narrative) critics presuppose a unitary text and attend primarily to the narrator and point of view, structure and plot, setting and character, rhetorical tropes, and repeated language/symbols (in contrast to historical criticism's traditional focus on the world behind the text or on reconstructing the units that seem to comprise the text).

An early scholarly work of literary criticism in a feminist register is Phyllis Trible's 1978 *God and the Rhetoric of Sexuality*, which combined literary innovations in form criticism[6] with interests informed by the feminist movement. Trible argued that the history of interpretation of Hebrew Bible images of God and of male and female was more androcentric than the text itself. Paying careful attention to structural patterns and the distinctive literary devices of texts such as Gen 2–3, Song of Songs, and Ruth, as well as the theme of the feminine divine throughout the Christian Old Testament canon, Trible

---

focus on the text (and sometimes the reader) while rhetorical criticism explores the relationship of the context, text, and reader. As will be discussed, ideology, understood as a symbolic system that encodes and produces the power relationships of a society, has been an important analytical tool for various kinds of feminist literary and rhetorical work.

5. For a review of the interaction of biblical studies with a range of literary theory (including reader-response theory, structuralism, formalism, semiotics, narratology, poetics, the New Rhetoric, and ideology critique), see The Bible and Culture Collective (George Aichele et al.), *The Postmodern Bible* (New Haven: Yale University Press, 1995).

6. Although feminists have been active in their development, literary and rhetorical approaches to the Bible made their way into the discipline primarily through mainstream scholarship. See the SBL presidential addresses of Amos N. Wilder (published as "Scholars, Theologians, and Ancient Rhetoric," *JBL* 75 [1956]: 1–11); and see Wilder, *The Language of the Gospel: Early Christian Rhetoric* (New York: Harper & Row, 1964), and James Muilenburg ("Form Criticism and Beyond," *JBL* 88 [1969]: 1–18). For literary criticism, see the introductions to David J. A. Clines and J. Cheryl Exum, eds., *The New Literary Criticism and the Hebrew Bible* (JSOTSup 143; Sheffield: JSOT Press, 1993); and Elizabeth Struthers Malbon and Edgar V. McKnight, eds., *The New Literary Criticism and the New Testament* (JSNTSup 109; Sheffield: Sheffield Academic Press, 1994). For rhetorical criticism in the Hebrew Bible in the tradition of Muilenburg, see Phyllis Trible, *Rhetorical Criticism: Context, Method, and the Book of Jonah* (Minneapolis: Fortress, 1994); and for the New Rhetoric in Christian Testament studies, see Burton L. Mack, *Rhetoric and the New Testament* (Minneapolis: Fortress, 1990).

demonstrated both the value of attending to topics raised by contemporary feminist critique of patriarchy and the hermeneutical power of close rereading from a feminist perspective.

Literary criticism has developed in the study of both testaments, particularly around the study of biblical narrative. This attention to *stories* marks a powerful connection to feminist theology and the larger feminist movement, which emphasize women's lives and thus their stories as a primary source of insight and authority. Feminist practices of midrash, storytelling, narrative preaching, and bibliodrama—all of which have lives in both religious communities and the academy—resonate with these critical literary methodologies developing in the academy. Feminist work on biblical stories often crosses between Christian theology and biblical studies, and church and academy. In her 1984 book, *Texts of Terror*, Trible tells the stories of violence against women such as Hagar, Tamar, the Levite's concubine, and Jephthah's daughter. The goal is not to redeem these stories of violence against women or to explicate method but to retell these stories as a memoriam and a call to social and ecclesial repentance.[7] Renita J. Weems's 1988 *Just a Sister Away* combines reclaiming stories of biblical women from both testaments with "the Afro-American oral tradition, with its gift for story-telling and drama" in order to facilitate discussion in women's Bible study groups about the complexity of women's relationships.[8] Feminists engaging the place of the female characters in the Markan narrative have debated their relevance to contemporary Christian women's discipleship and leadership.[9]

In the discipline, feminist work in narrative criticism has served a corrective function by focusing on underexplored women characters and feminine

---

7. Trible invites feminist preachers to take up these texts (*Texts of Terror*, xiii). Published ten years later in the same Fortress series, Overtures to Biblical Theology, Renita Weems's *Battered Love* demonstrates the developments in the feminist/womanist conversation around gendered metaphors of violence in the Bible. While Trible's work focuses closely on the text, Weems's work, also presented for a nonspecialist audience, draws on a mix of literary criticism, ideology critique, and gender criticism. See Renita J. Weems, *Battered Love: Marriage, Sex, and Violence in the Hebrew Prophets* (Minneapolis: Fortress, 1995).

8. Renita J. Weems, *Just a Sister Away: A Womanist Vision of Women's Relationships in the Bible* (San Diego, Calif.: LuraMedia, 1988), ix.

9. See Joanna Dewey, *Disciples of the Way: Mark on Discipleship* (Women's Division Board of Global Ministries, United Methodist Church, 1976); Marla Schierling (later Selvidge), "Women as Leaders in the Marcan Communities," *Listening* 15 (1980): 250–56; Winsome Munro, "Women Disciples in Mark?" *CBQ* 44 (1982): 225–41; and Elizabeth Struthers Malbon, "Fallible Followers: Women and Men in the Gospel of Mark," *Semeia* 28 (1983): 29–48.

images of God.[10] The following is a list of questions that a feminist narrative critic might raise:

▶ Is there a woman or a woman's point of view in this text?

▶ How are women portrayed in this text? Do they speak? Do we have access to their point of view?

▶ Who has the power in this text? How is power distributed? How do women get what they want (if they do)? What do the women want?

▶ How does the text represent uniquely female experiences, such as childbearing, or traditionally female experiences, such as childrearing?

▶ How have women's lives and voices been suppressed by this text? Are women made to speak and act against their own interests?

▶ What hidden gender assumptions lie behind this text?

▶ Whose interests are being served by this text?[11]

Recognizing that stories about women are embedded in texts that encode cultural values and presuppositions, feminist literary critics have also attended to sexual stereotypes and the textual construction of gender. For some critics, a literary-critical approach can risk over-privileging the text, wherein meaning is *intrinsic* to the text, and "proper analysis of form yields proper articulation of meaning."[12] This can allow the authority and value of the Christian

---

10. Because of the lack of texts ostensibly authored by women, the feminist interest in gynocriticism in literary studies has been less pronounced in feminist biblical studies. For this term, see Elaine Showalter, ed., *The New Feminist Criticism: Essays on Women, Literature, and Theory* (New York: Pantheon, 1985), 125–43 and 243–70. For innovative approaches to women's traditions and authorship, see Virginia Burrus, *Chastity as Autonomy: Women in Stories of Apocryphal Acts* (Lewiston: Edwin Mellen, 1987); Ilana Pardes, *Countertraditions in the Bible* (Cambridge: Harvard University Press, 1992); and Athalya Brenner and Fokkelien van Dijk Hemmes, *On Gendering Texts: Female and Male Voices in the Hebrew Bible* (Leiden: Brill, 1996). For a midrashic approach to revisioning the text, see Alicia Suskin Ostriker, *Feminist Revision and the Bible* (Oxford: Blackwell, 1993).

11. This list is slightly adapted from Cheryl Exum, "Feminist Criticism: Whose Interests Are Served?" in *Judges and Method: New Approaches in Biblical Studies* (ed. Gale Yee; 2nd ed.; Minneapolis: Fortress, 2007), 69. Exum suggests that these questions should be asked in literary criticism in general. The number of feminists works exploring biblical characters and gendered symbolism is too long to list, especially in Hebrew Bible scholarship. For bibliography, see Alice Bach, ed., *Women in the Hebrew Bible* (New York: Routledge, 1999), 523–32; the Feminist Companion series out of Sheffield Academic Press (Hebrew Bible) and Pilgrim Press (Christian Testament).

12. Trible, *God and the Rhetoric of Sexuality* (Philadelphia: Fortress, 1978), 8.

biblical canon to remain intact.[13] Thus, while a literary approach has clearly facilitated new or more wo/men-friendly readings, it can occlude both the role of the reader in producing meaning and the ideological power of the text to perpetuate domination and violence.

Esther Fuchs has consistently been less sanguine about feminist ability to productively reread the stories of women in the Bible. For Fuchs, female characters are neither heroines to be reclaimed (such as Deborah or Miriam) nor victims to be mourned (such as most of the women in Judges). Rather, they are literary-rhetorical constructs of patriarchal society. Theirs "are not only stories told *by* a man's world, but also *for* a man's world."[14] The Bible "is not merely a text authored by men—it also fosters a politics of male domination."[15] Because patriarchy both produces the text and is produced by the text, a distinctly political feminist analysis of biblical narrative is needed. Focusing primarily on the artistry or poetics of the biblical narratives, Fuchs contends, risks aestheticizing, naturalizing, and reinscribing the patriarchal politics of the text.[16]

Rather than choosing between recuperation and accusation, many feminists in the 1980s and 1990s turned to notions of countertraditions and/or counterreadings that take seriously the patriarchal politics of the text, and attempt to disrupt its power by exposing its multivocality, malleability, and self-deconstruction. For example, Cheryl Exum traces the gender ideology of biblical texts in order to "reveal strategies by which patriarchal literature excludes, marginalizes, and otherwise operates to subjugate women." This approach facilitates her stepping outside of, or reading against the grain of, the ideology of the narratives "in order to construct feminist (sub)versions of them."[17] A signal strategy of feminists working with the analysis of the ideol-

---

13. Alice Bach, "Reading Allowed: Feminist Biblical Criticism Approaching the Millennium," *CR:BS* 1 (1993): 191–215, here 197.

14. Esther Fuchs, "Status and Role of Female Heroines in the Biblical Narrative," *MQ* 23 (1982): 149–60. See also Pamela J. Milne, "The Patriarchal Stamp of Scripture: The Implications for a Structural Analysis for Feminist Hermeneutics," *JFSR* 5.1 (1989): 17–34.

15. Esther Fuchs, *Sexual Politics in the Biblical Narrative: Reading the Hebrew Bible as a Woman* (JSOTSup 310; Sheffield: Sheffield Academic Press, 2000), 11.

16. The Dutch feminist literary critic Mieke Bal has also critiqued the methods of mainstream literary criticism in the trajectory of Robert Alter and Meir Sternberg and the feminist use of them in that both idealize the text and thus risk perpetuating the ideological constructions of the biblical narrative. See Mieke Bal, *Femmes imaginaires: L'ancien testament au risqué d'une narratologie critique* (Utrecht: Hes, 1986); abridged English edition: *Lethal Love: Feminist Literary Readings of Biblical Love Stories* (Bloomington: Indiana University Press, 1987).

17. J. Cheryl Exum, *Fragmented Women: Feminist (Sub)versions of Biblical Narratives* (JSOTSup 163; Sheffield: Sheffield Academic Press, 1993), 9, 11.

ogy of narratives is to expose the ways that patriarchal texts also encode the strains of having to maintain patriarchy. In these suppressions, anxieties, and fragmentations, space can be made for recognizing, resisting, and reimagining patriarchal inscriptions of women's lives and voices.

The emphasis for Exum and others is less on producing a strongly coherent new reading of the text than it is on capitalizing upon its instability and anomalies to multiply possible readings. For example, Mieke Bal's reading of Judges exposes ways that the assumption of the book's literary and ideological coherence perpetuates the text's marginalization of women in the history of Israel. Bal proposes a countercoherence built on a series of anomalous factors in the stories of women. This countercoherence introduces many more themes of what the text is "about" than the dominant ones. But it does not do so to produce a new coherence so much as to multiply the text's themes (such as sex, obedience, and violence) so that they can be assessed comparatively in their "plurality and differences."[18] Danna Fewell and David Gunn's readings of the Pentateuch and Deuteronomistic History intentionally look from the "other side" of the implied (elite male) audience—that is, from the view of women and children. Yet their overall approach to the narratives seeks out "the different and discordant," and resists totalizing renarrations that suppress diversity and multivocality.[19]

3. RHETORIC AND CONTEXTS

In the mid-1980s, the publication of Trible's *Texts of Terror* and Elisabeth Schüssler Fiorenza's *The Book of Revelation: Justice and Judgment* mark two different ways that feminist rhetorical-critical scholarship develops. Whereas Trible emphasizes the text as literature and attends to rereading its structures and tropes, Schüssler Fiorenza situates her rhetorical approach at the intersection of historical and literary approaches, suggesting that historical criticism cannot do justice to the polysemous nature of language, while a wholly

---

18. Mieke Bal, *Death and Dissymetry: The Politics of Coherence in the Book of Judges* (Chicago: University of Chicago Press, 1988), 17. Bal's work has also significantly developed feminist notions of point of view and sought to open up the text to multiple subject positions. For a summative table of Bal's narratological method, see ibid., appendix 1. For a discussion of "difference and not coherence" as a feminist practice of reading, see Daniel Boyarin's review of Bal's *Lethal Love* in "The Politics of Biblical Narratology: Reading the Bible Like/As a Woman," *Diacritics* 20 (1990): 31–42. See also Mieke Bal, ed., *Anti-covenant: Counter-reading Women's Lives in the Hebrew Bible* (Sheffield: Almond, 1989).

19. Danna Nolan Fewell and David M. Gunn, *Gender, Power, and Promise: The Subject of the Bible's First Story* (Nashville: Abingdon, 1993), 13, 16.

literary approach does not consider that an author writes in a particular communicative context with theological and social interests.[20] Situated in the emergence of the New Rhetoric, Schüssler Fiorenza's work developed with an understanding of "rhetoric" not as stylistic ornamentation or formal features of a text but as an understanding of language as the art of persuasion.[21]

In her work on Revelation and 1 Corinthians, Schüssler Fiorenza explicates two important terms: *rhetorical strategy* and *rhetorical situation*. The rhetorical strategy consists of the literary forms and overall argument that make the text persuasive. This strategy should be a fitting response to a rhetorical situation, or the communicative context that called forth this particular rhetorical response. Since history is only available through texts that are themselves rhetorical-contextual, reconstructing a text's context is difficult. It must be evaluated as to how well it makes sense of a biblical text as a potentially persuasive response. Thus, the reconstituted rhetorical situation can serve as a tool for (cautiously) reconstructing the historical-communicative context of 1 Corinthians or other nonpoetic early Christian literature.[22] In order to encompass the entire range of communicative events from the production of texts to contemporary biblical interpretation (both academic and ecclesial), Schüssler Fiorenza has proposed a complex rhetorical model of interpretation.[23]

---

20. Elisabeth Schüssler Fiorenza, *The Book of Revelation: Justice and Judgment* (Philadelphia: Fortress, 1985), 15–25. The book is a collection of essays published between 1968 and 1985.

21. The term is taken from the title of the influential work: Chaim Perelman and Lucie Olbrechts-Tyteca, *The New Rhetoric: A Treatise on Argumentation* (tr. John Wilkinson and Purcell Weaver; Notre Dame, Ind.: Notre Dame University Press, 1969). See Mack, *Rhetorical Criticism*, 9–17; and Aichele, *Postmodern Bible*, 156–61.

22. This genre difference may be one reason that feminist work on the Gospels tends to be literary-critical and work on Pauline literature tends to be rhetorical-critical. See Mary Ann Tolbert, *Sowing the Gospel: Mark's Work in Literary-Historical Perspective* (Minneapolis: Augsburg Fortress, 1996), Elaine M. Wainwright, *Towards a Feminist Critical Reading of the Gospel according to Matthew* (Berlin: de Gruyter, 1991); Cynthia Briggs Kittredge, *Community and Authority: The Rhetoric of Obedience in the Pauline Tradition* (HTS 45; Harrisburg, Penn.: Trinity, 1998); and Joseph A. Marchal, *Hierarchy, Unity, and Imitation: A Feminist Rhetorical Analysis of Power Dynamics in Paul's Letter to the Philippians* (Atlanta: Society of Biblical Literature, 2006).

23. The steps of Schüssler Fiorenza's method of rhetorical analysis can be summarized as follows: (1) identify the interests, models, and social locations of contemporary interpretation; (2) delineate the rhetorical arrangement, features, and interests of the text; (3) outline the rhetorical situation implied in the text both in terms of the exigency to which the text is a fitting response and the rhetorical problem the author has to overcome; (4) reconstruct the common historical context and symbolic universe of the author and audi-

In terms of historical reconstruction, feminist rhetorical criticism is particularly amplified in the work of Antoinette Clark Wire. Her 1990 book *The Corinthian Women Prophets* sets out to "reconstruct as accurate a picture as possible of the women prophets in the church of first-century Corinth."[24] As neither Paul's rhetoric nor the dominant histories are interested in the women prophesying in Corinth (1 Cor 11:5), Wire's innovation in social history, not unlike that of feminist narrative criticism above, is to *change the question and focus of inquiry* in light of the feminist knowledge that women have always been present and active in history. The goal is not to multiply interpretations but to open up possibilities for imagining plausible, but alternative, histories. There has been ongoing debate among feminists utilizing literary and rhetorical methods, however, about the place of historical questions and the feasibility and value of moving from text to context (either ancient or contemporary).

Feminist narrative criticism has also developed in a way that takes interest in both "how the text means" and the social worlds that produce, reflect, and resist that meaning. Gale Yee, for example, explores the symbolization of woman as "the incarnation of moral evil, sin, devastation, and death in the Hebrew Bible and how this symbolization of a particular gender interconnects with issues of race/ethnicity, class, and colonialism during the times of its production."[25] Her work thus has two levels of analysis: an *extrinsic* one that draws on social-scientific methods for exploring the ways women's lives are constructed and constrained by the modes of production and ideologies in the societies that produce the Bible and an *intrinsic* analysis that investigates the rhetorical strategies of the text itself to see how text inscribes and reworks ideologies.[26] One challenge for bridging the social and literary worlds is that descriptions of social worlds are also "texts" produced in a time and place that have their own ideological assumptions and interests.

---

ence; (5) critically assess (in theological and/or ethical-political terms) the rhetoric of the text in terms of its function for the audience's self-understanding and community formation (*Rhetoric and Ethic*, 125–28).

24. Antoinette Clark Wire, *The Corinthian Women Prophets: A Reconstruction through Paul's Rhetoric* (Minneapolis: Fortress, 1990), 1.

25. Gale A. Yee, *Poor Banished Children of Eve: Women as Evil in the Hebrew Bible* (Minneapolis: Fortress, 2003), 1.

26. Ibid., 4–5. Yee defines her overall method as ideological criticism and utilizes feminist and Marxist-materialist ideology critique for her analysis. For a Christian Testament approach to fusing of literary and socio-historical methods, see Elaine M. Wainwright, *Women Healing/Healing Women: The Genderization of Healing in Early Christianity* (London: Equinox, 2006).

4. AUTHORITY AND THE READER

As women in the feminist movement claimed the authority of their experience and began to tell their stories, feminist biblical scholars began to attend more closely to the text-as-story and the interpreter as reader. It is apropos that a book proposing feminist reading strategies of biblical narrative is entitled: *She Can Read*.[27] Locating the meaning-making process among interpreters and their interactions with texts exposes the locatedness of authoritative readings and immediately raises the challenge of multiple interpretations, including a consideration of both differences and similarities among readers. Mainstream reader-response criticism constructs an implied ideal reader who is usually also an unacknowledged male elite reader. Many feminist and other ethnic-minority scholars have variously focused on actual, flesh-and-blood readers. This attention to readers has resulted in feminist interest in reception history, autobiographical criticism, and the use of diverse readers' stories to reread the biblical text for different contexts.

Reader-oriented feminist interpreters inquire after the experience of the reader in the communication event, attending to what the text *does*, or what effects it has.[28] In 1978, Judith Fetterly called attention to the effects of reading conventions on women, suggesting that patriarchal texts produce an "immas-culated" female reader who identifies with the implied male reader and there-fore internalizes the misogyny and androcentric privileging of the text.[29] For many interpreters, feminist conscientization provides a solution: "Once a woman is aware of immasculation, she can read as a feminist…. She recog-nizes that she and other feminists can resist or affirm the text, read it against the grain or transform it for feminist use."[30] The resisting feminist reader, therefore, is not a reader who simply rejects the text. Rather, she is a reader empowered to evaluate and revision the text. Janice Capel Anderson suggests that the female reader who self-consciously takes up the role of the implied

---

27. Emily Cheney, *She Can Read: Feminist Reading Strategies for Biblical Narrative* (Valley Forge, Penn.: Trinity, 1996).

28. Three questions explored by reader-response criticism: (1) What role does the reader or hearer of a text play in creating the meaning of a text? (2) Who is the reader/hearer? (3) What is the experience of reader or listening to a text like? (Elizabeth Struthers Malbon and Janice Capel Anderson, "Literary-Critical Methods," in *A Feminist Introduction* [vol. 1 of *Searching the Scriptures*; ed. Elisabeth Schüssler Fiorenza with Shelly Matthews; New York: Crossroad, 1993], 248).

29. Judith Fetterley, *The Resisting Reader: A Feminist Approach to American Fiction* (Bloomington: Indiana University Press, 1978); see also Eryl W. Davies, *The Dissenting Reader: Feminist Approaches to the Hebrew Bible* (Aldershot, U.K.: Ashgate, 2003).

30. Malbon and Anderson, "Literary-Critical Methods," 251.

reader in the Gospel of Matthew is "free to judge the ideological stances of the various character groups, male and female. In following the guidance of the narrative, the reader may also be led to judge some of the patriarchal assumptions implicit in their ideological viewpoints."[31]

The notion of a resisting or dissenting feminist reader has been influential in feminist biblical interpretation. However, it has also been a site of important debate. In her 1991 article on African American women's reading practices, Renita Weems explores the disjunction between the Bible's use in the subjugation of African Americans and its revered place in the lives of many African American women—a seemingly nondissenting readerly position. Drawing on reader-response criticism, Weems outlines how African American women's reading takes place in a sociohistorical context where the dominant reading practice requires bracketing personal experience and values in favor of "letting the text speak for itself." Weems recounts the story of Howard Thurman's grandmother claiming her right to reject or resist harmful parts of the text, and suggests that "the experience of oppression has forced the marginalized reader to retain the right, as much as possible, to resist those things within the culture and the Bible that one finds obnoxious or antagonistic to one's innate sense of identity and to one's basic instincts for survival."[32] As with claiming the right to read at all, reading in a way that defies dominant reading conventions—that is, by bringing one's own experience and needs into dialogue with the text—is a subversive act. This approach emphasizes the *extrinsically-*formed reading practices as constitutive to meaning rather than locating feminist (or womanist) reading in the orientation of the female reader to the implied/idealized reader.

Importantly, Weems also points out that both the process of immasculation and dissenting reading occur in contexts marked as much by class and race as by gender. Thus, the immasculation of a female reader means being taught/trained by the reading process to identify with "a certain kind of man."[33] Although white women's voices have been suppressed within the Euro-American tradition, white women have also benefitted from and contributed to the dominant culture.[34] As with the implied reader, neither the

---

31. Janice Capel Anderson, "Matthew, Gender, and Reading," *Semeia* 28 (1983): 3–27, here 23.

32. Renita J. Weems, "Reading *Her Way* through the Struggle: African American Women and the Bible," in *Stony the Road We Trod: African American Biblical Interpretation* (ed. Cain Hope Felder; Minneapolis: Augsburg Fortress, 1991), 57–77, here 63.

33. Ibid., 67.

34. Ibid. Thus the "implied she is really the implied 'Other' and might include subordinate men as well as women" (Aichele, *The Postmodern Bible*, 61).

"female" nor the "feminist" reader is an unlocated position. As a result of contributions such as Weems's (and Yee's, above), attention to located readers and to the intersections of systems of domination (such as race, class, status, etc.) is a critical requirement for what constitutes feminist theory and practice for many interpreters.

One of the results of reader-oriented criticism has been to introduce diversity and multiplicity as categories of critical deliberation. Can there be *one* meaning of a text? Can there be *a* feminist reading of a text? If the answer to both of these questions is no, then how does one choose among meanings? Are the possible effects of one's reading legitimate criteria? Where are these questions negotiated? Is biblical scholarship accountable to diverse reading communities within or outside it? Shifting to an understanding of meaning *produced in the reading process in diverse contexts* thus implicitly raises many questions of accountability.

5. The Rhetoric and Ethics of Interpretation

For many narrative and reader-oriented feminist critics, there is a decided turn away from historical questions, even those about ancient women's traditions, perspectives, or experiences. This is explained both in the shift away from understanding texts as windows onto reality as well as the recognition that historical-criticism is a located discourse—one that reflects Euro-American interests and questions. Historical questions have not been prominent among feminist (or non-white women) interpreters in Two-Thirds World and U.S. minoritized contexts.[35] An emphasis on questions about texts and readers rather than on ancient Israelite or Greco-Roman cultures allows for the biblical text to be relevant to women's lives in contemporary contexts, as well as for academic biblical studies to be opened up to a wider range of scholarly questions.[36] In part, the critique of historical criticism is part of the larger political critique of biblical studies' ethnocentric, Christian, and colonialist heritage and structures.

---

35. One of the risks of this turn away from historical questions is that the anti-Judaism of the Christian Testament (and its history of interpretation) is not always recognized and engaged. For a conversation among Jewish and Two-Thirds World women on this problem, see Amy-Jill Levine, "The Disease of Postcolonial New Testament Studies and the Hermeneutics of Healing," *JFSR* 20.1 (2004): 91–99.

36. Early on, Mary Ann Tolbert asked whether "*any* historical reconstruction can form the basis for Christian faith and practice" ("Defining the Problem: The Bible and Feminist Hermeneutics," *Semeia* 28 [1983]: 124).

While there is debate among feminists as to the extent to which feminist interpreters should continue to engage historical questions,[37] there is general recognition that the objective and scientific or value-free epistemological structures of the discipline are indefensible. No reading is context free or universal in its perspective. The production of knowledge about the Bible is a political practice. Because feminists and other minoritized scholars have frequently been forthright about their social location and interpretive interests, their work has often been classified as "ideological," a term that functions in this context as largely synonymous with "political."[38] While this naming correctly identifies the ethical-political nature of these kinds of interventions, relegating feminist and other minority criticisms to a subcategory of the discipline labeled "ideological" also masks the ideological-political nature of *all* interpretation and exempts supposedly nonideological interpretations from reflecting on their accountability to readers and the effects of their interpretations.

The most influential voice calling attention to the politics the field as a whole is Elisabeth Schüssler Fiorenza, whose 1987 Society of Biblical Literature presidential address drew on a rhetorical-political understanding of knowledge to call for a shift in how the discipline understands itself. Schüssler Fiorenza has pressed for a rhetorical understanding of the entire field that recognizes that "biblical interpretation, like all scholarly inquiry, is a communicative practice that involves interests, values, and visions."[39] Marking the rhetorical context of her own speaking as a woman in the academy, Schüssler

---

37. See Elisabeth Schüssler Fiorenza, "Re-visioning Christian Origins," in *Christian Origins: Worship, Belief, and Society* (ed. Kieran O'Mahoney; London: Sheffield Academic Press, 2003), 225–50.

38. In the two editions of *To Each Its Own Meaning*, only the essays on feminist and socioeconomic criticism are marked as political, with the titles: "Reading the Bible Ideologically: Feminist Criticism" and "Reading the Bible Ideologically: Socioeconomic Criticism." All of the other chapters in the book are simply labeled by their type of criticism. Apparently, such criticisms as source, canonical, social-scientific, or poststructuralist are not "reading ideologically." See Steven L. McKenzie and Stephen R. Haynes, eds., *To Each Its Own Meaning: An Introduction to Biblical Criticisms and their Application* (1993; 2nd ed.; Louisville: Westminster John Knox, 1999). In a nonpejorative sense, ideological critique requires that readers "own their own commitments and agendas, which can be difficult and uncomfortable" for many biblical scholars, given that "ideology is usually what the Other has" (Tina Pippin, "Ideology, Ideological Criticism, and the Bible" *CR:BS* 4 [1996]: 51–78, here 51).

39. Elisabeth Schüssler Fiorenza, "The Ethics of Biblical Interpretation: Decentering Biblical Scholarship," *JBL* 107 (1988): 3–17; cited in its reprinted version in *Rhetoric and Ethic*, 17–30.

Fiorenza challenged biblical scholars to adopt a new *rhetoric of inquiry*, one that recognizes and evaluates the prevailing epistemological and pedagogical frameworks of the discipline that mask its interests and values in scientific-objectivist terms. Whether or not they recognize it, all biblical scholars are part of contemporary meaning production about the Bible. Understanding the field itself as a rhetorical-political formation that shapes wo/men's lives and voices leads to analytical questions about how scholarly constructions perform ideological work, what questions are allowed and asked, and what categories, models, and images are used and to what effect.[40]

This interest in the politics of biblical interpretation is reflected in Schüssler Fiorenza's rhetorical method (see n. 23). Because *both* biblical texts and their interpretations produce kyriarchal conceptions of reality, the first stage of interpretation must be to articulate the social location and analyze the rhetoric of interpretations. Interpretations have rhetorical contexts and cannot simply produce a new scholarly-authoritative interpretation of the text; thus as a last step one must also evaluate and revision the theological and/or political-ethical visions and values of the text and the interpretation. Because the feminist movement challenges biblical scholarship to be account-able for its relationship to liberation struggles against kyriarchal oppressions, Schüssler Fiorenza views these steps as essential to rhetorical criticism with a feminist perspective. For this reason, she has critiqued literary and rhetorical approaches that remain with the text, do not critically reflect on the rhetori-cal context and political-ethical goals and effects of interpretation, or do not move to a constructive feminist revisioning.[41] The challenge is that feminist and other politically-engaged scholarship not simply produce new methods or readings, but transform the discipline and contribute to social change. These wide-scope interests are apparent in Schüssler Fiorenza's unfolding articulation of a rhetorical-emancipatory paradigm of biblical interpretation as a paradigm rooted in the social-political movements for change, which is theorized and practiced both at the micro-level of wo/men's lives and at the

---

40. See ibid., 196–97. For a summary, see Melanie Johnson-DeBaufre, *Jesus Among Her Children: Q, Eschatology, and the Construction of Christian Origins* (HTS 55; Cam-bridge, Mass.: Harvard University Press, 2006), 11–17.

41. See Elisabeth Schüssler Fiorenza, *But She Said* (Boston: Beacon, 1992), 34–40; and Schüssler Fiorenza, *Rhetoric and Ethic*, 83–104. For an example of a literary-critical reading that includes a feminist revisioning—in this case of the silence of the women in the Gospel of Mark—see Joan L. Mitchell, *Beyond Fear and Silence: A Feminist-Literary Reading of Mark* (New York: Continuum, 2001), 50–56, 108–113.

macrostructural levels of ideology, language, power relationships, and institutional practices.[42]

Notions of working for change, however, raise the issue of the diversity of feminist politics. For example, Elizabeth Castelli's examination of Paul's rhetoric of imitation exposes the tendency among biblical scholars to identify with and replicate Paul's authority, which is constructed on a model of privileging identification (but not equality) between leader and follower.[43] Castelli evaluates Paul's rhetoric of identity-as-sameness as part of a drive toward unity/universalism. Drawing on the postmodern critique of modernism (via Foucault and Derrida) and the challenges raised to feminism and liberation theology by minoritized and postcolonial critics, Castelli articulates a politics that affirms difference over a drive toward equality. In her reading of gender in Revelation using reader-response, postmodern, and Marxist-materialist literary criticism, Tina Pippin does not find humanist values and visions in the book's vision of the end of the world, but rather an "apocalypse of women" in which misogyny and violence are root features. Rather than translating Revelation for contemporary struggles, Pippin seeks to expose its misogyny and violence because "the Apocalypse is decolonizing literature that turns around and recolonizes."[44] The fact that the feminist scholars discussed in this article do not agree on the nature of feminist political values and goals suggests that feminist interpretation must routinely include deliberation and debate about the nature of feminist politics as much as a stated commitment to them.

This raises a final issue about accountability in interpretation. Accountability to whom? To the church? To the academy? To the poor and oppressed? To the feminist movement? To democratic society? Feminist interpreters have differed on their answer to these questions in ways that reflect their own locations of communication and the attendant exigencies of that context. For example, as this volume attests, the form, target audience, and content of feminist work is often shaped by the constraints and needs of the author's context. This suggests that once we have asserted that texts have social-ideological power and that readers participate in making meaning, the feminist discussion has just begun.

---

42. For the rhetorical-emancipatory paradigm, see Schüssler Fiorenza, *Rhetoric and Ethic*, 44–55.

43. Elizabeth Castelli, *Imitating Paul: A Discourse of Power* (Louisville: Westminster John Knox, 1991).

44. Tina Pippin, *Death and Desire: The Rhetoric of Gender in the Apocalypse of John* (Lousiville: Westminster John Knox, 1992), 47, 56.

Feminist Biblical Historiography

Shelly Matthews
Brite Divinity School, Texas Christian University

This essay considers methods employed in the writing of feminist biblical history in the late twentieth century along with issues of central concern in these historical narratives. The plethora of scholarship produced on this topic makes the undertaking both celebratory and daunting—celebratory, owing to the substantial nature of the corpus under consideration; daunting, owing to the necessity of shorthand in an article constrained by limitations of space.

Much historiographic energy in this time period has been devoted to the project of retrieval—of restoring wo/men[1] to the historical record. Thus, methods employed in these retrieval projects, beginning in the late 1970s and flourishing to the end of the twentieth century, receive considerable attention here. I will then consider other questions of power, identity, and ideology that feminist biblical scholars have engaged in their historical narratives.

1. Historical Retrieval: Documenting Wo/men's Roles, Contributions and Struggles in Ancient Israel, Second Temple Judaism, and the Early Christian Era

In this first and necessarily largest section, I outline key methods employed to document wo/men's presence in biblical periods, beginning with methods employed with particular efficacy in reading biblical texts. I then turn

---

1. I adopt the neologism wo/men, introduced by Elisabeth Schüssler Fiorenza as a means to signal that women are not all the same but rather experience the world differently owing also to structures of race, class, ethnicity, religion, sexuality, and colonialism. This neologism also signals the inclusion of subaltern men who in kyriarchal systems are seen "as wo/men." I also employ the neologism *kyriarchy*, coined by Schüssler Fiorenza as an alternative to *patriarchy*, as a means of signaling the multiplicative and intersecting structures of domination. See Elisabeth Schüssler Fiorenza, *Rhetoric and Ethic: The Politics of Biblical Studies* (Minneapolis: Fortress, 1999), ix.

to consider how feminist scholars engaged extrabiblical materials and also employed models from the social sciences in their reconstructive work. Finally, I introduce theoretical frameworks proposed by these scholars to account for wo/men's presence and prominence in various historical periods.

1.1. RETRIEVAL STRATEGIES FOCUSED ON THE BIBLICAL TEXT

1.1.1. Shifting Lenses to Find the Wo/men "in Plain Sight"

One of the legacies of kyriocentric biblical interpretation has been to occlude the presence and agency even of those wo/men who are acknowledged in biblical texts, and one strategy for restoring these women to history has been to adopt lenses that allow them to be seen. Feminist exegesis of Rom 16 illustrates both that some women in biblical history are hidden "in plain sight," and that a prerequisite for retrieving even these women leaders in the early Jesus movement is a scholarly imagination allowing for such a possibility.[2] In this final chapter of Romans, Paul greets several women as missionaries and coworkers. Consider Phoebe, hailed by Paul as *adelphēs, diakonos,* and *prostatēs* (Rom 16:1–2); and Junia, who, with Andronicus, is marked as "prominent among the apostles" (16:7). In traditional exegesis, Phoebe's leadership titles are diminished and mistranslated, so that instead of receiving the relatively high status of a "minister"[3] and "presider (or ruler),"[4] she becomes a "deaconess" and "benefactor," the rough equivalent of a member of a modern Christian ladies auxiliary. Furthermore, while the missionary partner of Andronicus, greeted in the accusative *Iounian,* was regarded by authors of the early church as Junia, the female partner of Andronicus, exegetes since the time of Aegidius of Rome (1245–1316 C.E.) began to insist that Paul was addressing a male, Junias, and not a female, Junia, with this apostolic title, in spite of the fact that the male name Junias is otherwise unattested in Greek or Latin inscriptions. For centuries after Aegidius, traditional scholarship simply

---

2. Bernadette Brooten, "Junia—Outstanding among the Apostles (Romans 16:7)," in *Women Priests: A Catholic Commentary on the Vatican Declaration* (ed. Leonard J. Swidler and Arlene Swidler; New York: Paulist, 1977), 141–44; Elisabeth Schüssler Fiorenza, "Missionaries, Apostles, Coworkers: Romans 16 and the Reconstruction of Women's Early Christian History," *WW* 6 (1986): 420–33.

3. Cf. this translation choice for the male *diakonos* Tychicus in Col 4:7 (NRSV); and see also Elizabeth Castelli, "*Les Belles Infidèles*/Fidelity or Feminism? The Meanings of Feminist Biblical Translation," in *A Feminist Introduction* (vol. 1 of *Searching the Scriptures*; ed. Elisabeth Schüssler Fiorenza; New York: Crossroad, 1993), 189–204.

4. Compare the NRSV translation of *ho proistamenos* at Rom 12:8 as "the leader" and the translation of *proestōtes presbyteroi* as "the elders who rule" at 1 Tim 5:17.

assumed that since women could not have been apostles, the apostolic partner of Andronicus could not have been a woman.[5] However, with the introduction of a feminist lens in the field of Christian Testament studies, the view of what was historically possible has again shifted, so that the leadership titles ascribed to these women are read as indications of a network of early believers in Jesus in which leadership is assumed by wo/men as well as men.

Uncovering wo/men in plain sight has also involved attention to the intersecting nature of gender, class, sexuality, and ethnicity, in order to privilege textual materials that have been neglected for reasons other than gender bias alone. Clarice Martin, for example, in writing of the Ethiopian chamberlain in Acts 8, refocuses on the chamberlain's ethnographic identity, analyzing how a "politics of omission has been operative in perpetuating a lack of familiarity with Ethiopians in antiquity and in contemporary culture."[6]

Of course, given the andro-kyriocentric nature of the biblical texts, most attempts at retrieving wo/men's history from the biblical periods have required more than a simple adjustment of lenses in order to foreground wo/men who are already featured within the text. As Elisabeth Schüssler Fiorenza has famously argued, visible wo/men in biblical texts should be considered as representing merely "the tip of the iceberg" in terms of wo/men's historical struggles and agency.[7] I turn now to strategies of reading kyriocentric biblical language against the grain and with a hermeneutics of suspicion in order to find traces of wo/men's agency and presence that are submerged beneath the text.

1.1.2. Recognizing the Rhetorical: Reading Biblical Texts as Prescriptive, Not Descriptive

Texts in both the Hebrew Bible and the New Testament seek to restrict wo/men's participation in cultic life, and either presume or explicitly exhort the submission of wo/men to their husbands, masters, or fathers.[8] Feminists have responded to this kyriarchal tendency in biblical texts by noting that this lan-

---

5. Brooten, "Junia."

6. Clarice Martin, "A Chamberlain's Journey and the Challenge of Interpretation for Liberation," *Semeia* 47 (1989): 105–35, here 105.

7. See, for example, Elisabeth Schüssler Fiorenza, *In Memory of Her: A Feminist Theological Reconstruction of Christian Origins* (New York: Crossroad, 1983), 54.

8. See, for example, Judith Plaskow, *Standing Again at Sinai: Judaism from a Feminist Perspective* (New York: HarperCollins, 1991), 25–74, on women's invisibility at the entry into the Sinai Covenant; Phyllis Bird, "The Place of Women in the Israelite Cultus," in *Women in the Hebrew Bible* (ed. Alice Bach; New York: Routledge, 1999), 3–20.

guage does not reflect social reality, but is rather the skewed attempt of an elite minority to prescribe exclusion and subordination. Feminists have worked to reconstruct historical narratives in which wo/men feature more centrally, both by drawing from extra-canonical texts and through employment of models from the social sciences inflected by gender concerns and reconstructive practices which will be elaborated more fully below.

Here I note that, even from reading the prescriptions in the biblical text alone, it has been possible to do some reconstructive work on the principle that the more shrill the authorial voice rings, the more plausible it is to assert the agency and/or leadership of wo/men that this voice opposes. On this principle, both Silvia Schroer and Susan Ackerman have read prophetic condemnations of goddess worship in the Hebrew Bible (e.g., Jer 7:16–20; 44:15–19, 25; Ezek 8:14) as signs of sixth-century Israelite women's religious practice apart from the Yahweh cult.[9] Or, as Linda Maloney has argued on the grounds that the Pastoral Epistles are patriarchal and androcentric "almost to the point of absurdity," the author of these epistles is "a frightened would-be authority on the defensive against powerful and intelligent opponents who are *not* attackers from the outside, but are themselves … active leaders within their local communities." Reading against the grain of his proscriptions, insults and attacks, she posits communities of women who "preach, teach, prophesy, travel, preside at worship and preserve certain 'Pauline' traditions that are anathema to the author."[10]

1.1.3. Recognizing the Rhetorical: Decentering Biblical Authors to Reconstruct Other Voices within the Text

Recognizing that all biblical texts are "rhetorical … multivoiced, and tensive-conflictive"[11] makes it possible to employ rhetorical criticism in order to reconstruct competing views of those to whom the text is addressed. This reading strategy has been employed to particularly good effect on the Pauline correspondence. Such decentering provides a hearing for participants in the

---

9. Silvia Schroer, "Diachronic Sections," in *Feminist Interpretation: The Bible in Women's Perspective* (ed. Luise Schottroff et al.; Minneapolis: Fortress, 1998), 109–44; Susan Ackerman, *Under Every Green Tree: Popular Religion in Sixth-Century Judah* (Atlanta: Scholars Press, 1992).

10. Linda Maloney, "The Pastoral Epistles," in *A Feminist Commentary* (vol. 2 of *Searching the Scriptures*; ed. Elisabeth Schüssler Fiorenza; New York: Crossroad, 1994), 361–80, here 361–62.

11. Schüssler Fiorenza, *Rhetoric and Ethic*, 196.

early *ekklesia* beyond "that Man, Paul," who has been granted colossal status in mainstream Christian tradition. [12]

One way of decentering Paul has been to assess pre-Pauline creeds, prayers, and hymns contained within the Pauline epistles, apart from Paul's own employment of them. Because these liturgical formulas are not authored by Paul, but rather represent earlier communal theological expressions that Paul subsequently incorporated into his letters, feminist scholars regard them as resources for reconstructing a multivoiced *ekklesia* in which Paul is but one speaker among many.[13]

The most well-known pre-Pauline formula related to questions of gender, status, and agency in the early *ekklesia* is the baptismal formula preserved in Gal 3:28, proclaiming that, among those who have been baptized into Christ, "there is no longer Jew or Greek; there is no longer slave nor free, there is no longer male and female; for all of you are one in Christ Jesus." By detaching the formula from its rhetorical context in Galatians, feminist scholars have shifted the focus concerning the formula's significance from the question of "what Paul really meant" by these words, and related debates about whether Paul himself had egalitarian tendencies to the question of how it might have functioned in other settings.

Reading Gal 3:28 apart from Paul's use of it is one tool in Antoinette Wire's arsenal as she subjects the whole of 1 Corinthians, a letter in which sex, gender, and authority are key points of contestation, to rhetorical criticism. In her work, Wire dislodges Paul as an oracular figure and places the women prophets of Corinth at the center of the debate. This enables her to acknowledge the role of Gal 3:28 in shaping resistance to Paul in Corinth

---

12. Cynthia Briggs Kittredge, "Rethinking Authorship in the Letters of Paul: Elisabeth Schüssler Fiorenza's Model of Pauline Theology," in *Walk in the Ways of Wisdom: Essays in Honor of Elisabeth Schüssler Fiorenza* (ed. Shelly Matthews et al.; Harrisburg, Penn.: Trinity, 2003), 318–33. The method of decentering has also been applied in Gospel studies by those who shift focus away from Jesus as central, and toward the communal *basileia movement* which included wo/men such as Mary Magdalene and Mary and Martha of Bethany. See Mary Rose D'Angelo, "Reconstructing 'Real' Women from Gospel Literature: The Case of Mary Magdalene," in *Women and Christian Origins* (ed. Ross Kraemer and Mary Rose D'Angelo; New York: Oxford University Press, 1999), 105–28. On decentering Jesus, see also Melanie Johnson-DeBaufre, *Jesus among Her Children: Q, Eschatology, and the Construction of Christian Origins* (HTS 55; Cambridge: Harvard University Press, 2005); and Elisabeth Schüssler Fiorenza, *Jesus: Miriam's Child, Sophia's Prophet: Critical Issues in Feminist Christology* (New York: Continuum, 1994).

13. On the implications of decentering the pre-Pauline Christ hymns, see Cynthia Briggs Kittredge, *Community and Authority: The Rhetoric of Obedience in the Pauline Tradition* (HTS 45; Harrisburg, Penn.: Trinity, 1998).

in the matter of head coverings and women's prophecy. It also allows her to reconstruct empathetic and plausible theological viewpoints articulated by women, apart from Paul, on matters of wisdom, celibacy, women's authority, and the resurrection.[14]

1.2. Retrieval Strategies That Move beyond the Canon

1.2.1. Extracanonical Texts

Another avenue for retrieving wo/men's history from the biblical period has been to consider roughly contemporary texts that stand outside of the kyriarchal-androcentric canonization process.[15] In her history of female homoeroticism in the ancient world, Bernadette Brooten casts a wide net beyond the one verse commonly associated with such sexual practices (Rom 1:26), considering sources as disparate as Greek erotic spells, astrological texts, artistic representations, and medical texts.[16] A number of contributors to *Women Like This* also work to reconstruct Jewish women's history in the Greco-Roman world through reading extrabiblical narratives such Ben Sira, Tobit, Judith, and the Maccabees.[17]

Because of the prominence of their female protagonists, the Gospel of Mary and the Apocryphal Acts have also been scrutinized by feminist interpreters. Though the Gospel of Mary is generally dated no earlier than the last decade of the first century, and other so-called "gnostic" traditions in which Mary Magdalene features date even later, these traditions remember Mary as an authoritative figure, a primary confidant of Jesus, and a teacher and comforter of the disciples in his absence. Karen King, Jane Schaberg, and Ann Brock have used these texts to supplement and challenge canonical traditions concerning Mary, making the case that Mary was revered in many early Christian circles.[18]

---

14. Antoinette Clark Wire, *The Corinthian Women Prophets: A Reconstruction through Paul's Rhetoric* (Minneapolis: Fortress, 1990). See also Schüssler Fiorenza, *Rhetoric and Ethic*, 149–73.

15. See Denise Buell in this volume.

16. Bernadette Brooten, *Love Between Women: Early Christian Responses to Female Homoeroticism* (Chicago: University of Chicago Press, 1996).

17. Amy-Jill Levine, ed., *"Women Like This": New Perspectives on Jewish Women in the Greco-Roman World* (Atlanta: Scholars Press, 1991).

18. Jane Schaberg, *The Resurrection of Mary Magdalene: Legends, Apocrypha, and the Christian Testament* (New York: Continuum, 2004); Karen L. King, *The Gospel of Mary of Magdala: Jesus and the First Woman Apostle* (Santa Rosa, Calif.: Polebridge, 2003); Ann

The Apocryphal Acts have been a significant retrieval site, owing to the prominence of their elite female heroines, who serve as the focal point of resistance in defying kyriarchal institutions of household and city. Of these texts, the Acts of Thecla is particularly salient to feminist New Testament scholars, because of its relatively early date and the thematic relationship between it and the Pastoral Epistles. While noting that the Thecla text might be dated to the late second century, Dennis McDonald posited an oral *Vorlage* dating to the time of the Pastoral Epistles. He argued that the Acts of Thecla, read against the Pastoral Epistles, bears witness to a second-century Christian struggle over the legacy of Paul in which gender and authority are key points of contestation. The Thecla text, through its depiction of Paul as authorizing a woman's self-baptism and her subsequent teaching ministry, stands against the rival assertion that "Paul," the pseudonymous author of 1 and 2 Timothy and Titus, prescribes marriage, childbearing, and women's silence in church. McDonald also made the historical argument that women were responsible for the oral transmission of Thecla stories, and were also the primary audience for these tales.[19]

1.2.2. Retrieval Strategies Incorporating Nontextual Materials and Methods from the Social Sciences

A number of feminists engaged in reconstructive projects have turned to the disciplines of anthropology, sociology and social history, along with archeological and epigraphical materials, to provide a profile of women's agency and presence in the biblical period unattainable from textual sources alone.

Some have focused on epigraphic materials, considering these sources less beholden to the androcentric-kyriarchal interests of narrative prose. Relying primarily on inscriptional evidence from Hellenistic and Roman periods (along with synagogue archeology), Bernadette Brooten argues that leadership titles associated with women in the ancient synagogue, including "leader," "elder," "mother," and "priest" should be understood as functional

---

Graham Brock, *Mary Magdalene, the First Apostle: The Struggle for Authority* (Cambridge: Harvard University Press, 2003).

19. Dennis Ronald MacDonald, *The Legend and the Apostle: The Battle for Paul in Story and Canon* (Philadelphia: Westminster, 1983). See also Steven L. Davies, *The Revolt of the Widows: The Social World of the Apocryphal Acts* (Carbondale: Southern Illinois University Press, 1980); and Virginia Burrus, *Chastity as Autonomy: Women in the Stories of Apocryphal Acts* (Lewiston, N.Y.: Mellon, 1987). For a summary of these women-centered accounts of the Apocryphal Acts, and subsequent response, see Shelly Matthews, "Thinking of Thecla: Issues in Feminist Historiography," *JFSR* 17.2 (2001): 39–55.

rather than honorific.[20] Others who have worked with inscriptions and papyri to supplement and counter the androcentric-kyriarchal canonical perspective on Jewish women in antiquity include Ross Kraemer and Tal Ilan.[21] In the field of early Christian studies, Ute Eisen has turned to epigraphical evidence from tombstone inscriptions, along with a selection of papyri, to supplement texts that document women office holders in the early church. She has retrieved epigraphic attestation to women serving in the church as apostles, prophets, teachers of theology, presbyters, enrolled widows, and even bishops.[22]

Carol Meyers has been a pioneer in using archeological remains along with models from social anthropology to sketch the roles of women and gender relationships in premonarchical Israelite society. Focusing on rural village settlements in the highlands of Israel, Meyers has argued that because the household was the central economic unit in these societies, women's roles in this subsistence economy were substantial, and included responsibilities for food preparation and allocation, the making of subsistence crafts, and the nurturing and education of children (including the teaching of at least rudimentary literacy). While conceding that gender hierarchies, so pronounced in the monarchical period, may have existed in "incipient" forms in these village societies, she argues: "Female power deriving from the various roles ... played by women in the complex peasant households enabled them to minimize or offset whatever formal authority was held by males. Assumptions of male dominance and female subservience in ancient Israel ... may be part of the 'myth' of male control masking a situation of male dependence."[23]

Others who have turned to the social sciences in their projects of retrieval include Ross Kraemer, who adopted the group-grid model first articulated by anthropologist Mary Douglass to account for women's status and roles in

---

20. Bernadette Brooten, *Women Leaders in the Synagogue* (Atlanta: Scholars Press, 1982). Brooten's work demonstrates also the importance of the feminist lens in retrieving women "in plain sight." Though many of the inscriptions treated in her work were long known, the leadership titles associated with women in them were routinely dismissed as merely honorific.

21. See, for example, Ross S. Kraemer, "Hellenistic Jewish Women: The Epigraphical Evidence," *SBLSP* 25 (1986): 183–200; Kraemer, "Non-Literary Evidence for Jewish Women in Rome and Egypt," in *Rescuing Creusa: New Methodological Approaches to Women in Antiquity* (ed. Marilyn B. Skinner; Lubbock: Texas Tech University Press, 1987) = *Helios* 13 (1986): 85–101; Tal Ilan, *Jewish Women in Greco-Roman Palestine* (Peabody, Mass.: Hendrickson, 1995), 37–40.

22. Ute Eisen, *Amtsträgerinnen im frühen Christentum: Epigraphische und literarische Studien* (Göttingen: Vandenhoeck & Ruprecht, 1996).

23. Carol Meyers, *Discovering Eve: Ancient Israelite Women in Context* (New York: Oxford, 1991), 181.

religions of the ancient Mediterranean; Kathleen Corley, who made use of anthropological insights concerning the cultural symbolism of food in her arguments about women and meals in the synoptic tradition; and Kathleen Torjeson, who employed the dualistic framework of honor and shame from anthropological studies of Mediterranean cultures to account for resistance to women's leadership in early churches.[24]

Finally, I note here retrieval projects falling under the rubric of social history. Both Luise Schottroff and Ivoni Richter Reimer have contributed social histories of early Christian women, with special attention to material circumstances of everyday life in the Roman world. This focus on women's work in the ancient world, including details of bread making and working in textile shops, and the obligations of slave women, shed light on questions of class and status among early Christians.[25] More recently, Carolyn Osiek and Margaret Macdonald have authored a social history of women in early Christian house churches, considering questions such as infant care, the vulnerability of female slaves, and wo/men's leadership within the household structure.[26]

1.3. Articulating a Theoretical Framework through Which Egalitarian and/or Utopian Impulses in Various Periods of Biblical History Might Be Traced

Hand in hand with the work of retrieving wo/men as agents and actors in biblical history has been the work of accounting for this presence, and particularly in accounting for shifts in wo/men's status and privilege across historical time periods and from various social locations.

Concerning women in ancient Israel, Carol Meyers characterized the premonarchical period as one in which the importance of women's work to the economic success of the village household resulted in a relatively high

---

24. Ross S. Kraemer, *Her Share of the Blessings: Women's Religions Among Pagans, Jews, and Christians in the Greco-Roman World* (New York: Oxford University Press, 1992); Kathleen Corley, *Private Women, Public Meals: Social Conflict in the Synoptic Tradition* (Peabody, Mass.: Hendrickson, 1993); Karen Jo Torjesen, *When Women Were Priests: Women's Leadership in the Early Church and the Scandal of Their Subordination in the Rise of Christianity* (San Francisco: HarperCollins, 1993).

25. Luise Schottroff, *Lydias ungeduldige Schwestern: Feministische Sozialgeschichte des frühen Christentums* (Gütersloh: Gütersloher, 1994); Schottroff, *Befreiungserfahrungen: Studien zur Sozialgeschichte des Neuen Testaments* (Munich: Kaiser, 1990); Ivoni Richter Reimer, *Frauen in der Apostlegeschichte des Lukas: Eine feministische-theologische Exegese* (Gütersloh: Gütersloher, 1992).

26. Carolyn Osiek and Margaret Y. MacDonald, with Janet H. Tulloch, *A Woman's Place: House Churches in Earliest Christianity* (Minneapolis: Fortress, 2006).

social status for women. This economic situation accounts for the measure of "gender unity" in biblical affirmations of household roles from this time period. She noted significant decreases in this status and privilege as Israel shifted politically from a tribal league of agricultural settlements to a monarchy with a centralized government focused on urban settlement of Jerusalem.[27]

Claudia Camp, in her study of wisdom literature of the postexilic period, pursuing a historical explanation for the prominence of the symbol of Woman Wisdom in Proverbs, proposed a shift in social situation among Israelite women after the exile. Like Meyers, she posited that the Israelite monarchy was a time of decreased social status and privilege for most Israelite wo/men. She then suggested that as those returning from exile faced difficulties in reestablishing their society, need for the "wise" wife and mother to anchor the household again became particularly keen.[28] Thus she read the prominence of both the wise woman and of the feminine, divine Sophia in Proverbs as suggestive of an elevated status for Israelite wo/men during the restoration.

In an elaborate theory of wo/men's relative prominence in Christian beginnings, Schüssler Fiorenza situated the early Jesus movement within Jewish reform movements of Palestine, a movement inspired by prophetic and wisdom traditions focusing on wholeness and holiness, in solidarity with the most powerless in society.[29] The theoretical model posited by Schüssler Fiorenza to account for these egalitarian influences was not (contrary to a frequent misreading of this work) one of pristine origins followed by patriarchal decline, but rather one of struggle between communities that argued for accommodation to patriarchal structures and mores of society and those that resisted such accommodation. As a sign of early Christian debate and struggle concerning conformity versus resistance, for example, she noted that the exhortations in the household codes to adopt the master/lord/father societal hierarchy are written at a time roughly contemporary with the Gospels of Mark and John (the last third of the first century C.E.). These Gospels, in contrast to Colossians, Ephesians, and 1 Peter, accord women "apostolic and ministerial leadership" while counseling that sufferings and persecution are an inevitable part of the countercultural *basileia* movement.

---

27. Meyers, *Discovering Eve.*

28. Claudia Camp, *Wisdom and the Feminine in the Book of Proverbs* (Decatur, Ga.: Almond, 1985).

29. Schüssler Fiorenza, *In Memory of Her.* For assessment of the breadth of Schüssler Fiorenza's contribution to the project of reconstructing early Christian history, and especially of the value of her insights into the epistemological challenges to the field, see Hal Taussig, "The End of Christian Origins? Where to Turn at the Intersection of Subjectivity and Historical Craft," *RBL* 13 (2011): 1–46.

While Schüssler Fiorenza's *In Memory of Her* specifically, and feminist biblical historiographical work in general, has been dismissed as anachronistically projecting contemporary egalitarian ideals back into the first century, this work from the early 1980s could be characterized as sober and cautious about the relative nature of the egalitarian and utopian impulses it traces.[30] The models posited by these scholars to account for social situations in which women of the biblical period experienced a relative status increase and/ or achieved positions of authority and leadership were not naively utopian; rather, they presume the strong influence of androcentric and patriarchal currents standing in tension with these egalitarian traces.

2. Other Questions of Power Relations Engaged by Feminist Historiography

While the project of retrieving wo/men as historical agents and actors has been central to much feminist historiographical work in the twentieth century, feminists have also turned spotlights on the power dynamics of category construction (including gender construction), and other hegemonizing modes of employing historical narrative.

2.1. Critiquing Concepts of Essential, Orthodox, and Normative Religious Identity

One dualistic category that has been criticized in feminist historiography is the binary orthodoxy/heresy, along with the related employment of categories such as "pagan," "Canaanite religion," "goddess worshipper," "gnostic," and "heretic" as terms of derision. These scholars share the conviction that the imposition of normative categories on ancient religious practice diminishes the range of religious practice that becomes part of the historical record, and further, that the religious practices often on the "chopping block" of normativizing history are those from persons resisting androcentric-kyriarchal forces.

Susan Ackerman has been instrumental in arguing that goddess worship, performed mainly by women, was an integral part of popular religion in sixth-century Judah, and thus should be considered in accounts of Israelite religious practice. Through these arguments she joins a number of scholars of Israelite religion who emphasize the Canaanite fabric of these practices, as

---

30. See Mary Ann Beavis, "Christian Origins, Egalitarianism, and Utopia," *JFSR* 23.2 (2007): 27–49.

well as the religious pluralism of the period.[31] Elaine Pagels and Karen King scrutinize early Christian texts traditionally categorized as "Gnostic," putting human faces on members of the communities in which these texts were cherished, as a means of countering traditional Christian historiography in which they are vilified and dehumanized. They have also pointed to the gender politics of early anti-gnostic polemic, which served to diminish possibilities for wo/men's leadership.[32]

2.2. FEMINISM AND ANTI-JUDAISM

Anti-Judaism is inherent in traditional, malestream Christian assertions of supersessionism and superiority formulated against the foil of an inferior Judaism, and continues to be a problem in Christian feminist historiography as well. One indication of the intractability of the problem is that Christian feminists often unwittingly reproduce such formulations, even when they are sensitive to the problem and attempt to avoid it.

Jewish scholars such as Judith Plaskow and Amy-Jill Levine have long challenged attempts of feminist Christians to frame Jesus and /or early Christian tradition as unique and liberatory, over and against an intractably oppressive Jewish backdrop. They have raised devastating critiques, for example, against scholarship which erroneously caricatures Jewish ritual, and against the notion that Jesus' prohibition of divorce is somehow more liberating for women than practices of divorce in first-century Judaism.[33] The challenge for feminist scholars who wish to claim New Testament traditions as liberatory resources, without reinscribing anti-Judaism, as Elisabeth Schüssler Fiorenza has argued, is to "articulate a model of historical reconstruction that does not continue to assert Jesus' superiority or uniqueness but also does not deny

---

31. Ackerman, *Under Every Green Tree*. See also Susan Ackerman, "At Home with the Goddess," in *Symbiosis, Symbolism, and the Power of the Past: Canaan, Ancient Israel, and Their Neighbors from the Late Bronze Age through Roman Palaestina* (ed. William G. Dever and Seymour Gitin; Winona Lake, Ind.: Eisenbrauns, 2003), 455–68.

32. Elaine Pagels, *The Gnostic Gospels* (Random House: New York, 1979); Karen King, ed., *Images of the Feminine in Gnosticism* (Philadelphia: Fortress, 1988); King, *What is Gnosticism?* (Cambridge: Harvard University Press, 2003).

33. See, for example, Judith Plaskow, "Anti-Judaism in Christian Feminist Interpretation," in *A Feminist Introduction* (vol. 1 of *Searching the Scriptures: A Feminist Introduction*; ed. Elisabeth Schüssler Fiorenza with the assistance of Shelly Matthews; New York: Crossroad, 1993), 117–29; Amy-Jill Levine, "Anti-Judaism and the Gospel of Matthew," in *Anti-Judaism and the Gospels* (ed. William Farmer; Harrisburg, Penn.: Trinity, 1999), 9–36.

either his particularity, nor our common—i.e., feminist—yet different Jewish and Christian struggles to transform kyriarchal relations of domination."[34]

The problem of Christian, including feminist Christian, anti-Judaism becomes even more complex when viewed through the prism of global Christianity and postcolonial biblical interpretation, as a roundtable discussion in the *Journal of Feminist Studies in Religion* indicated.[35] The history of Christian anti-Judaism is tied specifically to the West, and redressing the problem has become acute in the European and North American contexts in the wake of the Holocaust. One aspect of redressing this problem has been for these scholars to avoid dualistic assertions of Christian "goodness" over Jewish "badness." For liberationist Christians from other parts of the globe, however, problems of most urgency include oppression of wo/men, the AIDS epidemic, and poverty. Political violence nearer to home, including genocide in Africa, resonate in these contexts with more urgency than the European Holocaust. In this context, those seeking to utilize the Christian Bible as an emancipatory resource may highlight Jesus' goodness as a means to critique oppressive Christian leaders and practices. The anti-Jewish framing of the gospels themselves points to the complexity of how the gospel narratives are recontextualized to other historical contexts. This conversation is ongoing, and contentions are still not assuaged. Kwok Pui-lan has offered the hopeful insight that postcolonial theory, because of its emphasis on the complexity of multiple and competing perspectives, might offer a way out of the impasse.[36]

2.3. SLAVERY IN THE BIBLICAL PERIOD

While the institution of slavery was integral to the cultures of the biblical periods, malestream scholarship on the subject has either tended to ignore the implications of that social fact or to argue that the institution in these periods was relatively benign.[37] Both Clarice Martin and Jennifer Glancy have been unwavering in their attention to slaves and the historical implications of the numerous prescriptions concerning slavery in the biblical text in order to raise questions concerning the subjectivity of slaves in early Christianity and to

---

34. Schüssler Fiorenza, *Jesus: Miriam's Child*, 72–73.

35. Roundtable Discussion, "Anti-Judaism and Postcolonial Biblical Interpretation," *JFSR* 20.1 (2004): 91–132. See also Lawrence M. Wills, "A Response to the Roundtable Discussion 'Anti-Judaism and Postcolonial Biblical Interpretation,'" *JFSR* 20.1 (2004): 189–92.

36. Round Table Discussion, "Anti-Judaism," 99–106.

37. Clarice Martin, "The Eyes Have It: Slaves in the Communities of Christ Believers," in *Christian Origins* (ed. Richard Horsley; Minneapolis: Fortress, 2005), 221–39.

expose the harshness of the institution.[38] This work has also demonstrated the merits of a framework acknowledging the intersecting nature of oppressions, rather than a dualistic frame which assumes only that women are oppressed by men. Adopting this more complex framework, Glancy has reminded us that Lydia of Acts 16, often celebrated for her role as an independent woman, is depicted also as a slave-owning head of household. Attention to the historical data suggesting that slaves were frequently used as sexual objects, along with the importance of sexual purity in the *ekklesia*, at least as this *ekklesia* is imagined by Paul, has raised troubling questions about whether, and on what terms, slaves could possibly take part in early Christian worshipping communities.

2.4. Using Women "To Think With": Reading Female Characters as Ciphers for Androcentric Ideological Agendas

Other feminist scholars analyze women characters in narratives not for the purpose of retrieving women as historical figures, but for assessing how these characters function as ciphers, used by male authors to think through the ideological problems of a particular historical period.

Under the umbrella of ideological criticism, attuned to interrelationships of material modes of production and societal ideologies, and employing social-scientific models to shed light on ancient historical circumstance, Gale Yee teases out the historical circumstances of various periods of the Hebrew Bible that lead to depictions of evilness in the female gendered body. For example, she concludes that depictions of gender relations in Gen 2–3, including the depiction of Eve as source of evil, are truly displaced class conflicts owing to shifts in modes of production from the tribal to the monarchic period.[39] She notes that the story of domination of Adam over Eve (Gen 3:16b) provides the theological rationale for the division between upper and lower classes: "As the king ruled over the farmer, so would a husband rule over his wife."[40] Likewise, the pornographic depictions of Samaria and Jerusalem as adulterous wives in Ezekiel 23 "furnish a way for the prophet to deal with the

---

38. Clarice Martin, "Polishing the Unclouded Mirror: A Womanist Reading of Revelation 18.13," in *From Every People and Nation: The Book of Revelation in Intercultural Perspective* (ed. David Rhoads; Minneapolis: Fortress, 2005), 82–109; Jennifer Glancy, *Slavery in Early Christianity* (New York: Oxford University Press, 2002).

39. For more on Gen 1–3, see Schüngel-Straumann in this volume.

40. Gale Yee, *Poor Banished Children of Eve: Woman as Evil in the Hebrew Bible* (Minneapolis: Fortress, 2003), 161.

personal and collective trauma of the conquest and exile of the Judean royal and priestly aristocracy."[41]

Elizabeth Clark, an early church historian deeply engaged in issues of language and representation raised by poststructuralist theory, argued in 1998 for a turn from projects of historical retrieval toward analyzing how gender and women are constructed in the text, and what these constructions might reveal about these texts' "social logic." Thus, for example, she shows how Gregory of Nyssa's portrayal of his sister undergirds his own theology of creation, or serves to shame his male readers who have not attained her degree of rationality and wisdom.[42] Clark's turn to analyzing the social logic of gender construction is coupled with an expressed pessimism about the future of retrieval projects, especially insofar as those projects focus on women who function as characters in ancient narratives. Yet she also acknowledges that "the lady" [sic] need not entirely "vanish" from the work of modern historians, since she "leaves her traces, through whose exploration, as they are imbedded in a larger social-linguistic framework, she lives on."[43]

3. CONCLUDING REMARKS: CONSENSUS AND CONTENTION

Although a variety of methods, social locations, and interests inform feminist historical scholarship—a phenomenon that Elizabeth Castelli has aptly celebrated as "Heteroglossia"[44]—it is possible to discern common principles undergirding it. A broad consensus holds that the Bible in its final form is a kyriocentric/androcentric text constructed in a kyriarchal/androcentric social world. Thus, feminists have devoted their energies to documenting the patriarchal/kyriarchal strategies of the biblical narrative, on the one hand, and to retrieving submerged voices and countercultural impulses, on the other. Feminists also widely repudiate Enlightenment frameworks positing objectivity and disinterestedness, acknowledging instead that all interpreters are socially located and that all interpretations have political effects. For many, this presupposition is articulated in terms of theological commitments—

---

41. Ibid., 162.

42. Elizabeth Clark, "The Lady Vanishes: Dilemmas of a Feminist Historian after the Linguistic Turn," *CH* 67 (1998): 1–31, here 28–30.

43. Ibid., 31. For further debates concerning the historical significance of women characters in the apocryphal acts, see Kate Cooper, *The Virgin and the Bride: Idealized Womanhood in Late Antiquity* (Cambridge: Harvard University Press, 1996); Matthews, "Thinking of Thecla."

44. Elizabeth A. Castelli, "Heteroglossia, Hermeneutics, and History," *JFSR* 10.2 (1994): 73–98.

commitments articulated with particular force in feminist scholarship emerging in the 1970s and 1980s—though increasing numbers of feminist scholars articulate their ideological investments apart from theological discourse.[45]

While these two principles are points of consensus, they might also be acknowledged as sites of contention. For instance, those dedicated to mapping out and condemning the kyriarchal/androcentric nature of the biblical world worry that retrieval projects shade into biblical apologetics.[46] Feminists situated outside of theological contexts have argued that those within hold to biases that skew the results of their research; the counter argument holds that those eschewing theological commitments themselves are adhering to a notion of scientific disinterestedness they purport to avow.[47] With Elizabeth Castelli, however, I see these and other points of contention among feminist historiographers signaled above not as reasons for distress, but rather as signs of the vigor of the intellectual discipline as it enters the twenty-first century.

---

45. On the significance of connections between historical and theological questions pertaining to feminist work on biblical materials, see ibid., 80–92.

46. Esther Fuchs, "The Literary Characterization of Mothers and Sexual Politics in the Hebrew Bible," in *Women in the Hebrew Bible: A Reader* (ed. Alice Bach; New York: Routledge, 1999), 127–39, here 127.

47. Castelli, "Heteroglossia," 80–82.

Different Feminist Methods and Approaches: Biblical Women's Studies

Marinella Perroni
Pontificio Ateneo S. Anselmo, Rome

1. Introduction[1]

Taking stock of the present situation of biblical women's studies involves something more than a mere glance at the numerous and often disparate works that have come into existence in practically every linguistic region of the planet, particularly during the second half of the twentieth century. Since recognition of women's studies in the most diverse academic settings is not a fait accompli, and our way of examining it and evaluating its importance is not without certain ambiguities, it is important to revisit several basic questions that are still of current interest, including those specifically pertaining to biblical studies. I hope that a review of this type can help to keep alive the internal debate within feminist biblical studies as a whole in the twenty-first century.

I consider such a discussion to be an indispensable condition to ensure the possibility of survival of feminist exegesis and its ability to establish itself

---

1. I shall refer exclusively to bibliographies that came into being during those decades. Worthy of note is Mercedes Navarro Puerto, "Boletin Bibliográfico: Biblia, mujeres, feminismo. I Parte: Biblia Hebrea," *'Ilu: Revista de Ciencias de las Religiones* 14 (2009): 231–83; and "Boletín Bibliográfico: Biblia, mujeres, feminismo. II Parte: El Nuevo Testamento y el Cristianismo primitivo," *'Ilu: Revista de Ciencias de las Religiones* 15 (2010): 205–86. This work reports on exegetical research in Spanish and Italian as well as in German and English. I have dealt with this subject in Perroni, "Lettura femminile ed Ermeueutica Feminista del NT: Status Quaestionis," *RivB* 41 (1993): 315–39; Perroni, "L'interpretazione Biblica Femminista tra Ricerca Sinottica ed Ermeneutica Politica," *RivB* 45 (1997): 439–67; Perroni, "Cent'anni di Solitudine: La Lettura Femminista della Scrittura," *Servitium* 150 (2003): 21–34.

institutionally, given that the epistemological maturity of an area of research is in direct proportion to its internal scientific debates. The internal debates within every science are rooted in speculations that are already very abstract, and they are reopened each time an effort is made to consider a theoretical or practical reality not merely as incidental or cyclical but rather as structural. Particularly because of its flexibility, women's studies must be considered a core of feminist biblical epistemology, a core that is cyclical and indispensable. Above all, to focus on its singularity means positioning it within a method-ological debate that helped to impart a scientific status to the feminist point of view during the twentieth century and to accord feminist biblical research a dialectically interlocutory specificity.

It is not insignificant that feminist thought was articulated and developed in the twentieth century. With respect to the history of the episteme, the last century was important in many ways. I shall mention two factors that seem extremely decisive. First, from the point of view of criteriology, the require-ments of political theology and liberation theory encouraged the awareness that contextual theologies do not become mere adaptations, but require the development of critical paradigms.

Second, in terms of methodology, investigative research is now charac-teristic even in theology; in addition, it provides concepts and criteria that are "open," flexible, and functional, and offers a comprehensive form of engage-ment among more disciplines. The conviction that theological reflection by Christian scholars can henceforth only be ecumenical, at least in terms of per-spective, with all that this involves not only in terms of overcoming contro-versial opposition but also from the point of view of dialogical comparison, is not underrated. We shall see the broader nuances and the importance of this statement in the course of this essay.

A final preliminary comment is indispensable because, even if in all probability it springs from resentment of my personal situation as an Ital-ian woman, it nevertheless makes it possible to identify a problem that, in a number of ways and with varying intensity, exists in other cultural circles as well. Lexically, I use the word "feminist" to indicate a broad area of research. I am well aware that this involves a certain risk, because for many scholars it could be an unwelcome classification. However, the tendency—widespread in Italy—to prefer the word "feminine" is as insidious as ever, because it is charged with ideological content that is even stronger, and for that reason more underhanded, than the content that may be attributed to the word "feminist." The preference, particularly in clerical circles, for all the variants of the term "feminine," including even "in a feminine way," reminds us that no word is "innocent." Generally speaking, therefore, I view as "feminist" all those studies that reveal—admittedly in a wide variety of approaches—a critical intentionality with respect to any kind of monocratic male system, be it linguistic or sociopolitical, material or spiritual, atheist or religious.[2]

2. Biblical Women's or Gender Studies: Some Identity Marks?

As I have already mentioned, my point of view is closely connected with my situation as a Roman Catholic, Italian, female exegete. A reading of the interesting online debate that for years has occupied scholars in various disciplines on the subject of "women's studies versus gender studies"[3] has subsequently confirmed my conviction that the distance between the English-speaking world, particularly the United States, and the Latin world, particularly Italy, is characterized by both a great diversity of horizons and a wealth of cultural intersections that are encouraged by the positioning of theological research within multidisciplinary academic circles.[4] In the United States, ideas circulate and are modified at great speed. In the Latin countries, the reactivity of scholars to, or even their participation in, the international cultural debate has in contrast slowed considerably, at least with respect to humanistic and theological studies in particular. A small number of Catholic exegetes from southern Europe have sought to encourage the importation of some subjects and problems that have been under discussion across the Atlantic, but always *iuxta modum* ("with reservations") and not without a certain perplexity. There has not been much traffic in the opposite direction. It is true that there is genuine and characteristic censorious resistance, rather than perplexity, in our academic and ecclesiastical circles. But this does not mean that the debate has not been beneficial nonetheless: no separatism, whether elitist or censorious, can henceforth be useful to any cause, still less to the cause of women.

Thus, if we compare the energy of the online debate on the implications of the transition from women's studies to gender studies, which has been

---

2. In this connection I agree with the presentation of the premises of feminist theology by Teresa Forcades i Vila, *La Teología Feminista en la Historia* (Barcelona: Fragmenta, 2011), 13–40.

3. This is just one of the innumerable voices that contribute to in-depth discussions of the *status quaestionis* of women's studies in its various articulations and possibilities, complete with suggested bibliographies. WMST-L, a veritable trove of information, is an international electronic forum for teachers, researchers, librarians, and webmasters who are involved in the study of questions concerning the academic aspect of women's studies [WMST-L File Collection].

4. In Italy, schools of theology are not part of the civil academic network. They operate under the authority of the churches. The Catholic schools of theology are under the authority of the Vatican via the pontifical schools; the others are under that of the Episcopal Conference; and the one Protestant school of theology operates under the Waldensian Church.

developing in the U.S. for years, with what has occurred in Italy, for example, we are struck by the difference even in the fundamental terms of the debate itself. In the U.S., in engaging with a subject of reflection by scholars in various disciplines on a crossdisciplinary question, such as that of the development of women's studies, we encounter a basic assumption: that the transition from women's studies to gender studies implies a denaturing loss of political drive. As soon as the word "women" disappears from women's studies, thanks to an operation of inclusion via gender, both men and women are made the center of interest. The subversive political focus on women that characterized women's studies from the beginning is indisputably weakened.

In Italy we experience a complete reversal of perspective: the practice of women's studies is academically accepted precisely because, with respect to feminist biblical studies or gender studies, it is considered free of any ideological or political implications. Often this goes hand in hand with a strong resistance to the assumption of theoretical benchmark horizons, and even more to cases of transformation characteristic of the "American" formulation, whether feminist or gender-related—frankly stated, a refusal to submit to a form of cultural colonialism considered theologically misleading.

True, it is not by accident that in Italy only a Protestant publishing house (Claudiana) refrained from posing preliminary questions to openly feminist publications, while various Catholic publishing houses cited explicit reservations concerning the publication of the series La Bibbia e le Donne (The Bible and Women), which were specifically motivated by contributions from the other side of the Atlantic. On the other hand, it is true that in Italy the small size of the biblical studies market does not allow any venturesome choice. In addition, Catholic teaching exercises an explicit or implicit pressure over editorial policies.

Some will point out that this situation is limited solely to a single country, Italy. This is only partly true. The "active resistance" to feminist exegesis is in fact more Catholic than Italian. Even when questions of principle are involved, it is not always easy to draw a clear line between what is Catholic and what is Italian. There is no doubt, however, that theoretical arguments extend far beyond the confines of a single nation, and establish themselves throughout the world with varying degrees of moderation, but nevertheless pervasively. This rings true even if, like Italy, that country is considered emblematic for Catholicity. And, starting from the closing decades of the last century, the various feminisms or questions surrounding the sex/gender binary have been presented as load-bearing elements of Catholic religious ideology.

On the other hand, resistance from academia, and not only male academia, in discussing the differences between feminist studies, women's studies, and gender studies is still widespread. In Latin countries this is not always and not only because of an ideological allergy to any discussion of the status quo that is presumably neutral and thus considered unquestionable. During the twentieth century, the tumultuous development of feminist biblical science led to the emergence of a range of hermeneutical views, with its roots in political militancy within and outside the churches. Its ideological charge, both its geo-cultural and confessional circles of dissemination, as well as its meta-confessional and meta-religious openings are aimed at a broad spectrum of revision of the traditional exegetical system. Added to this, and cutting across the various feminist approaches, is the heavy charge of methodological and also ideological "official suspicion" with respect to traditional exegesis, a suspicion that has generated aversion toward biblical scholars from Origen to Bultmann. We need only to recall the statements of Luise Schottroff that articulate the challenge to the historical-critical method in order to understand that feminist exegesis seeks to unmask the ideology/methodology nexus against any presumption of neutrality, including the neutrality ascribed to research methods and tools.[5] Paradoxically, however, this precisely reinforced official Catholic theology had always looked to the historical-critical method with great reservations.

However, while to some extent a more historiographic, political, or sociological connotation makes it possible to define the differences between women's studies, gender studies, and feminist critical theory, it is also true that in addition to being different and sometimes even divergent, they also overlap in part—at least in their intentions—since they share the same concern with (re)discovery or (re)determination of the participation of women in biblical history, with particular attention to early Christianity, an attention that goes beyond "archaeo-historical" recovery and implies instead expectations of transformation for the future.

What Teresa Forcades states with respect to feminist theology is also true for exegesis: It is a critical position that starts from an experience of contradiction, and it requires one to take a personal stance that does not necessarily signify estrangement from institutions, but instead anticipates the possibility of influencing their transformation.[6] Whatever their approach, both the theologians and the exegetes have taken up the principle of *tua res agitur*—"this concerns you"—that Rudolf Bultmann indicated as the existential purpose of any critical exegesis, and have made it at least the motivational basis for their biblical research.

---

5. Luise Schottroff, Silvia Schroer, and Marie-Theres Wacker, eds., *Feminist Interpretation: The Bible in Women's Perspective* (Minneapolis: Fortress, 1998).

6. Forcades, *La teología*, 19–20.

On the other hand, women's studies and gender studies diverge with respect to the positions they assume regarding recognition of the difference and the assessment of expression concerning the sex/gender difference. I am deliberately using the dual term "sex/gender" because it reminds us of the internal polemic surrounding gender studies with respect to the meaning to be attributed to male/female difference. This conflict, which centers on the question of whether to consider the body as a product of nature or as a social construct, is far from resolved, and it hinders the comparison of the various feminisms, namely, the feminisms of equality, distinction, and difference.[7]

The basic premises of the sex/gender difference, on the other hand, cannot always be easily identified and described, because they involve an epistemological arc that ranges from the neurosciences to jurisprudence, from physiology to anthropology, from philosophy to psychology and sociology. When documentary attention was brought to the type of historiographic research aimed at historicosocial reconstruction of contexts, it imparted great dynamism to its own analytical point of view and became more attentive to social nexi and comparisons, even if this did not necessarily include an explicit assumption of political requirements.

3. Women's Studies, Biblical Feminist Studies, and Gender Studies in Italy and Southern Europe: Identification and Critical Contestation

Despite possible simplifications, I will attempt to delineate the specific scope of women's studies, starting with what distinguishes it from biblical feminist studies and gender studies, at least through our understanding of this field of research in Italy and, as I have discovered, in other countries of southern Europe as well. What normally passes for feminist critical theory is the tendency toward a systemic development of the male/female conflict and the possibility of moving beyond it. Gender studies in turn are understood to be the application of the sociological method that involves a mirror reading from social gender roles to biblical text interpretation, thereby leaving to women's studies the task of rediscovering the figures of women present in the scriptural texts and in the interpretive traditions of scripture, without depriving such topical research of its specific critical strength. Precisely because the concept of "gender" tends to dissolve the difference between the sexes, and feminist

---

7. In this connection, see Adriana Cavarero, *Le Filosofie Femministe: Due Secoli di Battaglie Teoriche e Pratiche* (ed. Adriana Cavarero and Franco Restaino; Milan: Bruno Mondadori, 2009).

critical theory looks to an ideological approach directed toward the overcoming of sex-based oppression, it seems fundamental that historiographic recognition is obligated to ensure a useful dialectical circularity between the different approaches, and consequently rejects a position of neutrality.

Let us therefore take as the first identity mark of women's studies—as it is understood in Italy—the broad scope of topical research. In its most rigorous performance, topical research of this type has had, and continues to have, a very important function as long as its basic system is secured by the use of historical criticism or a convincing literary analysis. It makes it possible to bring a large quantity of data to light, and to reveal a network of elements that until now has remained buried under a *Wirkungsgeschichte* (history of activity) of texts markedly stamped by monosexism and directed essentially toward the centuries-old preservation of the patriarchal order among various Christian churches.[8]

The limits of a topical approach are obvious, however. The fact that this area of research often opens the way to apologetics and has been enthusiastically put to the test by male exegetes who consider it a neutral operation is an embarrassing proof. Nevertheless, because of the variety and multiplicity of results that are dependent upon various levels of exegetical competencies as well as bibliographic output, the topical approach to biblical studies enjoyed considerable dissemination at the close of the last century even in Italy. Such widespread dissemination has the merit of having helped to liberate the *topos* of "women in the Bible" from the spiritual, ascetic, or pastoral manipulations that fill both early and recent ecclesiastical tradition. Furthermore, this exposure has restored "women in the Bible" to a specific historical and literary dignity.

However, the possibility of an acknowledged dissemination of the results of this type of research is another story. Basically, the current acritical validation of postmodern theories causes women to disappear from history yet again by reducing everything to a purely textual reality. While at first it represented a favorable alternative to biblical research on women, it could be considered in the long run a more serious danger than people have often been willing to admit.[9]

---

8. In this connection the volume edited by Adriana Valerio, *Donne e Bibbia: Storia ed esegesi* (La Bibbia nella storia 21; Bologna: Dehoniane, 2006), can also be considered indicative for the Italian public.

9. On this point I am in complete agreement with Elisabeth Schüssler Fiorenza when she warns feminists of this danger in her concise critical presentation of feminist christological research in *Jesus: Miriam's Child, Sophia's Prophet: Critical Issues in Feminist Christology* (New York: Continuum, 1994), 67–87. See also the critical review of the book by

In addition to its positioning within the scope of historical research, biblical women's studies in Italy is also characterized by three other traits. First of all, this field has received academic credence, admittedly after varying degrees of effort, in the various disciplines in which increasing attention is now being paid to the integrative function of a topical reading concerned with the presence of women in history. When it is done, however, it is done in the name of an historical research free of ideological commitments. Any type of specific or systematic critical analysis is therefore omitted. Often, moreover, even for women in academia, the search for vindication represents a specific and very real struggle.

A second identity mark that attests to the growing importance of biblical women's studies is its commercial usability. For very obvious reasons, the publishing market considers subjects relating to women to be an important sales vector even in biblical circles. The attention to women figures in the Bible has had a major popular impact because it coincides with increasing access of women to biblical literacy, and also because it does not propose any explicit vindication or demand radical transformations of existing social and ecclesiastical structures. It nonetheless represents a possibility for empowerment that is well suited to new forms of feminist awareness.

There is a third identity marker of biblical research on women that can be ascribed to the area of women's studies as understood in Italy: ecclesiastical credibility. In this regard, the Italian situation offers a useful perspective. The attention paid to the subject of women in the Hebrew and Christian Scriptures, or even to a "feminine reading" of the sacred text—which is increasing even in the Italian scientific and publishing worlds—has gradually come face to face with extremely strong resistance in relation to feminist critical hermeneutics. This resistance is part of what has been defined as "the burgeoning of new theologies that has characterized and continues to characterize thinking on faith and the life of the church in Central Europe and the Americas ... theologies that also include new biblical hermeneutics and in the face of which Italy has remained a spectator."[10] The question of the relationship between theology and faith, which is often relegated to the margins of much theological and scientific exegetic output, is instead postulated as a determining factor.

Romano Penna in *RivB* 4 (1998): 496–500. The comprehensive and intelligent presentation of her thought and work by the American exegete Elizabeth Green, *Elisabeth Schüssler Fiorenza* (Novecento Teologico; Brescia: Morcelliana, 2006) is also important in this connection.

10. See Giuseppe Betori, "Tendenze attuali nell'uso e nell'interpretazione della Bibbia," in *La Bibbia nell'epoca moderna e contemporanea, La Bibbia nella storia* (ed. R. Fabris; Bologna: Dehoniane, 1992), 247–91, here 257.

Added to this is the fact that the perspective of gender is considered completely incompatible with the fundamental principles of Catholic theology. Catholic teaching has been set forth in extremely censorious terms that, at various levels of authority, leave no possibility for discussion. This situation cannot be underestimated. While in no way limited to the subject of women, it in fact calls into question the very nature of exegesis. I mention it here because I feel it represents the basis on which feminist exegesis, and particularly women's studies, are called upon to prove themselves not just in Italy but around the globe.

4. BIBLICAL WOMEN'S STUDIES: A THEOLOGICAL DISCIPLINE?

The reference here to Catholic teaching serves to focus on theological formulations that feminist research must take into account, and not only in Latin countries with a Catholic tradition. In reality, it is the theological paradigm that has strong pervasive power among women—a paradigm that is shared by other churches or is current in interfaith circles, but rarely within feminist critical theory or certain liberationist approaches. It may be painful to admit this, but it is a fact. For this reason it is important not to dismiss it as undue self-importance, but rather to discuss both its theoretical premises and its ecclesiastical functions. From this perspective, precisely women's studies, understood above all as historical research, can serve as a useful Trojan horse. In Catholic circles, the document that embodied the acceptance of feminist exegesis by the Pontifical Biblical Commission—an acceptance that positioned it among contemporary hermeneutic approaches—was a pivotal event.[11] Inasmuch as it is a document with restricted pedagogical value, the mere fact that the term "feminist" was used, and moreover was used without being coupled with detailed explanations or criticisms, was completely unexpected, and continues to some extent to have positive effects. The comprehensive document, which referred to the historical-critical method as the "progenitor of all methods," put an end to the exhausting and painful story of Catholic biblical exegesis, and finally legitimized its intersection with the historical and human sciences. That is, it put an end to any lingering antimodernism, and this is why it was so important.

In this vein, it is not arbitrary to view this document as a clear and firm reaction to the position of the then-Prefect of the Congregation for the Doctrine of the Faith, Joseph Ratzinger, who sought instead to provide orienting guidelines for an overturning of historical criticism and a return to the pri-

---

11. Pontificia Commissione Biblica, *L'interpretazione della Bibbia nella Chiesa, 1993.*

macy of dogma, including in scriptural interpretation. The text of his guidelines was widely disseminated because it was translated into a number of languages and triggered extensive debate in the world of international exegetics.[12]
It overturned the standpoint set forth in *Dei Verbum*, the Dogmatic Constitution on Divine Revelation in which Vatican II had approved the opening of
Catholic exegesis to historical research, and thus made a striking contribution
to a specific project aimed at standardization of Council guidelines. Today, as
is evident from the first two volumes of *Gesù di Nazaret* by Benedict XVI, that
text very clearly appears to be indicative of a specific program.

Ratzinger stated that feminist exegesis, together with materialist exegeses, was "a symptom of the breakdown of interpretation and hermeneutics,"
because it considers "no longer truth but rather only that which can serve as a
practice," conducted in such a way that "the contribution of religious elements
reinforces the rush to action." Feminist exegesis therefore cannot "be an interpretation of the text and its intentions,"[13] and it poses a fundamental problem
that is much more serious and radical.

These statements speak for themselves. They call out for commentary
a further discussion. When Ratzinger rejects feminist exegesis, along with
any other exegesis directed toward social transformation, the very nature of
exegesis requires, even if only involuntarily, that the discussion turn to the
heart of the problem: What is the nature of biblical exegesis, the factor that
precedes and guides any methodological choice? The answer is clear, but rich
in implications: it is the ability to understand the intentions of the text. Let us
ignore the fact that for a theologian of his stripe the intention is to identify the
"truth," and the assumption that there is complete correspondence between
truth and Church doctrine. These are assumptions that are not very useful
from an exegetical point of view.

Among exegetes, the discussion is very different, and not restricted to
finding the *intentio auctoris* and/or the *intentio textus*, the intention of the
author or the intention of the text. Biblical scholarship has problematized
such an assumption on methodological and hermeneutical grounds. Above
and beyond this problem, however, exegesis, including the exegesis of biblical
women's studies, can place the question of the meaning of the text within the
theological sciences.

Absence of a desire to subject biblical interpretation to doctrinary or
pietistic stereotyping cannot signify abstention from research into the theo-

---

12. In Italian, see Joseph Ratzinger, "L'interpretazione Biblica in Conflitto: Problemi
del Fondamento ed Orientamento Dell'esegesi Contemporanea," in *L'esegesi Cristiana Oggi*
(Casale Monferrato: Marietti, 1991), 93–125.

13. Ibid., 97.

logical meaning internal to the text, that is, abstention from evaluation of the nature of religious texts or the value of theological texts. Nor can topical research on women in Scripture be considered exempt from such research. Thus, it is precisely here that its transformational impetus can take root.

The composition and writing of the biblical texts accords with "pastoral" needs, that is, must be directed toward establishing specific community practices. Thus the interpretation of these texts also has to meet needs that are equally concrete with respect to the life of the churches. The risk of instrumentalization is not present in political exegeses any more than it is in spiritual exegeses. Exegesis that searches for the intention of texts cannot be accused of instrumentalization with fundamentalist intent. Respecting the intention of the texts in fact means also establishing whether, and on what terms, the adherence of the biblical texts to the reality of the time in which they were written opens or closes off their intrinsic potentiality for faith today. In my opinion, interpreting texts always includes the implicit but responsible assumption of a "theological pedagogy," and therefore it is not possible to cut Scripture and its interpretation off from the life of faith of the churches.

If, precisely for this reason, the defense of the theological dimension of biblical women's studies is of necessity mediated by a comprehensive critical theory, the problem is all the more difficult. I glimpse possibilities here, but also risks. As in the case of other attempts to use systematic theoretical models, I ask, first of all, whether these models can serve in the interpretation of such complex texts as the Bible, which cannot be reduced to any omni-comprehensive system and must remain nonreducible. Basically, I am asking whether such systems are an important heritage from the twentieth century, but are difficult to apply in the new century. Time will tell.

Queer Studies and Critical Masculinity Studies in Feminist Biblical Studies

Joseph A. Marchal
Ball State University

1. Introduction and Initial Context

In the previous and current centuries, feminist studies has taken many forms, made both wide and specific impacts, and interacted with a range of allied or affiliated areas of study (as evidenced by the contributions within this volume). The development of queer studies and critical studies of masculinity reflect these feminist forms, impacts, and areas of study. Indeed, the relationship among these approaches has been a fraught one, with occasionally competing (or even clashing) timelines, even as there were also striking confluences between feminist, queer, and critical masculinity studies. Certainly feminisms influenced both of these academic developments, as will become evident over the course of this survey. Yet it is useful to think of queer studies and critical masculinity studies (themselves oddly paired here), or at least the most compelling parts of them, as specific kinds of feminist studies. Their development and practices were and are particular feminist projects. These confluences and compelling connections are at least partially mirrored in the development of queer studies and critical masculinity studies within biblical studies.

2. Queer Studies (Outside of Biblical Studies)

The coining of the term "queer theory" is frequently attributed to a key essay by feminist Teresa de Lauretis, in which she calls for lesbian and gay studies to pay greater critical attention to differences within sexual minority communities in light of dynamics of gender, race, class, and geography.[1] Queer studies,

---

1. Teresa de Lauretis, "Queer Theory: Lesbian and Gay Sexualities: An Introduction," *differences: A Journal of Feminist Cultural Studies* 3 (1991): iii–xviii.

then, does not simply "belong" to lesbian and gay activists and scholars; from its beginnings, queer scholarship sought to complicate such claims to identity in parallel to the various ways in which feminist scholars were required to complicate any straightforward notions of how the category "woman" was constructed and deployed in light of womanist and *mujerista* critiques, among others. Another feminist and a founding figure for queer studies, Judith Butler, will argue in a similar vein, insisting that there is no "proper object" for queer theories. Though it has historical and topical ties to lesbian and gay studies, queer studies are not confined to the study of sexual minorities or the topic of sexuality.[2] In short, queer studies does not equal sexuality studies. Such a division of labor actually inhibits any attempt to interrogate how certain norms are created and enforced (an important aim for queer studies), particularly given how people socially construct the meaning of something like "sexuality" differently with and through gender, race, ethnicity, class, religion, age, ability, and national or colonial factors. From its inception, then, but increasingly as queer studies makes inroads and examines its own practices, intersectional forms of analysis are needed, modes that grapple with how multiple factors of power and identification intersect and reinforce each other.

The theories and perspectives that would come to define queer studies coalesced in response to and out of a number of different movements and practices in the last two decades or so of the twentieth century. Various queer theories draw promiscuously from a range of partners and participants, including feminists inside and outside of the academy, as well as historians of sexuality, scholars in lesbian and gay studies, theorists adapting poststructuralist and psychoanalytic concepts, and activists attending to a range of issues, including lesbian feminisms, rights for sexual minorities, and the AIDS crisis (many of whom adapted feminist strategies and concepts). Drawing upon the theoretical articulations of feminist standpoint epistemology, queer theory can involve a kind of eccentric subjectivity or positionality connected to lesbian and gay studies.[3] Yet queer theoretical work also tends to trouble the function of identity categories, aiming rather to identify and subvert compulsory processes of normalization and naturalization. Butler's *Gender Trouble*, for instance, is a momentous work for late twentieth-century feminist theory and an early landmark in queer theory for the ways in which it interrogated

---

2. For an interrogation of a "division of labor" in which feminists study gender and queer theorists study sexuality, see Judith Butler, "Against Proper Objects," *differences: A Journal of Feminist Cultural Studies* 6.2–3 (1994): 1–26.

3. See Teresa de Lauretis, "Eccentric Subjects: Feminist Theory and Historical Consciousness," *Feminist Studies* 16 (1990): 115–50; and David M. Halperin, *Saint Foucault: Toward a Gay Hagiography* (New York: Oxford University Press, 1995), 56–73.

such processes of identification.[4] Butler reinforces key feminist work on the social construction of both gender and sexuality, while questioning the way the category "woman" functions to stabilize problematic gender concepts and support a heteronormative framework for subjectivity.

Queer studies, then, has deep and significant roots in feminist theoretical work. This is further reflected by many, even most, of its most prominently cited and deployed thinkers: de Lauretis, Butler, Eve Kosofsky Sedgwick, and Gayle Rubin each explicitly name and work toward feminist aims.[5] More controversially for feminist scholars, though, is the influence and impact of Michel Foucault, another pivotal thinker for queer studies, whose perspective and utility are much debated between feminists of various theoretical and practical commitments.[6] Foucault's attention to the construction of discourses and their powerful effects on bodies certainly corresponds with a number of feminist trajectories, though his persistent inattention to women within such interests is admittedly curious. Nevertheless, his work has proven adaptable for both feminist and queer purposes, particularly in the ways that queer studies focuses not on stable subjectivities, but on how various subjects are disciplined by calls to be, behave, or become normal or natural.

Indeed, the relation of queer to regimes of the normal and the natural is crucial for the development of queer activism and the parallel forms it takes in the academy. The selection of this particular word is purposeful, given queer's previous (and often still current) pejorative or derogatory uses. As a term that aims to pathologize or marginalize its targets, queer means odd, abnormal, or perverse. It has been used both as slang for homosexuals and as a homophobic term aimed at those who apparently do not adequately fit (enough) with dominant points of view. Therefore, its use for a different purpose indicates a spirit

---

4. Judith Butler, *Gender Trouble: Feminism and the Subversion of Identity* (New York: Routledge, 1990).

5. See previously cited works, as well as Butler, *Bodies That Matter: On the Discursive Limits of "Sex"* (New York: Routledge, 1993); Butler, *Undoing Gender* (New York: Routledge, 2004); and Eve Kosofsky Sedgwick, *Between Men: English Literature and Male Homosocial Desire* (New York: Columbia University Press, 1985); Sedgwick, *Epistemology of the Closet* (Berkeley: University of California Press, 1990); and Gayle S. Rubin, *Deviations: A Gayle Rubin Reader* (Durham, N.C.: Duke University Press, 2011). Sedgwick's work is also influential in critical masculinity studies.

6. See, for instance, Irene Diamond and Lee Quinby, eds., *Feminism and Foucault: Reflections on Resistance* (Boston: Northeastern University Press, 1988); Jana Sawicki, *Disciplining Foucault: Feminism, Power, and the Body* (New York: Routledge, 1991); Lois McNay, *Foucault and Feminism: Power, Gender, and the Self* (Cambridge: Polity, 1992); and Susan J. Hekman, ed., *Feminist Interpretations of Michel Foucault* (University Park: Pennsylvania State University Press, 1996).

of reclamation and even defiance in the face of insult and injury. The force, and often the excitement, of this term comes from the resignifying, even the reversal in its evaluation. Those groups and scholars who have reclaimed this word will not dispute that it connotes abnormality or nonconformity. Rather, they will dispute that such a contrary relation to "the normal" and often "the natural" is a negative thing. Queer, then, can indicate a challenge to regimes of the normal, a desire to resist and contest such a worldview. In this sense, then, queer is less an identity and more a disposition, a mode of examining the processes that cast certain people and practices into categories of normal and abnormal and then of interrogating the various effects of such processes. Queer can also work more like a verb or adverb: to "queer" an arrangement of power and privilege, or to interpret queerly by attending to certain dynamics. This is mostly how I use the term (as one might have noted by the description thus far).

Queer studies, then, can mean the study of those processes called "normalization" which have often been used against LGBTIQ people, but not only. Foucault is helpful in describing normalization as those exercises in power that perform and combine five particular operations by (1) comparing activities; (2) differentiating between them; (3) arranging them into a hierarchy of value; (4) imposing a homogenized category to which one should conform (within this hierarchy); and (5) excluding those who differ, and are thus abnormal.[7] As Foucault's various works on power and sexuality became available in English translations,[8] such techniques for analysis found wider audiences and contributed to the rise of queer theories in the 1980s and 1990s.

Such techniques reflect the resistance that many queer theorists show toward defining their tasks to one set of limited questions and concerns, indicating the mobility of a term such as *queer*. Instead of being a source of frustration, this quality of queer theories makes it quite useful, given how it adapts to new contours and critically reflects on its own practices. Since the queer is arrayed in a contesting relation with and against the normal, there is an underlying suspicion about imposing only one meaning or insisting that there is only one task for a queer thinker and activist. Thus, it is important to keep in mind that no definition and description of queer theories can be exhaustive; in fact, any claim to be giving the final and definitive version of what queer theories are or do would itself be *un*-queer! My introduction of such concepts and practices, then, will by necessity need to struggle with this aspect of queer

---

7. Michel Foucault, *Discipline and Punish: The Birth of the Prison* (trans. Alan Sheridan; New York: Vintage, 1979), 182–84.

8. See especially Foucault, *An Introduction* (vol. 1 of *The History of Sexuality*; trans. Robert Hurley; New York: Vintage, 1978).

theories, even as I strive to indicate briefly only *some* of the unique and useful directions queer interpretations can and do take.

Ironically, even as queer theories direct us to interrogate basic assumptions and critique received narratives, a standardized story is beginning to be told about what queer theories are and what they do. In fact, by beginning with thinkers like Butler and Foucault, I have at least initially reproduced one such common narrative. If the queer impulse to contest normativity is to be maintained, then one must recognize that there are other ways to organize and describe queer sorts of approaches and analyses. A questioning disposition to ideas, practices, and presumptions that seem foundational or fundamental to any of our social structures—particularly what we call normal or natural—hones both critical reflection and intersectional analysis for queer theorists. Such a disposition highlights that other stories can be told about work that, for instance, precedes Foucault and exceeds his focus. One of the longest critical engagements of the operations of sexuality as it intersects with a wide range of social dynamics can be found in the work of "women of color feminists" like Audre Lorde, Barbara Smith, and Gloria Anzaldúa.[9] Queer theories meet their critical potential when they recognize how the subjects of gender and sexuality are not fixed, but are enmeshed and moving in trajectories within and between intersecting differences and multiple dynamics of power. When queer modes fail to recognize this and, in turn, reinforce certain normalizing trajectories, it is justifiable to ask "what's queer about queer studies now?"[10] The charge to think and work in increasingly intersectional ways might just be recalling one of the impulses behind de Lauretis's first use of queer theory (precisely at a time when feminists had themselves been grappling with differences within and between women). Such multiple genealogies for queer studies suggest that readers and users of this volume would be wise to attend to and mix insights from those entries that engage critical feminist approaches to gendered, sexual, racial, ethnic, economic, class, colonial, and national dynamics, among others.

---

9. See Audre Lorde, *Sister Outsider: Essays and Speeches* (Berkeley: Crossing, 1984); Lorde, *I Am Your Sister: Collected and Unpublished Writings of Audre Lorde* (ed. Rudolph P. Byrd et al.; Oxford: Oxford University Press, 2009); Barbara Smith, ed., *Home Girls: A Black Feminist Anthology* (New York: Kitchen Table: Women of Color, 1983); and Gloria Anzaldúa, *Borderlands: The New Mestiza-La Frontera* (San Francisco: Aunt Lute, 1987); and Anzaldúa, *The Gloria Anzaldúa Reader* (ed. AnaLouise Keating; Durham: Duke University Press, 2009). See a similar critique in Roderick A. Ferguson, *Aberrations in Black: Toward a Queer of Color Critique* (Minneapolis: University of Minnesota Press, 2004).

10. David L. Eng et al., "Introduction: What's Queer about Queer Studies Now?" *Social Text* 23.3–4 (2005): 1–17.

Queer studies, then, develops and proceeds in ways similar to feminist studies, since queer studies aims to counter oppression and pathologization, while interrogating the arguments about the "normal" and the "natural" that buttress such dynamics. Feminists, for instance, counter the oppression of women by challenging sexist arguments and institutions that claim that females (and males) have certain essential, biological, or "natural" traits. Their targets are similar and even interrelated, as contesting heterosexism requires contesting sexism (and, to be honest, vice versa). Feminists must work to recognize and resist the androcentrism that constructs a (certain elite pale) male point of view as normal, just as queer scholars do likewise with heteronormativity, both aiming to displace oppressive claims about what is essential and valued, what should be seen as natural and normal. Works like Butler's *Gender Trouble*, then, are signal efforts for both queer and feminist studies not only because gender and sexuality are so closely and mutually constructed, but also because the interrogation of gender categories is crucial for resisting the forms of exclusion and domination they encounter.

3. Masculinity Studies (Outside of Biblical Studies)

Even as masculinity had been an intermittent subject of previous feminist analyses, the final decades of the century marked a change in approach by some feminist and feminist-allied scholars. This change can be followed through both the continuing expansion of subjects for feminist analysis and the differentiating response to the emergence of many "men's movement" groups. Such groups frequently subscribe to gender essentialist and outright antifeminist viewpoints that are irreconcilable with the aims of feminist studies (in or outside of biblical studies).[11] It is important, then, to separate those who claimed some sort of parallel "men's liberation" or "masculinist" identity from those male supporters of and advocates for women's rights, and then, further, both of these groups from those scholars and activists who turned a specifically feminist lens upon masculinity as a construction and practice. Indeed, the second of these groups go back to what we might call "first wave feminism," when activists like Frederick Douglass reflected on the intertwined histories of abolitionist and women's rights efforts.[12] Yet the role of males in feminist efforts and communities will remain controversial for over a century,

---

11. For some responses and dialogues between such groups and males allied with feminists, see Michael S. Kimmel, ed., *The Politics of Manhood: Profeminist Men Respond to the Mythopoetic Men's Movement (and the Mythopoetic Leaders Answer)* (Philadelphia: Temple University Press, 1995).

12. Scholars often also highlight the central role of certain males in political philoso-

as reflected even in debates about what such males should call themselves: profeminist, antisexist, feminist-allied, but seldom simply feminist. Such concerns over the presence of, names for, or alliances with, males in movements for women's rights tended to be lower among groups, like women of color feminists, socialist feminists, or lesbian feminists, when they saw the importance of working across gendered lines in order to fight intersecting structures of oppression: sexism alongside and within racism, capitalism, or heterosexism (see, e.g., the Combahee River Collective).[13]

Still, there is an important difference between males in feminist studies and the feminist (or at least feminist-influenced) analysis of masculinity.[14] Feminists have long interrogated how masculinity has been defined, or at least men have, in contrast to women. Often, as in the work of Simone de Beauvoir, this was done to trace how woman has historically been conceived as the "other" to the man—conceived as the stable, typical, and reliable subject, the "one" who is rational and therefore naturally essential and superior to his "other."[15] While feminists have powerfully interrogated this picture of women for many decades, it is only in the last three decades that the subject of masculinity as a powerful and problematic construction has received sustained attention. Critical masculinity studies, then, begins by viewing masculinity as a result of specific cultural representations and social practices.

In fact, critical masculinity studies takes as its focus not a singular object, masculinity, but rather plural masculinities, recognizing that such concepts and practices take many different forms. One of the more influential conceptualizations of these plural masculinities by R. W. Connell begins by acknowledging the concentration of social power among males.[16] This concentration is maintained through a culturally dominant ideal or norm for masculinity, or hegemonic masculinity. Hegemonic masculinity refers not to males' essential place in the sociopolitical order, but to the practices

---

phy (like John Stuart Mill and Friedrich Engels) for contributing key arguments about women's rights.

13. Combahee River Collective, "A Black Feminist Statement," in *The Second Wave: A Reader in Feminist Theory* (ed. Linda Nicholson; New York: Routledge, 1997), 63–70.

14. Two helpful resources for sorting the roles of feminisms and feminist theories within masculinity studies are Judith Kegan Gardiner, ed., *Masculinity Studies and Feminist Theory: New Directions* (New York: Columbia University Press, 2002); and Peter F. Murphy, ed., *Feminism and Masculinities* (Oxford: Oxford University Press, 2004).

15. Simone de Beauvoir, *The Second Sex* (trans. H. M. Parshley; New York: Vintage, 1989; first published 1949).

16. Raewyn W. Connell, *Masculinities* (Berkeley: University of California Press, 1995). See also Connell, *Gender and Power* (Stanford, Calif.: Stanford University Press, 1987); and Connell, *The Men and the Boys* (Cambridge: Polity, 2000).

that position certain males in the highest rungs of a gender hierarchy. When tracing this form of masculinity, then, masculinity studies grapples with certain practices among those socialized to be masculine, including aggression, competition, and even violence; authority, paternalism and heterosexuality; emotional control or remoteness, physical strength or resilience, and economic production. Such practices give certain males greater social clout in order to exercise dominance, even as (or perhaps because) hegemonic masculinity as an ideal is nearly impossible to achieve or quite simply be. Its comic unattainability is compatible with many of Butler's arguments about the inherent instability of gender as performative: it is panicked in its need to be repeatedly practiced and constantly reinforced, all in order to appear natural. This is one aspect of its power, but also a place from which it can be denaturalized and destabilized.

The plurality of masculinities, though, indicates that there is more than just hegemonic masculinity to consider, reinforcing the possibilities for subverting or resisting hierarchically arranged norms, as well as maintaining or even reinforcing them. Unfortunately, the next category in Connell's gender hierarchy reflects the effectiveness of hegemonic masculinity, even given its ostensible "failures." Complicit forms of masculinity occur when males benefit from the patriarchally arranged gender order by at least partially corresponding to or aspiring to participate along the lines of the ideal represented by hegemonic masculinity. (The layered complicities and interwoven aspects of this hierarchy might remind feminist biblical scholars of Elisabeth Schüssler Fiorenza's conceptualization of kyriarchy.[17]) Those who conform even less to the features of this norm are described in terms of subordinated masculinities. The most prominent examples of these include racially and sexually minoritized males, indicating that this gender hierarchy differentiates between several different kinds of males, not just between males and females.

Nevertheless, in Connell's conceptualization, all of these masculinities are still more hierarchically valued than femininity. Most males benefit in one way or the other from the subordinated place of females and femininities. Thus, Connell is not simply identifying a range of gender differences, or even different masculinities, but stressing male dominance as supported by claims about male difference(s). The aim of critical masculinity studies, so conceived, is not just to catalogue the forms masculinity takes; rather, it moves from identifying to interrogating and critiquing the impacts of these forms. In this way, critical masculinity studies destabilizes the claims made by many "men's movement"

---

17. See, for instance, Elisabeth Schüssler Fiorenza, *Rhetoric and Ethic: The Politics of Biblical Studies* (Minneapolis: Fortress, 1999), ix.

figures, particularly when those figures assert some sort of natural role or even biological grounding for a "real" and monolithic masculinity. Masculinity studies aims to denaturalize gender, both masculinity and femininity, contesting hegemonic conceptions of masculinity and the accompanying, oppressive views of femininity. Further, it demonstrates the ways that these hegemonic conceptions discipline and damage males (even while providing some significant cultural and political capital to most).[18] Indeed, hegemonic masculinity's structural support for elite, heteronormative pale males can be troubled and undermined by alternative masculinities, not only those enacted by racially and/or sexually minoritized males, but even by masculine females.[19] In that light, masculinity does not simply "belong" to "biological men."

Critical masculinity studies, then, is an extension of or simply just one particular exercise within feminist analysis. The analytic practices of masculinity studies show its clear conceptual debts to the social constructionism that is characteristic of a great deal of both feminist and queer scholarly work. Its aim to interrogate the construction of masculinities in forms of domination and oppression is compatible with a range of feminist practices, while its examination of alternative masculinities overlaps with queer studies' challenges to heteronormativity. Such interconnections are inevitable once a field of study grasps how masculinity was and is defined in opposition to females and queer males (among others). Hegemonic masculinity is not only misogynist in its devaluation of femininity, but also homophobic in its flight from certain kinds of male contact (particularly with those males who are ostensibly too closely associated with femininity).

As the current century began, some of the potential tensions and concerns previously articulated by feminist scholars about their colleagues in masculinity studies (particularly in the 1980s) have settled into the mostly uncontroversial current consensus about feminist kinds of and collaborations with(in) masculinity studies.[20] Whereas masculinity was previously unmarked, masculinity studies highlights how masculinity is indeed a gender, quite often tied

---

18. See Michael S. Kimmel, *Manhood in America: A Cultural History* (New York: Free, 1996).

19. See Judith Halberstam, *Female Masculinity* (Durham, N.C.: Duke University Press, 1999).

20. For an important expression of these initial concerns about males participating in feminist academic enterprises (and particularly literary criticism), see Alice Jardine and Paul Smith, eds. *Men in Feminism* (New York: Methuen, 1987). For further elaboration on the current consensus, see Judith Kegan Gardiner, "Introduction," in *Masculinity Studies and Feminist Theory* (ed. Judith Kegan Gardiner; New York: Columbia University Press, 2002), 1–29, especially 11–15.

to the distribution of power and privilege to certain kinds of males. Though forces work to make it appear essential and natural, masculinity is neither stable nor monolithic, but constructed, contingent, and changing according to a variety of conditions and contexts. Feminist, queer, and masculinity studies often share similar starting points about social constructions, accounting for their suspicion of any essentializing conception that claims that a sex, gender, or sexuality is natural, unchanging, or even crosscultural. Finally, for social change around any of these topics to be possible, scholarly and political collaboration between feminist, queer, and masculinity studies is necessary and useful. Despite previous debates about who can participate in which fields and movements, males have contributed to feminist studies, females to masculinity studies, and heterosexuals to queer studies. As queer studies and critical masculinity studies developed, it became incumbent to recognize that none of these fields are the exclusive property of only particular identity groups, but are organized around certain commitments and practices. If nothing else, the prominent contributions of a feminist scholar like Eve Sedgwick (who identified neither as a lesbian nor as male) within both queer studies and critical masculinity studies makes this evident.

To be clear, then, critical masculinity studies are engaged in interrogating and resisting hegemonic masculinity—constructions of masculine identification and differentiation that maintain sexism and heterosexism, for example—not defending or recuperating it. Understood in this fashion, critical studies of masculinities are not antifeminist but rather part of a very particular exercise of or within a larger feminist project.

4. Impacts and Practices within Feminist Biblical Studies

Thus, as the twentieth century drew to a close, the academic environments were rather different from the contexts in which feminist biblical studies first emerged. As the Bible and Culture Collective noted in its own moment: "In the 1990s, feminist studies finds sometime allies in gender studies, gay and lesbian studies, men's studies, and studies of sexuality."[21] The feminist alliances and interconnections described thus far outside of biblical studies (including

---

21. The Bible and Culture Collective, "Feminist and Womanist Criticism," in *The Postmodern Bible* (New Haven: Yale University Press, 1995), 225–71, here 269. The conclusion to this entry also notes that, though scholars might be using different (if allied) terms in feminist, gender, black, ethnic, postcolonial, and sexuality studies, for example, cultural forces of regulation and domination do not discriminate between these: *any* critical reflection upon gender or its intersections with sexuality, race, ethnicity, economy and empire is treated as a threat.

its feminist forms) will eventually be reflected and even crystallized in biblical interpretation influenced by queer studies and critical masculinity studies, two areas that also share elements but are not exactly identical to each other either. Queer work in biblical studies will be more voluminous than work that interrogates the constructions of masculinity, likely because of the prominent and persistent ways biblical images, arguments, and ideas are still used to target LGBTIQ people in various political and ecclesial contexts.

Such a tendency is less marked than in the neighboring discipline of classical studies, in which the interested reader can find a veritable explosion of research on Greek and Roman masculinities. Given the porous or even parasitical relationship between classical studies and New Testament and early Christian studies, it is not surprising to find relatively more focus on masculinity in these areas than in Hebrew Bible studies. The masculine self-fashioning described by Maud Gleason's *Making Men*, for instance, proves influential for a number of contributions, starting perhaps with Virginia Burrus's *"Begotten, Not Made": Conceiving Manhood in Late Antiquity*.[22] The ancient forms, arguments, and practices of masculinity delineated in classical studies, then, reinforce key claims about the construction and contextualization of masculinity, while providing the point of contact and contrast for scholars resituating and reconsidering the various forms of masculinity in New Testament and early Christian texts.[23] This methodological tendency to begin with the similarities and differences from the surrounding, often dominant culture, is reflected in the range of contributions to Janice Capel Anderson and Stephen D. Moore's *New Testament Masculinities*, up to and through Col-

---

22. Maud W. Gleason, *Making Men: Sophists and Self-Presentation in Ancient Rome* (Princeton: Princeton University Press, 1995); Virginia Burrus *"Begotten, Not Made": Conceiving Manhood in Late Antiquity* (Stanford, Calif.: Stanford University Press, 2000). Other important works in classical approaches to masculinity include Carlin Barton, *The Sorrows of the Ancient Romans: The Gladiator and the Monster* (Princeton: Princeton University Press, 1993); Jonathan Walters, "'No More Than a Boy': The Shifting Construction of Masculinity from Ancient Greece to the Middle Ages," *Gender and History* 5 (1991): 20–33; Walters, "Invading the Roman Body: Manliness and Impenetrability in Roman Thought," in *Roman Sexualities* (ed. Judith P. Hallett and Marilyn B. Skinner; Princeton: Princeton University Press, 1997), 29–43; and Craig A. Williams, *Roman Homosexuality: Ideologies of Masculinity in Classical Antiquity* (New York: Oxford University Press, 1999).

23. For a helpful, if initial, charting of masculinity studies in New Testament studies, including its debts to classics and differences from "men's movements," see Stephen D. Moore, "'O Man, Who Art Thou...?': Masculinity Studies and New Testament Studies," in *New Testament Masculinities* (ed. Stephen D. Moore and Janice Capel Anderson; SemeiaSt 45; Atlanta: Society of Biblical Literature, 2003), 1–22.

leen Conway's more recent *Behold the Man*.[24] Such scholarship traces the ways these texts present figures and standards for conduct that match as well as fail to conform to the idealized forms of masculinity (what Connell might call hegemonic masculinity). While these interpretations are often too optimistic about figures like Jesus or Paul, they at least conceive such marginalized or resistant practices of masculinity as aligned against the patriarchy, ethnic privilege, and/or imperialism of its time, finding common cause with or as feminist scholarship.

What masculinity studies in Hebrew Bible tend to lack in amount are more than balanced by efforts at systematization, particularly in the efforts of David J. A. Clines.[25] Clines has repeatedly attempted to delineate what qualities have been attached to masculinity, in both the ancient context of stories surrounding figures like David and the more modern context in which biblical figures are received as conforming to more recent norms for masculinity. The David narratives reflect his superior masculinity through such qualities as fighting, persuasion, beauty, male-bonding, womanlessness, and musicality.[26] The association between masculinity and violence, of both the military and sexual varieties, has been a recurrent concern for feminist scholars like Renita J. Weems, particularly when engaging with troubling aspects of the prophetic literature.[27] The tight, even synonymous connection between violence and manliness in the Hebrew Bible has been most acutely articulated by Harold C. Washington, whose work follows closely on the heels of an important collection by Claudia Camp and Carole Fontaine.[28]

------

24. Moore and Anderson, *New Testament Masculinities*; and Colleen Conway, *Behold the Man: Jesus and Greco-Roman Masculinity* (Oxford: Oxford University Press, 2008). Conway's second chapter is even titled "How to Be a Man in the Greco-Roman World."

25. David J. A. Clines, "David the Man: The Construction of Masculinity in the Hebrew Bible," in *Interested Parties: The Ideology of Writers and Readers of the Hebrew Bible* (Sheffield: Sheffield Academic Press, 1995), 212–43; Clines, "*Ecce Vir*, or, Gendering the Son of Man," in *Biblical Studies/Cultural Studies* (ed. J. Cheryl Exum and Stephen D. Moore; Sheffield: Sheffield Academic Press, 1998), 352–75; and Clines "He-Prophets: Masculinity as a Problem for the Hebrew Prophets and Their Interpreters," in *Sense and Sensitivity: Essays on Reading the Bible in Memory of Robert Carroll* (ed. Alistair G. Hunter and Philip R. Davies; London: Sheffield Academic Press, 2002), 311–27. For a more recent contextualization of critical masculinity studies, particularly in relation to feminist and queer approaches to the Hebrew Bible, see Deryn Guest, *Beyond Feminist Biblical Studies* (Sheffield: Sheffield Phoenix, 2012).

26. In fact, these qualities make up the headings of the first half of Clines, "David the Man."

27. See Renita J. Weems, *Battered Love: Marriage, Sex and Violence in the Hebrew Prophets* (Philadelphia: Fortress, 1995).

28. See Harold C. Washington, "Violence and the Construction of Gender in the

Clines's efforts are also intriguing for the way they provide an academically autobiographical (though contested) rationale for a critical approach to masculinity in biblical interpretation. As he narrates it:

> One day, feeling a little marginalized by the impact of feminist biblical criticism, I asked Cheryl Exum, in the words of Peter, What shall this "man" do?, feeling sure that feminist criticism could be no business of mine. I got a one-word answer: Masculinity; and I have gone in the strength of that word forty days and forty nights.[29]

This brief anecdote reveals the feminist impulses behind work like Clines as well as common mistakes about the division of labor between and within feminist, queer, and masculinity studies. Indeed, as I have already noted, scholars who happen to be female and, more relevantly, feminist have done important work in masculinity studies (in and outside of biblical studies), and scholars who happen to be male and, again more relevantly, feminist have contributed to feminist studies (again, in and outside of biblical studies).[30] The lines between feminist, masculinity, and queer studies are so blurry that policing any apparent boundaries among (or within) them seems unnecessary and even counterproductive.

Indeed, many works traverse not only the lines between feminist and masculinity studies, but also those that ostensibly differentiate queer and masculinity studies. In a series of articles, Brigitte Kahl, for example, has reflected upon the emphasis on masculinity as well as the potential gender trouble in Paul's letter to the Galatians.[31] Kahl asserts that this letter is the

---

Hebrew Bible: A New Historicist Approach," *BibInt* 5 (1997): 324–63; Claudia V. Camp and Carol R. Fontaine, eds., *Women, War, and Metaphor: Language and Society in the Study of the Hebrew Bible* (*Semeia* 61 [1993]).

29. Clines, "*Ecce Vir*," 353.

30. Since this chapter has already highlighted several instances of the former, it might be relevant to point out instances of the latter. Washington coedited an important feminist volume, *Escaping Eden: New Feminist Perspectives on the Bible* (ed. Harold Washington et al.; New York: New York University Press, 1999), and has made several useful feminist contributions besides; and I would be remiss not to point out my own commitments and contributions. (In fact, it is telling that, though my previous work has seldom if ever explicitly interrogated masculinity per se, my assigned contribution to the present volume was meant to include masculinity studies alongside queer studies.)

31. Brigitte Kahl, "Der Brief an die Gemeinden in Galatien: Vom Unbehagen der Geschlechter und anderen Problemen des Andersseins," in *Kompendium feministischer Bibelauslegung* (ed. Luise Schottroff and Marie-Theres Wacker; Gütersloh: Gütersloher, 1998), 603–11; Kahl, "Gender Trouble in Galatia? Paul and the Rethinking of Difference," in *Is There a Future for Feminist Theology?* (ed. Deborah F. Sawyer and Diane M. Collier;

most phallocentric in the Second Testament: "Nowhere else have we so much naked maleness exposed as the centre of a deeply theological and highly emotional debate: foreskin, circumcision, sperm, castration, to name only some of the relevant terms."[32] At times, Kahl's argument proceeds via rather traditional approaches, conducting a literary analysis of the letter through word statistics and stressing the recurrence in several chapters of terminologies such as sonship and oneness. Yet these articles make quite nontraditional claims that Paul is mitigating masculine authority, subverting hierarchical binaries, and delegitimizing biological categories. Explicitly feminist, yet focused on masculinity, Kahl underscores how such Pauline arguments manage also to reconceptualize femininity and motherhood through their different readings of the creation, kinship, and circumcision accounts in Genesis.[33] In fact, to Kahl's eyes, this Paul appears rather queerly, as a transgendered maternal figure in labor pains (4:19).[34] Kahl's explication of the "gender trouble" in Galatia allows her to read Paul's letter as a critical interrogation of masculinity, and yet also an apostolic transformation away from it.

Still, even as one of the titles of these articles echoes Butler's famous work *Gender Trouble*, Kahl's analyses reflect, but manage also to obscure, the influence of queer studies outside of biblical studies. Kahl does not explicitly cite or reflect upon key concepts like Butler's gendered performativity, Foucault's disciplinary power, or either of their reflections on practices of the self. Those biblical scholars who will engage such concepts tend also to be those with extensive backgrounds or interactions with literary theory and cultural studies.

A touchstone work in this regard, with a searing focus on hypermasculinity in biblical texts and interpreters (and the cultures that love them), is Moore's *God's Gym*.[35] In this work, Moore interrogates broader cultural fixations around violence, control, and masculinity by juxtaposing the tortured male body of Jesus and the spectacularly perfected biblical bodies of the divine, in general, alongside and akin to the bodies treated by butch-

---

Sheffield: Sheffield Academic Press, 1999), 57–73; and Kahl, "No Longer Male: Masculinity Struggles behind Galatians 3.28?" *JSNT* 79 (2000): 37–49.

32. Kahl, "Gender Trouble," 57; cf. Kahl, "Der Brief an die Gemeinden," 604; and Kahl, "No Longer Male," 40–41.

33. Kahl, "Gender Trouble," 68–73; and Kahl, "No Longer Male," 42–43, 48–49.

34. See Kahl, "Gender Trouble," 60, 68; and Kahl, "No Longer Male," 43, 49; cf. Beverly R. Gaventa, "The Maternity of Paul: An Exegetical Study of Galatians 4.19," in *The Conversation Continues: Studies in Paul and John in Honour of J. Louis Martyn* (ed. Robert R. Fortna and Beverly R. Gaventa; Nashville: Abingdon, 1990), 189–210.

35. Stephen D. Moore, *God's Gym: Divine Male Bodies of the Bible* (New York: Routledge, 1996).

ers, autopsies, and body-builders. As anachronistic and idiosyncratic as this technique might be (particularly in biblical studies), Moore's analysis remains incisively relevant and revelatory about the impact of interpretive histories, borrowing and adapting frequently from Foucault's sense of disciplinary power. The central symbol of Jesus' dead body prepares its viewers to be docile bodies for normalization. The wrath of God—cast as "'roid rage"—highlights that one is in the presence of a hegemonic hypermasculinity that opposes and attempts to expel anything feminine.[36] Just as feminist scholars have focused upon gendered pronouns, Moore highlights how the insistent barrage of masculine pronouns buries and all but extinguishes the female metaphors scholars like Phyllis Trible found for the deity.[37] With clear links to cultural studies approaches, including those of feminists, Moore's work reminds readers that if a figure is embodied, it is also hauntingly and potentially horrendously gendered.

In this sense, Moore's narrations of biblical views on masculinity are far less optimist than Kahl's: the divine is foreboding, even threatening, a kind of troubling that is not positively transformative. Yet, both types of analysis are often quite different, even opposed to, malestream biblical criticism, and are allied and interconnected with many feminist and queer approaches. Such work is poised to make vital contributions to feminist, critical masculinity, and queer approaches to biblical interpretation.[38] Thus, simultaneously, such studies also anticipate and/or participate in the development of queer approaches to biblical interpretation.

Queer approaches similarly depart from traditional methodologies and perspectives, while sharing concerns and strategies with feminist approaches. As was the case outside of biblical studies, inside biblical studies many, even most, of the first scholars working in queer approaches are also committed to or connected with feminist strategies and goals. Like queer studies, in general, queer biblical interpretation also has debts to and departures from gay liberationist and critical sexuality studies. Such studies have often, by necessity, been shaped by the contemporary use of certain "clobber passages" from the

---

36. Ibid., 96–101.

37. Ibid., 102, where he also quotes and cites the admission of Phyllis Trible, *God and the Rhetoric of Sexuality* (OBT; Philadelphia: Fortress, 1978), 23 n. 5. For further reflections on the masculinity of the deity, see Howard Eilberg-Schwartz, *God's Phallus and Other Problems for Men and Monotheism* (Boston: Beacon, 1994).

38. Moore's later, more (?) queerly inflected collection demonstrates this continued overlap, given that his targets for analysis and subversion include both compulsory heterosexuality and hegemonic masculinity (see Moore, *God's Beauty Parlor: And Other Queer Spaces in and around the Bible* [Stanford, Calif.: Stanford University Press, 2001], 17).

Bible against lesbian, gay, bisexual, and transgendered people (among others) in both ecclesial and political contexts. Evoking Trible's earlier feminist work, Robert Goss justifiably labeled these passages as further "texts of terror."[39]

From this particular religious and cultural context, then, three kinds of strategies developed. The first attempted to recuperate other, more gay-affirmative biblical traditions, such as David and Jonathan, Ruth and Naomi, or Jesus and the "beloved disciple."[40] A second set of responses, more frequently practiced by professionalized academic biblical scholars, insisted on properly placing biblical texts and cultures in their ancient historical contexts.[41] Such contextualizations often highlight that those bashing passages that are ostensibly "about homosexuality" are built upon and reflect the asymmetries of ancient gender roles.[42] Sex acts are closely tied to status claims, thus marking and creating differences in gender, geography, ethnicity, economy, and age.[43] At the close of the twentieth century, these kinds of strategies found greater purchase than the third resistant response developing in conversation with wider sets of queer studies and theories.

A more queerly resistant strategy to biblical interpretation will often be ambivalent or in tension with more recuperative-affirmative or historical-contextual approaches. In her foreword to the volume *Take Back the Word* (2000), Mary Ann Tolbert echoed the tensions and ambivalences she sounded for feminist hermeneutics in 1983, only now in the context of queer readings.[44] Given how the same text that can be read in creatively destabilizing ways is

---

39. Robert E. Goss, *Jesus ACTED UP: A Gay and Lesbian Manifesto* (San Francisco: Harper San Francisco, 1993), 90–94; referencing Phyllis Trible, *Texts of Terror: Literary Feminist Readings of Biblical Narratives* (OBT; Philadelphia: Fortress, 1984).

40. See, for example, Nancy L. Wilson, *Our Tribe: Queer Folks, God, Jesus, and the Bible* (San Francisco: Harper San Francisco, 1995).

41. See especially Bernadette J. Brooten, *Love Between Women: Early Christian Responses to Female Homoeroticism* (Chicago: University of Chicago Press, 1996); and Martti Nissinen, *Homoeroticism in the Biblical World: A Historical Perspective* (trans. Kirsi Stjerna; Minneapolis: Fortress, 1998).

42. See also, for example, Ken Stone, "Gender and Homosexuality in Judges 19: Subject-Honor, Object-Shame?" *JSOT* 67 (1995): 87–107.

43. See, for example, Randall C. Bailey, "'They're Nothing But Incestuous Bastards': The Polemical Use of Sex and Sexuality in Hebrew Canon Narratives," in *Social Location and Biblical Interpretation in the United States* (vol. 1 of *Reading from This Place*; ed. Fernando Segovia and Mary Ann Tolbert; Minneapolis: Fortress, 1995), 121–38; and Ken Stone, "The Hermeneutics of Abomination: On Gay Men, Canaanites, and Biblical Interpretation," *BTB* 27/2 (1997): 36–41.

44. Mary Ann Tolbert, "Foreword: What Word Shall We Take Back?" in *Take Back the Word: A Queer Reading of the Bible* (ed. Robert E. Goss and Mona West; Cleveland: Pilgrim, 2000), vii–xii.

also susceptible to "a barrage of killing interpretations," queer interpreters "must take it back in a new way, a way that attempts to obviate its potential for harm while engaging its message of liberation and love."[45] In continuity with at least some feminist approaches (and in a similarly ambivalent spot), queer interpretations will need to develop different strategies of resistance to the processes of normalization and naturalization. In doing so, these interpretations can draw upon facets of the two other responses: shifting attention to texts besides the four typical bashing passages (like the recuperative-affirmative strategy) and to multiple power dynamics and historical specificities (like the historical-contextual strategy).

For an example of a queer reading that identifies and challenges normativities, sexual or otherwise, this entry ends where many of the first feminist interventions into biblical studies began: with concerns about the creation accounts of Genesis. As Ken Stone highlights in his analysis, both popular and scholarly interpretations of these accounts reflect what de Lauretis and Monique Wittig have alternately called the "heterosexual presumption" or the "heterosexual contract."[46] Indeed, Trible's reading of Gen 1:27 potentially bolsters the assumption of this obligatory relation, given her emphasis on the binary division of the sexes as foundationally defining for humans. Such a vision could provide a stronger compulsory naturalization of heteronormative gender and sexual roles than supposedly condemnatory texts. Yet, a focus on the arguments of these accounts need not necessarily reinstall or make inevitable their success. Rather, Stone asserts that "Butler's work encourages us to focus upon instabilities and ambiguities in those texts, instabilities and ambiguities that might represent weak spots in the biblical foundation of the heterosexual contract and, hence, openings for a queer contestation."[47] Thus, the delay in the text's specification that the female human's desire will be for the male (until 3:16b) could be showing the always incomplete and unstable effort to make certain relations of desire "natural" and compulsory.

---

45. Ibid., ix, xi. This parallels her previous characterization of the tense and paradoxical place of feminist hermeneutics in Mary Ann Tolbert, "Defining the Problem: The Bible and Feminist Hermeneutics," *Semeia* 28 (1983): 113–26, here 126 (see also 120–21). The terminology of "taking back" should also be familiar to various feminist communities on college campuses (Take Back the Night events) and in biblical studies (Trible, "Take Back the Bible," *RevExp* 97 [2000]: 425–31).

46. See Teresa de Lauretis, "The Female Body and Heterosexual Presumption," *Semiotica* 67:3–4 (1987): 259–79; and Monique Wittig, *The Straight Mind and Other Essays* (Boston: Beacon, 1992), 32–45; as utilized in Ken Stone, "The Garden of Eden and the Heterosexual Contract," in Goss and West, *Take Back the Word*, 57–70.

47. Ibid., 63.

Indeed, in the narrative sequence of the second creation account, the Edenic existence of humanity and their sex-gender differentiation precede this delineation of female desire. Unlike the first creation account, then, the normalizing assumption of heterosexual desire is not present "from the start." This heterosexual presumption is perhaps not entirely inscribed in these texts, suggesting that they are less "obviously about" heteronormative marriage ("Adam and Eve, not Adam and Steve"), among other commonly taken-for-granted ecclesial and cultural claims. Nevertheless, Stone still clarified that the purpose and outcome of this reading was not recuperation to find a "queer-positive text."[48] In fact, one reason why the text cannot operate as an alternative foundation for queer hermeneutics is because this text and interpretations of it have been implicated in the domination of women.[49] What this reading can do, though, is undercut and subvert the foundations—religious, social, and political—that naturalize and normalize certain constricted roles of gender and sexuality (to start). Such strategies are less concerned with solving the meaning of a text or resolving its incoherencies and ambiguities than with resisting the operation of such texts in biblical and biblically-styled arguments by exposing the insecurities and instabilities of the texts and the arguments that use them.

Such work demonstrates that the troubling that queer reading strategies provide, then, cannot be reduced to a focus on masculinity. Critical masculinity studies and queer studies might overlap and influence each other, but they are not identical. Even as Stone's article also considered the potential homosocial discomfort at the heart of the second creation account, the article clearly draws upon feminist work in and outside of biblical studies, often to explicitly focus upon the role of the female human ("Eve").[50]

5. Conclusion

This entry (and readings like Stone's) complicates any simplified narratives about the relations and connections between feminist, masculinity, and

---

48. Ibid., 67.

49. Ibid. Such a stance reflects how queer hermeneutics often are (or at least can be) forms of feminist critique, while further reminding that women are among queer folk, and queer folk are often treated "as" women.

50. Ibid., 64–67. Aside from the feminist (and queerly feminist) theorists described above, Stone's work regularly engaged a number of feminist biblical scholars, including Trible and Exum (among others). For the connections between Stone's queer approach and Schüssler Fiorenza's feminist approach, see Joseph A. Marchal, "Responsibilities to the Publics of Biblical Studies and Critical Rhetorical Engagements for a Safer World," in *Secularism and Biblical Studies* (ed. Roland Boer; London: Equinox, 2010), 101–15.

queer approaches.[51] Critical masculinity studies and queer studies need not be framed as completing or competing with feminist approaches; rather, they are mostly particular kinds of feminist approaches. The participants in such studies often learned critical perspectives and approaches as, with, and/or from feminists. In the end, this work surveys just two of the ways that feminist biblical studies developed and impacted approaches in the twentieth century.

These two forms of feminist biblical studies are important for scholars in the twenty-first century to consider and critique, adapt and practice. Queer studies and critical masculinity studies suggest the complicated kinds of accountability that feminist biblical scholars must address if we are to remain reflexively critical about our prior and ongoing projects. These confluences and meeting points will be crucial to examine, particularly if feminist biblical studies will be able to reflect contemporary dynamics and ethical demands of, for instance, movements around and for transgender and intersex people. As we pause to look back on the previous century and the current contours of biblical studies, feminists will have to make difficult and honest assessments about unexamined heterosexism or the often heteronormative frames used (as Stone's work highlights about Trible's) when interrogating and working to change women's roles in religion and society. Indeed, such reflective projects like this collection would do well to consider what kind of disciplinary role normativity plays as the various contributions select ways of narrating the histories, presents, and prospects of feminist biblical studies. Is it, for instance, possible to have norms without normalization?

I opened this entry by positing that the most compelling parts of queer studies and critical masculinity are specific kinds of feminist studies. One might not have noticed this because, at times, feminists in biblical studies have acted hesitantly in the face of such projects. In efforts to reform communities by reaching less committed or convinced publics, feminists with various religious or political commitments were worried about appearing too radical. If one imagines that the sole focus of these projects was on sexuality, this might even seem problematic to efforts that sought to counteract the ways women were historically reduced to (certain constrained) sexual roles. Yet it remains vital to interrogate the naturalization in such argumentation, and to critique how certain forms of masculinity were enacted as the unexamined norm (here and elsewhere). Perhaps, then, to reorder my opening, the still

---

51. For two recent but rather different explications of the relation between queer and feminist approaches to biblical interpretation, see Guest, *Beyond Feminist Biblical Studies*; and Joseph A. Marchal, " 'Making History' Queerly: Touches across Time through a Biblical Behind," *BibInt* 19 (2011): 373–95.

most compelling kinds of feminist studies to come will also be queer and/or critical masculinity projects.

Postcolonial Feminist Biblical Criticism: An Exploration

Tan Yak-hwee
Taiwan Theological College and Seminary

Let me begin with my social location, which has in many respects informed my interest in exploring postcolonial feminist biblical criticism. I was born when Singapore was still a British colony, and even though Singapore gained its independence in the late 1950s, the education system was still very British in orientation. Since I went to a Christian missionary school, I learned more about the Bible, British history, and English literature than about Chinese history and literature. As a result, my identity and status were influenced by such lenses—a form of discursive colonialism of the mind had taken place. Such a narration of my encounter with the West explains the production of a "mixed" Yak-hwee—an "in-between" person. My reality is no longer fixed or essentialized, because I embody a conflicting disposition of classes, nationalities, religions, and ethnicities. Having taught in a theological college in Singapore for six years, I have now moved to Taipei, Taiwan to teach in Taiwan Theological College and Seminary.[1] Thus, the political, socioeconomic, and cultural environments of Taiwan further inform my social location.[2]

---

1. In 1872, the Canadian Presbyterian George Mackay initiated a training program that eventually became Taiwan Theological College and Seminary. Taiwan Theological College and Seminary is one of the Presbyterian seminaries affiliated with the Presbyterian Church in Taiwan.

2. The aborigines of Taiwan (formerly known as the Formosa) lived in peace for thousands of years until settlers from China and Japan occupied certain parts of the island in the sixteenth century. The political history of Taiwan is very eventful: the region was occupied by foreign powers (Dutch, Japanese, and Chinese) for approximately three hundred years. In 1949, the Nationalist regime was defeated by the Chinese Communist Party and expelled from China. Since then, Taiwan has been forced under the rule of the Republic of China. Taiwan was under martial law for thirty-eight years, and it was only in 1987 that this was lifted. In 1991 and 1992, the Taiwanese were finally able to elect their own repre-

In June 2010, the government of Taiwan signed the Economic Co-operation Framework Agreement (ECFA) with China. While the signing of the agreement was meant to be positive for the financial industries on both sides, many Taiwanese were wary that China might have political designs that extended beyond economic benefit, especially since China saw Taiwan, and continues to see it, as a renegade province.[3] The reality of the empire, whether in literary texts or in contemporary life, was and continues to be overwhelming for the Taiwanese. Although I am a "female guest worker" in this institution and country, this imperial context encompasses almost every facet of my life. In light of my past and current political, socioeconomic, and religious contexts, I find the hermeneutical lens of feminist postcolonial criticism particularly relevant. Postcolonial criticism allows me to analyze and critique the empire that permeates politics, economics, and society in general; the feminist aspect allows me to analyze the repression of women within these systems and to interrogate and resist such oppression.

Postcolonial feminist biblical criticism is a political activity that is interested not only in authors and texts, but also in readers of ancient texts, namely the Bible. On the one hand, it looks at the author's intentions in his/her writing to the original audience as situated within political and social realities, particularly in relationship to women. On the other hand, it also seeks to bring to the fore the ideals and aspirations of the real, flesh-and-blood readers who engage with the Bible, readers like me, a colonial/postcolonial feminist.

In this exploratory essay, I will first briefly chart the theoretical framework of postcolonial studies in general. Second, I will examine its impact upon the field of biblical studies, especially feminist biblical criticism. Third, I will delineate the works of some biblical scholars who have used such a strategy in their readings of the biblical texts. As a conclusion, I will add some comments regarding the challenges and opportunities postcolonial feminist biblical criticism could offer to the field of biblical criticism.

---

sentatives to congress and the legislative body. Economically, Taiwan is capitalist and state-owned. Most of the people are affiliated with Buddhism and Chinese religions (Taoism, Confucianism, and folklore). Christianity constitutes 2–3 percent of the population. See Yang-en Cheng, "Taiwan," in *A Dictionary of Asian Christianity* (ed. Scott W. Sunquist.; Grand Rapids: Eerdmans, 2001), 815–17.

3. See n. 1.

1. Postcolonial Criticism and Postcolonial Biblical Criticism

Postcolonial studies has its origins in literary criticism, so it is not surprising that leading postcolonial theorists come from that field. These leading theorists include Edward Said, Homi Bhabha, and Gayatri Chakravorty Spivak.

Greatly influenced by a Foucauldian understanding of "discourse," Edward Said's *Orientalism* demonstrates the close relationship between the production of Western knowledge and the non-Western world.[4] He asserts that "Orientalism" is a discourse whereby European culture manages and produces the Orient.[5] That is to say, the representation of the civilization and culture of the Orient is ideologically constructed through writings, doctrines, vocabulary, and scholarship in various disciplines of academic institutions and colonial bureaucracies.[6] Paradoxically, the encounter between the West and the Orient brought about a "dangerously unOtherable" native and, in the words of Rey Chow, "The native is no longer available as the pure, unadulterated object of Orientalist inquiry—she is contaminated by the West."[7] In short, the native is "hybridized."

According to Homi Bhabha, "hybridity" is an ambivalent space of tension created by the "splitting" of different facets within different cultures. This "split" identity suggests that one's identity is inevitably doubled, that is, the individual is never fully colonizer or fully colonized, but always shifting.[8] There is neither a One nor the Other, but "something else besides."[9] In other words, "hybridity" renders the possibility of "resistance mingled with complicity, and domination with its own disruption."[10]

Gayatri Chakravorty Spivak pushes the boundaries of postcolonial studies by raising the issue of the invisibility of women in the writings of subaltern studies, an enterprise in the rewriting of previous histories of India by colo-

---

4. Michel Foucault, *Discipline and Punishment: The Birth of the Prison* (trans. Alan Sheridan; New York: Pantheon, 1997), 27. Foucault advances the notion that knowledge and power are interdependent, serving and reinforcing each other. He states, "There is no power relation without the correlative constitution of a field of knowledge, nor any knowledge that does not presuppose and constitute at the same time power relations."

5. Edward W. Said, *Orientalism* (New York: Vintage, 1979), 1–9.

6. Ibid., 7, 23.

7. Rey Chow, *Writing Diaspora: Tactics of Intervention in Contemporary Cultural Studies* (Bloomington: Indiana University Press, 1993), 12.

8. Homi K. Bhabha, *The Location of Culture* (London: Routledge, 1994), 85–92, 107.

9. Ibid., 97.

10. Tat-siong Benny Liew, "Postcolonial Criticism: Echoes of a Subaltern's Contribution and Exclusion," in *Mark and Method: New Approaches in Biblical Studies* (ed. Janice Capel Anderson and Stephen D. Moore; 2nd ed.; Minneapolis: Fortress, 2008), 220.

nial British and elite Indian scholars. She comments that the participation of females did not surface in the face of colonial uprisings against imperialism.[11] The "figure" of woman, both as object of colonialist historiography and as subject of revolution, has been kept at bay as "the ideological construction of gender keeps the male dominant."[12] While Spivak must be credited for bringing to the fore the gender question in postcolonial studies, like Said and Bhabha, she restricts her investigations within literary criticism.

Similarly, the Bible is seen a discourse in which the dominant presence of empire is overarching with respect to the lands and people of their colonies. The imperial settings of the Hebrew Bible were the empires of Egypt, Assyria, Babylonia, and Persia.[13] Likewise, the dominant Roman Empire provides the political framework for every first-century Christian and every New Testament text by and about the Christian disciples.[14]

Many biblical scholars, such as Mark G. Brett and Tat-siong Benny Liew, have broached the field of postcolonial biblical criticism.[15] However, two foremost biblical critics, Fernando F. Segovia and R. S. Sugirtharajah, are to be particularly noted, because they have charted the path of the criticism. Segovia and Sugirtharajah proposed their method and theoretical frameworks for the analysis of the biblical texts. Segovia calls for a reading strategy that takes into account the sociopolitical and cultural reality of the "world of antiquity," "the world of modernity," and the "world of today" in which the biblical texts are constructed.[16] In a similar vein, in his initial work on postcolonial bibli-

---

11. Gayatri Chakravorty Spivak, "Can the Subaltern Speak?" in *Colonial Discourse and Post-colonial Theory: A Reader* (ed. Patrick Williams and Laura Chrisman; New York: Columbia University Press, 1994), 82.

12. Ibid.

13. Jon L. Berquist, "Postcolonialism and Imperial Motives for Canonization," *Semeia* 75 (1996): 15. Berquist alleges that the early stages of Hebrew Bible canonization are "an imperial production of ideology during the reign of the Persian Empire over colonial Yehud."

14. Richard J. Cassidy, *Christians and Roman Rule in the New Testament: New Perspectives* (New York: Crossroad, 2001), 1. See also Cassidy's book, *Paul in Chains: Roman Imprisonment and the Letters of St. Paul* (New York: Crossroad, 2001), in which he argues that Paul's letters, especially Rom 13:1–7 and Philippians, disclose the world of the Roman Empire and its ramifications for Paul, a believer in Jesus Christ.

15. See Mark G. Brett, *Decolonizing God in the Tides of Empire* (Sheffield: Sheffield Phoenix, 2008); and Brett, *Genesis: Procreation and the Politics of Identity* (New York: Routledge, 2000). See Tat-siong Benny Liew, *Politics of Parousia: Reading Mark Inter(con)textually* (Leiden: Brill, 1999); see also Liew, *What Is Asian American Biblical Hermeneutics: Reading the New Testament* (Hawaii: University of Hawaiʻi Press, 2008).

16. Fernando F. Segovia, *Decolonizing Biblical Studies: A View from the Margins* (Maryknoll, N.Y.: Orbis, 2000), 119–32.

cal criticism Sugirtharajah suggests some markers for a reading strategy, such as looking for protest voices in the text, looking for structural realities that collaborate with the victimization of characters, and addressing current questions that people face.[17]

The methods and theoretical frameworks of Segovia and Sugirtharajah are helpful for engaging with biblical texts. But, like Said, Bhabha, and Spivak, they confine their engagement to the literary texts—though they have raised the importance of social location in such an investigation. The issue of gender in postcolonial biblical studies has been taken up by Musa W. Dube.

1.1. POSTCOLONIAL FEMINIST BIBLICAL CRITICISM

While Musa W. Dube concurs with Segovia and Sugirtharajah that biblical texts are colonizing narratives that validate traveling and taking possession of foreign lands and people, her work brings gender especially to the fore of such investigations. This is seen in the authorization of travel through divine claims, the representation of the superiority of the colonizers, and the gender representations used to construct the colonizers' claims.[18]

Dube proposes a decolonizing feminist postcolonial reading that she calls "Rahab's Reading Prism," which highlights "the historical fact of colonizing and decolonizing communities inhabiting the feminist space of liberation practices."[19] As such, postcolonial feminist critics need to develop a decolonizing posture against colonial destruction, and to articulate their voices boldly, refusing to privilege the colonizing narratives of patriarchal oppression as well as imperial claims of cultural, economic, and political superiority. Such a stance will provide new postcolonial spaces that promote "native and international relations of equity, difference and liberation."[20] Dube's "Rahab's Reading Prism" could be elucidated in a number of ways, but I will limit myself to underlining two aspects.

One aspect is the "contact zone," which is the space where the colonizers and the colonized, whose relationship is usually disparate, encounter and grapple with each other.[21] According to Kwok Pui-lan, the "contact zone" is

---

17. R. S. Sugirtharajah, *Asian Biblical Hermeneutics and Postcolonialism: Contesting the Interpretations* (Maryknoll, N.Y.: Orbis, 1998), 20–24.

18. Musa W. Dube, *Postcolonial Feminist Interpretation of the Bible* (St. Louis: Chalice, 2000), 117–18.

19. Ibid., 122.

20. Ibid.

21. Mary Louise Pratt, *Imperial Eyes: Travel Writing and Transculturation* (New York: Routledge, 1992), 4.

one of the foci of postcolonial feminist critics who pay "special attention to the biblical women in the contact zone and present reconstructive readings as counternarrative."[22] Rahab, for example, finds favor with the Israelites after she helps them with the capture of Jericho, and her citation in the genealogy of Jesus confirms that she is highly regarded because of her heroic behavior on behalf of Israel (Matt 1; cf. Heb 11:31; Jas 2:25). Rahab, the Canaanite Other, stands in the "contact zone" and represents a counternarrative.

Another aspect of postcolonial feminist criticism is the role of the real, flesh-and-blood readers, that is, the social background of its practitioners from both academic and ordinary readership. For Dube, ordinary readers include those of the Third World who are often at the margins and excluded by the political and economic structures of society, such as the women from the African Independent Churches with whom she is involved and whose reading approach tends to be community-based.[23]

Postcolonial feminist criticism must broaden its investigation of the poetics and politics of the text to include the politics of location. Tolbert argues that the politics of location emphasizes the "multiplicity, complexity, and contextuality of human experience," and raises questions concerning the writing of the text, its ideology, and so forth. On the other hand, the *poetics* of location analyzes the text understood as "constitutive reality," raising the question of the language of power and the construction of positive or negative representations of others.[24] This brings one to the consideration of the complexity of social location, and also to the crossroads of different approaches used to analyze the texts.

Many postcolonial feminist critics are aware of their multiple identities, both as oppressors and oppressed.[25] With respect to Asia, Kwok acknowledges that there is no single, homogenous identity of the oppressed women of Asia because of the multiplicity of oppressed people in the Third World. As such,

---

22. Kwok Pui-lan, *Postcolonial Imagination and Feminist Theology* (Louisville: Westminster John Knox, 2005), 82.

23. Musa W. Dube, "Readings of *Semoya*: Botswana Women Interpretation of Matt. 15:21–28," *Semeia* 73 (1997): 111–29.

24. Mary Ann Tolbert, "The Politics and Poetics of Location," in *Reading from This Place: Social Location and Biblical Interpretation in the United States* (ed. Fernando F. Segovia and Mary Ann Tolbert; Minneapolis: Fortress, 1995), 305–17.

25. Sharon H. Ringe, "Places at the Table: Feminist and Postcolonial Biblical Interpretation," in *The Postcolonial Bible* (ed. R. S. Sugirtharajah; Sheffield: Sheffield Academic Press, 1998), 136–51. Ringe speaks of the ambivalent situation of feminists in the United States who find themselves both colonizers and colonized. She raises the importance of such consciousness that women in the West live in the "betweenness," that of the dominant culture and also being dominated on the basis of gender.

she concludes that to identify racial minority, economic disparity, or sexism as the only mark of "otherness" traps us into a privileged position of exploiting others. Kwok advocates that one must be aware of the cross sections of different cultures and religious traditions of Asian women's lives, and that "there is always the Other within the Other."[26] Therefore, postcolonial feminist critics "have to work to mitigate the practice of colonial authority and to share table fellowship with others for greater inclusiveness."[27]

To achieve this "greater inclusiveness," postcolonial feminist criticism should address the various forms of oppression of women, such as the issues of race, class, and sexuality, as argued by Elisabeth Schüssler Fiorenza.[28] That is, other aspects of domination and subordination must be addressed in addition to the issues of gender and empire, as these forms of oppression are interconnected with each other. Schüssler Fiorenza coined the term *kyriarchy*, a combination of two words, *kyrios* and *archein*, asserting the multiple and mutual relationships of gender with other facets of domination.[29]

2. Doing Postcolonial Feminist Biblical Criticism

To further focus on feminist postcolonial criticism, I will now outline the works of three biblical scholars and/or theologians, Musa W. Dube, Kwok Pui-lan, and Joseph A. Marchal, who engage with the biblical text from postcolonial feminist perspective. The initial practice of postcolonial feminist biblical criticism has attracted biblical scholars and theologians who are "women from the West; men and women from outside the West as well as from ethnic and racial minorities in the West."[30] However, with the end of formal colonialism, the rise of postcolonialism, and the continued impact of imperial culture everywhere in the form of neocolonialism, postcolonial feminist biblical criticism attracts a diverse group of interested biblical scholars using multifaceted approaches to interrogate imperial reality in its different forms and guises.

---

26. Kwok, *Postcolonial Imagination*, 82–83.

27. Ibid., 84.

28. Elisabeth Schüssler Fiorenza, *The Power of the Word: Scripture and the Rhetoric of Empire* (Minneapolis: Fortress, 2007), 125.

29. Elisabeth Schüssler Fiorenza, *But She Said: Feminist Practices of Biblical Interpretation* (Boston: Beacon, 1992), 115–17, 122–25; Schüssler Fiorenza, *Wisdom Ways: Introducing Feminist Biblical Interpretation* (Maryknoll, N.Y.: Orbis, 2001), 118–22.

30. Segovia, "Biblical Criticism and Postcolonial Studies," 130.

2.1. Musa W. Dube

In her reading of John 4:1–42, Dube states that residing within the Johannine text is the colonial ideology that sanctions the cultural subjugation of foreign lands and peoples.[31] Dube highlights some colonial innuendos in the text that warrant the intrusion into and subjugation of the territory of the "Other," the Samaritans. The mention of Pharisees, Jesus, and John the Baptist highlights the intense struggle for power directly related to imperialist occupation (4:1). With the disciples of Jesus losing control and power to the Pharisees, they extend their influence to Samaria, accentuating the characterization of Jesus as superior and authoritative (4:42) vis-à-vis the ignorant Samaritans (4:10, 22). The Samaritans' cultural and religious values are advanced as inferior, and must be replaced by the values of Jesus and his disciples. Moreover, Dube shows that the Fourth Gospel constructs Jesus' highly exalted christology and his place of origin vis-à-vis the world (1:1–4, 29; 8:58; 17:5, 24; 5:19–20; 20:28). In other words, Jesus' origin is outside this world. Furthermore, the "spatial origins" and authority of Jesus override all other religious figures, including Nicodemus, a representative of the leadership of Israel (3:1–12). Therefore, the colonizing ideology of the Fourth Gospel is unraveled in the light of Jesus' claims over earthly spaces, cultural figures, and his own elevated status. Furthermore, his disciples are asked to emulate his actions, and to go into other people's lands. Jesus not only permits, but also orders them to do so (4:34, 38; 17:18, 21–22; 20:21b).

These colonizing ideologies, insists Dube, must be decolonized. Using Mositi Totontle's *The Victims*[32] as her intertext, Dube discusses how Totontle rereads John 4:1–42, interrogating the oppressive constructions of gender, race, geography, and religion. Totontle's rereading attempts to feature a female character in the place of Jesus in order to take hold of the gender superiority enacted in the text. The article also attempts to describe the Samaritan woman as "sent." Therefore, she has the same status as that conferred upon the male disciples. Furthermore, Totontle's Samaritan woman, Mmapula, was offered living water from her own well on her own land, a decolonization of geographical hierarchy. Dube acknowledges that, in her rewriting of John 4:1–42, Totontle rewrites the Samaritan identity for postcolonial subjects and time. She does not deny her Samaritan race. Totontle's Samaritan woman, Mmapula

---

31. Musa W. Dube, "Reading for Decolonization (John 4:1–42), in *Voices from the Margin: Interpreting the Bible in the Third World.* (rev. ed.; ed. R. S. Sugirtharajah; Maryknoll, N.Y.: Orbis, 2006), 297–318.

32. Mositi Totontle, *The Victims* (Gaborone: Botsalo, 1993).

"comes to the reality of who she is—a mixture of many different things: a despised heretic and an outcast half-breed."[33]

2.2. KWOK PUI-LAN

In her article "Finding Ruth a Home: Gender, Sexuality, and the Politics of Otherness," Kwok uses "finding a home" as a metaphor and heuristic device in order to question the meaning of the term "home" from a postcolonial perspective.[34] "Home" is significant, as it discloses the issues of identity and a person's desire to belong. Kwok argues that looking at "home" from the angle of kinship demonstrates that Ruth is the foreign woman who stands in the contact zone of different cultures: the culture of the Moabites and that of the Jews. In her marriage to Boaz, Naomi's kinsman, Ruth secures economic and political protection for herself and Naomi, on the one hand, but on the other hand, her "foreignness" is obliterated in the Davidic patrilineal genealogy. In short, Ruth is the "boundary marker" of the two cultures.[35]

Furthermore, Kwok asserts that feminist scholars have focused upon female friendship, decent/indecent female sexual behavior as well as lesbian love[36] instead of focusing on the important roles of ethnicity, race, and nation of the protagonists. These perspectives have overlooked, silenced, and suppressed the role of patriarchal and heterosexual power. Kwok argues that "a romantic tale about Ruth and Naomi can equally cover up ethnic differences, as well as the difficulties of maintaining an interethnic or interracial relationship."[37] Besides, the story of Ruth has been read as a model of compassion and hospitality extended to strangers as Boaz protects and even marries Ruth, an enemy of his people. However, Kwok argues that such a romantic reading disguises the fact that the reality is otherwise, and "people at home do not accept all strangers equally."[38] A closer examination of the marriage between Boaz and Ruth reveals that it is a marriage for the continuation of Boaz's family line and that of his kin, Naomi.[39] Therefore, Ruth is a "surro-

---

33. Dube, "Reading for Decolonization," 314.
34. Kwok, *Postcolonial Imagination,* 100–121.
35. Ibid., 107.
36. Ibid., 108–11. Kwok cites works such as Phyllis Trible's, *God and the Rhetoric of Sexuality* (Philadelphia: Fortress, 1978); Ruth Anna Putnam, "Friendship," in *Reading Ruth: Contemporary Women Reclaim a Sacred Story* (ed. Judith A. Kates and Gail Twersky Reimer; New York: Ballantine, 1994), 44–54; and Rebecca Alpert, "Finding our Past: A Lesbian Interpretation of the Book of Ruth," in Kates and Reimer, *Reading Ruth,* 91–96.
37. Kwok, *Postcolonial Imagination,* 111.
38. Ibid.
39. Ibid., 114–15. Regina Schwartz argues that scarcity and kinship are attached to

gate" mother. In the face of group stability, the identity of the foreigner or the stranger is being undermined and the question of infliction of violence upon the foreign woman's identity who is "finding a home" is raised.

In highlighting some of these trajectories, Kwok states that the question of identity is complex. On the one hand, the colonizers are interested in the colonized (the "Other") by means of power through cultural and sexual means. On the other hand, there is the desire on the part of the colonized (the "Other") to imitate the colonizers, the "Pocahontas Perplex." The encounter between the "Self" and "Other" reveals, as in the case of Boaz and Ruth, "the complexity of interethnic and interreligious encounters … fruitfully interpreted with the help of the theories of the contact zone."[40]

The theories of the contact zone are also used by Joseph A. Marchal in his analysis of Paul's letter to the Philippians. Thus I shall now turn to his postcolonial feminist interpretation.

2.3. JOSEPH A. MARCHAL

At the outset of his book *The Politics of Heaven,* Marchal states that he will use a variety of sources to develop postcolonial feminist analysis of Paul's letters and Pauline interpretation.[41] As a feminist scholar, Marchal notes that the discussion of feminism should include the treatment of the structures of empire, but should also grapple more broadly with the "intersecting dynamics of gender, sexuality, ethnicity, and empire" and the way they functioned in the ancient world of Paul's writings as well as in our contemporary world.[42] In his multiaxial approach, he looks for the gaps in the rhetoric of the text so as to show the "complicated picture of colonial and communal dynamics in terms of agency, resistance, reinscription, and/or co-optation" in Paul's "cross-ethnic, cross-gendered imperial context."[43]

Therefore, using Paul's letter to the Philippians and the notions of travel and contact zone, Marchal reconstructs the role of Euodia and Syntyche, "who struggled alongside" Paul (Phil 4:3). Scholars have argued that Euodia and

---

monotheism, and this is illustrated in the book of Ruth, with the adoption of Ruth to the God of Israel. See Regina M. Schwartz, *The Curse of Cain: The Violent Legacy of Monotheism* (Chicago: University of Chicago Press, 1997), ix–x, 90–91.

40. Kwok, *Postcolonial Imagination,* 119.

41. Joseph A. Marchal, *The Politics of Heaven: Women, Gender, and Empire in the Study of Paul* (Minneapolis: Fortress, 2008).

42. Ibid., 3.

43. Ibid., 13.

Syntyche are missionaries[44] or leaders[45] who are not working together. However, Marchal questions the nature of their role with regard to their struggling together as well as with Paul.

Marchal locates Euodia and Syntyche, possibly freed slaves, spatially in the "coercion and asymmetry of the kyriarchally colonized contact zone."[46] On the one hand, Paul recognized them as his coworkers, and possibly they were converted as a result of Paul's missionary journey to Philippi. These "unconverted native women" have through their conversion become "heroes of anti-imperial or anti-kyriarchal liberation."[47] While Paul might expect them to be in agreement with him regarding the issue of life conditioned by suffering as favorable, Euodia and Syntyche think otherwise. They had experienced suffering because of Roman kyriarchical occupation and oppression based on their gender, ethnicity, slavery, and status. They refuse to be manipulated or coerced, because coercion is precisely the means by which their colonizers maintained their power.[48] Hence, they are both resistant and complicit. Their conflicted status, one that is conditioned by the realities of the Roman Empire as well as their gender and ethnicity, becomes the "contact zone" as they "struggle alongside" Paul's authority in their lives and in the Philippian community.

With reference to Euodia and Syntyche, Marchal argues that to engage with postcolonial feminist criticism is to consider the complex and multifaceted dynamics regarding methodology in its analysis and interpretation and also its ramifications for the political and ethical significance in which women and empire have been characterized in the past, present, and future.

2.4. SUMMARY

The three scholars cited illustrate the deployment of postcolonial feminist criticism in different settings and for different purposes. In some measures, they reflect the evolution of postcolonial biblical criticism from one that initially highlights the issue of gender in light of empire to an understanding of the multifaceted dimensions introduced by text and methodological approach.

---

44. Mary Rose D'Angelo, "Euodia," in *Women in Scripture: A Dictionary of Named and Unnamed Women in the Hebrew Bible, the Apocryphal/Deuterocanonical Books, and the New Testament* (ed. Carol Meyers et al; Grand Rapids: Eerdmans, 2000), 79. See also D'Angelo, "Syntyche," in Meyers et al., *Women in Scripture*, 159.

45. Ibid., 79, 159.

46. Marchal, *The Politics of Heaven*, 103.

47. Ibid., 107.

48. Ibid.

However, they all call for the liberation and transformation of women with respect to the realities of empire, gender, and status as articulated in the texts as well as in the approaches undertaken in the field of biblical criticism.

3. Some Thoughts on Future Explorations

The state of the world we live in is currently *glocal* in nature. *Glocal* is a term used in "global and transnational cultural studies to indicate the notion of how the local and global are co-complicit, each implicated in the other."[49] What happens in the local affects the international and vice-versa. Our lives are intertwined. Hence, to set these boundaries as exclusive is bound to be met with challenge and resistance. The voices of scholars who use postcolonial feminist criticism in their approaches to reading biblical texts are primarily influenced by social locations that are often conditioned by the reality of imperialism.

Furthermore, the question of gender is especially foregrounded in these studies. Such is the opportunity set before the field of biblical criticism, to expand and transform its horizons. It is a *dis-cover(y)*. However, such expansion will be met with challenges and will create *dis-ease*. For transformation to take place, *dis-ease* is necessary. Just like a chrysalis that has to undergo some discomfort and uneasiness in its shell before transforming into a butterfly, so I see postcolonial feminist criticism, currently in a transformative stage that challenges the field of biblical criticism by questioning its political and ethical implications.

---

49. Susan Stanford Friedman, "Locational Feminism: Gender, Cultural Geographies, and Geopolitical Literacy," in *Feminist Locations: Global and Local, Theory and Practice* (ed. Marianne Dekoven; New Brunswick, N.J.: Rutgers University Press, 2001), 31.

Canons Unbound

Denise Kimber Buell
Williams College, U.S.A.

> Feminist biblical scholarship cannot remain within the limits drawn by the established canon. Rather it must transgress them for the sake of a different theological self-understanding and historical imagination.
>
> — Elisabeth Schüssler Fiorenza[1]

> [T]he point of discussing the canon as a politically conservative force is to change its status—from self-evident power to a phenomenon to analyze, and thereby, by definition, to transform.
>
> — Mieke Bal[2]

1. Canons: What Are They, and How Do Feminists Transgress Them?

All feminist biblical interpreters call for some kinds of transformations, within Judaism or Christianity, within academic practices, or in contemporary politics. Feminist biblical interpreters have demonstrated that canons are of political and ethical concern to religious and nonreligious folks alike; biblical canons are not simply authoritative texts conveying the content from which Jewish or Christian identities are constituted, nor is canon simply the law that regulates legitimate religious identities. Making canon an object of scrutiny enables feminists to critique the relationship between collective identities (especially, but not only, religious ones), texts, and reading practices.

---

1. Elisabeth Schüssler Fiorenza, "Introduction: Transgressing Canonical Boundaries," in *A Feminist Commentary* (vol. 2 of *Searching the Scriptures*; ed. Elisabeth Schüssler Fiorenza with the assistance of Ann Brock and Shelly Matthews; New York: Crossroad, 1994), 8.
2. Mieke Bal, "Religious Canon and Literary Identity (Plenary lecture Nijmegen, Conference 'Literary Canon and Religious Identity')," *Lectio difficilior: European Electronic Journal for Feminist Exegesis* 2 (2000); online: http://www.lectio.unibe.ch/00_2/2-2000-r.pdf.

The term "biblical canon" refers to either the Tanak or the Christian Bible, collections associated with and often understood to index Jewish and Christian identities respectively. Defining canon in terms of texts with special religious or cultural authority is familiar outside of biblical and religious studies, too. Religious and nonreligious feminists have critically interrogated the formation of literary canons (including biblical ones) and engaged the claims made in the name of these texts. But "canon" has additional meanings. Within Roman Catholicism, canon continues to refer especially to the authority of tradition, echoing the ancient Christian definition of a canon as a "rule" or standard for interpretation. For feminist biblical interpreters, this understanding of canon has been adapted to critique the power-saturated process of interpretation and to advance feminist hermeneutics. Some feminist interpreters embrace an alternative "canon" or standard for interpretation, one that claims contemporary individual and collective wo/men's struggles for liberation as an authoritative countersite from which to evaluate canon.[3] This kind of standard is used to evaluate interpretations with reference to their ability to contribute to liberation of oppressed wo/men. It may be employed to read texts within conventional literary canonical boundaries, to revise and expand the notion of what counts as scripture or the sites and forms of revelation and authority in this world, or to redefine the significance of biblical texts. Other feminists are more wary of adopting alternative canons, promoting instead approaches that continue to make biblical canons a site of critical examination and transformation.

1.1. Canon as Site of Authority

Identifying biblical texts as the privileged container of divine authority has a mixed record. The contents of these texts have been experienced as lifegiving by many, but also as oppressive for many others. Biblical texts have been invoked to support oppressive practices such as slavery, colonialism, Christian supremacy over other religious identifications, exclusion of wo/men from leadership roles, authority of men over women in heterosexual marriage, and heterosexism, even as they have been invoked to challenge many of these forms of oppression. Thus, central problems that feminist biblical interpreters address with respect to canon have included: (1) Is the content of biblical canons, as a literary collection, itself the problem? If so, how to resolve it?

---

3. I employ the term "wo/men" here, following Elisabeth Schüssler Fiorenza, to indicate both "the instability in the meaning of the term but also … to include subordinated men" (*Jesus and the Politics of Interpretation* [New York: Continuum, 2000], 4 n. 10).

If not, how can the interpretation and application of canon avoid oppressive outcomes? (2) Can a different understanding of canon address the issues of authority and power, boundary-marking and collective identity formation? (3) What kind of critique of canon is adequate for analyzing the Christian-centric character of biblical studies in order to avoid perpetuating "Christian" as the unmarked form of the Bible (in religious and literary canons)?

The idea of canon as a fixed group of texts has informed biblical studies especially by way of Protestant forms of Christianity. Nonetheless, approaches to canon within Roman Catholicism and Judaism have also been very important for many feminist biblical interpreters as a way to speak about how canon can denote both a collection of texts and the ways these texts are interpreted (further raising the questions of by whom, for whom, and in what contexts). The ancient Christian definition of canon as a "rule" or standard for interpretation is echoed in Roman Catholicism's understanding and practice of canon as the "traditions" authorized by and also serving to reinforce kyriarchal ecclesial structures. Nonetheless, many Catholic feminists also build upon an understanding of canon as a standard for interpretation of biblical texts, arguing for alternative traditions and sites for determining what counts as authoritative, such Silvia Regina's call to "begin with life not orthodoxy."[4] Within Judaism, the centrality of oral Torah as well as midrashic and halakhic commentaries underscores that biblical texts function only in relationship to other traditions and interpretation.[5] Feminists need not be Catholic, Jewish, or religiously affiliated to benefit from these alternative understandings of canon.

Elisabeth Schüssler Fiorenza has built upon but altered the notion of canon as rule or standard by suggesting we view the Bible as a "historical prototype, or as a formative root-model," with specific reference to what it means to be Christian.[6] The idea of a prototype imbues biblical texts with value, but challenges the notion that the Bible's content alone is authoritative

---

4. See Elsa Tamez, "Feminist Biblical Studies in Latin America and the Caribbean," in this volume, citing Silvia Regina, "Fe y Axe: Sanació como experiencia de encuentro con la fuerza que nos habita," in *Ecce mulier: Homenaje a Irene Foulkes* (San José: SEBILA, 2005), 231–45.

5. See, e.g., Bonnie Devora Haberman, "Praxis-Exegesis: A Jewish Feminist Hermeneutic," in *Women's Sacred Scriptures* (ed. Kwok Pui-lan and Elisabeth Schüssler Fiorenza; London: SCM, 1998), 91–101; see also the contribution by Cynthia Baker in this volume.

6. See Elisabeth Schüssler Fiorenza, *Bread Not Stone: The Challenge of Feminist Biblical Interpretation* (Boston: Beacon, 1984), 16; and Claudia V. Camp, "Feminist Theological Hermeneutics: Canon and Christian Identity," in *A Feminist Introduction* (vol. 1 of *Searching the Scriptures*; ed. Elisabeth Schüssler Fiorenza with the assistance of Shelly Matthews; New York: Crossroad, 1993), 158–59. See also Schüssler Fiorenza, "The Will to Choose or

for or determinative of Christian doctrine and practice. This view enables those who wish to preserve Christian religious identifications to continue to invest biblical texts with special, but not exclusive, value, because it can foreground the creative engagement with biblical texts as received and used in specific contexts; it can highlight "the subversive reading and imaginative use of the Bible by people who are subjugated and colonized" and foreground the multiplicity of voices who continuously produce truth through discussion and creative dialogue.[7]

Such a stance can be useful for inter- or multifaith dialogue as well as for crafting decolonizing/anti-imperialist forms of Christianity, because it allows nonbiblical texts, traditions, and wo/men's experiences to be understood as possible sites for divine revelation, liberating ethics, and wisdom.[8] A few feminist biblical interpreters have called for a transformation of feminist New Testament studies that decenters the status of the New Testament texts by approaching *all* scriptures of the world as sites of potentially liberating knowledge, and by "disavow[ing] the colonialist model of comparative literature that sought to subject all other cultural/religious narratives to the literary corpus of the empire."[9]

1.2. CANON AS BOUNDARY

The definition of canon as a group of texts clearly involves the marking of boundaries. These texts have special, if not exclusive authority, for Jews or Christians (or for English curricula, and so on). And when defined as a rule or standard, a canon also marks the boundary of legitimate interpretation and/

---

to Reject: Continuing Our Critical Work," in *Feminist Interpretation of the Bible* (ed. Letty M. Russell; Philadelphia: Westminster, 1985), 135–36.

7. Kwok Pui-lan, *Discovering the Bible in the Non-Biblical World* (Maryknoll, N.Y.: Orbis, 1995), 40–43, here 42. In this context, Kwok actually critiques the prototype in favor of the notion of the Bible as a "talking book," a concept from African-American biblical hermeneutics. Nonetheless, I see more similarity than discrepancy between the notion of the Bible as a prototype creatively engaged by later readers and that of the "talking book."

8. See, e.g., the essays in Pui-lan and Schüssler Fiorenza, *Women's Sacred Scriptures*, especially Musa W. Dube, "Scripture, Feminism, and Post-Colonial Contexts," 45–54; Elsa Tamez, "Women's Lives as Sacred Texts," 57–64; Saroj Nalini Arambam Parratt, "Women as Originators of Oral Scripture in an Asian Society," 74–80; and Yuko Yuasa, "Performing Sacred Texts," 81–90. See also Tamez in this volume.

9. Musa W. Dube, "Rahab Is Hanging Out a Red Ribbon: One African Woman's Perspective on the Future of Feminist New Testament Scholarship," in *Feminist New Testament Studies: Global and Future Perspectives* (ed. Kathleen O'Brien Wicker et al.; New York: Palgrave MacMillan, 2005), 192.

or practice. Feminist biblical interpreters have exposed and problematized these boundary-marking processes and their often kyriarchal contexts and applications; they have also embodied challenges to various kinds of established boundaries. That is, feminist biblical interpreters in the twentieth century have also been the *who* of canonical boundary transgression when we claim a place in the academy, religious communities, or public conversations. In the late nineteenth century, first-wave feminist biblical interpretation took place largely outside of academic institutional structures, sometimes within specific religious communities and sometimes from their fringes. While feminist biblical interpretation continues in these non-academic locations across the globe,[10] starting in the 1960s, second-wave feminists in Western Europe and North America gained voices inside seminaries, divinity schools, as well as colleges and universities. Inside the academy, feminists often employ interpretive frameworks and methods in tension with the majority of their departmental and institutional peers. Thus, feminist biblical interpreters have devised or adapted a range of strategies to challenge and transform dominant methodological canons of philological, textual, and historical positivism. To the extent that there remain even implicit canonical boundaries for becoming a fully licensed biblical interpreter or academic, feminist biblical interpreters may transgress by our very presence.

At the same time, feminists of all religious backgrounds as well as nonreligious feminists must negotiate the way that the academic study of biblical texts echoes Protestantism's prime edict of *sola scriptura* ("scripture alone") by prioritizing analysis of biblical texts and contexts over the history of interpretation, including contemporary communities of interpreters. Feminist biblical interpretation undertaken outside of academic contexts now exists in varying degrees of contact and alliance or tension with academic feminist biblical work. Because feminist biblical interpreters are located both inside and outside of academia, we potentially challenge a privileging of academic training and affiliation over other sites of knowledge.[11] But feminists within the academy also risk choosing professional validation over allegiance to grassroots activism, inside and outside of religious communities.

While feminist biblical interpreters may be from any religious or nonreligious location, the term "biblical" conjures a boundary between nonreligious literary canons and all others that might also be considered scriptural.[12] That

---

10. See, in this volume, discussions by Dora Mbuwayesango and Monica Melanchthon.

11. Judith Plaskow, "We Are Also Your Sisters: The Development of Women's Studies in Religion," *WSQ* 1.2 (1997): 199–211; first published in 1993.

12. The term "scripture" is itself complicated; for discussion, see Pui-lan and Schüssler Fiorenza, *Women's Sacred Scriptures*, especially 1–3 and 105–12; and Vincent Wimbush,

is, "biblical" may appear to be a descriptive term for Jewish and Christian scriptures, but it is also a rhetorical-ideological concept. The rhetorical-ideological functions of "Bible" and "biblical" regularly include a preference for a literary canon linked with Christian supersessionism as well as colonial missionizing.[13] For example, feminists could do more to analyze and critique the histories of the use of the "Bible" in ways that imply only the *Christian* Bible. Indeed, such a line of analysis has been articulated especially in contexts where multiple religious traditions flourish or where Christianity has been practiced as a missionary religion linked with colonialism and imperialism. But this line of analysis is also salient for Euro-American histories of anti-Semitism. Canaan Banana has argued for a "radical rewriting" of what constitutes the Bible based on the understanding that divine revelation is not limited to the historical Christian Bible, but is found also in the "religious shrines and traditions of the peoples of Asia, Africa, Europe, the Caribbean, and Latin America."[14] Such a position is compatible with feminist views of the canon as prototype.

2. Accepting Biblical Canons
While Transgressing Interpretive Canons

> Scripture does not authorize its own interpretations all by itself.
> — Margaret Adam[15]

For many Jewish and Christian feminists active in religious communities, the Bible constitutes a limited, authoritative group of texts with which they want to continue to wrestle.[16] In these cases, feminist biblical interpreters may

---

ed., *Theorizing Scriptures: New Critical Orientations to a Cultural Phenomenon* (New Brunswick, N.J.: Rutgers University Press, 2008). This essay focuses on the question of canon in relationship to biblical texts. As Zayn Kassam's essay in this volume indicates, the Qur'ān is canonical scripture for Muslims; while Tanak and the Christian Testament are both intertextually referenced in the Qur'ān, neither has canonical status for Muslims.

13. See Cynthia Baker's contribution in this volume concerning Christian-centeredness of feminist biblical interpretation.

14. Canaan S. Banana, "The Case for a New Bible," in *Voices from the Margin: Interpreting the Bible in the Third World* (ed. R. S. Sugirtharajah; 2nd ed.; London: SPCK, 1995), 71, 73.

15. Margaret B. Adam, "This is *My* Story, This is *My* Song…: A Feminist Claim on Scripture, Ideology and Interpretation," in *Escaping Eden: New Feminist Perspectives on the Bible* (ed. Harold C. Washington et al.; New York: New York University Press, 1999), 225.

16. Certainly, nonreligious feminists also regularly engage the consensus canons of the Tanakh and the Christian Bible, and often in transgressive ways, but they do not view the texts under consideration as authoritative for themselves, so the stakes differ.

acknowledge the historical process of delimiting a limited group of texts as scripturally authoritative as a development fraught with gendered and other kinds of power-saturated dimensions, but the focus of biblical interpretation remains the end product, the consensus canon for Jews (Tanak) and Christians (the two-Testament Bible).

Although not situating her remarks as a feminist, Loveday Alexander effectively distills the issue that feminist biblical interpreters face who continue to value their Bibles: "The problem is not *what* we are to read but *how*."[17] Feminists articulate responses to this "how" especially in terms of authority. Jewish feminist Naomi Graetz, "respect[s] the authority inherent in the traditional text," viewing her feminism as "inseparable from [her] religious orientation."[18] Even as Graetz grants the biblical texts "inherent" authority, she insists that the feminist interpreter also has authority: "authority evolves out of the dialectic process of closely studying a text and simultaneously interpreting its meaning in terms of our own feminist and religious consciousness."[19] Writing about Christian feminist biblical interpreters, Claudia Camp has argued that "the authority of the text is always an embodied authority: persons must authorize the text, even as it authorizes them." Similarly to Graetz's dialectic process, Camp suggests that

> True authority has a *dialogical* quality ... in order to grant authority to someone or something else, one must first *have* the authority to do so. Legitimate or uncoerced granting occurs from a position of strength, not weakness. This granting is, moreover, reciprocal. For a text to have this dialogical authority, it must continually create new persons to participate in this ongoing interaction. In other words, a truly authoritative text will have a generative, life-giving quality.[20]

As Camp emphasizes, this approach authorizes both the Bible and the interpreter in lifegiving ways that require not simply celebration of the text's content but also critique, "for sometimes the authority of scripture that is embodied in persons will call for the destruction of the existing coercive institutions

---

17. Loveday Alexander, "God's Frozen Word: Canonicity and the Dilemmas of Biblical Interpretation Today," *ExpTim* 117 (2006): 238.

18. Naomi Graetz, *Unlocking the Garden: A Feminist Jewish Look at the Bible, Midrash, and God* (Piscataway, N.J.: Gorgias, 2005), 4.

19. Ibid.

20. Claudia V. Camp, "Feminist Theological Hermeneutics: Canon and Christian Identity," in *A Feminist Introduction* (vol. 1 of *Searching the Scriptures*; ed. Elisabeth Schüssler Fiorenza with the assistance of Shelly Matthews; New York: Crossroad, 1993), 162–63, emphasis original.

that have usurped authority," that is, institutions that have prevented some persons from being able to engage scripture with authority. From Camp's perspective, "The act of interpretation becomes the bringing together of biblical traditions with present circumstances to create life for the present and future."[21] Some womanist biblical scholars such as Renita Weems and Raquel St. Clair embrace an approach to scripture along these lines.[22]

This approach may not lead to a questioning of the canonical status of biblical texts.[23] Nonetheless, it can offer an effective feminist basis for challenging and transforming both what count as authoritative interpretations of biblical texts and how such interpretations are enacted in moral, ethical, social, and institutional arrangements. For example, in her powerful insistence on interpretive communities as the place where all biblical interpreters, including feminists, "find the authority to make sense of and defend our biblical interpretations," Margaret Adam urges feminists to continue to wrestle with passages such as Eph 5:22: "Wives, be subject to your husbands as you are to the Lord," not simply to denounce it, soften it, or explain it away, but to highlight its anomalousness and conflict with "what we know about our story of God-with-us" and "many other New Testament passages that recount the primacy of communal, grace-filled interaction over hierarchical social convention."[24]

A dialogical approach to biblical texts need not reinforce canonical boundaries, however. In a postcolonial register, Kwok Pui-lan has proposed a "dialogical model of interpretation [that] imagines the Bible as a talking book, engendering conversations and creating a polyphonic theological discourse," one that does not specifically privilege the biblical texts, but in which multivalent meanings are produced in collective and religiously pluralistic contexts.[25]

---

21. Ibid., 163.

22. See, e.g., Renita J. Weems, "Reading *Her* Way Through the Struggle: African American Women and the Bible," in *Stony the Road we Trod: African American Biblical Interpretation* (ed. Cain Hope Felder; Minneapolis: Fortress, 1991), 57–77; Raquel St. Clair, "Womanist Biblical Interpretation," in *True to Our Native Land: An African American New Testament Commentary* (ed. Brian K. Blount; Minneapolis: Fortress, 2007), 54–62.

23. Loveday Alexander describes a comparable interpretive process, based on a dialogical interrelation between the ancient canonical text and the contemporary experience of the interpreter who seeks to make the text meaningful for her present: " 'Learning from tradition' … is a complex interactive dialogue with the text, in which it is the task of the skillful interpreter to incorporate new discoveries into the text. But this ongoing process of adaptation and creative interpretation does not detract from the canonic status of the text: if it wasn't authoritative, it wouldn't be worth interpreting" (Alexander, "God's Frozen Word," 239).

24. Adam, "This is *My* Story," 226, 229–30.

25. Kwok Pui-lan, *Discovering the Bible*, 32, but see 36–70.

One literary form that such dialogical interaction can take is commentary writing. Biblical commentary often reproduces canonical boundaries, yet feminists have used it both to destabilize them and to advance "canon within a canon" kinds of critiques. Elizabeth Cady Stanton's *The Woman's Bible* is a touchstone of first-wave feminism, explicitly honored in the multi-author *Women's Bible Commentary* and in the two-volume *Searching the Scriptures*.[26] Athalya Brenner and Amy-Jill Levine have edited additional multiauthor and multivolume feminist commentary collections.[27] Both Stanton's project and the *Women's Bible Commentary* emphasize the authority of women to challenge the content and interpretations of biblical texts deemed to be androcentric, patriarchal, or kyriarchal. For its part, *Searching the Scriptures* consists of one volume of essays addressing feminist interpretive approaches and one volume of short commentaries on a range of texts associated with Christian tradition, both canonical and noncanonical, thus foregrounding associations of canon with prototype.[28] Feminists have also participated in the creation of *The Torah: A Woman's Commentary* and composed feminist midrash.[29]

3. Historicizing Literary Canons

Evidence for the canon of Scripture and its precise limits can only be found *outside* the canon![30]

— Mary Ann Tolbert

---

26. Elizabeth Cady Stanton, *The Woman's Bible* (Boston: Northeastern University Press, 1993; first published 1895); Carol A. Newsom and Sharon H. Ringe, eds., *The Women's Bible Commentary* (Louisville: Westminster John Knox, 1992). See also Luise Schottroff and Marie-Theres Wacker, eds., *Kompendium feministische Bibelauslegung* (3rd ed.; Gütersloh: Gütersloher, 2007; first published 1998).

27. See their Feminist Companion series, with volumes published by Sheffield Academic Press, Pilgrim, and T&T Clark.

28. Schüssler Fiorenza specifies that the inclusion of noncanonical texts alongside canonical ones does not signal a gesture toward a new literary canon ("Introduction," 8). Rather, the inclusion of noncanonical texts and the variety of interpretive considerations and approaches in volume 1 embody her notion of historical prototype—contemporary engagement with an expanded range of historical "root-models."

29. Tamara Cohn Eskenazi and Andrea L. Weiss, eds., *The Torah: A Woman's Commentary* (New York: Women of Reform Judaism, URJ, 2008); Ellen Frankel, *The Five Books of Miriam: A Woman's Commentary on the Torah* (New York, Putnam, 2006); Athalya Brenner, *I Am...: Biblical Women Tell Their Own Stories* (Minneapolis: Fortress, 2005). See also Baker in this volume.

30. Mary Ann Tolbert, "Reading the Bible with Authority: Feminist Interrogation of the Canon," in Washington et al., *Escaping Eden*, 146.

Another way that feminist biblical interpreters have interrogated canonical boundaries is by emphasizing that the Bible was the result of a process of centuries of use, interpretation, negotiation, and debate. This line of argument, developed primarily among scholars of Christianity, challenges claims that the texts of the Christian Bible are authoritative by divine fiat. Instead, as Karen King puts it: "The New Testament and Nicene Creed were not the starting points but the end products of debate and dispute, the result of experience and experimentation."[31] From a postcolonial or decolonizing angle, feminist biblical interpreters have called for attention also to the historical introduction and impact of the Christian Bible in colonial missionary contexts, often at the expense of other oral and literary resources. Less work has been done to assess the kinds of reading strategies that helped to produce "Christian" forms of identification in the Roman Empire through literary and hermeneutical differentiation from "Jewish" forms.

This mode of transgressing canonical boundaries has had greatest significant impact on early Christian historiography, including outside of feminist circles, as an increasing number of scholars reconstruct early Christian history without privileging canonical sources over noncanonical ones.[32] And while the identification of most Christian testament texts as historically Jewish texts is not controversial, none of these texts has become canonical in any Jewish communities.

In her writings on the Gospel of Mary, Karen King makes two kinds of arguments that destabilize canonical boundaries: first, experiment and struggle over all matters—including canon and creed—characterize earliest forms of Christianity, so this is a model for contemporary Christians to embrace.

---

31. Karen L. King, *The Gospel of Mary of Magdala: Jesus and the First Woman Apostle* (Santa Rosa, Calif.: Polebridge, 2003), 161. See also Silke Petersen, "Die Evangelienüberschriften und die Entstehung des neutestamentlichen Kanons," *ZNW* 97 (2006): 250–74. For some useful nonfeminist discussions of the historical process of Bible formation, see, e.g., James L. Kugel, *Traditions of the Bible: A Guide to the Bible As It Was at the Start of the Common Era* (Cambridge: Harvard University Press, 1998); David L. Dungan, *Constantine's Bible: Politics and the Making of the New Testament* (Minneapolis: Fortress, 2007); Lee Martin McDonald, *The Formation of the Christian Biblical Canon* (rev. ed.; Peabody, Mass.: Hendrickson, 1995); Aleida Assmann and Jan Assmann, *Kanon und Zensur: Beiträge zur Archäologie der literarischen Kommunikation II* (Munich: Wilhem Fink, 1987); Hans von Campenhausen, *The Formation of the Christian Bible* (trans. J. A. Baker; Philadelphia: Fortress, 1972).

32. See also the programmatic statement by Elizabeth A. Castelli and Hal Taussig, "Drawing Large and Startling Pictures: Reimagining Christian Origins by Painting like Picasso," in *Reimagining Christian Origins: A Colloquium Honoring Burton L. Mack* (ed. Elizabeth A. Castelli and Hal Taussig; Valley Forge, Penn.: Trinity, 1996), 3–20.

Second, the soteriology, anthropology, and ethics she discerns in the Gospel of Mary exist not simply in this noncanonical writing but also within those texts and practices that have persisted "inside of Christianity ... down to the present day," implicitly calling into question the notion that canonical boundaries mark the difference between authentic and authoritative teachings and their opposite.[33] The first argument is a variation on a long-standing Protestant argument for the origins of Christianity to serve as a warrant for current reform inside Christianity, even as her argument does not rely on appeal solely to writings that became canonical. While King never calls for contemporary Christian communities to add the Gospel of Mary to the biblical canon, her second argument opens the door for its ideas to serve as a basis for highlighting submerged elements within Christian tradition.

Jane Schaberg's work on Mary Magdalene offers a related kind of important feminist approach, one that examines "the texts of the canonical Gospels through the lens of their *Nachleben* or afterlife as well as their prelife."[34] Her work is also explicitly concerned with contemporary theological-political feminist transformations, as she aims to articulate a "Magdalene Christianity" as "an alternative and challenge to Petrine Christianity, which has never been able to silence it."[35] Thus, like King, Schaberg's engagement with canonical and noncanonical sources offer a historiographical approach to "Christian origins" as one of struggle and experimentation. Furthermore, both argue that this struggle and diversity has persisted over time, inside canonical texts and traditions, even if in asymmetrical and muted ways.

As Mary Ann Tolbert observes, the literary canon exists only because it has been designated so—individuals and communities had to formulate and debate interpretive standards before the scriptural canon could be secured. This insight underscores how any discussion of canon, feminist or not, must attend to both the *what* and the *how* of biblical interpretation. The canon is never simply the text. In the twenty-first century, feminist biblical interpreters may find more ways to articulate the possible relationships between these historiographical interventions and the decolonizing challenges to scriptural boundaries explored in the next section.

---

33. King, *The Gospel of Mary of Magdala*, see esp. 155–90.

34. Jane Schaberg, *The Resurrection of Mary Magdalene: Legends, Apocrypha, and the Christian Testament* (New York: Continuum, 2004), 8.

35. Ibid., 19.

4. Bursting Canonical Boundaries

> Mutual criticism and openness to the critique of women from other faith
> traditions is essential. Such critical engagement with one another is neces-
> sary if women of all faith traditions are to work together for the liberation
> and well-being of all women.
>
> — Kwok Pui-Lan[36]

As was noted above, feminist biblical interpreters have consistently transgressed
the "rules" for interpretation and sometimes also the literary boundaries of biblical canons. These two kinds of canonical boundary crossing are sometimes
explicitly conjoined to advance feminist theological understandings of religious
identity as resonating with texts classically defined as biblical, but not limited to
or determined by these texts. We see this especially in the notion of the Bible as
exemplar or prototype, as suggested by Schüssler Fiorenza:

> What leads us to perceive biblical texts as providing resources in the struggle
> for liberation from patriarchal oppression, as well as models for the transfor-
> mation of the patriarchal church is not some special canon of texts that can
> claim divine authority. Rather, it is the experience of women themselves in
> their struggle for liberation. I have therefore suggested that we understand
> the Bible as a structuring prototype of women-church rather than as a defi-
> nite archetype.[37]

Indeed, as this quotation indicates, when feminist biblical interpreters transgress canonical boundaries (literarily and/or methodologically), they must
also articulate the implications of these transgressions for religious identifications: "Such a notion of the Bible not as mythic archetype but as a historical prototype provides women-church with a sense of its own ongoing history as well as Christian identity."[38] In her introduction to the commentary
volume of *Searching the Scriptures*, Schüssler Fiorenza suggests that there is a
tension between what she underscores as a necessary "deconstructive, transgressive method" of feminist biblical interpretation and "a positive image
for the function of scripture in feminist struggles to transform religion and
society."[39] She finds just such an image in the figure of divine Wisdom, identifying it as a figure that appears in those classical canonical texts but also

36. Kwok Pui-lan, *Introducing Asian Feminist Theology* (Sheffield: Sheffield Academic
Press, 2000), 50.

37. Schüssler Fiorenza, "The Will to Choose or to Reject," 135.

38. Ibid., 136.

39. Schüssler Fiorenza, "Introduction," 11.

one that "permeates the whole world" and, in her view, "does not allow for an understanding of canonical authority as exclusive and commanding."[40] By identifying an image found in biblical texts, divine Wisdom, Schüssler Fiorenza enacts her position that the Bible is the heritage and legacy for Christian-identified feminists in their efforts for liberative transformation of Christianity. She also presents it as an image conducive to addressing the theological, social, and political problem of boundary marking, as she does not proclaim that Wisdom is limited to or contained by the content of biblical texts.[41]

Searching the Scriptures is carefully framed as a project that engages "inherited Christian socioreligious boundaries." Its contributors are not all Christian, and some explicitly speak to the need for biblical texts to be interpreted "from the perspective of other faith traditions."[42] In making this point, Kwok Pui-lan and other feminist biblical interpreters such as Chung Hyun Kyung call for critically engaging the biblical canon along with the religious traditions of one's home context as one strategy for addressing the long history of the Christian Bible's use as a canon of colonialism in Africa, Asia, the Americas, and elsewhere.[43]

Musa Dube not only calls for feminist biblical interpreters to consider all world scriptures in their scope, but also urges the expansion of a feminist "oral-Spirit place," which she calls a "Semoya place," from which wo/men "hear anew God speaking to them about the well-being of women and all the oppressed."[44] The urgency of this kind of analysis arises as a matter of intrareligious struggle, as members of a transnational religious identification such as "Christian" work to enact locally and globally what it means to hold this identification. But it also matters for how feminist struggles can

---

40. Ibid.

41. This topic exceeds the question of canon. Issues considered include: when and what kinds of feminist reforms might result in the production of a new religious tradition no longer understood as "Jewish," "Christian," and so on (e.g., Judith Plaskow, *Standing Again at Sinai: Judaism From a Feminist Perspective* [New York: HarperCollins, 1991]); conditions for productive interfaith and multifaith alliances and exchange (e.g., Kwok Pui-lan, *Introducing Asian Feminist Theology*) and the status of monotheism in feminist theology and praxis (e.g., Laurel Schneider, *Beyond Monotheism: A Theology of Multiplicity* [London: Routledge, 2008]).

42. Schüssler Fiorenza, "Introduction," 5; and Kwok Pui-lan, "Racism and Ethnocentrism in Feminist Biblical Interpretation," in Schüssler Fiorenza, *A Feminist Introduction*, 110.

43. See Chung Hyun Kyung, *Struggling to be the Sun Again: Introducing Asian Women's Theology* (Maryknoll, N.Y.: Orbis, 1990); and Kwok Pui-lan, *Introducing Asian Feminist Theology*, 42–62.

44. Dube, "Rahab Is Hanging Out a Red Ribbon," 187–88.

be enacted across and between religious identifications in various local and supralocal contexts. This kind of critical engagement can occur in academic contexts or in boundary crossing contexts, such as the Ecumenical Association of Third World Theologians, comprised of academics, lay people, and religious professionals.[45]

Biblical canonical boundaries do not simply pertain to religious affiliation. Within literary studies, the notion of a canon and the challenging of the boundaries of literary canons is a familiar one that is often linked to "culture wars" over gender, race, ethnicity, and national identity (though less often religious affiliation).[46] Indeed, the Christian Bible has functioned as a kind of canonical text along the lines of other literary works, such as Shakespeare's plays. That is, the Christian Bible is a widely circulated literary document with extensive intertextual and cultural influence in Christian-dominated parts of the world that is linked with histories of colonialism. In a multifaith, globally interconnected world with a range of transnational forms of alliance and activism, it is especially important for feminists of various locations to tackle and to transform the legacy of the Christian Bible as a literary canon whose effects include but also exceed the theological.[47]

------

45. See, e.g., discussion by Teresa Okure, "Feminist Interpretations in Africa," in Schüssler Fiorenza, *A Feminist Introduction*, 76–85; and María Pilar Aquino, "'The Dynamics of Globalization and the University': Toward a Democratic-Emancipatory Transformation," in *Toward a New Heaven and a New Earth: Essays in Honor of Elisabeth Schüssler Fiorenza* (ed. Fernando F. Segovia; Maryknoll, N.Y.: Orbis, 2003), 385–406.

46. See e.g., Harold Bloom, *The Western Canon: The Books and School of the Ages* (New York: Harcourt Brace, 1994).

47. Non-Christians may thus view the two-Testament Bible as canonical for nontheological reasons and wish to transgress or challenge its boundaries or uses in order to achieve feminist aims, including decolonization or civil rights for queer people. Nonetheless, the bulk of academic biblical interpreters were raised as Christians. Jewish feminists such as Judith Plaskow, Ross Kraemer, Amy-Jill Levine, and Susannah Heschel have made important contributions to the study of Christian Testament materials; some of their work indirectly suggests that canon formation interacts with the production of differences between "Christian" and "Jewish" identifications. See, e.g., Judith Plaskow, "Feminist Anti-Judaism and the Christian God," *JFSR* 7.2 (1991): 99–108; Ross Kraemer, "Jewish Women and Christian Origins: Some Caveats," in *Women and Christian Origins* (ed. Ross Kraemer and Mary Rose D'Angelo; New York: Oxford University Press, 1999), 35–49; Amy-Jill Levine, "Women in the Q Communit(ies) and Traditions," in Kraemer and D'Angelo, *Women and Christian Origins*, 150–70; Susannah Heschel, "Jesus the Theological Transvestite," in *Judaism Since Gender* (ed. Miriam Peskowitz and Laura Levitt; New York: Routledge, 1997), 188–99. As Cynthia Baker cautions, however, attention to the *Jewishness* of Christian Testament interpreters, as opposed to their interpretive approaches, is problematic, especially given the history of Christian anti-Judaism; see Baker in this volume.

PART 4
WORKING FOR CHANGE AND TRANSFORMATION

WHERE DO YOU COME FROM?
WHERE ARE YOU GOING? FEMINIST INTERRELIGIOUS
BIBLIODRAMA IN A GERMAN CONTEXT

Leony Renk
Pastor; TCI graduate; Laase Conference Centre (Wendland), Germany

1. INTRODUCTION

"What is in the past of the Jews, the Turks have ahead of them." I read this horrific prediction on a house wall in Berlin at the beginning of the 1980s and was deeply shocked. This graffiti reminded me of the disturbing events in my village at the end of the war in 1945, when I was six years old, the depressing, stultifying silence that followed our children's questions, and the disconsolate phrase: "One is powerless here." Alongside wartime and postwar memories, however, were also the liberating experiences during the student revolts at the end of the 1960s, when the great silence was broken and the myth of powerlessness radically questioned.

At this point in time I had already developed bibliodrama as a method, which in addition to the text and its effective history includes the reality of the participants in all its aspects (individually, socially, politically). The experiences at the beginning of the 1980s led me to develop an interreligious bibliodrama concept. From the beginning, my bibliodrama concept can be understood only within the humanistic concept of Theme-Centered Interaction (TCI).

1.1. LEARNING PROCESSES IN THE ENCOUNTER WITH TCI

I met Ruth C. Cohn, the developer of TCI, for the first time in the mid-1970s. Her method, based on humanist psychology, was developed as a way of counteracting the horrors of the Nazi period. Her original and pivotal approach was to make those belonging to different nationalities, professional groups, and social grassroots movements aware of their partial power and to increase their autonomy. As a result, it would be possible for them to resist emerging hierarchies and dictatorships by way of common, networked activities. The inspiration for this approach lay in her own experiences as a Berlin Jew in the Third Reich and in the U.S., where she fled after 1933.

Ruth Cohn had returned for a seminar in Berlin in order to establish a "Workshop Institute for Living Learning" (WILL)[1] in collaboration with other Jewish leaders committed to TCI in Germany. I have to thank Ruth especially and foremost, as well as a few other TCI instructors such as Elisabeth Tomalin and Helga Aschaffenburg, for giving me the essential drive during my educational learning process of many years[2] to develop an interreligious concept of bibliodrama that focuses on gender, religion, and social justice.

Influenced as I was by the mechanisms of denial and repression in postwar German society at the end of the 1950s, I would normally have rejected the graffiti mentioned at the beginning of this article. Due to my longstanding learning process, I am today able to accept my involvement in the dreadful history of anti-Semitism and racism, because I am not the guiltless woman I would like to be. I, like everyone in our society, live in contexts shaped by an anti-Semitic history. Thus, the political contexts in which I, and all people, live must be considered and incorporated into my work.

Ruth Cohn introduced me to an ultra-democratic theory of education. She based her philosophy on the fact that every group learning process is defined by four factors: (1) the individual person (I); (2) the group and group interaction (We); (3) the subject or the task (It or, in bibliodrama, the text); and (4) the context in a narrow and wider sense (the Globe).[3] TCI works on the assumption that all four of these factors are important and must be incorporated in a dynamic balance.

The TCI method includes, among others, the following postulates, which provide a new understanding of leadership and the role of participants.[4]

1. "I am my own chairperson." Each person is her or his own leader and takes responsibility for oneself and one's part in the group event.

---

1. Since 2002 it has borne the name: Ruth Cohn Institute for TCI International (www .ruth-cohn-institute.com).

2. It is typical for TCI that the training takes a minimum of three years, and to take ten years to receive the diploma is nothing extraordinary.

3. The English term "globe" was also taken over as a specialist TCI expression for the entire German-speaking area.

4. See the introduction to the TCI model by Ruth Cohn and Alfred Farau, *Gelebte Geschichte der Psychotherapie: Zwei Perspektiven* (Stuttgart: Klett Cotta, 1984), 351–70.

Therefore, each individual is involved in the leadership and the responsibility for the success of a seminar.

2. "I am autonomous *and* interdependent." This factor involves recognizing our connectedness with others in our various living, learning, and unlearning processes.

3. The postulate "I am not all-powerful; I am not completely powerless; *I am powerful in part*" highlights the individual's ability to take countermeasures when networked with others when a potential for social risk becomes apparent. The inclusion of the religious/cultural, social, political, and economic context and of the globe[5] is particularly important because "anyone who does not take the globe seriously is devoured by it."[6]

1.2. Developing Feminist Interreligious Bibliodrama

Feminist theology and bibliodrama emerged in Germany around the same time.[7] Bibliodrama and feminist theology aim to take into account every facet of the context.[8] Both understand women or participants as subjects of interpretation, and both are committed to justice. In dealing with biblical texts, both movements seek the marginal and marginalized clues in the text, and they use many different methods to do so.[9]

---

5. The importance of the globe must constantly be remembered in the TCI setting. The majority of the I-You-We-It levels overlap with the meaning of the political dimensions. When creating WILL America, the political dimension was even deleted again from the Articles of Association. See Leony Renk, "Die dringlichste Frage: Erinnerung an Ruth C. Cohn," *Schlangenbrut* 109/110 (2010): 51–53.

6. Cohn and Farau, *Gelebte Geschichte*, 355.

7. An in-depth examination of the relationships between bibliodrama and feminist theology is still pending. Uta Pohl-Patalong depicts the relationship of both as a "Kritische Freundschaft" (critical friendship) in her article of the same title in *Bibliodrama: Theorie–Praxis–Reflexion* (ed. Elisabeth Naurath and Uta Pohl-Patalong; Stuttgart: Kohlhammer, 2002), 30–37.

8. In bibliodramatic practice, the focus is usually on the individual (I), and often too little consideration is given, unfortunately, to the other factors (the context/globe and the group), even when the theory states otherwise.

9. In the Protestant history of women's Bible study, this has a long tradition only the rudiments of which have been researched. See on this Heike Koch, " 'Wichtig ist es, dass die Frauen lernen, "zwischen den Zeilen zu lesen" ': "Der Beitrag Maria Weigles für die Bibelarbeit der Evangelischen Frauenhilfe," in *100 Jahre Evangelische Frauenhilfe in Deutschland: Einblicke in ihre Geschichte* (ed. Christine Busch; Düsseldorf: Archive of the Protestant Church in the Rhineland, 1999), 171–204. An investigation could also be undertaken as to what differences can be identified between Protestant and Catholic female bibliodrama-

In the 1980s, German feminist theology became aware of how it was caught up in its own history. "The anti-Semitism debate in Germany placed Christian feminists in their most profound social, cultural, religious and historical context."[10] This observation is still valid and places before us a specific challenge: the tradition of Christian anti-Semitism shapes the way in which we deal with biblical texts.[11]

In developing my interreligious bibliodrama concept, I have tried to take up the aforementioned challenges as a significant part of my work in continuous education on the parish level and in other community venues.[12] In doing so, I have learned much from the field of humanistic psychology in the U.S., which was developed mainly by Jewish psychotherapists. At the point at which the unconscious and our inner creative strengths and imaginative capacities separate, they saw the impetus for destructive thought and action.

The theologian Ernst Lange also underlined the need for play, for aimless experimentation, and for exploring possibilities: "Without playing with possibilities, there is no recognition that reality needs not remain as it is, that it can be changed, improved. Play in our lives represents our utopian strengths, our capacity for visualizing a better world, for going beyond our limits."[13] With respect to bibliodrama, this means: "We express only what would otherwise remain inside … in music, in dealing with symbols, in dance, in play, in physical movement, what moves us inwardly and what inner movement there may be in the text…. God is given a living place in space and time."[14]

Working in such a holistic way requires more time than the traditional Bible class does. A bibliodrama seminar ideally lasts five days. There should

---

tists. See Klara Butting, "Bibel: Hermeneutik," in *Wörterbuch der Feministischen Theologie* (ed. Elisabeth Gössmann et al; Gütersloh: Gütersloher, 2002): 64–66, here 64.

10. Britta Jüngst, "Kontexte," in *Was Ist Feministische Theologie?* (ed. Claudia Rakel and Britta Jüngst; Gelnhausen: Arbeitsstelle Fernstudium EKD, 2004): 67–136, here 100.

11. See Antje Röckemann and Kathrin Winkler, "Christlich-feministische Theologie, Antijudaismus und jüdisch-christlicher Dialog," in *Feministische Theologie: Initiativen, Kirchen, Universitäten—eine Erfolgsgeschichte* (ed. Gisela Matthiae et al.; Gütersloh: Gütersloher, 2008), 344–50.

12. Until I retired in 2000, I led the Arbeitsstelle for Gemeinde- und Religionspädagogische Aus-, Fort- und Weiterbildung (Workplace for Community and Religious Training, Continuing and Further Education). Since 1990, I have been responsible for the Berlin and Brandenburg area and, prior to this, for West Berlin alone.

13. Ernst Lange, *Sprachschule für die Freiheit: Bildung als Problem und Funktion der Kirche* (Munich: Kaiser, 1980), 52.

14. Gerhard Marcel Martin, in the introduction to Walter Wink, *Bibelarbeit: Ein Praxisbuch für Theologen und Laien* (Kohlhammer: Stuttgart, 1982), 12. First published as *Transforming Bible Study* (Nashville: Abingdon, 1981).

be between ten and twenty people in the group, and it should be led by at least two people.

1.3. The Need for Liberating Biblical Interpretation

When we experience the dangers in our society with all our senses, we are often seized by both fear and crippling resignation. I am convinced that in these situations we need the liberating potential of biblical traditions so that courage and resistance can grow within the community of other resisters on our long way through the desert. I regard the biblical writings in my German context as an important "school of justice"[15] and assume that "the suspicion has been unproven that Scripture and feminist experience cannot be mediated."[16] This does not in any way indicate an uncritical approach. On the contrary, it means exposing not only the violent, misogynistic biblical texts but also the encouraging biblical narrative threads and those that liberate from structures of oppression. It means developing new democratic methods and educational concepts that nurture experiences of freedom and positively reinforce awareness and action for change.

2. Bibliodrama as a Holistic, Experiential, and Contextual Democratic Praxis of Biblical Interpretation

A contextual engagement with the Bible that will liberate women in such a way that they are able to perceive injustices can be nothing other than experiential and holistic. Biblical language in many places is already full of sensuality and physicality, even where it involves humiliating and depressing experiences between human beings (see, e.g., the texts about Sarah and Hagar). The body aspect of biblical language, however, is usually overlooked in conventional exegetical processes.[17]

---

15. Luise Schottroff, *Lydias ungeduldige Schwestern: Feministische Sozialgeschichte des frühen Christentum* (Gütersloh: Gütersloher, 1994), 11. Translated into English as *Lydia's Impatient Sisters: Feminist Social History of Early Christianity* (Louisville: Westminster John Knox, 1995).

16. Klara Butting, *Prophetinnen gefragt: Die Bedeutung der Prophetinnen im Kanon aus Tora und Prophetie* (Biblisch-feministische Texte 3; Wittingen: Erev-Rav, 2001), 205–6.

17. The theologian Antje Röckemann has developed a continuing education course from these considerations with the dance teacher Gabriela Jüttner: "Studying the Bible with Your Body" (www.theologie-in-bewegung.de).

2.1. Bibliodrama: Holistic Reading of Biblical Texts

Holistic experiences with all the senses, with heart and mind, with the whole body, inspire confidence and relation even with "outsiders"—in an entirely different way from cognitively disseminated information—and they change deeply internalized attitudes. "The body has its own language.… it makes the invisible visible—without words. When we translate its nonverbal language into a verbal one, we increase our understanding."[18]

In my first bibliodrama seminars, I was introduced to trainers who had trained intensively with Katya Delakova, a Jewish dance teacher who has had an enormous influence on bibliodrama in Germany. Motion and physical exercises make other experiences and perceptions possible and put our observational considerations into perspective. We become aware of differences, and even initial skeptics are captivated after some time.

Each bibliodrama, therefore, includes bodily awareness. Since we have not learned in our society to observe the body and include it in our learning processes, we need preparatory exercises. After an intensive exercise phase, the participants encounter the biblical text in a different way. The development of nonverbal gestures toward individual words of a text facilitate highly individual access—in approval or rejection, in experiencing intimacy or alienation. Out of the gestures, short scenes can be developed in small groups, which can change the meaning entirely or suggest new relationships between parts of the text. Bodily oriented play alternates with periods of reflection and periods of silence. Bibliodrama should therefore be seen as a process of body awareness; it is exegesis with the body.

In bibliodramatic work, the history of the impact of a biblical text often becomes apparent, too, through this alienation effect. Each bibliodrama can produce a practical implementation of the "hermeneutic of suspicion" (Elisabeth Schüssler Fiorenza). Each text is critically examined through the experiences of the bibliodramatists, and a lively resymbolization can be achieved in the readaptation process during the play. The text can thus be retold and a nonproductive history of its effects can be removed or its significance eliminated. Biblical texts come alive again as women become aware of their own roots in a new way. In doing so, all the participants become competent biblical interpreters, whether they are theologians or not, whether they are Jewish, Christian, Muslim, religious, or nonreligious women. "Bibliodrama is there-

---

18. Ruth Cohn, *Von der Psychoanalyse zur Themenzentrierten Interaktion: Von der Behandlung Einzelner zu einer Pädagogik für alle* (Stuttgart: Klett-Cotta, 2009), 202.

fore a democratic, nonacademic, interpretive feminist method that inspires and empowers women to appreciate their own theological authority."[19]

2.2. BIBLIODRAMA: THE CONTEXTS ARE CO-READERS

I live and work in a multicultural and multireligious society in Germany. A multireligious group in a bibliodrama is a great opportunity as well as a challenge for participants and for the leadership, because we have not had sufficient practice at being aware of our differences.[20]

Working with the body is also a great help here in developing a sense of the fact that we are all different. There is not just one globe for all, but each participant in a bibliodrama brings her own globe with her. This applies to all bibliodrama but more particularly to interreligious bibliodramatic work.

Differing globe perceptions also have an impact on leadership interventions in relation to the weighing of the themes of the individual participants (I level), their interactions (We level), and the significance of the respective biblical text (It level). There is a difference when I lead a bibliodrama group alone as a member of a Christian[21] majority as opposed to when I work as part of a leadership team in which a member of the small Jewish minority and/or the larger Muslim minority participates. Along with the religious background, the context also includes the collective patterns of reception that influence individuals, such as anti-Semitism and nationalism. It is essential that the globe should also be included in bibliodrama work.

My experiences with the Leitura Popular da Bíblia, particularly in Brazil itself, have once again reinforced for me the significance of the globe, which—as already suggested—is not adequately considered in the TCI movement. Experiences in Brazil have made me aware of the fact that the globe of the individual participants—with their hopes, dreams, strengths, and weaknesses—is determined by the social globe.

---

19. Antje Röckemann,"In Spiralen fliegen: Bibliodrama und TZI interkulturell," in *In Spiralen fliegen: Bibliodrama und TZI [Themenzentrierte Interaktion] interkulturell* (ed. Margarete Pauschert and Antje Röckermann; Münster: Schlangenbrut, 1999), 7–13, here 12.

20. Annette Mehlhorn therefore demands new educational concepts that also convey a "differential competence," in "Feministische Theologie und Praxis unter globalisierten Bedingungen: Thesen," in *Feministische Theologie: Initiativen, Kirchen, Universitäten—eine Erfolgsgeschichte* (ed. Gisela Matthiae et al.; Gütersloh: Gütersloher, 2008), 367–72, here 369.

21. In this text I include those with a Christian socialization in the term "Christian," even when some actually might have left their church.

The Leitura Popular da Bíblia gives considerable weight to the detailed analysis of political, social, economic, and cultural-religious aspects of the context of the participants, just as it does to the perception of these aspects in the historical biblical texts; the bibliodrama's strength lies in the appreciation of the individual and physical awareness.[22]

Latin American Bible study is marked by basic processes such as the pedagogy of the oppressed (Paulo Freire) and the theater of the oppressed (Augusto Boal). They understand the experiences of women in the so-called "social underclasses" and their religious ideas but also take into account their material living conditions. Freire's approach has also become familiar in Europe and Germany through theologian and educational theoretician Ernst Lange.

My concept of bibliodrama is based on TCI and inspired by the experiences with the Leitura Popular da Bíblia in Brazil. With it, I would like to overcome the gaps between thinking and feeling, between the personal and the factual, the private and the public, in order to bring areas that have diverged back together again. In this model, biblical texts will have more relevance in the long run in the public sphere and play a role in interreligious, intercultural contexts as "discussion partners" to be taken seriously. The division between the personal and political can be removed in this model by including the personal themes as well as themes of the globe. In this concept, a bibliodrama group is not a closed system but is defined by events in the outside world. My major concern is to raise awareness of the conditions of the social frameworks under which we all live. These include historical events whose impacts define the legacy we have inherited.

I see my experiences in the development of an interreligious bibliodrama as one step along the path to perceiving our diversity as enrichment rather than as threat. I understand bibliodrama as an open, creative process of interaction between a biblical text (It level) and the participants from different religions and cultures with their resulting different essential issues (I-You-We levels). The social and religious backgrounds of the participants and the particular context of the biblical text (globe) meet each other in this process of interaction. These encounters provide another view of individual participants' own life circumstances and a further opportunity to observe the "unfamiliar

---

22. See on this Mônica Ottermann, "The Blessing of the Canaanite Woman: Bibliodrama and *Leitura Popular*: Ten Years of Working with Bibliodrama in Brazil," *Bulletin Dei Verbum* 66/67 (2003): 11–15. Ottermann talks about a "love relationship" between bibliodrama and *leitura popular* (12). Articles on bibliodrama in Asia and the Pacific region can also be found in this edition of *Bulletin Dei Verbum*, a quarterly journal in German, English, French, and Spanish.

other." This fundamental experience is an important prerequisite for unlearning anti-Semitism and relearning how to live together from an interreligious and intercultural point of view.

2.3. Bibliodrama: The Text Pleads Its Own Case

In my own theological education, I had learned that I need to hold on to the *skopos* (Greek for goal, intention, aim, purpose) of the texts that I have exegetically defined. In my lengthy TCI education, on the other hand, I learned that I can liberalize the *skopos* of the text.[23] I have preferred attending seminars led by Jewish women who, based on their tradition, have a profound belief that the truth will in no way be lost even if extreme positions are expressed. My experience is that theological positions that also appear extreme to me are put into perspective in the play of bibliodrama and in the reflection following the debate.

We can learn from the midrashic tradition in Jewish exegetical history to allow different interpretations to stand side by side. We can rely on the fact that the message of the text prevails between all the extreme positions. For me, this is the profound meaning of this originally Jewish word from the tradition: "When two or three are gathered together in my name, the Shekinah is there in their midst."[24] The belief that the Shekinah is there in our midst gives me inner peace.

The bibliodrama method used by Peter and Susan Pitzele from the U.S. operates within the midrashic tradition. In the rabbinic tradition the black fire (the text itself, the characters) and the white fire (the spacing, the exegesis) belong together. This means that creative and imaginative exegesis makes the text complete. "The texts of the Bible stories (black fire) represent half of whole stories and are turned into whole stories by interpretation (white fire)."[25] For various reasons the term "bibliolog" was introduced for the Pitzeles' form of bibliodrama in German-speaking areas.[26]

---

23. A good exegetical preparation, as intensive and multifaceted as possible, is still important, of course.

24. Shekinah comes from the Hebrew verb *šākan* "to dwell" and can be translated as "in the presence of God." The Jewish word from m. Avot 3:2 reads: "when two sit together and concentrate on the words of the Torah, the Shekinah dewlls among them."

25. Michael Ellendorf, "Bibliolog im KU," *Lernort Gemeinde* 2 (2002): 49.

26. The Pitzeles' method refers primarily to language; physical work is not planned, and it is heavily focused on performance. This is precisely because the bibliolog is better suited to certain contexts, however, than bibliodrama, as shown by the latest Pohl-Patalong publications. See on this Andreas Pasquay, "'I Need You, to Participate the Story': Bib-

In the Christian tradition, we are exhorted to find *the* truth. The fact that there are several "truths" and, as a result, there can be different perspectives that are equally legitimate is cognitively easy to understand, but it is difficult actually to embrace this knowledge in Christian terms. The body work in a bibliodrama is helpful here, because we are able to learn in practical terms that there is no right or wrong. Each person has a different (physical) perception due to one's particular situation, physical, and spiritual constitution.

The acceptance of different opinions and different interpretations relating to the "truth" of biblical texts is also substantially more difficult. This is also true as a rule for the leadership. Leaders are also influenced by their purported correct understanding of a text. Their own hurts and vulnerabilities, however, are a disruptive factor and prevent participative leadership. In order to obviate these disruptions by the leadership, regular supervision or counseling and, if possible, a team leadership of two are very important.

3. Interreligious Bibliodrama in Practice

In Jewish-Christian bibliodrama workshops we are confronted—often very decisively—with the globe of Jewish-Christian-German relations, still largely unresolved. These form the background and provide the obvious answer to the question: "Why don't most Jews actually want any religious contact with us?"[27] The globe of the "mountain of collective Holocaust memories"[28] that has not yet become dissolved and its trauma are also consistently being highlighted in the second and third generations as the major problem between Jews and Christians. This "mountain of Holocaust memories" often torpedoes specification and organization of topics and ideas and at times makes any play or ritual impossible. Auschwitz as the collective tragedy in our country, as a violation of civilization, is neither adequately lamented nor thoroughly studied. This task of psychological work is still necessary for the mainstream in our society and our churches.

3.1. Bibliodrama on Genesis 12 (Kirchentag 2001)

Permit me to give an example of how the globe is present and at work in a Jewish-Christian bibliodrama. At the Deutscher Evangelischer Kirchentag in

---

liodrama/Bibliolog im christlich-jüdischen Gespräch"; online: http://www.judentum.net/dialog/bibliolog.htm.

27. Heiner Aldebert, "Bibliodrama und interreligiöser Dialog," in Naurath and Pohl-Patalong, *Bibliodrama*, 38–45, here 44.

28. Ibid.

2001, I led a Jewish-Christian bibliodrama workshop together with Iris Weiss, a Jewish bibliodrama leader.[29] Twenty-five women and men had gathered, all of them Christian. The only Jewish woman in the room was therefore one of the leaders. After a period of body exercises in silence, the individual participants were asked to answer the question: What kind of experiences with Jewish people or Judaism do I bring with me to the conversation?

Some talked about very enlightening discoveries in Jewish-Christian discussions, in connection with Aktion Sühnezeichen: Friedensdienste (Action Reconciliation: Service for Peace)[30] or in educational events put on by Protestant academies.[31] Most, however, had not had any personal encounter with a Jewish person. Instead, they had heard a great deal about Judaism and had adopted, usually unconsciously, an anti-Jewish attitude. All this was uncritically expressed by comments along a spectrum from "subject to the law" and "dim," because it was not illuminated by the bright light of the gospel, to stating that "Jews are arrogant."

We had not counted on so many anti-Jewish attitudes at the preliminary stages of the bibiliodrama. Therefore, after this conversation I put on hold our idea to approach Gen 12:1–11 with body exercises. I spontaneously suggested that they all change places on the stools and take on the role of a Jewish woman or man in order to react to what they had just heard as judgments about Jewish people. In doing so, they were not to look for any counterarguments but to observe what hearing these prejudices had unleashed within them. I asked the participants to take a few steps "in Jewish shoes" and to let the observation sink in without evaluating it. A deep dismay began to spread. After a long silence, a few voiced what they had experienced: "I need to question my so-called Christian identity, due to what I have just experienced." "As a woman, I regret my lack of wisdom when I think of what I have said before about Jewish people. I think I was very hurtful." "Perhaps this change in perspective I have just experienced is the start of a new Jewish-Christian understanding."

---

29. Deutscher Evangelischer Kirchentag [German Protestant Church Day] is a lay movement and independent organization that, in cooperation with the Protestant churches, organizes a biannual five-day event. It is something between a congress and a festival and attracts up to a hundred thousand participants. See www.kirchentag.de.

30. Aktion Sühnezeichen [Action Reconciliation] was founded in 1958 by members of the Synod of the Protestant Church in Germany. Acknowledging Germany's guilt for Nazi crimes, they set out with volunteer programs toward reconciliation in many European countries and Israel. See www.asf-ev.de.

31. See www.evangelische-akademien.de.

The dynamics of the text of Gen 12:1–11 began to work in a mysterious way even before it was realized. A performance "exodus from the errors" took place among a few of the participants at this stage, as a midrash interprets the text.[32] Perhaps a segment of spiritual strength has had an impact in this inspired internal Jewish-Christian encounter, which also made it possible to recognize the truth of the Jewish internal counterpart. "All understanding grows out of relation," according to Martin Buber. A relationship according to the mutuality principle was imagined through role reversal, even though only a single Jew was present.

3.2. Bibliodrama on Genesis 16 (Second European Women's Synod 2003)

I had a completely different experience in a similar situation. Together with Ewa Alfred, a Jewish Feldenkrais teacher and lawyer, I led an interreligious bibliodrama at the Second European Women's Synod in Barcelona in 2003. We set out a circle of chairs for the twenty-five participants expected, and the Jewish participants were "absent" again. Using Hagar's text, which we "translated" in gestures, our perception of the "empty chairs" was sharpened. In identifying with Hagar, the participants experienced an emotional change that led, for instance, to one participant coming out as Jewish in the course of the seminar and another participant revealing to me as leader that she was "actually" Jewish.

The fact that Hagar is "seen" changes her and her view of her own worth. The fact that Hagar is seen also changed participants' awareness, and they were able to grasp what it meant to trust others in the group and name their own identity. This moment was a gift for us. It was a moving moment at the end of the seminar. With a sharper perception of the room in which we were working, we realized that the "unoccupied chairs" had stayed empty for good reason: the absent Jewish women were absent because they had been murdered in the Shoah. Those who were present needed to remember those who were absent.[33]

---

32. With regard to Gen 12, a midrash explains that the threefold request "move out" also means that every man and woman must move out of the errors of the homeland, of the family, and of friends.

33. See Margarete Pauschert, "Der Stuhl bleibt frei: Die Präsenz der Abwesenden im Bibliodrama," in *Interreligiöses Bibliodrama: Bibliodrama als neuer Weg zur christlich-jüdischen Begegnung* (ed. Leony Renk; Schenefeld: EB, 2005), 135–43.

3.3. Bibliodrama on Genesis 21 (Women's Trialogue 1996)

In 1996, the secular association Goldnetz initiated a major women's trialogue in Berlin.[34] For the bibliodrama workshop that I offered at the trialogue, I chose the expulsion of Hagar, whose dramatic story plays a significant role in all three religions.[35] Jewish, Christian, Muslim, and nonreligious women were able to identify at different levels with Hagar and with her history. We saw that in all three religions of the book there are stories of women that tell of depression and oppression, of not being seen and not being valued.

In the bibliodramatic play we saw Hagar screaming in the desert from grief, loneliness, and anger because she was oppressed by Sarah. She found no support and without further ado was declared a nonperson—she was simply a slave. Hagar did not remain the speechless object in the play. Her suffering in and at the hands of the desert changed her. She became a strong woman, conversing with God: "You, God, have seen me." "Hagar, the first theologian," said the Muslims, "have you noted that?"

One participant, a radio broadcast editor, said in the feedback round: "We have acted out a 'book drama'—a story in a Jewish, Christian, and Muslim version in a way that indiscernibly backed up our approach. A word from the text stands out. From the word we form a gesture, from the gesture a movement and then, together, a play, a drama. We talk about how we experience it, our play and the play of others. We laugh, we open up, we appreciate one another."[36] "I got to know Hagar today," said an Israeli woman later, "as the mother of a nation."

This experience is evidence of the relation-generating, interreligious opportunity for communication in bibliodrama. Here, where thoughts *and* feelings come into play in the dealings with the holy scriptures, a willingness to change prejudgments about members of other religions can grow. It is crucial that the leaders provide space for individual religiosity. Exchanging these experiences within the group can become important for developing the important gift of a resilient solidarity for public culture.

---

34. See on this Rita Unruh and Waltraud Thiel, "Frau sein–Fremd sein–Offen sein: Mit t.a.n.g.o. zum ersten Frauen-Trialog in Berlin," in Pauschert and Röckermann, *In Spiralen fliegen*, 33–34.

35. In a Jewish-Christian-Muslim project, the term "Bible" in bibliodrama is, of course, no longer used solely for the Christian Bible, but textual bases on an equal footing are the Torah and the Qur'ān.

36. On August 29, 1996, the SFB (Sender Freies Berlin) broadcast this to commemorate the first interreligious women's trialogue in Berlin.

The discussions with the theme of religion and with the texts that have emerged in this field have a public and political dimension that is revealed in our play sequences. In the subsequent discussion, the subject was broached regarding the problematic understanding of religion in the singular and the resulting claims of exclusivity that have been made throughout the history of religions. The claim of absoluteness consequently led to delusional thinking in every area and was conducive to oppression and expulsion of heretics. This thinking has led to genocide. In the experiences of the participants, it became clear that religion in the singular attacked not only heretics or nonbelievers but also all those who attempted to juxtapose several alternative interpretations in their own religion.

4. "Hermeneutics of Suspicion" in Bibliodrama

The engagement with interreligious bibliodrama practices can change the European bibliodrama movement, which has to date been predominantly focused on Christian participants. In a Jewish-Christian bibliodrama, becoming aware of and understanding the "presence of those who are absent" will lead to a more critical interaction with presentations of the traditionally "holy text authorities" and the typologies derived from them.[37]

In both respects we need to sharpen our senses for a "hermeneutics of suspicion." On the one hand, it is essential to name clearly the claim of absoluteness in the traditional Christian interpretation of the Bible and to recognize how sublimely it is sometimes expressed and how deeply anchored it is in the collective Christian unconscious. This exegetical tradition has a monologist structure and is therefore inappropriate for a dialogue in interreligious bibliodrama seminars as well as in other interreligious contexts. In order to perceive one's own blind spots, it is always wise to have two leaders for mutual correction.

On the other hand, this "hermeneutics of suspicion" needs, in ideological-critical terms, to question the controlling interests of current interpretations, the history of exegesis, and the impact of biblical texts as to whether, for example, non-Christians, Jewish, or Muslim women and men are defamed, marginalized, or made invisible. Whenever the holy scriptures also are a document of the historical victors—speaking at the expense of the dignity of the

---

37. Examples include the presentation of the so-called "wicked" Pharisees (it has long since been established that Jesus was probably attached to the Pharisaic movement as well) and the ostensive opposition of law and gospel, about which complaints continue to be made, showing evidence of Christian ignorance of the Jewish understanding of the law.

defeated—we are expressly asked to distance ourselves from these texts and their exegetical history.[38]

Aside from the fact that bibliodrama seminars of the three religions of the book challenge us to reflect our religious identity to a considerable extent, the following basic rule for interreligious dialogue must be applied if bibliodrama is to succeed: "We need to represent our own tradition with integrity and conviction in interreligious dialogue, but this integrity and conviction must include and not exclude self-criticism."[39] Without self-criticism and without self-assurance of one's own cause, there cannot be successful dialogue.

5. CONCLUSION

In summary, my feminist interreligious bibliodrama seeks:

1. to make a contribution to a gender-just, experience-related, holistic, and creative interpretation of the Bible;
2. to develop a model of understanding that takes seriously the context both of the particular biblical ancient text as well as today's context in equal measure; and
3. to make conscious and to present the controlling interests of all those involved in the process of interpretation. Even unconscious interests thus become apparent, creating opportunities to expand self-awareness and textual awareness.

Understood in this way, bibliodrama is an ultra-democratic[40] group, teaching, and learning model in which theologians and scholars, alongside those who have not studied and those socialized as Christian alongside those of other faiths and no faith can participate as subjects in the process of understanding biblical texts and can thereby deepen and extend the resonating sphere within the text. Given the many and varied challenges that we can tackle only as a community in this globalized world, feminist interreligious and intercultural bibliodrama based on TCI can help in moving away from the errors of culture,

---

38. For example, "Satan's synagogue" (Rev 2:9–3:9) is still part of the pericope series. Reference is seldom made to this in sermons themselves; instead, this point is ignored. How such a text can be handled in bibliodrama is the question that should be raised.

39. Leonard Swidler, "Grundregeln für den interreligiösen Dialog," in his *Die Zukunft der Theologie* (Regensburg: Lang, 1994), 31.

40. See Elisabeth Schüssler Fiorenza, *Wisdom Ways: Introducing Feminist Biblical Interpretation* (Maryknoll, N.Y.: Orbis, 2001), 23–24.

religion, and generation and in starting the necessary unlearning processes.[41] At best, new learning processes can then begin, and the Bible will become a book of life, encouraging us to take political action.

---

41. See Antje Röckemann, "'Erbsünde gibt es bei uns nicht': Jüdisch-christliches Bibliodrama als Chance für Ver-Lernprozesse," in Renk, *Interreligiöses Bibliodrama*, 125–33.

Wo/men in Liturgy and Art on Wisdom's Paths

Regula Grünenfelder
Schweizerischer Katholischer Frauenbund

A police officer appeared at the break of dawn and quietly carried off the school satchel of our neighbor's boy. The refugee family was deported unannounced to an unknown destination. Many in the small Swiss village reacted with dismay and signed a letter of protest to the authorities. The children's education was not even considered. The Swiss children cried and wrote farewell letters to their schoolmates and their parents, as a teacher reported, "whom they would never see again." Three days later, the refugee family was back again. The police had taken them out of the country and left them at a European airport with no contact, money, food, or shelter. In their need and despair, they had one thing in mind: to get back to their home. Their arrival was a celebration organized by the community mixed with anger and especially fear—fear of further police action and fear of rendering themselves liable to prosecution by caring for the family. They fed and accommodated the hungry, exhausted people in various homes. A group organized further support and sent out invitations for a public meeting that same evening using posters, emails, and phone calls.

In the evening the church where the meeting took place was full. The Muslim couple and a friendly translator—a refugee recognized by Switzerland—were there. People from different parties, denominations, and those of no faith, young and old had come. A wide range of people rose to speak and share what they knew or to ask questions. Together we struggled to understand what was happening and what our duty was now as a village community. In preceding days, children had clearly voiced their belief that the family was one of us. Now they urgently wanted their questions answered and their demands heard. The following morning, the refugee family had to go with their children to the very office where the injustice had taken place. People offered to go with them and provide civil protection. In the meantime, others were organizing legal and psychological aid, food, shelter, and clothing.

That evening the church turned into a forum of wisdom: a place where the openness and solidarity that our village dreamt of began. It was a period of struggling to understand and to take the right action. It was a community in which children and outsiders had a voice and shared a common concern for serving justice and human kindness.

An unusually high number of people attended the harvest festival two weeks later. The refugee family had brought apples from "their" garden. We celebrated an interdenominational and interreligious Eucharist with apple slices in thanksgiving for salvation and for the community. Two years later, the family was finally recognized as refugees in Switzerland—a wonder, stated their lawyer at the party which the family gave for all supporters and friends.

1. "Wisdom Is Feminist"

I began this essay with an example of how wisdom is at work among people today who seek for justice and friendship. I did so in order to tell the story of wisdom/Wisdom as rediscovered by feminist theology and biblical interpretation.

The notion of wisdom is ancient and is at home in many religious traditions. Wisdom is the experience and longing for well-being and for all to be able to make their own contributions. Wisdom is the joy of living in harmony—therefore righteously—with oneself, with others, and with creation as a whole. Wisdom is also reflecting on wisdom and formulating wisdom-filled thoughts and actions. Wisdom is a space for wise interaction. Counter-experiences are also ancient: confusion, stupidity, domination, injustice, fixed ideas, and dogma about wisdom that are not always connected with wise and wisely shared experiences. Wisdom is a process, and it changes according to need, experience, and association, just as it does with patterns of domination and violence that oppose its development. Wisdom is also the One, the Goddess,[1] the custodian of justice with many names: Ma'at, the ancient Egyptian Goddess of a just human and cosmic order and its biblical, Jewish and Christian "daughters and granddaughters" Chokhma, Sophia, Shekhina, Christ and "sister" Goddesses of wisdom of many religious traditions, such as the American Pachamama, the Tibetan green Tara, and the Indian Saraswati. There are wisdom theologians in all religions and in every period. As creation

---

1. The spelling G*d indicates the provisional nature of human language to name the Divine. It was introduced to feminism by Elisabeth Schüssler Fiorenza, *Jesus: Miriam's Child, Sophia's Prophet: Critical Issues in Feminist Christology* (New York: Continuum, 1994).

theologians, they consider the just order that encompasses everything and provides space for all creatures, and admits all wo/men.

2. FEMINIST BIBLICAL RESEARCH AND CELEBRATION IN THE CONTEXT OF WO/MEN'S LIBERATION MOVEMENTS

Nelle Morton (1905–1987), church activist and feminist theologian, who saw wisdom with biblical roots and everyday practical sustenance at work in the wo/men's liberation movements stated, "Wisdom is Feminist."[2] This means that wisdom is available at present to those who wish to find it—irrespective of gender, origin, or other affiliations. It calls everyone alike to its table. Wisdom is therefore an internationally and interreligiously unifying project. It is also a female image of G*d that empowers wo/men to share in the vision and struggle for global justice. Many feminists have begun to nurture their spiritual and intellectual strength in Wisdom-Chokhma-Shekhina-Sophia's name, whom they need for their political work of liberation.

In the 1970s, Christian feminist biblical scholars began conducting research on the biblical traditions of wisdom and making the old stories of female images of G*d and "wise living" available to liberation movements worldwide. In books, lectures and seminars, they have shared stories that tell of justice, quality of life, and education for all wo/men.

At that time, some Jewish feminists embraced the Shekhina with the same goals: liberation and equality. Marcia Falk as well as Susan Sered[3] criticized the inherent polarity of gendered religious symbols. If G*d is conceptualized and addressed as "other" (creator, savior, Lord, even in feminine terms), as opposite to the "world," they argued, we are not able to speak of and create equal relations. Hence, Marcia Falk, author of a liturgical classic among Jewish feminists, does not use Shekhina as an appropriate term for the Divine.

> The dilemma of monotheism for feminist Jews is more profound than at first we may have thought. It is not just that monotheism has been perverted, throughout Jewish (as well as Christian and Moslem) history, to mean male monotheism; this problem would be relatively easy to correct. We would add female images to our language, change "he" into "she" and "God" into "Goddess" (at least part of the time), and substitute Shekinah for Adonai in

---

2. Nelle Morton, *The Journey Is Home* (Boston: Beacon, 1985), 175.

3. See Susan Sered, "Jewish Wo/men and the Shekhina," in *In the Power of Wisdom: Feminist Spiritualities of Struggle* (ed. Elisabeth Schüssler Fiorenza and Pilar Aquino; Concilium 5 (London: SCM, 2000) 78–90.

our prayers—or come up with new feminine names for Divinity. Would it be so easy![4]

This objection of Jewish feminists, which is in line with the tradition of the biblical ban on images (the ban of only *one* image), is a warning not to misunderstand Wisdom-Chokhma-Shekhina-Sophia as a dogmatic concept rather than as empowering elements in a multifocal dynamic process of liberation.

The antagonism between prophetic and wisdom-filled biblical texts stirred up by German feminist exegetes indicates how necessary such a multifocal, political focus is. A wisdom-filled reading is opposed to a fixed or mandatory dogmatic access to wisdom. The figure of Chokhma-Sophia-Shekinah-Sapientia may be read as "Lady Wisdom," as a fantasy of the Eternal Feminine by elitist educated men and therefore inappropriate for the practice of wo/men's liberation.[5] This finding was duplicated by analyses of the "female outsider" in Prov 1–9, which was seen in light of the kyriarchal dualist opposition of saints and whores in Sacred Texts[6] and anti-Semitic studies of the New Testament.[7] Wo/men researching feminist wisdom objected to this interpretation and demonstrated that the figure of biblical wisdom bears hardly any traits of a macho fantasy. It speaks and calls out to the public, organizes feasts, asks rulers to take the right action, is friendly with all those who seek it, and does not assume any privileges. A wise approach to any text, whether it belongs to prophetic or wisdom literature, whether it is old and sacred or the latest media report, needs to consider the complex power relationships inscribed in the texts as well in the community of producers and readers.[8]

Justice as a vision and wo/men's work in progress are common to the prophetic and wisdom traditions of the Hebrew Bible and the Second Testament. Critical study of all texts is necessary in order for the kyriarchal mechanisms

---

4. Marcia Falk, "Toward a Feminist Jewish Reconstruction of Monotheism," *Tikkun* 4 (July–August 1989): 53.

5. E.g., Luise Schottroff, "The Sayings Source Q," in *A Feminist Commentary* (vol. 2 of *Searching the Scriptures*; ed. Elisabeth Schüssler Fiorenza; New York: Crossroad, 1994), 510–34.

6. Christl Maier, *Die "fremde Frau" in Proverbien 1–9: Eine exegetische und sozialgeschichtliche Studie* (OBO 144; Göttingen: Vandenhoeck & Ruprecht, 1995).

7. Angelika Strotmann, "Weisheitschristologie ohne Antijudaismus? Gedanken zu einem bisher vernachlässigten Aspekt in der Diskussion um die Weisheitschristologie im Neuen Testament," in *Von der Wurzel getragen: Christlich-feministische Exegese in Auseinandersetzung mit Antijudaismus* (ed. Luise Schottroff and Marie-Theres Wacker; Leiden: Brill, 1996), 153–75.

8. Elisabeth Schüssler Fiorenza, *Wisdom Ways: Introducing Feminist Biblical Interpretation* (Maryknoll, N.Y.: Orbis, 2001).

and anti-Semitisms inscribed in biblical texts and their exegetical histories to be interrupted. With texts of biblical prophecy and biblical wisdom, the work of emancipation is the same, because both traditions convey kyriarchal relations, and these are reenlisted in exegesis, liturgy, and representative art or music, and thereby contribute further to the alienation and marginalization of wo/men. It is not whether and which sacred texts or any other texts are used, but *how they are used* that decides whether they are violent or empower a commitment to the liberation and well-being of all.

3. A Feminist Biblical Wisdom Hermeneutics and Politics for Wo/men's Liberation

Elisabeth Schüssler Fiorenza, feminist theologian, New Testament scholar, collaborator in feminist movements and projects, teacher and guest in countless "grassroots movements," developed the dance of wisdom in the last quarter of the twentieth century, enabling wo/men's movements to conceive a spirituality of wisdom, to think about justice in extremely complex relationships, to point out unjust situations and privileges, and to work to achieve moments of wisdom in a shared existence in society. Schüssler Fiorenza has coined a term for vision and experience in radical democratic collaboration with the oxymoron *ekklesia* of wo/men[9] (wo/men church), which has been adopted in analytical discussions as well as in rituals and practices of liberation movements.

The image of the spiral dance of wisdom of the wo/men's *ekklesia* links the multidimensional experiences of dissonance, thought processes, relations of dominance and their criticism, reference texts such as the Bible and the implication of their interpretations, privileges and unjust relationships, liturgical and artistic forms of expression. This Wisdom dance has the following hermeneutical steps, which are not linear but spiral: hermeneutics of experience and social location, of kyriarchal structural analysis, of suspicion, evaluation, imagination, remembering, and transformation. It seeks to meet, methodically,[10] the goal of wisdom first articulated by Nelle Morton:

---

9. *Ekklesia*: democratic assembly in the city states of ancient Greece. "Because throughout history, full citizenship and democracy were limited to elite men, it is necessary to qualify the term ekklesia with the term wo/men to overcome the kyriocentric certainty of this term" (Elisabeth Schüssler Fiorenza, *Wisdom Ways*, 297). See the detailed justification there.

10. In contrast to instructions establishing the "method," as in a "practice" book bordering on plagiarism by Luzia Sutter Rehmann and Kerstin Rödiger, *Der springende Punkt: Anleitung zur Bibellektüre in sieben Schritten* (Gütersloh: Gütersloher, 2010).

"Hearing into speech,"[11] so that wo/men may engage in conversation and dialogue, think critically, write poetry and music about their experiences and their ideas about liberation, act on them and nurture themselves "dancing" with others at wisdom's table.

4. Liturgy in Wisdom's Ways

Feminist Bible studies have turned academic biblical studies into an object of public, political debate as well as into a forum of Wisdom. The Wisdom liturgy movements enrich the forum of Wisdom with a particular emphasis. They have politicized liturgy and examined their liturgical experience and development. As with the term *ekklesia,* so also is the community and authority of wo/men addressed with the word *leitourgia,* or "public work" and "service of the people and for the people." Furthermore, the *ekklesia* must be specified as *ekklesia of wo/men* in order not to reproduce the marginalization of wo/men who find themselves at the bottom of the kyriarchal pyramid of power. "The recognition of the feminist political position and the impacts of the liturgy is necessary."[12]

Jewish feminist theologians, poets, and liturgists as well as Jewish ritual groups also see liturgy as a test case as to whether wo/men with their experiences feel themselves to be actually part of a group that is understood to be egalitarian. Marcia Falk highlights important moments in wo/men's lives for which there is no blessing even in liberal Judaism, for example the menarche.[13]

Because of its political impact, it is dangerous to occupy the squares and dance in the streets with Wisdom. This was demonstrated, for instance, at the plenary meeting of the Ecumenical Council in Canberra in 1991, where the theologian and Shaman Dr. Kyung Chung Hyun addressed the sacred spirit in the form of the Goddess Kwan Yin, the Goddess of compassion and wisdom in the Korean tradition. She issued an invitation to the assembly to take part

---

11. "We experienced G*d as Spirit—hearing human beings to speech—to new creation. The Word came as human word, the human expression to humanness. The creative act of the Spirit was not Word speaking, but hearing—hearing the created one to speech" (Morton, *Journey*, 82).

12. Christine Schaumberger, "Wir lassen uns nicht länger abspreisen! Überlegungen zur feministischen Suche nach Liturgie als Brot zum Leben," in *Meine Seele sieht das Land der Freiheit: Feministische Liturgien—Modelle für die Praxis* (ed. Christine Hojenski et al.; Münster: edition liberación, 1990), 43–58, here 51.

13. Marcia Falk, "Notes on Composing New Blessings," in *Weaving the Visions: Patterns in Feminist Spirituality* (ed. Judith Plaskow and Carol P. Christ; San Francisco: Harper & Row, 1989), 128–38.

in transforming power dynamics in the church and world. She was accused of blasphemy and regarded thereafter as disruptive to ecumenism.[14]

In 1993, the Re-imagining Conference organized by Protestant wo/men in Minneapolis led to enormous negative professional consequences for the wo/men who gave featured lectures and invoked and celebrated Wisdom in prayer and liturgy. Malestream Protestantism in the U.S.A. reacted so violently that one promoter lost her church job and others had to face tremendous difficulties.[15] This conference had a vital impact on the development of Divine Chokhma-Sophia-Wisdom the*logy, liturgy, and politics around the globe.

Liturgy in the house of wisdom is interreligious like the wisdom in numerous sacred texts of religions. Liturgies, prayers and songs, collections of liturgies, suggestions for the creation of liturgy and ritual, prayer, and song books, as well as numerous offerings on the Internet, provide materials and support for preparing and conducting feminist liturgies. Teresa Berger underscores, however, the problem that ensues when texts are taken over and become formulaic without the involvement of wisdom communities:

> Collections of liturgical material alone, however, invariably serve to decontextualize and dehistoricize, since by only reproducing the liturgical text, these collections occlude the particular material realities that produced the liturgies and determined their meaning in the first place.[16]

She emphasizes that the numinous, creative, and linear-rational unseizable dimension of the liturgy does not justify any precritical or uncritical handling of liturgy, but rather calls for a critical contextualization:

> Contrary to the popular assumption that ritual is a precritical activity, reflexivity is a prominent element in many of the new wo/men's liturgies themselves: a phase of reflecting on the liturgy is common for many wo/men-identified communities and in some cases is built into the ritualizing process itself.[17]

---

14. See Chung Hyun Kyung, *Struggle to Be the Sun Again: Introducing Asian Women's Theology* (Maryknoll, N.Y.: Orbis, 1990).

15. See Nancy J. Berneking and Pamela Carter Joern, eds., *Re-membering and Re-imaging* (Cleveland: Pilgrim, 1995).

16. Teresa Berger, "Introduction," in *Dissident Daughters: Feminist Liturgies in Global Context* (ed. Teresa Berger; Louisville: Westminster John Knox, 2001), 14.

17. Berger, "Introduction," 15. Likewise, as a reflection of one's own practice, see Christine Hojenski et al., "Feministische Liturgien: Suchbewegungen–Erfahrungen–Reflexionen," in *Meine Seele sieht das Land*, 59–75.

Berger's anthology of self-reflections on feminist liturgies around the world shows how wo/men have had to struggle with the conviction that religion and feminism do not go together. In the Peruvian context of militarism, wo/men created wisdom liturgies in which they articulated the tensions of their diverse engagement and were able to point out their commitment, their dilemmas, and their convictions. *Talitha Cumi* created its own liturgical space in Lima.

> The liturgical space felt like an oasis, a place and space that I longed for: no orthodoxy, no right formulas or words, time of silence, times of no words if we did not find any.[18]

In this space, they take the liberty of including indigenous symbols such as the ears of corn as a sign of unity, the Chicha drink and coca leaves together with the biblical symbols of light, dark, salt, and bread. The gatherings enable the wo/men to live with their overlapping faith and feminism, to study them and to construct them well. Liturgies are an essential and supportive part of their commitment. The gatherings combine eating, working, and ritualizing together.

Wisdom liturgy movements arose out of wo/men's movements for change. Hence, critical voices have even been loudly raised in Europe to continue asking whether wisdom liturgies distract from the struggles for self-determination, liberation, and solidarity. Christine Schaumberger thus designates the aim of a wo/men's liturgy in the subjunctive:

> Bread of life, in contrast, would need to awaken the memory, sharpen awareness and sorrow, keep the flame of the longing for salvation burning and re-ignite the power of resistance and the strength to fight.[19]

5. Wisdom Art

In the space of Wisdom, music, paintings, sculptures, and poems do not simply depict Wisdom. Furthermore, Wisdom liturgies, rituals, pictures and music are not simply illustrative, but "difficult art." They instigate to action and engender new perceptions. According to Christine Schaumberger:

> What is most important is that I experience such "difficult" art by perceiving, by changing from a first impression and many others, with the presentiment,

---

18. Rosanna Panizo, "Women Rise Up, Close Ranks! *Talitha Cumi* in Lima Peru," in Berger, *Dissident Daughters*, 51.

19. Schaumberger, "Wir lassen uns nicht länger abspreisen," 49.

with the impact on seeing further … and that I learn how controlled and limited my perceptions are and how difficult it is to have a clear perception.[20]

To this end, works that have so far only been incorporated to a limited extent in feminist Bible studies can become important, such as, for example, the water color "Wisdom is bought with blood" by Maria Lassnig (1981).[21]

This "difficult" art does not illustrate, does not look back, does not explain, does not offer to mean something to reflect the viewer(s), and does not allow the viewer(s) to peek through. In the wisdom dance, these idiosyncrasies shatter familiar perceptions and behavior and break rigidly-held opinions. Difficult wisdom art would be respite, for instance in hospitals. Pulheim and Schaumberger assert that difficult art involves

> facing difficulties and staying standing, constantly seeing anew and differently and learning to understand. This would break a viewing habit that makes the magnitude of the difficulties dependent on success and function and leads to the difficulties and struggles themselves being acknowledged… not becoming accustomed to sighs, but hearing and respecting them.[22]

Illustrative practical artwork in an open forum of wisdom can also open up new perspectives and possible courses of action. In the wisdom dance, for example, a picture that is meant in an entirely different way may suddenly set free critical impulses such as the web icons of the blond, delicate, beautiful Lady Wisdom embracing the earth.[23]

Students have recognized in it the clichés and marginalizations of wo/men associated with it in spiritual representations of wisdom: the countless wisdom images in the picture of the "white lady" embody the cosmic dimension and healing power of g*dly wisdom in the racist equation of "white" and "good," and assign to "the woman at the side of the warrior" the power to

---

20. Christine Schaumberger, in an email of June 2010, said: "Das Wichtigste ist, dass ich mit solcher 'schwieriger' Kunst Erfahrungen mit Wahrnehmen mache, mit dem Wechsel vom ersten Eindruck und vielen weiteren, mit dem Ahnen, mit den Auswirkungen auf das weitere Sehen … und dass ich lerne, wie beherrscht und begrenzt meine Wahrnehmungen sind und wie mühsam es ist, genau wahrzunehmen."

21. See http://www.artnet.com/artists/maria-lassnig.

22. Peter Pulheim and Christine Schaumberger, "Mit Figuren von Hans Steinbrenner leben," in Hans Steinbrenner zum 70. Geburtstag (ed. Helmut Dreiseitl; Cologne: Galerie Dreiseitl, 1998), 29.

23. Pamela Matthews, Sophia: Peace through Wisdom. See further, Katia Romanoff, "Sophia: Goddess of Wisdom and God's Wife"; online: http://www.northernway.org/sophia.html.

support the task of putting right and restoring what he destroys. Such images of the great embrace are applied to reflection and identification and almost call out to them to go against the grain so that the complicity of privileged wo/men is not glorified in systems of injustice.[24] Perhaps the development of ideas has a transforming effect on the healing power of wisdom. For this to be the case, the iconography would need to be more diverse.

Sophialogy is an important discipline in orthodox the*logy, and iconography provides new opportunities in the twentieth century for commemorating and valuing wo/men. The following icon thus shows the orthodox theologian, mother, and religious sister Maria Skobtsova, who looked after female employees in Paris eating houses and helped Jewish people to escape in Vichy's France. Mother Maria was murdered in 1945 in the Ravensbrück Concentration Camp. (On Holy Saturday in 1945, she took the place of a Jewish woman who was going to be sent to the gas chamber, and died in her place.) She is represented on the icon to the left with her thick spectacles, her simple robe, but (exceptionally) without a cigarette. [25] The table at which she is represented with her colleagues is presided over by Sophia.

The Indian artist Lucy de Souza, who has a Christian background, also creates illustrative wisdom art, representing, for example, the interreligious aspect of Sophia, in which she pictures wisdom as Mary of Bethany with the attributes of the goddess Saraswati, the goddess of wisdom, language, the intellect, and art, who is traditionally accompanied by a swan and a musical instrument.[26]

Religious art also includes cultural objects as they are produced in their own right or purchased in online stores and educational establishments, for example this Passover tambourine with the dancing and drumming wo/men at the Red Sea, as well as statues of g*ddesses or icons of the Pachamama.[27]

---

24. See Kwok Pui-lan, *Discovering the Bible in the Non-biblical World* (Maryknoll, N.Y.: Orbis, 1995), esp. 84–95.

25. Ivanka Dymyd, *St. Maria of Paris with those Glorified with Her.* Reproduced from Jim Forest, "St. Maria of Paris with those Glorified with Her," n.p. [cited 13 August 2013]. Online: http://www.flickr.com/photos/jimforest/158061160/in/set-72157594152181792/lightbox/. "This is an icon painted by Ivanka Dymyd, the composition of which is probably inspired by Rublev's Holy Trinity icon. At the head of the altar-like table is an angelic figure identified (in French) as "Saint Sophia, the Wisdom of God." At the lower left is Mother Maria Skobtsova. The others at the table are, going clockwise, Father Alexis of Ugine, Ilya Fundaminsky, the figure representing Holy Wisdom, Mother Maria's son Ilya, and finally Father Dimitri Klepinine."

26. See http://www.lucy-art.de.

27. The Tambourine: http://www.allthingsjewish.com/browseproducts/Miriam-Tambourine.html). See also http://www.elcaminodeladiosa.com.ar/pachamama.htm. In traditional Andean culture, there are no images of Pachamama.

Sophia has also become famous as a guest at the "Dinner Party" (1974–1979). Thirty-nine place settings on the three-piece table recall thirty-nine famous wo/men figures. Nine hundred ninety-nine names of other well-known wo/men are arranged in gold letters on the carpet in front. The "Dinner Party" is a milestone of feminist art and is part of a permanent exhibition in the Elizabeth A. Sackler Center for Feminist Art (Brooklyn, New York). The artist is sending a message with her artwork: "Our earth is our power."[28]

Wisdom art by wo/men, like wisdom liturgy, refers not only to representations of Sophia, but also to artistic contributions that inspire, support, irritate, and assimilate Wisdom's Dance in an open forum. The motif of Jesa Christa could rank as an entire category, which various wo/men artists have devised.[29] The motif is neither a New Age nor a Western one. The crucified wo/men are particularly provocative. Many male and female artists in the twentieth century used the motif inside and outside church contexts, including "the Canadian Almuth Lutkenhaus, the US American James M. Murphy, the Indian Lucy de Souza, the English woman Margaret Argyle, the Korean woman Kim Yong Lim."[30]

Awareness of feminist biblical Studies is demonstrated in the paintings of the German artist and art critic Gisela Breitling (b. 1939), who turns her attention to the nameless wo/men in Matthew's Gospel in sixteen pictures that can be found in the tower of the church of St. Matthäus in Berlin. One painting shows the Canaanite wo/man picking up chunks of bread, straddle-legged, from the ground, while well-heeled contemporary churchmen sit at table and watch her.[31]

Sophia is expressed in creative, bold works of art such as Elizabeth Tarr's "Black Virgin Lets Rip,"[32] which plays with the attributes of the Madonna/Black Goddess and brings them out of the motionlessness of the pure maidservant into a completely new, playful dynamic, balancing with the golden

---

28. "Sadly, most of the 1038 women included in The Dinner Party, are unfamiliar, their lives and achievement unknown to most of us. To make people feel worthless, society robs them of their pride; this has happened to wo/men. All the institutions of our culture tell us—through words, deeds and even worse silence—that we are insignificant. But our heritage is our power!" (Judy Chicago, *The Dinner Party: A Symbol of Our Heritage* [Garden City: Doubleday, 1979], 241. Online: https://www.brooklynmuseum.org/exhibitions/dinner_party).

29. See Claudia Kolletzki, "*Christus ist unsere wahre Mutter*": Feminine Konnotationen *für Christus in Denken der Julian von Norwich* (FTS 36; Frankfurt: Knecht,1997).

30. Martin Leutzsch, "The Vision of a Female Christ," in *Soziale Rollen von Frauen in Religionsgemeinschaften* (ed. Siri Fuhrmann et al.; Münster: LIT, 2003), 25–38, here 33.

31. Online: http://www.stiftung-stmatthaeus.de/die-kirche/kunstwerke.

32. Online: http://www.elizabethtarr.com/gallery.html.

apple and her ancient, Gothic face on the history of salvation. A transfer from art here could be related back to the wisdom texts and inspire anew the interpretation of the dynamic wisdom of Prov 7.

Traces of wisdom can also be found in animated images, for example *Antonias Line* (1995, by Marleen Gorris), which recounts a banquet of wo/men celebrating together and discovering and exchanging their truths at a large table.

6. Wisdom's Music

Like improvisations, songs and instrumental pieces express experiences, stories, and emotions, and play an important part in wo/men's liturgies. Wisdom liturgy groups find various sources throughout the world: their own compositions or redrafts of existing songs, traditional pieces, songs from wo/men's movements, indigenous songs, and songs which they have come to know from other wo/men's groups through celebrating together or through songbooks. Artists such as Colleen Fulmer and Carolyn McDade[33] have a supportive effect with spiritual Sophia music, as well as singers such as Mercedes Soza, who has inspired and sustained numerous wo/men's liberation movements in Latin America and beyond, as well as many other female singers of various musical styles:

> Ring us round O ancient circle,
> Great Mother dancing free,
> Beauty, strength and Holy Wisdom,
> Blessing you and blessing me.[34]

Too little consideration has thus far been given in feminist Bible studies to the various aspects of music, for example, experiences in states of trance or contributions of "difficult music" in a wisdom forum. Like difficult representative art, it could break the habits of listening and obeying in tonal ranges and make new perceptions possible.

7. Outlook on Wisdom's Ways

The wisdom dance of wo/men is as old as wisdom, and yet is new and amazingly open, each time wo/men resolve to collaborate in interpreting sacred texts and in shaping liturgies celebrating their own lives, their relationships,

---

33. See http://www.carolynmcdademusic.com.
34. Colleen Fulmer, *Dancing Sophia's Circle*, CD from: Loretto Spirituality Network.

and global links. The forum of g*dly wisdom invites us to change kyriarchal relationships into "grassroots movements," which throw whatever they have into the pot: bread and apple slices, borrowed prayers and prayers they have written themselves, liturgies and stories that connect us with others way beyond the barriers of culture and religion. They invite us likewise to share the grape juice in the forum of wisdom and to teach our children about sharing and accepting, recounting and about being connected. Talking *about* wisdom is therefore meaningless. Being filled with wisdom is about creating, protecting, and organizing spaces in which we wo/men listen to one another speaking and moving together. Since wisdom is always calling and dancing all over the world, wisdom's action for justice is a daily and lifelong invitation.

> Wisdom was there a long time ago. Wisdom was there and it was present everywhere in all its intensity and with all its desire in everything that was. And when the word was spoken, it, and it alone, plunged into the spaces between the words and blessed the silence, bringing forth new worlds. Now, as it was in the beginning, wisdom hears the whole of creation speaking. It alone knows something of the possibilities of such talk.[35]

The refugee family in Greppen, Switzerland, has obtained the right of residency from the Federal Administrative Court—the deportation was an official act against the Convention on Human Rights and therefore against Swiss law. Yet "we are only able to save a few people," the Jewish poet and refugee Hilde Domin stated in an interview in Romero-Haus, Luzern. Let us do that with all our wisdom and, likewise, let us occupy the streets and dance together wisdom's wonderful wild and loud dance. So also let our whole existence express it in wisdom's terms: well-being as the birthright of all beings!

---

35. Lucy Tatman, "Wisdom," in *An A to Z of Feminist Theology* (ed. Lisa Isherwood and Dorothea McEwan; Sheffield: Sheffield Academic Press, 1996), 236–40, here 238.

A Long History of Sowing, from Which Miracles Occasionally Grow: Bible Translations in Language That Is Just

Claudia Janssen and Hanne Köhler
Bibel in gerechter Sprache Editorial Group Members[1]

Bible translations do not appear out of nowhere, but emerge under certain social conditions and from within specific power networks. Furthermore, translations are always influenced by preconceptions and by the theologies of those involved, as well as other contextual factors.[2] These include economic considerations, images of the Bible as a cultural asset,[3] and issues of theological/church teaching and authority.[4] Since the Bible was, and is, often perceived

---

1. Both authors were involved at the origin of the German inclusive language Bible translation "Bibel in gerechter Sprache," a title invoking notions of justice. A comparative analysis of Bible translations that also considers the development in all areas of the world and in languages of differing structures and gender designations has yet to be undertaken. See, however, Satoko Yamaguchi, "Father Image of G*d and Inclusive Language: A Reflection in Japan," in *Toward a New Heaven and a New Earth: Essays in Honor of Elisabeth Schüssler Fiorenza* (ed. Fernando F. Segovia; Maryknoll, N.Y.: Orbis, 2003), 199–224.

2. Translation scholar Heidemarie Salevsky refers both to a network of antinomies and to a wealth of influences that are significant for biblical translation and its evaluation; see Heidemarie Salevsky, "Auf der Suche nach der Wahrheit bei der Bibelübersetzung: Ein Beitrag aus translationswissenschaftlicher Sicht am Beispiel der Hagar-Geschichte (Gen 16; 21; 25)," in *Heidemarie Salevsky: Aspekte der Translation. Ausgewählte Beiträge zur Translation und Translationswissenschaft* (ed. Ina Müller; Frankfurt: Peter Lang, 2009), 19–20; Heidemarie Salevsky (collaborating with Ina Müller and Bernd Salevsky), *Translationswissenschaft: Ein Kompendium* (Frankfurt: Peter Lang, 2002), 337–38.

3. This applies in particular to languages in which individual translations were widely distributed and culturally influential, such as the King James Bible and the Luther Bible.

4. The Roman Catholic Fifth Instruction for the Right Implementation of the Constitution on the Sacred Liturgy of the Second Vatican Council–Liturgiam Authenticam of 7.5.2001 makes this clear. Some Protestants also consider authorization of translations by the church in compliance with dogmatic teaching as necessary. See the statement of

as an important document for independent faith and for legitimizing religious institutions, the history of Bible translation is marked by conflict. These conflicts, which at times have been life-threatening for translators, continue today as translators are accused of heresy.[5] Bible translations appear to serve as crystallization points for different debates and for opening up a wealth of conflicting emotions. The increasing public awareness of Bible translations offers the opportunity to discuss topics and positions in depth beyond those groups that are invested in "pure" theological sciences, particularly those interested in feminism, social sciences, liberation theology, or Christian-Jewish dialogue.

1. From Antidiscrimination Legislation to New Bible Translations

The use of "inclusive language"[6] in the United States is connected with the civil rights movement and especially the women's movement. In 1972 and 1973, the U.S. American National Organization for Women made contact with Catholic, Protestant, and Jewish Bible translation projects in order to bring its influence to bear on the deletion of an unjustifiable masculinization in Bible translations.[7] UNESCO also has issued guidelines for combating sexist and discriminatory language.[8] These guidelines are based on the view

---

Rat der Evangelischen Kirche in Deutschland (EKD) (Council of Protestant Churches in Germany) on the "Bibel in gerechter Sprache" (March 31, 2007); online: http://www.ekd. de/presse/pm67_2007_bibel_in_gerechter_sprache.html.

5. See Martin Leutzsch, "Bibelübersetzung als Skandal und Verbrechen," in *Bibel-Impulse: Film–Kunst–Literatur–Musik–Theater–Theologie* (ed. Rainer Dillmann; INPUT 5: Berlin, 2006), 42–57. See further the discussion surrounding the "Bibel in gerechter Sprache," particularly the accusation of heresy by Ulrich Wilckens, "Theologisches Gutachten zur 'Bibel in gerechter Sprache,'" in *epd-Dokumentation* 17/18 (2007): 24–38. For the rejection of this accusation, see Luise Schottroff, "Stellungnahme zum theologischen Gutachten von Ulrich Wilckens zur Bibel in gerechter Sprache," in *epd-Dokumentation* 31 (2007): 34–37.

6. The term was and is variable, depending on which aspects of discriminatory language are to be avoided. Comprehensive current guidelines are, e.g., the University of Wisconsin at Madison's *A Guide to Bias-Free Communication: A Reference for Preparing Official University Publications;* online: http://academicaffairs.ucsd.edu/_files/aps/adeo/ Article_Guide_to_Bias-Free_Communications.pdf.

7. Martin Leutzsch, "Inklusive Sprache in der Bibelübersetzung" in *Die Bibel–übersetzt in gerechte Sprache? Grundlagen einer neuen Übersetzung* (ed. Helga Kuhlmann; Gütersloh: Gütersloher, 2005), 202.

8. The UNESCO Guidelines for English and French were issued in 1987 and subsequently revised. The third revised edition of 1999 is available online under the modified title *Guidelines on Gender-Neutral Language/Pour l'egalite des sexes dans le langage* at http:// unesdoc.unesco.org/images/0011/001149/114950mo.pdf. These guidelines are the basis

that a modified pattern of language also creates a corresponding change in personal attitudes towards discriminated groups of the population. Equivalent standards for Bible translation were also being demanded in this regard. In 1974, the Division of Education and Ministry of the National Council of the Christian Churches in the U.S.A. set up a "Task Force on Sexism in the Bible" with women who had a proven academic track record. One result was the publication in 1976 of *The Liberating Word: A Guide to Non-Sexist Interpretation of the Bible*.[9] In addition to key questions on hermeneutics, it also referred to the connection between linguistic modification and church reform.[10]

The suggestions of the task force were adopted by the "Inclusive Language Lectionary" (ILL), which appeared in 1983.[11] The translation committee had the task of revising the Revised Standard Version (RSV), considered to be the standard scientific translation at that time, "only in those places where male-biased or otherwise inappropriately exclusive language could be modified to reflect an inclusiveness of all persons."[12] This was carried out in reference to human language as well as in reference to the language about Christ and God.

Parallel to the work on the ILL, a revision of the RSV was initiated. In the New Revised Standard Version (NSRV), which appeared in 1990,[13] change

---

of the version published by the German UNESCO Committee in 1993; see http://www. unesco.de/fileadmin/medien/Dokumente/Bibliothek/eine_sprache.pdf. A Spanish version *Recomendaciones para un uso no sexista del lenguaje* is online at: http://unesdoc.unesco. org/images/0011/001149/114950so.pdf. The versions are not translations but are adapted to the corresponding language and cultural grouping.

9. Letty M. Russell, ed., *The Liberating Word: A Guide to Nonsexist Interpretation of the Bible* (Philadelphia: Westminster John Knox, 1977). The German translation neither uses inclusive language nor mentions the organizational context: Letty M. Russell, ed., *Als Mann und Frau ruft er uns: Vom nicht-sexistischen Gebrauch der Bibel* (Munich: Pfeiffer, 1979).

10. See Letty M. Russell, "Sprachveränderung und Kirchenreform," in Russell, *Als Mann und Frau ruft er uns*, 70–84.

11. National Council of the Churches of Christ in the United States of America, Division of Education and Ministry, ed. *An Inclusive Language Lectionary: Readings for Year A* (Atlanta: John Knox, 1983); *Readings for Year B* (1984); *Readings for Year C* (1985). This lectionary was compiled by Robert A. Bennett, Dianne Bergant, Victor Roland Gold (chairperson), Thomas Hoyt Jr., Kellie C. Jones, Patrick D. Miller Jr., Virgina Ramey Mollenkott, Sharon H. Ringe (vice-chairperson), Susan Thistlethwaite, Burton H. Throckmorton Jr., and Barbara A. Withers.

12. National Council of the Churches of Christ in the United States of America, Division of Education and Ministry, ed., *Readings for Year A,* under "Preface."

13. National Council of the Churches of Christ in the United States of America, Division of Christian Education, ed. *New Revised Standard Version Bible: The Holy Bible Containing the Old and New Testaments with the Apocryphal/Deuterocanonical Books* (Nashville: Thomas Nelson, 1989). At the time of the publication of the NRSV, the translation

was restricted entirely to the language about human beings and limited to cases in which, according to the opinion of the translation committee, inclusive language could be used without altering passages that would be appropriate to the patriarchal historical context. Androcentric language continues to be used in reference to God in the NRSV. These moderate changes of the English translation tradition, however, were met with vehement criticism. For example, the authorization of the NRSV in the Roman Catholic Church was countermanded because of the inclusive language used by the Vatican's Congregation for the Doctrine of the Faith at the end of 1994.[14] Inclusive language with respect to humans was also taken up in other Bible translation projects and was successful to varying degrees, although criticized by conservative groups.[15]

The New Testament and Psalms: An Inclusive Version,[16] published by six of the eleven members of the ILL committee, is based on the NRSV but goes beyond it insofar as it uses not only gender but also race, class, or disability

---

committee consisted of thirty people, including a Jewish man and four women; see "Frequently Asked Questions" (http://www.nrsv.net/about/faqs/).

14. See Catherine Wessinger, "Key Events for Women's Religious Leadership in the United States: Nineteenth and Twentieth Centuries," in *Religious Institutions and Women's Leadership: New Roles Inside the Mainstream* (ed. Catherine Wessinger; Columbia: University of South Carolina Press, 1996), 347–401.

15. See, e.g., New Century Version (1986, 1987, 1988), New American Bible (1988, 1990), The Message (1993), The New International Reader's Version (1994, 1996), Contemporary English Version (1995), New International Version Inclusive Language Edition (1995), New Living Translation (1996, 2004, 2007), New English Translation (1998), Today's New International Version (2002 NT, 2005 entire Bible). Each of these translations has its own guidelines regarding inclusive language. See, e.g., the webpage for the New Living Translation at www.newlivingtranslation.com/05discoverthenlt/faqs.asp?faq=12#go12. An examination of these respective guidelines, their changes, and the particular translation practice would require its own research work. For the discussion within the evangelical area in the U.S.A. alone, see Nancy A. Hardesty, *Inclusive Language in the Church* (Atlanta: John Knox, 1987); Donald A. Carson, *The Inclusive-Language Debate: A Plea for Realism* (Grand Rapids: Baker, 1998); Mark L. Strauss, *Distorting Scripture? The Challenge of Bible Translation and Gender Accuracy* (Downers Grove, Ill.: InterVarsity Press, 1998); Wayne A. Grudem and Vern S. Poythress, *The Gender-Neutral Bible Controversy: Muting the Masculinity of God's Words* (Nashville: Broadman & Holman, 2000); Mark L. Strauss, "Current Issues in the Gender-Language Debate: A Response to Vern Poythress and Wayne Grudem," in *The Challenge of Bible Translation: Communicating God's Word to the World* (ed. Glen G. Scorgie et al.; Grand Rapids: Zondervan, 2003), 115–41; Wayne A. Grudem and Vern S. Poythress, *The TNIV and the Gender-Neutral Bible Controversy* (Nashville: Broadman & Holman, 2004).

16. Victor Roland Gold et al., eds. *The New Testament and Psalms: An Inclusive Version* (New York: Oxford University Press, 1995).

in order to underscore that all are addressed by the New Testament and the Psalms. Furthermore, in contrast to the NRSV, this translation uses inclusive metaphors for God.[17]

Independently of the translation projects mentioned so far, Priests for Equality, a Catholic reform movement established in the U.S.A. compiled its own translation of the Bible in 1975.[18] In light of the official policy of the Roman Catholic Church, it soon became clear to Priests for Equality, who from the outset were committed to nonsexist language, that a change in language needed to be supported by a grassroots movement. As a result, Priests for Equality completed a translation of the New Testament in 1994, followed shortly by translations of the Psalms and the Old Testament with the apocryphal/Deuterocanonical writings found in the Roman Catholic Bible by 2007. In the first partial editions, the Tetragrammaton[19] was rendered "Adonai," which was transcribed after 2004 as "YHWH," with the following recommendation:

> When you approach the four-lettered name of God, you pause for a moment in prayerful reflection. When reading the scriptures aloud, you may choose to pronounce the Name as "Yahweh," or substitute such epithets as Holy One, Our God, the Most High, Ha-Shem, the I Am, or other names that speak to your heart and communicate your understanding of the Divine Mystery. Whatever you choose, however, choose with reflection and reverence.[20]

Introductions, particularly to the partial editions, provide information on procedures, aims, contributors, and bases of the translation. The intention is to make the Bible accessible to all, particularly to those for whom sexist language is sometimes an insurmountable barrier to their life of faith. It is emphasized, however, that there are sections of the Bible that cannot be translated into inclusive language, but require theological revision. The contributors agreed on a series of guidelines, which they followed from the first to the

---

17. Ibid., viii–xi.

18. The starting point was a charter originally signed by seventy-five Roman Catholic priests in which they campaigned for equal opportunities in society and in the Roman Catholic Church, including women's ordination to the priesthood.

19. On the Tetragrammaton, see Georg Howard, "The Tetragram and the New Testament," *JBL* 96 (1977): 63–76; Kristin De Troyer, "The Names of God, Their Pronunciation and Their Translation: A Digital Tour of Some of the Main Witnesses," *lectio difficilior* 2/2005; online: http://www.lectio.unibe.ch/05_2/troyer_names_of_god.htm; De Troyer, "The Choice is Yours! On Names of God," *JESWTR* 14 (2006): 53–66.

20. Priests for Equality, *The Prophets* (vol. 2 of *The Inclusive Hebrew Bible*; Lanham, Md.: AltaMira, 2004), xxii.

last partial volume. The intention to create a critical feminist biblical interpretation of scripture that is inclusive both in terms of content and style remained constant.

Around the same time, David E. S. Stein published a New Jewish Publication Society's (NJPS) translation of the Torah in 2006 entitled *The Contemporary Torah: A Gender-Sensitive Adaptation of the JPS Translation* (CJPS), which adapts a well-known English Jewish translation in terms of gender.[21] The CJPS attempts to delineate how the original target group would have understood a text, as grammatically masculine terms did not necessarily suggest the male gender. Using the example of ʿish, Stein illustrates how the lexical findings are also misleading, as the term usually translated as "man" does not necessarily refer to a "male adult" but rather concerns social roles and positions.[22] In addition to this sensitivity in relation to language about people, the translation focuses on the fact that gender-specific terms are dispensed with when referring to God:

> In the absence of contextual indications that gender was germane, I rendered the Torah's references to divine beings in gender-neutral terms.... In practice, such a rendering meant recasting NJPS to avoid gendered pronouns for God.[23]

The Tetragrammaton is expressed in unpunctuated Hebrew letters in the English text. The reading instructions in the foreword state: "We invite those who read this translation aloud to pronounce the name via whatever term that they customarily use for it."[24] This means that both the Priests for Equality and the CJPS think users are capable of reading God's name in an appropriate form at any time without directly dictating how this should be done.

---

21. In addition to David E. S. Stein as revising editor, Adele Berlin, Ellen Frankel, and Carol L. Meyers are listed as consulting editors, whose collaboration is described in more detail in the foreword; see David E. S. Stein, *The Contemporary Torah: A Gender-Sensitive Adaptation of the JPS Translation* (Philadelphia: Jewish Publication Society, 2006), i and xx.

22. Ibid., xxiv–xxv, xxxi, xxxv n. 31, as well as the entry under ʿish in the "Dictionary of Gender in the Torah," 394–95, which states at the beginning: "The present translation takes as the primary sense of ʾish (and its effective plural, ʾanashim), 'a representative member of a group: a member who serves as a typical or characteristic example.'" On the translation of ʾish, see also the detailed background material under the title "What Does It Mean to Be a 'Man'? The Noun ʾish in Biblical Hebrew: A Reconsideration" (http://scholar. davidesstein.name/Memoranda.htm).

23. See Stein, *Contemporary Torah*, xxvii–xxviii, here xxvii. On the classification of the changes, see xxviii.

24. Ibid., xxvii.

2. "INCLUSIVE LANGUAGE" TRANSLATIONS IN GERMANY

The lectionary (ILL) in particular, but also the inclusive translations of the New Testament and the Psalms, have encouraged women in Germany to translate the Bible into language that is just. The Evangelische Frauenarbeit in Deutschland e. V. (EFD) (Federation of Protestant Women's Organizations in Germany) provided a brochure entitled "Gerechte Sprache in Gottesdienst und Kirche" (Language That Is Just in Worship and the Church) for the Deutscher Evangelischer Kirchentag (German Protestant Church Convention) in 1987 in Frankfurt, which contained "three Bible study texts for the church convention in inclusive versions."[25]

> The translation was modified in places in which specifically male terms and images ("Lord," "Father") or male pronouns (he, his) were used for God.... Women are presumably included, but not named ("brother," ... "he") or designated by a deprecatory word ("Weib") according to today's linguistic sensitivity or have fewer opportunities for identification than men (brothers, men of God...). Believers of other religions ("heathens") or people with disabilities ("the blind") are discriminated against linguistically.[26]

The foreword states that, despite the reference to the Inclusive Language Lectionary of the National Council of Churches of Christ in the United States, the term "inclusive language" could not be adopted because it is easily misunderstood. "Indeed, we do not want any kind of language that 'includes' and designates women in male terms."[27] The group chose the designation language that does justice to women (*frauengerecht*). Women are not a minority alongside others who are deprived of justice in our society, but comprise more than half of society as a whole and even more than half of the church.

> "Frauengerecht" (just to women) is a language that refers to women and men as being of equal value and equal before the law. It makes the existence and significance of women linguistically visible and recognizes the need of women for self-respect, identity, and encouragement. This language exposes injustice and motivates women to perceive their rights and the rights of other people and to take an active role in the community and church.[28]

---

25. Evangelische Frauenarbeit in Deutschland, *Gerechte Sprache in Gottesdienst und Kirche: Mit Bibeltexten zum Frankfurter Kirchentag in frauengerechter Sprache* (Frankfurt: Evangelische Frauenarbeit in Deutschland, 1987), 3.

26. Ibid.

27. Ibid.

28. Ibid. For an argument against the term "geschlechtergerechte Sprache" (language

The seven general guidelines under the caption: "Language That Is Just Heals—
Unjust Language Divides: How Can I Speak 'Justly' in an Unjust World?"
demonstrates that the focus was broader than justice only for women.[29]

> A basic distinction was made between the reading of biblical texts in wor-
> ship (lectionary), which as proclamation to the assembled congregation
> cannot exclude anyone, and Bible translation. Worship requires a lectionary
> that "unveils anew in each case the liberating closeness of God."[30]

An accurate translation should not disguise the Bible's patriarchal precon-
ditions. On the other hand, it must not be overlooked that biblical translations and their effects in church tradition are much more patriarchal than the
Hebrew or Greek text. The booklet met with a broad response.[31] Alternative
versions of Bible texts were printed in the program booklets from the Twenty-
Third German Protestant Church Convention (DEKT) from 1989 onward.
They were based on the Luther revision current at the time, and modified
in places "in which God is referred to in masculine terms and grammatical
forms and women are not referred to, or not referred to on equal terms with
men."[32] From the Twenty-fourth German Protestant Church Convention
from 1991 onward, translations were compiled by Bible scholars and printed
in the program booklet, usually alongside the current Luther revision. In the
beginning the Tetragrammaton was rendered with "GOTT" (GOD) and since
1995 as "Adonaj." Numerous commentaries have used the inclusive language
in these Bible translations and have become ever more linguistically articulate and sophisticated in their translation solutions. The introduction to the
translations in the DEKT program booklet in 1999 points out that "in other
(particularly Anglo-American) countries, the effort made to produce inclusive language when translating biblical texts has a long tradition and has been

---

that is just concerning gender), see Senta Trömel-Plotz, "Sprache: Von Frauensprache
zu frauengerechter Sprache," in *Handbuch Frauen- und Geschlechterforschung: Theorie,
Methoden, Empirie* (ed. Ruth Becker and Beate Kortendiek; Wiesbaden: Verlag für Sozialwissenschaften, 2004), 749.

29. Evangelische Frauenarbeit, *Gerechte Sprache*, 5.

30. Hanne Köhler, "Frauengerechte Sprache in Gottesdienst und Kirche," in Evangelische Frauenarbeit, *Gerechte Sprache*, 30. See further 23–31.

31. The booklet appeared in January 1987. Although not available at bookstores, more
than seven thousand copies were sold by November, and many were also circulated in
photocopied form.

32. 23. Deutscher Evangelischer Kirchentag Berlin 1989, *Programmheft des 23.
Deutschen Evangelischen Kirchentages Berlin, 7.–11. Juni 1989* (Berlin) 13. This version was
provided by the Federation of Protestant Women's Organizations in Germany.

tried and tested in numerous forms,"[33] whereas in the German-speaking area there are scarcely any role models, and the church convention translations are therefore of an innovative nature, but have had far-reaching effects. The contextual nature of the church convention translations, as of all other translations, has been emphasized:

> There is no such thing as a correct translation; a decision constantly has to be made as to what should be emphasised and where the weight needs to be placed in this particular instance.[34]

The first ecumenical church convention in 2003 was a step backward regarding Bible translations in inclusive language. However, the DEKT resumed the tradition of church convention translations in 2005 and explained:

> Twenty years ago, when theologians began to translate the Biblical texts for the church conventions with the aim of producing them in more just language, this was a new venture in the German-speaking area. Translations of the Bible texts of nine church conventions had become available in the meantime and this work led to other, larger projects.
>
> The church convention translations attempt to meet the following criteria:
>
> 1. The translation should be true to the wording of the biblical texts in their Hebrew or Greek original version. These are therefore translations of the Hebrew Bible and the Greek New Testament and not new versions or even "translations" of the Luther Bible.
>
> 2. Translation should be in inclusive language. The women referred to, or not expressly referred to but included in the texts themselves, should be visible, and women should be recognizable as addressed today.
>
> 3. Such translation should be mindful of Jewish-Christian dialogue and show respect for the Jewish reading of scripture.
>
> 4. It should have a mutually comprehensible language. This language must be "easy on the ear." Yet, when the text itself is cumbersome or ambivalent, this should also be discernible in the translation.

These criteria should also be applied to language about God. God is not a man in the Bible, and the notion of the maleness of God is a violation of the aniconism in the Ten Commandments. Nor should God be discussed predominantly in grammatically male forms. How to handle God's proper name written in the Hebrew Bible with the consonants y-h-w-h is an issue continually discussed since biblical times, and every Bible translation has to find its

---

33. 28. Deutscher Evangelischer Kirchentag Stuttgart 1999, *Programmheft des 28. Deutschen Evangelischen Kirchentages Stuttgart, 16.–20. Juni 1999* (Stuttgart), 14.

34. Ibid.

own solution. The church convention translations render God's name by the description of authority, "Adonaj."[35]

Today the church convention translations are a fixture of the DEKT. With the generational change of contributors in recent years, the question has also come up as to how innovation can be institutionalized so that the wheel does not continually have to be reinvented. The Federation of Protestant Women's Organizations in Germany (EFD) has not only activated church convention translations, but has been trying to work from the outside toward consideration of an inclusive language in the revision of the Good News Bible. Women's groups were formed for this purpose in 1988 at the initiative of the Theological Consultant of the EFD. They worked intensively in an honorary capacity over a period of eighteen months on revision proposals and made them available to the German Bible Society, which holds the rights to the *Gute Nachricht Bibel* (Good News Bible). A detailed final report with general notes and a wealth of practical proposals for revision from the working groups was introduced by Hildburg Wegener in December 1989 at a conference of German-speaking Bible societies in East Berlin, and subsequently been published.[36] Reactions were cautious to begin with, but the German Bible Society subsequently decided to consider the aspect of inclusive language in relation to people, insofar as they thought it justifiable. Beginning in 1993, two women (Renate Jost and Monika Fander) were therefore invited to sift through the German texts submitted by the exclusively male translators and make suggestions for changes. Since there was no obligation to adopt or agree to their proposals, the two female biblical scholars were only able to achieve a few changes.

The *Gute Nachricht Bibel*, however, has been promoted since it appeared in 1997 as being the first German Bible translation to consider inclusive language.[37] Hildburg Wegener stated in her review that a great deal of work

---

35. 30. Deutscher Evangelischer Hannover 2005, *Programmheft des 30. Deutschen Evangelischen Kirchentages Hannover, 25.–29. Mai 2005* (Hannover), 24–25. Jürgen Ebach is listed as the author. After 2005, the Exegetical Outlines with Explanatory Notes on the Translations were no longer published internally but were made generally accessible and decisions made more transparently in a separate issue to the journal *Junge Kirche*.

36. See Siegfried Meurer, "Foreword," in *Die vergessenen Schwestern: Frauengerechte Sprache in der Bibelübersetzung* (ed. Siegfried Meurer; Jahrbuch der Deutschen Bibelgesellschaft [Yearbook of the German Bible Society]: Stuttgart, 1993), 10; and Hildburg Wegener, "Allen die Bibel, die sie brauchen," in Meurer, *Die vergessenen Schwestern*, 13–36.

37. See Hannelore Jahr, "Foreword," in *Die neue Gute Nachricht Bibel* (ed. Hannelore Jahr; Stuttgart: Deutsche Bibelgesellschaft, 1998), 11: "The fact that for the first time in a German Bible translation, the aspect of "inclusive language" was systematically considered is, however, of fundamental significance." This sentence is almost word for word on the

remained but that the German Bible Society had shown courage, because it had "performed truly pioneering work with the *Gute Nachricht Bibel* in (tempered) inclusive language for the German-speaking context and, in so doing, had hopefully started a process that will continue in the Bible Society, in the churches, and in academic theology."[38] Evidently Hildburg Wegener's critical remarks had an impact on the continuing revision of the *Gute Nachricht Bibel*, because some of the phrasing she criticized is no longer included in the later edition of 2000, without this being pointed out in the paratexts.[39]

In 2001, as an independent project, a lectionary with the Bible sections needed for Protestant services of worship was published as a fourth volume of a series of liturgical texts in just and inclusive language.[40] It expressly refers both to the Inclusive Language Lectionary as well as to the Hildburg Wegener's publications. The Tetragrammaton is rendered in the lectionary as $\frac{\text{Adonaj}}{\text{Gott}}$ and it was suggested that either "God" or, in the tradition of church convention translations, "Adonaj" should be read. Rendering it with $\frac{\text{Adonaj}}{\text{Gott}}$ makes it immediately recognizable in the text where the Tetragrammaton is in Hebrew.

The *Bibel in gerechter Sprache* (Bible in Inclusive German), which began in 2001 and was published in 2006, bases its theory and contributors on the experiences with the aforementioned lectionary and church convention translations.[41] It comprises the Old Testament/Hebrew Bible, Apocryphal/

---

webpage of the German Bible Society in the abstract of the *Gute Nachricht Bibel* (http://www.die-bibel.de/online-bibeln/gute-nachricht-bibel/ueber-die-gute-nachricht-bibel). Another modified version of it has appeared in the meantime: Evangelisches Bibelwerk/ Katholisches Bibelwerk e.V. Stuttgart/ Österreichisches Katholisches Bibelwerk/ Schweizerisches Katholisches Bibelwerk, eds., *Gute Nachricht Bibel: Altes und Neues Testament: Mit den Spätschriften des Alten Testaments (Deuterokanonische Schriften/Apokryphen)* (rev. ed.; Stuttgart: Deutsche Bibelgesellschaft, 2000).

38. Hildburg Wegener, "'…Und macht die Menschen zu meinen Jüngern und Jüngerinnen': Die Revision der Gute Nachricht Bibel in gemäßigt 'frauengerechter Sprache,'" in Jahr, *Die neue Gute Nachricht Bibel*, 73–74.

39. Wegener had demanded, for example, that the translation of Luke 1:38 "be modified as a matter of urgency in view of the discussion on theological aspects of the direct and indirect violence used against women and girls" (ibid., 71). This has happened in the meantime, and instead of "I belong to the Lord, I am entirely at His disposal," it is now "I belong to the Lord, I am ready."

40. Erhard Domay and Hanne Köhler, eds., *Der Gottesdienst: Liturgische Texte in gerechter Sprache, Band 4: Die Lesungen* (Gütersloh: Gütersloher, 2001). For the translation guidelines, the contributions and individual translation decisions, on which this lectionary is based, see Hanne Köhler, *Gerechte Sprache als Kriterium von Bibelübersetzungen: Von der Entstehung des Begriffs bis zur gegenwärtigen Praxis* (Gütersloh: Gütersloher, 2012).

41. The Bible is edited by Ulrike Bail, Frank Crüsemann, Marlene Crüsemann, Erhard Domay, Jürgen Ebach, Claudia Janssen, Hanne Köhler, Helga Kuhlmann, Martin Leutzsch,

Deuterocanonical writings, and the New Testament. The German title of this project, "Bibel in gerechter Sprache," encompasses the outlook of the entire program, and this vision can be expressed as the central biblical theme of articulating justice in many different respects. Feminist and liberation theological discourses as well as discussions of Christian anti-Semitism have been considered in addition to historical-exegetical and literary approaches. All translations attempt to be true to the original text, and offer a comprehensible language. The *Bibel in gerechter Sprache* comes in addition to the numerous existing German translations. It distinguishes itself not only in its profile, but also because it has disclosed this from the outset, not only in numerous accompanying publications,[42] but also with a programmatic introduction and a detailed glossary. Therefore the theological bases and theoretical issues of the translation process have been the subject of fierce debate since its publication.

The history of this translation[43] makes clear that the *Bibel in gerechter Sprache* is the product of a movement. Many aspects have been democratically decided by the translators at conferences, including the representation of God's name, the names of biblical books, and the selection of glossary terms. The individual books of the Bible were translated by fifty-two commentators, who are actually listed by name in the respective introductions to the books of the Bible.[44] Many of the contributors were already involved in the translations for

---

and Luise Schottroff. In 2007, the editorial group was expanded for further work to include Kerstin Schiffner, Johannes Taschner, and Marie-Theres Wacker. Ulrike Bail and Erhard Domay retired. In 2006 there were two editions, and a third appeared in 2007 (total circulation of over 70,000). A revised fourth edition appeared in 2011. For further information, see www.bibel-in-gerechter-sprache.de.

42. Erhard Domay and Hanne Köhler, eds., *Gottesdienstbuch in gerechter Sprache: Gebete, Lesungen, Fürbitten und Segenssprüche für die Sonn- und Feiertage des Kirchenjahres* (Gütersloh: Gütersloher, 2003); Erhard Domay and Hanne Köhler, eds., *Werkbuch gerechte Sprache in Gemeinde und Gottesdienst: Praxisentwürfe für Gemeindearbeit und Gottesdienst* (Gütersloh: Gütersloher, 2003); Erhard Domay et al., eds., *Singen von deiner Gerechtigkeit: Das Gesangbuch in gerechter Sprache* (Gütersloh: Gütersloher, 2005). Christiane Thiel, ed.; *Tageslesebuch: Bibel in gerechter Sprache für jeden Tag des Jahres* (Gütersloh: Gütersloher, 2008); Isa Breitmeier and Luzia Sutter Rehmann, *Gerechtigkeit lernen: Seminareinheiten zu den drei Grundkategorien von Gerechtigkeit* (Gütersloh: Gütersloher, 2008); Martina Gerlach and Monika Weigt-Blattgen, eds., *Gottes Antlitz hülle dich in Licht ... Andachten für Frauen mit der Bibel in gerechter Sprache* (Gütersloh: Gütersloher, 2009); Luise Metzler and Katrin Keita, *Bibel in gerechter Sprache: Fragen und Antworten* (Gütersloh: Gütersloher, 2009).

43. See Köhler, *Kriterium*.

44. In translations in inclusive language it is made clear who is responsible for the translation and who has contributed. Many other translations do not contain equivalent details.

DEKT or the Protestant lectionary. This explains the Protestant background of the majority of translators. However, there were some Catholic theologians involved also. The translators of the *Bibel in gerechter Sprache* are scholars of the Old and New Testaments, who base their translations on dissertations, postdoctoral theses, and other research work. This working process was intensive, as the translations were discussed both in small interdisciplinary groups relating to the books of the Bible (e.g., the Torah group and the group on Paul's letters), as well as in a full plenary session. In addition to this, they have opened themselves up with their still tentative results to an intensive practical test, and have also repeatedly revised the results of their translation in an internal reading process. Over three hundred groups and individuals were involved in this creative process, or "practical review." They have used tentative translations in Bible groups, in teaching or in their own readings, and have fed their experiences back to the translators.

This work was accompanied by an advisory council that publicly supported the project. A basic precondition for the project was that for five years the Protestant regional church in Hesse and Nassau provide a clergy person to organize the entire project. The work was supported by the Gütersloher Verlagshaus (publisher), which prefinanced the conferences. The project was, however, funded solely by donations from individuals and groups, which made it possible for this translation to be financially independent.[45] In addition, the unusual route of carrying out a Bible translation as a project meant that many people were able to identify with it.

Feedback indicates that, beyond the actual translations, many users attribute changes in congregations and social structures to the *Bibel in gerechter Sprache*. Even people at the margins of the church see a movement represented in the *Bibel in gerechter Sprache* that is present in many places. Incidentally, this point is also made clear by the vehement rejections of the project in the press.[46] The *Bibel in gerechter Sprache* inspires people and provokes reactions. The introduction to the *Bibel in gerechter Sprache* embraces this

---

45. The voluntary work of the Donations Officer, Luise Metzler, made a significant contribution to this.

46. A collection of the press reactions can be found at www.bibel-in-gerechter-sprache.de. Three publications of the Protestant news service contain the controversial discussion in 2007; see *epd Dokumentation* 17/18; 23; and 31 (2007). Reviews predominantly in opposition to the project are available in Elisabeth Gössman et al., eds., *Der Teufel blieb männlich: Kritische Diskussion zur "Bibel in gerechter Sprache" Feministische, historische und systematische Beiträge* (Neukirchen-Vluyn: Neukirchener, 2007); Ingolf Dalferth and Jens Schröter, eds., *Bibel in gerechter Sprache? Kritik eines misslungenen Versuchs* (Tübingen: Mohr Siebeck, 2007); Walter Klaiber and Martin Rösel, *Streitpunkt Bibel in gerechter Sprache* (Leipzig: Evangelische Verlagsanstalt, 2008).

process of discussion of biblical texts and their translation into a contemporary understandable language appropriate to the original texts, and points to the temporary nature of each translation:

> The *Bibel in gerechter Sprache* already required revision the moment it was published.... We see this Bible translation as our contribution to a constantly new understanding of Biblical texts that have also had impact on our lives and continue to challenge us. This translation is therefore a preliminary stop on a never-ending path. The *Bibel in gerechter Sprache* has reached its goal when people are encouraged to take this library of books of the Bible into their own hands, read, and discuss them with others.[47]

Since the *Bibel in gerechter Sprache* appeared, interest in theological issues has grown, particularly in the church fellowships and among nonacademic readers of the Bible. In 2011, a revised edition appeared, incorporating the results of the multifaceted discussions and practical experiences with the texts.

Commitment to more inclusive language in Bible translations exists not only in Germany but also in other countries, although such commitment is difficult to demonstrate, given the incomplete publication of decision-making processes which have not so far been published in full. Thus, information on the Zürich Bible in 2007 is available only on a very scattered basis,[48] but shows what efforts have been made to exclude contributions by female theologians and female New Testament scholars. For instance, the decision to render God's name with "Herr" was criticized beyond Switzerland.[49] Because a women's group has published alternative translation proposals, the counterarguments against numerous decisions by the New Testament section of the Zürich Bible's translation committee (2007) are available in print (no collaboration was formed with the Old Trestament translation committee).[50] Why the translation committee did not act on these recommendations is difficult for outsiders who have no access to the internal documents to understand.

---

47. Ulrike Bail et al., *Bibel in gerechter Sprache* (4th ed.; Gütersloh: Gütersloher, 2011), 26.

48. See the compilation and the literature in Köhler, *Gerechte Sprache als Kriterium*; also Ute E. Eisen, "'Quasi dasselbe?' Vom schwierigen und unendlichen Geschäft des Bibelübersetzens–Neuere deutsche Bibelübersetzungen," *ZNT* 26 (2010): 4–6.

49. See, e.g., the statement of the 9th International Conference of the European Society for Women in Theological Research (ESWTR) in Salzburg, which was adopted on August 23, 2001. See http://www.eswtr.org/de/konferenz_2001 salzburg_stellungnahme.html.

50. Ursula Sigg-Suter, Esther Straub, and Angela Wäffler-Boveland, "... *und ihr werdet mir Söhne und Töchter sein*": *Die neue Zürcher Bibel feministisch gelesen* (Zürich: Theologischer Verlag Zürich, 2007).

Why, for example, did the New Testament committee translate two different Greek verbs in Luke 22:25–26 with the same German verb "to rule over," when the women's reading group had suggested different terms ("to demand," "to head/lead")?[51] Since these translation decisions were challenged by the women's reading group, one can only assume that they were made deliberately.

The rendering of God's name in *De Nieuwe Bijbelvertaling* was also controversial.[52] This Dutch translation had undertaken to avoid exclusive language, among other things, but after controversial discussions[53] on the traditional rendering of God's name, they had decided to adhere to "HEER" in print but pointed out alternative suggestions on how to read it.[54]

3. Every Translation Is an Interpretation

Translation scholar Heidemarie Salevsky describes translation as a process of transformation that must take into account different causal connections: firstly, the content and meaning of the source text defined by a specific context and the understanding of those that have written it and, secondly, the content and meaning of the target text. Again, translation is influenced by

---

51. See Sigg-Suter et al., *Söhne und Töchter,* 76.

52. Nederlands Bubelgenootschap, *De Nieuwe Bijbel Vertaling (NBV)* (Haarlem: Nederlands Bijbelgenootschap, 2004). The corrections compiled since it appeared are online at www.nbv.nl/correcties only occasionally concern inclusive language (e.g., when it now states in Luke 17:3: "Indien een van je broeders of zusters zondigt, spreek die dan ernstig toe; en als ze berouw hebben, vergeef hun." [If one of your brothers or sisters sins, rebuke them; and if they repent, forgive them]. The current status is available http://www.biblija.net/biblija.cgi?l=nl.

53. See Anneke de Vries and Manuela Kalsky, "Ein Name, der ein Geheimnis bleibt," *Junge Kirche* 63 (2002): 22–25; Annette Birschel, "Bibel wurde neu ins Niederländische übersetzt," *Evangelische Kirche in Deutschland* (2004): online: www.ekd.de/aktuell_presse/news_2004_10_27_1_niederlaendische bibel.html; Lambert Wierenga, "'Jahwe' versus 'HEER': niets opgelost," *Nederlands Dagblad* (December 4, 2001); Caroline Vander Stichele, "The Lord Can No Longer Be Taken for Granted: The Rendering of JHWH in the New Dutch Bible Translation," in *Women, Ritual and Liturgy—Ritual und Liturgie von Frauen—Femmes, rituel et liturgie* (ed. Susan K. Roll et al.; JESWTR Yearbook 9; Leuven: Peeters, 2001), 179–87; Vander Stichele, "Der Herr? Das geht nicht mehr! Die Wiedergabe des Tetragramms in der neuen niederländischen Bibelübersetzung," in *"Gott bin ich, kein Mann": Beiträge zur Hermeneutik der biblischen Gottesrede* (ed. Ilona Riedel-Spangenberger and Erich Zenger; Paderborn: Schöningh, 2006), 318–27.

54. See http://www.nbv.nl/achtergrondinfo/godsnaam. Caroline Vander Stichele explains here that, in contrast to the German, the Dutch article "de" is grammatically gender neutral. Hence "de Einige" (Only One), for example, can refer both to a male as well as to a female person" (Vander Stichele, "Der Herr," 323 n. 14).

various factors determined by the translator and her/his specific context is incorporated into the objective. Added to this is the fact that a translation also has its own objective, which is dependent on its historical context: "it involves both reading and rereading as well as writing and re-writing and finally re-translating. Claims that it alone is the truth would have to be excluded from the outset."[55]

Translation does not take place without loss and change. Anyone who has ever tried to translate a text into his or her own language knows how difficult it is to convey the manifold possibilities of word choice and to communicate the limitations of language that has a specific meaning in one cultural area into a different cultural area. According to translation scholar Fritz Paepcke, "Translation is the communication between two languages at the level of the text."[56] Anyone who translates something needs to appropriate it in the source language and communicate it in the target language. Because translators always contribute something of themselves in a translation, every translation is an interpretation and thus tensions are inevitable. The translation of biblical texts faces particular challenges due to the temporal and cultural differences as well as the long history of exegesis and its impact. Ulrike Bail, one of the editors of the *Bibel in gerechter Sprache*, summarizes this, stating, "Every translation moves in a grey area between text and interpretation, between faithfulness and betrayal, loss and gain, the literal and metaphorical, between the deep ambiguity of the text and the translation decision."[57]

This insight is easily suppressed, particularly in cultural areas in which a definite Bible translation is almost normative. A few harsh reactions to translations that are candid about their criteria, such as the *Bibel in gerechter Sprache*, show that people are so familiar with some translations that these are regarded as "the original," assumed to be objective, and that changes distort the perceived "purity" of the original.[58] Our experience in working with groups is that the diversity and the coexistence of different translations enables serious discussion of the biblical texts. Such diversity also enriches one's own faith.

---

55. Heidemarie Salevsky, "Auf der Suche nach der Wahrheit bei der Bibelübersetzung: Ein Beitrag aus translationswissenschaftlicher Sicht am Beispiel der Hagar-Geschichte (Gen 16; 21; 25)," in Kuhlmann, DIE BIBEL, 111.

56. Fritz Paepcke, "Die Sprache im Zusammenleben der Völker," in *Im Übersetzen leben: Übersetzung und Textvergleich* (ed. Klaus Berger and Hans-Michael Speier: Tübingen: Narr, 1986), 22.

57. Ulrike Bail, "Wenn Gott und Mensch zur Sprache kommen…: Überlegungen zu einer Bibel in gerechter Sprache," in Kuhlmann, DIE BIBEL, 62.

58. This general misconception is being advanced in Germany by the German Bible Society's publicity campaign for the current Luther revision, among others, under the slogan "The Original." See http://www.ekd.de/reformationstag/wissenswertes/lutherbibel.html.

4. THE *BIBEL IN GERECHTER SPRACHE* UNDERSTANDS POLYPHONY AS OPPORTUNITY

The Bible is a library of books that emerged in different contexts over many hundreds of years and were written down by diverse people and groups with differing political concerns. These books were also revised to some extent before being assembled into today's canon. In addition, they were written in different languages—Hebrew, Aramaic, and Greek—by people with varying language skills. In the context of the *Bibel in gerechter Sprache*, the individual books of the Bible were translated by different people who tried to choose words that take the features of each biblical book into account. For instance, in his translation of the Revelation of John, Martin Leutzsch points out several places that the language derives from an author whose mother tongue was not Greek, and who therefore made many mistakes in sentence construction. The intentional polyphony of the translations in the Bible in inclusive German corresponds to the polyphony of the books of the Bible.

There has nevertheless been a consensus to select language that is inclusive and that avoids anti-Semitism and the linguistic exclusion of marginalized groups. All those involved were influenced by changes in theological thought in recent decades—Christian-Jewish dialogue, feminist theology, the rediscovery women's significant roles, liberation theology, and also a focus on the poor as historical subjects in the biblical texts. In each of these movements, the Bible has been reread and its importance reiterated for the present. Central to this is the struggle for justice. Some of the trademarks of the *Bibel in gerechter Sprache* are: as follows the biblical name of God is continually highlighted and a range of reading options offered (Eternal [male/female] One, Adonaj, GOD, Living One [male/female], etc.);[59] women are always explicitly mentioned wherever the intention of the text, the context, or the

---

59. Attentiveness to God's name is expressed in the *Bibel in gerechter Sprache* in a particularly graphic designation: the places in the Old Testament in which God's proper name appears have a grey background and are framed by the Hebrew letters *yod yod*. In between is a reading suggestion, e.g., ʾAdonaj. There is also a header on each double page with further reading suggestions in alternating rows. For the New Testament, the grey background is framed with the Greek letters *kappa* and *sigma*, making it transparent that it is a translation of the Greek *kyrios*, for example ˟the Eternal One˟. This designation is used if the substitute word *kyrios* was selected for God's name in quotations from the Old Testament and in New Testament texts where *kyrios* translated back into the Hebrew would result in God's name. The translators have taken different approaches here. See Jürgen Ebach, "Zur Wiedergabe des Gottesnamens in einer Bibelübersetzung, oder: Welche 'Lösungen' es für ein unlösbares Problem geben könnte," in Kuhlmann, *Die Bibel–Übersetzt in gerechte Sprache*, 150–58; and Christine Gerber et al., *Gott heißt nicht nur Vater: Zur Rede über*

research results of social history demonstrate that they are included in masculine terms; the order of the books of the Old Testament corresponds to the Jewish canon; and references within the canon are recognizable.[60]

5. JUSTICE

The Reformation is identified with the biblical terms for justice: ṣədāqâ (Hebrew), and *dikaiosynē* (Greek).[61] God's justice is shown in fundamental acts of salvation and liberation such as the exodus, through which God virtually defines Godself as God (Exod 20:2). The praying women and men of the psalms of lamentation expect salvation through God's action, and even sinners hope for justice (Ps 51:16) that includes forgiveness. The coming messianic age is described as the coming of God's ṣədāqâ (Jer 56:1). God's justice is permanently attached to the Torah: God will speak impartially to those who live as directed by God. The way they behave expresses their relationship to God and their response to God's justice. The name *Bibel in gerechter Sprache* does not claim that this translation is more just or fair than others, only that the attempt is being made to comply with the basic biblical theme of justice in a particular way and, in so doing, actively to turn against biased, unjust, discriminatory, militaristic, and sexist language. This was and is enormously effective—both in Christian theology and in Bible translations.

What is understood in the *Bibel in gerechter Sprache* by "gerechte Sprache" will be outlined below in a few examples. As will be demonstrated, the "dominant" theological interpretation is challenged in many cases by other translations, and another theology emerges as biblically based.[62] The fact that many perceive this as a threat and react emotionally is hardly surprising.

Gott in den Übersetzungen der "Bibel in gerechter Sprache" (Göttingen: Vandenhoeck & Ruprecht, 2008).

60. See Frank Crüsemann, *Kurzdarstellung,* online: http://www.bibel-in-gerechter-sprache.de/downloads/hgundandere/kurzdarstellung.pdf.

61. See Frank Crüsemann and Luise Schottroff, "Gerechtigkeit," glossary article in *Bibel in gerechter Sprache* (ed. Ulrike Bail et al.; Gütersloh, Gütersloher, 2006), 2347–49.

62. The examples refer to the *Bibel in gerechter Sprache* because the authors are well versed in relation to this translation. The translation decisions in the other listed and unlisted translations likewise convey insights that confound theological constructions and are opposed (sometimes vehemently) for this reason.

5.1. The Criterion of Doing Justice to the Text

The Bibel in gerechter Sprache should and will do justice primarily to the particular source text. It is a translation in its own right from the Hebrew, Aramaic, and Greek. All translations are based on an intensive scholarly engagement with the source text. Therefore, widely differing translation solutions were found in order to do justice to particular texts and their language. The *Bibel in gerechter Sprache* dispenses with additional interpretive subheadings. The glossary gives an account of the basic understanding and the translation options of all key biblical terms, thus allowing for discoveries that are otherwise only possible for people who have learned the ancient languages.

5.2. The Criterion of Gender Equality

Gerechte Sprache is a specialized term that has been in use in Germany since the 1980s as a rendering of the term "inclusive language" used in North America. Can a language be "just" or "unjust"? What criteria are there for this?[63] To answer these questions, Helga Kuhlmann, a systematic theologian who was part of the *Bibel in gerechter Sprache* editorial group, examined the act of speaking in itself:

> Relational structures between individuals, between groups, families, social environments, classes and larger institutions are reflected in the linguistic communication of these groups and maintain them at the same time by the speech patterns, the grammar and the linguistically explicit hierarchies. The structures of the gender ratio ... are also shown in the language and constantly reproduced by language or procedurally changed.[64]

Since the 1980s, feminist linguists such as Luise Pusch and Senta Trömel-Plötz have pointed out that androcentric language with masculine forms has a particular dominance in everyday German usage.[65] Since women now occupy important offices, changes have been made for the better. For instance, masculine terms are less commonly used to address women. In many churches there are now women priests, deacons, and even bishops.

---

63. See Helga Kuhlmann, "In welcher Weise kann die Sprache einer Bibelübersetzung 'gerecht' sein," in Kuhlmann, *Die Bibel*, 77–98, here 77–78.

64. Ibid., 77.

65. Luise F. Pusch, *Das Deutsche als Männersprache* (Frankfurt: Suhrkamp, 1984); Senta Trömel-Plötz, ed., *Gewalt durch Sprache: Die Vergewaltigung von Frauen in Gesprächen* (Frankfurt: Fischer Taschenbuch, 1984).

Finally, the election of a female German chancellor has challenged people to think about language use.

The Bible comes from a patriarchal world, and often speaks grammatically in masculine terms of "sons of Israel" and of "male disciples." Feminist social historical analyses have shown that women were involved in the events and experiences of biblical times.[66] Then, as now, androcentric texts refer to women. This fact shapes the translation of the *Bibel in gerechter Sprache*. Thus, a two-stage procedure was developed for the translations:

1. A question was raised with regard to social history: Did women in antiquity have this profession and did women carry out these activities?

2. It was asked what evidence there is that they were referred to in the text to be translated.

The reasons for this procedure are clear in an example from Mark 15:40–41. Here Mark's Gospel still only mentions women because the men were no longer present. It states: "They had followed Jesus in Galilee … and many other women, who had gone with him to Jerusalem." This sentence assumes that women were among those who had followed Jesus from Galilee, and the *Bibel in gerechter Sprache* therefore translates *mathētai* from Mark 1 onward as female and male followers.

Were there actually women shepherds, fisherwomen, women prophets, women Pharisees, or women disciples? These questions were raised many times after the *Bibel in gerechter Sprache* appeared, and they provided the opportunity to present to an interested wider public the results of over thirty years of feminist and social-historical research on the Bible. Criticisms of many translation decisions make clear that the corresponding research results are relatively unknown, and that it is possible in many cases to teach and to study at theological faculties without learning about such research. This concern about gender-fair language causes us to ask further questions regarding the context and roles of women in first-century Judaism.

---

66. On this, see also Elisabeth Schüssler Fiorenza, *In Memory of Her: A Feminist Theological Reconstruction of Christian Origins* (New York: Crossroad, 1983); Luise Schottroff, *Lydias ungeduldige Schwestern: Feministische Sozialgeschichte des frühen Christentums* (Gütersloh: Gütersloher, 1994); Elisabeth Schüssler Fiorenza, ed., *A Feminist Commentary* (vol. 2 of *Searching the Scriptures*; New York: Crossroad, 1994); Ute E. Eisen, *Amtsträgerinnen im frühen Christentum: Epigraphische und literarische Studien* (Göttingen: Vandehoeck & Ruprecht, 1996); Luise Schottroff and Marie-Theres Wacker, eds. *Kompendium Feministische Bibelauslegung* (Gütersloh: Gütersloher, 1998).

5.3. The Criterion of Jewish-Christian Dialogue

The *Bibel in gerechter Sprache* is a Christian translation that attempts to learn from Jewish-Christian dialogue. In recent decades it has been widely recognized how much the New Testament that emerged from a Jewish base has been read and translated in an anti-Semitic manner.[67] The so-called "antitheses" of the Sermon on the Mount are one example, in which the translation "but I say to you" must not be understood in the sense of Jesus' turning against the Jewish tradition.[68] In the *Bibel in gerechter Sprache*, Matt 5:21–22 reads: "You have heard that God said to earlier generations: thou shalt not kill.…" *I interpret this for you today as.…*" The Hebrew or Aramaic words corresponding to the Greek *egō de legō hymin* (in Matt 5:22, 28, 32, 34, 39, 44) introduce, as they did among other rabbis in Jesus' time, a biblical interpretation that differs from that of other scholars (e.g., Bereshit Rabbah 55:3). More recent research has emphasized this.[69] Jesus' interpretation of scripture in Matthew's Sermon on the Mount (5:21–48) should not be understood as a fundamental disagreement with the Torah, as the headline "antitheses" suggests. It is instead Jesus' contemporary interpretation of the Torah, intended to apply the will of God to the society of the time.

The emphasis on Jesus' Jewishness in the *Bibel in gerechter Sprache* was the subject of emotional discussions after it appeared. Some accused it of a "Judaization of Christianity,"[70] while others emphasized that what it meant had become clear to them for the first time—Jesus, Mary, Paul and many of the other followers were and remained Jews. The recognition of Christianity's being deeply rooted in Judaism is of great significance, particularly for interreligious discussions.

---

67. See also Leonore Siegele-Wenschkewitz, *Verdrängte Vergangenheit, die uns bedrängt: Feministische Theologie in der Verantwortung für die Geschichte* (Munich: Kaiser, 1988); Judith Plaskow, "Anti-Judaism in Feminist Christian Interpretation," in *A Feminist Introduction* (vol. 1 of *Searching the Scriptures*; ed. Elisabeth Schüssler Fiorenza; New York: Crossroad, 1993), 117–29; Luise Schottroff and Marie-Theres Wacker, eds., *Von der Wurzel getragen: Christlich-feministische Exegese in Auseinandersetzung mit Antijudaismus* (Leiden: Brill, 1996); Dagmar Henze et al., *Antijudaismus im Neuen Testament? Grundlagen für die Arbeit mit biblischen Texten* (Gütersloh: Kaiser, 1997).

68. See Luise Schottroff, "Votum zur Bibel in gerechter Sprache in Zürich 9.11.2006" (http://www.bibel-in-gerechter-sprache.de/downloads/schottroffzuerich.pdf).

69. See Martin Vahrenhorst, *"Ihr sollt überhaupt nicht schwören": Matthäus im halachischen Diskurs* (Neukirchen-Vluyn: Neukirchener, 2002), 218–34; Peter Fiedler, *Das Matthäusevangelium* (THKNT 1; Stuttgart: Kohlhammer, 2006), 122–58.

70. Johan Schloeman, "Und die Weisheit wurde Materie," *Süddeutsche Zeitung* (23–24 December 2006).

5.4. The Criterion of Social Justice

Liberation theology, feminist kyriarchal critique, postcolonial studies and the discussion of empire have shown that biblical texts and their exegetical history are also determined by power structures. They allude to the close association of androcentrism, colonialism, racism, militarism with other relationships of exploitation. Elisabeth Schüssler Fiorenza stated this in programmatic terms in 1983:

> Historical interpretation is defined by contemporary questions and horizons of reality and conditioned by contemporary political interests and structures of domination. Historical "objectivity" can only be approached by reflecting critically on naming one's theoretical presuppositions and political allegiances.[71]

Translating biblical texts into the contemporary German language context means seeking language that is appropriate to the history of Western Christianity. The New Testament uses many words that were used in the language of the Roman imperial ideology and propaganda.[72] For example: *euangelium* means "God's good news" as well as the good news of the emperor's birth; *parousia*, "advent of Christ," also meant the arrival of the emperor for a visitation rewarding the allegiance of a dominion or a city. The term *kyrios*, "Lord," or "Lord of the world," referred to God's authority as well as to the global dominance of Rome.[73] In the Jewish tradition of the first century c.e. when the New Testament was emerging, this language was language critical of authority. It communicated that believers listened to this lord and no other. The words contradicted the claim to power of political and social rulers, and were also understood by them in this way. These words and images were subsequently changed into authoritarian language, now itself legitimizing the language of an ideology, authority, and power. Images of dependence, obedience, and submission are therefore associated with the word "lord" in a democratic cultural sphere. Many words of the Bible have become unusable, as long as contem-

---

71. Elisabeth Schüssler Fiorenza, *In Memory of Her*, xvii. She describes hereafter how the androcentric perspective influences Bible translations and interpretations; see further 43–48.

72. See below Luise Schottroff and Claudia Janssen, "Übersetzungsfragen zu Herrschaft und Sklaverei," in Kuhlmann, *Die Bibel*, 212–21.

73. See Adolf Deissmann, *Licht vom Osten: Das neue Testament und die neuentdeckten Texte der hellenistisch-römischen Welt* (Tübingen: Mohr Siebeck, 1909), 184–298.

porary biblical interpretation does not help to develop awareness of their critique of hegemony and life force.

The following examples from Matt 11:5 and Luke 7:22 demonstrate what it means to understand social justice as a major criterion of translation. The presupposition that poor people are primarily objects of the New Testament message and not subjects of its proclamation has in many cases defined the exegesis of these texts and their translation. Thus the conventional translation reads: "the gospel is preached to the poor." In the Greek this is *ptōchoi euangelizontai*. Traditionally, this form of the verb "to proclaim" is interpreted as passive voice here, but it is in the middle voice, in the *genus verbi*, which in its meaning is between active and passive voice and is usually understood in the active: to proclaim the gospel.[74] This active meaning of the middle voice is also present in Jer 61:1 (LXX), a verse that is quoted in Luke 4:18: God's messenger proclaims the good news to the poor (dative: *ptōchois*). Luke 7:22 and Matt 11:5 also pick up Jer 61:1 but change the syntax. Now the poor *(ptōchoi)* are in the nominative: the poor proclaim the gospel; they turn into subjects of the proclamation. The literary context in Matt 11:5 and Luke 7:22 reinforces this version, since a series of subjects (in the nominative) are listed here that become active in relation to Jesus: the blind, the lame, and the deaf. This parallelism is broken up in the conventional interpretation if the verb is interpreted as passive voice, turning the subjects into objects. The *Bibel in gerechter Sprache* translates in terms that do justice to the text: "The blind see, the lame walk, the lepers become clean and the deaf can hear. The dead are raised and the poor bring the good news."

5.5. BIBLICAL CHRISTOLOGY IN INCLUSIVE GERMAN

The translation of the word *kyrios*, when it relates to Jesus, is a particular challenge. How can its meaning as critical of authority be rendered in a language that has been using it for centuries to legitimize authority? The translations in *The Bibel in gerechter Sprache* do not offer any standard solution. Some consciously avoid the word "Herr" and paraphrase in order to express the meaning of the term *kyrios*. In order to express the nature of belonging to Jesus as *kyrios*, the word is rendered many times with "(to) whom we belong." Other

---

74. See Walter Bauer, *Griechisch-deutsches Wörterbuch zu den Schriften des Neuen Testaments und der frühchristlichen Literatur* (6th ed.; ed. Kurt and Barbara Aland; Berlin: de Gruyter, 1988), 643. In addition to Matt 11:5 and Luke 7:22, he refers solely to one other place in the New Testament where the verb is of passive significance: Heb 4:2, 6. Here the statement is expressed by using a participle.

solutions are: "Jesus, the Christ, in whose power we trust," "in whose protective power we have entrusted ourselves," or "liberator."

In the translation of the letter to the church in Rome, Claudia Janssen has usually rendered *kyrios,* when it relates to Jesus or the Messiah, with "to whom we belong." The concern behind this is to make the Christology of Paul accessible to a contemporary understanding.[75] This translation reflects a Christology of relationship based on reciprocity, not on authoritarian power. The Messiah represents the hope of an entire people and their suffering in the present. "Christ," however, is no longer the christological "title of sovereignty" in the sense of the 1960s.[76] The title "son" or "child of God" (e.g., Rom 8:16, 17) does not separate Jesus from other people as unique, because they, too, are called the daughters and sons of God.[77]

Paul has summarized this Christology: "the firstborn among many brothers and sisters" (Rom 8:29). Christology in this sense means finding encouragement, empowerment, and comfort in a relationship with God, the Messiah, and in fellowship with other people who see themselves as brothers and sisters. The translations of the *Bibel in gerechter Sprache* are based here on the drafts of women theologians who have been describing Christology since the 1980s under the category of relationship and its perpetuation.[78]

---

75. On the Christology in 1 and 2 Corinthians, see Luise Schottroff, "'... Damit im Namen Jesus sich jedes Knie beuge': Christologie in 1 Kor und in Phil 2:9–11," in *Christus und seine Geschwister: Christologie im Umfeld der Bibel in gerechter Sprache* (ed. Marlene Crüsemann and Carsten Jochum-Bortfeld; Gütersloh: Gütersloher, 2009), 81–94; and Marlene Crüsemann, "Trost, Charis und Kraft der Schwachen: Eine Christologie der Beziehung nach dem zweiten Brief an die Gemeinde in Korinth," in Crüsemann and Jochum-Bortfeld, *Christus und seine Geschwister,* 111–37.

76. See Ferdinand Hahn, *Christologische Hoheitstitel: Ihre Geschichte im frühen Christentum* (5th ed.; Göttingen: Vandenhoeck & Ruprecht, 1995).

77. See Claudia Janssen, "Christus und seine Geschwister (Röm 8,12–17.29f)," in Crüsemann and Jochum-Bortfeld, *Christus und seine Geschwister,* 64–80.

78. See also Carter Heyward, *Und sie rührte sein Kleid an: Eine feministische Theologie der Beziehung* (Stuttgart: Kreuz, 1986); Doris Strahm and Regula Strobel, eds., *Vom Verlangen nach Heilwerden: Christologie in feministisch-theologischer Sicht* (Fribourg: Edition Exodus, 1991); Renate Jost and Eveline Valtink, eds., *Ihr aber für wen haltet ihr mich? Auf dem Weg zu einer feministisch-befreiungstheologischen Revision von Christologie* (Gütersloh: Kaiser, 1996). See, however, Elisabeth Schüssler Fiorenza, *Jesus: Miriam's Child, Sophia's Prophet: Critical Issues in Feminist Christology* (New York: Continuum, 1994).

6. There Is Life on the Road to Justice

Bible translations in "gerechte Sprache," or inclusive language, are widely received and at the same time continue to be developed. They are already shaping the spirituality of many women and men today who are encouraged to advocate greater justice in their communities and churches as well as in local social projects.

The Institutionalization of Feminist Biblical Studies in Its International and Ecumenical Contexts (Dossier)*

Renate Jost
Kirchliche Hochschule Neuendettelsau

Feminist biblical studies, as a fundamental component of the feminist movement in theology and religion, has accomplished much in the last thirty years worldwide. Its influence on scholarship and on church and religious history is a source of pride, and its contributions must be recognized. It is particularly important in times of conservative reaction not to retreat behind what has been accomplished.

The goal of this contribution is to collect some of the fundamental components of the institutionalization of feminist biblical studies. My primary focus is on institutions rather than persons, because they offer a context for further development. This focus is further defined by my academic context in Germany. In my introduction to *Feministische Theologie*, I adapted and used Anthony Gidden's definition of *institution* as a set of wide-ranging, extensive, longstanding practices with four discernible aspects: "(1) It is constituted by a common, unifying idea; (2) consists of a group of people who assume a predetermined set of tasks; (3) follows rules and norms that are accepted by all; and (4) it has a 'material component,' that is, objects and areas that are included in the institution."[1] According to this definition, religious communities, secondary schools, and universities are institutions, but so are other networks and independent groups working on feminist biblical interpretation.

Feministische Theologie is the first book to record the institutionalization of feminist theology in the German-speaking context. The editors are

---

* Translated by Richard Ratzlaff.

1. Renate Jost, "Erfolgsgeschichte Feministische Theologie—Initiativen, Kirchen, Universitäten: Einführung," in *Feministische Theologie: Initiativen, Kirchen, Universitäten— eine Erfolgsgeschichte* (ed. Gisela Matthiae et al.; Gütersloh: Gütersloher, 2008), 15.

convinced that the forty-year history of feminist theology has been a success worldwide. In order to learn from mistakes and avoid breaks with tradition, feminist theology also needs a culture of remembering that remains aware of its own past and deliberately makes it relevant in the present, so that it can become ever more part of the mainstream.[2] In *Feministiche Theologie* we present successful initiatives and processes of institutionalization in Germany. More than sixty women in various disciplines have described a rich variety of successful projects without ignoring the problems and difficulties that arose. While the largely Protestant perspective of the contributions is a function of the origins of the book, many contributors discuss ecumenical and interfaith perspectives.[3]

Because the first stirrings of feminist theology in Germany originated in women's movements in churches,[4] the first chapter is dedicated to various initiatives, networks, and projects.[5] The second chapter offers examples of how feminist theology became influential in church groups, structures, and associations. Feminist exegesis plays an especially important role in proclamation; in this context it is noteworthy that women have been leading worship in Protestant churches for forty years and in Old Catholic churches for twenty years, thus giving a new profile to this traditional role in the congregation.[6] The third chapter focuses on the process of institutionalization in universities. The fourth chapter presents developments in the Roman Catholic Church, the Old Catholic Church, and the international ecumenical movement. The final chapter focuses on Jewish feminists in the land of Shoah and on Muslim feminist theologies.[7] The appendix offers important data for the history of feminist theology in Germany, from the time of the earliest women's movement (ca. 1860).[8]

---

2. Bärbel Wartenberg-Potter, *EFD-Mitteilungen* 434 (2006): 42.

3. Renate Jost called for a volume collecting successful models of feminist theology at a symposium of "*tempo!* Aktionsbündnisses zur Institutionalisierung Feministischer Theologie" that took place in 2004 at the Women's Studies and Training Centre of the EKD (Evangelical Church in Germany) (see Jost, "Erfolgsgeschichte Feministische Theologie," 16).

4. In Germany, these stirrings were inspired by the works of Mary Daly (*The Church and the Second Sex*; *Beyond God the Father*), Elisabeth Moltmann-Wendel (see Schüngel-Straumann's chapter in this volume), Catharina Halkes (see Schüngel-Straumann), and Elisabeth Schüssler Fiorenza (*In Memory of Her*; *Bread Not Stone*).

5. Jost, "Erfolgsgeschichte Feministische Theologie," 19.

6. Ibid. For a discussion of feminist theology in Switzerland, see Dorothee Dieterich, "Hurra—Wir leben noch! Feministische Theologie heute," *FAMA* 16 (2000): 1–19.

7. Jost, "Erfolgsgeschichte Feministische Theologie," 19.

8. See "Daten zur Geschichte Feministischer Theologie in Deutschland," in Matthiae et al., *Feministische Theologie*, 386–90.

In the context of the astonishingly rich initiatives, institutionalization, and research presented in this book, I would like to focus in the rest of this chapter specifically on feminist biblical scholarship, taking international and interfaith academic contributions more fully into consideration. Because the organization of faith communities in many countries is much more diverse than in Germany, and because of the lack of materials documenting the influence of feminist exegesis in these contexts,[9] I propose to focus on publications, academic organizations, and initiatives of faith communities. A complete distinction between academic and nonacademic publications and organizations seems to me to be even less possible or relevant in the international context than it would be in the German context, as the people involved and the topics covered often overlap. After all, one goal of feminist theology from the beginning was to overcome this very separation between academia and lived religion.[10]

1. Professorships, Doctoral Programs, Centers, Selected Academic Organizations, and Grassroots Initiatives

Feminist biblical scholars have been active in universities internationally since the 1970s.[11] During the 1971 Atlanta meetings of the two large scholarly associations of the U.S., the American Academy of Religion (AAR) and the Society of Biblical Literature (SBL), the first thematic women's groups were formed.[12] Carol Christ (AAR) and Elisabeth Schüssler Fiorenza (SBL) were elected co-chairs of the Women's Caucus Religious Studies, the women in religion section was established, and Chris Downing was elected president of the AAR. There were far fewer women professors in SBL, the largest and oldest society for biblical scholarship in the U.S., working on feminist issues. At that time, they included, among others, Phyllis Bird, Phyllis Trible, Elisabeth Schüssler Fiorenza, Winsome Monroe, Antoinette Clark Wire, and Mary Wakeman.

---

9. On the situation in Argentina and Brazil, see in this volume Wanda Deifelt and Mercedes Navarro Puerto; in Eastern Europe, see Jutta Hausmann.

10. When feminist exegesis has reached a certain degree of differentiation and scholarly weight, a distinction between the two realms will become possible.

11. Compare Scholz, Plaskow, Baker, in this volume. For the years before this in the German context, compare also Schüngel-Straumann with her emphasis on Catholic women scholars. A Protestant scholar worthy of mention is the Anna Paulsen, whose biblical interpretation of the "particular pastoral role of women" is not without controversy and whose 1924 dissertation "Overcoming Protestant Scriptural Principles through Historical Revelation" was the second by a woman in Germany (after Carola Barth's, in 1904).

12. For further developments, see Scholz and Plaskow, in this volume.

In the 1970s in Germany, the English-language books of Mary Daly, Rosemary Radford Ruether and Letty M. Russell were widely read.[13] In the late 1970s and early 1980s, many groups both within and outside of universities began to study critically the biblical texts from a feminist point of view.[14] The *Handbuch Feministische Theologie*, edited by Christine Schaumberger and Monika Massen and published in 1986, was one of the results of this activity. The Dutch scholar Catharina Halkes was also influential in Germany in both Protestant and Catholic circles.[15] Even more influential was Elisabeth Schüssler Fiorenza, who is German but lives and works in the U.S. and whose publications have made pivotal contributions in both countries to ecclesial and academic work.[16]

The work of Elisabeth Moltmann-Wendel was also especially important for German feminist biblical interpretation, and reached women readers far beyond academia. In 1974, she published a collection entitled *Menschenrechte für die Frau: Christliche Initiative zur Frauenbefreiung* (Human Rights for Woman: Christian Initiatives for the Liberation of Women), which included contributions on biblical scholarship by Krister Stendhal, Leonard Swidler, and Rosemary Radford Reuther. In the same year the World Council of Churches Consultation on "Sexism in the 1970s" took place in Berlin. The discussion papers prepared for this consultation laid important groundwork arguing for complete equality for women pastors and, later, processes of institutionalization in Protestant churches and seminaries.[17] In 1980, Moltmann-Wendel published the book *Ein eigener Mensch werden: Frauen um Jesus*, in which

---

13. See Matthiae et al., *Feministische Theologie*, 236–40. Mary Daly's works included *The Church and the Second Sex* (New York: Harper & Row, 1968), published in German as *Kirche, Frau und Sexus* (Olten: Walter, 1970); and *Beyond God the Father* (Boston: Beacon, 1973), published in German as *Jenseits von Gottvater, Sohn und Co.* (Munich: Frauenoffensive, 1980). Compare Plaskow and Scholz, in this volume. See also Rosemary Radford Ruether, ed., *Religion and Sexism: Images of Woman in the Jewish Christian Traditions* (New York: Simon & Schuster, 1974); and Letty Russell, ed., *The Liberating Word: A Guide to Nonsexist Interpretation of the Bible* (Philadelphia: Westminster John Knox, 1977), published in German as *Als Mann und Frau ruft er uns: vom nicht-sexistischen Gebrauch der Bibel* (Munich: Pfeiffer, 1979).

14. Matthiae et al., *Feministische Theologie*, 236–40.

15. See Elisabeth Schüssler Fiorenza, "Celebrating Feminist Work by Knowing It," *JFSR* 27.1 (2011): 97–127.

16. See, for example, Elisabeth Schüssler Fiorenza, *Bread Not Stone: The Challenge of Feminist Interpretation* (Boston: Beacon, 1984), published in German as *Brot statt Steine: Die Herausforderung einer feministischen Interpretation der Bibel* (Freiburg: Edition Exodus, 1988).

17. See Matthiae et al., *Feministische Theologie*, 209–34.

she attempts to portray New Testament women as people liberated by Jesus. The year 1983 saw the publication of Elisabeth Schüssler Fiorenza's ground-breaking book *In Memory of Her*.[18] Her analysis had a significant impact on subsequent discussions in biblical scholarship.[19]

Toward the end of the 1980s two of Germany's first women professors of biblical studies, Luise Schottroff (New Testament) and Helen Schüngel-Straumann (Old Testament), also began to publish important work.[20] In 1971 Schottroff was appointed adjunct professor in Mainz, then professor in 1973, teaching and researching there until 1986. From 1986 until 1999 she held the chair in New Testament at the University of Kassel. Together with Christine Schaumberger she founded and shaped the summer university program in feminist and liberation theology in Hofgeismar and published numerous feminist studies on the social history of the New Testament.[21] Helen Schüngel-Straumann, the first Catholic woman Old Testament scholar appointed to a chair of biblical studies (in Kassel, 1987–2000) is the founder of the Helen Straumann-Stiftung für Feministische Theologie in Basel.[22] In the Netherlands, important contributions were made by Katharina Halkes,[23]

---

18. Elisabeth Schüssler Fiorenza, *In Memory of Her: A Feminist Theological Reconstruction of Christian Origins* (New York: Crossroad, 1983), published in German as *Zu ihrem Gedächtnis: Eine feministisch-theologische Rekonstruktion der christlichen Ursprünge* (Munich: Kaiser, 1988).

19. Lone Fatum, "Image of God and Glory of Man: Women in the Pauline Congregations," in *Image of God and Gender Models in Judaeo-Christian Traditions* (ed. Kari Elisabeth Børresen; Oslo: Solum, 1991), 56–137; Fatum, "1 Thessalonians," in *A Feminist Commentary* (vol. 2 of *Searching the Scriptures*; ed. Elisabeth Schüssler Fiorenza; New York: Crossroad, 1994), 250–62; Fatum, *Kvindeteologi og arven fra Eva* (Gyldendal Intro; Köpenhamn: Nordisk, 1992). I am grateful to Hanna Stenström for these references.

20. For the earlier period, see Schüngel-Straumann, in this volume.

21. Important books include Luise Schottroff and Dorothee Sölle, *Jesus von Nazareth* (Munich: Deutscher Taschenbuch, 2000); Luise Schottroff, *Lydias ungeduldige Schwestern: Feministische Sozialgeschichte des frühen Christentums* (Gütersloh: Gütersloher, 1994).

22. Important publications include Helen Schüngel-Straumann, *Die Frau am Anfang: Eva und die Folgen* (3rd ed.; Münster: LIT, 1999); Schüngel-Straumann, *Rûah bewegt die Welt: Gottes schöpferische Lebenskraft in der Krisenzeit des Exils* (SBS 151; Stuttgart: Katholisches Bibelwerk, 1992); Schüngel-Straumann, *Denn Gott bin ich, und kein Mann: Gottesbilder im Ersten Testament—feministisch betrachtet* (Mainz: Matthias-Grünewald, 1996). For more information on the Helen Schüngel-Straumann foundation, see Antje Röckemann, "Helen Straumann-Stiftung für Feministische Theologie," in Matthiae et al., *Feministische Theologie*, 56–57.

23. Professor from 1983 to 1986, with an emphasis on feminism and Christianity, at the Katholieke Universiteit Nijmegen, where she had been active as a scholar since 1967. See also Schüngel-Staumann.

the first professor of feminist theology in the world, and by Fokkelien van Dijk Hemmes, Old Testament scholar and assistant professor in the Faculty of Theology in Tilburg. New Testament scholar Lone Fatum was active in Copenhagen, Denmark, where she was assistant professor from 1981 to 2001.

The activities of these women and others led to the founding in 1986 of the European Society of Women in Theological Research (ESWTR), whose goal was to connect women working in academic theology in Europe and to promote and support exchange, conversation, cooperation, and research. National branches of the society were formed in several countries, but the German branch is the largest, with three hundred members. Since 1991, a New Testament group within the German section has been meeting semiannually; since 1995 an Old Testament group has been meeting annually. International conferences and national meetings are crucial in order to maintain the vibrancy of the ESWTR, because it is here that the organizational work and networking take place, rejuvenating the ESWTR. National meetings which take place biennially, provide opportunities for scholarly exchange on selected topics, serve as a venue for conversations on research projects, and promote further networking. An international newsletter has existed since the beginning, to which several national branches also contribute.

Together with the journal *Schlangenbrut* and the various conference centers of the Protestant Church,[24] the ESWTR was an important forum in Germany for the debate that began in 1987 concerning anti-Semitism in feminist theology and biblical interpretation.[25] The lectures and publications of American Jewish feminists such as Judith Plaskow and Susannah Heschel[26] were important for prompting the debate. They pointed to the dangerous anti-Semitic clichés present in German biblical scholarship since the nineteenth century, which inhere in the thesis of an original matriarchy suppressed by a patriarchal Jewish YHWH, and a pro-women Jesus who distinguished himself from a Judaism that discriminated against women. An understanding of the role of women in Judaism was deepened through the work on rabbinic scriptural exegesis from a feminist perspective by Jewish scholar Pnina Nave Levinson, co-founder and professor (until 1986) at the Hochschule für jüdische Studies in Heidelberg.[27]

---

24. Leonore Siegele-Wenschkewitz, *Verdrängte Vergangenheit, die uns bedrängt: Feministische Theologie in der Verantwortung für die Geschichte* (Munich: Kaiser, 1988).

25. See on this Wacker, Winkler, Schaumberger, in this volume.

26. See Plaskow, in this volume; Susannah Heschel, *On Being a Jewish Feminist: A Reader* (New York: Schocken, 1983).

27. Pnina Navè Levinson, *Was wurde aus Saras Töchtern? Frauen im Judentum* (Gütersloh: Gütersloher, 1989).

Feminist organizations with scholarly agendas emerged in other regions of the world as well, both within and outside of existing faith communities, occupied with critical scriptural exegesis.[28] For example, the Korean Association of Feminist Theologians (KAFT), founded in 1985, became a member of the Korean Association of Christian Studies in 1987. Founded in 1986 in Spain, the Seminario en Fey Secularidad sobre Teologia Feminista established the School of Feminist Theology at the University of Barcelona in 2006.

Sisters in Islam was founded in 1988 in Malaysia. The mission of Sisters in Islam is to promote "the rights of women within the framework of Islam as based on the principles of equality, justice and freedom enjoined by the Qur'an."[29] Sisters in Islam organizes public conferences, creates national and international Muslim women's networks, and publishes responses to contested issues such as polygamy.

The Circle of Concerned African Women Theologians (The Circle) was founded in 1989. Also founded in 1989 was the Britain and Ireland School of Feminist Theology (BISFT). Conspirando was founded in Chile in 1991, as well as the Asociación Teólogas Españolas (ATE). In addition to these, other organizations that are more or less or aligned with feminism offer a forum in various ways to feminist biblical scholars, depending. their need to work within their faith communities. Beginning in the mid-1980s, initiatives were undertaken in various locations (e.g., São Leopoldo, Graz, Harvard, Neuendettelsau, and Münster[30]) to create permanent opportunities for feminist research and to promote them widely.

In 1991, the Universidad Luterana in *São Leopoldo established a chair for feminist theology. This chair was held by Old Testament scholar Elaine Neuenfeldt from 2004 until her appointment in Geneva. Notable in this context is the requirement of a course in feminist theology for all theology students. The* Universidad Biblica Latinoamericana in Costa Rica and the Universidad Metodista de *São* Paulo also actively promote feminist biblical scholarship.[31]

In 1994 in Graz, Women's Studies and Gender Studies were established as subjects in reaction to the papal letter *Ordinatio sacerdotalis*, which forbade the ordination of women as priests, and in 1997 Anne Jensen was appointed as first professor, holding her position until 2008. Since then, the Catholic faculty has become an indispensable part of the curriculum of the Interdisciplinary Women's and Gender Studies program at the University of Graz. The

---

28. This section draws on the contributions of many of the authors in this volume.

29. See https://www.facebook.com/officialSIS/info.

30. On Neuendettelsau, see Matthiae et al., *Feministische Theologie*, 241, 249; on Münster, 249.

31. See Tamez, in this volume.

fruits of research at that institution can be seen in the impressive number of theses on feminist topics.[32] Further, the appointment of Graz-trained Irmtraud Fischer to the Chair for Theological Women's Studies at the Catholic Theology Faculty at the University of Bonn, a position established in 1997, reflects the international reputation of scholarship at Graz.[33] Upon her return to take up the Chair for Old Testament Studies, she chaired the Curriculum Commission on Women's and Gender Studies, which under her leadership developed an M.A. in Graz as well as a joint M.A. in Gender Studies with Ruhr University Bochum. Both programs include an in-depth module on feminist theology, which includes courses in biblical studies. As vice-rector of the university, Fischer initiated the development of doctoral programs, including one established in Women's and Gender Studies. Furthermore, she established an international doctoral and post-doctoral forum for theological women's and gender studies which took place for the first time in 2010. Although it is directed especially to those addressing gender-related theological issues in their doctoral or postdoctoral work, participants from other theological areas who are studying gender-specific issues are also welcome (e.g., the reception of biblical texts in literature or art history).[34]

In 1988 at Harvard, Margaret Miles, Clarissa Atkinson, Constance Buchanan, Bernadette Brooten, and Sharon Welch launched a Th.D. program in Religion, Gender, and Culture. Miles was the chair until 1996, when Elisabeth Schüssler Fiorenza took over and continued to develop the program until it was also recognized as a Ph.D. program in 1997. Important dissertations of feminist theology and gender studies have been produced by this program. Another Ph.D. program in Women's Studies and Religion that includes feminist biblical scholarship is offered at the Claremont University Graduate School of Religion.

While some German women biblical scholars accepted university posts in the U.S. in the early 1990s,[35] a few others, despite the difficulties already

---

32. However, to date there have been no Habilitationen.

33. Important publications include Irmtraud Fischer, *Erzeltern Israels: Feministisch-theologische Studien zu Genesis 12–36* (BZAW 222; Berlin: de Gruyter, 1994); a trilogy that includes Fischer, *Gottesstreiterinnen: Biblische Erzählungen über die Anfänge Israels* (Stuttgart: Kohlhammer, 1995); Fischer, *Gotteskünderinnen: Zu einer geschlechter-fairen Deutung der Prophetie in der Hebräischen Bibel* (Stuttgart: Kohlhammer, 2003); and Fischer, *Gotteslehrerinnen: Weise Frauen und Frau Weisheit im Alten Testament* (Stuttgart: Kohlhammer, 2006), which has now also been published in French (Paris: Cerf). The first volume has also been published in English. See also Fischer, *Rut* (HThK; Freiburg: Herder, 2000).

34. Applications for travel expenses and additional information should be directed to vizerektorin.forschung@uni-graz.at.

35. In the 1990s a growing number of female theologians aimed for permanent

mentioned, have been appointed since the late 1990s to positions in Old Testament[36] and New Testament studies in German-speaking universities. These appointments were made possible especially in places where years of active scholarship by women had prepared the way for the selection of an appropriately qualified woman scholar.[37] Chairs specifically in women's theological studies and feminist theology were also established. The importance of feminist biblical scholarship in Germany is due in part to the fact that the earliest positions in Catholic theological women's studies were filled with Old Testament/Hebrew Bible scholars working from a feminist perspective: Irmtraud Fischer in 1997 in Bonn, and Marie-Theres Wacker in 1998 in Münster. The only permanent Protestant professorial chair in feminist theology and theological women's studies, at the Augustana Hochschule of the Evangelical Lutheran Church in Neuendettelsau, Bavaria, has also been held since 2003 by a feminist biblical scholar, Renate Jost, who began there as a Lecturer in 1997.[38] Because of this appointment, the Augustana was able to include a required course in feminist theology in its curriculum, and to build an exceptional specialized library collection. In 2008 Renate Jost, Susannah Heschel, and Elisabeth Schüssler Fiorenza founded the International Institute for Feminist Theology and Religious Studies at the Augustana, which also has a focus on biblical scholarship.

Even when the challenges of establishing an academic position in feminist studies are met, the position does not always last or ends up changing direction. Moreover, such positions are often limited-term or part-time. For instance, the professorial chair held by Catharina Halkes, who was appointed in 1983 to the Chair for Feminism in Christendom at Radboud University Nijmegen, the first chair anywhere in the world for feminist theology, was created for her personally. After she retired in 1985, it was held for two years

---

academic positions. Some of them moved to the U.S., where feminist exegesis was more accepted. One example is Angela Bauer-Levesque (born 1960), who has served on the faculty of Episcopal Divinity School in Boston since 1994. Another example is Susanne Scholz, who also has been teaching in the U.S. since the mid-1990s. Since 2009 she has been a professor of Old Testament at the Perkins School of Theology at Southern Methodist University in Dallas.

36. Sylvia Schroer was appointed in 1997 to the Chair for Old Testament and Its Environment in Berne.

37. I note especially here the Catholic Old Testament scholar Silvia Schroer, who was appointed to the Chair for Old Testament and Its Environment in Berne, when it was still the Protestant Faculty of Theology. Through her work on Wisdom and feminist interpretation of ancient Near Eastern iconography and religion, she has considerably enriched feminist biblical scholarship.

38. Matthiae et al., *Feministische Theologie*, 241–48.

each by Mary Grey and Athalya Brenner. Not until the appointment of Maaike de Haardt in 1998 did it become a permanent chair, but it remains as before only a part-time position.

The second chair established in the Netherlands for Women's Studies and Practical Theology was held by Riet Bons-Storm at Groningen University from 1990 until 1998 and was paid for by Reformed Church of the Netherlands, albeit for only one day a week. When Bons-Storm retired, the chair was not filled immediately. Kune Biezeveld, who taught systematic theology at Leiden University from 2002 to 2008, can be seen as her successor, but after her death in 2008, no one was appointed to this position; it is not clear, therefore, if the position still exists (I owe this information to Maaike de Haardt).

The professor for Feminist Theology at São Leopoldo was held from 1991 until 2004 by the systematic theologian Wanda Deifelt, to whom I am grateful for the following information. When her successor Elaine Neuenfeldt became the director of WICAS (Women in Church and Society) of the Lutheran World Federation, in Geneva, the financial support of the Reformed Church of the Netherlands came to an end. The chair became a program in Gender and Feminist Theology, and the required course in Feminist Theology has since been taught by Carlos Nusskopf, who holds the Chair for Gender and specializes in Queer Theology.

The chair for Theological Women's Studies in Bonn was converted to an academic research position in the area of Church History (see *Feministische Theologie*) when Irmtraud Fischer left in 2004. The chair for Theological Women's Studies at Münster was combined with the chair for Old Testament.[39] The professor for Theological Women's Studies/Feminist Theologie at the Augustana is dedicated fulltime to these subjects; since 2008 it has been a permanent C2 Professorship and in contrast to the C4 teaching positions at the same University it is much more poorly paid and has fewer resources.

At present, feminist theology and gender studies is taught as a distinct discipline at only a few universities in the world, and even there is not granted the same long-term institutional commitment as other disciplines.[40]

---

39. See Gisela Matthiae and Renate Jost, "Bonn," in Matthiae et al, *Feministische Theologie*, 271–72.

40. In 2011 the following are known to me, in addition to those held by women biblical scholars in Münster and Neuendettelsau: assistant professor (i.e., appointed for six years, without the Habilitation) in Feminist Theology with a concentration in ecumenism in Wuppertal (Germany) (Heike Walz) (see also Matthiae et al., *Feministische Theologie*, 251–52); assistant professor for Theological Gender Studies in Berlin, Germany (Ulrike Auga) (253–56); Chair for Religion and Gender (since 2003; previously Feminisme en Christendom) with a concentration in Systematic Theology and Empirical Theology, i.e.,

Nevertheless, feminist content is taught in courses in biblical studies,[41] and in some places is integrated into the curricula of programs in gender studies. Examples of this integration can be found at the universities in Oslo and in Sarajevo.[42] The feminist biblical scholar Jorunn Økland heads the Center for Gender Research in Oslo. Since 2006 Sarajevo and Novi Sad have had a program in gender studies, to which was added the specialized program in gender studies in Bosnia and Hercegovina in 2010. In Sarajevo, the Muslim scholar Zilka Spahic-Siljak has been teaching courses in gender and religion, comparing Jewish, Christian, and Islamic traditions. Works of feminist biblical scholarship such as the books of Elisabeth Schüssler Fiorenza play an important role in these comparative studies.[43]

In spite of many obstacles, women scholars have produced an almost unimaginable wealth of research and doctoral work on numerous areas of biblical scholarship in many parts of the world.[44] The large number of dissertations

---

Religious Studies, in Nijmwegen (Netherlands, Maaike de Haardt); Professor for Religion, Gender and Modernity (since 2009; previously, from 1999 to 2009, Women's Studies/ Theology for one day per week), Faculty of Humanities, Utrecht University (Netherlands, Anne-Marie Korte) Chair in Interdisciplinary Theological Gender Studies (Gender, Theology, and Religion) in the Theology Faculty in Oslo (Norway; since 2005, Jone Salomonson, who also heads up the bilateral research project between South Africa and Norway, Broken Women/Healing Traditions); Chair in Systematic Theology with a concentration on Feminist Theology at the University of Iceland (Arnfidur Gudmundsdottir).

41. See the chapters in this book and Matthiae et al., *Feministische Theologie*.

42. For Barcelona, see also Navarro, in this volume.

43. See Svenka Savic (University of Novi Sad, Serbia), *Feminist Theology* [Serbian] (Novi Sad: Futura publikacije, 1999). Other books include Rebeka Anic, *Women in Church in the Twenty-First Century in Croatia* [Croatian] (Vienna: LIT, 2004); Zilka Spahic-Siljak and Rebeka Anic, *Women Believers and Citizens* [Bosnian] (Sarajevo: TPO Foundation, 2009), Zilka Spahic-Siljak, *Women, Religion, and Politics* (Sarajevo: IMIC Zajedno, 2010).

44. An overview of the results up to 1995 of the research of feminist biblical scholars writing in German can be found in Matthiae et al., *Feministische Theologie*. Hanna Stenström lists a number of publications in the Nordic countries. There are some works by Lone Fatum, the Danish voice in international feminist biblical scholarship, who worked at the University of Copenhagen and is now retired; Inger Ljung (University of Uppsala), *Silence or Suppression* (Stockholm: Uppsala, 1989), which must be the first book in Old Testament feminist scholarship published in Sweden; Talvikki Mattila (University of Helsinki), *Citizens of the Kingdom* (Göttingen: Vandenhoeck & Ruprecht, 2002), as far as I know the first dissertation in feminist biblical scholarship in Finland; Jorunn Økland (University of Oslo), *Women in Their Place* (Edinburgh: T&T Clark, 2004), a Norwegian contribution to international feminist biblical scholarship; Lilian Portefaix (University of Uppsala), *Sisters Rejoice!* (Stockholm: Almqvist & Wiksell, 1988), the first dissertation on a New Testament topic with a feminist perspective in Sweden but formally in history of religions; Turid Karlsen Seim (University of Oslo), *The Double Message* (Nashville: Abingdon, 1994), the

shows the growing acceptance of feminist work by those who direct doctoral research, even though they themselves are not involved in feminist theological research. This acceptance is particularly evident in Norway, although less scholarship is produced there than in Germany,[45] no doubt due to the smaller population. However, statistics on doctoral students, postdoctoral scholars, and professors show that women are by far underrepresented at these levels, including, for example, in Germany in 2010.

Although currently more than 50 percent of students in the humanities and cultural studies are women, only 7–12 percent of all C4/W3 academic positions are held by women. This is true as well for feminist biblical studies. A comparison of hiring practices shows that a specialization in feminist biblical scholarship has become a criterion for exclusion. A feminist perspective is regarded as narrow, although it touches on all areas of biblical scholarship and thus broadens the perspective of the whole.[46] Nevertheless, in schools and universities in Germany beyond those already noted where feminist scholarship is institutionally supported, there are women professors in various areas of biblical scholarship also working from a feminist perspective[47] who give lectures with on various themes of biblical scholarship with explicitly feminist theological content.[48] When these women professors retire, however, they are

---

first feminist dissertation in New Testament in Norway and a contribution to the international discussion; Mikael Sjöberg (University of Uppsala), *Wrestling with Textual Violence* (Sheffield: Sheffield Phoenix, 2006), the first feminist Old Testament dissertation in Sweden written by a man who identifies as a feminist scholar; Hanna Stenström (University of Uppsala), *The Book of Revelation: A Vision of the Ultimate Liberation or the Ultimate Backlash? A Study in 20th Century Interpretations of Rev 14:1–5, with Special Emphasis on Feminist Exegesis* (Uppsala: Uppsala University Press, 1999), the first feminist New Testament dissertation in Sweden; the issue of *Studia Theologica* mentioned above; Rut Törnkvist (University of Uppsala), *The Use and Abuse of Female Sexual Imagery in the Book of Hosea: A Feminist Critical Approach to Hos 1–3* (Uppsala: Uppsala University Library, 1998), the first feminist Old Testament dissertation in Sweden. To the list of "firsts" may be added the first dissertation using queer theory in biblical studies in Sweden, and as far as I know it is the first in all five Nordic countries using this perspective: Malin Ekström, *Allvarsam parodi och möjlighetens melankoli: En queerteoretisk analys av Ruts bok* (Uppsala: Uppsala University Press, 2011).

In India dissertations at the following universities are especially encouraged: Senate of Serampore College (University); the United Theological College, Bangalore; Gurukul Lutheran Theological College, Chennai; Tamilnadu Theological Seminary, Madurai. I am grateful to Monica Melanchthon for this information.

45. I am grateful to Jorunn Økland for this information.

46. Matthiae et al., *Feministische Theologie*, 236–37.

47. Ibid.

48. Asnath Natar of Indonesia describes the situation as follows: There are only two

not always succeeded by professors who work from a feminist point of view. In Kassel, Helen Schüngel-Straumann was replaced by the feminist exegete Ilse Müllner, but this proved to be an exception.

The situation in most northern European countries appears to be similar,[49] except that in some countries, such as Norway, feminist issues are more integrated into society than in Germany.[50] On the other hand, as in Germany, so also in many places in the world, feminist theologians hold important positions in Protestant churches and are relatively successful at integrating their concerns.[51] This integration has been facilitated by the numerous church centers and organizations of women theologians formed since the end of the 1980s.[52] In some places feminist women theologians have created momentum through conferences and publications. Thus, the Asian Women's Resource Center for Culture and Theology, founded in Hong Kong in 1988 and now operating in Yogyakarta, mobilizes and supports Asian women in the development of feminist perspectives, whether they are theologically trained or not.[53] At the Women's Studies and Training Center founded by the German Protestant Church in 1993, Renate Jost was Director of Studies until 1997, a position held by Claudia Janssen since 2007.[54] Japan's Center for Feminist

---

faculties of theology with courses in feminist theology: the Duta Wacana Theological Faculty in Yogyakarta and Tomohon Theological Faculty in Manado. In the other theological faculties and postsecondary schools, feminist theology is only an aspect of other courses: in New Testament, Old Testament, and systematics. The Satya Wacana Faculty of Theology in Salatiga has courses in gender studies.

49. See Hanna Stenström, in this volume.

50. See on this Matthiae et al., *Feministische Theologie*, 98–235, 241–49.

51. For Germany, see Matthiae et al., *Feministische Theologie*. Jorunn Økland describes the situation in Norway: "Kari Børresen. She has been the most international pioneer and led a range of projects, including EU projects. Sometimes they have been based in Norway, other times not. She is by far the most important person; Solveig Fiske, bishop of Hamar, was its former leader; Turid Karlsen Seim, former dean of theology and very active in ecumenical contexts (faith and order, etc.); Helga Byfuglien, also a former member of Norsk kvinnelig teologforening, Jone is professor of feminist theology at the Faculty of Theology (University of Oslo); Ingrid Vad Nielsen, former CEO of Norges kristne råd, now executive position in the Ministry for Church and Education."

52. For example, Der Konvent Evangelischer Theologinnen in der Bundesrepublik e.V. 1925 (The Convention of Protestant Women Theologians in the Federal Republic, incorporated in 1925; see also Matthiae et al., *Feministische Theologie*, 191–208) and The Norwegian Women's Theologian Association (NKTF), which published the book *Feminist Theology* in Norway in 1999.

53. See Melanchthon, in this volume.

54. See on this issue Janssen and Köhler, in this volume.

Theology and Ministry, founded in 2000, is led by two women biblical scholars, Satoko Yamaguchi and Hisako Kinukawa.[55]

While there are a large number of autonomous initiatives, I will describe only two examples. The Women's Alliance for Theology, Ethics, and Ritual (WATER) was founded in 1983 by Mary E. Hunt and Diann L. Neu, who continue to lead this initiative. It is a training center and network for those seeking justice. Its goal is to apply feminist values in the work for social and religious change. For twenty-five years, WATER has offered publications, consultations, workshops, and spiritual retreats, through which it has supported thousands of people striving to build inclusive social and faith communities.[56]

The Foundation for the Promotion of Women (FrauenFörderungsFonds) of the Erev-Rav Association has existed since 1996. Erev-Rav is a network of European Christians united in collaborative work on a liberation theology in a European context. "Erev Rav" is the biblical Hebrew word for the vast human swarm of non-Jewish people who accompanied Israel on the exodus from slavery to freedom (Exod 12:38). The association's name identifies its goal: to remember the experience of liberation but also the need for the church to walk together with the Jewish people. With this goal in mind, Erev-Rav organizes international ecumenical meetings, runs a press that publishes, among other things, the journal *Junge Kirche* and has a fund for the promotion of women.[57]

In short, globally there are attempts to institutionalize feminist biblical studies in almost every country, although many obstacles are still encountered. Let me provide two examples. First, with respect to Hungary, Jutta Hausmann explains that the sparseness of feminist literature in Hungarian libraries is a sign not only of a lack of interest but also a lack of money. When one has only about €700–800 annually to buy books on Old Testament scholarship, as I have had for some years at our university, one must buy first the general standard literature, and it is not at all enough for this. So special feminist literature is only from time to time on the list of the books to buy. It is more or less the same situation in the other institutions. That being said, even if there were more money, the lack of interest in feminist exegesis would often be the reason for not finding more feminist literature.

What about feminist exegetical literature written in Hungarian? When I look closely, I find fewer than a dozen articles. There is one exception: when after Eszter Andorka's death some friends collected and published her unfinished and unpublished papers, sermons, and articles, everyone realized how

---

55. See Melanchthon, in this volume.
56. See http://waterwomensalliance.org.
57. See www.erev-rav.de; Matthiae et al., *Feministische Theologie,* 52–53.

much she was involved in feminist research. Eszter Andorka was a Ph.D. student working on Mark and was very engaged in social issues. She combined in a pronounced way theological research and her sense of responsibility for those living as marginalized people. She was aware that theology and life are not divided, that theological work is dynamic and has the means to change one's life and the lives of others. Eszter Andorka was able to motivate students and to irritate colleagues in her work as pastor in a parish as well as in her work at the university, which she confronted with her sometimes inconvenient theological perspectives. The death of Eszter Andorka was a significant setback for the development of Hungarian feminist exegesis. At this point we can alos mention Márta Cserháti (Budapest), who is integrating feminist hermeneutics into her work and, more and more, Rita Perintfalvi and Gyöngyi Varga (both in Budapest) as well as Korinna Zamfir (in Cluj).

Second, Asnath Natar describes the situation of feminist theology in Indonesia. There are many theologians working on feminist theology, one of whom is Marianne Katoppo, who became known through her book *Compassionate and Free: An Asian Woman's Theology*, in which she describes the experiences of Asian Christian women, who are widely regarded as "others" by the churches.[58]

Another feminist scholar is K. A. Kapahang-Kaunang, author of a book of contextual theology from the perspective of Minahasa women.[59] Nunuk P. Murniati is a Catholic woman who has written several articles and books about feminist theology, among them "Peran Perempuan dalag Gereja" (The Role of Women in the Church). She criticizes the lack of roles for women in the Catholic churches.

In addition to the women writing on theology, there are also several men who write on feminist theology, among them J. B. Banawiratma, a pastor. One of his books is entitled *Gender dan Tali temalinya* (Gender and Its Relationship to Other Problems). He argues that gender injustice in the church is connected to other issues such as church tradition, power, and capitalism. Another male theologian is E. G. Singgih, who has also written several articles about feminist theology, for example, "Implikasi Gender dalam lembaga pendidikan Teologi" (The Impact of Gender at the Institute for Theological Education). In this article he criticizes the fact that there are few women teaching in the theology faculties and postsecondary schools.

---

58. Marianne Katoppo, *Compassionate and Free: An Asian Woman's Theology* (Maryknoll, N.Y.: Orbis, 1980).

59. K. A. Kapahang-Kaunang, *Perempuan: Pemahaman Teologis tentang Perempuan dalag Konteks Budaya Minahasa* (Jakarta: BPK Gunung Mulia, 1993).

Feminist approaches to theology have been developed as well by Elga Sarapung, Asnath N. Natar, Indriani Bone, Sientje Marentek-Abrah, Hendrietta Hutabarat-Leban, Margarethe Hendrik-Ririmase, and others. It is regrettable that many of them have taken over the ways of thinking and theology of women in the West and have written little about theology within an Indonesian context.

2. JOURNALS

The successful institutionalization of feminist biblical scholarship is evident worldwide in the wealth of journals that document the long-standing collaboration of feminist biblical scholars. The diverse and increasingly differentiated goals of the journals presented in this section reflect the changing discussions and emphases within the feminist theology movement. They reflect both the changing political and social discussions and situations and the possibilities of new technological developments. Furthermore, it must be noted that in the earlier writings there is little distinction between scholarly and nonscholarly publications, and it is not until the new millennium that exclusively exegetical journals appear.

One of the first journals of feminist theology was *Lilith: The Independent Jewish Magazine*. It was established in 1976 by a small group of Jewish[60] women working with Susan Weidman Schneider. The publication's name honors Adam's first wife, Lilith. Although she is not mentioned in the Bible, according to some Jewish scholars she was expelled from paradise because she was unwilling to obey Adam in all things, particularly in sexual matters. She is the paradigm of the rebellious, disobedient wife. By naming their journal for this figure, the founders wanted to identify with all women who are prepared to take risks in their struggle for gender equality. The journal's focus is on religious and social issues, but economic and political discussions are also featured. Appearing sporadically in its early years, the journal is now published quarterly and has a readership estimated to be more than 25,000.[61]

The progressive international Catholic journal *Concilium* includes numerous articles on feminist theology and with Elisabeth Schüssler Fiorenza as coeditor published twelve volumes on feminist theology between 1984 and 2002. *Concilium* had the largest number of women readers in Europe; in many respects it introduced feminist theology to France, Spain, and Latin America. Le Groupement International Femmes et Hommes dans

---

60. See Baker for a discussion of the question what constitutes "Jewish."
61. See Anne Lapidus Lerner at http://jwa.org/encyclopedia/article/lilith-magazine.

l'église (The International Association of Women and Men in the Church) was founded in 1970 in Brussels, Belgium, and Paris, France. This group introduced itself in a call to action in the September 1970 issue of the journal *Concilium*.[62] Serious internal discussions led finally to the first explicitly feminist volume of this journal in 1985.[63]

In God's Image: Journal of the Asian Women's Resource Centre for Culture and Theology has been published quarterly since 1981 with the intention to reflect the life situations, struggles, and hopes of Christian women in Asia.[64] The authors of the articles come from a range of Asian countries such as India, Japan, Taiwan, and New Zealand, and their work shows the cultural richness of Asia.[65] In prose and poetry the journal presents internationally relevant themes such as feminist expressions of God from various Asian perspectives,[66] theology of the body, and abuse and sexual violence in the church. More specific issues are also addressed, such as "On the Road to Freedom: The Saga of Karenni Women," by Eunice Barbara C. Novio, from the Philippines.[67] Since the early 1980s, the newsletter *Stee* of the All India Council for Christian Women (AICCW) has appeared regularly.[68] The growing number of women authors writing from a feminist perspective is also evident in the exegetical journal *Revista de Interpretación* (Latin American Biblical Interpretation Review–RIBLA). It has published the work of women biblical scholars from all of the Latin American countries since 1982.[69] Particularly notable is the fiftieth edition of this journal, containing the ground-breaking proceedings of a meeting of feminist exegetes in São Leopoldo in 2004.[70]

In May of 1983, the first issue of *Schlangenbrut*, a journal for women interested in religious subjects, was published. Because there were only very limited possibilities for biblical feminists to publish their writings in the early 1980s, this journal offered them excellent opportunities. From the journal's very beginning, certain special editions concentrated on feminist biblical interpretation. The first special edition in 1999 by Sabine Bäuerle and Elis-

---

62. My thanks to Mercedes Navarro Puerto for this information.

63. My thanks to Elisabeth Schüssler Fiorenza for this information.

64. For further information on the journal, contact: igi@awrc4ct.org. For a critical deconstruction of the term "Asian," see Melanchthon, in this volume.

65. See on this issue Melanchthon, 105–19, above, as well as the table of contents of *In God's Image* 29.1 (2010).

66. On the critical issues with these terms, see Melanchthon, 105–19.

67. Eunice Barbara C. Novio, "On the Road to Freedom: The Saga of Karenni Women," *In God's Image* 29.1 (2010).

68. Melanchthon, 112.

69. See Tamez, 35–52, in this volume.

70. See Tamez, in this volume.

Please supply exact pages to Tamez's chapter.

abeth Müller was about eulogies from a feminist biblical perspective. The second special edition of that year was in honor of Leony Renk, whose work focused on intercultural and inter-faith bibliodrama. The third special edition was published by the AG Feminismus und Kirchen in honor of Elisabeth Schüssler Fiorenza's sixty-fifth birthday. For this event, a collection of articles was also published in *FAMA*, where the feminist liberation theory of Elisabeth Schüssler Fiorenza was presented. Women wrote about how it had influenced their personal and professional lives and how feminist exegesis could be institutionalized.

Fortunately, *Schlangenbrut* already existed when the debate began on anti-Jewish feminist exegesis in Germany. Most of the articles discussing this issue were published in the 1987 volume of the journal, the year when the public debate started. The many quotations from these volumes in academic work confirm the important role that *Schlangenbrut* played. Since this debate, the journal has tried to include articles written by women of different cultural and religious backgrounds, especially Jewish women.[71] In 1984 in Switzerland, seven women theologians founded the association FAMA and its eponymous journal. It was preceded by the *Bulletin der theologischen Frauen-Web- und Werkstatt*, which was published quarterly in a small print run in 1983 and 1984.

The oldest interdisciplinary, interreligious feminist academic journal, the *Journal of Feminist Studies in Religion*, has been published twice annually since 1983. *JFSR* has two communities of accountability: the academy, in which it is situated; and the feminist movement, from which it draws its nourishment and vision.[72] Its editors are committed to rigorous thinking and analysis in the service of the transformation of religious studies as a discipline and the feminist transformation of religious and cultural institutions. *JFSR*'s national and international editorial boards are dedicated to diversity: diversity of religions, races, and cultures. It publishes contributions that focus not only on women's experience and on gender as a category of analysis but also that work within a feminist theoretical framework that analyzes the intersections of gender, race, class, and other structures of domination.[73] The founders and long-time coeditors, Judith Plaskow and Elisabeth Schüssler Fiorenza, as well as the current coeditor Melanie Johnson-DeBaufre, are well versed in interreligious dialogue and biblical scholarship. Thus, this journal also offers a wealth

---

71. Matthiae et al., *Feministische Theologie*, 27–31.
72. See "About Us" at http://www.fsrinc.org/jfsr/about-us.
73. Ibid.

of feminist exegetical research.[74] In 2007, *JFSR* established a prize for upcoming feminist scholars to foster feminist research.

Founded in 1990 by Ruth Atkin, Adrienne Rich, Elly Bulkin, Clare Kinberg, Rita Falbel, Ruth Kraut, and Laurie White, *Bridges: A Journal for Jewish Feminists and Our Friends* is another journal that originated in traditional Jewish values of justice and the resulting call to change in the world, as well as in the experiences of the gay and lesbian movement. The poems, prose, essays, graphic art, and reviews in *Bridges* take a stand against racism and discrimination based on class, gender, and sexual orientation in a variety of Jewish languages and in translation. Admittedly, the women authors are primarily from the Ashkenazi Jewish tradition, but increasingly the Sephardic tradition is also represented, for example by Rita Arditti and Loolwa Khazzoom, and by Jewish women from Latin American countries such as Marjorie Agos'n (Chile), Ruth Behar (Cuba), Renée Epelbaum (Argentina), and Aurora Levins Morales (Puerto Rico), and finally women converts to Judaism. When required by certain themes, contributions of non-Jewish women and men were published as well.[75] Unfortunately, due to financial reasons *Bridges* had to cease publication and no longer appears in print.

In March of 1992 the first issue of the journal *Con-spirando: Revista latinoamericana de Espiritualidad, ecofeminsmo y teología* was published by the Chilean group of the same name.[76] *Conspirando* offers a space for women from various contexts to document and exchange views on ethical, spiritual, and ecofeminist issues, processes, and struggles. The journal thus serves to connect various worlds: academic thought, feminism, church, spirituality, body, memory, internal and external.[77] In the context of these concerns, several other journals should be mentioned because they publish the work of women

---

74. Some examples: Yerra Sugarman, "Pharaoh's Daughter/King Solomon's Wife: Fragments from Her Diaries; Pharaoh's Daughter/King Solomon's Wife: A Letter Home; From King Solomon's Journal: Fragment of an Unsent Letter (Date Unknown)," *JFSR* 23. (2007): 43–53; Roundtable Discussion: Feminist Biblical Studies, *JFSR* 25.2 (2009): 93–143 (there were nine articles dedicated to this theme); Katherine B. Low, "The Sexual Abuse of Lot's Daughters: Reconceptualizing Kinship for the Sake of Our Daughters," *JFSR* 26.2 (2010): 37–54; Julia Watts Belser and Melanie S. Morrison, "What No Longer Serves Us: Resisting Ableism and Anti-Judaism in New Testament Healing Narratives," *JFSR* 27.2 (2011): 153–70.

75. Themes included, for example, the Holocaust, incest, Jewish women's rituals, and the relationship between Israel and Palestine. For contributions of non-Jewish women and men, see http://jwa.org/encyclopedia/article/bridges-journal-for-jewish-feminists-and-our-friends.

76. For more details on this group, see below in the section on organizations.

77. See http://www.conspirando.cl.

authors from all over Latin American countries: *Mandrágora*, published by an interdisciplinary group of scholars in the Gender and Religion program of the Methodist University of Sao Paolo, which has produced sixteen issues on various themes such as Christianity and feminism, ecofeminism, gender and images of God, homosexuality, and abortion;[78] *Aportes Biblicos* in Costa Rica; and *Alternativas* in Nicaragua.[79]

The journal *Feminist Theology* was also founded in 1992, the first of its kind published in Britain. Its goal is to give a voice to women in religion and theology in Britain and Ireland. It is academically oriented, but strives to be readable for men and women without training in theology. Its women editors aim to have the journal reflect feminism and its principles of experience, commonality/mutuality, creativity, respect, joy, education as learning accessible to all, and listening to the voices of women. Finally, from 1992 to 2008, the Iranian journal *Zanan* published research in gender hermeneutics and feminist interpretation of the Qur'ān. *Zanan* made space for a variety of diverse perspectives but was discontinued under the Ahmadinejad regime.[80]

In 1993 Luise Schottroff and Annette Esser edited the first volume of the annual Yearbook of the ESWTR,[81] entitled *Feministische Theologie im europäischen Kontext*. The yearbooks have since appeared regularly, published by Peeters in Belgium, with contributions in German, English, and French. The titles of the individual volumes reflect discussions within specific, mostly Christian disciplines such as pastoral theology, as well as a variety of other discussions taking place in Eastern, Western, and Southern Europe. Since the mid-1980s, feminist scholars in Asia have been active as well on the national and international level, working closely together to publish their research, primarily in English.[82] The journal *Feminist Theological Thought* was established in 1987 in Korea, focusing regularly on women in the Bible in subsequent years.[83] In 1995 the Ehwa Institute for Women's Theological Studies in Korea published the first volume of *Ehwa Journal of Feminist Theology*.[84]

In 1998, international cooperation between the Schechter Institute of Jewish Studies (Jerusalem, Israel) and the Hadassah-Brandeis Institute (Waltham, Massachusetts, U.S.A.) led to the first issue of *Nashim*, an international, interdisciplinary journal for Jewish women's and gender studies. This

---

78. See https://www.metodista.br/revistas/revistas-ims/index.php/MA.
79. See Tamez, 40, in this volume.
80. See Kassam, in this volume.
81. For details on its founding and goals, see below in the section on organizations.
82. I thank Monika Melanchthon for this information.
83. Melanchthon, 110.
84. See ibid.

journal is a semiannual academic forum for articles on literature, exegesis, anthropology, archeology, theology, and current discussions on sociology, art, and other topics.[85]

The e-journal *lectio difficilior: Europäische Zeitschrift für Feministische Exegese* was first published in 2000 in Bern, Switzerland. Originally edited by Silvia Schroer and Caroline Vander Stichele, it is currently edited by Silvia Schroer and Tal Ilan. Issues appear twice a year with two to five feminist biblical articles published in German, English, and French. The journal is free, nondenominational, and interfaith, and it provides a forum for exegetical research.

In 2013 a journal for Muslim women, *Azizah*, appeared in the United States, publishing Qur'ān interpretation by Muslim feminist scholars as well as others. Other publications focusing on women in Islam include *Karamah: Muslim Women Lawyers for Human Rights* as well as *The International Network for the Rights of Female Victims of Violence in Pakistan*. According to Zayn Kassam, "Both continue to publish on issues pertaining to gender in Muslim societies, and both argue that the Qur'ān is a scriptural text that offers women dignity and rights that Muslim societies have not always allowed, despite the fact that women are ontologically equal to men in the qur'ānic perspective."[86]

3. Dictionaries, Introductions, Commentaries, Edited Collections, and Series

As in the case of journals, the edited collections chosen as exemplary reveal the growing sophistication and scholarly importance of feminist biblical studies.

In 1980 the second volume of *Traditionen der Befreiung: Sozialgeschichtlichte Bibelauslegung, Frauen in der Bibel* appeared, edited by Wolfgang Stegemann and Willy Schottroff. With important contributions by Luise Schottroff, Elisabeth Schüssler Fiorenza, Renate Wind, Eva Loss, and others,[87] it was the first German-language publication to make available the results of feminist biblical interpretation.

The collection edited by John S. Pobee and Bärbel von Wartenberg-Potter, *New Eyes for Reading: Biblical and Theological Reflections by Women from the Third World*,[88] which came out of the work done by the World Council of

---

85. Managing Editor: Deborah Greniman; academic editor: Renée Levine Melammed; see http://www.schechter.edu/women/journal.htm.

86. See Kassam, 183, in this volume.

87. Willy Schottroff and Wolfgang Stegemann, eds., *Frauen in der Bibel* (vol. 2 of *Traditionen der Befreiung: Sozialgeschichtliche Bibelauslegungen*; Munich: Kaiser, 1980).

88. John S. Pobee and Bärbel Wartenberg-Potter, eds., *New Eyes for Reading. Biblical*

Churches, is credited with documenting for the first time the results of international feminist biblical interpretation within the context of ecclesial praxis.[89] This was followed in 1988 by the first edition of *With Passion and Compassion: Third World Women Doing Theology*, edited by Virginia Fabella and Mercy Amba Oduyoye.[90]

Feminist biblical interpretation entered the public eye as part of a larger movement in Germany in the same year, 1989, with the appearance of the two volumes of *Feministisch gelesen*,[91] a group project edited by Eva Renate Schmidt, Mieke Korenhof, and Renate Jost. In these volumes, intended for congregational work in preaching as well as biblical studies, there are interpretations of more than sixty biblical texts by many women and some men who work with these texts on a practical level. In 1991, the first edition of the *Wörterbuch der Feministischen Theologie* was published in German. Both editions of the *Wörterbuch* attempt to the present the *status quaestionis* of current feminist theology, largely in a German-language context. In addition to many definitions of terms, the dictionary also contains longer entries written by women exegetes that outline the state of the debate in feminist biblical studies (OT/NT). The second edition is significantly larger, in terms of number of pages, entries, and index entries. A new feature is the index not only of biblical texts but also of extracanonical Jewish and early Christian literature.[92]

The year 1992 saw the publication of *The Will to Arise: Women, Tradition and the Church in Africa*, edited by Musimbi R. A. Kanyoro and Mercy Amba Oduyoye, as well as *Clamor por la vida: Teologia latinoamericana desde la perspectiva de al mujer*, edited by Pilar Aquino.[93] Both collections contain exemplary feminist biblical interpretation from Africa and Latin America,

---

and Theological Reflections from Women of the Third World (Geneva: World Council of Churches, 1986).

89. For an important predecessor of feminist Biblical interpretation, see the two-volume work *The Women of Israel*, by Grace Aguilar (ed. Mayer I. Gruber; Piscataway, N.J.: Gorgias, 2011); first published in 1851 by Appleton. This Sephardic Jewish woman was born in England and is buried in Frankfurt am Main; on Auilar, see Baker, in this volume. See also, in this volume, Scholz, Plaskow, and the literature cited in Schüngel-Straumann.

90. See Mbuwayesango, in this volume.

91. Eva Renate Schmidt, Mieke Korenhof, and Renate Jost, eds., *Feministisch gelesen* (2 vols.; Stuttgart: Kreuz, 1989).

92. Elisabeth Gössmann et al., eds., *Wörterbuch der feministischen Theologie* (Gütersloh: Gütersloher, 1991). The second fully revised and substantially expanded edition was edited by Elisabeth Gössmann, Helga Kuhlmann, Elisabeth Moltmann-Wendel, Ina Praetorius, Luise Schottroff, Helen Schüngel-Straumann, Doris Strahm, and Agnes Wuckelt (Gütersloh: Gütersloher, 2002).

93. Musimbi R. A. Kanyoro and Mercy Amba Oduyoye, eds., *The Will to Arise:*

respectively. The first work with the sole aim of documenting systematically the results of feminist biblical interpretation is the *Women's Bible Commentary*, edited by Carol Newsom and Sharon Ringe, which also appeared in 1992.[94] The entries, written by women living and teaching in North America, include short commentaries on all of the books of the Protestant Bible, two articles with historical overviews, and two contributions dealing with groups of early Jewish and early Christian literature.

Since 1993, Athalya Brenner has been editing the series Feminist Companion to the Hebrew Bible.[95] There are nineteen volumes that are mostly devoted to the Hebrew Bible and one devoted exclusively to methodological questions.[96] These volumes include feminist essays by authors from a range of social, religious, and ethnic backgrounds, who write from a variety of hermeneutical and methodological perspectives:, social scientific, history of religions (some with a background in ancient Near Eastern studies), literary/intertextual or biblical/intertextual. They represent a broad spectrum of feminist biblical interpretation.

In 1994 and 1995 two volumes edited by Elisabeth Schüssler Fiorenza appeared, entitled *Searching the Scriptures*.[97] These volumes, published to celebrate the centennial anniversary of the appearance of two volumes of the *Woman's Bible* (1895/1898), offer methodological and hermeneutical foundations (vol. 1), as well as short commentaries on all of the books of the New Testament and other works of early Christian literature and of early Jewish literature that are not part of the Hebrew Bible (vol. 2). The first volume deals with themes such as liberation theology and includes essays by black, white, and indigenous Americans as well as women from all five continents. This fulfills the aim of the work, to document the great diversity of feminist engagement with the Bible and to encourage more of the same.

The collection *Feministische Exegese: Forschungserträge zur Bibel aus der Perspektive von Frauen* was also published in 1995.[98] The title *Feministische*

Women, Tradition and the Church in Africa (Maryknoll, N.Y.: Orbis, 1992); See further Mbuwayesango. On *Clamor por la vida*, see Tamez, in this volume.

94. See also Scholz, in this volume.

95. The first volume was Athalya Brenner, ed., *A Feminist Companion to Judges* (Sheffield: Sheffield Academic Press, 1993).

96. Athalya Brenner and Carole Fontaine, eds., *A Feminist Companion to Reading the Bible: Approaches, Methods and Strategies* (Sheffield: Sheffield Academic Press, 1997).

97. Elisabeth Schüssler Fiorenza, ed., *Searching the Scriptures* (2 vols.; New York: Crossroad, 1994–1995). See also Scholz, in this volume.

98. Luise Schottroff et al., eds., *Feministische Exegese: Forschungserträge zur Bibel aus der Perspektive von Frauen* (Darmstadt: Wissenschaftliche Buchgesellschaft, 1995; 2nd ed., 1997).

Exegese does not fully reveal the wide range of approaches adopted by contributors to the volume. Christian feminist engagement with the Bible is contextualized historically, classified hermeneutically, developed methodologically, and given concrete application. The focus is on developments and the current state of the debate among those writing in German, but feminist scholarship by European and American biblical scholars is also included. The authors stress the importance of taking greater account of the work of liberation theologians from other continents as well as Jewish scholarship on the Bible.

Von der Wurzel getragen: Christlich-feministische Exegese in Auseinandersetzung mit Antijudaismus, edited by Luise Schottroff and Marie-Theres Wacker, also appeared in 1995.[99] It documents the extent to which exegetes writing in German have engaged constructively with the criticism of Christian anti-Jewish scholarship.

The *Dictionary of Feminist Theologies*,[100] edited by Letty Russell and Shannon Clarkson and published in 1996, is, like the *Wörterbuch Feministische Theologie*, a reference work defining the central concepts of feminist theology. The editors made conscious efforts to include the widest possible range of feminist orientations. The entries do focus primarily on Christian theology, but take other religions into account as well. The editors deliberately invited as many authors as possible whose ethnic background was not white American.

In 1997 *Reading the Bible as Women: Perspectives from Africa, Asia, and Latin America* appeared.[101] The thirteen contributions are united not by a common theme but rather by the gender and social location of the authors, which had previously excluded them from the scholarly debate in North America and thus also from the possibility of pursuing scholarly biblical interpretation. The contributors are aware of the challenges of dominance and subordination in the context of the Two-Thirds world but seek nevertheless to overcome them. For the authors, there is a real tension between the methodological and conceptual tools of Western biblical exegesis and the contexts of their countries of origin. None of the contributions can be taken, therefore, as representative of the country or culture of origin of the author.

Whereas the primary focus of the two-volume work *Searching the Scriptures* is hermeneutical and methodological feminist discussions, on the one hand, and transcanonical commentaries, on the other, the *Kompendium*

---

99. Louise Schottroff and Marie-Teres Wacker, eds., *Von der Wurzel getragen: Christlich-feministische Exegese in Auseinandersetzung mit Antijudaismus* (Leiden: Brill, 1996).

100. Letty Russell and Shannon Clarkson, eds., *Dictionary of Feminist Theologies* (Louisville: Westminster John Knox, 1996).

101. Phyllis Bird, ed., *Reading the Bible as Women: Perspectives from Africa, Asia and Latin America* (*Semeia* 78; Atlanta: Scholars Press, 1997).

Feministische Bibelauslegung, the first edition of which appeared in 1998, strives to develop further the work done in the past.[102] It presents pluralist, contextual feminist exegesis that deals in new ways with the issue of canon, which is markedly different in the Protestant, Catholic, and Jewish traditions. Prominent concerns of feminist discussion are addressed, primarily those from the German context, and biographical influences are made clear. The collection also contains several useful indexes.[103]

In 2000 *The Women's Torah Commentary* appeared, a collection of interpretations by women rabbis designed for sermons on the Torah readings.[104] Since 2001, Amy-Jill Levine has edited a series of companion volumes to the Feminist Companion to the Hebrew Bible (Feminist Companion to the New Testament). Each of the volumes in this series deals with one book of the New Testament (Gospel, letter of Paul, etc.) and thoroughly investigates it by the criteria of feminist theology. Various authors investigate either passages from the book or address larger theological themes or concerns.

Also in 2001 the volume *Other Ways of Reading: African Women and the Bible* appeared, edited by Musa Dube. In it are published the results of African biblical interpretation.[105] In 2002, Musimbi R. A. Kanyoro edited *Introducing Feminist Cultural Hermeneutics: An African Perspective,*[106] a volume intended to be a group history of the communal theology of African women. Kanyoro analyzes the cultural treasures, experiences, and practices of women in Africa and interrogates especially the role of a cultural hermeneutics for understanding the Bible and the increased possibilities for liberation for women in Africa that will follow from that understanding. The book of Ruth is at the heart of the book, as well as the theme of the responsibilities of the church, women's organizations in the church, and African women theologians.

The Cambridge Companion to Feminist Theology, which appeared in 2002, also has a contribution on feminist hermeneutics of the Bible.[107] In 2003 a volume edited by Silvia Schroer and Sophia Bietenhardt appeared, entitled

---

102. Luise Schottroff et al., eds., *Kompendium Feministische Bibelauslegung* (3rd ed.; Gütersloh: Kaiser, 2007).

103. Ibid., "foreword," xiv–xv.

104. On this point see Baker, in this volume.

105. On this point see Mbuewayesango, in this volume.

106. Musimbi R. A. Kanyoro, *Introducing Feminist Cultural Hermeneutics: An African Perspective* (Cleveland: Pilgrim, 2002).

107. Susan Frank Parsons, ed., *Cambridge Companion to Feminist Theology* (Cambridge: Cambridge University Press, 2002). The chapter by Bridget Gilfillan Upton is entitled "Feminist Theology as Biblical Hermeneutics" (97–113).

Feminist Interpretation of the Bible and the Hermeneutics of Liberation.[108] This collection brings together papers given at an international symposium of female theologians from around the world, with diverse Christian and Jewish backgrounds. The theme of the symposium, held in Tessin, Switzerland in July 2000, was feminist exegesis and the hermeneutics of liberation. The participants explored to what extent a feminist theological exegesis could be liberating, and how the categories "gender," "feminism," and "liberation" could be critically grounded. The volume includes the plenary presentations, and the resulting discussions are highlighted at the center of the book and presented in narrative form. Finally, the international character of the symposium is reinforced with the inclusion of eight reflections written after the conference and reflecting the geographic diversity of the participants.

The 2003 publication of *New Testament Masculinities*, edited by Stephen D. Moore and Janice Capel Anderson, introduced a new voice into the discussion.[109] The essays in this book investigate the ideas and constructions of masculinity in the writings of the New Testament. The background of many of the contributions is in the discipline of masculinity studies and its efforts to uncover and change the implicit structures of male power. There are two introductory essays followed by thirteen contributions that shed light on the theme from many angles. The individual Gospels are examined, as is the title "son of man" and the theology of Paul.

At the heart of the many contributions to *On the Cutting Edge: The Study of Women in Biblical Worlds*, a Festschrift for Elisabeth Schüssler Fiorenza edited by Jane Schaberg, Alice Bach, and Esther Fuchs, is the encouraging and forceful energy of woman in the past.[110] Several texts take up directly thoughts of Schüssler Fiorenza (e.g., *ekklêsia* of wo/men). Others respond to her hermeneutical theories or build on some of her central themes, such as violence against women, remembrance, or the reconstruction of women's history. Many of the contributions in the Festschrift edited by Fernando Segovia, *Toward a New Heaven and a New Earth*, clearly base themselves on her foundational work, which transformed biblical scholarship.[111]

---

108. Silvia Schroer and Sophia Bietenhard, eds., *Feminist Interpretation of the Bible and the Hermeneutics of Liberation* (London: Sheffield Academic Press, 2003).

109. Stephen D. Moore and Janice Capel Anderson, eds., *New Testament Masculinities* (SemeiaSt 45; Atlanta: Society of Biblical Literature, 2003).

110. Jane Schaberg et al., eds., *On the Cutting Edge: The Study of Women in Biblical Worlds* (New York: Continuum, 2004).

111. Fernando Segovia, ed., *Toward a New Heaven and a New Earth: Essays in Honor of Elisabeth Schüssler Fiorenza* (Maryknoll, N.Y.: Orbis, 2003).

The 2005 volume edited by Kathleen O'Brien Wicker and others, *Feminist New Testament Studies: Global and Future Perspectives (Religion/Culture/Critique)*, brings together engaged and thought-provoking essays on contemporary feminist biblical theology.[112] The authors read the New Testament through the lens of their own social, cultural, religious background and against the backdrop of globalization. These contributions to biblical interpretation regard the relationships of gender/sex, race, class, and power, as structures that determine the context as well as the contents of the New Testament texts. A special concern in this respect is to bring together feminist sociological engagement with academic and ecclesial theology.

Another collection published in the same year, *Her Master's Tools? Feminist and Postcolonial Engagements of Historical-Critical Discourse*, edited by Caroline Vander Stichele and Todd Penner, has a similar goal, to enhance traditional historical-critical debates with a variety of feminist perspectives.[113] Thus there are feminist, gender-critical, and postcolonial points of view, with the focus on methodological reflections and applications to individual texts of the Old Testament (Joshua, Sarah and Hagar, Lamentations, Ruth, and Ezra-Nehemiah) and New Testament (Philippians, Paul).

The first edition of *Die Bibel in gerechter Sprache* appeared in 2006 and not only enriched the spectrum of German translations of the Bible but also documented the results of feminist exegesis and hermeneutics.[114] By virtue of its special concern for justice, it brings a variety of discourses together. Alongside the goal of every translation to be faithful to the text, there is a concern for gender justice and justice with respect to Jewish-Christian dialogue—in other words, a translation that deliberately avoids anti-Jewish interpretations. In so far as social realities become visible in the language of the translation, there is also a concern for social justice.[115]

In 2007 Todd Penner and Caroline Vander Stichele edited another collection, *Mapping Gender in Ancient Religious Discourses*, which focuses on role of the category gender in the religious debates in antiquity, early Christianity,

---

112. Kathleen O'Brien Wicker et al., eds., *Feminist New Testament Studies: Global and Future Perspectives (Religion/Culture/Critique)* (New York: Palgrave Macmillan, 2005).

113. Caroline Vander Stichele and Todd Penner, eds., *Her Master's Tools? Feminist and Postcolonial Engagements of Historical-Critical Discourse* (Global Perspectives on Biblical Scholarship 9; Atlanta: Society of Biblical Literature, 2005).

114. A fully revised pocket edition of the Bible in inclusive language appeared in 2011. See also Claudia Janssen, "Bibel in gerechter Sprache," in Matthiae et al., *Feministische Theologie*, 182–84; and Janssen and Köhler, in this volume.

115. See Janssen and Köhler, in this volume.

Judaism and the Greco-Roman world.[116] The contributors investigate the connections between sex/gender, rhetoric, power, and ideology, and their roles in the creation of "identity" in the ancient world. One particular focus is on the construction of sex and sexuality in religious discourses. The chapters deal both with broader themes and with particular texts. Also in 2007, Susanne Scholz published an introduction to the First Testament entitled *Introducing the Women's Hebrew Bible*, in which she presented the history, biblical characters, methods and main themes of the Old Testament.[117]

In 2008, *The Torah: A Women's Commentary* was published.[118] That same year, the first entries of the *Wissenschaftlichen Bibellexikons* (*WiBiLex*) were published. This is a project of the German Bible Society to make freely available on the Internet a Bible dictionary prepared by scholars. The dictionary is not yet complete; through 2013 approximately 1,000 of the planned 3,000+ entries are accessible, most of them dealing with the Old Testament. It is edited by Michaela Bauks and Klaus Koenen (Old Testament) and Stefan Alkier (New Testament); among the more than three hundred scholars specializing in a range of disciplines (e.g., theology, ancient history, ancient Near Eastern studies) are numerous feminist biblical scholars who present the results of their research in their articles and thus share their most important work with a larger public.[119]

The *Sozialgeschichtliche Wörterbuch zur Bibel* appeared in 2009 and is edited by Frank Crüsemann, Kristian Hungar, Claudia Janssen, Rainer Kessler, and Luise Schottroff. Its primary focus is on the living conditions of the time in which the biblical traditions arose and in the generations in which they were handed down and developed. The results of feminist biblical scholarship have been incorporated into most of the entries.

New Jewish Feminism: Probing the Past, Forging the Future, appeared in 2009 and was edited by Rabbi Elyse Goldstein. This book and *New Feminist Christianity: Many Voices, Many Views*, which appeared in 2010 and was edited by Mary E. Hunt and Diann L. Neu, were both published by the Jewish Lights Publishing House.[120] Both include valuable contributions to biblical

---

116. Todd Penner and Caroline Vander Stichele, eds., *Mapping Gender in Ancient Religious Discourses* (Leiden: Brill, 2007).

117. Susanne Scholz, *Introducing the Women's Hebrew Bible* (New York: T&T Clark, 2007).

118. Tamara Cohn Eskenazi and Andrea L. Weiss, eds., *The Torah: A Women's Commentary* (New York: Women of Reform Judaism/URJ Press, 2007).

119. See www.wibilex.de.

120. Mary E. Hunt and Diann L. Neu, eds. *New Feminist Christianity: Many Voices, Many Views* (Woodstock, Vt.: SkyLight Paths, 2010).

interpretation. In 2011, Sheila Briggs and Mary McClintock edited *The Oxford Handbook of Feminist Theology*.[121] It makes clear the relevance of globalization and the debates within gender studies and religious studies for feminist theology in the twenty-first century beyond the global North, and investigates new areas within the discipline.

Work is currently underway on an exegetical, cultural-historical encyclopedia of the Bible, The Bible and Women: An Encyclopaedia of Exegesis and Cultural History, edited by Irmtraud Fischer (Austria), Mercedes Navarro Puerto (Spain), Adriana Valerio (Italy), and Jorunn Økland (Norway). This multivolume series, of which this volume is a part, is being published in four languages (English, Spanish, Italian, and German) and presents interdisciplinary research using art history, archaeology, and music history.[122] The Bible is studied as a book of occidental culture. There is an awareness of obligations to the "larger ecumene" that includes Judaism and a desire to present the female contribution to history and thus to write history anew.

The Wisdom Commentary Series, which is in preparation, was initiated and is being edited by Barbara Reid. It will be published by Liturgical Press. In this commentary series, all of the biblical books will be interpreted from a feminist perspective. The title reflects both the importance of biblical figure Wisdom and the wisdom that women and men inspired by feminism can bring to the process of interpretation. Although questions about the role of gender will be at the center, questions of power and authority, ethnicity, race, and class will be examined as well in the interpretation. Questions such as these show how important it is to take account of the social location of the interpreter and that there can be no definitive feminist interpretation of a text. The primary audience for the series includes preachers, pastors, instructors, and students. In order that the series reach not only readers in the so-called First World, who will probably be the majority of those who buy the printed volumes, exegetes from many other parts of the world will be among the contributors, and the entire series will be made available online.

The organizations, journals, and books presented here provide impressive, albeit fragmentary, documentary evidence of the institutionalization of feminist biblical scholarship. However, it remains to be seen whether it sur-

---

121. Sheila Briggs and Mary McClintock Fulkerson, eds., *The Oxford Handbook of Feminist Theology: Oxford Handbooks in Religion and Theology* (Oxford: Oxford University Press, 2012).

122. The first English volume, edited by Irmtraud Fischer and Mercedes Navarro Puerto, with Andrea Taschl-Erber, *Torah*, appeared in 2011, published by the Society of Biblical Literature. The German edition, *Tora*, was published by Kohlhammer in 2010.

vives the founding generations, since feminist biblical scholarship has not been able to create and financially sustain its own independent institutions.

Bibliography

Prepared by Kelsi Morrison-Atkins

Abbey, Rose Teteki. "I Am the Woman." Pages 23–36 in *Other Ways of Reading: African Women and the Bible*. Edited by Musa W. Dube. Atlanta: Society of Biblical Literature, 2001.

Abou El Fadl, Khaled. *The Conference of the Books*. Lanham, Md.: University Press of America, 2001.

———. *And God Knows the Soldiers: The Authoritative and Authoritarian in Islamic Discourses*. Lanham, Md.: University Press of America, 2001.

———. *The Great Theft: Wrestling Islam from the Extremists*. San Francisco: Harper San Francisco, 2005.

Ackerman, Susan. "At Home with the Goddess." Pages 455–68 in *Symbiosis, Symbolism, and the Power of the Past: Canaan, Ancient Israel, and Their Neighbors from the Late Bronze Age through Roman Palaestina*. Edited by William G. Dever and Seymour Gitin. Winona Lake, Ind.: Eisenbrauns, 2003.

———. *Under Every Green Tree: Popular Religion in Sixth-Century Judah*. Atlanta: Scholars Press, 1992.

Ackermann, Denise M. "Tamar's Cry: Re-Reading an Ancient Text in the Midst of an HIV and AIDS Pandemic." Pages 27–59 in *Grant Me Justice! HIV/AIDS and Gender Readings of the Bible*. Edited by Musa Dube and Musimbi Kanyoro. Maryknoll, N.Y.: Orbis, 2004.

Adam, Margaret B. "This is *My* Story, This is *My* Song…: A Feminist Claim on Scripture, Ideology and Interpretation." Pages 218–32 in *Escaping Eden: New Feminist Perspectives on the Bible*. Edited by Harold C. Washington, Susan Lochrie Graham and Pamela Thimmes. New York: New York University Press, 1999.

Agosín, Marjorie, ed. *Women, Gender, and Human Rights: A Global Perspective*. New Brunswick, N.J.: Rutgers University Press, 2001.

Aguilar, Grace. *The Women of Israel*. Edited by Mayer I. Gruber. Piscataway, N.J.: Gorgias, 2011. First published in 1851 by Appleton.

Ahmed, Durre S., ed. *Gendering the Spirit: Women, Religion, and the Postcolonial Response*. New York: Palgrave, 2002.

Akoto, Dorothy B. E. A. "Women and Health in Ghana and the *Trokosi* Practice: An Issue of Women's and Children's Rights in 2 Kings 4:1–7." Pages 96–110 in *African*

Women, Religion, and Health. Edited by Isabel Apawo Phiri and Sarojini Nadar. Maryknoll, N.Y.: Orbis, 2006.

Aldebert, Heiner. "Bibliodrama und interreligiöser Dialog." Pages 38–45 in *Bibliodrama: Theorie–Praxis–Reflexion.* Edited by Elisabeth Naurath and Uta Pohl-Patalong. Stuttgart: Kohlhammer, 2002.

Alexander, Loveday. "God's Frozen Word: Canonicity and the Dilemmas of Biblical Interpretation Today." *ExpTim* 117 (2006): 237–42.

al-Hibri, Azizah. "Islamic Herstory: Or, How Did We Get into This Mess." Pages 208–13 in *Women and Islam.* Edited by Azizah al-Hibri. London: Pergamon, 1981.

Ali, Syed Ameer. *The Spirit of Islam.* Piscataway, N.J.: Gorgias, 2001.

Alpert, Rebecca. "Finding our Past: A Lesbian Interpretation of the Book of Ruth." Pages 91–96 in *Reading Ruth: Contemporary Women Reclaim a Sacred Story.* Edited by Judith A. Kates and Gail Twersky Reimer. New York: Ballantine, 1994.

Amorós, Celia. "Pensar filosóficamente desde el feminism." *Debats* 76 (2002): 66–80.

Anderson, Cheryl B. *Ancient Laws and Contemporary Controversies: The Need for Inclusive Biblical Interpretation.* New York: Oxford University Press, 2009.

Anderson, Janice Capel. "Matthew, Gender, and Reading." Pages 25–51 in *A Feminist Companion to Matthew.* Edited by Amy-Jill Levine with Marianne Blickenstaff. Sheffield: Sheffield Academic Press, 2001. First published in *Semeia* 28 (1983): 3–27.

Anic, Rebeka. *Women in Church in the Twenty-First Century in Croatia* [Croatian]. Vienna: LIT, 2004.

Anzaldúa, Gloria. *Borderlands: The New Mestiza-La Frontera.* San Francisco: Aunt Lute, 1987.

———. *The Gloria Anzaldúa Reader.* Edited by AnaLouise Keating. Durham: Duke University Press, 2009.

Aparecida Felix, Isabel. "Anseio por dançar diferente: Leitura popular da bíblia na ótica da hermenêutica feminista crítica de libertação." Ph.D. diss. Universidade Metodista de São Paulo, 2010.

Aquino, María Pilar. "'The Dynamics of Globalization and the University': Toward a Democratic-Emancipatory Transformation." Pages 385–406 in *Toward a New Heaven and a New Earth: Essays in Honor of Elisabeth Schüssler Fiorenza.* Edited by Fernando F. Segovia. Maryknoll, N.Y.: Orbis, 2003.

———. *Our Cry for Life: Feminist Theology from Latin America.* Maryknoll, N.Y.: Orbis, 1993. Original publication: *Clamor por la vida: Teologia latinoamericana desde la perspectiva de la mujer.* San José: Departamento Ecumenico de Investigaciones, 1992.

Arana, María José, and María Salas. *Mujeres sacerdotes ¿por qué no?* Madrid: Claretianas, 1994.

Arendt, Hannah. "What Is Freedom?" Pages 143–72 in *Between Past and Future: Eight Exercises in Political Thought.* New York: Penguin, 1993.

Assmann, Aleida, and Jan Assmann. *Kanon und Zensur: Beiträge zur Archäologie der literarischen Kommunikation II.* Munich: Wilhem Fink, 1987.

Avalos, Hector. *The End of Biblical Studies.* Amherst, N.Y.: Prometheus, 2007).

Bach, Alice. "Reading Allowed: Feminist Biblical Criticism Approaching the Millennium." *CR:BS* 1 (1993): 191–215.

———, ed. *Women in the Hebrew Bible: A Reader*. New York: Routledge, 1999.

Bail, Ulrike. "Wenn Gott und Mensch zur Sprache kommen.… Überlegungen zu einer Bibel in gerechter Sprache." Pages 61–76 in *Die Bibel–Übersetzt in gerechte Sprache? Grundlagen einer neuen Übersetzung*. Edited by Helga Kuhlmann. Gütersloh: Gütersloher, 2005.

Bail, Ulrike, Frank Crüsemann, Marlene Crüsemann, Erhard Domay, Jürgen Ebach, Claudia Janssen, Hanne Köhler, Helga Johanes Taschner, and Marie-Theres Wacker. *Bibel in gerechter Sprache*. 4th ed. Gütersloh: Gütersloher, 2011.

Bailey, Randall C. "'They're Nothing but Incestuous Bastards': The Polemical Use of Sex and Sexuality in Hebrew Canon Narratives." Pages 121–38 in *Social Location and Biblical Interpretation in the United States*. Vol. 1 of *Reading from This Place*. Edited by Fernando Segovia and Mary Ann Tolbert. Minneapolis: Fortress, 1995.

Bailey, Randall C., Tat-siong Benny Liew, and Fernando F. Segovia, eds. *They Were All Together in One Place? Toward Minority Biblical Criticism*. Atlanta: Society of Biblical Literature, 2009.

Baker, Cynthia. *Rebuilding the House of Israel: Architectures of Gender in Jewish Antiquity*. Stanford, Calif.: Stanford University Press, 2002.

Bal, Mieke. *Death and Dissymetry: The Politics of Coherence in the Book of Judges*. Chicago: University of Chicago Press, 1988.

———. *Femmes imaginaires: L'Ancien testament au risqué d'une narratologie critique*. Utrecht: Hes, 1986. Abridged English edition: *Lethal Love: Feminist Literary Readings of Biblical Love Stories*. Bloomington: Indiana University Press, 1987.

———. "Religious Canon and Literary Identity (Plenary lecture Nijmegen, Conference 'Literary Canon and Religious Identity')." *lectio difficilior* 2 (2000): Online: http://www.lectio.unibe.ch/00_2/2-2000-r.pdf.

———, ed. *Anti-covenant: Counter-reading Women's Lives in the Hebrew Bible*. Sheffield: Almond, 1989.

Baltodano, Mireya, Gabriela Miranda García, and Elisabeth Cook, eds. *Género y Religión*. San José, Costa Rica: Universidad Bíblica Latinoamericana, 2009.

Banana, Canaan S. "The Case for a New Bible." Pages 69–82 in *Voices from the Margin: Interpreting the Bible in the Third World*. Edited by R. S. Sugirtharajah. London: SPCK, 1995.

Barazangi, Nimat Hafez. *Woman's Identity and the Qur'an: A New Reading*. Gainesville: University Press of Florida, 2004.

Barlas, Asma. "Amina Wadud's Hermeneutics of the Qur'an: Women Rereading Sacred Texts." Pages 97–123 in *Modern Muslim Intellectuals and the Qur'an*. Edited by Suha Taji-Farouki. London: Oxford University Press in association with The Institute of Ismaili Studies, 2004.

———. *"Believing Women" in Islam: Unreading Patriarchal Interpretations of the Qur'an*. Austin: University of Texas Press, 2002.

———. "Does the Qur'an Support Gender Equality? Or, Do I Have the Autonomy to Answer This Question?" Keynote delivered at the University of Groningen. November 24, 2006.

Baron, Dennis. *Grammar and Gender*. New Haven: Yale University Press, 1986.

Barton, Carlin. *The Sorrows of the Ancient Romans: The Gladiator and the Monster*. Princeton: Princeton University Press, 1993.

Barton, Mukti. "The Skin of Miriam Became as White as Snow: The Bible, Western Feminism, and Colour Politics." *Feminist Theology* 27 (May 2001): 68–80.

Basarudin, Azza. "In Search of Faithful Citizens in Postcolonial Malaysia." Pages 93–127 in *Women and Islam*. Edited by Zayn R. Kassam. Santa Barbara, Calif.: Praeger, 2010.

Baskin, Judith. *Midrashic Women: Formations of the Feminine in Rabbinic Literature*. Hanover, N.H.: Brandeis University Press, 2002.

Beauvoir, Simone de. *Le deuxième sexe*. Paris: Gallimard, 1949.

———. *The Second Sex*. Translated by H. M. Parshley. New York: Vintage, 1989.

Beavis, Mary Ann. "Christian Origins, Egalitarianism, and Utopia." *JFSR* 23.2 (2007): 27–49.

Belser, Julia Watts, and Melanie S. Morrison. "What No Longer Serves Us: Resisting Ableism and Anti-Judaism in New Testament Healing Narratives." *JFSR* 27.2 (2011): 153–70.

Berger, Teresa. *Dissident Daughters: Feminist Liturgies in Global Context*. Louisville: Westminster John Knox, 2001.

Bernabé, Carmen, Pilar de Miguel, Trinidad León, and Lucía Ramón. *La Mujer en la Teología Actual*. San Sebastián: Publicaciones Idatz, 1996.

Berneking, Nancy J., and Pamela Carter Joern, eds. *Re-Membering and Re-Imagining*. Cleveland: Pilgrim, 1995.

Berquist, Jon L. "Postcolonialism and Imperial Motives for Canonization." *Semeia* 75 (1996): 15–35.

Betori, Giuseppe. "Tendenze attuali nell'uso e nell'interpretazione della Bibbia." Pages 247–91 in *La Bibbia nell'epoca moderna e contemporanea, La Bibbia nella storia*. Edited by R. Fabris. Bologna: Dehoniane, 1992.

Beya, Marie Bernadette Mbuy. "Doing Theology as African Women." *Voices from the Third World: EATWOT* 13 (1990): 153–74.

Bhabha, Homi K. *The Location of Culture*. London: Routledge, 1994.

Bible and Culture Collective. "Feminist and Womanist Criticism." Pages 225–71 in *The Postmodern Bible*. Edited by the Bible and Culture Collective. New Haven: Yale University Press, 1995.

Binz, Stephen J. *Women of the Gospels: Friends and Disciples of Jesus*. Grand Rapids: Brazos, 2011.

———. *Women of the Torah: Matriarchs and Heroes of Israel*. Grand Rapids: Brazos, 2011.

Bird, Phyllis A. "Images of Women in the Old Testament." Pages 42–88 in *Religion and Sexism: Images of Women in the Jewish and Christian Traditions*. Edited by Rosemary Radford Ruether. New York: Simon & Schuster, 1974.

———. "'Male and Female He Created Them': Gen 1:27b in the Context of the Priestly Account of Creation." *HTR* 74 (1981): 129–59.

———. *Missing Persons and Mistaken Identities: Women and Gender in Ancient Israel*. Minneapolis: Fortress, 1997.

————. "The Place of Women in the Israelite Cultus." Pages 3–20 in *Women in the Hebrew Bible*. Edited by Alice Bach. New York: Routledge, 1999.

————, ed. *Reading the Bible as Women: Perspectives from Africa, Asia and Latin America*. Atlanta: Scholars Press, 1997.

Birschel, Annette. "Bibel wurde neu ins Niederländische übersetzt." *Evangelische Kirche in Deutschland. Evangelische Kirche in Deutschland.* Online: www.ekd.de/aktuell_presse/news_2004_10_27_1_niederlaendische bibel.html.

Bloom, Harold. *The Western Canon: The Books and School of the Ages*. New York: Harcourt Brace, 1994.

Bornemann, Ernst. *Das Patriarchat: Ursprung und Zukunft unseres Gesellschaftssystems*. Frankfurt: Fischer, 1991.

Børresen, Kari E. *From Patristics to Matristics: Selected Articles on Christian Gender Models*. Rome: Herder, 2002.

————. *Subordination et Equivalence: Nature et rôle de la femme d'après Augustin et Thomas d'Aquin*. Oslo: Universitetsforlaget, 1968.

Borsinger, Hilde Vérène. "Rechtsstellung der Frau in der katholischen Kirche." Ph.D. diss. Leipzig, 1930.

Bosetti, Elena. *Donne della Bibbia: Bellezza intrighi fede passione*. Assisi: Cittadella Editrice, 2010.

Bourdieu, Pierre. *Masculine Domination*. Translated by Richard Nice. Stanford, Calif.: Stanford University Press, 2001.

Bousquet, Marc. *How the University Works: Higher Education and the Low-Wage Nation*. New York: New York University Press, 2008.

Boyarin, Daniel. *Carnal Israel: Reading Sex in Talmudic Culture*. Berkeley: University of California Press, 1993.

————. *Intertextuality and the Reading of Midrash*. Bloomington: Indiana University Press, 1990.

————. "The Politics of Biblical Narratology: Reading the Bible Like/As a Woman." *Diacritics* 20 (1990): 31–42.

————. *A Radical Jew: Paul and the Politics of Identity*. Berkeley: University of California Press, 1994.

Branch, Robin Gallaher. *Jeroboam's Wife: The Enduring Contributions of the Old Testament's Least-Known Women*. Peabody, Mass.: Hendrickson, 2009.

Brancher, Mercedes. "De los ojos de Agar a los ojos de Dios, Gen 16:1–16." *RIBLA* 25 (1997): 11–27.

————. "La violencia contra las mujeres hechiceras." *RIBLA* 50 (2005): 61–64.

Breitmeier, Isa, and Luzia Sutter Rehmann. *Gerechtigkeit lernen: Seminareinheiten zu den drei Grundkategorien von Gerechtigkeit*. Gütersloh: Gütersloher, 2008.

Brenner, Athalya. *I Am …: Biblical Women Tell Their Own Stories*. Philadelphia: Fortress, 2005.

————. *The Intercourse of Knowledge: On Gendering Desire and "Sexuality" in the Hebrew Bible*. Leiden: Brill, 1997.

————. "Who's Afraid of Feminist Criticism? Who's Afraid of Biblical Humor? The Case of the Obtuse Foreign Ruler in the Hebrew Bible." *JSOT* 63 (1994): 38–55.

————, ed. *A Feminist Companion to Judges*. Sheffield: Sheffield Academic Press, 1993.

Brenner, Athalya, and Carole Fontaine, eds. *A Feminist Companion to Reading the Bible: Approaches, Methods, and Strategies*. Sheffield: Sheffield Academic Press, 1997.

Brenner, Athalya, and Fokkelien van Dijk Hemmes. *On Gendering Texts: Female and Male Voices in the Hebrew Bible*. Leiden: Brill, 1996.

Brett, Mark G. *Decolonizing God in the Tides of Empire*. Sheffield: Sheffield Phoenix, 2008.

———. *Genesis: Procreation and the Politics of Identity*. New York: Routledge, 2000.

Briggs, Sheila. "Can an Enslaved God Liberate? Hermeneutical Reflections on Philippians 2:6–11." *Semeia* 47 (1989): 137–53.

Briggs, Sheila, and Mary McClintock Fulkerson, eds. *The Oxford Handbook of Feminist Theology: Oxford Handbooks in Religion and Theology*. Oxford: Oxford University Press, 2012.

Brock, Ann Graham. *Mary Magdalene, the First Apostle: The Struggle for Authority*. Cambridge: Harvard University Press, 2003.

Brodbeck, Doris. *Hunger nach Gerechtigkeit: Helene von Mülinen (1850–1924)—Eine Wegbereiterin der Frauenemanzipation*. Zürich: Chronos, 2000.

———. *Unerhörte Worte: Religiöse Gesellschaftskritik von Frauen im 20. Jh*. Bern: eFeF, 2003.

Brodbeck, Doris, Yvonne Domhardt, and Judith Stofer, eds. *Siehe, ich schaffe Neues: Aufbrüche von Frauen in Protestantismus, Katholizismus, Christkahtolizismus und Judentum*. Bern: eFeF, 1998.

Bronner, Leila Leah. *From Eve to Esther: Rabbinic Reconstructions of Biblical Women*. Louisville: Westminster John Knox, 1994.

Brooten, Bernadette. "Early Christian Women and Their Cultural Context." Pages 65–91 in *Feminist Perspectives on Biblical Scholarship*. Edited by Adela Yarbro Collins. Chico, Calif.: Scholars Press, 1985.

———. "Jewish Women's History in the Roman Period: A Task for Christian Theology." *HTR* 79 (1986): 22–30.

———. "Junia—Outstanding among the Apostles (Romans 16:7)." Pages 141–44 in *Women Priests: A Catholic Commentary on the Vatican Declaration*. Edited by L. J. Swidler and Arlene Swidler. New York: Paulist, 1977.

———. *Love between Women: Early Christian Responses to Female Homoeroticism*. Chicago: University of Chicago Press, 1996.

———. *Women Leaders in the Synagogue*. Atlanta: Scholars Press, 1982.

Brown, Michael Joseph. "The Womanization of Blackness." Pages 89–119 in *Blackening of the Bible: The Aims of African American Biblical Scholarship*. Harrisburg, Penn.: Trinity, 2004.

Buell, Denise Kimber. *Making Christians: Clement of Alexandria and the Rhetoric of Legitimacy*. Princeton: Princeton University Press, 1999.

———. *Why This New Race? Ethnic Reasoning in Early Christianity*. New York: Columbia University Press, 2005.

Bührig, Marga. *Spät habe ich gelernt, gerne Frau zu sein*. Stuttgart: Kreuz, 1987.

Burrus, Virginia. *"Begotten, Not Made": Conceiving Manhood in Late Antiquity*. Stanford, Calif.: Stanford University Press, 2000.

———. *Chastity as Autonomy: Women in Stories of Apocryphal Acts.* Lewiston: Mellen, 1987.

———. "Mapping as Metamorphosis: Initial Reflections on Gender and Ancient Religious Discourse." Pages 1–10 in *Mapping Gender in Ancient Religious Discourses.* Edited by Todd Penner and Caroline Vander Stichele. Leiden: Brill, 2007.

Bussmann, Hadumond, and Renate Hof, eds. *Genus: Geschlechterforschung/Gender Studies in den Kultur- und Sozialwissenschaften: Ein Handbuch.* Stuttgart: Kröner, 2005.

Butler, Judith. "Against Proper Objects." *differences: A Journal of Feminist Cultural Studies* 6:2–3 (1994): 1–26.

———. *Bodies That Matter: On the Discursive Limits of "Sex."* New York: Routledge, 1993.

———. *Gender Trouble: Feminism and the Subversion of Identity.* New York: Routledge, 1990.

———. *Undoing Gender.* New York: Routledge, 2004.

Butting, Klara. "Bibel: Hermeneutik." Pages 64–66 in *Wörterbuch der Feministischen Theologie.* Edited by Elisabeth Gössmann, Elisabeth Gössmann, Helga Kuhlmann, Elisabeth Moltmann-Wendel, Ina Praetorius, and Luise Schottroff. Gütersloh: Gütersloher, 2002.

———. *Prophetinnen gefragt: Die Bedeutung der Prophetinnen im Kanon aus Tora und Prophetie.* Biblisch-feministische Texte 3. Wittingen: Erev-Rav, 2001.

Byron, Gay L. "The Challenge of 'Blackness' for Rearticulating the Meaning of Global Feminist New Testament Interpretation." Pages 85–102 in *Feminist New Testament Studies: Global and Future Perspectives.* Edited by Kathleen O'Brien Wicker, Althea Spencer Miller, and Musa W. Dube. New York: Palgave Macmillan, 2005.

———. *Symbolic Blackness and Ethnic Difference in Early Christian Literature.* New York: Routledge, 2002.

Calduch-Benages, Nuria. *Il profumo del vangelo: Gesù incontra le donne.* La parola e la sua ricchezza 11. Milan: Paoline, 2009.

Camp, Claudia V. "Feminist Theological Hermeneutics: Canon and Christian Identity." Pages 154–71 in *A Feminist Introduction.* Vol. 1 of *Searching the Scriptures.* Edited by Elisabeth Schüssler Fiorenza with the assistance of Shelly Matthews. New York: Crossroad, 1993.

———. "Review of *Texts of Terror: Literary-Feminist Readings of Biblical Narratives*, by Phyllis Trible." *JAAR* 54 (1986): 159–61.

———. *Wisdom and the Feminine in the Book of Proverbs.* Decatur, Ga.: Almond, 1985.

———. *Wise, Strange, and Holy: The Strange Woman and the Making of the Bible.* Sheffield: Sheffield Academic Press, 2000.

Camp, Claudia V., and Carole R. Fontaine, eds. *Women, War, and Metaphor: Language and Society in the Study of the Hebrew Bible. Semeia* 61 (1993).

Campenhausen, Hans von. *The Formation of the Christian Bible.* Translated by J. A. Baker. Philadelphia: Fortress, 1972.

Cannon, Katie Geneva. "The Emergence of Black Feminist Consciousness." Pages 30–40 in *Feminist Interpretation of the Bible.* Edited by Letty M. Russell. Philadelphia: Westminster, 1985.

———. *Katie's Canon: Womanism and the Soul of the Black Community.* New York: Continuum, 1995.

Cardoso Pereira, Nancy. "La mujer y lo cotidiano: La mujer y el niño en el ciclo del profeta Eliseo." *RIBLA* 14 (1993): 7–21.

———. "Prostitutas-madres-mujeres: Obsesiones y profecía en 1R3:16–28." *RIBLA* 25 (1997): 8–40.

———. "Las raíces afro-asiáticas de la Biblia hebrea: ¿Disfraz académico o corriente esotérica?" *RIBLA* 54 (2006): 7–16.

Carson, Donald A. *The Inclusive-Language Debate: A Plea for Realism.* Grand Rapids: Baker, 1998.

Cassidy, Richard J. *Christians and Roman Rule in the New Testament: New Perspectives.* New York: Crossroad, 2001.

———. *Paul in Chains: Roman Imprisonment and the Letters of St. Paul.* New York: Crossroad, 2001.

Castelli, Elizabeth. "The Ekklēsia of Women and/as Utopian Space: Locating the Work of Elisabeth Schüssler Fiorenza in Feminist Utopian Thought." Pages 36–53 in *On the Cutting Edge: A Study of Women in Biblical Worlds.* Edited by Jane Schaberg, Alice Bach, and Esther Fuchs. New York: Continuum, 2003.

———. "Heteroglossia, Hermeneutics, and History." *JFSR* 10.2 (1994): 73–98.

———. *Imitating Paul: A Discourse of Power.* Louisville: Westminster John Knox, 1991.

———. "*Les Belles Infidèles*/Fidelity or Feminism? The Meanings of Feminist Biblical Translation." Pages 189–204 in *A Feminist Introduction.* Vol. 1 of *Searching the Scriptures.* Edited by Elisabeth Schüssler Fiorenza with the assistance of Shelly Matthews. New York: Crossroad, 1993.

———, ed. *Women, Gender, and Religion: A Reader.* New York: Palgrave, 2001.

Castelli, Elizabeth A., and Hal Taussig. "Drawing Large and Startling Pictures: Reimagining Christian Origins by Painting like Picasso." Pages 3–20 in *Reimagining Christian Origins: A Colloquium Honoring Burton L. Mack.* Edited by Elizabeth A. Castelli and Hal Taussig. Valley Forge, Penn.: Trinity, 1996.

Cavarero, Adriana. *Le Filosofie Femministe: Due Secoli di Battaglie Teoriche e Pratiche.* Edited by Adriana Cavarero and Franco Restaino. Milan: Bruno Mondadori, 2009.

Chamorro, Graciela. "Maria en las culturas y religiones amerindias." *RIBLA* 46 (2003): 74–81.

Cheney, Emily. *She Can Read: Feminist Reading Strategies for Biblical Narrative.* Valley Forge, Penn.: Trinity, 1996.

Cheng, Yang-en. "Taiwan." Pages 815–17 in *A Dictionary of Asian Christianity.* Edited by Scott W. Sunquist. Grand Rapids: Eerdmans, 2001.

Chicago, Judy. *The Dinner Party: A Symbol of Our Heritage.* Garden City: Doubleday, 1979.

Choi, Hee An, and Katheryn Pfisterer Darr, eds. *Engaging the Bible: Critical Readings from Contemporary Women.* Minneapolis: Fortress, 2006.

Chopp, Rebecca S. *The Power to Speak: Feminism, Language, and God.* New York: Crossroad, 1989.

Chow, Rey. *Writing Diaspora: Tactics of Intervention in Contemporary Cultural Studies*. Bloomington: Indiana University Press, 1993.

chung, Hyun Kyung. *Struggle to Be the Sun Again: Introducing Asian Women's Theology*. Maryknoll, N.Y.: Orbis, 1990.

Clark, Elizabeth. "The Lady Vanishes: Dilemmas of a Feminist Historian after the Linguistic Turn." *CH* 67 (1998): 1–31.

Clines, David J. A. "David the Man: The Construction of Masculinity in the Hebrew Bible." Pages 212–43 in *Interested Parties: The Ideology of Writers and Readers of the Hebrew Bible*. Sheffield: Sheffield Academic Press, 1995.

———. "*Ecce Vir*, or, Gendering the Son of Man." Pages 352–75 in *Biblical Studies/Cultural Studies*. Edited by J. Cheryl Exum and Stephen D. Moore. Sheffield: Sheffield Academic Press, 1998.

———. "He-Prophets: Masculinity as a Problem for the Hebrew Prophets and Their Interpreters." Pages 311–27 in *Sense and Sensitivity: Essays on Reading the Bible in Memory of Robert Carroll*. Edited by Alistair G. Hunter and Philip R. Davies. London: Sheffield Academic Press, 2002.

Clines, David J. A., and J. Cheryl Exum, eds. *The New Literary Criticism and the Hebrew Bible*. JSOTSup 143. Sheffield: JSOT Press, 1993.

Code, Lorraine. "Patriarchy." Pages 378–79 in *Encyclopedia of Feminist Theories*. Edited by Lorraine Code. London: Routledge, 2000.

Cohick, Lynn H. *Women in the World of the Earliest Christians: Illuminating Ancient Ways of Life*. Grand Rapids: Baker Academic, 2009.

Cohn, Ruth. *Von der Psychoanalyse zur Themenzentrierten Interaktion: Von der Behandlung Einzelner zu einer Pädagogik für alle*. Stuttgart: Klett-Cotta, 2009.

Cohn, Ruth, and Alfred Farau. *Gelebte Geschichte der Psychotherapie.: Zwei Perspektiven*. Stuttgart: Klett Cotta, 1984.

Collins, Gail. *When Everything Changed: The Amazing Journey of American Women from 1960 to the Present*. New York: Little, Brown, 2009.

Combahee River Collective. "A Black Feminist Statement." Pages 63–70 in *The Second Wave: A Reader in Feminist Theory*. Edited by Linda Nicholson. New York: Routledge, 1997.

Connell, Raewyn W. *Gender and Power*. Stanford, Calif.: Stanford University Press, 1987.

———. *Masculinities*. Berkeley: University of California Press, 1995.

———. *The Men and the Boys*. Cambridge: Polity Press, 2000.

Conti, Cristina. "Infiel es esta palabra." *RIBLA* 37 (2000): 41–56.

Conway, Colleen. *Behold the Man: Jesus and Greco-Roman Masculinity*. Oxford: Oxford University Press, 2008.

Cook, Elisabeth. "Las mujeres extranjeras, victimas del conflicto e identidades." Pages 105–33 in *Ecce Mulier: Homenaje a Irene Foulkes*. Edited by Universidad Bíblica Latinoamericana. San José: Sebila, 2005.

Cooper, Kate. *The Virgin and the Bride: Idealized Womanhood in Late Antiquity*. Cambridge: Harvard University Press, 1996.

Cordoso, Nancy. "La mujer y lo cotidiano: La mujer y el niño en el ciclo del profeta Eliseo." *RIBLA* 14 (1993): 7–21.

Corley, Kathleen. *Private Women, Public Meals: Social Conflict in the Synoptic Tradition*. Peabody, Mass.: Hendrickson, 1993.

Craig, Kerry M., and Margaret A. Kristjansson. "Women Reading as Men/Women Reading as Women: A Structural Analysis for the Historical Project." *Semeia* 51 (1990): 119–36.

Crüsemann, Frank. "'… er aber soll dein Herr sein' (Genesis 3,16): Die Frau in der patriarchalischen Welt des Alten Testaments." Pages 13–106 in *Als Mann und Frau geschaffen: Exegetische Studien zur Rolle der Frau*. Edited by Frank Crüsemann and H. Thyen. Gelnhausen: Burckhardthaus, 1978.

Crüsemann, Frank, Marlene Crüsemann, Erhard Domay, Jürgen Ebach, Claudia Janssen, Hanne Köhler, Helga Kuhlmann, Martin Leutzsch, and Luise Schottroff, eds. *Bibel in gerechter Sprache*. Gütersloh: Gütersloher, 2006.

Crüsemann, Frank, Kristian Hungar, Claudia Janssen, Rainer Kessler, and Luise Schottroff. *Sozialgeschichtliches Wörterbuch zur Bibel*. Gütersloh: Gütersloher, 2009.

Crüsemann, Frank, and Luise Schottroff. "Glossarartikel 'Gerechtigkeit.'" Pages 2347–49 in *Bibel in gerechter Sprache*. Edited by Ulrike Bail, Frank Crüsemann, Marlene Crüsemann, Erhard Domay, Jürgen Ebach, Claudia Janssen, Helga Kuhlmann, Martin Leutzsch, and Luise Schottroff. Gütersloh: Gütersloher, 2006.

Crüsemann, Marlene. "Trost, Charis und Kraft der Schwachen: Eine Christologie der Beziehung nach dem zweiten Brief an die Gemeinde in Korinth." Pages 111–37 in *Christus und seine Geschwister: Christologie im Umfeld der Bibel in gerechter Sprache*. Edited by Marlene Crüsemann and Carsten Jochum-Bortfeld. Gütersloh: Gütersloher, 2009.

Dalferth, Ingolf, and Jens Schröter, eds. *Bibel in gerechter Sprache? Kritik eines misslungenen Versuchs*. Tübingen: Mohr Siebeck, 2007.

Daly, Mary. *Beyond God the Father*. Boston: Beacon, 1973. German edition: *Jenseits von Gottvater, Sohn und Co.* Munich: Frauenoffensive, 1980.

———. *The Church and the Second Sex, with a New Feminist Postchristian Introduction*. New York: Harper & Row, 1975. First published in 1968. German edition: *Kirche, Frau und Sexus*. Olten: Walter, 1970.

D'Angelo, Mary Rose. "Euodia." Page 79 in *Women in Scripture: A Dictionary of Named and Unnamed Women in the Hebrew Bible, the Apocryphal/Deuterocanonical Books, and the New Testament*. Edited by Carol Meyers, Toni Craven, and Ross S. Kraemer. Grand Rapids: Eerdmans, 2000.

———. "Reconstructing 'Real' Women from Gospel Literature: The Case of Mary Magdalene." Pages 105–28 in *Women and Christian Origins*. Edited by Ross Kraemer and Mary Rose D'Angelo. New York: Oxford University Press, 1999.

———. "Syntyche." Page 159 in *Women in Scripture: A Dictionary of Named and Unnamed Women in the Hebrew Bible, the Apocryphal/Deuterocanonical Books, and the New Testament*. Edited by Carol Meyers, Toni Craven, and Ross S. Kraemer. Grand Rapids: Eerdmans, 2000.

D'Angelo, Mary Rose, and Elizabeth Castelli. "Elisabeth Schüssler Fiorenza on Women in the Gospels and Feminist Christology." *RelSRev* 22 (1996): 293–300.

Daud, Wan Mohd Nor Wan. *The Concept of Knowledge in Islam and Its Implications for Education in a Developing Country*. London: Mansell, 1989.

Davies, Eryl W. *The Dissenting Reader: Feminist Approaches to the Hebrew Bible*. Aldershot, U.K.: Ashgate, 2003.

Davies, Steven L. *The Revolt of the Widows: The Social World of the Apocryphal Acts*. Carbondale: Southern Illinois University Press, 1980.

Day, Linda, and Carolyn Pressler, eds. *Engaging the Bible in a Gendered World: An Introduction to Feminist Biblical Interpretation in Honor of Katharine Doob Sakenfeld*. Louisville: Westminster John Knox, 2006.

Day, Peggy L., ed. *Gender and Difference in Ancient Israel*. Minneapolis: Fortress, 1989.

de Lima Silva, Silvia Regina. *En territorio de Frontera. Una lectura de Marcos 7:24–30*. San José: DEI, 2001.

———. "Fe y Axe: Sanación como experiencia de encuentro con la fuerza que nos habita." Pages 231–45 in *Ecce mulier: Homenaje a Irene Foulkes.*San José: Sebila, 2005.

———. "Hay zapatos viejos que hacen callos en los pies Ensayo re relectura bíblica a partir de la realidad afroamericana y caribeña." *RIBLA* 19 (1994): 37–45.

De Troyer, Kristin. "The Choice is Yours! On Names of God. " *JESWTR* 14 (2006): 53–66.

———. "The Names of God, Their Pronunciation and Their Translation: A Digital Tour of Some of the Main Witnesses." *lectio difficilior* 2/2005. Online: http://www. lectio.unibe.ch/05_2/troyer_names_of_god.htm.

Deissmann, Adolf. *Licht vom Osten: Das neue Testament und die neuentdeckten Texte der hellenistisch-römischen Welt*. Tübingen: Mohr Siebeck, 1909.

Devananda, Malini. "Women's Spirituality." *In God's Image: Journal of Asian Women's Resource Centre for Culture and Theology* 24.2 (June 2005): 2–4.

Devasahayam, V. *Biblical Perspectives on Women: Ten Bible Studies*. Chennai: AICCW, 1986.

Dewey, Joanna. *Disciples of the Way: Mark on Discipleship*. Women's Division Board of Global Ministries: United Methodist Church, 1976.

Días Marianno, Lilia. "¡Qué alegría! La palabra de Yahveh también vino a la mujer: Un análisis ecofeminista de Génesis 16." *RIBLA* 50 (2005): 49–52.

Dieterich, Dorothee. "Hurra—Wir leben noch! Feministische Theologie Heute," *FAMA* 16 (2000): 1–19.

Diamond, Irene, and Lee Quinby, eds. *Feminism and Foucault: Reflections on Resistance*. Boston: Northeastern University Press, 1988.

Dillmann, August. *Genesis*. 6th ed. Leipzig: Hirzel, 1892.

Doely, Sarah Bentley. "Introduction." In *Women's Liberation and the Church: The New Demand for Freedom in the Life of the Christian Church*. Edited by Sarah Bentley Doely. New York: Association, 1970.

Doetsch-Kidder, Sharon. *Social Change and Intersectional Activism*. New York: Palgrave, 2012.

Döller, Johannes. *Das Weib im Alten Testament*. Münster: Aschendorff, 1920.

Domay, Erhard, Burkhard Jungcurt, and Hanne Köhler, eds. *Singen von deiner Gerechtigkeit: Das Gesangbuch in gerechter Sprache*. Gütersloh: Gütersloher, 2005.

Domay, Erhard, and Hanne Köhler, eds. *Der Gottesdienst: Liturgische Texte in gerechter Sprache, Band 4: Die Lesungen*. Gütersloh: Gütersloher, 2001.

————, eds. *Gottesdienstbuch in gerechter Sprache: Gebete, Lesungen, Fürbitten und Segenssprüche für die Sonn- und Feiertage des Kirchenjahres*. Gütersloh: Gütersloher, 2003.

————, eds. *Werkbuch gerechte Sprache in Gemeinde und Gottesdienst: Praxisentwürfe für Gemeindearbeit und Gottesdienst*. Gütersloh: Gütersloher, 2003.

Douglas, Kelly Brown. "Marginalized People, Liberating Perspectives: A Womanist Approach to Biblical Interpretation." *ATR* 83.1 (2001): 41–47.

Dube, Musa W. "Consuming a Colonial Time Bomb: Translating *Badimo* into 'Demons' in Setswana Bible (Matt. 8:8–34, 15:2, 10:8)." *JSNT* 73 (1999): 33–59.

————. "Divining Ruth for International Relations." Pages 179–95 in *Other Ways of Reading: African Women and the Bible*. Edited by Musa W. Dube. Atlanta: Society of Biblical Literature, 2001.

————. "Fifty Years of Bleeding: A Storytelling Feminist Reading of Mark 5:24–43." Pages 50–60 in *Other Ways of Reading: African Women and the Bible*. Edited by Musa W. Dube. Atlanta: Society of Biblical Literature, 2001.

————. "Grant Me Justice: Towards Gender-Sensitive Multi-Sectoral HIV/AIDS Readings of the Bible." Pages 3–24 in *Grant Me Justice! HIV/AIDS and Gender Readings of the Bible*. Edited by Musa Dube and Musimbi Kanyoro. Maryknoll, N.Y.: Orbis, 2004.

————. "Introduction." Pages 1–19 in *Other Ways of Reading: African Women and the Bible*. Edited by Musa W. Dube. Atlanta: Society of Biblical Literature, 2001.

————, ed. *Other Ways of Reading: African Women and the Bible*. Atlanta: Society of Biblical Literature, 2001.

————. *Postcolonial Feminist Interpretation of the Bible*. St. Louis: Chalice, 2000.

————. "Rahab Is Hanging Out a Red Ribbon: One African Woman's Perspective on the Future of Feminist New Testament Scholarship." Pages 177–202 in *Feminist New Testament Studies: Global and Future Perspectives*. Edited by Kathleen O'Brien Wicker, Althea Spencer Miller, and Musa W. Dube. New York: Palgrave MacMillan, 2005.

————. "Reading for Decolonization (John 4:1–42)." Pages 297–318 in *Voices from the Margin: Interpreting the Bible in the Third World*. 3rd ed. Edited by R. S. Sugirtharajah. Maryknoll, N.Y.: Orbis, 2006.

————. "Readings of *Semoya*: Botswana Women Interpretation of Matt. 15:21–28." *Semeia* 73 (1997): 111–29.

————. "Scripture, Feminism, and Post-colonial Contexts." Pages 45–54 in *Women's Sacred Scriptures*. Edited by Kwok Pui-lan and Elisabeth Schüssler Fiorenza. London: SCM, 1998.

Dube, Musa W., Andrew M. Mbuvi, and Dora R. Mbuwayesango, eds. *Postcolonial Perspectives in African Biblical Hermeneutics*. Atlanta: Society of Biblical Literature, 2012.

Dungan, David L. *Constantine's Bible: Politics and the Making of the New Testament*. Minneapolis: Fortress, 2007.

Ebach, Jürgen. "Zur Wiedergabe des Gottesnamens in einer Bibelübersetzung, oder: Welche 'Lösungen' es für ein unlösbares Problem geben könnte." Pages 150–58 in *Die Bibel–übersetzt in gerechte Sprache? Grundlagen einer neuen Übersetzung.* Edited by Helga Kuhlmann. Gütersloh: Gütersloher, 2005.

Eilberg-Schwartz, Howard. *God's Phallus and Other Problems for Men and Monotheism.* Boston: Beacon, 1994.

———. *The Savage in Judaism: An Anthropology of Israelite Religion and Ancient Judaism.* Bloomington: Indiana University Press, 1990.

Eisen, Ute. *Amtsträgerinnen im frühen Christentum: Epigraphische und literarische Studien.* Göttingen: Vandenhoeck & Ruprecht, 1996.

———. "'Quasi dasselbe?' Vom schwierigen und unendlichen Geschäft des Bibelübersetzens–Neuere deutsche Bibelübersetzungen. " *ZNT* 26 (2010): 3–15.

Eisenbaum, Pamela. *Paul Was Not a Christian: The Original Message of a Misunderstood Apostle.* New York: Harper, 2009.

Ekström, Malin. *Allvarsam parodi och möjlighetens melankoli: En queerteoretisk analys av Ruts bok.* Uppsala: Uppsala University Press, 2011.

Elkin, Judith Laikin. "Imagining Idolatry: Missionaries, Indians, and Jews." Page 75–99 in *Religion and the Authority of the Past.* Edited by Tobin Siebers. Ann Arbor: University of Michigan, 1993.

Ellendorf, Michael. "Bibliolog im KU." *Lernort Gemeinde* 2 (2002): 49.

Elshtain, Jean Bethke. *Public Man, Private Woman: Women in Social and Political Thought.* Princeton: Princeton University Press, 1981.

Elvey, Anne F. *An Ecological Feminist Reading of the Gospel of Luke: A Gestational Paradigm.* Lewiston: Mellen, 2005.

Eng, David L., Judith Halberstam, and José Esteban Muñoz. "Introduction: What's Queer about Queer Studies Now?" *Social Text* 23/3–4 (2005): 1–17.

Eriksson, Anne-Louise. "Radical Hermeneutics and Scriptural Authority." *Yearbook of the European Society of Women in Theological Research* 12 (2004): 47–52.

Eskenazi, Tamara Cohn, and Andrea L. Weiss, eds. *The Torah: A Women's Commentary.* New York: Women of Reformed Judaism/URJ, 2008.

Eugene, Toinette M. "A Hermeneutical Challenge For Womanists: The Interrelation Between the Text and Our Experience." Pages 20–28 in *Perspectives on Feminist Hermeneutics.* Edited by Gayle G. Koontz and Willard Swartley. Elkhart, Ind.: Institute for Mennonite Studies, 1987.

Evangelische Frauenarbeit in Deutschland, ed. *Gerechte Sprache in Gottesdienst und Kirche: Mit Bibeltexten zum Frankfurter Kirchentag in frauengerechter Sprache.* Frankfurt: Evangelische Frauenarbeit in Deutschland, 1987.

Exum, J. Cheryl, ed. *Beyond the Biblical Horizon: The Bible and the Arts.* Leiden: Brill, 1999.

———. "Feminist Criticism: Whose Interests Are Served?" Pages 65–90 in *Judges and Method: New Approaches in Biblical Studies.* 2nd ed. Edited by Gale Yee. Minneapolis: Fortress, 2007.

———. *Fragmented Women: Feminist (Sub)versions of Biblical Narratives.* JSOTSup 163. Sheffield: Sheffield Academic Press, 1993.

———. *Plotted, Shot, and Painted: Cultural Representations of Biblical Women.* Sheffield: Sheffield Academic Press, 1996.

Falk, Marcia. "Notes on Composing New Blessings." Pages 128–38 in *Weaving the Visions: Patterns in Feminist Spirituality*. Edited by Judith Plaskow and Carol P. Christ. San Francisco: Harper & Row, 1989.

———. "Toward a Feminist Jewish Reconstruction of Monotheism," *Tikkun* 4 (July–August 1989): 53–56.

Faria, Stella, Corinne Scott, and Jessie B. Tellis Nayak, eds. *Biblical Women: Our Foremothers—Women's Perspectives by Anna Vareed Alexander*. Indore: Satprakashan Sanchar Kendra, 1997.

Farley, Margaret A. "Feminist Consciousness and the Interpretation of Scripture." Pages 41–49 in *Feminist Interpretation of the Bible*. Edited by Letty M. Russell. Philadelphia: Westminster, 1985.

Fatum, Lone. "1 Thessalonians." Pages 250–62 in *A Feminist Commentary*. Vol. 2 of *Searching the Scriptures*. Edited by Elisabeth Schüssler Fiorenza. New York: Crossroad, 1994.

———. "Image of God and Glory of Man: Women in the Pauline Congregations." Pages 56–137 in *Image of God and Gender Models in Judaeo-Christian Traditions*. Edited by Kari Elisabeth Børresen. Oslo: Solum, 1991.

———. *Kvindeteologi og arven fra Eva*. Gyldendal Intro. Copenhagen: Nordisk, 1992.

Ferguson, Roderick A. *Aberrations in Black: Toward a Queer of Color Critique*. Minneapolis: University of Minnesota Press, 2004.

Fetterley, Judith. *The Resisting Reader: A Feminist Approach to American Fiction*. Bloomington: Indiana University Press, 1978.

Fewell, Danna Nolan, and David M. Gunn. *Gender, Power, and Promise: The Subject of the Bible's First Story*. Nashville: Abingdon, 1993.

Fiedler, Maureen, and Dolly Pomerleau. "The Women's Ordination Movement in the Roman Catholic Church." Pages 952–53 in vol. 2 of *Encyclopedia of Women and Religion in North America*. Edited by Rosemary Radford Ruether, Rosemary Skinner Keller, and Marie Cantlon. 3 vols. Bloomington, Ind.: Indiana University Press, 2006.

Fiedler, Peter. *Das Matthäusevangelium*. THKNT 1. Stuttgart: Kohlhammer, 2006.

Fischer, Irmtraud. *Erzeltern Israels: Feministisch-theologische Studien zu Genesis 12–36*; BZAW 222. Berlin: de Gruyter, 1994.

———. *Gotteskünderinnen: Zu einer geschlechter-fairen Deutung der Prophetie in der Hebräischen Bibel*. Stuttgart: Kohlhammer, 2003.

———. *Gotteslehrerinnen: Weise Frauen und Frau Weisheit im Alten Testament*. Stuttgart: Kohlhammer, 2006.

———. *Gottesstreiterinnen: Biblische Erzählungen über die Anfänge Israels*. Stuttgart: Kohlhammer, 1995.

———. *Rut*. HThK. Freiburg: Herder, 2000.

Fischer, Irmtraud, and Mercedes Navarro Puerto, eds., with Andrea Taschl-Erber. *Torah*. Atlanta: Society of Biblical Literature.

Fonrobert, Elisheva Charlotte. "The Handmaid, the Trickster, and the Birth of the Messiah." Pages 245–75 in *Current Trends in the Study of Midrash*. Edited by Carol Bakhos. Leiden: Brill, 2006.

———. *Menstrual Purity: Rabbinic and Christian Reconstructions of Biblical Gender.* Stanford, Calif.: Stanford University Press, 2000.

Fontaine, Carole R. *With Eyes of Flesh: The Bible, Gender, and Human Rights.* Sheffield: Sheffield Phoenix, 2008.

Forcades i Vila, Teresa. *La Teología Feminista en la Historia.* Barcelona: Fragmenta, 2011.

Foskett, Mary F., and Jeffrey Kah-Jin Kuan, eds. *Ways of Being, Ways of Reading: Asian American Biblical Interpretation.* St. Louis: Chalice, 2006.

Foucault, Michel. *Discipline and Punish: The Birth of the Prison.* Translated by Alan Sheridan. New York: Vintage, 1979.

———. *An Introduction.* Vol. 1 of *The History of Sexuality.* Translated by Robert Hurley. New York: Vintage, 1978.

Foulkes, Irene. "Los códigos y deberes domésticos en Colosenses 3:18–31 y Efesios 5:22–6:9: Estrategias persuasivas, reacciones provocadas." *RIBLA* 55 (2006): 41–62.

———. "Conflictos en Corinto: Las mujeres en una iglesia primitiva." *RIBLA* 15 (1993): 107–22.

———. "Invisibles y desaparecidas: Rescatar la historia de las anónimas." *RIBLA* 25 (1997): 41–51.

———. "Praxis exegética feminista: Conceptos, instrumentos, procedimientos." *Alternativas* 36 (2008): 33–58.

———. *Problemas pastorales en Corinto.* San José: DEI, 1996.

Frankel, Ellen. *The Five Books of Miriam: A Woman's Commentary on the Torah.* San Francisco: Harper, 1996.

Friedman, Susan Stanford. "Locational Feminism: Gender, Cultural Geographies, and Geopolitical Literacy." Pages 13–36 in *Feminist Locations: Global and Local, Theory and Practice.* Edited by Marianne Dekoven. New Brunswick, N.J.: Rutgers University Press, 2001.

Frymer-Kensky, Tikva. *In the Wake of the Goddesses: Women, Culture, and Biblical Transformation of Pagan Myth.* New York: Free Press, 1992.

———. *Reading the Women of the Bible.* New York: Schocken, 2002.

Fuchs, Esther. "Biblical Feminisms: Knowledge, Theory, and Politics in the Study of Women in the Hebrew Bible." *BibInt* 16 (2008): 205–26.

———. "Jewish Feminist Approaches to the Bible." Pages 25–40 in *Women and Judaism: New Insights and Scholarship.* Edited by Frederick E. Greenspahn. New York: New York University Press, 2009.

———. "The Literary Characterization of Mothers and Sexual Politics in the Hebrew Bible." Pages 127–39 in *Women in the Hebrew Bible: A Reader.* Edited by Alice Bach. New York: Routledge, 1999.

———. "Points of Resonance." Pages 1–21 in *On the Cutting Edge: The Study of Women in Biblical Worlds.* Edited by Jane Schaberg, Alice Bach, and Esther Fuchs. New York: Continuum, 2004.

———. *Sexual Politics in the Biblical Narrative: Reading the Hebrew Bible as a Woman.* JSOTSup 310. Sheffield: Sheffield Academic Press, 2000.

————. "Status and Role of Female Heroines in the Biblical Narrative." *MQ* 23 (1982): 149–60.

Gafney, Wilda C. M. "A Black Feminist Approach to Biblical Studies." *Encounter* 67.4 (2006): 391–403.

Galarza, Heydi. "Agar e Ismael: Un estudio de Génesis 21:1–21." *Aportes Bíblicos* 9 (2009): 5–30.

García Bauchman, Mercedes. "Un rey muy viejo y una machacha muy linda." *RIBLA* 41 (2002): 50–57.

Gardiner, Judith Kegan, ed. *Masculinity Studies and Feminist Theory: New Directions.* New York: Columbia University Press, 2002.

Gaventa, Beverly R. "The Maternity of Paul: An Exegetical Study of Galatians 4.19." Pages 189–210 in *The Conversation Continues: Studies in Paul and John in Honour of J. Louis Martyn.* Edited by Robert R. Fortna and Beverly R. Gaventa. Nashville: Abingdon, 1990.

Gendler, Mary. "The Vindication of Vashti." *Response* 18 (summer 1973): 154–60. Also published as *The Jewish Woman.* Edited by Liz Koltun. Waltham, Mass.: Jewish Educational Ventures, 1973.

Gerber, Christine, Benita Joswig, and Silke Petersen. *Gott heißt nicht nur Vater: Zur Rede über Gott in den Übersetzungen der "Bibel in gerechter Sprache."* Göttingen: Vandenhoeck & Ruprecht, 2008.

Gerlach, Martina, and Monika Weigt-Blättgen, eds. *Gottes Antlitz hülle dich in Licht … Andachten für Frauen mit der Bibel in gerechter Sprache.* Gütersloh: Gütersloher, 2009.

Gifford, Carolyn De Swarte. "American Women and the Bible: The Nature of Woman as a Hermeneutical Issue." Pages 11–33 in *Feminist Perspectives on Biblical Scholarship.* Edited by Adela Yarbro Collins. Chico, Calif.: Scholars Press, 1985.

Glancy, Jennifer. *Slavery in Early Christianity.* New York: Oxford University Pres, 2002.

Gleason, Maud W. *Making Men: Sophists and Self-Presentation in Ancient Rome.* Princeton: Princeton University Press, 1995.

Gnanadason, Aruna, ed. *Towards a Theology of Humanhood: Women's Perspectives.* Delhi: ISPCK, 1986.

Gold, Victor Roland, Thomas L. Hoyt, Sharon H. Ringe, Susan Brooks Thistlethwaite, Burton H. Throckmorton, and Barbara Withers, eds. *The New Testament and Psalms: An Inclusive Version.* New York: Oxford University Press, 1995.

Goldstein, Rabbi Elyse, ed. *The Women's Torah Commentary.* Woodstock, Vt.: Jewish Lights, 2000.

Goss, Robert E. *Jesus Acted Up: A Gay and Lesbian Manifesto.* San Francisco: Harper San Francisco, 1993.

————. *Queering Christ: Beyond Jesus Acted Up.* Cleveland: Pilgrim, 2002.

Goss, Robert E., and Mona West, eds. *Take Back the Word: A Queer Reading of the Bible.* Cleveland: Pilgrim, 2000.

Gössmann, Elisabeth. *Das Bild der Frau Heute.* Düsseldorf: Haus der Katholischen Frauen, 1967.

————. *Eva, Gottes Meisterwerk.* Archiv für philosophie- und theologiegeschichtliche Frauenforschung 2. Munich: Iudicium, 1985; rev. ed., 2000.

———. "Gottebenbildlichkeit." Pages 95–97, 177–81 in *Wörterbuch der Feministischen Theologie*. Edited by Elisabeth Gössmann, Helga Kuhlmann, Elisabeth Moltmann-Wendel, Ina Praetorius, and Luise Schottroff. Gütersloh: Gütersloher, 1991.

———. *Ob die Weiber Menschen seyn oder nicht*. Archive for Women's Research into the History of Philosophy and Theology 4. Munich: Iudicium, 1988.

———. *Die streitbaren Schwestern: Was will die Feministische Theologie?* Freiburg: Herder, 1981.

———. *Die Verkündigung an Maria im dogmatischen Verständnis des Mittelalters*. Munich: Hueber, 1957.

Gössmann, Elisabeth, Helga Kuhlmann, Elisabeth Moltmann-Wendel, Ina Praetorius, Luise Schottroff, eds. *Wörterbuch der feministischen Theologie*. 2nd ed. Gütersloh: Gütersloher, 2002.

Gössmann, Elisabeth, Elisabeth Moltmann-Wendel, Herlinde Pissarek-Hudelist, Ina Praetorius, Luise Schottroff, and Helen Schüngel-Straumann, eds. *Wörterbuch der feministischen Theologie*. Gütersloh: Gütersloher, 1991.

Gössmann, Elisabeth, Elisabeth Moltmann-Wendel, and Helen Schüngel-Straumann, eds. *Der Teufel blieb männlich: Kritische Diskussion zur "Bibel in gerechter Sprache" Feministische, historische und systematische Beiträge*. Neukirchen-Vluyn: Neukirchener, 2007.

Graetz, Naomi. *Unlocking the Garden: A Feminist Jewish Look at the Bible, Midrash, and God*. Piscataway, N.J.: Gorgias, 2005.

Grant, Jacquelyn. "Black Theology and the Black Woman." Pages 323–38 in *Black Theology: A Documentary History, Vol. 1: 1966–1979*. Edited by James H. Cone and Gayraud S. Wilmore. Maryknoll, N.Y.: Orbis, 1993.

———. *White Women's Christ and Black Women's Jesus: Feminist Christology and Womanist Response*. Atlanta: Scholars Press, 1999.

Green, Elizabeth E. *Dal silenzio alla parola*. Turin: Claudiana, 1995.

———. *Elisabeth Schüssler Fiorenza*. Brescia: Morcelliana, 2006.

Green, Rayna. "The Pocahontas Perplex: The Image of Indian Women in American Culture." *MR* 16.4 (1975): 698–714.

Greenberg, Blu. "Woman and Judaism." Pages 1039–53 in *Contemporary Jewish Religious Thought*. Edited by Arthur A. Cohen and Paul Mendes-Flohr. New York: Scribner, 1987.

Greenberg, Steven. "Gender after Feminism." *Lilith* (fall 2009): 18–20.

———. *Wrestling with God and Men: Homosexuality in the Jewish Tradition*. Madison: University of Wisconsin Press, 2004.

Grenholm, Christina, and Daniel Patte, eds. *Gender, Tradition, and Romans: Share Ground, Uncertain Borders*. New York: T&T Clark, 2005.

Gross, Rita. *Feminism and Religion: An Introduction*. Boston: Beacon, 1996.

Gross, Rita, ed. *Beyond Androcentrism: New Essays on Women and Religion*. Missoula, Mont.: Scholars Press for the American Academy of Religion, 1977.

Grudem, Wayne A., and Vern S. Poythress. *The Gender-Neutral Bible Controversy: Muting the Masculinity of God's Words*. Nashville: Broadman & Holman, 2000.

——. *The TNIV and the Gender-Neutral Bible Controversy.* Nashville: Broadman & Holman, 2004.

Grünenfelder, Regula. *Frauen an den Krisenherden: Eine rhetorisch-politische Deutung des Bellum Judaicum.* Münster: LIT, 2003.

Grünenfelder, Regula, and Bernd Lenfers Grünenfelder. *Erde und Licht: Mit dem Johannesevangelium auf den Spuren unserer Lebenswünsche.* Stuttgart: Katholisches Bibelwerk, 2004.

Guest, Deryn. *Beyond Feminist Biblical Studies.* Sheffield: Sheffield Phoenix, 2012.

——. *When Deborah Met Jael: Lesbian Biblical Hermeneutics.* London: SCM, 2005.

Guest, Deryn, Robert E. Goss, Mona West, and Thomas Bohache, eds. *The Queer Bible Commentary.* London: SCM, 2006.

Gunkel, Hermann. *Genesis.* 4th ed. HKAT. Göttingen: Vandenhoeck & Ruprecht, 1917.

Haberman, Bonna Devorah. "'Let My Gender Go!' Jewish Textual Activism." Pages 429–42 in *Toward a New Heaven and a New Earth: Essays in Honor of Elisabeth Schüssler Fiorenza.* Edited by Fernando Segovia. Maryknoll, N.Y.: Orbis, 2003.

——. "Praxis-Exegesis: A Jewish Feminist Hermeneutic." Pages 91–101 in *Women's Sacred Scriptures.* Edited by Kwok Pui-lan and Elisabeth Schüssler Fiorenza. London: SCM, 1998.

Habermas, Jürgen. *Coneixement i Interès.* Barcelona: Editorial Acribia, 1996.

Hahn, Ferdinand. *Christologische Hoheitstitel: Ihre Geschichte im frühen Christentum.* 5th ed. Göttingen: Vandenhoeck & Ruprecht, 1995. First published in 1963.

Halberstam, Judith. *Female Masculinity.* Durham: Duke University Press, 1999.

Halkes, Catharina. *Gott hat nicht nur starke Söhne: Grundzüge einer feministischen Theologie.* Gütersloh: Gütersloher, 1980.

——. *Suchen, was verloren ging: Beiträge zur feministischen Theologie.* Gütersloh: Gütersloher, 1985.

Halmer, Maria, Barbara Heyse Schaefer, and Barbara Rauchwarter, eds. *Anspruch und Widerspruch.* Vienna: Klagenfurth, 2000.

Halperin, David M. *Saint Foucault: Toward a Gay Hagiography.* New York: Oxford University Press, 1995.

Hampson, Daphne. "On Not Remembering Her." *Feminist Theology* 19 (1998): 63–68.

Hardesty, Nancy A. *Inclusive Language in the Church.* Atlanta: John Knox, 1987.

Harnack, Adolf von. *Mission und Ausbreitung des Christentums.* 2 vols. Leipzig, 1902.

Harrison, Beverly W. "Review of *In Memory of Her*, by Elisabeth Schüssler Fiorenza." *Horizons* 11 (1984): 150.

Hasan-Rokem, Galit. *Web of Life: Folklore and Midrash in Rabbinic Literature.* Stanford, Calif.: Stanford University Press, 2000.

Hassan, Riffat. "Equal Before Allah? Woman-Man Equality in the Islamic Tradition." *Harvard Divinity Bulletin* 17 (January–May 1987): 2–14.

Hauptman, Judith. *Rereading the Rabbis: A Woman's Voice.* Boulder: Westview, 1998.

Heinzelmann, Gertrud. *Das grundsätzliche Verhältnis von Kirche und Staat in den Konkordaten.* Aarau: Sauerländer, 1943.

——. *Wir schweigen nicht länger: Frauen äussern sich zum II. Vatikanischen Konzil.* Zürich: Interfeminas, 1964.

Hekman, Susan J., ed. *Feminist Interpretations of Michel Foucault*. University Park: Pennsylvania State University Press, 1996.

Helminiak, Daniel A. *What the Bible Really Says about Homosexuality*. Tajique, N.M.: Alamo Square, 2000.

Henze, Dagmar, Claudia Janssen, Stefanie Müller, and Beate Wehn. *Antijudaismus im Neuen Testament? Grundlagen für die Arbeit mit biblischen Texten*. Gütersloh: Kaiser, 1997.

Heschel, Susannah. *The Aryan Jesus: Christian Theologians and the Bible in Nazi Germany*. Princeton, N.J.: Princeton University Press, 2008.

———. "Jesus the Theological Transvestite." Pages 188–99 in *Judaism Since Gender*. Edited by Miriam Peskowitz and Laura Levitt. New York: Routledge, 1997.

———. *On Being a Jewish Feminist: A Reader*. New York: Schocken, 1983.

Hewitt, Emily C., and Suzanne R. Hiatt. *Women Priests: Yes or No?* New York: Seabury, 1973.

Hewitt, Marsha A. "The Feminist Liberation Theology of Elisabeth Schüssler Fiorenza as a Feminist Critical Theory." Pages 443–58 in *Toward a New Heaven and a New Earth: Essays in Honor of Elisabeth Schüssler Fiorenza*. Edited by Fernando Segovia. Maryknoll, N.Y.: Orbis, 2003.

Heyward, Carter. *Und sie rührte sein Kleid an: Eine feministische Theologie der Beziehung*. Stuttgart: Kreuz, 1986.

Hill, Renee L. "Who Are We for Each Other? Sexism, Sexuality and Womanist Theology." Pages 345–51 in *Black Theology: A Documentary History Volume Two: 1980–1992*. Edited by James H. Cone and Gayraud S. Wilmore. Maryknoll, N.Y.: Orbis, 1993.

Hojenski, Christine, Birgit Hübner, Reinhild Hundrup, and Martina Meyer. "Feministische Liturgien: Suchbewegungen–Erfahrungen–Reflexionen." Pages 59–75 in *Meine Seele sieht das Land der Freiheit: Feministische Liturgien–Modelle für die Praxis*. Edited by Christine Hojenski, Birgit Hübner, Reinhild Hundrup, and Martina Meyer. Münster: Edition liberación, 1990.

Hole, Judith, and Ellen Levine. *Rebirth of Feminism*. New York: Quadrangle, 1971.

hooks, bell. *Yearning: Race, Gender, and Cultural Politics*. Boston: South End, 1990.

Howard, George. "The Tetragram and the New Testament. " *JBL* 96 (1977): 63–76.

Howell, Maxine. "Towards a Womanist Pneumatological Pedagogy: Reading and Re-reading the Bible from British Black Women's Perspectives." *Black Theology* 7 (2009): 86–99.

Hunt, Mary E., and Diann L. Neu, eds. *New Feminist Christianity: Many Voices, Many Views*. Woodstock, Vt.: SkyLight Paths, 2010.

Ilan, Tal. *Integrating Women into Second Temple History*. Tübingen: Mohr Siebeck, 1999.

———. *Jewish Women in Greco-Roman Palestine*. Peabody, Mass.: Hendrickson, 1995.

Isasi-Diaz, Ada Maria. "The Bible and *Mujerista* Theology." Pages 261–69 in *Lift Every Voice: Constructing Christian Theologies from the Underside*. Edited by Susan Brooks Thistlethwaite and Mary Potter Engel. Maryknoll, N.Y.: Orbis, 1998.

———. *En la lucha: In the Struggle: A Hispanic Women's Liberation Theology*. Minneapolis: Fortress, 1993.

Jacob, Benno. *The First Book of the Torah: Genesis*. Stuttgart: Calwer, 2000. First published in 1934 by Schocken.

Jahr, Hannelore, ed. *Die neue Gute Nachricht Bibel*. Stuttgart: Deutsche Bibelgesellschaft, 1998.

Janssen, Claudia. "Bibel in gerechter Sprache." Pages 182–84 in *Feministische Theologie: Initiativen, Kirchen, Universitäten—eine Erfolgsgeschichte*. Edited by Gisela Matthiae, Renate Jost, Claudia Janssen, Antje Röckemann, and Annette Mehlhorn. Gütersloh: Gütersloher, 2008.

———. "Christus und seine Geschwister (Röm 8,12–17.29f)." Pages 64–80 in *Christus und seine Geschwister: Christologie im Umfeld der Bibel in gerechter Sprache*. Edited by Marlene Crüsemann and Carsten Jochum-Bortfeld. Gütersloh: Gütersloher, 2009.

———. *Endlich lebendig: Die Kraft der Auferstehung erfahren*. Freiburg: Kreuz, 2013.

Jardine, Alice, and Paul Smith, eds. *Men in Feminism*. New York: Methuen, 1987.

Jeansonne, Sharon Pace. *The Women of Genesis: From Sarah to Potiphar's Wife*. Minneapolis: Fortress, 1990.

Jennings, Theodore W. *Jacob's Wound: Homoerotic Narrative in the Literature of Ancient Israel*. New York: Continuum, 2005.

———. *The Man Jesus Loved: Homoerotic Narratives from the New Testament*. Cleveland: Pilgrim, 2003.

Jervell, Jacob. "*Imago Dei*: Gen 1,26ff im Spätjudentum, in der Gnosis und in den paulinischen Briefen." Ph.D. diss., Göttingen, 1960.

Jewish Orthodox Feminist Alliance. "JOFA Bible Curriculum: Bereishit." Online: http://www.jofa.org/about.php/programs/jofabiblecur/bereishit.

John, Mary E. *Discrepant Dislocations: Feminism, Theory, and Postcolonial Histories*. Berkeley: University of California Press, 1996.

Johnson, Sylvester A. *The Myth of Ham in Nineteenth-Century American Christianity: Race, Heathens, and the People of God*. New York: Palgrave Macmillan, 2004.

Johnson-Debaufre, Melanie. *Jesus among Her Children: Q, Eschatology, and the Construction of Christian Orgins*. HTS 55. Cambridge: Harvard University Press, 2006.

Johnson-Debaufre, Melanie, and Jane Schaberg, eds. *Mary Magdalene Understood*. New York: Continuum, 2006.

Jones-Warsaw, Koala. "Toward a Womanist Hermeneutic: A Reading of Judges 19–21." *JITC* 22.1 (1994): 18–35.

Jost, Renate. *Feministische Bibelauslegungen: Grundlagen–Forschungsgeschichtliches–Geschlechterstudien*. IFFTR Befreiende Perspektiven 1. Münster: LIT, 2013.

———. *Frauenmacht und Männerliebe: Egalitäre Utopien aus der Frühzeit Israels*. Stuttgart: Kohlhammer, 2006.

———. *Gender, Sexualität und Macht in der Anthropologie des Richterbuches*. BWANT 164; Stuttgart: Kohlhammer, 2006.

Jost, Renate, and Klaus Rashchzok, eds. *Gender–Religion–Kultur–Biblische, interreligiöse und ethische Aspekte*. Theologische Akzente 6. Stuttgart: Kohlhammer, 2011.

Jost, Renate, and Eveline Valtink, eds. *Ihr aber für wen haltet ihr mich? Auf dem Weg zu einer feministisch-befreiungstheologischen Revision von Christologie.* Gütersloh: Kaiser, 1996.

Joy, Elizabeth, ed. *Lived Realities: Faith Reflections on Gender Justice.* Bangalore: JWP/CISRS, 1999.

Jüngst, Britta. "Kontexte." Pages 67–136 in *Was ist Feministische Theologie?* Edited by Britta Jüngst and Claudia Rakel. Gelnhausen: Arbeitsstelle Fernstudium EKD, 2004.

Junior, Nyasha. "Womanist Biblical Interpretation." Pages 37–46 in *Engaging the Bible in a Gendered World: An Introduction to Feminist Biblical Interpretation in Honor of Katharine Doob Sakenfeld.* Edited by Linda Day and Carolyn Pressler. Louisville: Westminster John Knox, 2006.

Juschka, Darlene M., ed. *Feminism in the Study of Religion: A Reader.* New York: Continuum, 2001.

Kahl, Brigitte. "Der Brief an die Gemeinden in Galatien: Vom Unbehagen der Geschlechter und anderen Problemen des Andersseins." Pages 603–11 in *Kompendium feministischer Bibelauslegung.* Edited by Luise Schottroff and Marie-Theres Wacker. Gütersloh: Gütersloher, 1998.

———. "Gender Trouble in Galatia? Paul and the Rethinking of Difference." Pages 57–73 in *Is There a Future for Feminist Theology?* Edited by Deborah F. Sawyer and Diane M. Collier. Sheffield: Sheffield Academic Press, 1999.

———. "No Longer Male: Masculinity Struggles behind Galatians 3.28?" *JSNT* 79 (2000): 37–49.

Kähler, Else. *Die Frau in den paulinischen Briefen unter Berücksichtigung des Begriffs der Unterordnung.* Zürich: Gotthelf, 1960.

Kang, Namsoon. "Who/What is Asian? A Postcolonial Theological Reading of Orientalism and Neo-Orientalism." Pages 100–117 in *Postcolonial Theologies, Divinities, and Empire.* Edited by Catherine Keller, Michael Nausner, and Mayra Rivera. St. Louis: Chalice, 2004.

Kanyoro, Musimbi R. A. "Biblical Hermeneutics: Ancient Palestine and the Contemporary World." *RevExp* 94 (1997): 363–78.

———. "Cultural Hermeneutics: An African Contribution." Pages 101–13 in *Other Ways of Reading: African Women and the Bible.* Edited by Musa W. Dube. Atlanta: Society of Biblical Literature, 2001.

———. *Introducing Feminist Cultural Hermeneutics: An African Perspective.* Cleveland: Pilgrim, 2002.

Kanyoro, Musimbi R. A., and Mercy Amba Oduyoye. *The Will to Arise: Women, Tradition, and the Church in Africa.* Maryknoll, N.Y.: Orbis, 1992.

Karim, Jamillah. "Voices of Faith, Faces of Beauty: Connecting American Muslim Women through Azizah." Pages 169–88 in *Muslim Networks from Hajj to Hip Hop.* Edited by Miriam Cooke and Bruce B. Lawrence; Chapel Hill: University of North Carolina Press, 2005.

Kellenbach, Katharina von. *Anti-Judaism in Feminist Religious Writings.* Atlanta: Scholars Press, 1994.

Kelley, Shawn. *Racializing Jesus: Race, Ideology, and the Formation of Modern Biblical Scholarship*. New York: Routledge, 2002.

Kern, Kathi. *Mrs. Stanton's Bible*. Ithaca, N.Y.: Cornell University Press, 2001.

Kidd, Colin. *The Forging of Races: Race and Scripture in the Protestant Atlantic World, 1600–2000*. New York: Cambridge University Press, 2006.

Kim, Jean Kyoung. *Woman and Nation: An Intercontextual Reading of the Gospel of John from a Postcolonial Feminist Perspective*. Boston: Brill, 2004.

Kim, Seong Hee. *Mark, Women and Empire: A Korean Postcolonial Perspective*. Sheffield: Sheffield Phoenix, 2010.

Kimmel, Michael S. *Manhood in America: A Cultural History*. New York: Free, 1996.

———, ed. *The Politics of Manhood: Profeminist Men Respond to the Mythopoetic Men's Movement (and the Mythopoetic Leaders Answer)*. Philadelphia: Temple University Press, 1995.

King, Karen L. *The Gospel of Mary of Magdala: Jesus and the First Woman Apostle*. Santa Rosa, Calif.: Polebridge, 2003.

———. *What Is Gnosticism?* Cambridge: Harvard University Press, 2003.

———, ed. *Images of the Feminine in Gnosticism*. Philadelphia: Fortress, 1988.

Kirschbaum, Charlotte von. *Die wirkliche Frau*. Zürich: Evangelischer Verlag, 1949.

Kittredge, Cynthia Briggs. *Community and Authority: The Rhetoric of Obedience in the Pauline Tradition*. HTS 45; Harrisburg, Penn.: Trinity, 1998.

———. "Rethinking Authorship in the Letters of Paul: Elisabeth Schüssler Fiorenza's Model of Pauline Theology." Pages 318–33 in *Walk in the Ways of Wisdom: Essays in Honor of Elisabeth Schüssler Fiorenza*. Edited by Shelly Matthews, Cynthia Kittredge, and Melanie Johnson DeBaufre. Harrisburg, Penn.: Trinity, 2003.

Klaiber, Walter, and Rösel Martin. *Streitpunkt Bibel in gerechter Sprache*. Leipzig: Evangelische Verlagsanstalt, 2008.

Köbler, Renate. *Schattenarbeit: Charlotte von Kirschbaum–Die Theologin an der Seite Karl Barths*. Köln: Pahl-Rugenstein, 1987.

Koch, Heike. "'Wichtig ist es, dass die Frauen lernen, "zwischen den Zeilen zu lesen"': Der Beitrag Maria Weigles für die Bibelarbeit der Evangelischen Frauenhilfe." Pages 171–204 in *100 Jahre Evangelische Frauenhilfe in Deutschland: Einblicke in ihre Geschichte*. Edited by Christine Busch. Düsseldorf: Archive of the Protestant Church in the Rhineland, 1999.

Köhler, Hanne. "Frauengerechte Sprache in Gottesdienst und Kirche." Pages 23–31 in *Gerechte Sprache in Gottesdienst und Kirche*. Edited by Evangelische Frauenarbeit. Frankfurt: Evangelische Frauenarbeit in Deutschland.

———. "Frauengerechte Sprache ist menschengerechte Sprache." *TP* 2 (1987): 151–62.

———. *Gerechte Sprache als Kriterium von Bibelübersetzungen: Von der Entstehung des Begriffs bis zur gegenwärtigen Praxis*. Gütersloh: Gütersloher, 2012.

Köhler, Ludwig. *Theologie des Alten Testaments*. Tübingen: Mohr Siebeck, 1947.

Kolletzki, Claudia. *"Christus ist unsere wahre Mutter": Feminine Konnotationen für Christus in Denken der Julian von Norwich*. FTS 36. Frankfurt: Knecht, 1997.

Koltun, Elizabeth. *The Jewish Woman: New Perspectives*. New York: Schocken, 1976.

Kopp, Barbara. *Die Unbeirrbare: Wie Gertrud Heinzelmann den Papst und die Schweiz das Fürchten lehrte*. Zürich: Limmat, 2003.

Kraemer, Ross S. "Hellenistic Jewish Women: The Epigraphical Evidence." *SBLSP* 25 (1986): 183–200.

———. *Her Share of the Blessings: Women's Religions Among Pagans, Jews, and Christians in the Greco-Roman World.* New York: Oxford University Press, 1992.

———. "Jewish Women and Christian Origins: Some Caveats." Page 35–49 in *Women and Christian Origins.* Edited by Ross Kraemer and Mary Rose D'Angelo. New York: Oxford University Press, 1999.

———. "Non-literary Evidence for Jewish Women in Rome and Egypt." In *Rescuing Creusa: New Methodological Approaches to Women in Antiquity.* Edited by Marilyn B. Skinner. Lubbock, Tex.: Texas Tech University Press, 1987 = *Helios* 13 (1986): 85–101.

———. *When Aseneth Met Joseph: A Late Antique Tale of the Biblical Patriarch and His Egyptian Wife, Reconsidered.* New York: Oxford University Press, 1998.

Kroeger, Catherine Clark, and Mary J. Evans, eds. *The IVP Women's Bible Commentary.* Downers Grove, Ill.: InterVarsity Press, 2002.

Kugel, James L. *Traditions of the Bible: A Guide to the Bible As It Was at the Start of the Common Era.* Cambridge: Harvard University Press, 1998.

Kuhlmann, Helga. "In welcher Weise kann die Sprache einer Bibelübersetzung 'gerecht' sein." Pages 77–98 in *Die Bibel: Übersetzt in gerechte Sprache? Grundlagen einer neuen Übersetzung.* Edited by Helga Kuhlmann. Gütersloh: Gütersloher, 2005.

Kvam, Kristen E., and Linda S. Schearing, eds. *Eve and Adam: Jewish, Christian, and Muslim Readings on Genesis and Gender.* Bloomington: Indiana University Press, 1999.

Kwok Pui-lan. *Discovering the Bible in the Non-biblical World.* Maryknoll, N.Y.: Orbis, 1995.

———. *Introducing Asian Feminist Theology.* Sheffield: Sheffield Academic Press, 2000.

———. *Postcolonial Imagination and Feminist Theology.* Louisville: Westminster John Knox, 2005.

———. "Racism and Ethnocentrism in Feminist Biblical Interpretation." Pages 101–16 in *A Feminist Introduction.* Vol. 1 of *Searching the Scriptures.* Edited by Elisabeth Schüssler Fiorenza with the assistance of Shelly Matthews. New York: Crossroad, 1993.

———. "Response." *JFSR* 20.1 (2004): 99–106.

Kwok Pui-lan and Elisabeth Schüssler Fiorenza, eds. *Women's Sacred Scriptures.* London: SCM, 1998.

Laffey, Alice L. *An Introduction to the Old Testament: A Feminist Perspective.* Philadelphia: Fortress, 1988.

Lambert, Gustave. "L'Encyclical 'Humani generis' et l'Ecriture Sainte." *NRTh* 73 (1951): 225–43.

Lange, Ernst. *Sprachschule für die Freiheit: Bildung als Problem und Funktion der Kirche.* Munich: Kaiser, 1980.

Laqueur, Thomas. *Making Sex: Body and Gender from the Greeks to Freud.* Cambridge: Harvard University Press, 1990.

Lauretis, Teresa de. "Eccentric Subjects: Feminist Theory and Historical Consciousness." *Feminist Studies* 16 (1990): 115–50.

―――. "The Female Body and Heterosexual Presumption." *Semiotica* 67:3–4 (1987): 259–79.

―――. "Queer Theory: Lesbian and Gay Sexualities: An Introduction." *differences: A Journal of Feminist Cultural Studies* 3 (1991): iii–xviii.

―――. *Technologies of Gender*. Bloomington: Indiana University Press, 1987.

Le Fort, Gertrud von. *Die ewige Frau*. Munich: Kösel & Pustet, 1960.

Lee, Dorothy. *Flesh and Glory: Symbol, Gender, and Theology in the Gospel of John*. New York: Crossroad, 2002.

Lee, Kyung Sook. "An Old Testament Interpretation in an Era of Globalization: From the Perspective of Korean Feminist Theology." Unpublished manuscript, 2009.

Lerner, Gerda. *The Creation of Feminist Consciousness: From the Middle Ages to Eighteen-Seventy*. New York: Oxford University Press, 1993.

Leutzsch, Martin. "Bibelübersetzung als Skandal und Verbrechen." Pages 42–57 in *Bibel-Impulse: Film– Kunst–Literatur–Musik–Theater–Theologie*. Edited by Rainer Dillmann. INPUT 5. Münster: LIT, 2006.

―――. "Inklusive Sprache in der Bibelübersetzung." Pages 200–209 in *Die Bibel–Übersetzt in gerechte Sprache? Grundlagen einer neuen Übersetzung*. Edited by Helga Kuhlmann. Gütersloh: Gütersloher, 2005.

―――. "The Vision of a Female Christ." Pages 25–38 in *Soziale Rollen von Frauen in Religionsgemeinschaften*. Edited by Siri Fuhrmann, Erich Geldbach, and Irmgard Pahl. Münster: LIT, 2003.

Levine, Amy-Jill. "Anti-Judaism and the Gospel of Matthew." Pages 9–36 in *Anti-Judaism and the Gospels*. Edited by William Farmer. Harrisburg, Penn.: Trinity, 1999.

―――. "The Disease of Postcolonial New Testament Studies and the Hermeneutics of Healing." *JFSR* 20.1 (2004): 91–99.

―――. "Multiculturalism, Women's Studies, and Anti-Judaism." *JFSR* 19.1 (2003): 119–28.

―――. "Response." *JFSR* 20.1 (2004): 125–32.

―――. "Women in the Q Communit(ies) and Traditions." Pages 150–70 in *Women and Christian Origins*. Edited by Ross Kraemer and Mary Rose D'Angelo. New York: Oxford University Press, 1999.

―――, ed. *"Women Like This": New Perspectives on Jewish Women in the Greco-Roman World*. Atlanta: Scholars Press, 1991.

Levinson, Pnina Navè. *Was wurde aus Saras Töchtern? Frauen im Judentum*. Gütersloh: Gütersloher, 1989.

Liew, Tat-siong Benny. *Politics of Parousia: Reading Mark Inter(con)textually*. Leiden: Brill, 1999.

―――. "Postcolonial Criticism: Echoes of a Subaltern's Contribution and Exclusion." Pages 211–31 in *Mark and Method: New Approaches in Biblical Studies*. 2nd ed. Edited by Janice Capel Anderson and Stephen D. Moore. Minneapolis: Fortress, 2008.

―――. *What Is Asian American Biblical Hermeneutics? Reading the New Testament*. Honolulu: University of Hawai'i Press, 2008.

Ljung, Inger. *Silence or Suppression.* Stockholm: Uppsala, 1989.

Löhr, Max. *Die Stellung des Weibes in Jahwe-Religion und -Kult.* Beiträge zur Wissenschaft vom Alten Testament 4. Leipzig: Hinrichs, 1908.

López, Mercedes. "Alianza por la vida: Una lectura de Rut a partir de las culturas." *RIBLA* 26 (1997): 96–101.

———. "Danzando en el universo: Proverbios 8:22–31." *RIBLA* 50 (2005): 65–86.

Lorber, Judith. *Paradoxes of Gender.* New Haven: Yale University Press, 1990.

Lorde, Audre. *I Am Your Sister: Collected and Unpublished Writings of Audre Lorde.* Edited by Rudolph P. Byrd, Johnetta Betsch Cole, and Beverly Guy-Sheftall. Oxford: Oxford University Press, 2009.

———. *Sister Outsider: Essays and Speeches.* Berkeley: Crossing, 1984.

Low, Katherine B. "The Sexual Abuse of Lot's Daughters: Reconceptualizing Kinship for the Sake of Our Daughters." *JFSR* 26.2 (2010): 37–54.

Lozano, Betty Ruth, and Bibiana Peñaranda. "Una relectura de Números 12 desde una perspectiva de mujeres negras." *RIBLA* 50 (2005): 114–16.

Ludeña, Digna. "La comida compartida: Una lectura de Marcos 6:30–44 en diálogo con la cultura Quechua–Andina." *Aportes Bíblicos* 3 (2006): 3–40.

Lutz, Helma, Maria Theresa Herrera Vivar, and Linda Supik, eds. *Focus Intersektionalität: Bewegungen und Verortungen eines vielschichtigen Konzepts.* Wiesbaden: VS, 2010.

Lykke, Nina. *Feminist Studies: A Guide to Intersectional Theory, Methodology, and Writing.* New York: Routledge, 2010.

MacDonald, Dennis Ronald. *The Legend and the Apostle: The Battle for Paul in Story and Canon.* Philadelphia: Westminster, 1983.

Mack, Burton L. *Rhetoric and the New Testament.* Minneapolis: Fortress, 1990.

Maier, Christl. *Die "fremde Frau" in Proverbien 1–9: Eine exegetische und sozialgeschichtliche Studie.* OBO 144. Göttingen: Vandenhoeck & Ruprecht: 1995.

Malbon, Elizabeth Struthers. "Fallible Followers: Women and Men in the Gospel of Mark." *Semeia* 28 (1983): 29–48.

Malbon, Elizabeth Struthers, and Janice Capel Anderson. "Literary-Critical Methods." Pages 241–54 in *A Feminist Introduction.* Vol. 1 of *Searching the Scriptures.* Edited by Elisabeth Schüssler Fiorenza with Shelly Matthews. New York: Crossroad, 1993.

Malbon, Elizabeth Struthers, and Edgar V. McKnight, eds. *The New Literary Criticism and the New Testament.* JSNTSup 109. Sheffield: Sheffield Academic Press, 1994.

Maloney, Linda. "The Pastoral Epistles." Pages 361–80 in *A Feminist Commentary.* Vol. 2 of *Searching the Scriptures.* Edited by Elisabeth Schüssler Fiorenza. New York: Crossroad, 1994.

Manona, Ncumisa. "The Presence of Women in Parables: An Afrocentric Womanist Perspective." *Scriptura* 81 (2002): 408–21.

Mansilla, Sandra. "Hermenéutica de los linajes políticos: Un estudio sobre los discursos en torno a las genealogías y sus implicaciones políticas." *RIBLA* 41 (2002): 83–92.

———. "Intuiciones para abrir la historia: Mujeres, conocimiento y Biblia." *RIBLA* 50 (2005): 150–52.

Mara Sampaio, Tania. "Consideraciones para una hermenéutica de género del texto bíblico." *RIBLA* 37 (2000): 7–14.

———. "El cuerpo excluido de su dignidad." *RIBLA* 25 (1997): 35–45.

———. *Movementos do corpo prostituido da mulher. Aproximações da profecia atribuida a Oséias*. São Paulo: Loyola, 1999.

Marchal, Joseph A. *Hierarchy, Unity, and Imitation: A Feminist Rhetorical Analysis of Power Dynamics in Paul's Letter to the Philippians*. Atlanta: Society of Biblical Literature, 2006.

———. "'Making History' Queerly: Touches across Time through a Biblical Behind." *BibInt* 19 (2011): 373–95.

———. *The Politics of Heaven: Women, Gender, and Empire in the Study of Paul*. Minneapolis: Fortress, 2008.

———. "Responsibilities to the Publics of Biblical Studies and Critical Rhetorical Engagements for a Safer World." Pages 101–15 in *Secularism and Biblical Studies*. Edited by Roland Boer. London: Equinox, 2010.

———, ed. *Studying Paul's Letters: Contemporary Perspectives and Methods*. Minneapolis: Fortress, 2012.

Mariano, Lilia Dias. "Profetisas en el antiguo Israel, interfiriendo en el transcurso de la historia." *RIBLA* 60 (2008): 131–46.

Marques, María Antonita. "Los caminos de sobrevivencia: Una lectura del libro de Rut." *RIBLA* 63 (2009): 66–72.

Martin, Clarice J. "A Chamberlain's Journey and the Challenge of Interpretation for Liberation." *Semeia* 47 (1989): 105–35.

———. "The Eyes Have It: Slaves in the Communities of Christ Believers." Pages 221–39 in *Christian Origins*. Edited by Richard Horsley. Minneapolis: Fortress, 2005.

———. "Polishing the Unclouded Mirror: A Womanist Reading of Revelation 18:13." Pages 82–109 in *From Every People and Nation: The Book of Revelation in Intercultural Perspective*. Edited by David Rhoads. Minneapolis: Fortress, 2005.

———. "Womanist Biblical Interpretation." Pages 655–58 in *Dictionary of Biblical Interpretation*. Edited by John H. Hayes. Nashville: Abingdon, 1999.

———. "Womanist Interpretations of the New Testament: The Quest for Holistic and Inclusive Translation and Interpretation." *JFSR* 6.2 (1990): 4–61.

Masenya, Madipoane J. "African Womanist Hermeneutics: A Suppressed Voice from South Africa Speaks." *JFSR* 11.1 (1995): 149–55.

Masuzawa, Tomoko. *The Invention of World Religions, or, How European Universalism Was Preserved in the Language of Pluralism*. Chicago: University of Chicago Press, 2005.

Matthews, Pamela. *Sophia: Peace through Wisdom*. Reproduced from Katia Romanoff, "Sophia: Goddess of Wisdom and God's Wife." Online: http://www.northernway.org/sophia.html/.

Matthews, Shelly. *The Acts of the Apostles: Taming the Tongues of Fire*. Sheffield: Sheffield Phoenix, 2013.

———. *First Converts: Rich Pagan Women and the Rhetoric of Mission in Early Judaism and Christianity*. Palo Alto, Calif.: Stanford University Press, 2001.

———. *Perfect Martyr: The Stoning of Stephen and the Construction of Christian Identity.* Oxford: Oxford University Press, 2010.

———. "Thinking of Thecla: Issues in Feminist Historiography." *JFSR* 17.2 (2001): 39–55.

Matthews, Shelly, Cynthia Briggs Kittredge, and Melanie Johnson-DeBaufre, eds. *Walk in the Ways of Wisdom: Essays in Honor of Elisabeth Schüssler Fiorenza.* Harrisburg, Penn.: Trinity, 2003.

Matthews, Victor H., Bernard M. Levinson, and Tikva Frymer-Kensky, eds. *Gender and Law in the Hebrew Bible and the Ancient Near East.* Sheffield: Sheffield Academic Press, 1998.

Matthiae, Gisela, Renate Jost, Claudia Janssen, Antje Röckemann, and Annette Mehlhorn, eds. *Feministische Theologie: Initiativen, Kirchen, Universitäten—eine Erfolgsgeschichte.* Gütersloh: Gütersloher, 2008.

Mattila, Talvikki. *Citizens of the Kingdom.* Göttingen: Vandenhoeck & Ruprecht, 2002.

Mbuwayesango, Dora R. "Canaanite Women and Israelite Women in Deuteronomy: The Intersection of Sexism and Imperialism." Pages 45–57 in *Postcolonial Interventions: Essays in Honor of R. S. Sugirtharajah.* Edited by Tat-siong Benny Liew. Sheffield: Sheffield Phoenix, 2009.

———. "Childlessness and Woman-to-Woman Relationships in Genesis and in African Patriarchal Society: A Zimbabwean Woman's Perspective (Gen. 16:1–16; 21:8–21)." *Semeia* 78 (1997): 27–36.

———. "How Local Divine Powers Were Suppressed: A Case of Mwari of the Shona." Pages 63–77 in *Other Ways of Reading: African Women and the Bible.* Edited by Musa W. Dube. Atlanta: Society of Biblical Literature, 2001.

———. "Zephaniah" Pages 202–3 in *The Africana Bible: Reading Israel's Scriptures from Africa and the African Diaspora.* Edited by Hugh R. Page. Minneapolis: Fortress, 2009.

Mbuwayesango, Dora R., and Susanne Scholz, "Dialogical Beginnings: A Conversation on the Future of Feminist Biblical Studies." *JFSR* 25.2 (2009): 93–103.

McDonald, Lee Martin. *The Formation of the Christian Biblical Canon.* Rev. ed. Peabody, Mass.: Hendrickson, 1995.

McKenzie, Steven L., and Stephen R. Haynes, eds. *To Each Its Own Meaning: An Introduction to Biblical Criticisms and Their Application.* Rev. and exp. Louisville: Westminster John Knox, 1999. First published in 1993.

McNay, Lois. *Foucault and Feminism: Power, Gender, and the Self.* Cambridge: Polity, 1992.

Mehlhorn, Annette. "Feministische Theologie und Praxis unter globalisierten Bedingungen: Thesen." Pages 367–72 in *Feministische Theologie: Initiativen, Kirchen, Universitäten—eine Erfolgsgeschichte.* Edited by Gisela Matthiae, Renate Jost, Claudia Janssen, Annette, Mehlhorn, Antje Röckemann. Gütersloh: Gütersloher, 2008.

Mena, Maricel. "¡Amen, Axe! ¡Sarava, aleluya!" *RIBLA* 46 (2003): 64–73.

———. "La herencia de las diosas: Egipto y Sabá en el tiempo de la monarquía salomónica." *RIBLA* 54 (2006): 34–47.

————. "Hermenéutica negra feminista: De invisible a intérprete y artífice de su propia historia." *RIBLA* 50 (2005): 130–34.

————. "Raíces afroasiáticas en el mundo bíblico: Desafíos para la exégesis y hermenéutica latinoamericana." *RIBLA* 56 (2006): 17–33.

Metzler, Luise, and Katrin Ketia. *Bibel in gerechter Sprache: Fragen und Antworten.* Gütersloh: Gütersloher, 2009.

Meurer, Siegfried, ed. *Die vergessenen Schwestern: Frauengerechte Sprache in der Bibelübersetzung.* Stuttgart: Jahrbuch der Deutschen Bibelgesellschaft, 1993.

Meyers, Carol. *Discovering Eve: Ancient Israelite Women in Context.* New York: Oxford University Press, 1991.

Meyers, Carol, Toni Craven, and Ross S. Kraemer, eds. *Women in Scripture.* Boston: Houghton Mifflin, 2000.

Mies, Maria. *Patriarchy and Accumulation on a World Scale: Women in the International Division of Labour.* New York: Palgrave, 1999.

Miguel, Pilar de. "La Biblia leída con ojos de mujer." Pages 47–72 in *La mujer en la teología actual.* Edited by Carmen Bernabé, Pilar de Miguel, Trinidad León, and Lucía Ramón. San Sebastián: Publicaciones Idatz, 1996.

————. "Los movimientos de mujeres y la teología feminista: Una visión panorámica desde nuestro contexto." *Xirimiri* 12 (2003). Online: http://www.ciudaddemujeres.com/articulos/Los-movimientos-de-mujeres-y-la

Militello, Cettina. *Donne e Chiesa.* Palermo: EdiOftes, 1985.

————. "Teologhe." Pages 194–205 in *Teologhe: In quale Europa.* Edited by Sandra Mazzolini and Marinella Perroni. Sui generis; Cantalupa-Torino: Effatá 2008.

Milne, Pamela J. "The Patriarchal Stamp of Scripture: The Implications for a Structural Analysis for Feminist Hermeneutics." *JFSR* 5.1 (1989): 17–34.

————. "Toward Feminist Companionship: The Future of Feminist Biblical Studies and Feminism." Pages 39–60 in *A Feminist Companion to Reading the Bible: Approaches, Methods, and Strategies.* Edited by Athalya Brenner and Carole Fontaine. Sheffield: Sheffield Academic Press, 1997.

Mitchell, Joan L. *Beyond Fear and Silence: A Feminist-Literary Reading of Mark.* New York: Continuum, 2001.

Moghadam, Valentine M. "Islamic Feminism and its Discontents: Towards a Resolution of the Debate." Pages 15–52 in *Gender, Politics, and Islam.* Edited by Therese Saliba, Carolyn Allen, and Judith A. Howard. Chicago: University of Chicago Press, 2002.

Mohanty, Chandra Talpade. *Feminism without Borders: Decolonizing Theory, Practicing Solidarity.* Durham, N.C.: Duke University Press, 2003.

————. "Under Western Eyes: Feminist Scholarship and Colonial Discourses." Pages 51–80 in *Third World Women and the Politics of Feminism.* Edited by Chandra Talpade Mohanty, Ann Russo, and Lourdes Torres. Bloomington: Indiana University Press, 1991.

————. "'Under Western Eyes' Revisited: Feminist Solidarity through Anticapitalist Struggles." Pages 221–51 in *Feminism without Borders: Decolonizing Theory, Practicing Solidarity.* Edited by Chandra Talpade Mohanty. Durham: Duke University Press, 2003.

Mollenkott, Virginia. *Women, Men, and the Bible*. Nashville: Abingdon, 1977.

Moltmann, Jürgen. "Henriette Visser't Hooft." Pages 169–79 in *Gotteslehrerinnen*. Edited by Luise Schottroff and Johannes Thiele. Stuttgart: Kreuz, 1989.

Moltmann-Wendel, Elisabeth. *Ein eigener Mensch werden: Frauen um Jesus*. Gütersloh: Gütersloher, 1981.

———. *Frauenbefreiung: Biblische und theologische Argumente*. Munich: Kaiser, 1978.

———. *Das Land, wo Milch und Honig fließt: Perspektiven einer feministischen Theologie*. Gütersloh: Gütersloher, 1985.

———. *Wer die Erde nicht berührt, kann den Himmel nicht erreichen*. Zürich: Benziger, 1997.

———. *The Women Around Jesus*. Translated by John Bowden. New York: Crossroad, 1982.

Moore, Stephen D. *God's Beauty Parlor: And Other Queer Spaces in and around the Bible*. Stanford, Calif.: Stanford University Press, 2001.

———. *God's Gym: Divine Male Bodies of the Bible*. New York: Routledge, 1996.

———. "'O Man, Who Art Thou…?': Masculinity Studies and New Testament Studies." Pages 1–22 in *New Testament Masculinities*. Edited by Stephen D. Moore and Janice Capel Anderson. SemeiaSt 45. Atlanta: Society of Biblical Literature, 2003.

Moore, Stephen D., and Janice Capel Anderson, eds. *New Testament Masculinities*. SemeiaSt 45. Atlanta: Society of Biblical Literature, 2003.

Morton, Nelle. *The Journey Is Home*. Boston: Beacon, 1985.

Muilenburg, James. "Form Criticism and Beyond." *JBL* 88 (1969): 1–18.

Munro, Winsome. "Patriarchy and Charismatic Community in 'Paul.'" Pages 189–98 in *Women and Religion*, rev. ed. Edited by Judith Plaskow and Joan Arnold Romero. Missoula, Mont.: Working Group on Women and Religion and Scholars Press, 1974.

———. "Women Disciples in Mark?" *CBQ* 44 (1982): 225–41.

Murphy, Peter F., ed. *Feminism and Masculinities*. Oxford: Oxford University Press, 2004.

Murphy-O'Connor, Jerome, Cettina Militello, and M. Luisa di Rigato. *Paolo e le donne*. Orizzonti biblici. Assisi: Cittadella Editrice, 2006.

Mwaura, Philomena Njeri. "Feminist Biblical Interpretation and the Hermeneutics of Liberation: An African Woman's Perspective." Pages 77–85 in *Feminist Interpretation of the Bible and the Hermeneutics of Liberation*. Edited by Silvia Schroer and Sophia Bietenhard. London: Sheffield Academic Press, 2003.

Nadar, Sarojini. "A South African Indian Womanist Reading of the Character of Ruth." Pages 159–75 in *Other Ways of Reading: African Women and the Bible*. Edited by Musa W. Dube. Atlanta: Society of Biblical Literature, 2001.

———. "'Texts of Terror': The Conspiracy of Rape in the Bible, Church, and Society: The Case of Esther 2:1–18." Page 77–95 in *African Women, Religion, and Health*. Edited by Isabel Apawo Phiri and Sarojini Nadar. Maryknoll, N.Y.: Orbis, 2006.

Nash, Jennifer C. "Rethinking Intersectionality." *Feminist Review* 89 (2008): 1–15.

Nasimiyu-Wasike, Anne. "Christology and African Woman's Experience." Pages 70–84 in *Faces of Jesus in Africa*. Edited by Robert J. Schreiter. Maryknoll, N.Y.: Orbis, 1995.

———. "Polygamy: A Feminist Critique." Pages 101–18 in *The Will to Arise: Women, Tradition, and the Church in Africa*. Edited by Mercy Amba Oduyoye and Musimbi R. A. Kanyoro. Maryknoll, N.Y.: Orbis, 1992.

National Council of the Churches of Christ in the United States of America, Division of Christian Education, ed. *New Revised Standard Version Bible: The Holy Bible Containing the Old and New Testaments with the Apocryphal/Deuterocanonical Books*. Nashville: Thomas Nelson, 1989.

National Council of the Churches of Christ in the United States of America, Division of Education and Ministry, ed. *An Inclusive Language Lectionary: Readings for Year A*. Atlanta: John Knox, 1983; *Readings for Year B*, 1984; *Readings for Year C*, 1985.

Naurath, Elisabeth, and Uta Pohl-Patalong, eds. *Bibliodrama: Theorie–Praxis–Reflexion*. Stuttgart: Kohlhammer, 2002.

Navarro Puerto, Mercedes. "Boletin Bibliográfico: Biblia, Mujeres, Feminismo. I Parte: Biblia Hebrea." *'Ilu: Revista de Ciencias de las Religiones* 14 (2009): 231–83.

———. "Boletin Bibliográfico: Biblia, Mujeres, Feminismo. II Parte: El Nuevo Testamento y el Cristianismo Primitivo." *'Ilu: Revista de Ciencias de las Religiones* 15 (2010): 205–86.

———. *Cuando la Biblia cuenta: Claves de la Narrativa Bíblica*. Madrid: Ed. PPC, 2003.

———, ed. *Diez palabras de Teología Feminista*. Estella, Spain: Editorial Verbo Divino, 1993.

———. "L'interpretazione biblica femminista tra ricerca sinottica ed ermeneutica politica." *RivB* 45 (1997): 439–67.

———. *Morir de vida. Mc 16,1-8: exégesis y aproximación psicológica a un texto*. Estella, Spain: Editorial Verbo Divino, 2011.

———. *Ungido para la vida: Exégesis narrativa de Mc 14,3-9 y Jn 12,1-8*. Estella, Spain: Editorial Verbo Divino,1999.

———. *Violencia, sexismo, silencio: In-conclusiones en el libro de los Jueces*. Estella, Spain: Editorial Verbo Divino, 2013.

Navia, Carmiña. "Violencia histórica contra María de Magdala." *RIBLA* 4 (2002): 107–16.

Nederlands Bubelgenootschap. *De Nieuwe Bijbel Vertaling (NBV)*. Haarlem: Nederlands Bijbelgenootschap, 2004.

Nelson, Cary, Paula A. Treichler, and Lawrence Grossberg. "Cultural Studies: An Introduction." Pages 1–22 in *Cultural Studies*. Edited by Lawrence Grossberg, Cary Nelson, and Paula A. Treichler. New York: Routledge, 1992.

Neufel, Elaine. "Volencia sexual y poder: El caso de Tamar in 2S 13:1–22." *RIBLA* 41 (2002): 39–49.

Newsom, Carol A., and Sharon H. Ringe, eds. *Women's Bible Commentary*. Louisville: Westminster John Knox, 1992; exp. ed., 1998.

Nieto, Genoveva. "El cuerpo femenino como texto: La curación de la mujer encorvada, Lc.13:10–17." *Aportes bíblicos* 1 (2005): 5–36.

Nissinen, Martti. *Homoeroticism in the Biblical World: A Historical Perspective*. Translated by Kirsi Stjerna. Minneapolis: Fortress, 1998.

Ntloedibe-Kuswani, Gomang Seratwa. "Translating the Divine: The Case of Modimo in the Setwana Bible." Pages 78–97 in *Other Ways of Reading: African Women and the Bible*. Edited by Musa W. Dube. Atlanta: Society of Biblical Literature, 2001.

Oakley, Ann. *Sex, Gender, and Society*. New York: Harper & Row, 1972.

O'Connor, Kathleen M. "The Feminist Movement Meets the Old Testament: One Woman's Perspective." Pages 3–26 in *Engaging the Bible in a Gendered World: An Introduction to Feminist Biblical Interpretation in Honor of Katharine Doob Sakenfeld*. Edited by Linda Day and Carolyn Pressler. Louisville: Westminster John Knox, 2006.

Oduyoye, Mercy Amba. *Daughters of Anowa: African Women and Patriarchy*. Maryknoll, N.Y.: Orbis, 1995.

———. *Hearing and Knowing: Theological Reflections on Christianity in Africa*. Maryknoll, N.Y.: Orbis, 1986.

———. *Introducing African Women's Theology*. Sheffield: Sheffield Academic Press, 2001.

———. "Violence against Women: Window on Africa." *Voices from the Third World* 18 (1995): 168–76.

Oduyoye, Mercy Amba, and Musimbi R. A. Kanyoro, eds. *Talitha Qumi! Proceedings of the Convocation of African Women Theologians*. Ibadan: Daystar, 1990.

———, eds. *The Will to Arise: Women, Tradition, and the Church in Africa*. Maryknoll, N.Y.: Orbis, 1992.

Økland, Jorunn. *Women in Their Place*. Edinburgh: T&T Clark, 2004.

Okure, Teresa. "Feminist Interpretations in Africa." Pages 76–85 in *A Feminist Introduction*. Vol. 1 of *Searching the Scriptures*. Edited by Elisabeth Schüssler Fiorenza with the assistance of Shelly Matthews. New York: Crossroad, 1993.

———. "Women in the Bible." Pages 47–59 in *With Passion and Compassion: Third World Women Doing Theology*. Edited by Virginia Fabella and Mercy Amba Oduyoye. Maryknoll, N.Y.: Orbis, 1989.

Osiek, Carolyn. "The Feminist and the Bible: Hermeneutical Alternatives." Pages 93–106 in *Feminist Perspectives on Biblical Scholarship*. Edited by Adela Yarbro Collins. Chico, Calif.: Scholars Press, 1985.

Osiek, Carolyn, and Margaret Y. MacDonald, with Janet H. Tulloch. *A Woman's Place: House Churches in Earliest Christianity*. Minneapolis: Fortress, 2006.

Ostriker, Alicia Suskin. *Feminist Revision and the Bible: The Unwritten Volume*. Oxford: Blackwell, 1993.

Ottermann, Mônica. "The Blessing of the Canaanite Woman: Bibliodrama and *Leitura Popular*: Ten Years of Working with Bibliodrama in Brazil." *Bulletin Dei Verbum* 66/67 (2003): 11–15.

Paepcke, Fritz. "Die Sprache im Zusammenleben der Völker." Pages 17–24 in *Im Übersetzen leben: Übersetzung und Textvergleich*. Edited by Klaus Berger and Hans-Michael Speier. Tübingen: Narr, 1986.

Pagels, Elaine. *The Gnostic Gospels*. Random House: New York, 1979.

———. "Paul and Women: A Response to Recent Discussion." *JAAR* 42 (1974): 538–49.

Pardes, Ilana. *Countertraditions in the Bible: A Feminist Approach*. Cambridge: Harvard University Press, 1992.

Parratt, Saroj Nalini Arambam. "Women as Originators of Oral Scripture in an Asian Society." Pages 74–80 in *Women's Sacred Scriptures*. Edited by Kwok Pui-lan and Elisabeth Schüssler Fiorenza; London: SCM, 1998.

Parsons, Susan Frank, ed. *Cambridge Companion to Feminist Theology*. Cambridge: Cambridge University Press, 2002.

Parvey, Connie. "The Theology and Leadership of Women in the New Testament." Pages 117–49 in *Religion and Sexism: Images of Women in the Jewish and Christian Traditions*. Edited by Rosemary Radford Ruether. New York: Simon & Schuster, 1974.

Pasquay, Andreas. "I Need You, to Participate the Story": Bibliodrama/Bibliolog im christlich-jüdischen Gespräch." Online: http://www.judentum.net/dialog/bibliolog.htm.

Pauschert, Margarete. "Der Stuhl bleibt frei: Die Präsenz der Abwesenden im Bibliodrama." Pages 135–43 in *Interreligiöses Bibliodrama*. Edited by Leony Renk. Schenefeld: EB, 2005.

Penner, Todd, and Caroline Vander Stichele, eds. *Mapping Gender in Ancient Religious Discourses*. Leiden: Brill, 2007.

Perelman, Chaim, and Lucie Olbrechts-Tyteca. *The New Rhetoric: A Treatise on Argumentation*. Translated by John Wilkinson and Purcell Weaver. Notre Dame, Ind.: Notre Dame University Press, 1969.

Perroni, Marinella. "Canone inverso: La rivoluzione femminista e la maternità di Maria." Pages 277–97 in *La maternità tra scelta, desiderio e destino*. Edited by Saveria Chemotto. Soggetti rivelati 25; Padua: Il poligrafo, 2009.

———. "Cent'anni di Solitudine: La Lettura Femminista della Scrittura." *Servitium* 150 (2003): 21–34.

———. "Cristo dice 'donna': La testimonianza del IV evangelo." Pages 100–122 in AA.VV., *Le donne dicono Dio: Quale Dio dicono le donne? E Dio dice le donne? Atti del decimo convegno di studio Progetto Donna, Milan, 26 November 1994*. Milan: Paoline, 1995.

———. "Discepole di Gesù." Pages 197–240 in *Donne e Bibbia: Storia ed esegesi*. Edited by Adriana Valerio. La Bibbia nella storia 21. Bologna: Dehoniane, 2006.

———. *I. L'unità letteraria e teologica dell'opera di Luca (Vangelo e Atti degli Apostoli)*. Padua: Istituto per la Storia Ecclesiastica Padovana, 2002.

———. "Il Cristo Maestro (Lc 10,38–42): L'apoftegma di Marta e Maria: Problemi di critica testuale." Pages 57–78 in *Mysterium Christi: Symbolgegenwart und theologische Bedeutung*. Edited by M. Löhrer and E. Salmann. Studia Anselmiana 115. Rome: Anselmiana, 1995.

———. *Il discepolato delle donne nel Vangelo di Luca: Un contributo all'ecclesiologia neotestamentaria*. Excerptum ex Dissertatione ad Doctoratum Sacrae Theologiae Assequendum in Pontificio Athenaeo S. Anselmi: Romae, 1995.

———. "L'annuncio pasquale alle/delle donne [Mc 16,1–8]: alle origini della tradizione kerygmatica." Pages 397–436 in *Patrimonium fidei: Traditionsgeschichtliches Verstehen am Ende?* Studia Anselmiana 124. Rome: Anselmiana, 1997.

———. "L'approccio ermeneutico della teologia femminista ai testi biblico-mariologici." Pages 409–40 in *L'ermeneutica contemporanea e i testi biblico-mariologici:*

Verifica e proposte. Edited by Ermanno M. Toniolo. Atti del XIII Simposio Internazionale Mariologico, Rome: 2–6 October 2001; Rome: edizioni Marianum, 2003.

———. "Le donne e Maria madre di Gesù in Luca." Pages 115–29 in *San Luca evangelista testimone della fede che unisce.* Edited by G. Leonardi and F. G. B.Trolese. Atti del Congresso Internazionale. Padua: Istituto per la Storia Ecclesiastica Padovana, 2002.

———. "Lettura femminile ed ermeneutica femminista del NT: Status quaestionis." *RivB* 41 (1993): 315–39.

———. "Lettura femminista e lettura spirituale della Bibbia." Pages 49–77 in *Istituto Superiore di Scienze Religiose delle Venezie. Sede centrale di Padova, Le prolusioni ai corsi degli anni accademici 1994–1996.* Padua: n.p., 1997.

———. "L'interpretazione biblica femminista tra ricerca sinottica e ermeneutica politica: una rassegna di recenti opere di esegesi femminista." *RivB* 45 (1997): 439–68.

———. "'Muriò y fue sepultado': La contribución de las discípulas de Jesús a la elaboracion de la fe en la resurreción." Pages 147–80 in *En el umbral: Muerte y Teología en perspectíva de mujeres.* Edited by Mercedes Navarro. Bilbao: Descléè de Brouwer, 2006.

———. "Per una pneumatologia femminista: Un contributo biblico." *Servitium* 156 (2004): 731–42.

———. "Una sessuazione non-segregante: Il 'terzo sesso' interpella la Bibbia." Pages 55–74 in *L'enigma corporeità: sessualità e religione.* Edited by Antonio Autiero and Stefanie Knauss. Scienze religiose. Nuova serie 24. Bologna: EDB, 2010.

———. "Una valutazione dell'esegesi femminista: verso un senso critico integrale." *StPat* 43 (1996): 67–92.

Pertuz, Maribel. "La evangelista de la resurrección en el cuarto evangelio." *RIBLA* 25 (1997): 69–76.

petersen, Silke. "Die Evangelienüberschriften und die Entstehung des neutestamentlichen Kanons." *ZNW* 97 (2006): 250–74.

Phiri, Isabel Apawo, Betty Govenden, and Sarojini Nadar, eds. *Her-Story: The Histories of Women of Faith in Africa.* Pietermaritzburg, South Africa: Cluster, 2002.

Pippin, Tina. *Death and Desire: The Rhetoric of Gender in the Apocalypse of John.* Lousiville: Westminster John Knox, 1992.

———. "Ideology, Ideological Criticism, and the Bible." *CR:BS* 4 (1996): 51–78.

Plaatjie, Gloria Kehilwe. "Toward a Post-Apartheid Black Feminist Reading of the Bible: A Case of Luke 2:36–38." Pages 114–42 in *Other Ways of Reading: African Women and the Bible.* Edited by Musa W. Dube. Atlanta: Society of Biblical Literature, 2001.

Plaskow, Judith. "Anti-Judaism in Christian Feminist Interpretation." Pages 117–29 in *A Feminist Introduction.* Vol. 1 of *Searching the Scriptures.* Edited by Elisabeth Schüssler Fiorenza with the assistance of Shelly Matthews. New York: Crossroad, 1993.

———. "Christian Feminism and Anti-Judaism." *Cross Currents* 33 (Fall 1978): 306–9.

———. *The Coming of Lilith: Essays on Feminism, Judaism, and Sexual Ethics 1972–2003.* Boston: Beacon, 2005.

------. "Feminist Anti-Judaism and the Christian God." *JFSR* 7.2 (1991): 99–108.

------. "Lilith Revisited." Pages 425–30 in *Eve and Adam: Jewish, Christian, and Muslim Readings on Genesis and Gender.* Edited by Kristen Kvam, Linda Schearing, and Valarie H. Ziegler. Bloomington: Indiana University Press, 1999.

------. *Sex, Sin, and Grace: Women's Experience and the Theologies of Niebuhr and Tillich.* Washington: University Press of America, 1980.

------. *Standing Again at Sinai: Judaism from a Feminist Perspective.* New York: HarperCollins, 1991.

------. "We Are Also Your Sisters: The Development of Women's Studies in Religion." *WSQ* 1/2 (1997): 199–211. First published in 1993.

Plaskow, Judith, and Joan Arnold Romero, eds. *Women and Religion.* Rev. ed. Missoula, Mont.: Working Group on Women and Religion and Scholars Press, 1974.

Plaskow Goldenberg, Judith, and Joan Arnold Romero, eds. *Women and Religion: 1973 Proceedings.* Tallahassee, Fla.: American Academy of Religion, 1973.

Pobee, John S., and Bärbel Wartenberg-Potter, eds. *New Eyes for Reading: Biblical and Theological Reflections from Women of the Third World.* Geneva: World Council of Churches, 1986.

Pohl-Patalong, Uta. "Kritische Freundschaft." Pages 30–37 in *Bibliodrama: Theorie-Praxis–Reflexion.* Edited by Elisabeth Naurath and Uta Pohl-Patalong. Stuttgart: Kohlhammer, 2002.

Portefaix, Lilian. *Sisters Rejoice!* Stockholm: Almqvist & Wiksell, 1988.

Prasad, Madhava. *The Ideology of Hindi Cinema: A Historical Construction.* Delhi: Oxford University Press, 1998.

Pratt, Mary Louise. *Imperial Eyes: Travel Writing and Transculturation.* New York: Routledge, 1992.

Priests for Equality. *The Prophets.* Vol. 2 of *The Inclusive Hebrew Bible.* Lanham, Md.: AltaMira, 2004.

Pulheim, Peter, and Christine Schaumberger. "Mit Figuren von Hans Steinbrenner leben." Pages 25–30 in *Hans Steinbrenner zum 70. Geburtstag.* Edited by Helmut Dreiseitl. Cologne: Galerie Dreiseitl, 1998.

Pusch, Luise F. *Das Deutsche als Männersprache.* Frankfurt: Suhrkamp, 1984.

Putnam, Ruth Anna. "Friendship." Pages 44–54 in *Reading Ruth: Contemporary Women Reclaim a Sacred Story.* Edited by Judith A. Kates and Gail Twersky Reimer. New York: Ballantine, 1994.

Ralte, Rini, Florence Robinson, Corinne Scott, and Nirmala Vasanthkumar. *Envisioning a New Heaven and a New Earth.* New Delhi: ISPCK, 1998.

Raming, Ida. *Der Ausschluss der Frau vom priesterlichen Amt: Gottgewollte Tradition oder Diskriminierung?* Köln-Wien: Böhlau, 1973.

Rashkow, Ilona N. *Taboo or Not Taboo: Sexuality and Family in the Hebrew Bible.* Minneapolis: Fortress, 2000.

Ratzinger, Joseph. "L'interpretazione Biblica in Conflitto: Problemi del Fondamento ed Orientamento Dell'esegesi Contemporanea." Pages 93–125 in *L'esegesi Cristiana Oggi.* Casale Monferrato: Marietti, 1991.

Regina, Silvia. "Fe y Axe: Sanació como experiencia de encuentro con la fuerza que nos habita." Pages 231–45 in *Ecce mulier: Homenaje a Irene Foulkes*. San José: SEBILA, 2005.

Rehmann, Luzia Sutter, and Kerstin Rödiger. *Der springende Punkt: Anleitung zur Bibellektüre in sieben Schritten*. Gütersloh: Gütersloher, 2010.

Reid, Barbara E. *Taking Up the Cross: New Testament Interpretations Through Latina and Feminist Eyes*. Minneapolis: Fortress, 2007.

Reimer, Ivoni Richter. *Frauen in der Apostlegeschichte des Lukas: Eine feministische-theologische Exegese*. Gütersloh: Gütersloher, 1992.

———. "Reconstruir historia de mujeres: Reconsideraciones sobre el trabajo y estatus de Lidia en Hechos 16." *RIBLA* 4 (1989): 47–64.

———. et al. "Respiros ... entre transpiración y conspiración: Documento final del encuentro de mujeres en San Leopoldo." *RIBLA* 50 (2005): 109–13.

Reinhartz, Adele. *Befriending the Beloved Disciple: A Jewish Reading of the Gospel of John*. New York: Continuum, 2001.

———. "Feminist Criticism and Biblical Studies on the Verge of the Twenty-First Century." Pages 30–38 in *A Feminist Companion to Reading the Bible*. Edited by Athalya Brenner and Carole Fontaine. Sheffield: Sheffield Academic Press, 1997.

———. "From Narrative to History: The Resurrection of Mary and Martha." Pages 161–84 in *"Women Like This": New Perspectives on Jewish Women in the Greco-Roman World*. Edited by Amy-Jill Levine. Atlanta: Scholars Press, 1991.

———. "Jewish Women's Scholarly Writings on the Bible." Pages 2000–2005 in *The Jewish Study Bible*. Edited by Adele Berlin and Marc Zvi Brettler. Oxford: Oxford University Press, 2004.

———. "Response." *JFSR* 20.1 (2004): 111–15.

Renk, Leony. "Die dringlichste Frage: Erinnerung an Ruth C. Cohn." *Schlangenbrut* 109/110 (2010): 51–53.

———, ed. *Interreligiöses Bibliodrama: Bibliodrama als neuer Weg zur christlich-jüdischen Begegnung*. Bibliodrama Kontexte 5. Schenefeld: EB, 2005.

Ricci, Carla. *Maria di Magdala e le molte alter: Donne sul cammino di Gesù*. Naples: D'Auria, 1991.

Richard, Pablo. "Hermenútica bíblica india: Revelación de Dios en las religiones indígenas y en la Biblia (Después de 500 años de dominación)." Pages 45–62 in *Sentido histórico del V Centenario (1492–1992)*. Edited by Guillermo Meléndez. San José: CEHILA-DEI, 1992.

Rigato, Maria-Luisa. *Discepole di Gesù*. Collana Studi biblici 63; Bologna: EDB, 2011.

———. Le figure femminili nel Vangelo secondo Giovanni." Pages 173–233 in *I laici nel popolo di Dio. Esegesi Biblica*. Edited by Vittorio Liberti. Rome: ED, 1990.

———. Gesù 'profumato' a Betania da una donna, nella redazione matteana." Pages 497–504 in *Donna e ministero: Un dibattito ecumenico*. Edited by Cettina Militello. Rome: ED, 1991.

———. *Giovanni: l'enigma il Presbitero il culto il Tempio la cristologia*. Bologna: EDB, 2007.

———. *Il Titolo Della Croce Di Gesù: Confronto tra i Vangeli e la Tavoletta-reliquia della Basilica Eleniana a Roma*. Tesi Gregoriana. Serie Teologia 100: Rome, 2005.

————. *I.N.R.I. Il titolo della Croce*. Bologna: EDB, 2010.

————. "Le figure femminili nel Vangelo secondo Giovanni." Pages 173–233 in *I laici nel popolo di Dio: Esegesi Biblica*. Edited by Vittorio Liberti. Rome: ED, 1990.

————. "'Lingue come di fuoco' e 'invio' di discepoli/e come profeti-testimoni (At 2,3–4 e Is 6,5–8)." Pages 81–106 in *Profezia: Modelli e forme nell'esperienza cristiana laicale*. Edited by Cettina Militello. Padua: CEDAM, 2000.

————. "Maria La Maddalena: Ancora riflessioni su colei che fu chiamata 'la Resagrande'" (Lc 8,2; 24,10; Gv 20,1.10–17). *Studia Patavina* 50 (2003): 727–52.

Ringe, Sharon H. "Places at the Table: Feminist and Postcolonial Biblical Interpretation." Pages 136–51 in *The Postcolonial Bible*. Edited by R. S. Sugirtharajah. Sheffield: Sheffield Academic Press, 1998.

Rizzante Gallazzi, Anna María. "La mujer sitiada: Lectura de Judit a partir de Dina." *RIBLA* 15 (1993): 47–58.

————. "Yo seré para él como aquella que da la paz." *RIBLA* 21 (1996): 91–101.

Rocha, Violeta. "Entre la fragilidad y el poder: Mujeres en al Apocalipsis." *RIBLA* 48 (2004): 95–104.

Röckemann, Antje. "'Erbsünde gibt es bei uns nicht': Jüdisch-Christliches Bibliodrama als Chance für Ver-Lernprozesse." Pages 125–33 in *Interreligiöses Bibliodrama*. Edited by Leony Renk. Schenefeld: EB, 2005.

————. "In Spiralen fliegen: Bibliodrama und TZI interkulturell." Pages 7–13 in *In Spiralen fliegen: Bibliodrama und TZI [Themenzentrierte Interaktion] interkulturell*. Edited by Margarete Pauschert and Antje Röckemann. Münster: Schlangenbrut,1999.

Röckemann, Antje, and Kathrin Winkler. "Christlich-feministische Theologie, Antijudaismus und jüdisch-christlicher Dialog." Pages 344–50 in *Feministische Theologie: Initiativen, Kirchen, Universitäten—eine Erfolgsgeschichte*. Edited by Gisela Matthiae, Renate Jost, Claudia Janssen, Annette Mehlhorn, and Antje Röckemann. Gütersloh: Gütersloher, 2008.

Roundtable Discussion. "Anti-Judaism and Postcolonial Biblical Interpretation." *JFSR* 20.1 (2004): 91–132.

Rubin, Gayle S. *Deviations: A Gayle Rubin Reader*. Durham, N.C.: Duke University Press, 2011.

Ruether, Rosemary Radford. "The Becoming of Women in Church and Society." *Cross Currents* 17 (1967): 418–26.

————. "Feminist Interpretation: A Method of Correlation." Pages 111–24 in *Feminist Interpretation of the Bible*. Edited by Letty M. Russell. Philadelphia: Westminster, 1985.

————. "Mother Earth and the Megamachine." *Christianity and Crisis* 31 (December 13, 1971): 267–72.

————. "Patriarchy." Pages 236–40 in *An A to Z of Feminist Theology*. Edited by Lisa Isherwood and Dorothea McEwan. Sheffield: Sheffield Academic Press, 1996.

————, ed. *Religion and Sexism: Images of Woman in the Jewish and Christian Traditions*. New York: Simon & Schuster, 1974.

————. *Sexism and God-Talk: Toward a Feminist Theology*. Boston: Beacon, 1993.

———. "Women's Liberation in Historical and Theological Perspective." Pages 26–36 in *Women's Liberation and the Church: The New Demand for Freedom in the Life of the Christian Church.* Edited by Sarah Bentley Doely. New York: Association Press, 1970.

Russell, Letty M. *Feminist Interpretation of the Bible.* Philadelphia: Westminster, 1985.

———. "Introduction: Liberating the Word." Pages 11–18 in *Feminist Interpretation of the Bible.* Edited by Letty M. Russell; Philadelphia: Westminster, 1985.

———, ed. *The Liberating Word: A Guide to Nonsexist Interpretation of the Bible.* Philadelphia: Westminster John Knox, 1977.

———. "Sprachveränderung und Kirchenreform." Pages 70–84 in *Als Mann und Frau ruft er uns: Vom nicht-sexistischen Gebrauch der Bibel.* Edited by Letty M. Russell. Munich: Pfeiffer, 1979.

Russell, Letty M., ed. *Als Mann und Frau ruft er uns: Vom nicht-sexistischen Gebrauch der Bibel.* Munich: Pfeiffer, 1979.

Russell, Letty M., and Shannon Clarkson, eds. *Dictionary of Feminist Theologies.* Louisville: Westminster John Knox, 1996.

Safrai, Chana, and Micah Halpern, eds. *Jewish Legal Writings by Women.* Jerusalem: Urim, 1998.

———, eds. *Women Out Women In* [Hebrew]. Tel Aviv: Yedioth Ahronoth, 2008.

Said, Edward W. *Culture and Imperialism.* New York: Vintage, 1994.

———. *Orientalism.* New York: Vintage, 1979.

Sakenfeld, Katharine Doob. "Feminist Uses of the Biblical Materials." Pages 55–64 in *Feminist Interpretation of the Bible.* Edited by Letty M. Russell. Philadelphia: Westminster, 1985.

———. "Old Testament Perspectives: Methodological Issues." *JSOT* 22 (1982): 13–20.

Salevsky, Heidemarie. "Auf der Suche nach der Wahrheit bei der Bibelübersetzung: Ein Beitrag aus translationswissenschaftlicher Sicht am Beispiel der Hagar-Geschichte (Gen 16; 21; 25)." Pages 5–30 in *Heidemarie Salevsky: Aspekte der Translation: Ausgewählte Beiträge zur Translation und Translationswissenschaft.* Edited by Ina Müller. Frankfurt: Lang, 2009.

Salevsky, Heidemarie, collaborating with Ina Müller and Bernd Salevsky. *Translationswissenschaft: Ein Kompendium.* Frankfurt: Lang, 2002.

Samartha, Stanley J. "The Asian Context: Sources and Trends." Pages 36–49 in *Voices from the Margin: Interpreting the Bible in the Third World.* London: SPCK, 1991.

Savic, Svenka. *Feminist Theology* [Serbian]. Novi Sad: Futura publikacije, 1999.

Sawicki, Jana. *Disciplining Foucault: Feminism, Power, and the Body.* New York: Routledge, 1991.

Scanzoni, Letha, and Nancy Hardesty. *All We're Meant to Be: A Biblical Approach to Women's Liberation.* Waco, Tex.: Word, 1974.

Schaberg, Jane. *The Illegitimacy of Jesus: A Feminist Theological Interpretation of the Infancy Narratives.* San Francisco: Harper & Row, 1987.

———. *The Resurrection of Mary Magdalene: Legends, Apocrypha, and the Christian Testament.* New York: Continuum: 2004.

Schaberg, Jane, Alice Bach, and Esther Fuchs, eds. *On the Cutting Edge: The Study of Women in Biblical Worlds.* New York: Continuum, 2004.

Schaller, J. B. "Gen 1.2 im antiken Judentum." Ph.D. diss. Göttingen, 1961.

Schaumberger, Christine. "Wir lassen uns nicht länger abspreisen! Überlegungen zur feministischen Suche nach Liturgie als Brot zum Leben." Pages 43–58 in *Meine Seele sieht das Land der Freiheit: Feministische Liturgien–Modelle für die Praxis.* Edited by Christine Hojenski, Birgit Hübner, Reinhild Hundrup, and Martina Meyer. Münster: Edition liberación, 1990.

Schierling, Marla. "Woman as Leaders in the Marcan Communities." *Listening* 15 (1980): 250–56.

Schloeman, Johan. "Und die Weisheit wurde Materie." *Süddeutsche Zeitung.* 23–24 December 2006.

Schmidt, Eva Renate, Mieke Korenhof, and Renate Jost. *Feministisch gelesen.* 2 vols. Stuttgart: Kreuz, 1989.

Schmidt, Wilhelm. "Die Uroffenbarung als Anfang der Offenbarung Gottes." Pages 479–632 in vol. 1 of *Religion, Christentum, Kirche.* Edited by Gerhard Esser and Joseph Mausbach. München, 1911.

Schneider, Laurel. *Beyond Monotheism: A Theology of Multiplicity.* London: Routledge, 2008.

Schneider, Tammi J. *Mothers of Promise: Women in the Book of Genesis.* Grand Rapids: Baker, 2008.

Schneiders, Sandra M. *Women and the Word.* New York: Paulist, 1986.

Scholz, Susanne, ed. *Biblical Studies Alternatively.* Upper Saddle River, N.J.: Prentice Hall, 2002.

———. "The Christian Right's Discourse on Gender and the Bible." *JFSR* 21.1 (2005): 81–100.

———, ed. *Feminist Interpretation of the Hebrew Bible in Retrospect: Biblical Books (Vol. 1).* Sheffield: Sheffield Phoenix, 2013.

———, ed. *God Loves Diversity and Justice: Progressive Scholars Speak about Faith, Politics, and the World.* Lanham, Md.: Lexington Books, 2013.

———. *Introducing the Women's Hebrew Bible.* London: T&T Clark, 2007.

———. *Rape Plots: A Feminist Cultural Study of Genesis 34.* Bern: Lang, 2000.

———. *Sacred Witness: Rape in the Hebrew Bible.* Minneapolis: Fortress, 2010.

Schottroff, Luise. *Befreiungserfahrungen: Studien zur Sozialgeschichte des Neuen Testaments.* Munich: Kaiser, 1990.

———. "'…Damit im Namen Jesus sich jedes Knie beuge': Christologie in 1 Kor und in Phil 2,9–11." Pages 81–94 in *Christus und seine Geschwister: Christologie im Umfeld der Bibel in gerechter Sprache.* Edited by Marlene Crüsemann and Carsten Jochum-Bortfeld. Gütersloh: Gütersloher, 2009.

———. *Lydias ungeduldige Schwestern: Feministische Sozialgeschichte des frühen Christentums.* Gütersloh: Gütersloher, 1994. English edition: *Lydia's Impatient Sisters: Feminist Social History of Early* Christianity. Louisville:Westminster John Knox, 1995.

———. "The Sayings Source Q." Pages 510–34 in *A Feminist Commentary.* Vol. 2 of *Searching the Scriptures.* Edited by Elisabeth Schüssler Fiorenza. New York: Crossroad, 1994.

————. "Stellungnahme zum theologischen Gutachten von Ulrich Wilckens zur Bibel in gerechter Sprache." in *epd-Dokumentation* 31 (2007): 34–37.

————. "Votum zur Bibel in gerechter Sprache in Zürich 9.11.2006." Online: http://www.bibel-in- gerechter-sprache.de/downloads/schottroffzuerich.pdf.

Schottroff, Luise, and Claudia Janssen. "Übersetzungsfragen zu Herrschaft und Sklaverei." Pages 212–21 in *Die Bibel–Übersetzt in gerechte Sprache? Grundlagen einer neuen Übersetzung.* Edited by Helga Kuhlmann. Gütersloh: Gütersloher, 2005.

Schottroff, Luise, Silvia Schroer, and Marie-Theres Wacker, eds. *Feministische Exegese: Forschungserträge zur Bibel aus der Perspektive von Frauen.* Darmstadt: Primus, 1995. English edition: *Feminist Interpretation: The Bible in Women's Perspective.* Minneapolis: Fortress, 1998.

Schottroff, Luise, and Dorothee Sölle. *Jesus von Nazareth.* Munich: Deutscher Taschenbuch, 2000.

Schottroff, Luise, and Marie-Theres Wacker, eds. *Kompendium Feministische Bibelauslegung.* 3rd ed. Gütersloh: Gütersloher, 2007.

————, eds. *Von der Wurzel getragen: Christlich-feministische Exegese in Auseinandersetzung mit Antijudaismus.* Leiden: Brill, 1996.

Schottroff, Willy, and Wolfgang Stegemann, eds. *Frauen in der Bibel.* Vol. 2 of *Traditionen der Befreiung: Sozialgeschichtliche Bibelauslegungen.* Munich: Kaiser, 1980.

Schroer, Silvia. "Diachronic Sections." Pages 109–44 in *Feminist Interpretation: The Bible in Women's Perspective.* Edited by Luise Schottroff, Silvia Schroer, and Marie-Theres Wacker. Minneapolis: Fortress, 1998.

Schroer, Silvia, and Sophia Bietenhard, eds. *Feminist Interpretation of the Bible and the Hermeneutics of Liberation.* London: Sheffield Academic Press, 2003.

Schüngel-Straumann, Helen. *Anfänge feministischer Exegese: Gesammelte Beiträge, mit einem orientierenden Nachwort und einer Auswahlbibliographie.* Münster: LIT, 2002.

————. *Denn Gott bin ich, und kein Mann: Gottesbilder im Ersten Testament–feministisch betrachtet.* Mainz: Grünewald, 1996.

————. "Die Frage der Gottebenbildlichkeit der Frau." Pages 63–76 in *Theologie des Alten Testaments aus der Perspektive von Frauen.* Edited by Manfred Oeming and Gerd Theissen. Münster: LIT, 2003.

————. *Die Frau am Anfang: Eva und die Folgen.* 3rd ed. Münster: LIT, 1999.

————. "Frauen in der Bibel." *Der evangelische Erzieher* 34 (1982): 496–506.

————. "God as Mother in Hosea 11," in *TD* 34 (1987): 3–8. First published as "Gott als Mutter in Hosea 11." *ThQ* 166 (1986): 119–34.

————. "Mann und Frau in den Schöpfungstexten von Genesis 1–3 unter Berücksichtigung der innerbiblischen Wirkungsgeschichte." Pages 142–66 in *Mann und Frau–Grundproblem theologischer Anthropologie.* Edited by Theodor Schneider. QD 121. Herder: Freiburg, 1989.

————. "On the Creation of Man and Woman in Genesis 1–3: The History and Reception of the Texts Reconsidered." Pages 53–76 in *A Feminist Companion to Genesis.* Edited by Athalya Brenner. Sheffield Academic Press, 1993.

————. *Rûah bewegt die Welt: Gottes schöpferische Lebenskraft in der Krisenzeit des Exils.* SBS 151. Stuttgart: Katholisches Bibelwerk, 1992.

———. *"Tamar–Eine Frau verschafft sich ihr Recht."* *BiKi* 39 (1984): 148–57.

. Schüssler Fiorenza, Elisabeth. *The Book of Revelation: Justice and Judgment.* Philadelphia: Fortress, 1985.

———. *Bread Not Stone: The Challenge of Feminist Biblical Interpretation.* Boston: Beacon, 1985. German edition: *Brot statt Steine: Die Herausforderung einer feministischen Interpretation der Bibel,* Freiburg: Ed. Exodus,1988.

———. *But She Said: Feminist Practices of Biblical Interpretation.* Boston: Beacon, 1992.

———. "Celebrating Feminist Work by Knowing It." *JFSR* 27.1 (2011): 97–127.

———. *Changing Horizons: Explorations in Feminist Interpretation.* Minneapolis: Fortress, 2013.

———. *Democratizing Biblical Studies: Toward an Emancipatory Educational Space.* Louisville: Westminster John Knox, 2009.

———. *Discipleship of Equals: A Critical Feminist Ekklesia-logy of Liberation.* New York: Crossroad, 1993.

———. *Empowering Memory and Movement: Thinking and Working across Borders,* Minneapolis: Fortress, 2014.

———. "The Ethics of Biblical Interpretation: Decentering Biblical Scholarship." *JBL* 107 (1988): 3–17. Cited in its reprinted version in *Rhetoric and Ethic,* 17–30.

———, ed. *A Feminist Commentary.* Vol. 2 of *Searching the Scriptures.* New York: Crossroad, 1994.

———, ed. *A Feminist Introduction.* Vol. 1 of *Searching the Scriptures.* New York: Crossroad, 1993.

———. "Gender, Sprache, und Religion: Feministisch-Theologische Anfragen." Pages 83–90 in *Erträge: 60 Jahre Augustana.* Neuendettelsau: Augustana Hochschule, 2008.

———. *Gesù, Figlio di Miriam, Profeta della Sofia: Questioni Critiche di Cristologia Femminista.* Sola Scriptura. Turin: Claudiana, 1996.

———. *Grenzen überschreiten: Der theoretische Anspruch feministischer Theologie.* Münster: LIT, 2004.

———. *In Memory of Her: A Feminist Theological Reconstruction of Christian Origins.* New York: Crossroad, 1983. German edition: *Zu ihrem Gedächtnis: Eine feministisch-theologische Rekonstruktion der christlichen Ursprünge* (Munich: Kaiser, 1988).

———. "Introduction: Exploring the Intersections of Race, Gender, Status, and Ethnicity in Early Christian Studies." Pages 1–23 in *Prejudice and Christian Beginnings: Investigating Race, Gender, and Ethnicity in Early Christian Studies.* Edited by Laura Nasrallah and Elisabeth Schüssler Fiorenza. Minneapolis: Fortress, 2009.

———. "Introduction: Transgressing Canonical Boundaries." Pages 1–14 in *A Feminist Commentary.* Vol. 2 of *Searching the Scriptures.* Edited by Elisabeth Schüssler Fiorenza with the assistance of Ann Brock and Shelly Matthews. New York: Crossroad, 1994.

———. *Jesus and the Politics of Interpretation.* New York: Continuum, 2000.

———. *Jesus: Miriam's Child, Sophia's Prophet: Critical Issues in Feminist Christology.* New York: Continuum, 1994.

———. *Jesus–Mirjams Kind, Sophias Prophet: Kritische Anfragen feministischer Christologie*. Gütersloh: Gütersloher, 1997.

———. "Missionaries, Apostles, Coworkers: Romans 16 and the Reconstruction of Women's Early Christian History." *WW* 6 (1986): 420–33.

———. *The Power of the Word: Scripture and the Rhetoric of Empire*. Minneapolis: Fortress, 2007.

———. "Reaffirming Feminist/Womanist Biblical Scholarship." *Enc* 67/4 (Autumn 2006): 361–73.

———. "Religion, Gender, and Society: Shaping the Discipline of Religious/Theological Studies." Pages 85–99 in *The Relevance of Theology*. Edited by Carl Reinhold Bråckenhielm and Gunhild Winqvist Hollman. Uppsala: Uppsala University Press, 2002.

———. "Re-visioning Christian Origins." Pages 225–50 in *Christian Origins: Worship, Belief, and Society*. Edited by Kieran O'Mahoney. London: Sheffield Academic Press, 2003.

———. *Rhetoric and Ethic: The Politics of Biblical Studies*. Minneapolis: Fortress, 1999.

———. *Sharing Her Word: Feminist Biblical Interpretation in Context*. Boston: Beacon, 1998.

———. "The Study of Women in Early Christianity: Some Methodological Considerations." Pages 30–58 in *Critical History and Biblical Faith: New Testament Perspectives*. Edited by Thomas J. Ryan. Villanova, Penn.: College Theology Society, 1979.

———. "Toward an Intersectional Analytic: Race, Gender, Ethnicity, and Empire in Early Christian Studies." Pages 1–24 in *Prejudice and Christian Beginnings*. Edited by Laura Nasrallah and Elisabeth Schüssler Fiorenza. Minneapolis: Fortress, 2009.

———. *Transforming Vision: Explorations in Feminist The*logy*. Minneapolis: Fortress, 2011.

———. "The Will to Choose or to Reject: Continuing Our Critical Work." Pages 125–36 in *Feminist Interpretation of the Bible*. Edited by Letty M. Russell. Philadelphia: Westminster, 1985.

———. *Wisdom Ways: Introducing Feminist Biblical Interpretation*. Maryknoll, N.Y.: Orbis, 2001.

———. "Women in the Early Christian Movement." Pages 84–92 in *Womanspirit Rising: A Feminist Reader in Religion*. Edited by Carol P. Christ and Judith Plaskow. New York: Harper & Row, 1979.

———. "Women in the Pre-Pauline and Pauline Churches." *USQR* 33 (1978): 153–66.

———. "Word, Spirit, and Power: Women in Early Christian Communities." Pages 30–70 in *Women of Spirit: Female Leadership in the Jewish and Christian Traditions*. Edited by Rosemary Radford Ruether and Eleanor McLaughlin. New York: Simon & Schuster, 1979.

———. "'You Are Not to Be Called Father': Early Christian History in a Feminist Perspective." *Cross Currents* 29/3 (1978): 301–23.

———. *Zu ihrem Gedächtnis: Eine feministisch-theologische Rekonstruktion der urchristlichen Ursprünge*. Translated by C. Schaumberger. Munich: Kaiser, 1988.

Schüssler Fiorenza, Elisabeth, and Kent Richards, eds. *Transforming Graduate Biblical Education: Ethos and Discipline.* SBLGPBS. Atlanta: Society of Biblical Literature, 2010.

Schwartz, Regina M. *The Curse of Cain: The Violent Legacy of Monotheism.* Chicago: University of Chicago Press, 1997.

Scroggs, Robin. "Paul and the Eschatological Woman." *JAAR* 40 (1972): 283–303.

———. "Paul and the Eschatological Woman: Revisited." *JAAR* 42 (1974): 532–37.

Sebastiani, Lilia. *Svolte: Donne negli snodi del cammino di Gesù.* Assisi: Cittadella, 2008.

———. *Tra/Sfigurazioni.* Brescia: Queriniana, 1992.

Sedgwick, Eve Kosofsky. *Between Men: English Literature and Male Homosocial Desire.* New York: Columbia University Press, 1985.

———. *Epistemology of the Closet.* Berkeley: University of California Press, 1990.

Segovia, Fernando F. *Decolonizing Biblical Studies: A View from the Margins.* Maryknoll, N.Y.: Orbis, 2000.

———, ed. *Toward a New Heaven and a New Earth: Essays in Honor of Elisabeth Schüssler Fiorenza.* Maryknoll, N.Y.: Orbis, 2003.

Segovia, Fernando F., and Mary Ann Tolbert, eds. *Social Location and Biblical Interpretation in Global Perspective.* Vol. 2 of *Reading from This Place.* Minneapolis: Fortress, 2000.

———, eds. *Social Location and Biblical Interpretation in the United States.* Vol. 1 of *Reading from This Place.* Minneapolis: Fortress, 1995.

Seim, Turid Karlsen. *The Double Message.* Nashville: Abingdon, 1994.

Sered, Susan. "Jewish Women and the Shekhina." Pages 78–90 in *In the Power of Wisdom: Feminist Spiritualities of Struggle.* Concilium 5. Edited by Elisabeth Schüssler Fiorenza and María Pilar Aquino. London: SCM, 200.

Sherwood, Yvonne. *A Biblical Text and Its Afterlives: The Survival of Jonah in Western Culture.* Cambridge: Cambridge University Press, 2000.

Showalter, Elaine, ed. *The New Feminist Criticism: Essays on Women, Literature, and Theory.* New York: Pantheon, 1985.

Siegele-Wenschkewitz, Leonore. *Verdrängte Vergangenheit, die uns bedrängt: Feministische Theologie in der Verantwortung für die Geschichte.* Munich: Kaiser, 1988.

Sigg-Suter, Ursula, Esther Straub, and Angela Wäffler-Boveland. *"… Und ihr werdet mir Söhne und Töchter sein." Die neue Zürcher Bibel feministisch gelesen.* Zürich: Theologischer Verlag Zürich, 2007.

Sjöberg, Mikael. *Wrestling with Textual Violence.* Sheffield: Sheffield Phoenix, 2006.

Smith, Andrea. "Heteropatriarchy and the Three Pillars of White Supremacy." Pages 66–73 in *The Color of Violence: The Incite! Anthology.* Edited by INCITE! Women of Color against Violence. Boston: South End, 2006.

Smith, Barbara, ed. *Home Girls: A Black Feminist Anthology.* New York: Kitchen Table: Women of Color, 1983.

Soavo, María. "Nosotras que tenemos alas y sabemos volar: Una hermenéutica ecofeminista de Isaías 34:8–17." *RIBLA* 41 (2002): 64–82.

Soto, Aida. "Lidia, la vendedora de púrpura, una alternativa de economía doméstica (experiencias bíblicas)." *RIBLA* 51 (2005): 102–5.

Spahic-Siljak, Zilka. *Women, Religion, and Politics.* Sarajevo: IMIC Zajedno, 2010.

Spahic-Siljak, Zilka, and Rebeka Anic. *Women Believers and Citizens* [Bosnian]. Sarajevo: TPO Foundation, 2009.

Spivak, Gayatri Chakravorty. "Can the Subaltern Speak?" Pages 66–111 in *Colonial Discourse and Post-Colonial Theory: A Reader*. Edited by Patrick Williams and Laura Chrisman. New York: Columbia University Press, 1994.

St. Clair, Raquel A. *Call and Consequences: A Womanist Reading of Mark*. Minneapolis: Fortress, 2008.

———. "Womanist Biblical Interpretation." Pages 54–62 in *True To Our Native Land: An African American New Testament Commentary*. Edited by Brian K. Blount. Minneapolis: Fortress, 2007.

Stanton, Elizabeth Cady. *The Woman's Bible*. Boston: Northeastern University Press, 1993. First published in 1895.

Stein, David E. S. *The Contemporary Torah: A Gender-Sensitive Adaptation of the JPS Translation*. Philadelphia: Jewish Publication Society, 2006.

Stein, Dina. "A Maidservant and Her Master's Voice: Discourse, Identity, and Eros in Rabbinic Texts." *JHS* 10 (2001): 375–97.

Stendahl, Krister. *The Bible and the Role of Women*. Philadelphia: Fortress, 1966.

Stenström, Hanna. *The Book of Revelation: A Vision of the Ultimate Liberation Or the Ultimate Backlash? A Study in 20th Century Interpretations of Rev 14:1-5, with Special Emphasis on Feminist Exegesis*. Uppsala: Uppsala University Press, 1999.

Stone, Ken. "The Garden of Eden and the Heterosexual Contract." Pages 57–70 in *Take Back the Word: A Queer Reading of the Bible*. Edited by Robert E. Goss and Mona West. Cleveland: Pilgrim, 2000.

———. "Gender and Homosexuality in Judges 19: Subject-Honor, Object-Shame?" *JSOT* 67 (1995): 87–107.

———. "The Hermeneutics of Abomination: On Gay Men, Canaanites, and Biblical Interpretation." *BTB* 27/2 (1997): 36–41.

———. *Practicing Safer Texts: Food, Sex, and Bible in Queer Perspective*. London: T&T Clark, 2005.

———. *Queer Commentary and the Hebrew Bible*. Cleveland: Pilgrim, 2001.

Strahm, Doris, and Regula Strobel, eds. *Vom Verlangen nach Heilwerden: Christologie in feministisch-theologischer Sicht*. Fribourg: Edition Exodus, 1991.

Strauss, Mark L. "Current Issues in the Gender-Language Debate: A Response to Vern Poythress and Wayne Grudem." Pages 115–41 in *The Challenge of Bible Translation: Communicating God's Word to the World*. Edited by Glen G. Scorgie, Mark L. Strauss, and Steven M. Voth. Grand Rapids: Zondervan, 2003.

———. *Distorting Scripture? The Challenge of Bible Translation and Gender Accuracy*. Downers Grove, Ill.: InterVarsity Press, 1998.

Stroher, Marga. "Caminos de resistencia, en las fronteras del poder normativo: Un estudio de las Cartas Pastorales en la perspectiva feminista." Ph.D. diss., Escola Superior de Teologia, Instituto Ecumenico de Pós-gradução, São Leopoldo, RS, 2002.

Strotmann, Angelika. "Weisheitschristologie ohne Antijudaismus? Gedanken zu einem bisher vernachlässigten Aspekt in der Diskussion um die Weisheitschristologie im Neuen Testament." Pages 153–75 in *Von der Wurzel getragen: Christ-*

lich-feministische Exegese in Auseinandersetzung mit Antijudaismus. Edited by Luise Schottroff and Marie-Theres Wacker. Leiden: Brill, 1996.

Sugarman, Yerra. "Pharaoh's Daughter/King Solomon's Wife: Fragments from Her Diaries; Pharaoh's Daughter/King Solomon's Wife: A Letter Home; From King Solomon's Journal: Fragment of an Unsent Letter (Date Unknown)." *JFSR* 23.1 (2007): 43–53.

Sugirtharajah, R. S. *Asian Biblical Hermeneutics and Postcolonialism: Contesting the Interpretations*. Maryknoll, N.Y.: Orbis, 1998.

———. *The Bible and the Third World: Precolonial, Colonial, and Postcolonial Encounters*. New York: Cambridge University Press, 2001.

Swidler, Leonard. "Jesus Was a Feminist." *Catholic World* (January 1971): 177–83.

Swidler, Leonard, and Arlene Swidler, eds. *Women Priests: A Catholic Commentary on the Vatican Declaration*. New York: Paulist, 1977.

Tamez, Elsa. *The Amnesty of Grace: Justification by Faith from a Latin Perspective*. Translated by Sharon Ringe. Nashville: Abingdon, 1993.

———. "The Bible and the Five Hundred Years of Conquest." Pages 13–26 in *Voices from the Margin: Interpreting the Bible in the Third World*. Rev. ed. Edited by R. S. Sugirtharajah. Maryknoll, N.Y.: Orbis, 2006.

———. *The Bible of the Oppressed*. Translated by Matthew J. O'Connell. Maryknoll, N.Y.: Orbis, 1979.

———. "Hermenéutica Feminista en América Latina y el Caribe: Una mirada retrospectiva." Pages 43–66 *Religión y género*. Vol. 3 of *Enciclopedia Iberoamericana de religiones*. Edited by Sylvia Marcos. Madrid: Trotta, 2004.

———. "Introduction: The Power of the Naked." Pages 1–14 in *Through Her Eyes: Women's Theology from Latin America*. Edited by Elsa Tamez. Translated by Jeltje Aukema. Maryknoll, N.Y.: Orbis, 1989.

———. "La mujer como sujeto de producción teológica," *Servir* 88/89 (1980): 461–78.

———. *Luchas de Poder en los orígenes del cristianismo: Un estudio de 1 Timoteo*. Santander: Sal Terrae, 2005. English Edition: *Struggles for Power in Early Christianity*. Maryknoll, N.Y.: Orbis, 2007.

———. "Pautas hermenéuticas para comprender Gálatas 3:28 y 1 Corintos 14:34." *RIBLA* (1993): 9–18.

———. *The Scandalous Message of James: Faith without Works Is Dead*. New York: Crossroad, 2002.

———. *Struggles for Power in Early Christianity: A Study of the First Letter of Timothy*. Maryknoll, N.Y.: Orbis, 2007.

———. "Women's Lives as Sacred Texts." Pages 57–64 in *Women's Sacred Scriptures*. Edited by Kwok Pui-lan and Elisabeth Schüssler Fiorenza. London: SCM, 1998.

———. "Women's Rereading of the Bible." Pages 48–57 in *Voices from the Margin: Interpreting the Bible in the Third World*. Edited by R. S. Sugirtharajah. Maryknoll, N.Y.: Orbis, 1995.

Tan Yak-hwee. *Re-presenting the Johannine Community: A Postcolonial Perspective*. New York: Lang, 2008.

Tatman, Lucy. "Wisdom." Pages 236–40 in *An A to Z of Feminist Theology*. Edited by Lisa Isherwood and Dorothea McEwan. Sheffield: Sheffield Academic Press, 1996.

Taussig, Hal. "The End of Christian Origins? Where to Turn at the Intersection of Subjectivity and Historical Craft." *RBL* 13 (2011): 1–46.

Thiel, Christiane, ed. *Tageslesebuch: Bibel in gerechter Sprache für jeden Tag des Jahres.* Gütersloh: Gütersloher, 2008.

Tolbert, Mary Ann. "Defining the Problem: The Bible and Feminist Hermeneutics." *Semeia* 28 (1983): 113–26.

———. "Foreword: What Word Shall We Take Back?" Pages vii–xii in *Take Back the Word: A Queer Reading of the Bible.* Edited by Robert E. Goss and Mona West. Cleveland: Pilgrim, 2000.

———. "The Politics and Poetics of Location." Pages 305–17 in *Reading from This Place: Social Location and Biblical Interpretation in the United States.* Edited by Fernando F. Segovia and Mary Ann Tolbert. Minneapolis: Fortress, 1995

———. "Reading the Bible with Authority: Feminist Interrogation of the Canon." Pages 141–62 in *Escaping Eden: New Feminist Perspectives on the Bible.* Edited by Harold C. Washington, Susan Lochrie Graham, and Pamela Thimmes. New York: New York University Press, 1999.

———. *Sowing the Gospel: Mark's Work in Literary-Historical Perspective.* Minneapolis: Augsburg Fortress, 1996.

Torjesen, Karen Jo. *When Women Were Priests: Women's Leadership in the Early Church and the Scandal of Their Subordination in the Rise of Christianity.* San Francisco: HarperCollins, 1993.

Törnkvist, Rut. *The Use and Abuse of Female Sexual Imagery in the Book of Hosea: A Feminist Critical Approach to Hos 1–3.* Uppsala: Uppsala University Library, 1998.

Totontle, Mositi. *The Victims.* Gaborone: Botsalo, 1993.

Tran, Mai-Anh Le. "Lot's Wife, Ruth, and Tô Thị: Gender and Racial Representation in a Theological Feast of Stories." Pages 123–36 in *Ways of Being, Ways of Reading: Asian American Biblical Interpretation.* Edited by Mary Foskett and Jeffrey Kahjin Kuan. St. Louis: Chalice, 2006.

Trible, Phyllis. "Depatriarchalizing in Biblical Interpretation." *JAAR* 41 (March 1973): 30–48.

———, ed. "The Effects of Women's Studies on Biblical Studies." *JSOT* 22 (1982): 3–71

———. "Eve and Adam: Genesis 2–3 Reread." *ANQ* 13 (1973): 251–58. Reprinted as pages 74–83 in *Womanspirit Rising: A Feminist Reader in Religion.* Edited by Carol P. Christ and Judith Plaskow. New York: Harper & Row, 1979.

———. "Feminist Hermeneutics and Biblical Studies." Pages 23–29 in *Feminist Theology: A Reader.* Edited by Ann Loades. Louisville: Westminster John Knox, 1990.

———. "Gegen das patriarchalische Prinzip in Bibelinterpretationen." Pages 93–117 in *Frauenbefreiung: Biblische und theologische Argumente.* Edited by Elisabeth Moltmann-Wendel. 2nd ed. Munich: Kaiser, 1978.

———. *God and the Rhetoric of Sexuality.* OBT. Philadelphia: Fortress, 1978.

———. *Rhetorical Criticism: Context, Method, and the Book of Jonah.* Minneapolis: Fortress, 1994.

———. "Take Back the Bible." *RevExp* 97 (Fall 2000): 425–31.

———. *Texts of Terror: Literary-Feminist Readings of Biblical Narratives.* OBT. Philadelphia: Fortress, 1984.

Trömel-Plötz, Senta. "Sprache: Von Frauensprache zu frauengerechter Sprache. " Pages 748–51 in *Handbuch Frauen- und Geschlechterforschung: Theorie, Methoden, Empirie*. Edited by Ruth Becker and Beate Kortendiek. Wiesbaden: Verlag für Sozialwissenschaften, 2004.

———, ed. *Gewalt durch Sprache: Die Vergewaltigung von Frauen in Gesprächen.* Frankfurt: Fischer Taschenbuch, 1984.

Tsokkinnen, Anni. "Elisabeth Schüssler Fiorenza on the Authority of the Bible." *Yearbook of the European Society of Women in Theological Research,* vol. 12 (2004): 133–42.

Tzabedze, Joyce. "Women in the Church (1 Timothy 2:8–15, Ephesians 5:22)." Pages 76–79 in *New Eyes for Reading Biblical and Theological Reflections by Women from the Third World.* Edited by John Pobee and Barbel von Wartenberg-Porter. Geneva: WCC, 1986.

Ukpong, Justine. "Developments in Biblical Interpretation in Africa: Historical and Hermeneutical Directions." Pages 11–28 in *The Bible in Africa: Transactions, Trajectories, and Trends.* Boston: Brill, 2001.

Unruh, Rita, and Waltraud Thiel. "Frau sein–Fremd sein–Offen sein: Mit t.a.n.g.o. zum ersten Frauen-Trialog in Berlin." In *In Spiralen fliegen: Bibliodrama und TZI [Themenzentrierte Interaktion] interkulturell.* Edited by Margarete Pauschert and Antje Röckermann. Münster: Schlangenbrut, 1999.

Upton, Bridget Gilfillan. "Feminist Theology as Biblical Hermeneutics." Pages 97–113 in *Cambridge Companion to Feminist Theology.* Edited by Susan Frank Parsons. Cambridge: Cambridge University Press, 2002.

Vaccari, Michela. *Lavoratrice del pensiero: Elisa Salerno, una teologa ante litteram.* Sui generis 7. Cantalupa-Torino: Effatà, 2010.

Vahrenhorst, Martin. *"Ihr sollt überhaupt nicht schwören": Matthäus im halachischen Diskurs.* Neukirchen-Vluyn: Neukirchener, 2002.

Valerio, Adriana. *Donne e Bibbia: Storia ed esegesi.* La Bibbia nella storia 21. Bologna: Dehoniane, 2006.

Vander Stichele, Caroline. "Der Herr? Das geht nicht mehr! Die Wiedergabe des Tetragramms in der neuen niederländischen Bibelübersetzung." Pages 318–27 in *"Gott bin ich, kein Mann": Beiträge zur Hermeneutik der biblischen Gottesrede."* Edited by Ilona Riedel-Spangenberger and Erich Zenger. Paderborn: Schöningh, 2006.

———. "The Lord Can No Longer Be Taken for Granted: The Rendering of JHWH in the New Dutch Bible Translation." Pages 179–87 in *Women, Ritual, and Liturgy—Ritual und Liturgie von Frauen—Femmes, rituel et liturgie.* Edited by Susan K. Roll, Annette Esser, and Brigitte Enzner-Probst. ESWTR Yearbook 9. Leuven: Peeters, 2001.

Vander Stichele, Caroline, and Todd Penner. *Contextualizing Gender in Early Christian Discourse: Thinking Beyond Thecla.* London: T&T Clark, 2009.

———, eds. *Her Master's Tools? Feminist and Postcolonial Engagements of Historical-Critical Discourse.* Atlanta: Society of Biblical Literature, 2005.

Ventura, Tirsa. *Cuerpos Peregrinos: Un estudio desde la opresión y resistencia desde el género, clase y etnia, Salmos 120–134.* San José: DEI, 2008.

———. "Un cusita habla ¡como el Dios del profeta!: Una lectura de Jeremías 38:7–13." *RIBLA* 54 (2006): 48–54.

Visser't Hooft, Henriette. *Eva, wo bist du? Frauen in internationalen Organisationen der Ökumene: Eine Dokumentation.* Gelnhausen: Burckhardthaus-Laetare, 1991.

Vries, Anneke de, and Manuela Kalsky. "Ein Name, der ein Geheimnis bleibt." *Junge Kirche* 63 (2002): 22–25.

Vriezen, Theodoor C. "Onderzoek naar de Paradijsvoorstelling bij de oude semietische Volken." Ph.D. diss. Utrecht, 1937.

Wacker, Marie-Theres. "Geschichtliche, hermeneutische und methodologische Grundlagen." Pages 3–79 in *Feministische Exegese: Forschungsbeiträge zur Bibel aus der Perspektive von Frauen.* Edited by Luise Schottroff, Silvia Schroer, and Marie-Theres Wacker. Darmstadt: Wissenschaftliche, 1995.

Wahlberg, Rachel Conrad. *Jesus According to a Woman.* New York: Paulist, 1975.

Wainwright, Elaine M. *Towards a Feminist Critical Reading of the Gospel according to Matthew.* Berlin: de Gruyter, 1991.

———. *Women Healing/Healing Women: The Genderization of Healing in Early Christianity.* London: Equinox, 2006.

Wakeman, Mary. "Biblical Prophecy and Modern Feminism." Pages 67–86 in *Beyond Androcentrism: New Essays on Women and Religion.* Edited by Rita Gross. Missoula, Mont.: Scholars Press for the American Academy of Religion, 1977.

Walby, Sylvia. *Theorizing Patriarchy.* Oxford: Basil, 1990.

Walker, Alice. *In Search of Our Mothers' Gardens: Womanist Prose.* San Diego: Harcourt Brace Jovanovich, 1983.

Walters, Jonathan. "Invading the Roman Body: Manliness and Impenetrability in Roman Thought." Pages 29–43 in *Roman Sexualities.* Edited by Judith P. Hallett and Marilyn B. Skinner. Princeton: Princeton University Press, 1997.

———. "'No More Than a Boy': The Shifting Construction of Masculinity from Ancient Greece to the Middle Ages." *Gender and History* 5 (1991): 20–33.

Wartenberg-Potter, Bärbel. *EFD-Mitteilungen* 434 (2006): 42.

Washington, Harold C. "Violence and the Construction of Gender in the Hebrew Bible: A New Historicist Approach." *BibInt* 5 (1997): 324–63.

Washington, Harold C., Susan Lochrie Graham, and Pamela Thimmes, eds. *Escaping Eden: New Feminist Perspectives on the Bible.* New York: New York University Press, 1999.

Way, Peggy. "Authority of Possibility for Women in the Church." Pages 77–94 in *Women's Liberation and the Church: The New Demand for Freedom in the Life of the Christian Church.* Edited by Sarah Bentley Doely. New York: Association Press, 1970.

Weber, Lynn. *Understanding Race, Class, Gender, and Sexuality: A Conceptual Framework.* 2nd ed. New York: Oxford University Press, 2010.

Weems, Renita J. *Battered Love: Marriage, Sex, and Violence in the Hebrew Prophets.* Minneapolis: Fortress, 1995.

———. "The Hebrew Women Are Not Like the Egyptian Women: The Ideology of Race, Gender, and Sexual Reproduction in Exodus 1." *Semeia* 59 (1992): 25–34.

————. *Just a Sister Away: A Womanist Vision of Women's Relationships in the Bible*. San Diego, Calif.: LuraMedia, 1988.

————. "Reading *Her Way* through the Struggle: African American Women and the Bible." Pages 57–77 in *Stony the Road We Trod: African American Biblical Interpretation*. Edited by Cain Hope Felder. Minneapolis: Fortress, 1991.

————. "Womanist Reflections on Biblical Hermeneutics." Pages 215–24 in *Black Theology: A Documentary History, Vol. 2: 1980–1992*. Edited by James H. Cone and Gayraud S. Wilmore. Maryknoll, N.Y.: Orbis, 1993.

Wegener, Hildburg. "Allen die Bibel, die sie brauchen." Pages 13–36 in *Die vergessenen Schwestern: Frauengerechte Sprache in der Bibelübersetzung*. Edited by Siegfried Meurer. Stuttgart: Jahrbuch der Deutschen Bibelgesellschaft, 1993.

————. "… Und macht die Menschen zu meinen Jüngern und Jüngerinnen: Die Revision der Gute Nachricht Bibel in gemäßigt 'frauengerechter Sprache.'" Pages 62–73 in *Die neue Gute Nachricht Bibel*. Edited by Hannelore Jahr. Stuttgart, 1998.

Wegner, Judith. *Chattel or Person? The Status of Women in the Mishnah*. New York: Oxford University Press, 1988.

Weiler, Lucía. "Jesús y la samaritana." *RIBLA* 15 (1993): 123–30.

Wessinger, Catherine. "Key Events for Women's Religious Leadership in the United States: Nineteenth and Twentieth Centuries." Pages 347–401 in *Religious Institutions and Women's Leadership: New Roles Inside the Mainstream*. Edited by Catherine Wessinger. Columbia: University of South Carolina Press, 1996.

West, Gerald. "(Ac)claiming the (Extra)Ordinary African 'Reader' of the Bible." Pages 29–47 in *Reading Other-Wise: Socially Engaged Biblical Scholars Reading with Their Local Communities*. Edited by Gerald O. West. Atlanta: Society of Biblical Literature, 2007.

Westermann, Claus. "*Ādām*." Pages 31–42 in vol. 1 of Theological Lexicon of the Old Testament. Edited by Ernst Jenni and Claus Westermann. Translated by Mark E. Biddle. 3 vols. Peabody, Mass.: Hendrickson, 1997.

"*Adam*." Pages 41–57 in vol. 1 of *Theologisches Handwörterbuch zum Alten Testament*. Edited by Ernst Jenni and Claus Westermann. 2 vols. Gütersloh: Gütersloher, 1994.

————. *Genesis 1–11*. Neukirchen: Neukirchener, 1974.

Wicker, Kathleen O'Brien, Althea Spencer Miller, and Musa W. Dube, eds. *Feminist New Testament Studies: Global and Future Perspectives (Religion/Culture/Critique)*. New York: Palgrave Macmillan, 2005.

Wierenga, Lambert. "'Jahwe' versus 'HEER': niets opgelost." *Nederlands Dagblad* (12.4.2001).

Wilckens, Ulrich. "Theologisches Gutachten zur 'Bibel in gerechter Sprache,'" in *epd-Dokumentation* 17/18 (2007): 24–38.

Wilder, Amos N. *The Language of the Gospel: Early Christian Rhetoric*. New York: Harper & Row, 1964.

————. "Scholars, Theologians, and Ancient Rhetoric." *JBL* 75 (1956): 1–11.

Williams, Craig A. *Roman Homosexuality: Ideologies of Masculinity in Classical Antiquity*. New York: Oxford University Press, 1999.

Williams, Delores S. "The Color of Feminism: Or, Speaking the Black Woman's Tongue." *JRT* 43 (1986): 42–58.

———. *Sisters in the Wilderness: The Challenge of Womanist God-Talk*. Maryknoll, N.Y.: Orbis, 1993.

———. "Womanist Theology: Black Women's Voices." Pages 265–72 in *Black Theology: A Documentary History [Volume 2: 1980–1992]*. Edited by James H. Cone and Gayraud S. Wilmore. Maryknoll, N.Y.: Orbis, 1993.

Wills, Lawrence M. *Not God's People: Insiders and Outsiders in the Biblical World*. Lanham: Rowman & Littlefield, 2008.

———. "A Response to the Roundtable Discussion 'Anti-Judaism and Postcolonial Biblical Interpretation.'" *JFSR* 20.2 (2004): 189–92.

Wilson, Nancy L. *Our Tribe: Queer Folks, God, Jesus, and the Bible*. San Francisco: Harper San Francisco, 1995.

Wimbush, Vincent L. "The Bible and African Americans: An Outline of an Interpretative History." Pages 81–97 in *Stony the Road We Trod: African American Biblical Interpretation*. Edited by Cain Hope Felder. Minneapolis: Fortress, 1991.

———. "Introduction: Reading Darkness, Reading Scriptures." Pages 1–43 in *African Americans and the Bible: Sacred Texts and Social Textures*. Edited by Vincent L. Wimbush, with the assistance of Rosamond C. Rodman. New York: Continuum, 2000.

———. "Introduction: TEXTureS, Gestures, Power: Orientation to Radical Excavation." Pages 1–20 in *Theorizing Scriptures: New Critical Orientations to a Cultural Phenomenon*. Edited by Vincent L. Wimbush. New Brunswick, N.J.: Rutgers University Press, 2008.

———, ed. *Theorizing Scriptures: New Critical Orientations to a Cultural Phenomenon*. New Brunswick, N.J.: Rutgers University Press, 2008.

———, ed., with the assistance of Rosamond C. Rodman. *African Americans and the Bible: Sacred Texts and Social Textures*. New York: Continuum, 2000.

Wink, Walter. *Bibelarbeit: Ein Praxisbuch für Theologen und Laien*. Kohlhammer: Stuttgart, 1982. Original publication: *Transforming Bible Study*. Nashville: Abingdon, 1981.

Winters, Alicia. "La Memoria Subversiva de una mujer, 2S 21: 1–13." *RIBLA* 13 (1992): 77–86.

Wire, Antoinette Clark. *The Corinthian Women Prophets: A Reconstruction through Paul's Rhetoric*. Minneapolis: Fortress, 1990.

Wittig, Monique. *The Straight Mind and Other Essays*. Boston: Beacon, 1992.

Yamaguchi, Satoko. "Father Image of G*d and Inclusive Language: A Reflection in Japan," Pages 199–224 in *Toward a New Heaven and a New Earth: Essays in Honor of Elisabeth Schüssler Fiorenza*. Edited by Fernando F. Segovia. Maryknoll, N.Y.: Orbis, 2003.

———. "From Dualistic Thinking toward Inclusive Imagination." Pages 53–71 in *Mapping and Engaging the Bible in Asian Cultures: Congress of the Society of Asian Biblical Studies 2008 Seoul Conference*. Edited by Yeong Mee Lee and Yoon Jong Yoo. Seoul: The Christian Literature Society of Korea, 2009.

Yee, Gale A. *Poor Banished Children of Eve: Woman as Evil in the Hebrew Bible.* Minneapolis: Fortress, 2003.

———. "Yin/Yang Is Not Me: An Exploration into an Asian American Biblical Hermeneutics." Pages 152–63 in *Ways of Being, Ways of Reading: Asian American Biblical Interpretation.* Edited by Mary Foskett and Jeffrey Kah-jin Kuan. Atlanta: Chalice, 2006.

Yegenoglu, Meyda. *Colonial Fantasies: Toward a Feminist Reading of Orientalism.* Cambridge: Cambridge University Press, 1988.

Yuasa, Yuko. "Performing Sacred Texts." Pages 81–90 in *Women's Sacred Scriptures.* Edited by Kwok Pui-lan and Elisabeth Schüssler Fiorenza. London: SCM, 1998.

Zine, Jasmine. "Between Orientalism and Fundamentalism: The Politics of Muslim Women's Feminist Engagement." *MWJHR* 3:1 (2006).

Contributors

Cynthia Baker is Associate Professor of Religious Studies at Bates College in Lewiston, Maine. She is the author of numerous publications in biblical studies and Jewish studies, including *Rebuilding the House of Israel: Architectures of Gender in Jewish Antiquity* (Stanford, Calif.: Stanford University Press, 2002) and a book on the word "Jew," forthcoming in Rutgers University Press's Key Words in Jewish Studies Series.

Rosa Cursach Salas has taught introduction to feminist exegesis and hermeneutics at EFETA (School of Feminist Theology Andalusia; www.efeta.org) and currently teaches high school philosophy and religion in Mallorca. She is a member of the Work, Sustainability, and Politics research group at the University of Balearic Islands (UIB) and collaborator of the Inequalities, Gender, and Public Policy research group at the UIB. She has been one of the directors of the Feminist Studies in Religion conference that has been organized every year since 2011. She has published and collaborated on various papers in a number of publications and is a member of the ESWTR (European Society of Women in Theological Research).

Regula Grünenfelder, Dr. theol., is responsible for education and training in the Swiss Catholic Women Association and is committed to civic involvement in issues of asylum in Switzerland and Europe. She has published *Frauen an den Krisenherden: Eine rhetorisch-politische Deutung des Bellum Judaicum* (Münster: LIT, 2003) and, together with Bernd Lenfers Grünenfelder, *Erde und Licht: Mit dem Johannesevangelium auf den Spuren unserer Lebenswünsche* (Stuttgart: Katholisches Bibelwerk, 2004).

Jacqueline M. Hidalgo is an Assistant Professor of Latina/o Studies and Religion at Williams College. Her research attends to the ways that U.S. Latina/o identities, gender, sexuality, colonialism, and race have shaped each other and have been shaped by and through utopian religious and scriptural traditions.

Claudia Janssen has studied theology at the universities of Kiel and Marburg. She is apl. Professor of New Testament at the Faculty of Theology at Marburg University and study leader of the "Studienzentrum für Genderfragen in Kirche und Theologie der EKD" in Hannover, an institute for gender studies in the German Protestant Church. Her specialized areas of study are feminist social history of early Christianity, Pauline theology, and gender studies. Along with others, she served as editor of a Bible translation in language that is just (*Bibel in gerechter Sprache* [Gütersloh: Gütersloher, 2006]) and a dictionary of social history of the Bible (*Sozialgeschichtliches Wörterbuch zur Bibel* [Gütersloh: Gütersloher, 2009]). She has recently published a book on resurrection (*Endlich lebendig: Die Kraft der Auferstehung erfahren* [Freiburg: Kreuz, 2013]). Her personal website is www.claudia-janssen.eu.

Melanie Johnson-DeBaufre is Associate Professor of New Testament and Early Christianity at Drew Theological School in Madison, New Jersey, USA. She is the author of *Jesus among Her Children: Q, Eschatology, and the Construction of Christian Origins* (HTS 55; Cambridge: Harvard University Press, 2006); and, with Jane Schaberg, *Mary Magdalene Understood* (New York: Continuum, 2006), as well as articles related to Christian beginnings, rhetorical-historical feminist interpretation, and material culture. She is also the coeditor of the *Journal of Feminist Studies in Religion*.

Renate Jost is the former Director of Studies at the Anna-Paulsen-House, the Center for Women's Studies and Education of the Protestant Church of Germany. She is presently Professor in Theological Women's Studies and Feminist Theology at the Augustana Hochschule in Neuendettelsau, as well as director of the International Institute for Feminist Research in Theology and Religion. Her recent books are *Feministische Bibelauslegungen: Grundlagen–Forschungsgeschichtliches–Geschlechterstudien* (IFFTR Befreiende Perspektiven 1; Münster: LIT, 2013); *Gender, Sexualität und Macht in der Anthropologie des Richterbuches* (BWANT 16; Stuttgart: Kohlhammer, 2006); and *Frauenmacht und Männerliebe: Egalitäre Utopien aus der Frühzeit Israels* (Stuttgart: Kohlhammer, 2006). With Klaus Raschzok she edited *Gender–Religion–Kultur: Biblische, interreligiöse und ethische Aspekte* (Theologische Akzente 6; Stuttgart: Kohlhammer, 2011); and, with Gisela Matthiae, Claudia Janssen, Anette Mehlhorn, and Antje Röckemann, *Feministische Theologie: Initiativen, Kirchen, Universitäten—eine Erfolgsgeschichte* (Gütersloh: Gütersloher, 2008).

Zayn Kassam is the John Knox McLean Professor of Religious Studies at Pomona College, where she teaches courses relating to Islam, gender, and the environment. Her current research focuses on Muslim feminist theologies, as well as migration, and she has published an introductory volume on Islam and edited a volume on women and Islam. Her most recent essays include a chapter on migration, on Muslim women and globalization, and on interreligious dialogue concerning Muslim women. Zayn Kassam serves on the editorial board of the *Journal of Feminist Studies in Religion* as well as the *Journal of Religion, Conflict, and Peace.*

Denise Kimber Buell is Professor of Religion at Williams College and senior member of its Women's, Gender, and Sexuality Studies Program. Her work appears in multiple articles as well in her books *Making Christians: Clement of Alexandria and the Rhetoric of Legitimacy* (Princeton: Princeton University Press, 1999); and *Why This New Race: Ethnic Reasoning in Early Christianity* (New York: Columbia University Press, 2005).

Hanne Köhler is pastor of the Protestant Church in Hesse and Nassau and author of numerous publications on liturgy and worship. She is one of the editors of *Bibel in gerechter Sprache* (Gütersloh: Gütersloher, 2006). Her doctoral thesis on Bible translations, *Gerechte Sprache als Kriterium von Bibelübersetzungen: Von der Entstehung des Begriffs bis zur gegenwärtigen Praxis* (Gütersloh: Gütersloher) was published in 2012.

Joseph A. Marchal is Associate Professor of Religious Studies and affiliated faculty in Women's and Gender Studies at Ball State University. His work explores, combines, and elaborates aspects of feminist, postcolonial, and queer approaches, crossing between biblical studies and critical theories of interpretation, the ancient world and its many contemporary echoes and impacts. Marchal is the author of *The Politics of Heaven: Women, Gender, and Empire in the Study of Paul* (Minneapolis: Fortress, 2008); *Hierarchy, Unity, and Imitation: A Feminist Rhetorical Analysis of Power Dynamics in Paul's Letter to the Philippians* (Atlanta: Society of Biblical Literature, 2006), and he is currently completing a guidebook on Philippians (for Sheffield Phoenix) and an examination of perversely feminized figures in Paul's letters through various queer approaches. He is also the editor of *Studying Paul's Letters: Contemporary Perspectives and Methods* (Minneapolis: Fortress, 2012); and the forthcoming *People beside Paul: The Philippian Assembly and History from Below* (Atlanta: Society of Biblical Literature).

Shelly Matthews is Associate Professor of New Testament at the Brite Divinity School, Texas Christian University. She is the author of *The Acts of the*

Apostles: Taming the Tongues of Fire (Sheffield: Sheffield Phoenix, 2013); *Perfect Martyr: The Stoning of Stephen and the Construction of Christian Identity* (Oxford: Oxford University Press, 2010); and *First Converts: Rich Pagan Women and the Rhetoric of Mission in Early Judaism and Christianity* (Stanford, Calif.: Stanford University Press, 2001). She is the coeditor, with Cynthia Kittredge and Melanie Johnson DeBaufre, of *Walk in the Ways of Wisdom: Essays in Honor of Elisabeth Schüssler Fiorenza* (Harrisburg, Penn.: Trinity Press International, 2003).

Monica Jyotsna Melanchthon is from India and is currently Associate Professor of Old Testament at the United Faculty of Theology, MCD University of Divinity, Melbourne, Australia. She has strong commitments to the marginalized and has contributed toward developing Dalit and Indian feminist hermeneutics and theologies and interpretation of biblical texts drawing on insights from the social biographies of these communities, their perspectives, and their lived experiences.

Mercedes Navarro Puerto, biblical scholar and psychologist, has taught Old Testament as well as Psychology and Religion at the U.P. of Salamanca. She is a founding member of the Association of Spanish Theologians (ATE) and of the School of Feminist Theology in Andalusia (EFETA). Her recent work includes: *Ungido para la vida: Exégesis narrativa de Mc 14,3–9 y Jn 12,1–8* (Estella, Spain: Editorial Verbo Divino, 1999); *Morir de vida: Mc 16,1–8: Exégesis y aproximación psicológica a un texto* (Estella, Spain: Editorial Verbo Divino, 2011); and *Violencia, sexismo, silencio: In-conclusiones en el libro de los Jueces* (Estella, Spain: Editorial Verbo Divino, 2013). With Irmtraud Fischer, she edited *Torah* (Atlanta: Society of Biblical Literature, 2011); and, with Marinella Perroni, *Los Evangelios: Narraciones e historia* (Estella, Spain: Editorial Verbo Divino, 2011).

Marinella Perroni has a doctorate in Philosophy and Theology. She is extraordinary professor for New Testament at the Pontificio Ateneo Sant'Anselmo and guest professor of the theological faculty at Marianum in Rome. She is past president of the Italian theological association (Coordinamento Teologhe Italiane, CTI) and the author of many studies of New Testament exegesis and biblical theology, among them "Lettura femminile ed Ermeueutica Femminista del NT: Status Quaestionis," *RivB* 41 (1993): 315–39; "L'interpretazione Biblica Femminista Tra Ricerca Sinottica ed Ermeneutica Politica," *RivB* 45 (1997): 439–67; "Cent'anni di Solitudine: La Lettura Femminista della Scrittura," *Servitium* 150 (2003): 21–34. With Mercedes Navarro Puerto she coedited *Evangelien: Erzählungen und Geschichte* (Stuttgart: Kohlhammer, 2012), the first New Testament volume of Bible and Women: An Encyclopedia of Exegesis and Cultural History.

Judith Plaskow is professor emerita of religious studies at Manhattan College. She is a Jewish feminist theologian who has been teaching, writing, and speaking about Jewish feminism and feminist studies in religion for over forty years. Cofounder and coeditor of the *Journal of Feminist Studies in Religion,* she is author or editor of several works in feminist theology, including *Standing Again at Sinai: Judaism from a Feminist Perspective* (New York: HarperCollins, 1991); and *The Coming of Lilith: Essays on Feminism, Judaism, and Sexual Ethics 1972–2003* (Boston: Beacon, 2005).

Leony Renk is a pastor, graduate of TCI (Theme-Centered Interaction, by Ruth C. Cohn), and instructor in religious and parish pedagogy. She has been director of the Institute for Religious and Parish Pedagogy of the regional church (Arbeitsstelle für gemeinde- und religionspädagogische Aus-, Fort- und Weiterbildung der Evangelischen Kirche in Berlin-Brandenburg) and is one of the founders of Bibliodrama within the concept of TCI. She is engaged in Jewish-Christian and Jewish-Christian-Muslim dialogue, one of the initiators of the interfaith women's initiative Sarah-Hagar (Berlin), and director of Laase Conference Centre (Wendland/Germany) for interreligious and intercultural encounter. She edited the volume *Interreligiöses Bibliodrama: Bibliodrama als neuer Weg zur christlich-jüdischen Begegnung* (Bibliodrama Kontexte 5; Schenefeld: EB, 2005).

Dora Rudo Mbuwayesango is the Iris and George E. Battle Professor of Old Testament Literature and Languages at Hood Theological Seminary. Her research interests include sexuality in the Hebrew Bible and postcolonial readings of the Torah and prophets. She is coeditor of *Postcolonial Perspectives in African Biblical Hermeneutics* (Atlanta: Society of Biblical Literature, 2012). She has contributed articles in journals and chapters in books including, most recently, "Canaanite Women and Israelite Women in Deuteronomy: The Intersection of Sexism and Imperialism," in *Postcolonial Interventions: Essays in Honor of R. S. Sugirtharajah* (ed. Tat-siong Benny Liew; Sheffield: Sheffield Phoenix, 2009), 45–57; "Zephaniah," in *The Africana Bible: Reading Israel's Scriptures from Africa and the African Diaspora* (ed. Hugh R. Page; Minneapolis: Fortress, 2009).

Susanne Scholz is Associate Professor of Old Testament at Perkins School of Theology in Dallas, Texas. Her research focuses on feminist hermeneutics, epistemologies and sociologies of biblical interpretation, and cultural and literary methodologies. Among her publications are *Sacred Witness: Rape in the Hebrew Bible* (Minneapolis: Fortress, 2010); *Introducing the Women's Hebrew Bible* (London: T&T Clark, 2007); and *Rape Plots: A Feminist Cultural Study of Genesis 34* (Bern: Lang, 2000). She is editor of *Feminist Interpretation of the Hebrew Bible in Retrospect: Biblical Books* (vol. 1; Sheffield: Sheffield Phoenix, 2013); *God Loves Diversity and Justice: Progressive Scholars Speak about Faith, Politics, and the World* (Lanham, Md.: Lexington, 2012); and *Biblical Studies Alternatively* (Upper Saddle River, N.J.: Prentice Hall, 2003).

Helen Schüngel-Straumann is a Swiss theologian and professor emerita of Old Testament Studies. From 1987 to 2001 she taught at various universities in Germany and was last professor of biblical theology at the University of Kassel. She founded the Stiftung Feministische Theologie, which sponsors the development of a feminist theological library in the Center for Gender Studies at the University of Basel, Switzerland. Her works include *Die Frau am Anfang: Eva und die Folgen* (3rd ed.; Münster: LIT, 1999); *Rûah bewegt die Welt: Gottes schöpferische Lebenskraft in der Krisenzeit des Exil* (SBS 151; Stuttgart: Katholisches Bibelwerk, 1992); and *Denn Gott bin ich, und kein Mann: Gottesbilder im Ersten Testament–feministisch betrachtet* (Mainz: Grünewald, 1996). She was also coeditor of the *Wörterbuch der Feministischen Theologie* (Gütersloh: Gütersloher, 1991).

Elisabeth Schüssler Fiorenza, Krister Stendahl Professor at Harvard University Divinity School, is the founding coeditor of the *Journal of Feminist Studies in Religion* and the Feminist The*logy issues of *Concilium*. She is past president of the Society of Biblical Literature and was elected in 2001 to the American Academy of Arts and Sciences. The list of her publications and translations of her work into other languages is extensive. They include *In Memory of Her: A Feminist Theological Reconstruction of Christian Origins* (New York: Crossroad, 1983); *Bread Not Stone: The Challenge of Feminist Biblical Interpretation* (Boston: Beacon, 1985); *Discipleship of Equals: A Critical Feminist Ekklesia-logy of Liberation* (New York: Crossroad, 1993); *But She Said: Feminist Practices of Biblical Interpretation* (Boston: Beacon, 1992); *Jesus: Miriam's Child, Sophia's Prophet: Critical Issues in Feminist Christology* (New York: Continuum, 1994); *Sharing Her Word: Feminist Biblical Interpretation in Context* (Boston: Beacon, 1998); *Jesus and the Politics of Interpretation* (New York: Continuum, 2000); *Rhetoric and Ethic: The Politics of Biblical Studies* (Minneapolis: Fortress, 1999); *Wisdom Ways: Introducing Feminist Biblical Interpretation* (Maryknoll, N.Y.: Orbis, 2001); *The Power of the Word: Scripture and the Rhetoric of Empire* (Minneapolis: Fortress, 2007); and *Democratizing Biblical*

Studies: Toward an Emancipatory Educational Space (Louisville: Westminster John Knox, 2009). She has edited *Searching the Scriptures* (2 vols.; New York: Crossroad, 1993–1994); and coedited *Transforming Graduate Biblical Educa- tion: Ethos and Discipline* (SBLGPBS; Atlanta: Society of Biblical Literature, 2010). Her essays are collected in *Grenzen überschreiten: Der theoretische Anspruch feministischer Theologie* (Münster: LIT, 2004); *Transforming Vision: Explorations in Feminist The*logy* (Minneapolis: Fortress, 2011); *Changing Horizons: Explorations in Feminist Interpretation* (Minneapolis: Fortress, 2013); and *Empowering Memory and Movement: Thinking and Working across Borders* (Minneapolis: Fortress, 2014). In recognition of her work she has received several honorary doctorates from European universities and Ameri- can colleges and divinity schools.

Elsa Tamez is Emeritus Professor of the Latin America Biblical University (Costa Rica). Among her books translated into English are *The Bible of the Oppressed* (trans. Matthew J. O'Connell; Maryknoll, N.Y.: Orbis, 1979); *The Scandalous Message of James: Faith without Works Is Dead* (rev. ed.; New York: Crossroad, 2002); *The Amnesty of Grace: Justification by Faith from the Latin American Perspective* (trans. Sharon Ringe; Nashville: Abingdon, 1993); and *Struggles for Power in Early Christianity: A Study of the First Letter of Timothy* (Maryknoll, N.Y.: Orbis, 2007).

Tan Yak-hwee is the Programme Secretary for Reflection and Research of Council for World Mission, Singapore. Prior to her current position, she taught New Testament Studies and Theology at Taiwan Theological College and Seminary, Taipei, Taiwan. She is the author of *Re-presenting the Johannine Community: A Postcolonial Perspective* (New York: Lang, 2008). Her research interests are Johannine literature, biblical theology, feminist criticism, postco- lonial criticism, and ecological hermeneutics.

CPSIA information can be obtained at www.ICGtesting.com
Printed in the USA
BVOW07s0345230614

356993BV00002B/2/P